FOOD SECURITY, DIVERSIFICATION AND RESOURCE MANAGEMENT: REFOCUSING THE ROLE OF AGRICULTURE?

T0383992

FOOD SECURITY, DIVERSIFICATION AND RESOURCE MANAGEMENT: REFOCUSING THE ROLE OF AGRICULTURE?

PROCEEDINGS
OF THE
TWENTY-THIRD
INTERNATIONAL CONFERENCE
OF AGRICULTURAL ECONOMISTS

Held at Sacramento, California
10–16 August 1997

Edited by
G.H. Peters, International Development Centre,
Queen Elizabeth House, University of Oxford, England
and
Joachim von Braun, Centre for Development Research,
University of Bonn, Germany

INTERNATIONAL ASSOCIATION OF
AGRICULTURAL ECONOMISTS
QUEEN ELIZABETH HOUSE
UNIVERSITY OF OXFORD

1999

Routledge
Taylor & Francis Group

LONDON AND NEW YORK

First published 1999 by Ashgate Publishing

Reissued 2018 by Routledge
2 Park Square, Milton Park, Abingdon, Oxon, OX14 4RN
711 Third Avenue, New York, NY 10017, USA

Routledge is an imprint of the Taylor & Francis Group, an informa business

Publisher's Note
The publisher has gone to great lengths to ensure the quality of this reprint but points out that some imperfections in the original copies may be apparent.

Disclaimer
The publisher has made every effort to trace copyright holders and welcomes correspondence from those they have been unable to contact.

A Library of Congress record exists under LC control number: 98051290

Typeset by Manton Typesetters, 5-7 Eastfield Road, Louth, Lincs, LN11 7AJ, UK.

ISBN 13: 978-1-138-31392-7 (hbk)
ISBN 13: 978-1-138-31395-8 (pbk)
ISBN 13: 978-0-429-45732-6 (ebk)

CONTENTS

Contents vii

CONTRIBUTED PAPERS – TRADE AND TRADE EFFECTS

PREFACE

This volume reports the bulk of the Proceedings of the 23rd International Conference of Agricultural Economists held at Sacramento, California, USA, during August 1997. The gathering was attended by 780 participants from 81 countries. It was the first time that the Association had met in the United States in many years, the last occasion being in East Lansing, Michigan, in 1955.

The theme of the conference was 'Food Security, Diversification and Resource Management: Refocusing the Role of Agriculture?'. The global food and agriculture system is changing dramatically, hence the conference addressed a range of important research and policy issues likely to challenge that system well into the 21st century. These included the implications of rapidly expanding food demand in the presence of natural resource constraints and rapid urbanization; the likely adjustments of markets and trade due to the diversification of diets in quickly developing nations, and also recent and current trade liberalizations; the economic opportunities presented by development in biological and information technologies; and region-by-region examination of the interface between food security, diversification and resource management.

The 23rd conference had a number of new features. We shortened it to less than one week, starting after lunch on Sunday and ending at noon on Saturday, with there being fewer arranged papers and twice as many competitively selected contributed papers as in recent meetings. Computer-based presentations and software demonstrations supplemented poster sessions, while invited panels were an innovation that fostered open discussion and bringing a regional perspective to the themes that ran through the conference.

A meeting of this size would not be possible without the creativity and hard work of many people. Vice President Joachim von Braun (then of the University of Kiel, Germany) deserves high praise for the intellectual and organization leadership he brought to the programme. He also brought a number of well-received innovations to the conference. Peter Hazell (British, but a member of staff of the International Food Policy Research Institute, Washington, DC) led the heroic task of peer review of the large number of contributed paper submissions and reducing them to the 111 selected for presentation at the conference. He was also responsible for editing the special issue of the IAAE journal, *Agricultural Economics*, which contains half the contributed papers selected for publication, and writing a masterly introduction to it. Arie Oskam (Wageningen Agricultural University, The Netherlands) organized the poster sessions. He was in charge of selection as well as being responsible for broadening the concept to include computer-based presentations. Larry Sivers (National Agricultural Statistics Service, United States Department of Agriculture) organized the workshops and symposia. The tireless efforts of these individuals, and all who made presentations in Sacramento, provided the programme with a rich substantive content.

Organizing the logistics for a major conference requires a huge effort by the host country. Jerry Siebert (University of California at Berkeley) provided outstanding leadership of the local arrangements in Sacramento, while Nicole Ballenger (Economic Research Service, United States Department of Agriculture) chaired the country Organizing Committee. Bud Stanton (Cornell University, USA) led the successful effort which raised funds to foster participation by more agricultural economists from foreign exchange-constrained countries than ever before. During the meeting he was also responsible for editing the daily newsletter, *Cowbell*, which has a unique place in each conference.

The home institution of all these organizers made a significant in-kind contribution of their time, and often covered major items of expense, which helped towards the success of the meeting. In addition, substantial support was provided by the University of California (through the Berkeley and Davis campuses), the Giannini Foundation, the United States Department of Agriculture, the American Agricultural Economics Association and the Farm Foundation.

I wish to thank my fellow Executive Committee members for their efforts on behalf of the International Association of Agricultural Economists: President Elect Douglas D. Hedley (Agriculture and Agri-Food, Canada); Past President Csaba Csaki (Hungary, working at the World Bank); Vice President (Programme) Joachim von Braun (University of Kiel); Secretary-Treasurer Walter Armbruster (Farm Foundation, Chicago); and Members, Ruvimbo Chimedza (University of Zimbabwe) and Yang-Boo Choe (Office of the President, Republic of Korea). Finally, but in no sense least, all members of the International Association owe a great debt of gratitude to its editors who are responsible for publications: George Peters (Oxford University, United Kingdom) for this Proceedings volume, and Stanley Johnson (Iowa State University, USA) for the journal, *Agricultural Economics*. Their diligence and editorial care ensure that the intellectual contributions of the Association become valued additions to the literature of agricultural economics. For the largely uncompensated investments of time and resources made by them and their home institutions, the entire membership is most appreciative.

ROBERT L. THOMPSON
Immediate Past President

GEORGE H. PETERS AND JOACHIM VON BRAUN[1]

Introduction: The 23rd Conference and the Association

INTRODUCTION

The 23rd Conference of the International Association of Agricultural Econo-mists was held at the Hyatt Regency Hotel and Convention Centre in Sacramento, California, USA, in August 1997, around the theme of 'Food Security, Diversification and Resource Management: Refocusing the Role of Agriculture?'. Regular conference attenders, or indeed those who are in the less fortunate position of being simply readers of this *Proceedings* volume, will recognize the similarity between the format of the congress and that of its recent predecessors, though they will also note some evolutionary changes in the programme and in the manner of our reporting.

Both of these latter elements are important. Briefly, at this stage, it can be noted that the Conference was shorter than hitherto (beginning on Sunday afternoon and ending by lunch time on the following Saturday), with innova-tion in the programme (the introduction of Panel Sessions, the dropping of what were known as 'Invited papers' and a different method of handling 'Contributed paper' sessions. A shortened version of the programme appears as an appendix. On reporting, the publications from the meeting now consist of what is often called the '*Blue Book*' (that is, this volume) and a special issue of our journal, *Agricultural Economics*. Some of these points will eventually be spelled out in greater detail. There is one further matter to notice. At the end of the Introduction there is a report on business of the International Association, which includes biographical sketches of the new life members elected in Sacramento.

ORGANIZING THE LOCATION

The on-site organizing work was again performed by a local committee, headed by Professor Jerry Siebert, Department of Agricultural Economics, University of California-Berkeley. At a parallel level the United States Organizing Com-mittee was chaired by Dr Nicole Ballenger (United States Department of Agriculture). Since much work had to be done, the two groups are too large for their members, and responsibilities, to be named individually. They are simply assured of our gratitude for their collective efforts.

Apart from the complexity of organizing a meeting attended by 762 profes-sionals, the local committee set up a full programme of associated events, including a series of tours and events for 'accompanying persons'. The day tour was to the Kautz Ironstone Vineyard and Winery in the 'Gold Country' of California State, a site which was able to accommodate (and feed) over 800 people. To add to that there was a selection of post-conference tours, which included the beauty of Yosemite and the Monterrey area and provided an opportunity to visit farms, processing plants and research stations to observe the sheer efficiency of California agriculture at first hand.

The local and national committees received massive financial and material support from the United States Department of Agriculture, from organizations serving California agriculture, and from universities, foundations and commercial undertakings. It was also notable that money could be raised to provide grants, which facilitated attendance by colleagues from low-income and transforming economies (handled through the 'Fund for the International Conference of Agricultural Economists') from governments and official aid agencies in Denmark, Germany, The Netherlands, United Kingdom, Switzerland and the United States. Help was also forthcoming from the Rockefeller and Ford Foundations and the Japan branch of the Association. The Fund is administered by Professor B.F. Stanton (Cornell University, USA).

As can be seen from the programme appendix, Professor Csaba Csaka (Budapest University of Economic Science, Hungary and World Bank) took the chair at the opening ceremony. This is the traditional task of the Past President of IAAE. Other speakers included Jerry Siebert, Nicole Ballenger and our own Secretary–Treasurer, Dr Walter Armbruster, though he was appearing on this occasion as the President of the American Association of Agricultural Economists. The opening address was given by Richard Rominger, Deputy Secretary, United States Department of Agriculture, who is also a Californian farmer. It was a memorable speech which ranged across the agricultural spectrum, from the challenges of policy making at a national and international level to the realities of financing a farm and doing farm work.

Traditionally International Association conferences include at least part of a day devoted to local agriculture. Prior to the Wednesday tour, which is part of that segment, talks were presented. The organizers were Professors Daniel Sumner and Frank Buck (University of California-Davis). Speakers included Susan Offutt (Administrator, Economic Research Service, US Department of Agriculture[2]), Ann Veneman (Secretary, California Department of Food and Agriculture) and 'local academics' (if that is an allowable designation of colleagues with a far higher profile) Alan Olmstead, Warren Johnston, Roberta Cook and David Sunding.

ORGANIZING THE PROGRAMME

In accordance with the accepted practice of the International Association of Agricultural Economists the task of evolving a theme and an array of speakers fell to the Vice-President (Programme), Joachim von Braun. He was ably assisted by Gerta Gedess, Katinka Weiberger, Detlef Virchow and Ulf Stolzke, all at that time from the University of Kiel. Their presence in Sacramento contributed substantially to the smooth running of an extremely complex and full programme.

The contents pages and the appendix provide information on the form of the programme. There is a certain amount of inevitable duplication involved, though it was the view of the Executive Committee that it would be worthwhile to record the depth and complexity of the programme and the extent to which it covered so many issues of great contemporary importance.[3] To draw attention to the familiar elements, the *Opening Session*, in addition to the various speeches of welcome already noted, included the Presidential Address (Robert Thompson, President and Chief Executive Officer of Winrock International) and the Elmhirst Memorial Lecture (Professor Yair Mundlak, Hebrew University of Jerusalem and University of Chicago).

At the core of subsequent days were four *Plenary Sessions*, each consisting of three papers, with discussion openings and participation from the floor. As a professional organization, the IAAE obviously has 'agriculture' in the forefront of its activities. In fact, however, the relevant agenda is always tending to broaden, a process reflected in a theme which embraces the issues of 'food security, diversification and resource management'. The Vice-President, after much consultation with the membership, took a leading role in setting out the highlights of the programme. Traditionally, however, some of the organizational work is delegated, in this case to Ruvimbo Chimedza (University of Zimbabwe), Alain de Janvry (University of California-Berkeley), Clem Tisdell (University of Queensland, Australia) and Michel Petit (World Bank, Washington, DC). Apart from their superb efforts in arranging speakers and discussion openers, they took the chair for the appropriate Plenary Session and did much to foster a stimulating atmosphere devoid of rigid formalism. Shortened comments of discussion openers, compiled with the help of the rapporteurs, are included within the session reports.[4] It is impossible to record details of the floor debate or the closing comments of the main speakers, though it is worth noting that discussion was always vigorous and that there was competition to catch the eye of the chair.

In previous conferences it has been customary to supplement the plenary papers with further 'invited papers' relating to each sub-theme, as well as organizing an open competition for a place on the programme as the presenter(s) of a 'contributed paper'. At Sacramento there was a substantial modification. It has always been understood that contributed papers can cover any issue of interest within our subject and that relevance to the main theme and sub-themes was not a requirement for acceptance. To allow a wider element of freedom, 'invited' papers, which had been 'themed', were dropped and there was a single competition for a large number of contributed paper slots. The organiser was Dr Peter Hazell (International Food Policy Research Institute, Washington, DC, USA). In selecting over 100 papers for floor presentation, from submissions of about three times that number, he was assisted by a panel of appraisers. As explained later, there was then a further selection for publication either in this volume or in *Agricultural Economics* (vol. 19, Sept. 1998).

The next elements in the *Proceedings* are a mixture of the new and the traditional. The Panel Discussions were an innovative feature. Under the general direction of the Vice-President Programme they were organized by leaders in the profession to provide opportunity for more open discussion, especially with users of the results of agricultural economics research. Several included a methodological focus, while some concentrated on themes (or sub-themes) of the conference in relation to particular developing country regions. Platform speakers were asked to introduce topics, rather than to present formal papers, and then to participate in open discussion in relatively small groups. We have been reminded by one of our older members, Professor John Raeburn,[5] that an early aim of Association conferences was to mix together academic 'golf' and academic 'tennis'. In the former, one persons fires off the shots and others watch (or rather listen in the context of conferences); in the latter, there is an exchange 'over the net' as shot is matched with shot. Reports of the interchanges are included below.

It must not, of course, be thought that wide participation was secured only by changing the format of contributed papers and introducing panel sessions. There was continuance of *Discussion Groups and Mini-symposia*, so ably organized by Dr Larry Sivers (United States Department of Agriculture, Washington, DC) and of *Poster Paper Sessions*, where Professor Arie Oskam (Wageningen Agricultural University, The Netherlands) undertook the daunting task of putting together a large number of posters. There were three long sessions, which proved exceedingly popular. On this occasion it was also decided to add to the attractiveness of informal presentations by including computer-based sessions designed to provide methodological guidance. Enormous efforts were made by Arie Oskam, as organizer, to make a success of the innovation. Help in guiding the discussion was provided by a team of colleagues (G. Nagarajan, Z. Hassan, W. Florkowski, M. Trueblood, S. Makki, J. Kola, R. Huirne, L. Unnevehr, A. Burrell, M. Veeman, M. Reed, H. Guoyomard, V. Sukhatme, K. Olson, E-A. Nuppenau, O. Bergland, H. de Gorter, G. Schiefer, S. Lerman, A. Kuyvenhoven, W. Masters, D. Colman, J. Peerlings, Q. Paris, H. Jansen, H.P. Witzke, G. Meester, B. Mills, M. Lyne and W. Heijman). It is regretted that more extensive reporting is not possible.

The conference had its traditional ending, which makes up the final component of the *Proceedings*, namely the *Synoptic View* by the President-Elect, Dr Douglas Hedley, the senior official of the Policy Branch of Agriculture and Agri-Food Canada, Ottawa.

ORGANIZATION OF PUBLICATIONS

The basic format of post-conference reporting has remained virtually standardized over seven conference periods. Each meeting resulted in the appearance of a hardback *Proceedings* volume (or *Blue Book*), a paperback *IAAE Occasional Paper* containing the contributed papers and poster paper abstracts,[6] and a less formal *Members' Bulletin* (distributed from the Editorial Office in Oxford), with the reports on discussion groups and mini-symposia, plus short biographies of new life members elected at the conference. This latter publication will no longer appear; the material is incorporated into the *Proceedings*. The *Occasional Paper* series is also abandoned, though effectively it is replaced rather than abolished. The poster abstracts appear below, as does a selection of contributed papers, with 20 others included in a special issue of the Association journal, *Agricultural Economics*. Part of the motivation was to make the journal more central to the affairs of IAAE by having it include papers from our main triennial event.

As indicated earlier, the Association has long experience of running a 'contributed paper competition'. On this occasion, however, it also had to decide on how many papers to publish either in the *Proceedings* or in *Agricultural Economics*. To be brief, the first stage of selecting 'floor papers' was done in the normal way; but there was then a 'second competition' involving colleagues from the review panel of the journal, as well as others in attendance at Sacramento, to make a further selection on the basis of standard 'journal referee' processes. Authors were then allowed some time to revise their material in the light of referee comment. The process was organized by Peter Hazell, Stanley Johnson (Iowa State University, editor of *Agricultural Economics*) and George Peters. Indispensable assistance was given by Ellen Balm, the journal editorial assistant.

There are a number of points which emerge. First, it was desperately difficult to make a cut from 'floor papers' to a smaller group (about 70 were sent to referees), and then to refine the list to 40 selected for publication, with half in each publication. We are expecting many of those not selected to be resubmitted to the journal, or to appear in other publications. Second, it was decided that the division of papers should allow the special issue to have a 'theme', the one chosen being *Agricultural Growth, Poverty and the Environment*. In the programme appendix, which lists all of the contributed paper sessions, those which appear in the special issue are labelled (S). The papers which appear below (labelled as P) are then grouped into the four sections shown in the contents page.[7] Because of space constraints, discussion openings, unfortunately, do not appear.

There are many people who assisted in book preparation. Notable among these were Ellen Balm, who has already been mentioned, and Geralyn Unterberg (University of California-Berkeley) who found time to organize much of the paperwork for the editors in Sacramento as well as acting as assistant to Jerry Siebert. Katinka Weinberger dealt with the organization of Panel reports. In Oxford, a debt is owed to Denise Watt and Roger Crawford, who did a great deal to help the editorial process, and to the library staff of Queen Elizabeth House, University of Oxford (notably Sheila Allcock, Bob Townsend, Gill Short and Dawn Young), who can always find the details of misquoted references. Larry Sivers, in addition to organizing so much, also provided the report on the discussion groups. A major part was played by Judith Peters, who took the bulk of the responsibility for editing the poster abstracts and also checked over much of the text for the types of problem which inevitably appear, even in the work of the most careful of authors. The staff of Ashgate Publishing Company (notably John Irwin, Ann Newell and Sonia Hubbard) were again enthusiastic, constantly helpful and extremely patient.

ASSOCIATION BUSINESS

A conference *Proceedings* volume is not the place in which to engage in long discussion of the business affairs of the International Association. For members that purpose is served by the Newsletter and the Internet.[8] During conference weeks, pride of place is taken by 'Cowbell' (the daily conference newsletter), edited with incomparable style by Bud Stanton. A feature of the work of the Council, which can only meet at a conference venue on a triennial basis, is the election of Life Members of the Association. Those elected at Sacramento in 1997 were Michele de Benedictis (Italy), John Dillon (Australia), Yujiro Hayami (Japan), Michel Petit (France) and Vijay Vyas (India). Brief biographies are appended.

CONCLUSION

Three standard observations must now be made. First, the International Association records its debt to the many organizations and universities which have lent 'in-kind' support to its activities. Second, the views expressed in this book are not necessarily those of the IAAE nor of the institutions to which the various authors are affiliated. Third, the IAAE is an organization without any form of political affiliation and the use of geographical descriptions is simply a matter of convenience. The points may appear formal, but they are of vital significance to the Council, the Executive Committee and the Membership at large.

NOTES

[1]George Peters, Research Professor in Agricultural Economics, University of Oxford, International Development Centre, Queen Elizabeth House, and Wolfson College, is Editor of Proceedings of the IAAE. Joachim von Braun, Vice-President Programme, at the time of the 1997 meeting was with the University of Kiel, Germany, but is currently Director of the Centre for Development Research at the University of Bonn.

[2]Included among the useful material distributed was Economic Research Service, USDA (1997), *Forces Shaping U.S. Agriculture: A Briefing Book* (Washington, DC: USDA). This was a helpful compilation prepared specially for the conference.

[3]The appendix does not list the Panel Sessions, or the Discussions Groups and Mini-Symposia, both of which appear in detail in later sections of this volume. Some details of the administration of the poster sessions are also excluded.

[4]The inclusion of the programme means that the names of chairpersons and rapporteurs are recorded. This is not repeated. They will understand how vital their role is both at the meetings and for the preparation of proceedings.

[5]The opportunity appears here of reminding readers of an important book, whose title speaks for itself: J.R. Raeburn and J.O. Jones (1990), *A History of the International Association of Agricultural Economists: Toward Rural Welfare Worldwide* (Aldershot: Dartmouth). Neither author is able now to attend conferences but both are a constant source of advice and encouragement to the Editor of Proceedings.

[6]The last in the series contained material from the Harare, Zimbabwe, meeting of 1994. It appears as R. Rose, C. Tanner and M. Bellamy (eds) (1997), *Issues in Agricultural Competitiveness: Markets and Policies*, IAAE Occasional Paper Number 7, Aldershot: Dartmouth. The Proceedings volume from that meeting is G.H. Peters and D.D. Hedley (eds) (1995), *Agricultural Competitiveness: Market Forces and Policy Choice*, Aldershot: Dartmouth.

⁷Slotting papers into groups is inherently difficult – some could fall into more than one category – and it is done as a means of providing readers with *some* guidance as to content. The programme classification was not used since it was designed for the guidance of those attending the meeting. It was quickly decided that the poster papers could not usefully be handled on any sort of thematic basis; hence they are arranged in a way which depends heavily on nothing more complex than geography.
⁸The newsletter is distributed to members twice a year. The website is http://www.ag.iastate.edu.

BIOGRAPHIES OF NEW LIFE MEMBERS

Michele De Benedictis

Michele De Benedictis was born in Asmara in 1927 and earned his bachelor's degree in agricultural studies at the University of Naples in 1952, gaining a PhD in agricultural economics from Iowa State University in 1957. As a professor at the University of Rome, La Sapienza – from which he is expected to retire next year – his contributions to agricultural economics are numerous. He was responsible in the 1960s and 1970s for the successful spread, among the profession in Italy, of the use of quantitative analysis. Many Italian agricultural economists received their training in the post-graduate programme in Portici, Naples, an institution he has been associated with for more than 20 years.

Michele is the only agricultural economist to be elected to membership of the Italian 'Lincei' Academy. His research contributions range from the early seminal application of programming to farm and sector problems, to the most recent analyses of the nature of the reform processes of the Common Agricultural Policy of the European Union. Some will remember the brilliant paper (written with Fabrizio de Filippis and Luca Salvatici) delivered at the European Association meeting in The Hague in 1990, in which he steered carefully between Scylla and Charibdis or, in our context, protectionism and free trade in agriculture.

Michele de Benedictis was a founding member of the Editorial Board of the journal of our Association, *Agricultural Economics*, rendering devoted and efficient service.

John L. Dillon

An active member of the IAAE since the late 1960s, John Dillon's discussion opening on Academician Rustaeov's paper (Minsk, 1970) is still remembered with mixed, but cordial, feelings. That capacity for frank, fearless and constructive criticism remained a valuable asset during his long service on the Editorial Committee of *Agricultural Economics*. John Dillon has now retired from the University of New England, where he served variously as Foundation Professor of Farm Management, Head of the Department of Agricultural Economics, Dean of the Faculty of Economic Studies and Pro-Vice Chancellor. He supervised a multinational network of graduate students from Chile, Brazil,

India and Australia. He retains an office in the Department but restricts his activities to guiding a few graduate students.

The published work on which his international reputation is based includes Heady and Dillon (1961) *Agricultural Production Functions*, his 1968 *Analysis of Response in Crop and Livestock Production* and his joint work with Anderson and Hardaker, *Agricultural Decision Analysis* (1977). He is currently involved in work on a book for FAO.

John is highly regarded in the international agricultural science community, playing an active role in the Consultative Group on International Agricultural Research, where he has served on more Boards of Trustees than perhaps anyone else, and being a prominent participant in many Centre reviews. Professional recognition has come in many forms, with election to fellowship of several learned societies, including the American Agricultural Economics Association. He has a number of honorary doctorates, a Distinguished Alumnus Award from his PhD alma mater, Iowa State University and, most recently, he received the highest national honour, Member of the Order of Australia. John Dillon is one of the most committed and distinguished internationalists of our profession.

Yujiro Hayami

Yujiro Hayami's first degree was in liberal arts at the University of Tokyo, from which he proceeded to a PhD from Iowa State University, where he was a Rockefeller Foundation Scholar. He began his career at Japan's National Research Institute of Agricultural Economics and this was followed by positions at Tokyo Metropolitan University (Professor and Council member), the International Rice Research Institute (Philippines) and Aoyoma Gakuin University (Tokyo), where he continues as Director of the Centre for International Studies. He has served as visiting professor or fellow at the University of Minnesota, the University of the Philippines, the Australian National University, the Institute for Economic Growth in Delhi, the Economic Growth Centre at Yale, and as T.H. Lee Professor of World Affairs at Cornell.

Yujiro received international acclaim for work with Vernon Ruttan on induced technological innovation (*Agricultural Development: An International Perspective*). Further books on Japan, Taiwan, Korea, the Philippines and the revised 1985 edition of the induced innovation hypothesis constitute a valuable corpus of work in agricultural economics. Other important publications include *Anatomy of a Peasant Economy* and *Japanese Agriculture Under Siege*. He continues to publish on Japanese and Asian agrarian issues.

There have been many academic honours, including the Distinguished Research Award from the Agricultural Economics Society of Japan, the Outstanding Published Research Award of the American Agricultural Economics Association, the Outstanding Economic Book Award from Nikkei Shinbun, the Best Journal Article in the *American Journal of Agricultural Economics* on two occasions, the Award for Enduring Quality Publication from the AAEA, the Tohata Memorial Award from the National Institute for Research Advancement in Japan and the Award for Quality of Research Discovery by the AAEA. He is a Fellow of the American Agricultural Economics Association, Honorary Professor of Tokyo Metropolitan University and he was the Elmhirst Lecturer at the IAAE Conference in Buenos Aires, 1988.

He has served with the Consultative Group on International Agricultural Research, the Technical Advisory Committee to the CGIAR, has been a board member of the UN ESCAP Regional Centre for Research and Development of Coarse Grains, Pulses, Roots and Tubers in Bogor, Indonesia, a board member of IFPRI, and a member of the Executive Committee of the International Economic Association. He has been a member of the editorial boards of numerous publications including the *American Journal of Agricultural Economics*, the *Journal of the Japan Society of Agricultural Economics* and of *Agricultural Economics* since its inception.

Michel Petit

Michel Petit was elected President of the IAAE at the Malaga Conference in 1985, as an individual who had come to his professional maturity in three different cultures. First, he was a French 'agronome', a former student of René Dumont and Denis Bergmann, educated in the tradition of the grassroots agronomists (who celebrated farmer contact and knowledge of all technical aspects of agriculture). Michel was also the intellectual offspring of Michigan State University. This second culture was much concerned with discovering the policy and social implications of microeconomic observation and analysis. He obtained his PhD thesis under the supervision of Glenn Johnson, also a former IAAE President and Honorary Life Member. The examination was actually held during the 1964 IAAE Conference at Lyons, France, in a room of the university, which for the occasion had been given the extraterritorial privilege of being deemed part of the Michigan State University campus for the day. His third cultural source was India, where he was appointed programme advisor for agriculture and rural development for the Ford Foundation. For two years from 1975, he saw at first hand the realities of developing economies in Asia.

Apart from the time in India, Michel was a researcher and teacher at Lyons from 1964 to 1988, becoming well known for his pioneering work in applying linear programming models to the study of local and regional development. Subsequently, during a stay at IFPRI in 1983–4, he shifted his interests to the study of agricultural policies and he is famous for his analysis of the worldwide consequences of European agricultural policies. As a teacher, he was responsible for the economic education of most of the higher-level staff in the French Ministry of Agriculture, where he is particularly well received. He was among the founders of the *European Review of Agricultural Economics*, of which he was for many years the associate editor, in charge of Spain and France.

In the late 1980s, Michel's career took him more deeply into administration and management, when he was appointed head of the agricultural branch of the World Bank in Washington, though he did not forget his primary research interests, since he has continuously published in academic journals and participated in professional conferences. At the Bank his latest work has been especially concerned with the development of agricultural research around the world. When his contract with the Bank expires, it is no surprise to learn, he intends to resume his research career in Paris.

Vijay S. Vyas

Vijay Shankar Vyas is Director of the Institute of Development Studies (IDS) in Jaipur, India. Prior to this, Professor Vyas was the senior advisor in the agricultural and rural development department of the World Bank in Washington. In 1983–4, he was awarded an IDRC Senior Research Fellowship and was a visiting scholar at the Asian Studies Centre of Boston University. From 1978 to 1982, he was Director of the Indian Institute of Management at Ahmedabad.

After receiving his PhD in economics from the University of Bombay in 1958, Professor Vyas was on the faculty of Bombay University, Sardar Patel University and the Indian Institute of Management. He has extensive experience in the field of rural development and agricultural policy in India and abroad. He was a member of the Agricultural Prices Commission of the Government of India and served as chairman or member of other commissions and committees set up by the Union and the State governments.

Vijay has acted as a consultant to the United Nations and other international institutions and has served on the Board of the International Centre for Tropical Agriculture (CIAT) in Colombia. He was a member of the Governing Council of the Institute of Development Studies at Sussex University and now occupies a place on the governing boards of several academic and non-governmental institutions in India.

He has written extensively on various aspects of agricultural development and policies, and has been honoured by the academic community of India and abroad for his contributions. Professor Vyas delivered the Elmhirst Lecture at the Tokyo Conference of the IAAE in 1991.

APPENDIX: PROGRAMME INFORMATION*

Sunday, 10 August 1997

13:00–13.45   Opening, Convention Center (Chairperson: Csaba Csaki, Past President IAAE)
Welcome to the 23rd Conference of IAAE
   Nicole Ballenger, Chair, US Organizing Committee, Walter J. Armbruster, President of AAEA
Introduction to the Programme and Conference Theme
   Joachim von Braun, Vice President Programme, IAAE
Opening Address
   Richard Rominger, Deputy Secretary, US Department of Agriculture

13:45–14:30   Presidential Address, Convention Center
Robert Thompson, President IAAE

14:30–15:30   Elmhirst Lecture, Convention Center: 'The Dynamics of Agriculture'
Yair Mundlak, The Hebrew University of Jerusalem, Israel, University of Chicago, USA

15:30–16:00   Break

16:00–18:30   Panel Session 1 (5 concurrent)

19:30–21:30   Reception, Regency Ball Room

Monday, 11 August 1997

8:30–10:30   Plenary Session 1, Regency ABC: 'Security and Demand Challenges: Global Level and National Policy Issues, Household Consumption Improvement'
Chairperson: Ruvimbo Chimedza, University of Zimbabwe
Rapporteur: Kizito Langha, Rural Development Resource Centre, Cameroon

Food Security: A Global Perspective
Per Pinstrup-Andersen, Rajul Pandya-Lorch, IFPRI
Discussion opener: Eugenia Muchnik de Rubinstein, CEPAL, Chile
National Food Security: a Policy Perspective for India
C.H. Hanumantha Rao, University of Hyderabad, R. Radhakrishna, Indian Council of Science Research, India
Discussion opener: Anthony Ikpi, University of Ibadan, Nigeria

---

*Papers below marked (P) appear in this volume; those marked (S) appear in a special issue of *Agricultural Economics*.

Food Security and the Household
Ben Senauer, Terry Roe, University of Minnesota, USA
Discussion opener: Luciano Venturini, Universita Catolica Piacenza, Italy

10:30–11:00   Break

11:00–12:30   Poster/Computer Presentation 1

12:30–14:00   Lunch and visit to posters at leisure

14:00–15:30   Contributed Paper Session 1 (5 concurrent)

CPS 1-1: Emerging Supply Shifts in World Agriculture Markets
Chairperson: Nicole Ballenger, USA
(1)   Prospects for China's grain security in the new millennium
      Liming Wang (UK) and John Davis (UK)
(2)   Declining agricultural productivity in developing countries? (S)
      Lilyan E. Fulginiti (USA) and Richard K. Perrin (USA)
(3)   The impact of agricultural productivity increases in the Former Soviet
      Union and Eastern Europe on world agriculture markets
      Silvia Weyerbrock (USA)
Discussion opener: Kelley White, USA

CPS 1-2: Price Stabilization Policies for Food Markets
Chairperson: Shoichi Ito, Japan
(1)   The optimal quantity of official rice purchase in Taiwan under trade
      liberalization
      Rhung-Jieh Woo (Taiwan) and Yih-Bey Lin (Taiwan)
(2)   A study of optimal rice policy changes in Taiwan
      Chin-Cheng Chang (Taiwan) and Shih-Hsun Hsu (Taiwan)
(3)   Storage–trade interactions under production uncertainty: implications for
      food security
      Shiva S. Makki (World Bank), Luther G. Tweeten (USA) and Mario J.
      Miranda (USA)
Discussion opener: Stan Thompson, USA

CPS 1-3: Food Demand Analysis
Chairperson: Michio Kanai, Japan
(1)   Changing food demand under transition in Slovenia
      Emil Erjavec (Slovenia), George Mergos (Greece), Leonard Mizzi (Bel-
      gium) and Jernej Turk (Slovenia)
(2)   Will European diets be similar? A cointegration approach (P)
      A. Gracia (Spain), A.M. Angulo (Spain), and José M. Gil (Spain)
(3)   Analysis of domestic food demand in Costa Rica
      Hans G.P. Jansen (Costa Rica), Jorgen M. Geurts (Netherlands) and Aad
      van Tilburg (Netherlands)
Discussion opener: Ben Senauer, USA

CPS 1-4: Targeting Food Assistance for the Poor
Chairperson: Sisay Asefa, Senegal
(1) Determinants of diversification of urban Sahel diets into maize: a contingent valuation study of processed maize demand in Mali (P)
     Duncan Boughton (UK), Thomas Reardon (USA) and Jeffrey Wooldridge (USA)
(2) Can targeting work in food security programmes? A study of consumer behaviour and the fair price shop system for food in India
     Vasant P. Gandhi (India) and Abraham Koshy (India)
(3) Estimating the demand for calories in India
     P.J. Dawson (UK) and Richard Tiffin (UK)
Discussion opener: Per Pinstrup-Anderson, IFPRI

CPS 1-5: Socioeconomic Issues at the Household Level
Chairperson: Patrick Webb, Germany
(1) Intra-household resource allocation in Ghana: the impact of the distribution of asset ownership within the household (P)
     Cheryl R. Doss (USA)
(2) Welfare impacts of technological change on women in Mali (S)
     Nina Lilja (Côte d'Ivoire) and John H. Sanders (USA)
(3) Some socioeconomic and health problems of urinary schistosomiasis in Benin State, Nigeria
     J. Chinedu Umeh (Nigeria), O. Amali (Nigeria) and E.U. Umeh (Nigeria)
Discussion opener: Agnes Quimsuming, IFPRI

15:30–16:00   Break

16:00–17:30   Contributed Paper Session 2 (5 concurrent)

CPS 2-1: Public Policy and Agricultural Growth in Developing Countries
Chairperson: Kirit S. Parikh, India
(1) External adjustment, production subsidies and agricultural growth in Brazil (P)
     Joaquim Bento de Souza Ferreira Filho (Brazil)
(2) Assessing impact of government policies on rural development: an explorative study for Bangladesh
     Abdul Bayes (Bangladesh) and Mahabub Hossain (Bangladesh)
(3) Planning, investments and exports in Malaysia's economic development
     Thamir Saleh (USA) and Dale Colyer (USA)
Discussion opener: Michel Griffon, France

CPS 2-2: Policy Issues in Transition Economies
Chairperson: Natalija Kazlauskiene, Lithuania
(1) Official and effective liberalization in the Former Soviet Union: the example of Ukrainian agriculture
     Stephan von Cramon-Taubadel (Germany) and Ulrich Koester (Germany)
(2) Consolidation of the Russian budget: a general equilibrium analysis
     Peter Wehrheim (Germany) and Manfred Wiebelt (Germany)

(3) Economic assessments of the social costs of food security of the econo-
     mies in transition: the case of Bulgaria and Romania
     Nedka Ivanova (Bulgaria)
Discussion opener: Csaba Forgacs, Hungary

CPS 2-3: Agricultural Issues in Transition Economies
Chairperson: Sergey V. Kiselev, Russia
(1) The economics of agricultural decollectivization in Central and Eastern
     Europe (P)
     Erik Mathijs (Belgium) and Johan F.M. Swinnen (Belgium)
(2) The roads of agricultural decollectivization: the case of Eastern Europe
     Volker Beckmann (Germany) and Konrad Hagedorn (Germany)
(3) Competitiveness of agriculture and the food industry in Central and East-
     ern European Association countries (CEAs)
     Monika Hartmann (Germany)
Discussion opener: Zhu Ling, China

CPS 2-4: New Directions in Agricultural Policy Analysis
Chairperson: Markus Hofreiter, Austria
(1) Transfer efficiency of agricultural policies: a review
     David S. Bullock (USA), Jukka Kola (Finland) and Klaus Salhofer (Vi-
     enna)
(2) Sunk costs and resource mobility: implications for economic and policy
     analysis (P)
     Bradford L. Barham (USA) and Jean-Paul Chavas (USA)
(3) Economic development, rurality and minority cultures
     T.N. Jenkins (UK) and G.O. Hughes (UK)
Discussion opener: Bruce Gardner, USA

CPS 2-5: Domestic and International Agricultural Pricing Issues
Chairperson: Lio da Rocha, Brazil
(1) Lessons from the coffee market on political economy in developing coun-
     tries
     Mary Bohman (USA) and Lovell Jarvis (USA)
(2) Does China discriminate among origins in the pricing of its wheat im-
     ports? (P)
     Kevin Z. Chen (Canada), Jianguo Hui (USA) and Peter Chen (Canada)
(3) The effects of food aid on maize prices in Mozambique (P)
     Cynthia Donovan (Senegal), Robert Myers (USA), David Tschirley (USA)
     and Michael Weber (USA)
Discussion opener: David Harvey, UK

17:30–19:00   Discussion Groups/Mini-symposia 1 (27 concurrent)

18:30–20:00   IAAE Council Meeting

20:00–22:00   CWAE Reception

Tuesday, 12 August 1997

8:30–10:30 Plenary Session 2: 'Agricultural Diversification and New Technology'
Chairperson: Alain de Janvry, University of California-Berkeley, USA
Rapporteur: Akinwumi A. Adesina, IITA, Cameroon
Diversification and International Trade
Alex McCalla and Alberto Valdés, World Bank
Discussion opener: Hassan Sergini, University of Hassan II, Morocco
Rural Economy and Farm Income Diversification in Developing Countries
Chris Delgado, IFPRI and Ammar Siamwalla, Thailand Development Research Institute
Discussion opener: Michael Carter and Bradford Barham, University of Wisconsin, USA
Agricultural Biotechnology: Economic and International Perspectives
David Zilberman and Cherisa Yarkin, University of California-Berkeley, USA, Amir Heiman, Hebrew University of Jerusalem, Rehovot, Israel
Discussion opener: Rafael Posada, CIAT

10:30–11:00 Break

11:00–12:30 Poster/Computer Presentation 2

12:30–14:00 Lunch and visit to posters at leisure

14:00–15:30 Contributed Paper Session 3 (5 concurrent)

CPS 3-1: Agricultural Marketing
Chairperson: Cornelis J. van der Meer, The Netherlands
(1) Food quality, reputation and price: the case of wine
     Silke Gabbert (Germany), Günter Schamel (Germany) and Harald von Witzke (Germany)
(2) Trade, labels and consumer information: the case of hormone-treated beef
     Jean-Christophe Bureau (France), Stephan Marette (France) and Alessandra Schiavina (France)
(3) The competitive position of farmers' food processing cooperatives: the German case
     C.-Hennig Hanf (Germany)
Discussion opener: Roley Piggott, Australia

CPS 3-2: Spatial Issues in Food Marketing and Processing
Chairperson: Margherita Chang Ting Fa, Italy
(1) Development of an optimizing system with fully-connected neural networks for marketing of vegetables
     Yasushi Sembokuya (Japan), Daisuke Takeshima (Japan), Yoshinori Fujii (Japan) and Kozo Kasahara (Japan)

15:30–16:00   Break

16:00–17:30   Contributed Paper Session 4 (5 concurrent)

CPS 4-1: Trade and the Environment
Chairperson: Gordon Rausser, USA
(1)   Have structural adjustment programmes compromised efforts to sustainably intensify African agricultural production? Empirical evidence from Senegal
       Valerie Kelly (USA), Thomas Reardon (USA), Bocar Diagana (Senegal), Matar Gaye (Senegal) and Maniivel Sene (Senegal)
(2)   Growth, trade, pollution and natural-resource use in Chile: evidence from an economy-wide model (S)
       Dominique van der Mensbrugghe (France), David Roland-Holst (USA), Sebastien Dessus (France) and John Beghin (Belgium)
(3)   Environmental regulation and trade: exploring the time dimension
       Ki-Ju Han (Korea) and John B. Braden (Korea)
Discussion opener: Don MacLaren, Australia

CPS 4-2: Land Tenure and Security
Chairperson: Peter Rieder, Switzerland
(1)   Rights to land and farmer investment incentives in China (S)
       Guo Li (USA), Scott Rozelle (USA) and Loren Brandt (USA)
(2)   Tenure security and productivity in small scale agriculture in Zimbabwe: implications for South Africa
       G.M. Moore (South Africa) and W.L. Neiuwoudt (South Africa)
(3)   A game theoretical model of land contract choice
       Americo M.S. Carvalho Mendes (Portugal)
Discussion opener: Klaus Deininger, World Bank

CPS 4-3: Induced Innovation and Nature Resource Management
Chairperson: Hans Binswanger, World Bank
(1)   Population pressure, technological change and agricultural growth in sub-Saharan Africa: the farming systems evolution approach, evidence and issues
       Kizito Langha (Cameroon)
(2)   Population growth, agricultural intensification, induced innovation and natural resource sustainability: an application of neoclassical growth theory (S)
       John L. Pender (IFPRI)
(3)   Induced innovation in natural resource management: example from a community case study in the Honduras hillsides
       Sara J. Scherr (IFPRI), Gilles Bergeron (IFPRI), John Pender (IFPRI) and Bruno Barbier (IFPRI)
Discussion opener: Simeon Ehui, ILRI

CPS 4-4: Agricultural and Greenhouse Gas Emissions
Chairperson: Rafael Posada, CIAT

(1) Food security and environmental sustainability: an economic evaluation of CO_2 mitigation strategies
     R.P.S. Malik (India)
(2) Farming systems models on the reduction of greenhouse gas emissions in crop and dairy farms
     Jürgen Zeddies (Germany) and Konrad Lothe (Germany)
(3) Economies of tropical forest land use and global warming
     Paula Horne (Finland)
Discussion opener: Pierre Crosson, USA

PS 4-5: Trees and Agriculture
Chairperson: Scott Rozelle, USA
(1) Agricultural development with rainforest conservation: methods for seeking best bet alternatives to slash-and-burn, with applications to Brazil and Indonesia (S)
     Thomas P. Tomich (ICRA), Meine van Noordwijk (ICRA), Stephen Vosti (IFPRI) and Julie Witcover (IFPRI)
(2) Policy and competitiveness of agroforestry-based technologies for maize production in the western highland of Cameroon: an application of policy analysis matrix (S)
     Akinwumi Adesina (IITA) and Ousmane N. Coulibaly (IITA)
(3) Woodland clearing and forest policy: the Ethiopian case
     Tassew Woldehanna, (Ethiopia), Erwin Bulte (The Netherlands) and Wim Heijman (The Netherlands)
Discussion opener: Steve Franzel, ICRAF

17:30–19:00   Discussion Groups/Mini-symposia 2 (27 concurrent)

20:00   Ad hoc meetings and reunions

Wednesday, 13 August 1997

08:30–10:00   Contributed Paper Session 5 (5 concurrent)
CPS 5-1: Water Management Policies
Chairperson: Mona Nour El Din, Syria
(1) Water conveyance, spatial technology choice and rents
     Ujjayant Chakravorty (USA) and Chieko Umetsu (USA)
(2) Water pricing policies, public decision making and farmers' response: implications for water policy (S)
     Consuelo Varela-Ortega (Spain), José M. Sumpsi (Spain), Alberto Garrido (Spain), Maria Blanco (Spain) and Eva Iglesias (Spain)
Discussion opener: Mark Rosegrant, IFPRI

CPS 5-2: Determinants of Adoption of Soil Conservation
Chairperson: Boubakar T. Thabet, Tunisia
(1) A microeconomic analysis of adoption of soil conservation in the Philippine uplands
     Ma. Lucila A. Lapar (IRRI) and Sushil Pandey (IRRI)

(2) Determinants of farmers' indigenous soil and water conservation investments in semi-arid India (S)
John L. Pender (IFPRI) and John M. Kerr (IFPRI)
(3) Poverty, market imperfections and time preferences: of relevance for environmental policy?
Stein T. Holden, (Norway), Bekele Shiferaw (Norway) and Mette Wik (Norway)
Discussion opener: Peter Matlon, UNDP

CPS 5-3: Household and Community Models of Soil Management Decisions
Chairperson: Antonio Cipiriano Pinheiro, Portugal
(1) Induced innovation and land degradation: results from a bioeconomic model of a village in West Africa (S)
Bruno Barbier (IFPRI)
(2) Technology, market policies and institutional reform for sustainable land use (S)
Arie Kuyenhoven (The Netherlands), Ruerd Ruben (The Netherlands) and Gideon Kruseman (The Netherlands)
(3) Agricultural policy reform and smallholder soil fertility management
Steven Were Omamo (The Netherlands) and Gerdien Meijerink (The Netherlands)
Discussion opener: Ruud Huirne, The Netherlands

CPS 5-4: Pest Management
Chairperson: Jürgen Zeddies, Germany
(1) Economic and environmental implications of pesticide use on vegetable production
Latha Nagarajan (India), Shiva S. Makki (World Bank) and M.S. Swaminathan (India)
(2) Pesticide productivity, host-plant resistance and China's battle against insects and diseases (S)
David Widawsky (IRRI), Scott Rozelle (USA), Songqing Jin (China) and Jikun Huang (China)
Discussion opener: Mahabub Hossain, IRRI

CPS 5-5: Rangeland Management in the Sahel
Chairperson: Kwadwo Asenso-Okyere, Ghana
(1) Economic analysis of mixed-species grazing and implications for sustainable livestock production in semi-arid West Africa
Timothy O. Williams (ILRI), Salvador Fernandez-Rivera (ILRI) and Pierre Hiernaux (ILRI)
(2) Pasture taxes and agricultural intensification in Southern Mali (S)
Timothy J. Dalton (Côte d'Ivoire)
Discussion opener: Jock Anderson, World Bank

10:00–10:30　Break

10:30–12:30　Special Plenary Session US/California Agriculture

Organizer: Daniel A. Sumner, Director, Agricultural Issues Center, University of California
Chairperson: Frank H. Buck, Jr. Professor, Department of Agricultural and Resource Economics, University of California-Davis, USA
(1)   The US agricultural economy
      Susan Offutt, Administrator, Economic Research Service, US Department of Agriculture, USA
(2)   A welcome from California agriculture
      Ann Veneman, Secretary, California Department of Food and Agriculture, USA
(3)   A historical perspective on California agriculture
      Alan Olmstead, Department of Economics, University of California-Davis, USA
(4)   A geographic survey of California agriculture
      Warren Johnston, Professor Emeritus, Department of Agricultural and Resource Economics, University of California-Davis, USA
(5)   Marketing of fruits and vegetable crops in California
      Roberta Cook, Cooperative Extension Specialist, Department of Agricultural and Resource Economics, University of California-Davis, USA
(6)   Resource and environmental issues in California agriculture
      David Sunding, Cooperative Extension Specialist, Department of Agricultural and Resource Economics, University of California-Berkeley, USA
(7)   Government policy and California agriculture
      Daniel A. Sumner, University of California, USA

12:30–13:00   Break

13:00   Load buses for tour (with box lunch on board)

17:00–19:00   Barbecue

Thursday, 14 August 1997

8:30–10:30   Plenary Session 3: 'Resource Management in Agriculture: Water and Land, Biodiversity, Agriculture and Climate'
Chairperson: Clem Tisdell, University of Queenland, Australia
Rapporteur: R.P.S. Malik, University of Delhi, India
Water and Land Resources and Global Food Supply
Mark Rosegrant, IFPRI, Claudia Ringler, IFPRI, Roberta Gerpacio, IFPRI
Discussion opener: Anthony H. Chisholm, La Trobe University, Australia
Impacts of Global Warming on Agriculture
Darwin Hall, California State University, USA
Discussion opener: Prabhu L. Pingali, IRRI
The Management of Genetic Resources for Agriculture: Ecology and Information, Externalities and Policies
Tim Swanson, Cambridge University, UK
Discussion opener: P.S. Ramakrishnan, Jawaharlal Nehru University, India

10:30–11:00   Break

11:00–12:30   Poster/Computer Presentation 3

12:30–14:00   Lunch and visit to posters at leisure

14:00–15:30   Panel Session 2 (5 concurrent)

17:30–19:00   Discussion Groups/Mini-symposia 3 (27 concurrent)

20:00   Ad hoc meetings and reunions

Friday 15 August 1997

08:30–10:30   Plenary Session 4: 'Economics of Policy and Institutional Change'
Chairperson: Michel Petit, World Bank
Rapporteur: Nedka Ivanova, Ministry of Agriculture, Bulgaria
Institutional and Organizational Forces Shaping the Agricultural Transformation Process: Experiences, Causes and Implications
P. Michael Schmitz, Cornelia Noeth, University of Giessen, Germany
Discussion opener: Ewa Rabinowicz, University of Uppsala, Sweden
Policy and Institutional Change for Agriculture in China: Production, Consumption and Trade Implications
Ke Bingsheng, China Agricultural University
Discussion opener: Mahabub Hossain, IRRI
Regionalism in World Food Markets: Implications for Trade and Welfare
Thomas Hertel, William Masters, Purdue University, USA, Mark Gehlhar, ERS/USDA, USA
Discussion opener: Alexander Sarris, University of Athens, Greece

10:30–11:00   Break

11:00–12:30   Contributed Paper Session 6 (5 concurrent)

CPS 6-1: Agricultural Effects of the North American Free Trade Agreement
Chairperson: Mauro De Rezende Lopes, Brazil
(1)   NAFTA in a changing policy environment
        Mary E. Burfisher (USA), Daniel Plunkett (USA), Sherman Robinson (IFPRI) and Karen Thierfelder (USA)
(2)   Impact of the Uruguay Round agreement and NAFTA on the Mexican economy
        Erly Cardoso Teixeira (Brazil)
(3)   Agricultural effects of a North American customs union: a game theoretic analysis
        P. Lynn Kennedy (USA) and Karol W. Hughes (USA)
Discussion opener: Ruben Echeverria, IDB

(3) Testing the induced innovation hypothesis: an error correction model of South African agriculture (S)
Colin Thirtle (UK), Robert Townsend (South Africa) and Johann van Zyl (South Africa)
Discussion opener: Awudu Abdulai, Switzerland

12:30–14:00 Lunch, ad hoc meetings and reunions

14:00–15:30 Contributed Paper Session 7 (4 concurrent)

CPS 7-1: Determinants of Agricultural Exports
Chairperson: Hassan Sergini, Morocco
(1) An econometric analysis of US broiler exports
Crispin Mutshipayi Kapombe (USA) and Dale Coly (USA)
(2) A Bayesian analysis of trade in processed food products: an application to France
Nadine Herrard (France), Yves Le Roux (France) and Yves Surry (France)
(3) US–Mexico fresh vegetable trade: policy intervention and technological change
Jaime E. Malaga (USA), Gary W. Williams (USA) and Stephen W. Fuller (USA)
Discussion opener: Ralph Lattimore, New Zealand

CPS 7-2: Agricultural Research Policy
Chairperson: Prabhu Pingali, CIMMYT
(1) Organizational models for management of research and extension: the case of New Zealand
R.W.M. Johnson (New Zealand)
(2) The rise and fall of public sector plant breeding in the United Kingdom: a recursive model of basic and applied research and diffusion (S)
Colin Thirtle (UK), P. Bottomley (UK), P. Palladino (UK) and D. Schimmelpfennig (USA)
(3) An empirical study of the determinants of public research investment and commodity policies in agriculture
Johan F.M. Swinnen (Belgium), Harry De Gorter (USA) and Gordon C. Rausser (USA)
Discussion opener: Dina Deininger-Umali, World Bank

CPS 7-3: Impact of Agricultural Research
Chairperson: Charles Mataya, Malawi
(1) The contribution of genetic resources and diversity: the case of wheat productivity in the Punjab of Pakistan
Jason Hartell (Belgium), Melinda Smale (CIMMYT), Paul Heisey (CIMMYT) and Ben Senauer (USA)
(2) Agricultural research priority setting under multiple objectives: an example from Zimbabwe
Gladys Mutangadura (USA) and George W. Norton (USA)

(3) The impact of agricultural research in Africa: aggregate and case study evidence (S)
     William A. Masters (USA), Touba Bedingar (Mali) and James F. Oehmke (USA)
Discussion opener: Derek Byerlee, World Bank

CPS 7-4: Policies for Promoting Technology Adoption among Smallholders
Chairperson: Guenther Dresruesse, Germany
(1) Getting technology and the technology environment right: lessons from maize development in Southern Africa
     Julie A. Howard (USA), Lawrence Rubey (USA) and Eric W. Crawford (USA)
(2) Market access by smallholder farmers in Malawi: implications for technology adoption, agricultural productivity and crop income (S)
     Manfred Zeller (IFPRI), Aliou Diagne (IFPRI) and Charles Mataya (Malawi)
(3) Technology and farm performance: paths of productive efficiencies over time
     Kali Kalirajan (Australia) and Ric Shand (Australia)
Discussion opener: Truman Phillips, Canada

15:30–16:00   Break

16:00–18:30   Panel Session 3 (5 concurrent)

18:00–19:30   IAAE Council Meeting, Big Sur

19:30   Conference Dinner, Regency Ball Room

Saturday, 16 August 1997

8:30–10:00   Contributed Paper Session 8 (4 concurrent)

CPS 8-1: Agricultural and Economic Growth
Chairperson: Kohei Kobajashi, Japan
(1) Agriculture and economic growth in a market economy: analysis of the French postwar experience
     Xavier Irz (USA) and Terry Roe (USA)
(2) The Asian path of agricultural development: patterns of development of structural input–output relationships
     Cid L. Terosa (Philippines), Katshuhiko Demura (Japan) and Akio Ito (Japan)
(3) The place of agriculture in the development of Poland and Hungary: lessons of a computable general equilibrium model with risk considerations (P)
     Jean-Marc Boussard (France) and Ane Kathrine Christensen (Denmark)
Discussion opener: Alexander Sarris, Greece

CPS 8-2: Agricultural Sector Modelling Methods
Chairperson: Ralph Lattimore, New Zealand
(1)   The mixed-complementarity approach to specifying agricultural supply in computable general equilibrium models (P)
Hans Löfgren (IFPRI) and Sherman Robinson (IFPRI)
(2)   MATA Africa: a model to study the impacts of agricultural policies
D. Deybe (France) and P. Castella (France)
(3)   Reform of the CAP: empirical evidence for the new Länder of Germany
D. Kirschke (Germany), H. Lotze (Germany), S. Noleppa (Germany) and H. von Witzke (Germany)
Discussion opener: Jean Marc Boussard, France

CPS 8-3: Management with Imperfect Information
Chairperson: C.-Henning Hanf, Germany
(1)   Imperfect information in contracts between farm contractor and farm: interpretation by extensive-form game
Fumio Osanami (Japan), Xiu Zhenjie (Japan) and Takumi Kondo (Japan)
(2)   Hazard and the household microenterprise: evidence from Guyana, South America
Edward W. Bresnyan (USA)
(3)   Putting economics into dairy farm management: a Scottish experience
David D. Mainland (UK)
Discussion opener: Michael Murphy, UK

CPS 8-4: Estimation Methods
Chairperson: Gunter Fisher, The Netherlands
(1)   Amending profit function models with farm structure information
H. Peter Witzke (Germany)
(2)   A two-constraint AIDS model of recreation demand and the value of leisure time
Douglas M. Larson (USA), Sabina L. Shaikh (USA) and John B. Loomis (USA)
(3)   Environmental degradation and mortality increase. Estimation of the value of a statistical life in developing economies
Brad J. Bowland (USA) and John C. Beghin (USA)
Discussion opener: Gunter Fisher, The Netherlands

10:00–10:30   Break

10:30–12:00   Conference Synthesis
Chairperson: Douglas Hedley, President Elect, Canada
Statements of Panellists
Food Security and Demand Challenges
Ruvimbo Chimedza, University of Zimbabwe, Harare
Agricultural Diversification and New Technology
Alain de Janvry, University of California-Berkeley, USA
Resource Management in Agriculture
Clem Tisdell, University of Queensland, Australia

Economics of Policy and Institutional Change
Michel Petit, World Bank

Conference Synthesis: Douglas Hedley, President-Elect, IAAE

12:00   Adjourn and Departure

13:00   Post-conference tours departure

OPENING SESSION

PRESIDENTIAL ADDRESS

ROBERT L. THOMPSON*

Technology, Policy and Trade:
The Keys to Food Security and Environmental Protection

I am deeply honoured to deliver the 23rd Presidential Address to the International Association of Agricultural Economists. During my three years of office I have been privileged to visit over 40 countries on all continents, except Antarctica! This experience, involving both research and innumerable conversations (too numerous to cite individually) with agricultural economists, government officials and other well informed observers, forms the basis of my presentation.

I intend to address the problems of hunger and poverty in the world's rural areas in the light of the growing need and demand for food, linking that with farmers' potential to raise production to satisfactory levels without either substantially increased real prices or unacceptable environmental damage. I then turn to a highly stylized regional review of agricultural demand and supply potential, drawing inferences about the need for investment in agricultural research and necessary changes in both public policy and the global agricultural trading environment.

HUNGER AND POVERTY

Of the world's 5.8 billion people, an estimated 800 million suffer hunger. At the individual level, food insecurity is mainly caused by poverty. In no country do the rich go hungry except in times of war, natural disaster or politically imposed famine.

There are 1.3 billion people who subsist on an income of less that one United States dollar per day. The World Bank calculates that 80 per cent of the world's poor live in rural areas, where the bulk of the people earn their living from farming. Half of the poor live in less favoured areas. To understand the roots of the problems of poverty and hunger in rural areas, it is important to recognize that no country in the world has solved the problem of rural poverty by focusing exclusively on agriculture. Certainly, by raising farm productivity the lot of rural people can be improved, food availability can be increased and the real price of food reduced. But availability is not enough. It takes

*Winrock International Institute for Agricultural Development, Morrilton, AR, USA.

purchasing power to gain access to food needs above a family's own production. And there is not enough land per person in most rural areas for everyone who is trying to make a living from agriculture to grow enough to feed their family adequately and have sufficient left to sell to raise the family income above the poverty line.

The countries which have substantially reduced rural poverty have created off-farm employment opportunities, either within the rural communities or in distant cities. In the highest income countries today, the majority of farm families earn more than half of their income from non-farm sources. One or more members of the family work full-time or part-time off the farm. Some of these jobs are in agricultural input supply or in adding value to the raw products of the land. Many, however, are in cottage industries and other businesses completely unrelated to agriculture.

In many developing countries the only option for rural people to escape poverty is to move to distant cities. In 1990, there were four cities of over 10 million people in the world, and it is projected that by 2010 there will be 21 cities of this size, 13 of which will be in Asia. The diseconomies of supplying safe drinking water and social services and of removing garbage and sewage from cities of this size are overwhelming. While urbanization is a trend that is unlikely to be reversed, it could be slowed down if there were more attractive opportunities in rural areas. To do this will require much larger investments in roads, communications, education, health care and putting the necessary pre-conditions in place for employment and enterprise growth. These investments in infrastructure and human capital are also important for successful agricultural development.

The world's population continues to grow rapidly, though the growth rate is falling faster than many analysts expected. Each year the United Nations' median projection of the world population is revised downwards. Much that is written about the ability of the world's farmers to feed this population adequately and without environmental damage focuses on the number of mouths to be fed. Certainly, population growth creates additional need for food, but whether that need is translated into effective demand depends on purchasing power.

While the rise in numbers attracts most of the media attention, what has been much less noted is the broad-based economic growth which has been empowering millions of poor people with the means to upgrade the quality of their diets. As families gain more income, the first thing they do is modify their diet, usually by including more fruits, vegetables, animal protein, edible oils and sweets. This income effect accounts for more of the recent growth in global demand for food than population growth. While there are hundreds of millions of people in the world who have been left behind by this economic growth, many millions more are participating, particularly those living in urban areas. Much of the growth is export-led and is in East and Southeast Asia. Much also is associated with privatization and moves to a market economy.

The combined effects of population and income growth are expected to double global food consumption in the next 30 years. This brings us to the question of aggregate global food security. At the national level, food security is a problem of availability. We ask whether a country's farmers can satisfy its food demand at competitive prices. Each country should use its arable land and agricultural production potential to the fullest extent that it can efficiently or without wasting resources, that is at a marginal rate of transformation which is lower in domestic production than in trade. It is important to recognize that investments in agricultural research can often modify the domestic marginal rate of transformation to create a comparative advantage in agriculture where it did not exist previously. If a country cannot efficiently produce its own food, it must either export other products to earn the foreign exchange to import its needs or hope that a dependable supply of food aid is available.

Food security at the global level is a question of whether the world's farm and food system can provide twice or even three times as much food as today, at no higher real cost, and do it in a manner that does not destroy the environment. There are only three ways to increase global availability: increase the land area planted, increase yield per hectare and reduce post-harvest losses. If we were to double food production by doubling the amount of land under cultivation, it would create massive environmental damage. It could only be done with large-scale destruction of forests and, with them, wildlife habitat and biodiversity. This would also reduce the carbon sink and destroy the homes of indigenous peoples.

This paper examines how much more fertile, well-watered, unforested, non-erodible land is available and where, and then draws inferences for research, public policy and international trade in ensuring food security without environmental damage. In the next section of the paper we will take a highly stylized tour of the continents addressing these questions.

ASIA

Asia has a much larger fraction of the world's population than of its arable land. Many parts have made significant investments in agricultural research and in education. A number of countries of East and Southeast Asia have been experiencing very fast economic growth with rapid creation of non-agricultural employment, often widely dispersed through the countryside. As per capita incomes rose from a low to a middle level, diets rapidly diversified. Despite significant growth in agricultural productivity, food consumption quickly exceeded internal food production capacity, and agricultural imports grew rapidly, particularly for feed grains and protein meals for livestock and poultry. As incomes have risen, rice consumption has fallen and that of wheat has grown.

The land–labour ratio in most of these countries is very low. Some of the highest income countries of East Asia introduced quite generous price supports and protectionist import policies for their most important traditional products. However, even with these policies, they could not provide parity of income to their farmers from their small landholdings. As a result, large off-farm migration has occurred, and part-time farming has become a common means of supplementing farm income.

With 1.2 billion people, China has 22 per cent of the world's population, but it has only 9 per cent of the arable land. Though population is expanding slowly, the economic growth rate of around 10 per cent per year is causing diets to alter rapidly, with large increases in poultry and pork consumption in particular. China experienced very rapid growth in agricultural output during the 1980s, following its economic reforms, but its future ability to feed itself has become an issue of great media attention and numerous academic conferences, including an IAAE interconference symposium last year. Until recently, there was significant doubt about how much productivity growth potential still existed. However, the recent announcement by the State Statistical Bureau that the land area under cultivation had been significantly underestimated means that crop yields per hectare are lower than previously thought. With larger investments in agricultural research and in technology transfer, it should be possible to raise yields considerably.

Over the last 20 years, China's public policy has varied, in the amount of support it has given to agriculture. The recent 'Grain Bag' policy, which encourages provincial self-sufficiency, has been a step backwards. In addition, the inadequate rural transport infrastructure reduces the ability of the international market to function efficiently. Some attention is being given to the need to increase the production of high-value plant and animal products in place of cereals, with the objective of not only supplying domestic demand, but also generating export revenue that could pay for imports of even more grain than could be grown on the same land. Consistent with this, the government of China has reduced its cereals self-sufficiency goal from 100 per cent to 92 per cent. China is likely to become the world's largest importer of maize and soybeans.

While China has received most of the recent media attention, we should also pay attention to India. Some demographers now project that by the middle of the next century India will have 1.5 billion people, and China, 1.4 billion. India has made large investments in agricultural research. The 'green revolution', which began in the late 1960s, satisfied the growth in food demand for at least one generation. It is important to remember that India has 250 million middle-class consumers, but also half a billion very low-income people. While India has been slow to abandon the socialist model and let market forces work, economic growth is starting to accelerate. If this becomes broad-based, diets are likely to change, and India could also place greater demands on the world food system. Consumption of dairy products is already large and with higher incomes Indian consumers are likely to eat considerably more poultry and sheep and goat meat.

Having so much more of the world's population than arable land, Asia is likely to become an even larger net food-importing region as per capita incomes rise, drawing much larger agricultural exports from other regions of the world.

AFRICA

Africa has experienced rapid population growth and slow economic advance. It is the one continent with declining per capita food production, which has been going on for three decades. Africa has the geologically oldest exposed land surface in the world and heavy weathering of its soils has left them with weak structure and very low nutrient content. Many regions have low annual rainfall with quite high variance, while some are prone to desertification. It is the continent with the greatest natural limitations to high-productivity agriculture. While there is a modest amount of additional land that could be brought into use, especially in the southern cone, much of this is subject to these same climatic and soil quality constraints.

There is a smaller cumulative stock of agricultural research results available in Africa than in other continents. This reflects an underinvestment by national governments and by the international system. Because the food staples are crops not widely grown in other parts of the world (for example, millet, sorghum, yams and sweet potatoes), there is also much less international research upon which to draw than for wheat, rice or maize. Nevertheless, the available research demonstrates that high yields are attainable in many regions of Africa with improved varieties, better soil management and applications of chemical fertilizers.

Many countries have had a pronounced anti-rural or anti-agricultural bias in their public infrastructure investments and agricultural price policies, enforcing price ceilings and accepting dumped food aid to keep food cheap in the cities. This, in turn, depresses farm prices. As a result of the terrible condition of most rural roads, the cost of transport is extremely high. This further depresses the farm-level prices of commodities and increases the cost of fertilizer and other purchased inputs. Such price-distorting effects have often been further accentuated by inefficient parastatal marketing monopolies. As a result, it is simply not profitable for farmers to adopt the improved technologies which are available to many parts of Africa.

Diffusion of improved technologies is impeded also by several other factors. The agricultural extension service is often weak and fails to recognize that working with the 70 per cent of African farmers who are women may require a different approach than working with men. The private sector serving agriculture is often not well developed because of inadequacies in the legal code or because of unfair competition from inefficient, but subsidized, public companies. Moreover, credit is often not readily available.

Agricultural productivity could be much higher than it is now in Africa, and somewhat more land could be brought into production without causing environmental damage. The continent could also produce much more of its food supply.

The anti-rural bias of many African governments is also reflected in the low priority which they place on agricultural and rural development projects when approaching foreign aid donors and the international development banks. There are often more resources available to Africa for agricultural and rural development than are taken up.

If and when faster economic growth occurs, it will cause food consumption to grow even faster. Therefore, even with some agricultural successes, I expect Africa to continue to be a net food importer from the rest of the world, on both a commercial and food aid basis, well into the 21st century.

WESTERN EUROPE

Western Europe is a mature, highly protected, high-income market, with limited expected growth in food consumption. Its high-income consumers are very quality conscious and are placing increasing demands upon their food system for organic foods and for labelling products for content and for indications of the processes used to grow the raw agricultural outputs involved.

Large investments in agricultural research and relatively high price supports have led to very high agricultural productivity levels by international standards. The European Union's price policy substantially stabilized the internal prices of most products, insulating farmers from international price shocks. Agricultural production has grown much faster than internal consumption over the past two decades, with substantial quantities being exported with the assistance of subsidies to offset the high internal support prices.

Government stocks have accumulated at various times as a result of price support operations and have often been donated as food aid to poor countries. A land set-aside programme and marketing quotas have been used to constrain overproduction stimulated by the high price supports. In response to both financial and political pressures, the EU's price support levels have been reduced significantly in recent years. Furthermore, in the Uruguay Round GATT agreement, the EU agreed to reduce its subsidies to agricultural exports.

Western Europe has had some of the most intensive crop and livestock production in the world in terms of livestock feeding rates and heavy fertilizer and agricultural chemical applications. This has led to adverse environmental consequences, especially in surface and ground water where nitrates and pesticide residues have accumulated. As a result, environmental activists have sought and achieved government regulations to reduce the adverse consequences of intensive farming.

In addition to environmental measures, a number of Western European countries also impose animal welfare regulations and other production process rules which prevent their farmers from adopting cheaper technologies available elsewhere in the world. Other regulations restrict the ability of European agricultural scientists to use certain powerful basic research tools to develop productivity-enhancing and cost-reducing technologies, or prevent European farmers from adopting such technologies developed in other countries. Biotechnology is a prime case in point. Such regulations tend to increase the unit cost of agricultural production and reduce the competitive position of European farmers. Their competitiveness has been further reduced as the value of price supports and marketing quotas has been capitalized into farm asset values, thereby raising the capital cost of farming in Europe relative to other countries.

An unanticipated consequence of the EU price supports was a loss in the domestic market for cereals in livestock rations. Imports of several cereal substitutes, in particular manioc, have been admitted free of tariffs. As a result, the relatively more highly priced cereals grown in Europe dropped out of least-cost ration formulations, to be replaced by manioc imported from Southeast Asia and by other cereal substitutes. This further increased the fraction of the EU's cereal production to be exported. As cereal price supports have been reduced in the last few years, more locally grown grain is going back into least-cost rations, reducing the quantity available for export.

As price supports have fallen and environmental regulations have been imposed, the intensity of agricultural input use has been reduced in Western Europe, and the volume of agricultural products available for export has fallen. As EU-grown cereals once again replace cereal substitutes in rations and as export subsidies are further reduced, this will limit agricultural export prospects. Therefore, despite the likely growth in world agricultural import demand in the next century, I expect that Western Europe's agricultural exports will be no larger, and will probably be smaller, than recently.

CENTRAL AND EASTERN EUROPE

Agriculture in Central and Eastern Europe underperformed relative to its potential under central planning during the socialist period. To appreciate the productive potential of this region, one has only to recall that the Ukraine, which has some of the world's most fertile soil, was the largest wheat-exporting country as recently as 1930. The former Soviet Union was a major cereals importer during the 1970s and 1980s.

During the socialist period, food consumption levels were quite high relative to other countries because of food price controls and large consumer subsidies for food. Processing was generally done by large-scale state monopolies, which paid little attention to consumer service or quality control.

Agricultural productivity levels have been low by international standards. This reflects inadequate economic incentives, weak applied research and technology transfer, and unreliable agricultural input supply systems. Production units were often extremely large, but with inadequate information-processing capacity and incentives available to manage effectively such large-scale units. Post-harvest losses were very large, with estimates as high as 40 per cent lost between the field and the consumer.

The agricultural sector of the former Soviet Union consistently performed weakly relative to its potential. While some observers point to the constraints imposed by its northern climate, such disadvantages have not prevented Canada, with a similar climate, having consistently been a major agricultural exporter. Basic agricultural science in the former Soviet Union was well respected by international standards but, by contrast, applied research and technology transfer was weak. For example, conversion rates of feed into meat were very low because rations were not balanced with enough protein. There needs to be a much stronger two-way flow of information between production agriculture and agricultural researchers, with stronger incentives to study real world problems of importance to the farm sector. Since the economic reforms, public investment in agricultural research has declined, and many formerly prestigious institutes have fallen on hard times.

Since the beginning of economic reforms in the former Soviet Union, per capita income has declined and the previously large food subsidies have been eliminated. As a result, food consumption has dropped. A reduction in agricultural production subsidies has resulted in output declining even more, especially in animal agriculture. The previously large periodic bulk commodity imports, particularly of feed, vanished. With the liberalization of imports, a number of high-value commodities, including meats and processed foods, are being imported. These could be produced in the region, but the consumers with purchasing power to buy such goods are dissatisfied with the domestically supplied items owing to lack of attention to customer service and quality control.

As the economies of Central and Eastern Europe have moved towards a market system, privatization of agriculture has begun, moving at varying speed. In many cases, property rights are still ill-defined, and not easily registered, protected, transferred or pledged as collateral against loans. Private input markets and sources of production credit have been slow to evolve. Rural roads and other marketing infrastructure, including bulk and refrigerated storage, have not been improved fast enough. Public monopolies have often replaced state monopolies, with no improvement in customer service or quality control. The old state-supported basic research system has collapsed for want to resources and has not been replaced by an effective applied research and technology transfer system. Public policy continues to reflect an anti-agricultural bias, with farm product prices depressed well below world market levels and farm input prices held well above world values.

Once the transition to a market economy is completed and these problems are addressed, there is no reason why the countries of Central and Eastern Europe cannot supply more of their internal consumption and be large exporters of a number of crop and animal products. The northern countries of Central Europe are well poised to do this soon, but those of the former Soviet Union and the southern countries of Central Europe appear to be a number of years away from achieving their potential. Nevertheless, as we contemplate the capacity of the world's farmers to produce twice or three times as much food as today at no higher price and without environmental damage, this region will have an important role to play.

SOUTH AMERICA

South America is the region of the world with the largest area of arable land available to be brought into agricultural production without causing deforestation or other environmental damage. While the destruction of the Amazon rain forests receives a great deal of media coverage, there is abundant non-erodible unforested land that can be brought into agricultural production in regions south of the Amazon. South America is a region of abundant land area relative to its population, and it has some of the world's most fertile soil in its southern cone. While it is an historically important agricultural exporting region, its performance has not matched its potential. Indeed, it has not done so for over 60 years. Many countries have had a strong anti-agricultural bias in their public policies, often failing to invest enough in rural services and infrastructure, and imposing heavy taxes on agricultural exports. Public policy so depressed returns in agriculture that it remained a very extensive industry with very low productivity per hectare. It was not profitable to adopt higher yielding varieties and to apply much fertilizer.

Exports have often been further taxed implicitly by overvaluation of exchange rates, and bouts of hyperinflation have caused flight of capital into agricultural land. Until recently, many countries followed import-substituting industrialization development strategies which created inefficient, but highly protected, non-agricultural sectors, which further increased farmers' costs. Recently, this situation has been changing rapidly in many Latin American countries. Economic reforms have liberalized their economics and an export-led growth strategy has been adopted. Agricultural export taxes have been cut, and several outstanding agricultural export success stories have occurred in the last 20 years, including soybeans and frozen concentrated orange juice in Brazil, fruits and wines in Chile, and cut flowers in Colombia.

Brazil, in particular, has made a major commitment to public investments in agricultural research. As a result, the huge *campo cerrado* region in the central west part of Brazil has been converted from an unproductive region of scrub vegetation to a highly productive producer of soybeans. This is but one example of how investments in agricultural research in the region are breaking natural bottlenecks to expansion of agricultural production to meet the growing world market demand.

It is important to recognize that the distribution of income and wealth is more skewed in South America than in other regions of the world. If an economic development strategy is adopted which successfully increases the incomes of the millions of poor people, there will be a large increase in demand for agricultural products within the continent, with a larger proportion of output being consumed internally rather than being exported. Nevertheless, the region is expected to supply a much larger volume of agricultural exports to satisfy the growing import demand in Asia and other areas in the 21st century.

OCEANIA

Oceania, which is dominated by Australia and New Zealand, has historically been a strong agricultural exporter, and is expected to continue to be in the future. In these mature, high-income markets, internal demand for agricultural products is growing slowly. Both the major countries have traditionally afforded their agriculture low levels of government assistance and New Zealand has now completely eliminated agricultural support. Historically, there has been strong investment in agricultural research, often paid for by taxes that farmers have imposed upon themselves. With high productivity levels, agricultural export potential is limited mainly by size and climatic constraints, in particular, low rainfall in much of Australia.

Both countries have significantly repositioned their agricultural sectors in recent years to take advantage of the rich and growing markets to the north, in Asia. Australia has experienced a large increase in dairy and cattle production, and New Zealand in dairy products and fruits. Both have shifted the balance of their exports from bulk commodities to higher-value agricultural exports whose demand is growing in the more affluent Asian markets. They will continue to be major agricultural exporters, but with limited expansion potential.

NORTH AMERICA

North America has a mature, high-income, slowly growing market for agricultural output. As a result, the region, which has invested large sums in agricultural research and is blessed with large expanses of fertile, well-watered soils and a relatively low-cost transport system, has become the largest agricultural exporter in the world. However, as in the other regions described, agriculture is also undergoing significant changes.

Canada has a large land area and sparse population. While agriculture might be expected to be constrained by its northerly climate, large investments in agricultural research and rural infrastructure made it possible for Canada to become a major agricultural exporter. Farming has also benefited from substantial government assistance. Prairie grain producers benefited from large subsidies to rail transport to ocean ports for almost a century, until two years ago, when the subsidy was eliminated. As a result, prairie agriculture is rapidly repositioning itself and has substantially increased the production of oilseeds, particularly canola, and fed livestock, particularly cattle and hogs, relative to wheat. The balance of exports has shifted towards higher-value products, particularly meats.

Canada has a highly protected segment of its agriculture which has been supported by production quotas, particularly dairy and poultry. The capitalized value of the quotas has raised the cost of production, and these sectors have stagnated technologically. As a result, they are not internationally competitive and are unable to expand to take advantage of growing international market opportunities. There are large political constraints to change in policies, though Canada has significantly reduced the assistance it provides to its agriculture and the sectors not subject to supply controls have responded quickly to greater world market opportunities, particularly in higher value products. We can expect Canada to be an even larger exporter of both bulk commodities and higher valued items in the future.

About half of the United States agriculture, in particular field crops and dairy, received significant levels of government support for more than 60 years, while the rest of American agriculture, including horticultural crops and the remainder of animal agriculture, was basically operating on free market principles. In 1996, Congress made the largest changes in agricultural policy since support began in 1933. Most subsidies linked to the volume of agricultural production were eliminated. This effectively removed the government from the business of stock holding. Set-asides associated with price supports were eliminated, except for long-term setting aside of erodible or environmentally fragile land in the Conservation Reserve Programme. Target prices and deficiency payments were eliminated. Even price supports to the dairy sector, which previously had been guarded by one of the most politically powerful lobbies, were cut. The effect of all of these changes was to move most of the previously protected parts of American agriculture to free market conditions. The changes have significantly increased farmers' planting flexibility and responsiveness to world market demand. While government programmes formerly provided substantial protection against risk, American farmers are well served by market institutions which permit them to manage risk at reasonable cost, in particular by means of well-developed futures markets.

While many parts of the United States are blessed with fertile soils and favourable climatic conditions, public and private investments in agricultural research and transport infrastructure account for significant parts of the international competitiveness of agriculture. In the last 20 years, public investments in agricultural research have declined in real terms, but there has been a large increase in private-sector efforts. In part, this reflects improvements in intellectual property protection which ensure that the private sector can reap the returns on its spending on research. Developments are focused particularly in biotechnology and in electronic sensors, information processing and geopositioning systems.

Another major recent innovation has been low-till agriculture or conversation tillage, which reduces labour and energy costs, conserves moisture and improves soil conservation. Applications of the electronic technologies in so-called 'precision farming' are starting to expand, and we are poised at the beginning of the biotechnology revolution in production agriculture. These technological changes are expected to increase productivity substantially and reduce unit costs of production, while having positive environmental effects as well. They should make it possible for the United States to further expand agricultural output and exports.

Several sectors of American agriculture are undergoing rapid structural change. While the transformation of the poultry industry lasted several decades, the corresponding process has occurred almost overnight in the pig industry and is occurring in parts of the dairy sector, particularly in the southwest. By bringing together state-of-the-art genetics, nutrition and disease control methods, with electronic sensors and information processing capacity, it has become possible to manage large-scale production units at high productivity and low unit cost. While animal waste disposal from large production units is a significant environmental challenge, there appears to be a comparative advantage in locating such units in wide open spaces away from concentrations of population.

In 1981, 90 per cent of agricultural exports were raw, bulk commodities. Today over half are high-value products like meats, fruits, vegetables, nuts and wine. I anticipate that in the future the United States will export a larger fraction of its maize and soybeans in the forms of meat and other animal products, including dairy products. It will also export large quantities of high-value products from the horticultural sector, but it will also continue to be a large exporter of food and feed grain and oilseeds.

GENERAL OBSERVATIONS

Simultaneously with rapidly growing demand for food due to population and income growth, the structure of demand is changing all over the world. In low-income countries, demand for meat and other animal products, fruits, vegetables, edible oils and sweets is expanding. In a number of high-income countries, consumers are wanting much more processing, packaging, food safety, nutrition, labelling of production processes and specialized products, like organic and vegetarian foods. This is requiring the marketing system to be able to preserve the identity of smaller lots of more differentiated products as they move through national and international markets. In any case, it is important to think of agriculture as part of a total food system, which exists to satisfy consumer demands.

A bifurcation of the size distribution of farms is occurring all over the world. We may soon reach the point where 20 per cent of the world's farms produce 80 per cent of the output. The high-producing segment will have high land–labour ratios and high capital–labour ratios. In fact, agriculture may be more capital-intensive than the rest of the economy. Such farms are generally in the more favourable agroclimatic zones. They use state-of-the-art production technologies and highly sophisticated management, including financial management, risk management and marketing strategies. Their unit cost of production is very low, and they earn their investors a competitive rate of return. These farms have the potential to increase output sharply at low unit cost of production.

The situation is very different for the 80 per cent of the world's farmers who collectively grow only 20 per cent of the output. They tend to be concentrated in areas of high population density, often in the less favourable agroclimatic zones. Many are located in hilly or mountainous areas. Typically, there is little physical capital in agriculture and little credit available. In many countries the governments have invested little in education, health or other rural social services. These areas are generally characterized by widespread poverty, with few non-agricultural income sources. There is simply not enough land per person available for everyone to grow enough for their own families' consumption and have enough more left to sell to provide a family income that exceeds the poverty level. Many of these regions can increase their food production. Increasing agricultural productivity can help, as can shifting their mix of products to high value per hectare crop and animal enterprises. However, without creating part- or full-time employment opportunities off the farm, difficult though that is, there is little hope of solving the problem of rural poverty and hunger in such areas. If their poverty is reduced, these rural areas may increase their food consumption at an even faster rate, reducing their food self-sufficiency. The transport and communications infrastructure necessary for successful rural economic development is also important to link local agricultural and food markets to national and international commerce.

Rapid changes are under way in national agricultural policies in many parts of the world. There is a widespread move to place greater reliance on market forces and to reduce the role of government. Many high-income countries are cutting the subsidies they have provided to their farmers, especially those that have been linked to the volume of production. They are making direct payments to farmers instead of distorting market prices. These measures are reducing inefficient production in high-cost producing areas and dumping of the resulting surpluses onto the world market. The availability of food aid is also falling. A number of low-income countries have reduced their government intervention in agriculture and permitted domestic agricultural prices to rise closer to world market levels. However, much more progress is needed to eliminate the anti-agricultural bias in their public policies.

In many low-income countries and economies in transition to a market economy, property rights are inadequately defined and protected. Many also lack an adequate commercial code and contract dispute settlement procedure for a well functioning private sector to emerge, create employment and contribute to agricultural and economic development.

Agricultural markets are becoming global in extent as the fraction of the world's agricultural output that moves through international markets grows. This has been facilitated by a tendency towards a freer and more open international trading environment. It was further advanced by the recent agreement under the Uruguay Round of multilateral trade negotiations under the GATT. This agreement officially acknowledged, for the first time, that domestic agricultural aid linked to the volume of production can distort trade, and it reduced and bound domestic subsidies. The agreement mandated a reduction in the volume and value of agricultural export subsidies and guaranteed a minimum access for imports to every market. The agreement also established that good scientific reasons must exist before sanitary and phytosanitary barriers can be imposed on imports.

With few exceptions, the agreement required that non-tariff barriers to imports be converted to tariffs, often referred to as 'tariffication'. This was important because quotas and other non-tariff barriers had effectively cut the link between internal and world market price in many countries. As a result, world prices were much more volatile in response to supply shocks than they would have been if all countries shared in the adjustment to the shocks. Tariffication fell short of its expectations in stabilizing world market prices, however, because the tariffs were set at prohibitively high levels under socalled 'tariff rate quotas'.

To achieve greater world market price stability, these tariff rates will have to be cut substantially and the quotas increased. The existence of undue international price instability makes countries less willing to rely on the world market for their food security. However, with modern global telecommunications and transport infrastructure, there is no reason why the world market should not be able to ensure national food security. For this to occur, countries have to be confident that they can be assured access to supply in any year, and that they can sell the goods in which they have a comparative advantage in the world market.

Today there is great public concern about protecting the quality of the environment. This often manifests itself in regulations which restrict agricultural production practices, particularly in the application of chemicals. It is unfortunate that sweeping generalizations are made concerning the environmental effects of chemical fertilizers and pesticides. Some are harmful, with long persistence in the environment and high mammalian and avian toxicity, yet many others are quite safe. Much of the modern chemistry is applied in small doses and quickly degrades into harmless by-products after it serves its purpose. Biological controls and integrated pest management are also important tools in controlling pests, but are not likely to suffice. Biotechnology, which some environmental activists also criticize, has great potential, not only to raise productivity, but also to breed in resistance to diseases, insects and other pests, reducing the need for chemical controls.

The greatest environmental danger, however, will occur if the best that science has to offer is not brought to bear on increasing productivity substantially from present levels. If we should attempt to double or triple agricultural production by doubling or tripling the area planted, this would require massive destruction of forests and, with them, wildlife habitat and biodiversity, and it would reduce the carbon sequestration capacity of the forests. The only acceptable alternative is to increase productivity on unforested fertile non-erodible soils and in animal production systems, and to reduce post-harvest losses.

Another important environmental problem of agriculture today is related to disposal of animal wastes without causing nitrate accumulation in the groundwater. A further constraint on production is likely to be the adequacy of water. Supply of water to farmers is often priced at zero. As a result, a great deal is wasted and there is little incentive to adopt water-saving technologies. Greater incentives for more efficient use will have to come in the 21st century, or water shortage will become a severe constraint on world food supply.

CONCLUSIONS

(1)   There is a limited amount of additional fertile, well-watered, non-erodible, unforested land available in the world that can be brought into agricultural production at low cost. This tends to be in North and South America and southern Africa. There is somewhat more land that can be brought into production with significant investment in reclamation or irrigation.

(2)   A great deal of much higher-productivity technology is available in the world than is at present in use. For example, there is widespread application of fertilizer with the wrong nitrogen–phosphorous–potash balance and frequent use of rations for poultry and livestock with a defective energy–protein mix. As a result, the productivity of input use is much below potential. In some cases, the technology transfer system is deficient, and farmers do not know better; in others, the marketing system, especially when it is in the public sector, does not make the proper inputs available. In many countries, public policy depresses output prices and increases input prices, so that it is not profitable to adopt higher-yielding technologies. Investments in transport infrastructure are essential to reduce the costs of input supply and product marketing. These observations are particularly appropriate for Africa and Eastern Europe.

(3)   We are living in the golden ages of the biological sciences and of information processing. There are numerous powerful research tools available to agricultural scientists to develop environmentally benign production technologies. However, just as these powerful tools were becoming available, the public sector often reduced its investments in agricultural research at both the national and international levels. The private sector has increased its spending, but not by as much as the public-sector cuts. In several countries, government regulations have restricted the ability of the private sector to apply some of the powerful new research tools, such as biotechnology. Many governments provide inadequate intellectual property protection, or so increase the cost of obtaining approval to sell the products of their research that the cost becomes prohibitive. Moreover, the private sector will not invest in minor products, or in regional staples of poor countries where there is a limited commercial market for the

products of research. Overall, there is substantial lack of investment in agricultural research relative to what is needed to raise productivity on fertile, non-erodible soils. Unless there is more effort, it will be necessary to expand production onto fragile lands, or currently forested lands, with great environmental damage. Additional investment in agricultural research should increase agricultural production potential on all continents and protect the environment.

(4)   It is important that governments which discriminate against their agricultural sectors reduce the anti-agricultural bias in their public policies. I am not advocating a policy of subsidizing agriculture. The experience of a number of high-income countries demonstrated that such policies have rarely helped the intended beneficiaries and have often resulted in unanticipated adverse environmental consequences. Rather, governments should give their farmers a level playing field in which they are not asked to pay more than the world price for their inputs and receive the world price for their outputs. There is an important role for public investments in rural infrastructure, human capital and agricultural research, and for government in registering and protecting property rights and providing a legal code and fair judicial system to support the efficient functioning of a market economy.

(5)   It is useful to note that very few countries in the world have solved the problem of rural poverty and food insecurity in agriculture. Increasing agricultural productivity can help, but it is not sufficient. It is necessary to augment farm income from non-farm sources either through part-time or full-time employment outside agriculture. Part of this can be in industries that supply inputs to farmers or add value to the raw products of the land. However, part of it needs to be in completely unrelated activity.

(6)   A larger fraction of the world's food production is likely to move through international trade in the 21st century. Research and technology transfer have the potential to raise agricultural productivity in all regions of the world. However, because the world's population and arable land are distributed among the continents in very different proportions, we expect that Asia, in particular, and Africa, to some extent, will be larger importers of food and agricultural products in the 21st century. North and South America and Central and Eastern Europe have the productive potential, if appropriately developed, to supply this import demand. As long as the international trading system is reasonably free, so that it openly transmits price signals to suppliers and demanders in all countries, there is no reason why the system cannot ensure food security to all.

ELMHIRST MEMORIAL LECTURE

YAIR MUNDLAK*

The Dynamics of Agriculture

Almost 50 years ago I read a report of a delegation of Israeli farmers and agronomists on their tour of United States agriculture. At the time, I was a young farm manager in a kibbutz and was very impressed by what I read about American productivity. This raised my curiosity and eventually resulted in my enrolment at the University of California. In the process I spent three semesters at Davis, near to our gathering, taking as many production courses in the various branches of agriculture as the system allowed me. Since then, I have spent a great deal of time thinking about the various aspects of productivity, gradually realizing that the subject is much broader in scope than the agrotechnical aspects of production and that the context of the discussion should be broadened accordingly. The factors affecting productivity also affect growth and are affected by growth – it is a two-way street. I have recently written a progress report on my efforts to understand the subject (Mundlak, forthcoming), and I am grateful for the honour and the opportunity to share some of the thoughts and findings spelled out in this volume with you.[1]

Agricultural economists are policy oriented. It is therefore appropriate to state at the outset that this is also the ultimate objective of this lecture, even though it may not be immediately obvious. To be faithful to this objective, we note that any policy recommendation should be guided by a target, and this raises the question about what we expect of agriculture. High on the list of public concerns are the following:

- food supply to meet the growing demand of a growing population;
- stability of food supply;
- low food prices to make food affordable to more people;
- maintaining future production capacity of agriculture (sustainability);
- protect the environment;
- provide farmers with 'fair' income and alleviate rural poverty;
- help the development of the economy at large;
- achieve it all efficiently.

*Hebrew University of Jerusalem, Rehovot, Israel and University of Chicago, USA. I am indebted to Rita Butzer, Donald Larson and Al Crego, all at the World Bank, for helping in our joint work on global agriculture. The more experience I have in empirical work, the more I learn to appreciate the impact of team effort on the final outcome.

How realistic and consistent are these objectives? I can think of only one way to answer this question, namely, to look at the evidence. It is on that basis that we can use our economic analysis to gain insight into the process. This should provide us with the foundation for understanding the dynamics of agriculture, needed for formulating a policy framework. To fully understand the process, it is not sufficient to look at global figures, because there is a considerable spread in performance among countries which conceals important information. This spread is not generated merely by a random process, so any relevant framework should be able to account for it. To present the evidence in a way that allows us to examine the changes over time, as well as the country spread, we will look at the empirical distribution of country performances. The number of countries on which the information was available varied with the measures of interest. The sample covers countries which account for most of the global food production and consumption and, as such, it is informative.

Given the time limitation, we will devote our lecture today to summarizing and organizing some pertinent evidence and ideas and to examining some of the important consequences. Any such undertaking builds on the evolution of our collective thinking that has been spanned by many writers. It is only natural that this evolution is selective in terms of what analysis survived and what has been shelved. However, it should be emphasized here that studies that have not stood the test of time have been valuable in helping us to choose the direction for our journey.

FOOD SUPPLY AND DEMAND

Beginning with supply, we look at agricultural production, summarized in Figure 1, which presents the distribution of the growth rates for 130 countries for the period 1967–92. We present two graphs, one giving equal weight to each country (uniform distribution), while the other assigns weights according to the country's production. The first one provides a straightforward picture of the cross-country spread, whereas the second one is an indicator of the global situation. During the sample period, output increased in practically all countries. The median growth rate was 1.92 per cent for the uniform distribution and 2.25 per cent for the weighted distribution. Thus 50 per cent of world output came from countries whose production grew at a rate of 2.25 per cent and higher. A comparison of the two graphs indicates that the growth rates were higher in countries with larger agricultural production. Some of the countries had a policy of curtailing production and, without it, their output would have increased even more. Thus the figures underestimate the production potential at the current prices.

From the point of view of demand, it is more meaningful to look at the growth in per capita output, presented in Figure 2. For the uniform distribution, the median growth rate per capita is –0.03 per cent. Taking into account the production weights, the median growth rate is 0.7 per cent. Output exceeded population growth in countries accounting for 81 per cent of world production.

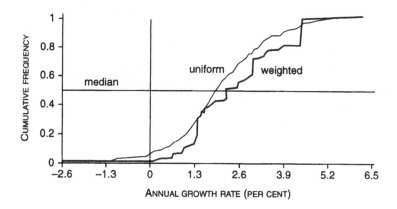

FIGURE 1   *Total agricultural production 1967–92 (130 countries)*

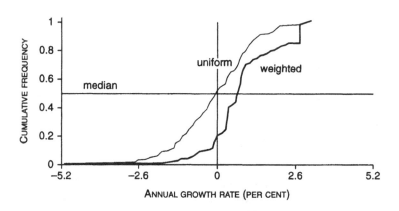

FIGURE 2   *Per capita agricultural production, 1967–92 (130 countries)*

Such a pronounced difference between the two distributions underlines the importance of distinguishing between country problems and global problems, as well as the danger of generalizing from a country performance to world performance: a trap that it is easy to fall into, as some writers and research institutes have demonstrated. Also the graphs in Figure 2 are steeper than the corresponding graphs in Figure 1, indicating that the variance of *total* growth rates is larger than that of *per capita* rates. This shows that many countries met a large part of growth in demand through home production. In fact, on the whole, production growth exceeded population growth somewhat because of the increase in demand due to the rise in income and fall of (real) prices. Clearly, this development is consistent with demand, rather than supply, derived production growth.

A more direct view of the role of demand is obtained by looking at the ratio of the growth rates of per capita agricultural output to that of total output, taken as a proxy measure for income. Figure 3 presents the distribution of such a ratio for 91 countries during 1960–92. The median values are 0.82 and 0.86 for the weighted and unweighted distributions, respectively. The spread of the distribution is smaller than that of Figure 2, implying that countries with a low growth rate in agriculture also suffered from a low growth rate in other sectors. This means that the factors contributing to poor performance were not necessarily agriculture-specific; hence the search for the remedy for poor performance should take us beyond the agronomy literature and our fixation with research.

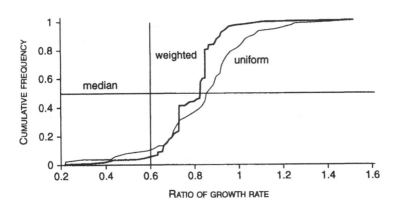

FIGURE 3   *Per capita GDP growth ratio agricultural to total, 1960–92 (91 countries)*

A fear of food shortage is well entrenched in the thinking of society. It is a subject of interest to economists as well as to other social scientists. Our comparative advantage is to use the crystal ball (not always a clean one) provided by economics. Placing it on the back mirror, what do we see? Has supply lagged demand, as some believe is a fate we have been cursed with? If this were the case, agricultural prices would have risen, but this did not

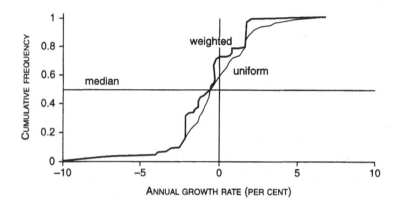

FIGURE 4   *Agricultural prices, 1967–92 (112 countries)*

happen, as can be seen in Figure 4, which presents the distribution of the rates of change of agricultural prices, deflated by the domestic consumer price indices. The median of the uniform distribution is –0.45 per cent per year, and, when we weigh the countries by their importance in world production, the median changes to –0.61 per cent per year. Note that the vertical line at a zero growth rate cuts the graph of the weighted distribution at 0.71, indicating that 71 per cent of the world total in the period 1967–92 was produced in countries where real prices fell.

Thus the recent experience, which generalizes well to the entire postwar period and beyond, is of faster growth in supply compared with demand.[2] To place this impressive performance into historical perspective, we note that world food supply sustained a world population of one-half of a billion in 1650, four billion in 1974 and is expected to support eight billion in 2020 (Fogel, 1997).

PRODUCTIVITY

The foregoing review reaffirms what is a common knowledge, that agriculture demonstrated a remarkable growth record in the postwar period. What determines the pace of this growth is a subject on which the unanimity disappears, but this is the real question on which we need an answer in order to form a judgment about the feasibility of repeating past performance in the foreseeable future. This lack of unanimity reflects measurement and conceptual problems in the interpretation of the data. Such a situation invites personal views and beliefs into the discussion. An improvement in the precision of our measure-

TABLE 1 *Summary information:[1] rates of growth[2]*

Variable	Countries	Uniform distribution Deciles			P(x=0) (per cent)	Weighted distribution Deciles			P(x=0) (per cent)
		1	5	9		1	5	9	
Output	130	0.37	1.92	3.87	6.1	0.93	2.25	4.44	0.5
Real price	112	−2.4	−0.45	2.21	59	−2.4	−0.61	1.58	71
Per capital output	130	−1.6	−0.03	1.4	51	−1.6	0.7	2.79	19
Output: ag/na[3]		0.82				0.86			
Labour/land	87	−3.2	0.04	1.75	49	−3.1	0.09	1.64	49
Output/land	87	−0.13	1.8	3.6	13	1.3	1.92	3.8	2
Output/labour	87	−0.5	2.0	4.6	16	0.8	2.6	4.9	13
Labour prod. na/ag	88	−4.6	−1.6	0.8	80	−3.9	−1.1	2.0	60

Variable	Countries	Uniform distribution Deciles			P(x=0) (per cent)
		1	5	9	
Land	132	−1.8	0.4	2.1	35
Labour	148	−3.3	0.56	2.1	40
Capital	56	−1.7	1.05	6.35	29
Fixed capital	56	−0.64	2.1	8.7	16
Fixed capital/labour	56	−2.62	2.93	8.5	27
Fixed capital/output	56	−1.7	1.6	4.9	27
Fixed capital/Labour (economy)	56	−0.6	2.25	7.9	13
Migration rates	148	0.5	1.97	3.8	1
Fixed capital	37	1.36	5.3	8.9	8
Land	37	−0.54	0.04	0.77	46
Labour	37	−3.55	0.29	2.7	43

Notes: [1]Unless indicated otherwise, the data are for agriculture. The sources are Mundlak, Larson and Crego (1997) and Mundlak, Larson and Butzer (1997).
[2]The growth rates were calculated from a regression of the logs of the variables on time. The data differ from those reported for the 56 countries in terms of deflators used to obtain constant terms. In the smaller sample, to convert from nominal to 1990 US dollars, the data are deflated by the US agricultural GDP deflator, whereas in the larger sample the US total GDP deflator was used. The growth rates from the agricultural GDP deflated capital are larger.
[3]Ag stands for agriculture, na stands for non-agriculture. Output ag/na is the output ratio of ag to na. Labour prod. is the average labour productivity.

ments of the underlying processes should help us in reducing the scope for a belief-rooted debate. It is therefore necessary to review what is at stake if we want to obtain a better understanding of the process.

A good starting point is to review the changes in inputs. Table 1 summarizes the information on the growth rates of the variables covered in the discussion. It provides information on the first, fifth (median) and ninth deciles as well as on the proportion of the observations with negative values. Thus, during 1960–92, cultivated land declined in 35 per cent of the countries and increased in the remainder, with a median annual growth rate of 0.4 per cent. The figures for agricultural labour are quite similar: a median growth rate of 0.56 per cent with 40 per cent of the countries displaying a decline in labour. Thus the slower growth of labour and land compared with that of output implies a growth of (partial) labour and land productivity. The weighted distribution of these two measures is presented in Figure 5 in order clearly to bring out the pervasiveness of the partial productivity growth.

The partial productivity improvement reflects changes in inputs and technology. The major input that is missing from the discussion so far, as well as from most of the writings on the subject, is capital. This omission can be attributed to the fact that information is limited and not much work has been done to nail down the importance of capital in agricultural production, particularly in cross-country comparisons. A recent effort to alleviate this deficiency resulted in a series for capital stock in agriculture for 56 countries (Crego *et al.*, 1997). The series presented here is that of fixed capital, mainly structures and equipment. It is not comprehensive, in that it does not contain capital which originated in agriculture, such as orchards and livestock. For this sample, the median growth rate of fixed capital in agriculture during 1960–92 was 2.1 per cent and only 16

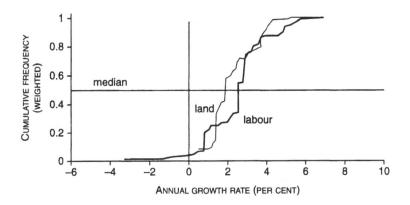

FIGURE 5   *Labour and land productivity, 1960–92 (87 countries)*

per cent of the countries realized a decline. It thus appears that capital grew faster than labour and land, as well as output. For this sample, the median growth rate of capital–output is 1.6 per cent and in only 27 per cent of the countries was this rate negative (namely, output grew faster than capital).

On the face of it, the big cross-country spread in the data poses two questions. First, what does it tell us about the sources of productivity growth, and second, what determines the spread of the inputs and their rate of change? We start with the first subject.

AGRICULTURAL PRODUCTION FUNCTIONS

Growth accounting requires aggregating the growth rates of all inputs, where the weights of the aggregation are the production elasticities. The elasticities are unknown and are therefore replaced either by estimates obtained from production functions or by factor shares, as originally used by Solow (1957). The common practice has been to use production function estimates. This is straightforward, possibly giving reasonably accurate results, when the technology is homogeneous and easily represented by a production function. The problem is that under heterogeneous technology the outcome can be very misleading, as we shall now argue and demonstrate.

In a world of heterogeneous technology, we have to explain how producers choose the techniques they actually employ (implemented technology) from the pool of all available techniques (available technology). This is the key issue for the empirical analysis and also for our thinking on the big issues of growth and development. The underlying premise is that producers at any time choose the techniques to be employed together with the inputs and outputs. The outcome of this optimization is a joint decision on the implemented technology and on the input allocation to the various techniques. The state variables that determine this choice can be grouped into environment (physical, political and so on), incentives (such as expected prices and risk), constraints (for example, capital goods, credit and infrastructure) and the available technology. Data are seldom reported by techniques and in general we estimate a production function from data aggregated over techniques. Such an aggregation creates an identification problem, because, apart from errors in optimization, the only way the inputs change is in response to changes in the state variables. But a change in those affects the choice of techniques and therefore may change the implemented technology. Thus the corresponding change in output is the result of the change in both the implemented technology and in the inputs. Hence the coefficients of the empirical production function reflect both changes.

To illustrate, consider the appearance of a new wheat variety whose performance is better than that of the traditional one. The variety requires irrigation, so that the marginal productivity of water function associated with the new variety is different from that of the traditional variety. Consequently, both the coefficient of water in an aggregate production function and the quantity of water used will alter with the variety composition of the sample. This is a metaphoric example of the more general case where the implemented technology is determined by the availability of capital.[3] But this is not the end of story.

The mere appearance of a new technique which is both capital-intensive and more productive raises the shadow price of capital. This in turn attracts investment to the sector and thus expands the capital stock. The additional capital increases the employment of the new varieties, thereby changing the implemented technology. When the sample consists of observations generated by different technologies, the coefficient of capital will not only capture the productivity of capital under a constant technology, but will also represent the change in technology. This is our problem, because the whole idea of growth accounting is to separate the contribution of inputs from that of technical change. The separation fails when the weights for the exercise are taken from an empirical aggregate production function.

Not independently, this view also sheds light on the pace of adoption of the new technique. If it dominated the traditional one, farmers would be expected to adopt the new variety once convinced that change could be profitable. But experience shows that it often takes a long time to shift to the new variety. Such a delayed response can be attributed to a lack of resources needed to implement the change. For instance, when the farmer does not have water or irrigation facilities, there is no chance of implementing the water-intensive technical change until the necessary investment is made. That clearly needs resources. This illustrates how the implemented technology depends on resource availability. A similar illustration can be offered to show the dependence on other state variables. It is thus clear that the implemented technology is not identical with the available technology. The first represents the current practice, whereas the latter represents the frontier. The movement to the frontier depends on resource availability as well as on the other state variables. We return to this below, but we first continue to trace the implications for empirical study.

In empirical analysis, there is a way out of the identification problem which (perhaps we should say, ironically) depends on errors in the optimization. Input variations, whether or not chosen optimally, trace the production function if they are generated by shocks, rather than by the state variables that affect the choice of techniques. The inputs trace a given technology and thereby solve the identification problem. In this case, given the implemented technology, the choice of inputs fails to fulfil the first-order conditions. An empirical application of this approach is carried out by approximating the implemented technology by a type of Cobb–Douglas production function where the coefficients themselves are functions of the state variables. In this formulation, a change in the state variables causes a change in the aggregate production function. However, errors in the optimization affect the level of inputs without having a similar effect on the implemented technology.

In estimating a production function we have to include variables that represent the level of technology, so that the input variations will allow us to estimate their pure contribution and not that of technology. The same applies to other state variables. The estimation of an aggregate production function where the coefficients are functions of the state variables requires knowledge of the factor shares. Such an application of the state variables requires knowledge of the factor shares. Such an application is demonstrated in analysis for Argentina, Chile and Colombia and we will return to this below.[4] Unfortunately, data on factor shares in agriculture are not readily available for most countries, and it is therefore impossible to apply the approach to cross-country studies in the same way that it was applied to the country studies. Thus, if we want to utilize the cross-country spread in the data, we will have to examine a second-best approach. This will also help us to reinterpret some known findings and conclusions in the literature.

Cross-country studies

Analysis of agricultural production functions began in 1944 with the work of Tintner (1944) and Tintner and Brownlee (1944), followed by Heady (1944), all of whom used farm data. Subsequent work was extended to cover aggregate data while, in 1955, Bhattacharjee presented the first analysis based on cross-country data. The underlying notion for these early studies was that all observations were generated from the same production function. In an effort to get a definitive view, Heady and Dillon (1961, ch. 17) compared the result of Bhattacharjee's study with numerous others and discovered that the notion of a homogeneous technology was elusive and they warned against the dangers associated with the use of a global production function (p. 633).

The use of cross-country data to estimate a global production function gained impetus with the work of Hayami (1969; 1970) and Hayami and Ruttan (1970) which sought to explore the causes of cross-country differences in agricultural productivity. Like most of the current work, the underlying assumption in these studies is that all countries use the same production function. As further evidence that this assumption does not hold, it is sufficient to follow Heady and Dillon and to realize that there are considerable disparities between the results obtained in such cross-country studies and those obtained in country studies.[5] To provide a numerical background to the discussion, Table 2 summarizes results obtained in a series of cross-country studies.[6] To anticipate what is coming, we recall that studies which use data for a single period are based on cross-country comparisons and as such provide estimates for the *between-country* regression for that particular year. Also studies which use panel data and introduce time dummies (*within-time* regressions) but not country dummies provide *between-country* regressions for the sample period. Studies with panel data which contain country dummies (with or without time dummies) provide estimates for the *within-country* (or *within-country and time*) regression.

In a nutshell, Table 2 shows that the between-country estimates of land elasticity are low in absolute terms and relative to estimates obtained from the within regression.[7] Two measures of capital have been used in most studies: machinery and livestock. The elasticity of machinery varies around 0.1 (a little higher for the between-country regression) and that of livestock concentrates in the range of 0.2–0.3.[8] The estimates for the labour elasticity are less stable. Why should be estimates vary accordingly to what dummy variables, if any, are introduced? The answer is that they should not, apart from statistical error, when the technology is homogeneous and shared by all countries throughout the sample period. However, they should vary if the technology is heterogeneous. In this case, the empirical regression is an estimate of the implemented

TABLE 2 *Comparison of results*

	Bhattacharjee	Hayami & Ruttan	Evenson & Kislev	Yamada & Ruttan	Antle	Hayami & Ruttan	Nguyen	Evenson & Kislev	Mundlak & Hellinghausen
Date of study	1955	1970	1975	1980	1983	1970	1979	1975	1982
Sample									
Number of countries	22	37	36	41	43	36	40*	36	58
Time period	1949	1960	1955, 60, 65, 68	1970	1965	1955, 60, 65	1955, 60, 65, 70, 75	1955, 60, 65, 68	1960, 65, 70, 75
Estimation method	OLS	OLS	OLS	OLS	PCR	OLS	OLS	OLS	PCR
Data specification	S, N	M, N	M, N	M, N	S, N	M, PW	M, N	M, N	M, N
Fixed effects included						year	year	country	country†
Elasticities									
Structures & equipment/ machinery/tractors		0.12	0.10	0.11		0.11	0.14	0.06	0.07
Livestock & orchards/livestock		0.23	0.30	0.23	0.14**				
Land	0.42	0.08**	0.04**	0.02**	0.16	0.28	0.33	0.35	0.19
Labour	0.28	0.41	0.23	0.33	0.38	0.07	0.02**	0.14	0.16
Fertilizer	0.29	0.12	0.10	0.24	0.07**	0.40	0.39	0.03**	0.46
Irrigation						0.14	0.10	0.09	0.11
Schooling/general education		0.32**		0.08**	0.25**	0.24	0.10**		0.01
Technical education		0.14	0.04	0.14		0.12	0.17	0.00**	
Research and extension			0.14		0.17			0.07	
Infrastructure					0.21				
Sum of input elasticities	0.99	0.96	0.77	0.93	0.75	1.00***	0.98	0.67	1.00***

Notes: *sample is not balanced, $n = 183$ for Nguyen study. ** not significant at $P = 0.05$ for one-tailed test. *** homogeneity constraint imposed. †Country effects on slopes and intercept. OLS and PCR are ordinary least squares and principal components regressions. S and M represent single year observations and multi-year averages. PW represents per-worker averages of national aggregated data; N represents national aggregates.

technology and consequently the coefficients are functions of the state variables which vary across countries and over time.

Numerical results

To illustrate this claim, we use results from Mundlak, Larson and Butzer (1997) where panel data were analysed covering 37 countries for the period 1970–90. The sample is a sub-sample of the 57 countries for which data were available on capital as well as on the other variables included in the analysis. For this sub-sample, the distribution of the growth rates of the three inputs is given in Figure 6. The median growth rate of fixed capital is 5.3 per cent, much higher than the rate for labour and land. Three regressions are estimated: between country (where the variables are country means), between time (the variables are year means, common to all countries) and within-country and time (the variables are deviations from the country and time means). The three groups of variables are orthogonal to each other and therefore the three regressions are estimated as a part of one regression.[9]

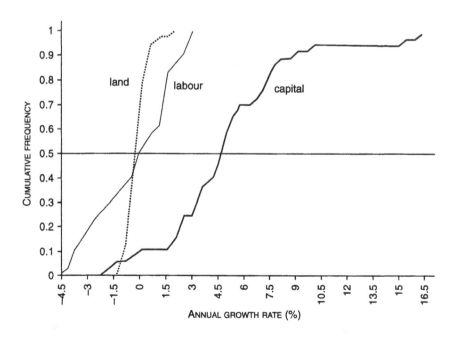

FIGURE 6   *Agricultural fixed capital, land and labour, 1970–90 (37 countries)*

A decomposition of the total sum of squares of the variables in the sample to the three components shows a remarkable result: the between-country variability accounts for about 97 per cent of the total variability in the inputs (Table 3). This explains the tendency of some writers to pay more attention to the between-country regression. This is a natural position to take when all countries use the same production function, but it is a wrong one to take when they do not. Indeed, the within-country and time deviations account for only 1–2 per cent of the total sum of squares of the inputs, but they also account for a similar fraction of the total output sum of squares. Thus there is no *a priori* reason to assume that the results are less precise, and this is backed up by the results which are presented in Table 4.

In addition to the inputs, three state variables to represent technology are included: *schooling*, measured by the mean years of education of the total

TABLE 3   *Growth rates and the decomposition of the sum of squares*

Variable	Average annual growth rate (%)	Decomposition of the sum of squares (expressed as a percentage of total)		
		SSB(t)	SSB(i)	SSW(it)
Output				
GDP	3.82	2.49	96.17	1.34
Inputs				
Capital	4.25	2.67	95.77	1.56
Structures & equipment	5.42	3.00	95.24	1.76
Livestock & orchards	2.17	0.96	97.83	1.21
Land	0.12	0.00	99.95	0.05
Labour	−0.04	0.01	99.35	0.64
Fertilizer	3.04	1.14	96.76	2.09
Technology				
Schooling	1.80	4.14	93.48	2.38
Peak yield	1.90	58.10	24.64	17.27
Development	−0.29	1.41	94.18	4.41
Yield gap		8.97	30.91	60.12
Prices				
Relative prices	−0.30	3.01	41.98	55.00
Price variability		2.48	15.78	81.75
Inflation		2.38	10.65	86.97
Per labour output and inputs				
GDP		2.67	95.00	2.33
Capital		2.14	95.46	2.40
Structure & equipment		2.17	95.86	1.98
Livestock & orchards		1.14	96.78	2.07
Land		0.01	99.41	0.58
Fertilizer		0.98	97.78	1.24

labour force (Nehru *et al.*, 1993); *peak yield*, a country-specific index of peak yield to represent the implemented agricultural technology; and *development*, the ratio of the country's total GDP per capita in US dollars to total US GDP per capita. The price block consists of the *relative price* calculated as the ratio of the agricultural GDP deflator to the manufacturing GDP deflator, lagged one period; *price variability* is a moving standard deviation of the *relative price* from the previous three years; and *inflation* is the rate of change in the total GDP deflator. The physical environment is represented by two measures, *potential dry matter* (PDM) and a measure of *water availability* (WPD). These are not critical for our current discussion and we therefore skip the description of their construction.

Table 4 consists of the three blocks. The first is the within-time and country regression. Taking deviations from time and country means implies that the observations are taken from the more stable, or core, technology pertinent to world agriculture for the relevant period. The second block presents the between-time estimates obtained from a short time-series of the sample means for each year. This represents the time-series component, common to all countries and as such it captures the impact of changes in the available technology. The last block presents the between-country estimates based on the between-country variations which constitute the major component of the total sum of squares. Statistical tests do not reject the hypothesis of constant returns to

TABLE 4   *Base model*

Variable	Within time and country Estimate	t-score	Between time Estimate	t-score	Between country Estimate	t-score
Inputs						
Capital	0.37	6.90	1.03	6.01	0.34	13.13
Land	0.47	3.78			−0.03	−2.82
Labour	0.08		−0.16	−0.16	0.26	13.67
Fertilizer	0.08	1.53	0.14	0.33	0.43	21.91
Technology						
Schooling	0.09	0.55	−0.28	−0.06	0.02	0.52
Peak yield	0.83	3.80	−0.32	−0.07	0.06	4.19
Development	0.52	3.36	−0.21	−0.33	0.31	2.97
Prices						
Relative prices	0.04	1.78	0.02	0.09	0.01	1.95
Price variability	−0.03	−0.97	−0.07	−0.26	−0.08	−2.82
Inflation	−0.00	−0.75	0.04	0.71	0.07	4.25
Environmental						
Potential dry matter					0.16	2.68
Water availability					0.44	7.96

Note: R-square for 777 obs. = 0.9696

scale. Also the hypothesis that one of the blocks of state variables (technology, incentives and environment) can be eliminated is rejected.

The results show clearly that the three blocks represent three different processes described by very different coefficients. Perhaps the more interesting result is the elasticity of capital, 0.37 in the *within* regression, 1.03 in the *between-time* regression and 0.34 in the *between-country* regression. The coefficient in the *between-time* regression is particularly high, and this is consistent with the important role of physical capital in the implementation of changes in the available technology. The land elasticity in the *within* regression is 0.47, which is relatively high. This gives no support for the idea, originally expressed by Schultz (1953) and echoed by others (for example, Kawagoe and Hayami, 1985) that land has lost importance in modern agriculture. Indeed, the land coefficient is basically zero in the between-country regression. This shows that the techniques used by the more productive countries were land saving. However, with a given technology, and this goes for modern technology as well, the contribution of land to output is substantive.[10]

The striking result is the big difference in the fertilizer elasticity between the between-country and the within regressions. A value of 0.08, obtained in the within regression for the elasticity of fertilizers, may seem to be low, but this is not the case. A point estimate of 0.08 means that about 8 per cent of the 'within' changes in agricultural output are attributed to fertilizers. This result is obtained for the aggregate agricultural output, whereas fertilizers are used only on plant products. It is likely that a production function for plant products alone would show a larger elasticity for fertilizers. Thus a value of 0.08 for aggregate output may even be rather high. One possibility is that fertilizers capture the impact of other chemicals and, more generally, the modern inputs, as indicated above. With this interpretation, the fertilizer elasticity obtained in the between-country regression is excessively high to represent a production elasticity of a given production function. Instead, it can serve as another illustration where a change in the variable is associated with a change in the implemented technology. That is, the improvement in the implemented technology is fertilizer using. At the same time, it is also capital using but land saving. However, it is less capital using than the core technology, in that its capital elasticity is somewhat lower.

The 'within' regressions were obtained under the constraint of constant returns to scale. The constraint was tested empirically and it is not rejected. The 'between' regressions are unconstrained, and it is interesting that the sum of elasticities of the inputs of the between-country regression is practically one. This is in contrast to the results of those cross-country studies which show increasing returns to scale (for instance, Kawagoe *et al.*, 1985, p. 120). This indicates that our specification succeeds in capturing the impact of cross-country differences in technology and thus eliminates the spurious result of increasing returns to scale.[11] Such results have led to erroneous calculations of the total factor productivity in cross-country, as well as in cross-state, studies.

Technology

The technology variables play a dual role in the analysis. First, they serve as technology shifters and as such reduce, or eliminate completely, the bias of the estimated input coefficients caused by the correlation of inputs and technology. Second, we can examine empirically how well they describe the data and thereby guide us in the search for appropriate technology indicators.

Turning to the individual components, the peak yield serves well as a shifter of the agricultural productivity, as measured by the core technology, with an elasticity of about 0.8. The level of development of the country relative to the United States is also an important explanatory variable of agricultural productivity. Note that the contribution of this variable is over and above that of the peak yield, which shows that the yield level is not the only indicator; first, the yield variable does not represent the productivity in livestock production which accounts for about one-third of output; and second, there is scope for improving efficiency under a given technology by coming closer to the frontier, as represented by the performance of the United States.

The between-time regression shows that none of the technology variables was important in accounting for the change in agricultural productivity over time. The work is done by physical capital. The implication is far reaching – even though schooling and peak yields increased with time, we find no evidence that they contributed directly to the benefits harvested from improvements in the available technology. It was capital availability that was crucial for the countries to take full advantage of the available technology. This sheds light on the importance of physical capital in accounting for the changes in agricultural productivity in the study period.

The results are different for the between-country regression, where the level of development is important in accounting for the productivity variations. This is a statement of the importance of the various attributes of the overall level of development of a country in determining the level of agricultural productivity. This may also be the reason for schooling appearing to be irrelevant. To the extent that schooling matters, it may have an indirect effect through the development variable. However, to what extent schooling matters and how it can be measured using aggregate data is still an open question, one recently highlighted by Pritchett (1996).

Prices

The test of the null hypothesis that the price block can be omitted from the analysis is rejected. However, the quantitative effect of prices is small and this reflects the fact that the channels for the price effect, the level of inputs and the choice of technology, are represented by explanatory variables. But these are affected by prices, as we shall see below, and consequently a major channel for the effect of prices on productivity is through the effect on the stock of inputs.

Two measures of market risk, inflation and relative price volatility, dampen agricultural production (as seen by the 'within' estimates); however, both effects are quantitatively small. The coefficient of the measure of price volatility is negative, but it is significantly different from zero only in the between-country regressions. The effect of inflation is ambiguous, in that it is negative but insignificant in the 'within' regression, and it is positive and significant in the between-country analysis.

Additional evidence

We can now compare the results in Table 4 to those in the literature as summarized in Table 2.[12] Most of the studies in Table 2 are strictly cross-country and as such are comparable to the between-country results in Table 4. The similarity is in the low land elasticity, and also the sum of the elasticities of machines and livestock is close in most cases to the value of 0.34 obtained for capital in the between-country regression. This similarity is consistent with our interpretation that these studies describe only the between-country changes; hence they provide a limited and incomplete picture of the production process. In any case, they do not provide coefficients of a stable production function and, consequently, do not provide the appropriate weights for growth accounting, as they were intended to do.

It is always useful to check the results against all available information. The Global Trade Analysis Project (GTAP) reported factor shares of land and labour in agriculture for 1992 for 24 regions (Hertel, 1997). The data needed to compute factor shares are not available for all countries. The more accessible data are on labour costs, and these were used as a pivot to generate the other shares relying on 'other sources' where available (ibid., p. 113). Mundlak, Larson and Butzer (1997) applied the appropriate regional data to the 37 sample countries and reported the empirical distributions. The median values of these distributions are 0.25 for land, 0.31 for labour and 0.42 for capital. Another source of information is the OECD, which reports 'compensation of employees' by sectors. Computing labour shares from these series for 19 countries for the period 1970–90 (for seven countries the period is somewhat shorter) yields a median value of 0.19. The labour share in these statistics is somewhat higher than the estimated elasticity from the within regression. Nevertheless, these values are conveniently close to the within estimates and are conspicuously far away from the between-country estimates. This seems to provide independent support for our interpretation.

TOTAL FACTOR PRODUCTIVITY

Using the within time and country elasticities from Table 4 and the median growth rates from Table 3, we infer that 'aggregate input' and 'total factor productivity residual technical change' account for about one half each of the total growth in output. This evaluation of the contribution of aggregate input is substantially smaller than the rate reported in the cross-country studies referred to above. These studies use the between-country estimates where the weight of fertilizers is high and that of land is low. The median growth rate of land in the sample was 0.12 per cent and that of fertilizers was 3.04. The difference in the elasticities of these two variables accounts for much of the difference in the growth accounting. In addition, the studies reporting increasing returns to scale overstate the role of inputs and understate the role of technical change.

How well do we capture the residual technical change in terms of the state variables included in the within regression? To answer this question, we multiply the median values of the rate of change of the state variables (Table 3) by their elasticities (Table 4) to show that the contribution to growth for schooling was 0.16 per cent and for peak yield 1.58 per cent, whereas the relative price and development had small negative effects. Obviously, the peak yield appears to be the main carrier of the technology. Perhaps we should recall the purpose of introducing the state variables, including the technology block. It was to capture the changes in the implemented technology in order to measure factor productivity net of the technical change. The results indicate that we have been quite successful. Thus the peak yield captures about 83 per cent of the residual, and only 0.37 percentage points of the total growth of 3.82 per cent (or 10 per cent) is not represented by variables in the regression.

A completely different picture is obtained by using the weights from the between-time regression. The elasticity of capital is 1.03 and thus, using the median growth rates, capital more than exhausts the growth in output. The over exhaustion is compensated for by a decline in the other variables. Thus the global picture is that the changes in the available technology did not constitute a constraint to growth in output. The pace of the implementation of the changes in the available technology was determined by the pace of capital accumulation. How do we account for the difference in the results between the two calculations? The exercise using the within estimates evaluated the contribution of the inputs along a 'stable' production function, whereas the exercise using the between-time estimates gave a mixed effect of changes on the production function and across production functions. The latter was dominating.

To have continuous progress in the implemented technology, it is necessary to have a change in the available technology. Deep in our minds (or hearts) we all know the means of achieving it: research and education. But our knowledge is more limited than we would like to admit. As economists, we would like to relate the results in output to inputs, and in this case the 'output' is innovations. Then we can apply our calculus and compute the social optimum for research. Unfortunately, it does not work this way when it comes to the production of new knowledge pertinent to changes in the available technology. In other words, there is no production function of knowledge, a concept that takes on different names, such as the innovation frontier. A basic property of a production function is that, apart from random variations, the relationship between inputs and output obtained in one sample can be reproduced in another. We refer to this as the repetitious property. It is this property which justifies the study of a production function using data from a given sample, because the results can be applied to other cases having the same underlying environment. But this property is absent when it comes to the production of innovations. It is not profitable (and hence makes no sense) to reinvent the wheel or other existing knowledge. New research aims at new discoveries, and therefore the input–output relationships of the past have no predictive power for the future.

Nevertheless, there is a basic property of production functions that is still pertinent here, namely 'monotonicity', but this is as far as we can go. Discoveries are to a large extent random and this is particularly true for such discoveries that move societies to new epochs, in the language of Simon Kuznets. Consequently, there is always a surprise element in the appearance of new techniques in a *given* year, and this is the reason for the fact that some of the technical change, involved in the way that we calculate the total factor productivity (TFP), appears as a residual.

To sum up, the more we invest in efforts to obtain new discoveries, the more likely it is that we will get a larger output, but the distribution of this relationship does not exist *ex ante*. However, once the new knowledge becomes available, we can encourage its implementation through resource use and the generation of a conducive environment for such an implementation. This then brings us to examine what affects factor supply.

FACTOR SUPPLY

The joint decision concerning implemented technology and factor demand assigns an important role to factor supply. When total resources are given, their supply to the various uses is determined by a convergence rule which, to emphasize its nature and implications, we name the 'economic law of gravity' (ELG). The weak (or static) version says that, other things equal, resources flow in the direction of higher returns. The strong (or dynamic) version says that the rate of flow is monotonically increasing in the income gap between the source and destination. This law, simple as it is, has far-reaching implications, and it is applicable to all factors and can be observed at all levels – firm, industry, sectoral, national and global. The statement is conditioned on 'other things equal', a condition that covers many factors such as risk, cost of mobility, friction, political and institutional settings, cultural differences and the like. These factors determine, not only the existence of the flow, but also its pace in the sense that the larger is the gap, the stronger is the flow. Thus we see capital flows to developing countries where the capital–labour ratio is low and therefore the rate of return is high. However, this flow stops way before the equalization of the capital–labour ratios across countries is accomplished. Furthermore, this is not a one-way street and capital also flows to high-income countries where the environment is more stable, investment is more secure, but also where high productivity more than offsets the high capital–labour ratio to result in higher returns. The same process holds true with respect to resource flow between agriculture and non-agriculture.

The validation of the ELG is a challenge to empirical analysis. Sometimes the process is obvious and in other cases it requires more sophisticated effort to unveil it. We know more about the mobility of labour than about that of capital. For instance, we explain the universal phenomenon of off-farm migration by citing the prospects of better living outside agriculture for the migrants or their children. A recent study based on all the available country data for the period 1950–90 reaffirmed previous findings that the pace of off-farm migration is determined by the income differential between agriculture and non-agriculture

(Larson and Mundlak, 1997). The larger is the gap, the faster is the migration rate. The importance of this study is in its wide country and time coverage, which makes the findings universal.

There are fewer studies on agricultural investment, let alone the intersectoral flow of capital. This reflects in part the lack of data on agricultural capital and in part the difficulties encountered in the econometrics of investment. The data shortage also restricts our knowledge of more basic facts related to agricultural capital, and it is therefore useful to look at some of the findings of Crego *et al.* (1997). Figure 7 presents the distribution of the ratio of fixed investment to output in agriculture, Figure 8 shows the share of agriculture in total fixed investment, Figure 9 has the ratio of fixed capital to output in agriculture, while Figure 10 deals with the distribution of the capital–labour ratio in agriculture.

Keeping in mind the preliminary nature of the data, we can summarize some of the evidence.

- The share of agriculture in total investment, and in total capital, is smaller than its shares in total output and in the labour force. This is an indication that the capital–labour ratio in agriculture is smaller than in non-agriculture. This is also consistent with the fact that the capital–output ratio in agriculture is smaller than that for the economy as a whole.
- The share of agriculture in total investment has been declining since 1970, the first year in the data base.
- As in agriculture, there is a decline in the share of manufacturing in total investment and the capital stock. This indicates that other sectors, probably services, have attracted increasing shares of investment.

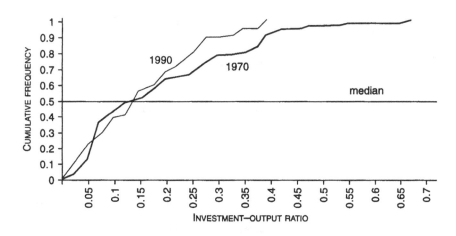

FIGURE 7   *Agriculture: fixed investment–output ratio (58 countries)*

Yair Mundlak

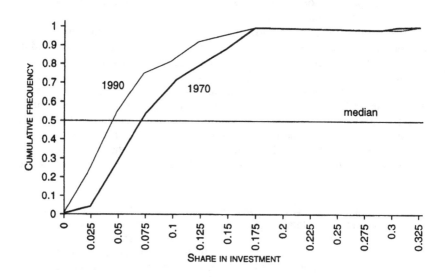

FIGURE 8   *Share of agriculture in total fixed investment (58 countries)*

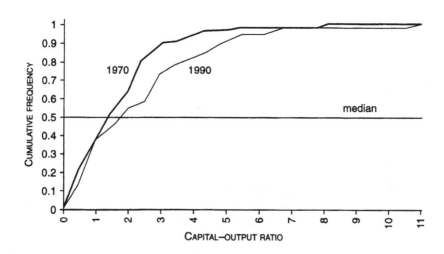

FIGURE 9   *Agriculture: fixed capital–output ratio (56 countries)*

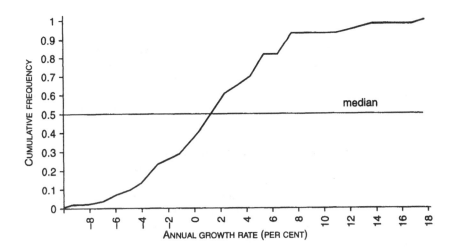

FIGURE 10   *Agriculture: fixed capital–labour ratio 1967–90 (56 countries)*

- In the study period, the capital–output ratio increased in agriculture and in the economy as a whole, indicating capital deepening.
- In most countries the capital–labour ratio has grown over time in the economy as a whole, and in agriculture.
- In general, the distributions of the various measures of investment and capital show a much larger spread in agriculture than in manufacturing or the rest of the economy.

How can we account for this evidence? The developments have taken place in response to changes in the economic environment. The tendency for a decline in the share of agriculture in total investment indicates that the expansion effect is dominating, since agriculture is the income-inelastic sector. On the other hand, non-agriculture net of manufacturing, to be referred to as 'services', is the income-elastic sector and the growth of its share in investment is the other side of the expansion effect. Similarly, an examination of the components of investment which are not shown here indicates a growth of components such as livestock or orchards which also reflects demand expansion. This outcome is consistent with the interpretation of the role of demand as a determinant of agricultural growth given at the beginning of our discussion.

The growth of other components of investment, such as machines, reflects changes in technology and factor supply. The increase of the capital–labour ratio in agriculture, to a large extent, reflects off-farm migration. The rise in the capital–output ratio indicates a shift to more capital-intensive techniques. The larger spread in the measures of agricultural investment, compared with the economy as a whole, may point to data inaccuracy, but it also suggests that there is a much larger spread in the implemented technology in agriculture than in the rest of the economy. This is the story of heterogeneous technology, a subject that should receive more attention in future research for both its substantive value and its methodological implications.

These changes in the economy take time because the process of resource allocation is time consuming. There are a number of reasons for this gradual response.

(1)   Changes involving stock buildings, such as an investment, are basically irreversible and therefore are not conducive to changing instantly with the change in the market environment.
(2)   There are costs involved in changes, so that the incentives to change should be sufficiently large to offset the costs.
(3)   Changes in the market environment that justify a response should last long enough to pay off the investment.

When the factors do not respond instantly to changes in the economic environment, it is common to find factor price differentials across sectors, often referred to as 'distortion' in factor markets. Such differentials indeed represent distortion when judged by *ex post* prices and the criterion of static optimization, but not necessarily when judged by expected prices and a dynamic criterion. One aspect of such a distortion is the difference in the two measures of capital intensity, which is implicit in our foregoing discussion. The direct measure of the capital–labour ratio, alluded to above, indicates that, in most countries, agriculture is labour-intensive. However, the factor share of labour in agriculture is lower than that in non-agriculture, indicating that by this measure (factor-cost intensity) agriculture is capital-intensive.

IMPLICATIONS

We can now return to the topics of interest listed at the beginning of the discussion. The main dynamic factors that have affected agriculture are population and income growth, on the demand side, and considerable improvements in the biological and mechanical processes, on the supply side. On the whole, supply grew faster than demand and this resulted in a downward trend in the relative price of agriculture. To get some perspective on the productivity growth in agriculture, we compare it to that in non-agriculture. As seen in Figure 11, the average labour productivity in agriculture exceeded that in non-agriculture in 80 per cent of the countries, and the difference in the rates at the median is 1.6 percentage points in favour of agriculture.[13]

Productivity growth reflects a continuous process of change in the available technology and in its implementation. The appearance of a new technology has an important random element in terms of its nature, magnitude and the timing

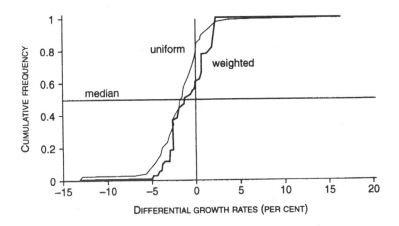

FIGURE 11   *Differential growth of labour productivity, 1960–92 (growth rates: non agricultural minus agricultural, 88 countries)*

of its appearance. To make this point concrete, we could ask each one of us to write down his or her vision (or better yet 'prediction', if there is framework to construct one) of agricultural technology to be available in 10 and 20 years from now. It is not necessary to wait until then to see the importance of the random element – it will suffice to compare all the answers to see the magnitude of their spread in order to illustrate that we lack an appropriate framework to come up with a precise prediction. I am willing to conjecture that the spread would not be smaller if we all took a month to prepare a more studious reply. The situation would have been completely different had the appearance of the new technology followed a deterministic path. Given this state of affairs, how can we expect to explain away the residual component of technical change that appears in productivity studies? Recall that empirical analysis is done with dated data which makes the timing of the appearance of the changes critically important. As is well known, and we have seen it above, the residual consti-tutes an important component of the total output growth.

However, not all that is known is used in production. Given the changes in the available technology, the implementation of the new productive techniques requires the flow of various forms of capital to agriculture and is encouraged by a supportive economic environment. We emphasize the implementation of available technology because this is largely the problem of the developing countries. They do not have to invest in moving the frontier, this is why they can grow faster. Thus production or, more to the point, the growth in produc-tion needed to meet the growing demand, can be sustained with the flow of new resources, in addition to technology, to agriculture.

But what happens if this view of the intermediate future is wrong and the flow of new technology is insufficient so that, at some point, the fortunes of this century will be reversed and supply will start to lag demand? To answer this question, recall that real agricultural prices declined in this century by more than a factor of two. Suppose that for some reason they doubled from here on – then what would happen to production and resource flows to agriculture? A poll on this issue would probably result in more unanimity than the one on technical change. To the resource flow, we can add more intensive research effort which, in line with the monotonicity property of the production of knowledge alluded to above, should foster, in a probability sense, further improvement in the available technology.

What about stability? This has more than one aspect. Secular stability of food supply is achieved if production is sustained. In the short term, basic agricultural production is subject to the mercy of the weather and other influences of the physical environment. The randomness associated with these factors is there to stay. This implies occasional declines in the available storage and short-lived price spikes. A litmus test for good economics is not to build on such fluctuations by changing the long-term strategy of anything – research investment and the like. Having said this, we note that, at the margin, capital-intensive agriculture with irrigation is less vulnerable to the environment, and with time more output will be more immune to the weather.

Welfare implications

In evaluating the impact of technical change on agriculture it is important to differentiate between agriculture as an economic activity, or a sector, and farmers. The welfare of the sector is measured by the returns to land, which is the factor specific to agriculture. The main welfare issue related to farmers is their income level and, to a lesser extent, its stability.

The returns to land are reflected in land prices.[14] Figure 12 shows the pattern of real agricultural land prices for the United States, Canada, South Africa and Japan for which we have longer time-series, reported as indices with 1986 = 1. The upper panel reports the distribution of the price in units of output (deflated by the price of the agricultural product) and the lower panel is of the distribution of the price in units of the consumption good (deflated by the consumer price index). Comparing the land prices at the end to those of the beginning of the period of each series, we see that the output measure is considerably higher, whereas the consumption measure hardly shows a change. On the whole, the prices in consumption units in the 1990s are historically relatively low, and it is remarkable that land prices today are not much different from those at the beginning of the century. Moreover, land prices reflect the subsidies to agriculture. If the effect of subsidies had been taken into account, we would have observed a substantive decline in land prices. Another striking observation is the high correlation between the prices for the countries plotted in Figure 12 as well as for most countries for which data were assembled. The correlation is stronger for the output measure than for the consumption measure. This indicates that much of the impact of the dramatic changes in agricultural

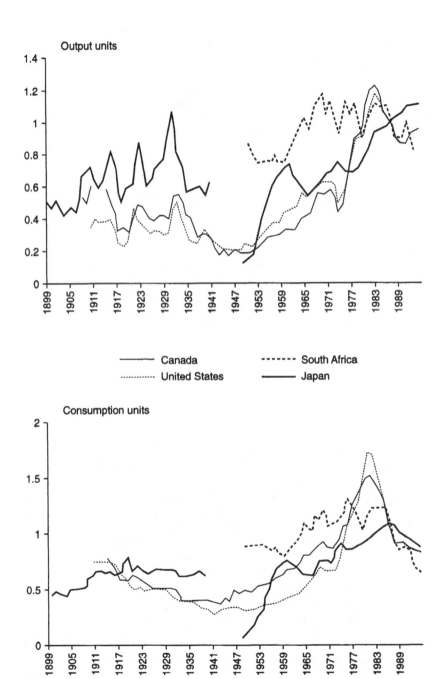

FIGURE 12   *Real land price*

technology was transmitted to the various countries (at least those observed here). However, the benefits were not captured by agriculture and eventually were distributed to the consumers. This was achieved through a decline in agricultural prices relative to prices of the other consumption goods.

The changes in the welfare of people in agriculture is a different, and a more complex, story. The income of farmers is the returns to labour and to other factors in their possession. Aside from the returns to land, discussed above, which apply mainly to land owners, labour income is the main income source for farm operators and primarily the only source for landless labour. The data on returns to labour are deficient and leave much to be desired. Therefore, we will look at the changes in the structural composition of the labour force to derive inferences about the impact of the changes in technology on labour.

Naturally, when labour income in agriculture is low, people will migrate to other sectors. Thus the off-farm migration is probably the most important single process that contributes to the alleviation of rural poverty. This result should be kept in mind in judging not only economic processes but also institutional and legal reforms. There is nothing more effective in improving people's welfare than allowing them to choose freely between opportunities and thus escape areas of hardship. The traditional exploitation of agricultural labour may have taken place because the migration opportunities were restricted either by institutional arrangement, by lack of infrastructure or by lack of outside opportunities. This is where economic growth comes in as a factor in the alleviation of agriculture-based poverty.

Agriculture and development

Technological change in agriculture had two important effects on the economy as a whole. First, it improved the overall food supply, while prices declined and thus improved consumers' welfare. Second, it made it possible to produce more output with relatively less labour and thus facilitated the development of non-agriculture. As a result of the migration, the share of agriculture in the total labour force declined. The median share of 148 countries declined from 70 per cent in 1950 to 33 per cent in 1990. There is hardly any single indicator that better describes the role of agriculture in economic development. It is the freeing of labour that is a necessary condition for development. The net outcome of the processes is a decline in the relative importance of agriculture in total output. The median share of the distribution of 67 countries declined from 30 to 8 per cent between 1950 and 1990.

To sum up, technological change in agriculture serves the rest of the economy by increasing supplies at lower prices and contributing labour to the development of non-agriculture. At the same time, in the longer run, none of the benefits are captured in agriculture. Who would stand to benefit from further increases in agricultural productivity in the future? There is no reason to think that the future will be any different from the past. This welfare conclusion has an important policy implication for the financing of agricultural research. Historically, much of it was publicly financed, because the fruits of the research cannot be internalized by the researcher. The foregoing discussion indicates that it is indeed in the interest of the public at large to promote research that will generate technological change in agriculture. Therefore the financing burden should be carried by the public at large and not by agriculture, which does not seem to capture and maintain the benefit from it. Furthermore, as the fruits of the research are eventually spread to all countries, there is a strong case to be made for international financing of a large part of the research. Countries can take a lead in advancing technology and benefit from it until the new technology spreads to other countries. Also, for countries to take advantage of global developments, they must have an active research programme. Thus there is a strong case for each country financing its own research as well.

On policy

All the progress in agricultural production was achieved in spite of the fact that many countries taxed agriculture. By the ELG, such policies deter investment in agriculture and consequently deter the implementation of the new productive capital-intensive techniques. The policies can be discussed at different levels. Much of the discussion on agricultural policies focuses on policies directed towards agriculture. There is more to it, though, because indirect policies, which appear under the title of macro and trade policies, appear to be sector-neutral, but this is not the case. Agriculture has a larger trade component than non-agriculture, and consequently suffers more from policies that cause an appreciation of the local currency, or alternatively cause a decline in the real exchange rate. Also, because agriculture is cost and capital-intensive, it is more sensitive than non-agriculture to changes in the rate of interest and less so to the cost of labour. Policies that cause a rise in the interest rate are more damaging to agriculture in general and to agricultural investment in particular. Going one level up, we can evaluate the damage caused by policies that caused countries to miss out on much of the economic growth that took place in the postwar period. This damaged agriculture as well as the whole economy, as in eastern Europe, Africa and Latin America.

Finally, assuming that we know more today about growth and the consequences of policies, will past mistakes be avoided in the future? They may be reduced, but not necessarily disappear. The reason is that governments, as pure as they come, are not the social planners of the kind that the theory often assumes. They differ in one fundamental respect from the community which they are supposed to serve; the difference is in the time horizon. It is not productive to ignore political survival as a major driving force in government decisions. You do not have to be a predator to want to survive. In this sense, there is less scope for overlapping generations and altruism in the government utility functions, and this may lead to decisions which are inconsistent with what we might think is conducive to long-term growth. This is also the source of variations in the data which, ironically, are helpful in empirical analysis.

All this has some important repercussions for policy-oriented research. Our comparative advantage as economists is not to compete with the agronomists in speculating about future yields. We can be most helpful in locating the bottlenecks and constraints to growth and suggest means to their alleviation. In this, we sometimes have to operate at the frontier of professional knowledge, often against the common wisdom of governments, but this is where the progress is to be made.

NOTES

[1] In doing this I am restricting reference to the literature to subjects of immediate concern. A recent overview by D. Gale Johnson (1997) deals with some of the issues discussed.

[2] Binswanger *et al.* (1987) report a declining trend of real prices of the basic agricultural products at an annual rate of 0.5 to 0.7 per cent for the period 1900–1984. It thus appears that, in real terms, agricultural prices at the end of the century will be less than one-half their level than at its beginning.

[3] This is the explanation given by McGuirk and Mundlak (1991) for the fact that it has taken many years to complete the shift to new varieties of rice and wheat in the Indian Punjab. This explanation shifts the weight of delayed transformation to new technology away from imperfect knowledge to capital constraints.

[4] Mundlak *et al.* (1989), Coeymans and Mundlak (1993) and Gomez *et al.* (forthcoming).

[5] For more details, see Mundlak (1997).

[6] We present only studies where the quantities of outputs and inputs are expressed either as country totals or in per worker terms. Studies which use quantities per farm are not quite comparable and introduce additional issues which are secondary to the discussion.

[7] Compare the two sets of results obtained by Evenson and Kislev (1975).

[8] For space limitations, we do not discuss the results. It should, however, be noted that the study by Bhattacharjee does not include any measure of capital items or shifters, technology or others, and therefore the results cannot be compared meaningfully with the other studies. The remaining studies have some technology shifters such as schooling, research and extension, infrastructure and the like.

[9] These three regressions form a canonical set, in the sense that any linear pooling of the date yields regression which can be expressed as a matrix-weighted combination of the canonical set.

[10] Land is not included as a variable in the between-time regression in view of the low variability over time, as indicated in Table 2.

[11] The claim of increasing returns to scale in cross-country analysis found justification in a similar finding by Griliches (1963) in cross-regions analysis for the United States. For more evidence, see Kislev and Peterson (1996).

[12] We ignore the early work of Bhattacharjee (1955) because it had no measure of capital or of state variables and is therefore not comparable with the other studies.

[13] This pattern is not shared by some of the big producers, including China. Hence the weighted distribution shows a more modest difference. It is still true that, in countries accounting for 60 per cent of output, average labour productivity has shown faster growth in agriculture.

[14] There is no readily available data set with time-series of land prices for the various countries. Rita Butzer has helped in finding material.

REFERENCES

Antle, J.M. (1983), 'Infrastructure and Aggregate Agricultural Productivity: International Evidence', *Economic Development and Cultural Change*, 31, 609–19.
Bhattacharjee, J.P. (1955), 'Resource Use and Productivity in World Agriculture', *Journal of Farm Economics*, 37, 57–71.
Binswanger, H., Mundlak, Y., Yang, M-C. and Bowers, A. (1987), 'On the Determinants of Cross-Country Aggregate Agricultural Supply', *Journal of Econometrics*, 36, 11–31.
Coeymans, J.E. and Y. Mundlak (1993), *Sectoral Growth in Chile: 1962–82*, Research Report 95, Washington, DC: International Food Policy Research Institute.

Crego, A., Larson, D., Butzer, R. and Mundlak, Y. (1997), *A New Database on Investment and Capital for Agriculture and Manufacturing*, Washington, DC: World Bank.

Evenson, R.E. and Kislev, Y. (1975), *Agricultural Research and Productivity*, New Haven: Yale University Press.

Fogel, R.W. (1997), 'Have the Extent and the Impact of Chronic Malnutrition been Underestimated? A Theory of Technophysio Evolution and its Implications for Nutritional Standards', in Y. Mundlak (ed.), *Contemporary Economic Issues, Volume 2, Labour, Food and Poverty*, New York: Macmillan.

Gomez, J., Garcia Garcia, J. and Mundlak, Y. (forthcoming), 'Agricultural Productivity in Colombia', mimeo.

Griliches, Z. (1963), 'Estimates of the Aggregate Agricultural Production Function from Cross-Sectional Data', *Journal of Farm Economics*, **45**, 419–28.

Hayami, Y. (1969), 'Sources of Agricultural Productivity Gap among Selected Countries', *American Journal of Agricultural Economics*, **51**, 564–75.

Hayami, Y. (1970), 'On the Use of the Cobb–Douglas Production Function in the Cross-Country Analysis of Agricultural Production', *American Journal of Agricultural Economics*, **52**, 327–9.

Hayami, Y. and Ruttan, V.W. (1970), 'Agricultural Productivity Differences Among Countries', *American Economic Review*, **60**, 895–911.

Heady, E.O. (1944), 'Production Functions from a Random Sample of Farms', *Journal of Farm Economics*, **26**, 989–1004.

Heady, E.O. and Dillon, J.D. (1961), *Agricultural Production Functions*, Ames: Iowa University Press.

Hertel, T. (1997), *Global Trade Analysis*, Cambridge: Cambridge University Press.

Johnson, D.G. (1997), 'Agriculture and the Wealth of Nations', *American Economic Review*, **87**, 1–12.

Kawagoe, T. and Hayami, Y. (1985), 'An Intercountry Comparison of Agricultural Production Efficiency', *American Journal of Agricultural Economics*, **67**, 87–92.

Kawagoe, T., Hayami, Y. and Ruttan, V.W. (1985), 'The Intercountry Agricultural Production Function and Productivity Differences among Countries', *Journal of Development Economics*, **19**, 113–32.

Kislev, Y. and Peterson, W. (1996), 'Economies of Scale in Agriculture: A Reexamination of Evidence', in J. Antle and D. Summer (eds), *The Economics of Agriculture: Papers in Honor of D. Gale Johnson, Volume 2*, Chicago: University of Chicago Press.

Larson, D. and Mundlak, Y. (1997), 'On the Intersectoral Migration of Agricultural Labor', *Economic Development and Cultural Change*, **46**, 295–319.

McGuirk, A. and Mundlak, Y. (1991), *Constraints Incentives and the Transformation of Punjab Agriculture: 1960–1980*, Research Report 87, Washington, DC: International Food Policy Research Institute.

Mundlak, Y. (1997), *Agricultural Production Functions: A Critical Survey*, working paper series, Rehovot, Israel: Centre for Agricultural Economic Research.

Mundlak, Y. (forthcoming), *Agriculture and Economic Growth*, Cambridge: Harvard University Press.

Mundlak, Y. and Hellinghausen, R. (1982), 'The Intercountry Agricultural Production Function: Another View', *American Journal of Agricultural Economics*, **64**, 664–72.

Mundlak, Y., Cavallo, D. and Domenech, R. (1989), *Agriculture and Economic Growth in Argentina, 1913–84*, Research Report 76, Washington, DC: International Food Policy Research Institute.

Mundlak, Y., Larson, D. and Butzer, R. (1997), 'The Determinants of Agricultural Production: A Cross-Country Analysis', paper read at the 7th International Conference on Panel Data, La Sorbonne, 19–20 June.

Mundlak, Y., Larson, D. and Crego, A. (1997), 'Agricultural Development: Evidence, Issues and Consequences', in Y. Mundlak (ed.), *Contemporary Economic Issues, Volume 2, Labour, Food and Poverty*, New York: Macmillan.

Nehru, V., Swanson, E. and Dubey, A. (1993), *A New Database on Human Capital Stock: Sources, Methodology, and Results*, Policy Research Working Paper 1124, Washington, DC: World Bank.

Nguyen, D. (1979), 'On Agricultural Productivity Differences among Countries', *American Journal of Agricultural Economics*, **61**, 565–70.
Pritchett, L. (1996), *Where Has All the Education Gone?*, Policy Research Working Paper 1581, Washington, DC: World Bank.
Schultz, T.W. (1953), *Economic Organization of Agriculture*, New York: McGraw-Hill.
Solow, R.M. (1957), 'Technical Change and the Aggregate Production Function', *Review of Economics and Statistics*, **39**, 312–20.
Tinter, G. (1944), 'A Note on the Derivation of Production Functions from Farm Records', *Econometrica*, **12**, 26–34.
Tintner, G. and Brownlee, O.H. (1944), 'Production Functions Derived from Farm Records', *Journal of Farm Economics*, **26**, 566–71 (see also the correction in *JFE*, February 1953, p. 123).
Yamada, S. and Ruttan, V.W. (1980), 'International Comparisons of Productivity in Agriculture', in J.W. Kendrick and B.N. Vaccara (eds), *New Developments in Productivity Measurement and Analysis*, Chicago: University of Chicago Press.

SECTION I

Security and Demand Challenges: Global Level and National Policy Issues,
Household Consumption Improvement

PER PINSTRUP-ANDERSEN AND RAJUL PANDYA-LORCH*

Food Security: A Global Perspective

INTRODUCTION

Although enough food is being produced today for nobody to have to go hungry, about 840 million people are chronically undernourished, around 185 million pre-school children are seriously underweight for their age, and illnesses resulting from, or exacerbated by, hunger and malnutrition are widespread (FAO, 1996a). As the world's population will also increase by an expected 80 million people every year over the next quarter-century (UN, 1996), attaining food security will be the central global challenge. Will there be enough food to meet the needs of current and future generations? And even if enough food is available, will all people have access to sufficient amounts to lead healthy and productive lives? Can, and will, global food security be attained or will food surpluses continue to coexist with widespread hunger and malnutrition, further destabilizing and polarizing the world? What will it take to ensure a world of food-secure people?

Following a brief discussion of food security concepts and an assessment of the current food security situation, this paper examines the major challenges to realizing a food-secure world, considers the prospects for global food security with special attention to whether Malthusian predictions may come true for sub-Saharan Africa and identifies key actions required to ensure global food security.

FOOD SECURITY CONCEPTS

The world would be food-secure when each and every person could be assured of access at all times to the food required for a healthy and productive life. Food security is jointly determined by availability of food and access to it. Availability does not guarantee access, but access to food is contingent on there being food available (von Braun *et al.*, 1992). National, regional or local availability of food is a function of food production, stockholding and trade. National access to food from international markets is determined by world food prices and foreign exchange availability. Household availability of food requires that food be available at local or regional markets, which is determined by market operations, infrastructure and information flows. The situation

*International Food Policy Research Institute, Washington, DC, USA.

51

for households and individuals is usually conditioned by income: the poor commonly lack adequate means to secure their access to food.

Food security at one level does not guarantee food security at any other level (ibid., 1992). For example, household food security does not necessarily mean that all individuals in that household have access to the needed food; some members may be denied their full share. Intra-household inequality in distribution of food, with women in particular eating less than their share, is observed quite often. Similarly, regional or national food security does not necessarily lead to household or individual food security; the available food may not be distributed according to needs and households, or individuals may not have equitable access to it. And, of course, global food availability does not mean universal food security. There may be marked national, regional, household and individual differences in access to food.

THE CURRENT WORLD FOOD SECURITY SITUATION

Despite impressive food production growth in recent decades, which means that enough food is available to meet the basic needs of each and every person in the world, not all people are food-secure. If available food could be evenly distributed, each person would be assured of 2700 calories a day, 20 per cent more than in 1961–3 (FAO, 1997). However, available food is neither evenly distributed nor fully consumed among or within countries. In all, 42 countries were unable to assure minimum requirements of 2200 calories per person per day for their populations during 1992–4, even if available food had been evenly distributed within each one (ibid.). Of these countries, 29 were in Africa, six in Asia, three in Latin America and the Caribbean, three in Eastern Europe and the former Soviet Union, and one in the Middle East.

In the developing world as a whole, about 840 million people – 20 per cent of the population – were chronically undernourished during 1990–92, lacking economic or physical access to sufficient food to lead healthy and productive lives (FAO, 1996a). East Asia was home to 32 per cent of the world's undernourished, South Asia to 30 per cent, and sub-Saharan Africa to 26 per cent (Table 1). China and India together accounted for 45 per cent of the world's undernourished people (FAO, 1996d). Progress is being made in reducing the magnitude and prevalence of undernourished people. There were about 80 million fewer undernourished people in 1990–92, compared with 1969–71 (Table 1), while an additional 1.5 billion people were being adequately fed. The share of undernourished people in the population declined in more than 55 countries between 1969–71 and 1990–92 (FAO, 1996d), contributing to a reduction in the share of the developing world's population from 35 to 21 per cent during this period (Table 1). Most of the improvements in food security have taken place in East Asia, where there was a fall in the numbers undernourished from 475 million in 1969–71 to 268 million in 1990–92. Nevertheless, with two-thirds of the developing world being affected, South and East Asia remain key areas of food security concern. Furthermore, a new 'flash-point' or locus of hunger and food insecurity has emerged in sub-Saharan Africa, where the number of undernourished people doubled between 1969–71 and 1990–92

TABLE 1   *Chronic undernutrition in the developing world, 1969–71, 1990–92 and 2010*

Region	Number of chronically undernourished people* (millions)			Share of region's population (per cent)			Share of total undernourished population (per cent)		
	1969–71	1990–92	2010	1969–71	1990–92	2010	1969–71	1990–92	2010
East Asia	475	268	123	41	16	6	52	32	18
South Asia	238	255	200	33	22	12	26	30	29
Sub-Saharan Africa	103	215	264	38	43	30	11	26	39
Latin America and the Caribbean	53	64	40	19	15	7	6	8	6
Middle East and North Africa	48	37	53	27	12	10	5	4	8
Total	917	839	680	35	21	12	100	100	100

Note: *Chronically undernourished people are those whose estimated annual food energy intake falls below that required to maintain body weight and support light activity.

Source: FAO (1996a).

to 215 million, and the proportion of the population rose from 38 to 43 per cent.

Child malnutrition is another indicator of food insecurity. The number of malnourished children rose during the 1980s from 164 million to 184 million, although as a result of population growth their share of the pre-school children population declined slightly, from 37.8 per cent to 34.3 per cent. One-third of all pre-school children in the developing world are still underweight. About 101 million underweight children are in South Asia, 44 million in East Asia and 28 million in sub-Saharan Africa. About 60 per cent of the pre-school children in South Asia are underweight, compared to 30 per cent in sub-Saharan Africa and East Asia, respectively, and 8 per cent in Latin America and the Caribbean.

Micronutrient deficiencies are also widespread in the developing world, even where caloric consumption is adequate. Micronutrient deficiencies have detrimental effects on human health and productivity. About 2 million people are affected by iron deficiency, around 1.6 billion people are at risk of iodine deficiency and 40 million children suffer from Vitamin A deficiency (FAO, 1996b).

In addition to those who are already food-insecure and show symptoms or consequences of food insecurity, there are many others worldwide who live with the risk of being affected: their incomes are so low that any sudden shock, such as loss of employment or price fluctuations, could tip them into food insecurity. These vulnerable people must also be taken into account when considering the world food security situation.

Earlier, it was noted that food security is jointly determined by availability of food and access to it. With regard to availability of food, production growth in recent decades has been impressive. Between 1961–3 and 1994–6, output increased by 119 per cent worldwide, while it rose 200 per cent in developing countries as a group, with particularly large increases in the developing countries of Asia. Even in those of Africa, where the problems of food security are greatest, production increased by 120 per cent during the period. Between 1961–3 and 1994–6, cereal production worldwide more than doubled to 1.97 billion tons and almost tripled in developing countries to 1.14 billion tons; meat production almost tripled worldwide to 208 million tons and quintupled in developing countries to 107 million tons; and production of roots and tubers doubled in developing countries, increasing to 436 million tons.

Worldwide, food production more than kept pace with population growth; per capita supply increased by 40 per cent between 1961–3 and 1994–6. In the developing countries, as a group, the increase was marginally higher, at 47 per cent. However, performance varied widely among developing countries; while per capita food production increased by 67 per cent in the developing countries of Asia, less was produced per person in the developing countries of Africa in the mid-1990s than in the early 1960s. Between 1961–3 and 1994–6, cereal production per person worldwide increased by 20 per cent, to 350 kilograms, while it increased by 28 per cent, to 252 kilograms, in the developing world; and meat production per person worldwide increased by 55 per cent to 37 kilograms, with figures of 242 per cent and 24 kilograms in the developing world (FAO, 1997).

There are indications that growth in food production has begun to lag in recent years. The annual rate for global cereal production dropped from 2.6 per cent during 1967–82 to 1.3 per cent during 1982–94, while cereal yields slowed from 2.3 per cent to 1.5 per cent between these two periods (Rosegrant *et al.*, 1997). After steadily increasing during the 1960s and 1970s, world grain production per person has fallen by about 1 per cent annually over the past decade (Brown *et al.* 1995). Yields of rice and wheat have been constant over the past few years in Asia, which is a significant producer (Pinstrup-Andersen, 1994). It is becoming increasingly difficult to maintain the yield gains already achieved, let alone to increase yields, in the high-potential or more-favoured areas, while in the less-favoured areas, which are home to many of the world's food-insecure people, yields are low and variable (Hazell, 1995).

Gains in availability of food have not been matched by corresponding gains in access to it. There were significant reductions in poverty during the 1960s and 1970s, particularly in East Asia, but the record was somewhat mixed during the 1980s and early 1990s, with reductions in the number of poor people in East Asia mitigated by increases in sub-Saharan Africa, South Asia and Latin America (World Bank, 1990; 1996b; FAO, 1987). The number of absolutely poor people – those with incomes of a dollar a day or less to meet food, shelter and other basic needs – increased between 1987 and 1993 from 1.23 billion to 1.30 billion, 29 per cent of the developing world's population (Table 2).

TABLE 2   *Poverty in the developing world, 1987 and 1993*

Region	Number of poor people* (millions)		Share of region's population (per cent)		Share of total poor population (per cent)	
	1987	1993	1987	1993	1987	1993
East Asia	464	446	29	26	38	34
South Asia	480	515	45	43	39	40
Sub-Saharan Africa	180	219	39	39	15	17
Latin America and the Caribbean	91	110	22	24	7	8
Middle East and North Africa	10	11	5	4	1	1
Total	1 225	1 301	30	29	100	100

Note: *People living on $1 a day or less.

Source: World Bank (1996b).

CHALLENGES TO A FOOD-SECURE WORLD

Among the major driving forces influencing, or challenging, access to sufficient food are income levels and economic growth, human resource development,
and population growth and movements. Investment in agricultural growth and
development, timely and reasonably priced access to agricultural inputs, the
condition of the natural resource base, existence of competitive markets and
functioning infrastructure, and domestic resource mobilization and external
assistance are among the key forces influencing or challenging availability of
food (IFPRI, 1995).

Income levels and economic growth

As noted earlier, about 1.3 billion people in the developing world are absolutely poor, while another 2 billion are only marginally better off. Income
levels vary considerably among developing regions, ranging from $320 per
person on average in South Asia to $460 in sub-Saharan Africa, $860 in East
Asia and $3340 in Latin America and the Caribbean (World Bank, 1996c).
Similarly, income growth rates also vary considerably. While East Asia and the
Pacific had an average growth in per capita GNP of 6.9 per cent during the
most recent decade for which information is available (1985–94), sub-Saharan
Africa and the Middle East and North Africa struggled with negative growth
rates of –1.2 and –0.4 per cent, respectively. Growth rates have picked up very
recently in sub-Saharan Africa (Sarbib, 1997; UN, 1997).
    Prospects for improvements over the next 10 years appear favourable, with
all regions projected to have positive and higher rates of economic growth
(World Bank, 1996a). However, unless significant and fundamental changes
occur in many developing countries, disparities in income levels and growth
are likely to persist. Without concerted action, poverty is likely to remain
entrenched in South Asia and Latin America and to increase considerably in
sub-Saharan Africa. Only in East Asia is absolute poverty expected to decline
substantially. Most of the world's poor are in rural communities and, even
when they are not engaged in their own agricultural activities, they rely on
non-farm employment and income that depend in some way or the other on
agriculture (Pinstrup-Andersen and Pandya-Lorch, 1995). Agricultural growth
and development must be vigorously pursued in low-income developing countries, not simply to produce more food but also to generate employment and
incomes for poor people within and outside agriculture.

Human resource development

Poor people have low productivity and lack secure access to productive resources and remunerative employment. Investments in health care, education,
clean water, sanitation and housing, which are essential for human resource
development, are far below required levels, especially in rural areas of low-
income developing countries. About 790 million people in the developing

world lack access to health services, 1.28 billion people to safe water and 2.53 billion people to sanitation services, while 850 million adults are illiterate. Public expenditures on health and education amount to 2 and 4 per cent, respectively, of the gross national product (GNP) of developing countries as a group. Underinvestment in the health and education of females is particularly severe. Poor nutrition and health in early childhood affect cognitive development, with consequent losses in productivity during adulthood. Poor, hungry, ill and uneducated people are handicapped in ensuring food security for themselves and others.

Population growth

During the next quarter-century, almost 80 million people are likely to be added to the world's population each year, increasing world population by 35 per cent to 7.67 billion in 2020 (UN, 1996). Most of this change (98 per cent) is expected to occur in developing countries, whose share of global population is projected to increase from 79 per cent in 1995 to 84 per cent in 2020. Over this period, the absolute population increase will be highest in Asia, at 1.15 billion, but the relative increase will be greatest in sub-Saharan Africa, where the population is expected to almost double from 0.59 billion to 1.12 billion.

Most of the population increase in developing countries during the next 25 years is expected in the cities. Rapid urbanization could double the developing world's urban population to 3.6 billion by 2020, by which time urban dwellers could outnumber rural dwellers (UN, 1995). Urbanization is associated with more diverse diets: increasing opportunity costs of women's time, changes in food preferences caused by changing lifestyles and changes in relative prices associated with rural–urban migration lead to shifts from basic staples such as sorghum and millet to cereals such as rice and wheat (which require less preparation), livestock products, fruits and vegetables, and processed foods. Changes in dietary patterns, particularly rapid increases in demand for livestock products, place strong pressures on the demand for cereals for feedgrain purposes. Rapidly growing urban populations also place severe pressures on food marketing systems, including transport, storage, processing and market information.

From its peak of 2.0 per cent in the late 1960s, the global annual population growth rate is expected to halve to 1.0 per cent by 2015–20 (UN, 1996). However, sub-Saharan Africa's projected annual population growth rate of 2.33 per cent will be more than double that in the other regions. Change of this magnitude will severely constrain efforts to increase income and improve welfare, while at the same time it will greatly increase the need for food. Should fertility rates not decline as expected in the next 25 years, and the annual population growth rate reach the United Nations high-variant projection of 1.3 per cent by 2015–20, there could be as many as 400 million more people by 2020 (UN, 1996).

Investments in agricultural growth and development

In most low-income developing countries, agricultural growth is a catalyst for broad-based economic growth and development (Pinstrup-Andersen and Pandya-Lorch, 1995). About 60 per cent of the developing world's labour force is engaged in agricultural activities (World Bank, 1996c). Moreover, agriculture's linkages to the non-farm economy generate considerable employment, income and growth in the rest of the economy. Very few countries have experienced rapid economic growth without agricultural growth either preceding or accompanying it. Economic growth is strongly linked to poverty reduction. While diversification out of agriculture will occur in the long term, in the short term many countries lack alternatives. Thus agricultural growth and development must be vigorously pursued in developing countries for at least four reasons: (1) to meet food needs driven primarily by population and income growth, (2) to alleviate poverty through employment creation and income generation, (3) to stimulate overall economic growth, and (4) to conserve natural resources since poverty forces many people to often overuse or misuse the natural resource base to meet their basic needs.

It is a matter for concern, then, that not only has the average annual growth rate for agriculture in low- and middle-income developing countries slowed down in the first half of the 1990s, to 2.0 per cent, compared to 3.1 per cent in the 1980s, but that in sub-Saharan Africa, a growing locus of food insecurity, the growth rate is low and falling, declining from 1.9 per cent in 1980–90 to 1.5 per cent in 1990–95. National investments in agriculture have declined in recent years, mainly because of structural adjustment (FAO, 1996c). In many countries, agriculture has been taxed implicitly and explicitly. As Figure 1 shows, international assistance to developing-country agriculture has also declined in recent years in real terms, driven primarily by reductions in bilateral assistance.

Agricultural research and technological improvements are crucial to increase agricultural productivity and returns to farmers and farm labour, thereby reducing poverty and meeting future food needs at reasonable prices without irreversible degradation of the natural resource base (Pinstrup-Andersen and Pandya-Lorch, 1995). Accelerated investment in agricultural research is particularly urgent for low-income developing countries, partly because they will not achieve reasonable economic growth and poverty alleviation without productivity increases in agriculture, and partly because appropriate technology is urgently needed. Low-income developing countries are grossly underinvesting in agricultural research compared to industrialized countries, even though agriculture accounts for a much larger share of their employment and incomes. Their public-sector expenditures on agricultural research are typically less than 0.5 per cent of agricultural gross domestic product, compared with about 1 per cent in higher-income developing countries and 2–5 per cent in industrialized countries (Pardey *et al.*, 1991; Pardey *et al.*, 1995). Growth has slowed considerably since the late 1980s, and research investments have begun to decline in real terms in many developing countries (Pardey and Alston, 1995). Low and declining levels of resources available per researcher are crippling agricultural research in many developing countries. In sub-Saharan Africa, which desper-

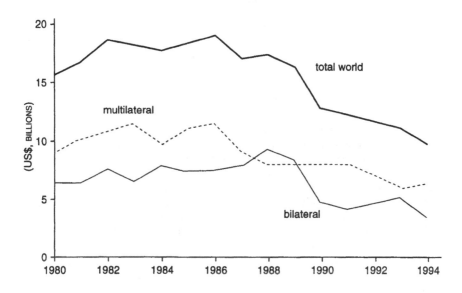

FIGURE 1 *External assistance to agriculture, 1980–94 (at 1990 constant prices)*

Source: FAO (1996c).

ately needs productivity increases in agriculture, real spending per researcher has fallen by 2.6 per cent per year sine 1961 (Pardey *et al.*, 1995). Similar trends are observed in Latin America (Echeverria *et al.*, 1996). Further reductions in public investment in agricultural research will have severe consequences for global food production by reducing yield growth. This, in turn, will result in increasing pressures to draw into agricultural production land that is less well-suited for agriculture, much of which is currently under forest. Failure to maintain high rates of yield growth will cause severe environmental degradation.

Very little investment in agricultural biotechnology is taking place in, or for, developing countries, although it is one of the most promising developments in modern science. It has considerable potential to raise productivity, increase resistance to pests and diseases, develop tolerance to adverse weather conditions, improve the nutritional value of some foods and enhance the durability of products during harvesting or shipping (Pinstrup-Andersen and Pandya-Lorch, 1996b). Most biotechnology research is occurring in private firms in industrialized countries and is geared towards the needs of farmers and consumers in those countries. It is essential that research, relevant to the needs of smallholder farmers in developing countries and to the conditions in those countries, is undertaken, and that the benefits are transmitted to farmers and consumers at affordable prices. Otherwise, farmers in developing countries will not only fail to share in the benefits of agricultural biotechnology, but will be seriously hurt as synthetic alternatives to their products are developed in the laboratories of industrialized countries. That is already happening with cocoa and vanilla.

Natural resources and agricultural inputs

Natural resources and agricultural inputs are critical determinants of food supply. Degradation of natural resources, such as soils, forests, marine fisheries and water, undermines production capacity, while availability of and access to agricultural inputs, such as water, fertilizer, pest control measures, research and technology, determine productivity and therefore production.

Since 1945, about 2 billion of the world's 8.7 billion hectares of agricultural land, permanent pastures and forests and woodlands have been degraded (Oldeman, 1992). Much of the degradation is taking place on agricultural lands: soil degradation has affected 74 per cent of agricultural lands in Central America, 65 per cent in Africa, 45 per cent in South America and 38 per cent in Asia. Overgrazing, deforestation and inappropriate agricultural practices account for most of the degradation. To a large extent, these result from or are exacerbated by inadequate property rights, poverty, population pressure, inappropriate government policies, lack of access to markets and credit, and inappropriate technology. Crop productivity losses from degradation are significant and widespread. In the absence of efforts to protect non-degraded soils and to restore currently degraded soils, increasing population and persisting poverty will hasten soil degradation.

Availability of water to support current and future food production is emerging as a serious challenge (Rosegrant, 1997). Although enough fresh water is available worldwide to meet needs for the foreseeable future, water is poorly distributed across countries, across regions within countries, and across seasons. There is growing competition for water between countries and between sectors within a country. New sources of water are increasingly expensive to exploit because of high construction costs for dams and reservoirs and concerns about environmental effects and displacement of people. Efficiency of water use is generally low because of inappropriate incentives.

Securing timely, reasonably priced access to modern inputs such as fertilizer in order to engage in sustainable food production is a key challenge across the developing world. In many of the developing countries, especially those of sub-Saharan Africa, fertilizer applications on smallholder farms tend to be insufficient, untimely and unbalanced, primarily because of high fertilizer prices, insecure supplies, inadequate agricultural extension systems, insufficient access to credit and greater risks associated with agricultural production in marginal environments (Pinstrup-Andersen and Pandya-Lorch, 1997). While negative environmental consequences of fertilizer use and production must be avoided, in most developing countries the problem is not excessive, but insufficient, fertilizer use. In sub-Saharan Africa, for instance, fertilizer use amounts to 10 kilograms per hectare (Bumb and Baanante, 1996). Depletion of soil nutrients is a critical constraint on food production in the region and a serious cause of soil degradation.

Crop production losses from pests are significant; reduction of these losses would contribute notably to improving food supplies. However, past practices of pesticide use cannot be sustained. Concerns are multiplying that pesticides compromise human health, contaminate soils and water and damage ecosystems, exterminate species, and lead to pesticide resistance, pest resurgence and evolution of secondary pests. Moreover, overuse of pesticides leads to decreased food production. Environmentally sound alternatives must be developed and adopted.

Markets and infrastructure

In addition to production and environmental issues, there are infrastructural and marketing challenges to ensuring a food-secure world. In many regions, especially sub-Saharan Africa, food marketing costs are extremely high (Ahmed and Rustagi, 1987). Lowering these costs through investment in improved transport and storage infrastructure and marketing facilities (which may also facilitate increased competition) may be as important in lowering food prices to consumers as increasing agricultural productivity. Many countries have made considerable improvements in recent years, but investments in infrastructure, especially transport and communications, are far below needed levels. Road, rail, port and storage facilities are inadequate, while telecommunications, electricity, piped water and sanitation systems reach only certain segments of the population. Past investments have tended to favour urban areas. Investments in creating and maintaining basic infrastructure lag far behind in African countries relative to Asian and Latin American countries.

The efficient functioning of markets, especially agricultural input and output markets, supported by governments that have the capacity to perform their role, is of critical importance. In recent years, many governments have embarked upon market reforms to move away from state-controlled or parastatal organizations towards reliance on private firms operating in free markets. While clearly desirable, such reforms must be undertaken with care, taking into account the organizational structure of the affected markets. In many cases, inefficient parastatals are being replaced by oligopolistic or monopolistic private firms, with little or no improvement in performance. The current and unprecedented transition from controlled to market economies has generated confusion about the appropriate role of government and weakened the capacity of governments to perform needed functions.

Domestic resource mobilization and international assistance

Without increased mobilization of domestic resources, developing countries will not be able to accelerate investment in economic growth and human resources. Many low-income countries are trapped in a vicious circle whereby low income leads to low savings, low investment, low growth, continued poverty and low savings. In sub-Saharan Africa, the share of GDP devoted to investment has fallen since 1980 from 23 to 17 per cent, while the domestic saving rate has fallen from 27 to 16 per cent (World Bank, 1996c). These levels are not high enough to have much effect in raising economic growth rates.

International assistance has an important role to play in supporting developing countries as they implement the actions required to ensure food security. Private flows to developing countries have increased substantially since the late 1980s (OECD, 1997). Most of these flows, however, go to a small number of medium-income, semi-industrial countries in Latin America and Asia. Poorer countries, especially in sub-Saharan Africa, are left out and depend much more on aid flows. However, official development assistance (ODA) to developing countries is slowing. At 1994 prices and exchange rates, bilateral and multilateral ODA from OECD countries has dropped, from $62.1 billion in 1992 to $53.6 billion in 1995 (OECD, 1997). Given observed trends in external assistance, developing countries are challenged to devise strategies to ensure food security with less aid.

In sum, there are several interconnected challenges to realizing a food-secure world: (1) widespread poverty and inadequate human resource development, which inhibit people's capacity to grow and/or purchase the needed food; (2) large increases in developing country populations, especially in urban areas, which will substantially increase food needs; (3) gross underinvestment in agricultural growth and development, particularly agricultural research, in developing countries; (4) inadequacies in availability of and access to agricultural inputs, such as water, fertilizer and pesticides, which leads to lagging yield increases, in more favoured areas and low and variable yields in less favoured areas; (5) degradation of natural resources, such as soils, forests and water, which undermines production capacity and productivity; (6) inefficient functioning of markets and inadequate infrastructure as well as weakened capacity of developing-country governments to perform their appropriate functions; and (7) insufficient domestic resource mobilization – savings and investment – and declining international assistance, which restrains economic growth and development.

PROSPECTS FOR GLOBAL FOOD SECURITY

Views differ about the prospects for future world food security (Brown, 1996; FAO, 1996a; IFPRI, 1995; Ingco *et al.*, 1996; Islam, 1995; Penning de Vries *et al.*, 1995; Rosegrant *et al.*, 1995; 1997). Some are complacent that future food needs will be met through technological advances that do not require any special effort, that the dangers of natural resource loss have been exaggerated and that global food surpluses are a sufficient guarantee of global food security, even for low-income countries and people. Others are cautiously optimistic that investment in agricultural development holds promise for ensuring global food security, not only by increasing food production but also by stimulating overall economic growth and raising incomes and employment, thereby enhancing economic access to food. And there are some who are convinced that the limits of food production are being reached, that new technologies will not be able to raise agricultural productivity and production sufficiently to keep up with growing food needs, and that natural resources are being degraded and lost at alarming rates.

Food insecurity is likely to continue to diminish rapidly in East Asia, but, without new and concerted action, it could persist in South Asia and, to a lesser extent, in Latin America, while it could accelerate substantially in sub-Saharan Africa and in the Near East and North Africa. FAO projections suggest that the number of chronically undernourished people could decline by 23 per cent between 1990–92 and 2010 to 680 million people, 12 per cent of the developing world's population (Table 1). By then, sub-Saharan Africans and South Asians could make up 70 per cent of the world's undernourished people, up from 56 per cent in 1990–92. In fact, sub-Saharan Africa's share of the world's undernourished population is projected to almost quadruple between 1969–71 and 2010, from 11 to 39 per cent. By 2010, every third sub-Saharan African is likely to be undernourished compared with every eighth person in South Asia and every twentieth person in East Asia.

Projections to the year 2020 suggest that, in the most likely or baseline scenario, the number of malnourished children could decrease to 155 million or 25 per cent of the population of pre-school children (Table 3). Large

TABLE 3   *Child malnutrition in developing countries, 1990 and 2020*

Region	Number of malnourished children (millions)			
	1990	2020		
		Baseline[1]	Low inv./ slow growth[2]	High inv./rapid growth[3]
Asia	137.62	97.64	128.12	70.27
Sub-Saharan Africa	28.61	42.67	52.75	33.61
Latin America and the Caribbean	11.71	8.12	13.23	3.12
West Africa and North Africa	6.76	6.30	11.05	1.87
Developing countries	184.33	154.73	205.14	108.88

Notes: [1]The baseline scenario incorporates the best assessment of future trends in population, income growth, urbanization, rate of increase in food production due to technological change and productivity growth, commodity prices and response of supply and demand to prices.
[2]The low investment/slow growth scenario simulates the combined effect of a 25 per cent reduction in the rate of non-agricultural income growth and reduced investment in agricultural research and social services.
[3]The high investment/rapid growth scenario simulates the combined effect of a 25 per cent increase in the rate of non-agricultural income growth and higher investment in agricultural research and social services.

Source: Rosegrant, Agcaoili-Sombilla and Perez (1995).

decreases in the number of malnourished children are expected in South and East Asia, but in sub-Saharan Africa their number could increase by 50 per cent, to reach 43 million. In South Asia, malnutrition rates are so high that, even with a projected reduction of 20 million in the number of malnourished children by 2020, two out of five pre-school children would remain malnourished. Simulations suggest that, under a scenario of more rapid income growth and higher investment in public goods such as education and health and in agricultural research, the number of malnourished children could decline by 40 per cent between 1990 and 2020, to 109 million children. However, reduced public investments in agricultural research and social services and slower income growth could lead to an increase in the number of malnourished children to 205 million in 2020. There are 'hot spots' of child malnutrition; South Asia is home to half of the developing world's malnourished children, and in sub-Saharan Africa, even under an optimistic scenario of more rapid income growth and investments in public goods such as education and health, the number of malnourished children is projected to increase between 1990 and 2020.

Meeting the increasing and changing food needs resulting from population growth, rising incomes and changing lifestyles will be a fundamental challenge. Global effective market demand for cereals is projected to increase by 40 per cent between 1993 and 2020, to 2.49 billion tons, for livestock products by 63 per cent to 306 million tons, and for roots and tubers by 40 per cent to 856 million tons (Table 4). These increases are large and will put tremendous pressures on agricultural production and marketing systems, particularly in developing countries, which are projected to increase their demand for cereals by 58 per cent, for meat by 118 per cent and for roots and tubers by 56 per cent. The changes in food demand vary considerably amongst developing-country regions, with the largest percentage increase in demand for cereals, and for roots and tubers, forecast for sub-Saharan Africa, with Asia leading for meat.

Per capita demand for cereals in developing countries as a group is projected to increase by 6.5 per cent to 255 kilograms, for meat by 47 per cent to 31 kilograms, and for roots and tubers by 5.4 per cent to 98 kilograms (Table 4). Because of more rapid population and income growth, market demand for food is projected to grow much faster in developing countries than in developed countries. Nevertheless, a developing-country resident is projected to demand only 40 per cent of the cereals and 38 per cent of the meat that a resident in a developed country is likely to demand by 2020, although developing countries will account for more than 80 per cent of the world's population.

To meet growing food needs, world cereal production is expected to grow on average by 1.3 per cent per year between 1993 and 2020, meat production by 1.8 per cent and production of roots and tubers by 1.3 per cent (Rosegrant *et al.*, 1997). Production growth rates are expected to be substantially higher in developing countries than in developed countries. Cereal production is projected to grow at an average annual rate of 1.5 per cent (compared to 1.0 per cent in developed countries), meat production at 2.7 per cent (compared to 0.8 per cent in developed countries), and production of roots and tubers at 1.7 per cent (compared to 0.4 per cent in developed countries) (ibid.).

Developing countries as a group are projected to increase their net imports of cereals (the difference between production and demand) from about 94

TABLE 4 *Total and per capita demand for cereals, meat, and roots and tubers, 1993 and 2020*

	Total demand (million tons)			Per capita demand (kilograms)		
	1993	2020	1993–2020 (per cent)	1993	2020	1993–2020 (per cent)
Cereals						
Developing countries	1 022.0	1 613.5	+58	239.1	254.5	+6.5
Asia	695.0	1 042.8	+50	237.7	261.9	+10.2
Sub-Saharan Africa	70.4	154.9	+120	137.1	147.9	+7.9
Latin America	128.8	199.1	+55	278.9	302.0	+8.3
West Africa and North Africa	127.1	215.4	+70	344.3	631.6	−2.1
Developed countries	751.0	877.2	+17	587.8	631.6	+7.5
World	1 773.0	2 490.7	+40	319.3	322.4	+9.7
Meat						
Developing countries	88.9	193.5	+118	20.82	30.56	+46.8
Asia	55.7	125.9	+128	19.07	32.54	+70.6
Sub-Saharan Africa	4.5	6.9	+53	8.84	10.65	+20.5
Latin America	21.2	37.6	+77	45.92	57.09	+24.3
West Africa and North Africa	7.3	14.8	+103	19.71	23.16	+17.5
Developed countries	99.3	112.4	+13	77.72	80.98	+4.2
World	188.2	305.9	+63	33.90	39.62	+16.9
Roots and tubers						
Developing countries	396.9	620.7	+56	92.9	97.9	+5.4
Asia	181.8	249.7	+37	71.1	71.7	+0.8
Sub-Saharan Africa	126.1	243.2	+93	245.4	232.1	−5.5
Latin America	45.9	65.0	+42	99.5	98.6	−0.9
West Africa and North Africa	14.1	22.0	+56	38.3	34.5	−9.9
Developed countries	213.9	234.8	+10	167.4	169.1	+1.0
World	610.8	855.5	+40	110.0	110.7	+0.6

Source: Rosegrant, Sombilla, Gerpacio, and Ringler (1997).

million tons in 1993 to 228 million tons in 2020 (ibid.). Maize is expected to constitute 27 per cent of net cereal imports in 2020 (compared to 19 per cent in 1993), wheat is expected to constitute 61 per cent (69 per cent in 1993), and rice is expected to constitute 0.2 per cent (0.22 per cent in 1993) (ibid.). All developing regions are projected to increase their net cereal imports between 1993 and 2020 – Asia by 425 per cent, primarily because of rapid income growth, and sub-Saharan Africa by 250 per cent, primarily because of continued poor performance in food production. During the same period, developing countries are projected to increase their net meat imports almost 20-fold. Rapid income growth is the primary driving force underlying the massive increases in demand for meat, especially in Asia. Net imports are a reflection of the gap between production and demand. The gap between production and need is likely to be even wider as many of the poor are priced out of the market, even at low food prices, and are unable to exercise their demand for necessary food. The better-off developing countries, notably those of Southeast Asia, will be able to fill the gap between production and demand through commercial imports, but the poorer countries will lack sufficient foreign exchange to import food in the necessary quantities. It is the latter group of countries, including most of those in sub-Saharan Africa and South Asia, that will remain a challenge and require special assistance to avert widespread hunger and malnutrition.

Where are world food prices headed? As expected, the recent rises in prices for wheat and maize were short-term blips, driven primarily by poor weather in North America, government set-aside programmes and reduced price subsidies in Western Europe and North America, declining food production in the former Soviet Union and large increases in food demand in China (Pinstrup-Andersen and Garrett, 1996). On average, world cereal prices are expected to decline by about 11 per cent between 1993 and 2020, meat prices by about 6 per cent, and prices for roots and tubers by 4 per cent (Rosegrant *et al.*, 1997). According to Rosegrant *et al.* (ibid.), 'these price declines are minuscule compared to the rate of decline in prices over the last several decades'.

SHADOWS OF MALTHUS

The writings of Malthus (1798) have been referred to frequently to argue that the world is headed towards global food shortages. Malthus' basic argument was that the world's natural resources would not be able to ensure expansions in food supply that would match population growth. As Figure 2 shows, there are no indications that Malthusian predictions will come true for Asia, where food production has increased at a rate much higher than the rate of population growth. The situation is quite different in sub-Saharan Africa where, as Figure 3 shows, the population growth rate has exceeded that for food production since the early 1970s. The gap is widening, resulting in declining food production per capita. Simple projections of the trends in population and food production growth since 1961 show a further increase in the gap between the two, which is exactly the type of thing predicted by Malthus. While he argued that the population would grow geometrically and food production would grow

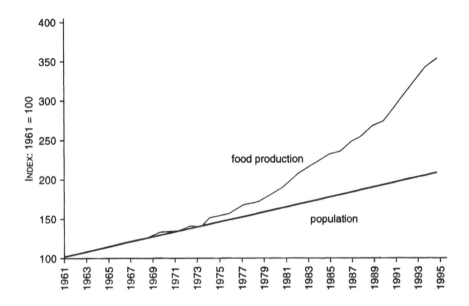

FIGURE 2   *Population and food production indices for developing countries in Asia, 1961–96*

Source: FAO (1997).

arithmetically, the projections shown in Figure 2 are both based on a regression equation with a square term. Such a function showed a better fit than linear functions for either of the two variables.

Malthus' predictions, made so long ago, grossly underestimated the potential of productivity-increasing technology. Where that has been effectively developed and utilized, as is the case in most of Asia, food production has expanded much faster than population. In sub-Saharan Africa, technological potential has yet to be realized. Maize yields for Africa, Asia and China were virtually the same in 1961, but since then they have tripled in Asia and quintupled in China, while they have remained at around 1 ton per hectare in Africa (FAO, 1997).

Does this mean that Malthus will eventually be proved correct in the developing countries of Africa? The answer lies in the extent of action taken to develop and ensure the use of appropriate technologies to expand the productivity of African soils and African farmers. There are encouraging signs that productivity-increasing technology is beginning to accelerate yield growth. For example, the introduction of improved maize varieties has resulted in productivity increases in West and Central Africa at rates as high as 4 per cent per year during the period

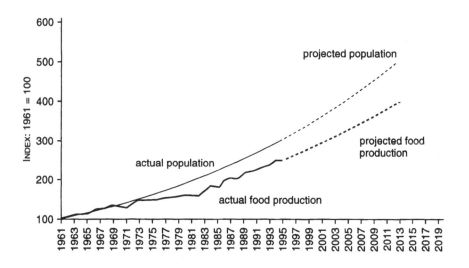

FIGURE 3   *Actual and projected population and food production indices for sub-Saharan Africa, 1961–2020*

Source: FAO (1997) and author's calculations

1983–92 (CGIAR, 1997). Some countries have experienced particularly high rates of growth in maize production during this period, including Burkina Faso (17.1 per cent), Ghana (8.3 per cent) and Mali (7.5 per cent). If Malthus is to be proved wrong, not only globally but also in Africa, a much greater effort must be made to ensure that farmers have access to appropriate production technology and that policies are conducive to expanded productivity in staple food crops. A continuation of the trends of the past 25 years will confirm Malthus' predictions. Therefore new initiatives and expanded support for agricultural development, including the development of appropriate technology and the implementation of appropriate policies, must be pursued.

REQUIRED ACTION

The action required to ensure a food-secure world is known. Much thought and effort has been expended to identify priority action at the individual, house-hold, community, national, regional and global levels. Most recently, at the World Food Summit convened by the Food and Agriculture Organization of the United Nations (FAO) in November 1996, leaders from around the world signed the Rome Declaration on World Food Security, reaffirming 'the right of every person to have access to safe and nutritious food, consistent with the right to adequate food and the fundamental right of everyone to be free from hunger' (FAO, 1996e). They pledged their 'political will and [their] common and national commitment to achieving food security for all and to an ongoing effort to eradicate hunger in all countries, with an immediate view to reducing the number of undernourished people to half their present level no later than 2015'. To this end, they made seven commitments.

(1) To ensure an enabling political, social and economic environment designed to create the best conditions for the eradication of poverty and for durable peace, based on full and equal participation of women and men, which is most conducive to achieving sustainable food security for all.
(2) To implement policies aimed at eradicating poverty and inequality and improving physical and economic access by all, at all times, to sufficient, nutritionally adequate and safe food and its effective utilization.
(3) To pursue participatory and sustainable food, agriculture, fisheries, forestry and rural development policies and practices in high- and low-potential areas, which are essential to adequate and reliable food supplies at the household, national, regional and global levels, and combat pests, drought and desertification, considering the multifunctional character of agriculture.
(4) To strive to ensure that food, agricultural trade and overall trade policies are conducive to fostering food security for all through a fair and market-oriented world trade system.
(5) To endeavour to prevent and be prepared for natural disasters and man-made emergencies and to meet transitory and emergency food requirements in ways that encourage recovery, rehabilitation, development and a capacity to satisfy future needs.
(6) To promote optimal allocation and use of public and private investments to foster human resources, sustainable food, agriculture, fisheries and forestry systems, and rural development in high- and low-potential areas.
(7) To implement, monitor and follow up this plan of action at all levels in cooperation with the international community (ibid.).

A detailed plan of action seeks to achieve the goals included in these seven commitments.

The International Food Policy Research Institute (IFPRI), in its initiative, *A 2020 Vision for Food, Agriculture and the Environment*, has developed the vision of 'a world where every person has access to sufficient food to sustain a healthy and productive life, where malnutrition is absent and where food originates from efficient, effective and low-cost food systems that are compatible with sustainable use of natural resources' (IFPRI, 1995). Sustained action is required in six priority areas to realize the 2020 vision.

(1) Strengthen the capacity of developing-country governments to perform appropriate functions.

(2) Enhance the productivity, health and nutrition of low-income people and increase their access to employment and productive assets.
(3) Strengthen agricultural research and extension systems in and for developing countries.
(4) Promote sustainable agricultural intensification and sound management of natural resources, with increased emphasis on areas with agricultural potential, fragile soils, limited rainfall and widespread poverty.
(5) Develop efficient, effective and low-cost agricultural input and output markets.
(6) Expand international cooperation and assistance and improve its efficiency and effectiveness.

The first priority area of action is selectively to strengthen the capacity of developing-country governments to perform appropriate functions, such as maintaining law and order, establishing and enforcing property rights, promoting and ensuring private-sector competition in markets and maintaining appropriate macroeconomic environments. Predictability, transparency and continuity in policy making and enforcement must be assured. The efforts of the past decade to weaken developing-country governments must be turned around. More effective local and national governments are essential for other partners, such as individuals, households, communities, non-governmental organizations (NGOs) and the private sector to contribute to food security. Governments must also be helped to relinquish those functions that are better performed by others such as NGOs. Governments should facilitate food security for all households and individuals, not by physically delivering needed foods to all citizens but by facilitating a social and economic environment that provides all citizens with the opportunity to ensure their food security.

The second priority area is to invest more in poor people in order to enhance their productivity, health and nutrition, and to increase their access to remunerative employment and productive assets. Governments, local communities and NGOs should ensure access to and support for a complete primary education for all children, with immediate emphasis on enhancing access by female and rural children; ensure access to primary health care, including reproductive health services, for all people; improve access to clean water and sanitation services; provide training for skill development in adults; and strengthen and enforce legislation and provide incentives for empowerment of women to gain gender equality. Improved access by the rural poor, especially women, to productive resources can be facilitated through land reform and sound property rights legislation, strengthened credit and savings institutions, more effective rural labour markets and infrastructure for small-scale enterprises. Social safety nets for the rural poor are urgently needed. Direct transfer programmes, covering poverty relief, food security and nutrition intervention, are needed in many countries at least in the short term and must be better focused on the poor. Efforts must be made to lower fertility rates and slow population increases. Strategies to reduce population growth rates include providing full access to reproductive health services to meet unmet demand for contraception; eliminating risk factors that promote high fertility, such as high rates of infant mortality or lack of security for women who are dependent on their children for support because they lack access to income, credit or assets; and providing young women with education. Female education is among the most important investments for ensuring food security.

The third area for action is to accelerate agricultural productivity by strengthening agricultural research and extension systems in and for developing countries. Agriculture is the life-blood of the economy in most developing countries; it provides up to three-quarters of all employment and half of all incomes. There are very strong links between agricultural productivity increases and broad-based economic growth in the rest of the economy; research from Africa and Asia shows that, for each dollar generated in agriculture, one to one-and-a-half dollars are generated in other areas of the economy (Hazell and Röell, 1983; Delgado *et al.*, 1995). Agriculture has long been neglected in many developing countries, resulting in stagnant economies and widespread hunger and poverty, yet there is considerable evidence, particularly from East Asia, that rapid economic growth is facilitated by a vibrant and healthy agricultural sector (World Bank, 1993). The key role of the agriculture sector in meeting food needs and fostering broad-based economic growth and development must be recognized and exploited. To make this happen, agricultural research systems must be mobilized to develop improved agricultural technologies, and extension systems must be strengthened to disseminate improved technologies.

While expanded agricultural research is urgently needed for all ecoregions, added emphasis should be placed on sustainable productivity increases in areas with significant agricultural potential but with fragile soils, low or irregular rainfall, and widespread poverty and natural resource degradation. Interaction between public-sector agricultural research systems, farmers, private-sector companies that conduct agricultural research, private-sector enterprises in food processing and distribution and NGOs should be strengthened to ensure relevance of research and appropriate distribution of responsibilities. Investments in strategic international and regional agricultural research with large potential international benefits should be expanded to better support national efforts. Biotechnology research in national and international research systems should be expanded to support sustainable intensification of small-scale agriculture in developing countries. Effective partnerships between developing-country research systems, international research institutions and private- and public-sector research institutions in industrialized countries should be forged to bring biotechnology to bear on the agricultural problems of developing countries. Developing countries can address funding and personnel constraints by providing incentives to the private sector to engage in such research, by collaborating with international research programmes, and by seeking private- and public-sector partners in industrialized countries. They should be encouraged to adopt regulations that provide an effective measure of biosafety without crippling the transfer of new products to small farmers.

The fourth priority area of action is to promote sustainable agricultural intensification and ensure sound management of natural resources. Public- and private-sector investments in infrastructure, market development, natural resource conservation, soil improvements, primary education and health care and agricultural research must be expanded in areas with significant agricultural potential, fragile soils and large concentrations of poverty to address effectively their problems of poverty, food insecurity and natural resource degradation before they worsen or spill over into other regions. In areas of low current productivity, but significant agricultural potential, public policy and public-sector investment should promote sustainable use of existing natural resources to enhance the productivity of agriculture and other rural enterprises. Farmers and local communities should be given incentives to invest in and protect natural resources and to restore degraded lands. Clearly specified systems of rights to use and manage natural resources, including land, water and forests, should be established and enforced. Local control over natural resources must be strengthened and local capacity for organization and management improved. Farmers and communities should be encouraged to implement integrated soil fertility programmes in areas with low soil fertility through policies to ensure long-term property rights to land, access to credit, improved crop varieties and information about production systems; through effective and efficient markets for plant nutrients, and investments in infrastructure and transport systems; and through temporary fertilizer subsidies where prices are high owing to inadequate infrastructure or poorly functioning markets. Integrated pest management programmes should be promoted as the central pest management strategy to reduce use of chemical pesticides, remove pesticide subsidies and increase farmer participation in developing effective and appropriate strategies of pest management. Water policies should be reformed to make better use of existing water supplies by providing water users with appropriate incentives, improving procedures for water allocation and developing and disseminating improved technology for water supply and delivery.

The fifth priority is to develop effective, efficient and low-cost agricultural input and output markets. To obtain gains from improved efficiency and reduced costs of marketing agricultural inputs and outputs, governments should phase out inefficient state-run firms in agricultural input and output markets and create an environment conducive to effective competition among private agents in order to provide producers and consumers with efficient and effective services. Governments should identify their role in agricultural input and output markets and strengthen their capacity to perform this role better while disengaging themselves from functions that should be undertaken by the private sector. Policies and institutions that favour large-scale, capital-intensive enterprises over small-scale, labour-intensive ones should be removed. Market infrastructure of a public goods nature, such as roads, electricity and communications facilities, should be developed and maintained by direct public-sector investment or effective regulation of private-sector investment. Governments should develop and enforce standards, weights and measures, and regulatory instruments essential for effective functioning of markets. Development of small-scale credit and savings institutions should be facilitated. Technical assistance and training could be provided to create or strengthen small-scale, labour-intensive competitive rural enterprises in trade, processing and related marketing activities.

The sixth requirement is to expand and realign international assistance. The current downward trend in international development assistance must be reversed, and industrialized countries allocating less than the United Nations target of 0.7 per cent of their gross national product (GNP) should rapidly move to that target. Official development assistance, which is only a small fraction of the resources required by developing countries, must be allocated to complement national and local efforts effectively. Official government-to-government assistance should be made available primarily to countries that have demonstrated commitment to reducing poverty, hunger and malnutrition, and to protecting the environment. International development assistance must be realigned to low-income developing countries, primarily in sub-Saharan Africa and South Asia, where the potential for further deterioration of food security and degradation of natural resources is considerable. In higher-income developing countries, concessional aid such as grants should be replaced by internationally available commercial capital, freeing resources for the low-income countries. To improve effectiveness of aid, each recipient country should develop a coherent strategy for achieving its goals related to food security, poverty and natural resources, and should identify the most appropriate uses of international assistance.

The action plans for the World Food Summit and IFPRI's 2020 vision are fully compatible and should be pursued to the fullest extent possible.

CONCLUSIONS

Food insecurity has long been perceived by some to be primarily a problem of insufficient food production rather than insufficient access to food. Yet, as enough food is being produced to meet the basic needs of every person in the world, it is evident that the persistence of food insecurity – with about 840 million chronically undernourished people and 185 million malnourished pre-school children – is increasingly attributable to difficulties in gaining access to sufficient food. Food-insecure people simply do not have the means to grow and/or purchase the needed food. Empowering every individual to have access to remunerative employment, to productive assets such as land and capital, and to productivity-enhancing resources such as appropriate technology, credit, education and health care is essential. Besides enabling every person to acquire the means to grow and/or purchase sufficient food to lead healthy and productive lives, ensuring a food-secure world calls for producing enough food to meet increasing and changing food needs and for meeting food needs from better management of natural resources.

With foresight and decisive action, we can create the conditions that permit food security for all people in the coming years. The action required is not new or unknown; for instance, we know that increased productivity in agricultural production helps, not only to produce more food at lower unit costs and make more efficient use of resources, but also to raise the incomes of farmers and others linked to agriculture and thus improve their capacity to purchase needed food. The action programme outlined earlier will require all relevant parties – individuals, households, farmers, local communities, the private sector, civil society, national governments and the international community – to work together in new or strengthened partnerships; it will require a change in behaviour, priorities and policies; and it will require strengthened cooperation between developing and industrialized countries and among developing countries. The world's natural resources are capable of supporting sustainable food security for all people, if current rates of degradation are reduced and replaced by appropriate technological change and sustainable use of natural resources (Pinstrup-Andersen and Pandya-Lorch, 1996a).

We have the means to ensure a food-secure world; let us act to make it a reality for each and every person.

REFERENCES

Ahmed, R. and Rustagi, N. (1987), 'Marketing and Price Incentives in African and Asian Countries: A Comparison,' in D. Elz (ed.), *Agricultural Marketing Strategy and Pricing Policy*, Washington, DC: International Bank for Reconstruction and Development.

Alexandratos, N. (ed.) (1995), *World agriculture: Towards 2010*, Rome: Food and Agriculture Organization of the United Nations.

Brown, L. (1996), *Tough Choices: Facing the Challenge of Food Scarcity*, New York: W.W. Norton.

Brown, L.R., Lenssen, N. and Kane, H. (1995), *Vital Signs 1995: The Trends That Are Shaping Our Future*, New York: W.W. Norton.

Bumb, B.L. and Baanante, C.A. (1996), *The Role of Fertilizers in Sustaining Food Security and Protecting the Environment to 2020*, Food, Agriculture and the Environment Discussion Paper 17, Washington, DC: International Food Policy Research Institute.

CGIAR (Consultative Group on International Agriculture Research) (1997), 'Phenomenal Increase in Maize Production in West and Central Africa', in *CGIAR News*, **4** (2), 1, 14, 15.

Delgado, C., Hopkins, J. and Kelly, V., with Hazell, P., Alfano, A., Gruhn, P., Hojjati, B. and Sil, J. (1995), 'Agricultural Growth Linkages in sub-Saharan Africa', mimeo, International Food Policy Research Institute, Washington, DC.

Echeverria, R.G., Trigo, E.J. and Byerlee, D. (1996), *Institutional Change and Elective Financing of Agricultural Research in Latin America*, World Bank Technical Paper 330, Washington, DC: World Bank.

FAO (Food and Agriculture Organization of the United Nations) (1987), *Agriculture Toward 2000*, Rome: FAO.

FAO (Food and Agriculture Organization of the United Nations) (1996a), *Food, Agriculture and Food Security: Developments Since the World Food Conference and Prospects*, World Food Summit Technical Background Document 1, Rome: FAO.

FAO (Food and Agriculture Organization of the United Nations) (1996b), *Food Security and Nutrition*, World Food Summit Technical Background Document 5, Rome: FAO.

FAO (Food and Agriculture Organization of the United Nations) (1996c), *Investment in Agriculture: Evolution and Prospects*, World Food Summit Technical Background Document 10, Rome: FAO.

FAO (Food and Agriculture Organization of the United Nations) (1996d), *Mapping Undernutrition – An Ongoing Process*, poster prepared for the World Food Summit.

FAO (Food and Agriculture Organization of the United Nations) (1996e), *Rome Declaration on World Food Security and World Food Summit Plan of Action*, Rome: FAO.

FAO (Food and Agriculture Organization of the United Nations) (1997), FAOSTAT database, <http://faostat.fao.org/default.htm>. accessed May.

Hazell, P. (1995), 'Technology's Contribution to Feeding the World in 2020', in *A 2020 Vision for Food, Agriculture and the Environment: Speeches Made at an International Conference*, Washington, DC: International Food Policy Research Institute.

Hazell, P.B.R. and Röell, A. (1983), *Rural Growth Linkages: Household Expenditure Patterns in Malaysia and Nigeria*, Research Report 41, Washington, DC: International Food Policy Research Institute.

IFPRI (International Food Policy Research Institute) (1995), *A 2020 Vision for Food, Agriculture and the Environment: The Vision, Challenge and Recommended Action*, Washington, DC: IFPRI.

Ingco, M., Mitchell, D.O. and McCalla, A. (1996), *Global Food Supply Prospects*, Washington, DC: World Bank.
Islam, N. (ed.) (1995), *Population and Food in the Early Twenty-First Century: Meeting Future Food Demand of an Increasing Population*, Washington, DC: International Food Policy Research Institute.
Malthus, T.R. (1798), *An Essay on Population*, London: J. Johnson.
OECD (Organization for Economic Cooperation and Development) (1997), *Development Cooperation 1997*, Paris: OECD.
Oldeman, L.R. (1992), 'Global Extent of Soil Degradation', in *Biannual Report 1991–1992*, Wageningen, The Netherlands: International Soil Reference and Information Centre.
Pardey, P.G. and Alston, J.M. (1995), *Revamping Agricultural R&D*, 2020 Brief 24, Washington, DC: International Food Policy Research Institute.
Pardey, P.G., Roseboom, J. and Anderson, J.R. (eds) (1991), *Agricultural Research Policy: International Quantitative Perspectives*, Cambridge: Cambridge University Press.
Pardey, P.G., Roseboom, J. and Beintema, N.M. (1995), *Investments in African Agricultural Research*, Environment and Production Technology Division Discussion Paper 14, Washington, DC: International Food Policy Research Institute.
Penning de Vries, F.W.T., van Keulen, H., Rabbinge, R. and Luyten, J.C. (1995), *Biophysical Limits to Global Food Production*, 2020 Brief 18, Washington, DC: International Food Policy Research Institute.
Pinstrup-Andersen, P. (1994), *World Food Trends and Future Food Security*, Food Policy Report, Washington, DC: International Food Policy Research Institute.
Pinstrup-Andersen, P. and Garrett, J.L. (1996), *Rising Food Prices and Falling Grain Stocks: Short-Run Blips or New Trends?*, 2020 Brief 30, Washington, DC: International Food Policy Research Institute.
Pinstrup-Andersen, P. and Pandya-Lorch, R. (1995), *Agricultural Growth is the Key to Poverty Alleviation in Low-Income Developing Countries*, 2020 Brief 15, Washington, DC: International Food Policy Research Institute.
Pinstrup-Andersen, P. and Pandya-Lorch, R. (1996a), 'Food for All in 2020: Can the World be Fed Without Damaging the Environment?', *Environmental Conservation*, 23, 226–34.
Pinstrup-Andersen, P. and Pandya-Lorch, R. (1996b), 'Using Modern Science to Assure Food Security', commentary in *IFPRI Report* (October), Washington DC: International Food Policy Research Institute.
Pinstrup-Andersen, P. and Pandya-Lorch, R. (1997), 'Farm Management Challenges in the Developing World', paper presented for the Eleventh International Farm Management Congress, Calgary, Canada, 9 June.
Rosegrant, M.W. (1997), *Water Resources in the Twenty-First Century: Challenges and Implications for Action*, Food, Agriculture and the Environment Discussion Paper 20, Washington, DC: International Food Policy Research Institute.
Rosegrant, M.W., Agcaoili-Sombilla, M. and Perez, N.D. (1995), *Global Food Projections to 2020: Implications for Investment*, Food, Agriculture and the Environment Discussion Paper 5, Washington, DC: International Food Policy Research Institute.
Rosegrant, M.W., Sombilla, M.A., Gerpacio, R.V. and Ringler, C. (1997), 'Global Food Markets and U.S. Exports in the Twenty-First Century', paper presented at the Illinois World Food and Sustainable Agriculture Program Conference on 'Meeting the Demand for Food in the Twenty-first Century: Challanges and Opportunities for Illinois Agriculture', Urbana-Champaign, 27 May, International Food Policy Research Institute, Washington, DC.
Sarbib, J.-L. (1997), 'Rural Development in Africa: The World Bank's Perspective', presentation on 1 May 1997 at the International Food Policy Research Institute, Washington, DC.
UN (United Nations) (1995), *World Urbanization Prospects: The 1994 Revisions*, New York: UN.
UN (United Nations) (1996), *World Population Prospects: The 1996 Revisions*, New York: UN.
UN (United Nations) (1997), *The World Economy at the Beginning of 1997*, note by the Secretary-General, New York: UN Economic and Social Council.
von Braun, J., Bouis, H., Kumar, S. and Pandya-Lorch, R. (1992), *Improving Food Security of the Poor: Concept, Policy and Programs*, Washington, DC: International Food Policy Research Institute.
World Bank (1990), *World Development Report 1990*, New York: Oxford University Press.

World Bank (1993), *The East Asian Miracle: Economic Growth and the Public Policy*, New York: Oxford University Press.
World Bank (1996a), *Global Economic Prospects and the Developing Countries 1996*, Washington, DC: World Bank.
World Bank (1996b), *Poverty Reduction and the World Bank*, Washington, DC: World Bank.
World Bank (1996c), *World Development Report 1996*, New York: Oxford University Press.

C.H. HANUMANTHA RAO AND R. RADHAKRISHNA*

National Food Security: A Policy Perspective for India

OVERVIEW OF PERFORMANCE AND EMERGING ISSUES

Achievement of national food security has been a major goal of development policy in India for half a century, since the country became independent. This was to be achieved by attaining self-sufficiency in the availability of food; by raising the purchasing power of the poor through the endowment of land and non-land assets and by generating employment opportunities so as to enable them to have adequate access to food; and through public intervention for stabilizing consumption, reducing the annual variations in the availability of food and providing subsidized food to the poorer and the vulnerable sections of the community.

The achievements have been substantial in terms of reaching near self-sufficiency in food and overcoming transient food insecurity through public procurement and distribution of foodgrains. However, despite a significant reduction in the incidence of poverty, chronic food insecurity persists, as a large proportion of the population is still below the poverty line. This is basically explained by the slow growth in gross domestic product (GDP) and, consequently, sluggish growth in employment. This has been exacerbated by the failure of land reforms to provide land for the landless poor in rural areas, the ineffective implementation of the poverty alleviation programmes and the universal nature of the public distribution of foodgrains with hardly any selectivity.

In terms of its performance, the food economy of India reveals three distinct phases. The first phase, from the beginning of planning to the mid-1960s, was characterized by severe imbalances between the demand for food and its domestic supply. Over the post-'green revolution' period, from about the mid-1960s to the close of the 1980s, the country achieved near self-sufficiency in the availability of food and experienced an improvement in effective food security insofar as there was a significant reduction in the incidence of poverty, especially in the 1980s. This second phase itself warrants sub-grouping into the 1970s, characterized by the emergence of interregional and inter-crop imbalances in agricultural growth, and the 1980s when crops like rice, oilseeds and pulses registered high growth, especially in the eastern and central regions where poverty is widespread, and which were largely bypassed in the early

*Centre for Economic and Social Studies, Hyderabad and Indian Council of Social Science Research, New Delhi, India, respectively.

phase of the 'green revolution'. The third phase is represented by the post-economic reform period of the 1990s, when measures for macroeconomic stabilization and structural adjustment were launched. The immediate, or short-run, consequences of these reforms for the food economy seem to have been adverse.

Foodgrain production in the pre-'green revolution' period barely kept pace with population growth, the annual growth rate of per capita output being negative in the 1960s. Output growth was achieved mainly through the extension of the area under cultivation by using traditional technology. Imports of foodgrains increased, reaching a level of 14 per cent of domestic availability in 1966. The droughts of 1965 and 1966, with the rising prices of food, highlighted the imbalance in India's food economy. There was sluggish growth in productivity, with a slow rise in the use of inputs such as high-yielding seeds, irrigation and fertilizers, in the face of growing demand for food on account of rapid growth of population and improving income.

This crisis prompted the government to give an overriding priority to the goal of achieving self-sufficiently in foodgrains by launching the 'green revolution'. Public investment in irrigation and agricultural research was stepped up. As a result of this and the rise in total factor productivity, the per capita growth rate in the output of foodgrains was close to 1 per cent in the first decade of the 'green revolution' and accelerated further, to slightly over 1.5 per cent, during the 1980s. Consequently, the dependence on imports declined in the post-'green revolution' period, when net imports of foodgrains were either negative or less than 1 per cent of domestic availability (Government of India, 1997). The relative prices of foodgrains declined after the mid-1970s (Figure 1) and there was a rise in real wages of farm labour.

In the post-reform period of the 1990s, however, the growth rate in foodgrains output, at 1.7 per cent, has been lagging behind the population growth rate of 1.9 per cent (ibid.). The rate of inflation has been high, at 10 per cent or more, for four consecutive years, with the rise in the prices of foodgrains being even greater, so that the relative price registered a steep rise. As a result there was an increase in poverty and inequality in the immediate post-reform period, with only a slow reduction in poverty thereafter (Gupta, 1995).

Public intervention in the foodgrain market assumed greater significance in the post-'green revolution' period, both for ensuring remunerative prices for farmers and for stabilizing consumption. Procurement of foodgrains by the government increased steadily, from well below 5 per cent of output over much of the pre-'green revolution' period to well above 10 per cent and 15 per cent in the 1980s and 1990s (Government of India, 1997). Correspondingly, the volume of public distribution of foodgrains increased markedly, exceeding 10 per cent of domestic availability in the post-'green revolution' period. As a result, prices were remunerative for producers of wheat and rice in better endowed regions, while price collapses were prevented in periods of bumper harvest (Radhakrishna and Rao, 1995). Thanks also to a series of good monsoons, the annual fluctuations in the per capita availability of foodgrains declined during the 1980s and 1990s when compared with the previous period, and there was a decline in the seasonal as well as regional variation in their prices (Bhalla, 1994).

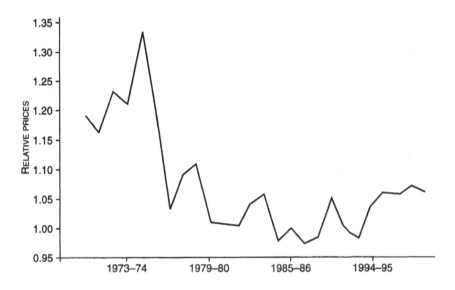

FIGURE 1   *Relative prices of foodgrains*

This overview suggests that the most important problem of food management in India is to overcome chronic food insecurity, by ensuring adequate nutrition for the whole population on a sustainable basis (Radhakrishna, 1996). This would require augmentation of food supplies to meet the expanding food basket which, as mentioned later, is becoming increasingly diversified on account of changing tastes and preferences. However, the real challenge is to ensure that there is adequate purchasing power in the hands of those suffering from chronic food insecurity. As argued in this paper, the current economic reforms, given appropriate content and sequencing, can be expected to generate productive employment necessary to overcome the insecurity problem. Public support for poverty alleviation programmes, as well as subsidized food for the vulnerable sections, will have to continue but, basically, it will be supplementary to the broad-based employment-oriented growth. The focus of such interventions in future should be on better designing and direction of the schemes and on cost-effective delivery systems.

FOOD TRENDS

The National Sample Survey (NSS) consumption data suggest that the per capita consumption of cereals in India is falling. Between 1970–71 and 1991–2, it declined by 0.52 per cent per annum in rural areas and by 0.23 per cent per annum in urban areas (Radhakrishna, 1996).[1] The decline is very prominent in Punjab and Haryana. What is striking is the low per capita intake of cereals in the most prosperous state of Punjab (12 kg. in rural areas and only 8.85 kg. in urban areas in 1991–2) and high consumption in the backward state of Orissa (17kg. in rural areas and 13.36 kg. in urban areas). Part of the explanation for this paradox lies in the diversification of the food basket in Punjab in favour of non-cereal food, particularly milk and milk products, meat, eggs, fish, vegetables and fruits. The wide coverage of the public distribution system (PDS) in Kerala, and the substantial increase in rice production in West Bengal and Orissa in the 1980s, may explain the rising trend in cereal consumption in these states.

The fall in cereal consumption was offset by an increase in the consumption of non-cereal food. In fact, when compared with 1972–3, the per capita food expenditure was higher in 1987–8, by 15.15 per cent in urban areas and by 14.70 per cent in rural areas (Table 1). However, these increases were not commensurate with the increase in per capita total expenditure. Despite this increase in food expenditure, the nutrient intake expanded at a slower rate; per capita calorie and protein intakes, respectively, grew by 5.15 and 3.51 per cent in rural areas and 8.59 and 5.56 per cent in urban areas. Considering the long timespan of 15 years (1972–3 to 1987–8), these improvements were negligible. Part of the explanation for this slower improvement in nutrient intake lies in the decline in the consumption of cereals, which is the cheapest source of calories. In the case of the lowest 30 per cent of the population, there has been hardly any improvement in the cereal and nutrient intakes in both rural and urban areas (Table 1). It seems that the improvement in economic access to cereal food did not result in higher consumption. The poorer section of the population fails to enjoy a diet which provides the required food energy, with adverse effects on health and nutritional status of both adults and children.

Among the poor, per capita cereal consumption did not alter despite a significant improvement in their real per capita expenditure and a decline in the relative cereal price. This counterintuitive result can be attributed to changes in preferences as a result of the increased availability of a wide variety of food and non-food items (Radhkrishna and Ravi, 1992; Rao and Gulati, 1994). There has also been a substantial diversification of the consumption basket of the poor in favour of non-cereal items, particularly non-food items. The question of topical interest is whether poor households are buying efficient diets from a nutritional perspective. It can be argued that, if the diversification of the consumption basket improves nutritional status, even though it may not add calories, there should be no cause for concern. However, while the implications of changes in dietary preferences on nutritional and health status may be important there is, unfortunately, hardly any work which throws light on the issue.

Given the changing structure of demand, any improvement in the nutritional intake levels of the poor would require a substantial increase in their incomes so that their choice of consumption basket would ensure adequate nutrients. In the absence of such a possibility in the near future, there is a need to increase the supply of subsidized food to the poor through the PDS and through em-

TABLE 1 *Per capita consumption expenditure and nutrient intake in 1972–3 and 1987–8 at 1987–8 prices*

	All classes					
	Rural			Urban		
Commodity group	1972–3	1987–8	Percentage change	1972–3	1987–8	Percentage change
(1)	(2)	(3)	(4)	(5)	(6)	(7)
Per capita expenditure (Rs/month)						
1. Cereal and cereal substitutes	22.23	21.36	3.91	19.41	19.37	0.21
2. Non-cereal food	19.43	26.61	36.95	35.47	43.58	22.86
3. All food	41.66	47.97	15.15	54.88	62.95	14.70
4. Non-food	18.78	26.72	42.28	39.34	56.71	44.15
5. Total expenditure	60.44	74.69	23.58	94.21	119.67	27.02
Nutrient intake						
Calories (kcal/day)	2 134	2 244	5.15	2 026	2 200	8.59
Protein (g/day)	57.00	59.00	3.51	54.00	57.00	5.56

	Poorest 30 per cent population					
	Rural			Urban		
Commodity group	1972–3	1987–8	Percentage change	1972–3	1987–8	Percentage change
(1)	(2)	(3)	(4)	(5)	(6)	(7)
Per capita expenditure (Rs/month)						
1. Cereal and cereal substitutes	16.41	16.50	0.55	15.59	16.36	4.94
2. Non-cereal food	8.87	12.71	43.29	15.17	21.25	40.08
3. All food	25.28	29.21	15.55	30.76	37.61	22.27
4. Non-food	6.98	11.19	60.32	10.81	16.19	49.80
5. Total expenditure	32.26	40.40	25.23	41.57	53.80	29.42
Nutrient intake						
Calories (kcal/day)	1 510	1 599	5.89	1 524	1 704	11.81
Protein (g/day)	41.25	42.98	4.19	40.23	46.00	14.34

Source: Radhakrishna (1996).

ployment programmes, as well as strengthening various nutrition programmes
to provide supplementation of the diets of vulnerable groups such as children,
and pregnant and lactating women.

NUTRITION INTAKE AND NUTRITIONAL STATUS

The National Nutrition Monitoring Bureau (NNMB, 1991) provides data on
diet and nutritional status of rural households in seven sample states for the
periods 1975–80 and 1988–90. The results do not reveal any increase in nutritional intake. Although the average daily intake of calories and protein was
found to have become closer to the standard requirements suggested by the
Indian Council of Medical Research, the lower socioeconomic strata can suffer
from protein–calorie deficiency as there are inter-state, inter-household and
intra-household (gender) inequalities in food intake. NNMB data also reveal
severe micronutrient (Vitamin 'A', Thiamine, Riboflavin and Niacin) deficiencies stemming from lack of variety in the diet.

The NNMB classified rural children, aged 1–5 years, into different nutritional grades based on weight for age. The results show that the percentage of
children in the standard normal range increased from 5.9 in 1975–9 to 9.9 in
1988–90, while those falling into the severe malnutrition range declined from
15.0 per cent to 8.7 per cent during the same period (Table 2). If those
classified in the moderate and severe malnutrition ranges are considered together, the percentage declined from 62.5 per cent in 1975–9 to 52.5 per cent
in 1988–90. It is clear, however, that even with some improvement in nutritional status, more than half of the rural children can be considered to be
suffering from malnutrition.[2]

In terms of the nutritional status of children, middle-income states such as
Kerala, Tamil Nadu and Andhra Pradesh performed better than those with
higher income, such as Gujarat and Maharashtra. Not surprisingly, lower-
income areas such as Madhya Pradesh and Orissa had the worst performance.
It is notable that calorie intake per consumer unit was very low in Kerala and
Tamil Nadu, where there was a high ranking in nutritional status. Inter-state
comparisons do not reveal any empirical association either between per capita
GDP and nutritional status, or between average calorie consumption per consumer unit per day and nutritional status. The state level mismatch between
food intake and nutritional status can be attributed to the differences in education, health, availability of safe drinking water and environmental sanitation,
which intervene between food and nutritional status. The better nutritional
status at a comparatively lower level of nutrient intake per consumer unit per
day, as observed in Kerala and Tamil Nadu, could be due to better health care
and nutritional intervention.[3]

Does all this imply that calorie intake hardly matters? Empirical evidence
tends to suggest a positive association between calorie intake and nutritional
status, though the relationship is likely to be affected by the prevalence of
disease. The nature of a desirable diet from a nutritional perspective still
remains unsettled, as does the extent to which malnutrition is due to an inadequate diet or to the general conditions of life.[4] But, given the fact that a

TABLE 2   *Percentage distribution of children (aged 1–5 years) according to nutritional grades*[1]

State	Period	Normal	Mild	Moderate	Severe
Kerala	1975–79	7.5	35.7	46.5	10.3
	1988–90	17.7	47.4	32.9	2.0
Tamilnadu	1975–79	6.2	34.2	47.0	12.6
	1988–90	8.0	42.0	45.8	4.2
Karnataka	1975–79	4.6	31.1	50.0	14.3
	1988–90	4.8	38.1	48.8	8.3
Andhra-Pradesh	1975–79	6.1	32.4	46.1	15.4
	1988–90	8.7	39.5	44.3	7.5
Maharashtra	1975–79	3.2	25.4	49.5	21.9
	1988–90	6.7	38.0	47.5	7.8
Gujarat	1975–79	3.8	28.1	54.3	13.8
	1988–90	7.3	33.9	45.8	13.0
Madhya-Pradesh	1975–79	8.4	30.3	45.1	16.2
	1988–90	17.7	27.4	38.9	16.0
Orissa	1975–79	7.5	35.9	41.7	14.9
	1988–90	8.1	34.6	46.6	10.7
All states[2]	1975–79	5.9	31.6	47.5	15.0
	1988–90	9.9	37.6	43.8	8.7

Notes: [1]Based on National Centre for Health Statistics (NCHS), USA standards.
[2]Pooled estimates for Kerala, Tamilnadu, Karnataka, Andhra-Pradesh, Maharashtra, Gujarat, Madhya-Pradesh and Orissa.

Source: National Nutritional Monitoring Bureau (1991), *Report of Repeat Surveys (1988–90)*, Hyderabad: National Institute of Nutrition.

sizeable section of the population is exposed to risk, food and nutrition interventions are required to supplement the normal effects of economic growth.[5]

FOOD PRODUCTION TRENDS

During the 1960s and 1970s total food production, including non-cereal food, barely kept pace with population growth. The growth rate per capita declined during the 1960s, but grew at a slow rate during the 1970s (Table 3). It was only during the 1980s that per capita output increased at a satisfactory rate of 1.6 per cent per annum. A similar pattern is discernible in the supply of calories and protein. The improved performance during the 1980s was mainly due to significant acceleration in non-foodgrain production, with oilseeds and livestock products as the principal engines of growth. The diversification of production more or less conforms to the growth patterns of domestic demand.

TABLE 3   *Annual compound growth rates for food and agricultural production (per cent per annum)*

Period	Food production		Agr. production	
	Aggregate	Per cap.	Aggregate	Per cap.
1961–63 to 1971–73	2.11	−0.21	2.03	−0.18
1971–73 to 1981–83	3.00	0.84	3.20	0.90
1981–83 to 1991–93	3.77	1.62	3.82	1.76
1961–63 to 1991–93	2.96	0.75	3.01	0.82
1971–73 to 1991–93	3.39	1.23	3.51	1.33

	Food supply (Per cent per annum)		
Period	K/cal p. cap./day	Protein gr. p. cap./day	Fat gr. p. cap./day
1961–63 to 1971–73	−0.14	−0.44	−0.52
1971–73 to 1981–83	0.51	0.44	1.45
1981–83 to 1990–92	1.05	0.81	2.08
1961–63 to 1990–92	0.45	0.25	0.96
1971–73 to 1990–92	0.76	0.62	1.75

Source: *The State of Food and Agriculture*, Rome: Food and Agriculture Organization.

The annual growth rate of foodgrain production improved from 2.3 per cent during the 1970s to 2.8 per cent during the 1980s. It is particularly noteworthy that real foodgrain prices were declining, as a result both of better production performance and of the long-term downward trend in per capita foodgrain consumption. Another positive feature of growth during the 1980s was its spread to hitherto lagging regions exposed to high risk of food insecurity: both the eastern region, where production had been stagnating,[6] and the slow growing central region showed a better performance.[7]

Agricultural growth has slowed down during the 1990s. It is disturbing that grain production has barely kept pace with population growth and the real price of foodgrains has moved into an upward trend.[8] Ironically, even with slow output growth, supply outstripped the effective market demand and the first half of the 1990s has seen a rapid increase in the stock of foodgrains held by the government. This coincided with a failure to continue the downward trend in poverty.

THE PUBLIC DISTRIBUTION SYSTEM

The PDS, in its present form of a producer price support mechanism allied to a consumer subsidy programme, has evolved in the wake of foodgrain shortages of the 1960s. The main emphasis until the late 1970s was on price stabilization, hence the PDS was mainly confined to urban areas and food deficit states. The welfare dimension has gained importance since the early 1980s, with coverage being extended to rural areas in some states, as well as to areas with a high incidence of poverty. The food subsidy cost accounted for 0.7 per cent of GDP in 1993–4. In the wake of economic reform, the PDS is perceived to be the main safety net to protect the poor from potential short-run, price-induced adverse effects.

PDS supplies

PDS supplies have increased rapidly since the mid-1960s, changing from 6.5 million tonnes per year during 1961–5 to 18.4 million tonnes during 1990–92. A noteworthy feature is the response of the government supply to fluctuations in production: it is higher in drought years than in normal ones. For instance, in 1979–80 and 1987–8, when grain production was low, government supplies were substantially higher than in normal years, even though procurement levels were lower. By means of the PDS and employment-generation programmes, famine deaths have been kept at a very low level during the past decade. This has been achieved despite PDS operations not being very sensitive to inflationary situations, with price stabilization measures being ineffective in combating the foodgrain price increases engineered, in part, by speculative trade practices. On the other side, however, price collapse in periods of bumper harvest has been prevented.

Pricing and subsidies

The recent large increases in procurement prices do not seem to be based on any economic rationale, hence the consequent upward revisions in the Central issue prices have had an adverse impact on the efficacy of the system. The minimum support price was raised by 69 per cent for wheat and 44 per cent for rice between 1990–91 and 1995–6. On the one hand, the price advantage to farmers has resulted in the Food Corporation of India (FCI) buying up more wheat and rice than it can manage. The reason is simply that the FCI is a parastatal which, ever since it was established in 1965, has had no choice but to buy whatever it is offered at the minimum support price. On the other hand, owing to large increases in the issue prices, the off-take of rice from the Corporation has declined from 9.9 million tonnes in 1991–2 to 8.0 million tonnes in 1994–5, with figures for wheat of 8.8 million tonnes declining to less than 5 million tonnes. Consequently, buffer stocks have reached uneconomic levels, far exceeding the norms suggesting by the technical group constituted by the government. This is unfortunate since withholding foodgrains from the market has adverse effects.[9] Withholding increases the open market price, which hurts the poor and has severe consequences for the very poor, not least because not all of those at risk are covered by the PDS. Even those who are covered depend on the open market for a major portion of their foodgrain requirements.

The sharp increases in the minimum support and issue prices explain the abnormal increase in the carrying cost of buffer stocks in 1993–4 and 1994–5. In the latter period the share amounted to 36 per cent of the food subsidy budget of Rs 51 000 million. The excess stock over the minimum norm is estimated to have involved an additional Central Government expenditure amounting to 19 per cent.

Despite the increasing trend of the central food subsidy budget, the consumer cereal subsidy (measured as the FCI cost minus its sales) has declined since 1992–3. What is more disquieting is the decline in the subsidy which has gone towards poverty alleviation programmes. Their share in 1994–5 was about 30 per cent of the government food subsidy, though even that is probably dispersed among people who do not need it.

PDS food access by the poor

It is important to ask whether the poor have benefited from the increased tempo of PDS operations and to question the efficiency of the scheme in distributing food to them. Many empirical studies have shown severe bias in the interregional distribution of the PDS supplies: states with a high incidence of poverty, such as Bihar, Orissa and Madhya Pradesh, receive a lower share. Further, with few exceptions, the PDS has remained a non-selective programme (Jha, 1991; Dev and Suryanarayana, 1991; Radhakrishna, 1996).

Contrary to the repeated assertion that the PDS is urban-biased, empirical evidence does not seem to support this as a major issue (Radhakrishna *et al.*, 1996). Out of the eight states (Andhra Pradesh, Gujarat, Jammu and Kashmir, Karnataka, Kerala, Maharashtra, Tamil Nadu and West Bengal) in which the PDS network has spread, only in Jammu and Kashmir, Karnataka, Maharashtra and West Bengal were the per capita purchases from the PDS higher in the urban areas. Bias only appears to have been extreme in Jammu and Kashmir and in West Bengal. The major issue, apart from the universal character of entitlement, is regional misallocation.

The system is not functioning at all in the states with a high concentration of the poor, owing to lack of initiative on the part of the state governments (ibid.). The prospect of these states providing safety nets to the poor on the basis of spending from their own resources would seem to be bleak, since they are facing severe fiscal austerity. The proposed new scheme of providing 10 kg per month to a poor household at half the issue price, if earnestly implemented, may help the poor to get access to food, provided the delivery systems in the poorer states are made to function properly, without leakages.

PDS reform

The PDS has remained an expensive and largely non-selective programme and its poverty-reducing effects are weak. Structural reforms need to be introduced against the background of the changing agricultural and institutional scene. Given these changes, and the weakness and constraints under which the FCI currently operates, it may be better to phase out government controls over grain markets and abolish all procurement operations. The FCI should then be allowed to compete in the market without budgetary support, but free from controls, with the added advantage of economies of scale. The new role of the FCI may be to stabilize prices within a range, provide a minimum support price and maintain strategic buffer stocks.[10]

The food subsidy cost saved could be distributed to the state governments and the Panchayat Raj institutions on the basis of the incidence of poverty.[11] The institutions should be entrusted with the responsibility of identifying the poor on the basis of household-specific characteristics. They, as well as state governments, should be free to buy grain, from the FCI or the open market, to meet their PDS requirements and distribute to the poor at a price lower than the purchase price, utilising the Central subsidy. In very poor states, where administrative structures and local institutions are weak, schemes which tie food distribution to wage employment programmes, nutrition programmes and welfare programmes for old and disabled persons should receive high priority.

THE FUTURE: POVERTY AND FOOD DEMAND

Poverty

Until the mid-1970s, the proportion of people below the poverty line remained above 50 per cent, with no declining trend being evident. Higher growth, supplemented by policies to enable the poor to achieve higher incomes, has subsequently contributed to the decline in poverty. The extent of that, however, has differed sharply among regions, with rural poverty being concentrated in the eastern and central regions, which have lagged behind in agricultural development. Urban poverty has been more general.

The declining trend in poverty incidence which ran on into the 1980s seems to have slowed down in the initial years of reform.[12] Whether the reforms have contributed to the slowdown, or what would have happened in the absence of reforms, is difficult to know.[13] The higher incidence of poverty in 1992 (the second year of the reform period) could be attributed to the rise in food prices as well as the decline in public expenditure on the social sector. In 1993–4, official estimates placed the proportion of poor at 36 per cent (37 per cent in rural areas and 32 per cent in urban areas). The incidence of poverty is high, despite the fact that India has long experimented with a number of poverty alleviation programmes (PAPs). In 1993–4, the amount spent by Central and State governments on the programmes, including the PDS, was 1.36 per cent of GDP (Radhakrishna *et al.*, 1996). Many of the schemes suffer from loose allocation, leakages and high income transfer costs, though this is less evident with employment programmes (particularly the Maharashtra Employment Guarantee Scheme[14]) and with nutrition programmes, both of which seem to be better directed because of self-selection.

Projections of poverty incidence

A growth rate of 6–7 per cent during the Ninth Plan Period is considered to be within reach, and there is a possibility of sustaining this growth rate into the future. Some of the main features are shown in Table 4. The projections are

TABLE 4   *Projected expenditure distribution*

Expenditure groups	Rural				Urban			
	Estimated distribution		Projected distribution		Estimated distribution		Projected distribution	
	1994	2000	2010	2020	1994	2000	2010	2020
Very poor	20	14	6	2	19	11	2	0
Moderately poor	18	15	9	5	14	10	4	1
Poor	38	29	15	7	33	21	6	1
Non-poor lower	29	28	23	16	25	22	12	4
Non-poor higher	33	43	62	77	42	57	82	95
Non-poor	62	71	85	93	67	79	94	99
All	100	100	100	100	100	100	100	100

Note: Persons below 75 per cent of the poverty line (Z) are defined as very poor; persons between 75 per cent of Z and Z as moderately poor; persons between Z and 150 per cent of Z as non-poor lower and above 150 per cent of Z non-poor high. Poverty lines are those of the Planning Commission given for the 1993–4 period. Using the log-normal distribution fitted to the 1993–4 NSS data, projections of expenditure distribution in the year 2000, 2010 and 2020 are made on the following assumptions: (1) aggregate private expenditure will grow at 5 per cent during 1994–2000 and at 6 per cent during 2000–2020; (2) the ratio of urban to rural per capita expenditure will increase at the historical rate; (3) the inequality in expenditure within rural and urban areas will remain the same as in 1993–4; (4) population figures are based on recent estimates released by the Registrar General of India.

Source: CESS Project on Food Demand.

made on the assumption that private consumption will grow at 5 per cent from 1994 to 2000, and at 6 per cent up to 2020,[15] that the rural–urban distribution of population and rural–urban differences in per capita expenditure will follow past trends, and that the inequality of expenditure distribution will remain constant at the 1993–4 levels in rural and urban areas. For rural areas, the projections suggest that 29 per cent will remain poor in 2000, though the figure will then drop to 15 per cent in 2010 and 7 per cent in 2020. In urban areas, 21 per cent will be poor in 2000, with a drop to 4 per cent in 2010 and 1 per cent in 2020. In absolute terms, the number of poor in India will decline from 377 million in 1994 to 266 million in 2000, 115 million in 2010 and, further, to 35 million in 2020. This decline will occur despite a projected increase in population from 909 million in 1994 to 1344 million in 2020. Of the projected 266 million poor in 2000, some 130 million, or about half, will be 'very poor'. The need to focus food security on that group will remain in the coming years. Provided that food transfers can be made without leakages, simple calculations show that it would require about 3 million tonnes of cereals to meet their chronic cereal deficiency in the year 2000, and 1 million tonnes in 2010. This suggests that the problem of chronic insecurity can be overcome in the next decade, though it has to be remembered that malnutrition may persist owing to other deprivations, even if broadly defined food security is achieved.

Food demand

Based on the above assumption, food demand is projected to increase at 4.41 per cent between the years 2000 and 2010, which is closer to the target agricultural growth rate in the Ninth Plan (Table 5). The projected annual rate of increase in household demand varies among the food items: it is more than 5 per cent for milk and milk products, 4–5 per cent for meat, eggs, fish, sugar, gur and edible oils, and less than 3 per cent for cereals items. These differential growth rates imply substantial diversification of the food basket in favour of non-cereal food. The contribution of population growth to rising cereal demand is very significant, as it accounts for more than three-quarters of the increase. Clearly, the shifts in tastes observed in the historical data have dampened the growth of cereal demand. Household demand for cereals in future will slow down, eventually levelling off at about the rate of the growth in population, which itself is likely to decline.

The other sources of demand for cereals are for seed, feed and for processing by industry; these together accounted for about 12.5 per cent of cereal production in 1993. Feed demand, which constituted about 6 per cent of production, is likely to be influenced by the growth rate of consumption of milk and milk products as well as meat, eggs and fish (that is, 4–5 per cent per annum). Since cereals may replace other types of feed, demand may grow at a higher rate than that of total feed demand. Taking all aspects into consideration, a maximum growth rate of 4.5 per cent can be assumed for non-household cereals demand, while the growth rate of national demand (household and non-household) can be assumed at 2.8 per cent during 2000–2010 and 2.5 per cent during 2010–2020. It is pertinent to note that the household cereal demand has

TABLE 5   *Projected annual growth rate in total household demand, by commodity groups, 1994–2020*

	1994–2000	2000–2010	2010–2020
Rice	2.66	2.58	2.23
Wheat	2.98	3.06	2.69
Other cereals	0.93	0.76	1.01
All cereals	2.49	2.49	2.24
Milk and milk products	5.34	5.80	5.21
Edible oil	3.96	4.40	4.26
Meat, egg and fish	4.61	5.05	4.74
Sugar and gur	4.11	4.55	4.15
Other food	4.58	5.26	5.21
All food	4.41	4.41	4.32
Non-food	6.55	7.81	7.37
Total	5.00	6.00	6.00

Note: Projections are based on an integrated demand model and on NSS rounds from 1977–8 to 1993–4, which includes the latest round. The projections are made at the relative prices of 1993–4 and the assumptions about the variables are those given in Table 4.

Source: CESS Project on Food Demand.

been projected on the assumption that the historical downward trend in per capita consumption of cereals due to change in taste will be reversed and food demand will depend only on population, per capita income, level of urbanization and income inequalities. Hence the estimated growth rate of 2.8 per cent is likely to be on the high side.

To match growing food demand, there is need for production to grow at a rate of 4.41 per cent, which implies a significant increase on the rate of 3.4 per cent achieved during the 1970s and 1980s. The objective of national food security requires that the deceleration in the growth rate experienced during the first half of the 1990s, as well as the weaknesses of the PDS, should be overcome. There is a long-term problem of sustaining a growth rate of about 2.8 per cent in cereal production during 2000–2010 and 2.5 per cent during 2010–2020, though these are lower than the rates achieved during the 1980s. As will be argued in the next section, the targets are within reach.

EMERGING PERSPECTIVES AND POLICY IMPERATIVES

Achievement of food security is integral to the process of alleviating poverty through employment generation. The experience across countries in Asia shows that the overall growth rate of the economy is the most important factor accounting for the alleviation of poverty (Quibria and Srinivasan, 1994). The Asian experience shows further that there are strong linkages between agriculture and the rest of the economy, with there being a significant correlation between agricultural growth and overall growth (ESACP, 1996).

The 'negative protection' of agriculture under the pre-liberalization strategy, with the implied subsidy to the consumers of food which it entailed, failed to reduce poverty to any marked extent. Clearly, the potential loss to the poor from the failure to generate productive employment through higher agricultural and overall growth was far greater than the 'gain' from cheaper food. However, it is equally clear from the Asian experience that the impact of post-liberalization growth on poverty reduction is greatest in situations where land reforms have been implemented effectively, and a high priority has been accorded to enlarging physical infrastructure and fostering agriculture and human resource development.

In several countries of East and Southeast Asia, in the 1970s and 1980s, the growth in GDP originating from agriculture was well over 1 per cent, or close to 2 per cent, per head. In India, on the other hand, the per head GDP growth originating from agriculture was negative in the 1970s and only around 1 per cent in the next decade. In countries like China, Indonesia and Thailand, the post-reform growth was spearheaded by agriculture, resulting in the speedy alleviation of poverty (ibid.). The experience of East and Southeast Asia suggests that India needs to aim at 4–4.5 per cent agricultural growth, or 2–2.5 per cent per head, together with an overall GDP growth rate of 7 per cent, if chronic food insecurity is to be overcome through the speedy alleviation of poverty.

At this level of development, agriculture would become diversified and its growth would increasingly consist of dairying and animal husbandry, fishing and horticulture. With this composition of output, agroprocessing industries in rural areas could receive special impetus, meeting domestic as well as export demand. Such activities would be labour-intensive and have strong linkages with manufacturing and service sectors. Thus, despite a significant decline in the share of agriculture in GDP in several of the East and Southeast Asian countries, the proportion of labour force engaged in the rural sector including agriculture is still quite high, exceeding, for example, 60 per cent of the total labour force in China and Thailand (ibid.). It is this broad-based labour-intensive, rural development, together with high levels of social development such as primary education and primary health services, which has triggered off a speedy demographic transition in many countries. Apart from leading to high rates of savings and investment, this process has activated 'trickle-down' mechanisms which have aided poverty reduction.

The experience with structural adjustment in several countries has demonstrated substantial benefits flowing to agriculture. Exchange rate liberalization and reduction in the rate of protection to industry are translated into improved terms of trade for agriculture. Quantitatively, these indirect benefits are far more significant than the direct benefits from reforms specific to agriculture. Thus the incentive framework for agriculture in India can be expected to improve vastly as a consequence of the current structural adjustment measures and new opportunities may be opened up as the existing restrictions on trade in agricultural commodities are phased out. Already private investment in agriculture has picked up considerably, not only recovering from the downward trend of the 1980s but recording in 1996 the highest level of real investment ever achieved (Government of India, 1997). However, the economic reforms so far have failed to ensure the necessary physical and institutional infrastructure to evoke a sufficient supply response from agriculture.

The target for reducing the fiscal deficit has been pursued, not so much by raising revenues or by reducing inessential expenditure, as by reducing capital expenditures. The tax ratio (net tax revenues as a proportion of GDP) is still lower by about 1 percentage point than the pre-reform level. The amount of hidden subsidies at the state level, represented by the non-recovery of irrigation charges and the favourable power tariff, is as high as in the pre-reform period and exceeds public investment in agriculture. The combined outlay of the centre and states on rural development and social services, at 6.7 per cent of GDP in 1994–5, was lower than even the immediate pre-reform level of 7.3 per cent (Guhan, 1995). There could have been a justification for a gradual rise in the farm gate prices of fertilizers in line with the rise in the procurement prices of crops but a sudden and steep fertilizer price rise, stemming from a reduction in subsidy, led to a significant decline in the demand for fertilizers (the growth rate in their use was less than half that of the 1980s). On account of the resulting decline in output and income, a large number of small and marginal farmers were pushed below the poverty line in the immediate post-reform period (Gupta, 1995). The decontrol of phosphatic and potassic fertilizers, with a doubling of prices, has accentuated the imbalance in the application of different nutrients, resulting in a decline in the productivity of fertilizers as a whole (Government of India, 1997).

As mentioned above, there are clear signs of a slowdown in agricultural growth in the post-reform period. Real public investment in agriculture continues to be lower than that realized in the early 1980s (Figure 2). As a result, there has been a significant shortfall in the achievement of the Eighth Plan's irrigation target, especially in the major and medium irrigation projects, where the achievement is less than half the target. There has also been a steep fall in the share of credit from the commercial banks allocated to farmers, despite an improvement in the recovery of loans advanced to them (Government of India, 1997). Thus the country has not been able to exploit fully the potential offered by a recent series of good monsoons. To achieve food security by taking advantage of the benefits of economic liberalization, a series of reforms in technology, infrastructure, dryland farming, farm credit and input delivery systems are needed to activate supply response from agriculture. A rise in agricultural productivity could hold the key to deriving full benefits from the opportunities for trade opened up by the Uruguay Round (ESCAP, 1996).

Stepping up investment in infrastructure through cost recovery is inextricably linked with the quality of services provided, and with the way in which infrastructure and other services are managed. Experience in India has shown that, in a democratic polity, farmers cannot be expected to pay heavier charges regardless of the quality and cost of the services provided, especially when the political parties have been practising competitive populism. Decentralized management of infrastructure, with less bureaucracy and political interference,

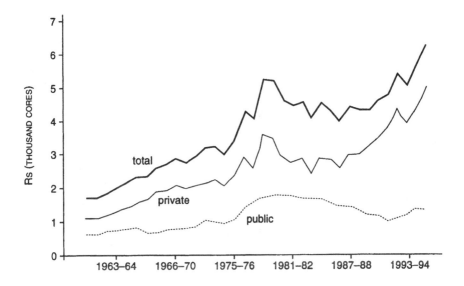

FIGURE 2   *Gross capital formation in agriculture (private, public and total)*

should, therefore, be at the top of the agenda of reform. In many cases, associations of farmers and non-government organizations could be entrusted with the responsibility for repairing and managing small irrigation works, especially if they were given the power to collect water rates and retain a share for maintenance and development. Further, the local elected institutions could be entrusted with similar functions, including the transmission and distribution of power. Investment in infrastructure by the private sector, including subscription to shares by farmers on a wide scale, could contribute a great deal towards augmentation and efficient management.

The experience with decentralization of services in Southeast Asia has shown that irrigated yields can be increased by at least 50 per cent and that farmers would be willing to pay service charges to the extent of at least one-quarter of the increment in the value of output, as the benefits from better management appear. Such payments by farmers in India would represent almost a tenfold increase over the existing levels. Some state governments in Gujarat, Karnataka and Andhra Pradesh have already taken steps towards decentralization.

The yields under seed-fertilizer technology have been hovering round their peak for some time. The tools of biotechnology offer significant possibilities for breaking these barriers, even in drought-prone areas. Biotechnology may contribute to the protection and regeneration of the environment by reducing the dependence on chemical inputs and by facilitating afforestation through tissue culture techniques. However, India is currently investing only about 0.3 per cent of its agricultural GDP in agricultural research, as against 0.7 per cent in the developing countries as a whole. Therefore, so far as India is concerned, there is considerable scope for diverting incremental outlays to the priority areas in research.

A large part of the unirrigated area is highly degraded and is characterized by low and uncertain rainfall, low wages and high poverty. The poor suffer intermittently from acute scarcity of food due to weather shocks. The current programmes for soil and moisture conservation in such areas need considerable strengthening through better planning of work on a watershed basis, by involving people and improving coordination between various departments. The integration of wage employment schemes with those for soil and moisture conservation is now being attempted with some success as new guidelines are adopted.

Institutional credit for agriculture has to expand at a faster rate than before because of the need to raise the growth rate and because the changing product mix will necessitate larger investments. It would be useful to phase out the concessionary rates of interest in order to improve the viability of credit institutions, especially as their normal rates are much lower than those charged in the informal market. There is also a need to ensure the timely availability of institutional credit to small farmers through appropriate rationing. Otherwise, the tendency of the commercial banks to reduce unit costs by serving a small number of big borrowers, rather than a large number of small ones, could result in limiting credit to the needy. Subject to such broad guidelines, the management of credit institutions should be accorded greater autonomy by abolishing administrative and political interference in their functioning.

The existing poverty alleviation programmes, including the public distribution of foodgrains, are essentially 'top-down' ventures heavily dependent on the bureaucracy. Whereas even small and marginal farmers, being decision makers in control of their resources, successfully participated in the 'green revolution', the management of poverty alleviation programmes has resulted in inefficiencies and large leakages. The beneficiaries need to be involved in the design and implementation of programmes through the local-level (Panchayati Raj) institutions, for which periodic elections have now become constitutionally mandatory. The recent agricultural breakthrough achieved in West Bengal points to the efficacy of decentralized management (Sen, 1993; Mukerji and Mukhopadhyay, 1995). It strongly suggests that the state governments have to muster the necessary political will to delegate vital decisions bearing on economic development and social justice to a lower level, to devolve adequate resources and confer greater power over administration.

NOTES

[1]More recent NSS material shows that, in 1993–4, the per capita monthly consumption of cereals was 13.4 kg. in rural areas and 10.6 kg. in urban areas, as against the corresponding figures of 15.4 kg. and 11.4 kg. in 1970–71.

[2]Children suffering from malnutrition do not achieve full genetic growth potential and are exposed to a greater risk of child mortality. Pelletier *et al.* (1995) show that malnutrition, by virtue of its synergistic relationship with infectious disease, has a powerful impact in India.

[3]Kerala and Tamil Nadu have better health care and educational facilities and coverage of PDS.

[4]Sekler (1982) observes that 'severe' malnutrition is caused by nutrient intake deficiency, while 'moderate' and 'mild' forms are due to environmental factors. He argues that the former problem calls for nutritional intervention and the latter for environmental intervention. There is, as yet, not much empirical basis for his proposition.

[5]Overcoming the problem of hunger is not the same as elimination of malnutrition. The former can be achieved through the intake of cereals, while the latter will demand non-cereal food as well as a better environment.

[6]It is pertinent to note the contribution of panchayats (local institutions) to the improvement in factor productivity in West Bengal (Mukerji and Mukhopadhyay, 1995). It is argued that the active role of panchayats in input delivery and in land and water management has a positive impact on agricultural productivity.

[7]In the rainfed region, Rajasthan and Madhya Pradesh, the yield increases more than compensated for the substantial decline in cropped area under foodgrains due to a shift in areas under coarse cereals to oilseeds (Sawant and Achuthan, 1995; Bhalla and Singh, 1996). The shift in area from low-yield and low-value coarse cereals to high-value oilseeds would improve the incomes of the poor.

[8]The upward trend in foodgrain prices can be partly attributed to the large increases in the minimum support prices and consequent upward revision in the ration prices.

[9]While foodgrain stocks reached uneconomic levels during 1993–6, they have fallen below the required stocks in 1997. The decline could be partly attributed to the shortcomings of food management. As the result of a failure to notice a decline in production, foodgrains were exported when international prices were low and domestic prices were on an upward trend.

[10]For arguments in favour of these reforms and other details, see Radhakrishna *et al.* (1996).

[11]For details, see Radhakrishna *et al.* (1996).

[12]Official estimates show that, while the proportion of poor in all of India declined from 51 to 39 per cent between 1978 and 1998, it remained at 36 per cent in 1993–4.

[13]The available data are inadequate to permit analysis of the complexities in the underlying relations. Empirical evidence, however, suggests a definite association between the poverty level and the inflation rate. Agricultural wages as well as wages in the unorganized sector do not adjust to inflation without a lag.

[14]Female participation is reported to be high in the Maharashtra Guarantee Scheme.

[15]The assumed growth rate in private expenditure is closer to the one assumed in the Ninth Five Year Plan, which has assumed a growth rate of 5.9 per cent during 1997–2002 under its accelerated growth scenario.

REFERENCES

Bhalla, G.S. (1994), 'Policies for Food Security in India', in G.S. Bhalla (ed.), *Economic Liberalisation and Indian Agriculture*, New Delhi: Institute for Studies in Industrial Development.

Bhalla, G.S. and Singh, G. (1996), 'Recent Developments in India Agriculture: A State Level Analysis', mimeo, New Delhi: Centre for the Study of Regional Development, Jawaharlal Nehru University.

Dev, Mahendra S. and Suryanarayana, M.H. (1991), 'Is PDS Urban Biased and Pro-Rich? An Evaluation', *Economic and Political Weekly*, XXVI, 2357–66.

Economic and Social Commission for Asia and the Pacific (ESCAP) (1996), *Rural Poverty Alleviation and Sustainable Development in Asia and the Pacific*, New York: United Nations.

Food and Agriculture Organization of the United Nations (FAO) (annual), *The State of Food and Agriculture*, Rome: FAO.

Government of India (1997), *Economic Survey (1996–97)*, New Delhi: Government of India.

Guhan, S. (1995), 'Social Expenditures in the Union Budget', *Economic and Political Weekly*, XXX, 1095–1101.

Gupta, S.P. (1995), 'Economic Reform and its Impact on the Poor', *Economic and Political Weekly*, **XXX**, 1295–1313.

Hanumantha Rao, C.H. and Gulati, A. (1994), 'Indian Agriculture: Emerging Perspectives and Policy Issues', *Economic and Political Weekly*, **XXIX**, A158–A169.

Jha, S. (1991), *Consumer Subsidies in India: Is Targeting Objective?*, Bombay: Indira Gandhi Institute of Development Studies.

Mukerji, B. and Mukhopadhyay, S. (1995), 'Impact of Institutional Change in a Small Farm Economy', *Economic and Political Weekly*, **XXX**, 2134–7.

National Nutritional Monitoring Board (1991), *Report of Repeat Surveys (1988–90)*, Hyderabad: National Institute of Nutrition.

Pelletier, D.L., Frongillo, E.A. Jr., Schroeder, G.D. and Habicht, J.P. (1995), 'The Effects of Malnutrition on Child Mortality in Developing Countries', *Bulletin of the World Health Organization*, **73**, 443–8.

Quibria, M.G. and Srinivasan, T.N. (1994), 'Introduction', in M.G. Quibria (ed.), *Rural Poverty in Developing Asia, Vol. 1: Bangladesh, India and Sri Lanka*, Manila: Asian Development Bank.

Radhakrishna, R. (1996), 'Food Trends, Public Distribution System and Food Security Concerns', *Indian Journal of Agricultural Economics*, **51**, 168–83.

Radhakrishna, R. and Hanumantha Rao, K. (1995), 'Food Security, Public Distribution and Price Policy', in N.S.S. Narayana and Anindya Sen (eds), *Poverty, Environment and Economic Development*, New Delhi: Interline Publishing.

Radhakrishna, R. and Ravi, C. (1992), 'Effects of Growth, Relative Price and Preferences on Food and Nutrition', *Indian Economic Review*, **XXVII**, 303–23.

Radhakrishna, R., Subbarao, K., Indrakant, S. and Ravi, C. (1996), *India's Public Distribution System: A National And International Perspective*, Draft, New Delhi: Indian Council of Social Science Research.

Sawant, S.D. and Achuthan, C.V. (1995), 'Agricultural Growth Across Crops and Regions', *Economic and Political Weekly*, **XXX**, A2–A13.

Sekler, D. (1982), 'Small but Healthy', in P.V. Sukhatme (ed.), *Newer Concepts in Nutrition and their Implications for Policy*, Pune: Maharashtra Association for the Cultivation of Science.

Sen, Abhijit (1993), *'Agriculture in Structural Adjustment'*, mimeo, Bombay: Indira Gandhi Institute of Development Research.

BEN SENAUER AND TERRY ROE*

Food Security and the Household

INTRODUCTION

Food security is widely defined as 'access by all people at all times to enough food for an active healthy life'. Food security is, therefore, ultimately a household and individual-level issue. Recent research has greatly enriched our understanding of household behaviour concerning food and nutrition. The key factors affecting household food security and individual nutritional status are shown in Figure 1. They are influenced by the availability of food, the ability and desire of the household to acquire it, its intra-household distribution and

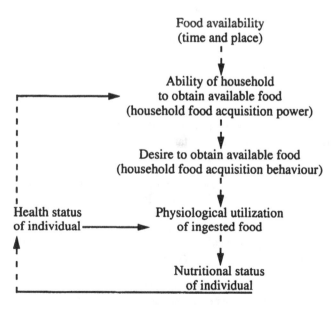

FIGURE 1 *Factors affecting household food security and individual nutritional status*

Source: Pinstrup-Andersen (1981)

*University of Minnesota, St. Paul, Minnesota, USA.

the physiological utilization of the ingested nutrients, which both affects and is affected by the person's state of health. The person's nutritional status also has a feedback effect on their productivity and the ability to acquire food.

INCOME AND PRICES

The general understanding has been that food insecurity and hunger are primarily the result of poverty. With economic growth and improved incomes, poor households will have the ability, and presumably the desire, to obtain an adequate diet, at least in terms of food energy (calories). By the mid-1980s, certain conclusions concerning the income elasticity for food seemed warranted since they were based on many different research studies. The income elasticities for staple foods are typically markedly higher for lower-income than for higher-income households. The income elasticity with respect to food expenditure (in value terms) considerably exceeds the elasticity for energy (calories) among poor households. Even people at low-income levels want to increase the variety and quality of their diets. The poor buy more expensive foods per calorie as their incomes rise.

However, the income elasticity for food energy (calories) was still substantial, varying across several studies from a low of 0.10 for poor urban households in Brazil to 0.60 for poor rural households in Sri Lanka. Most calorie–income elasticities were in the range of 0.30 to 0.40 (Alderman, 1986; Senauer, 1990). A 10 per cent increase in household income would lead to a 3 to 4 per cent increase in calorie consumption.

Several studies in the late 1980s and early 1990s challenged these conclusions and seemed to indicate that the income elasticity for calories might be very low and even close to zero (Behrman and Deolalikar, 1987; Bouis and Haddad, 1992; Bouis, 1994). Behrman and Deolalikar (1987) concluded that 'increases in income will not result in substantial improvements in nutrient intakes'. Hence economic growth and improved income among the poor would not lead to substantial reductions in hunger and malnutrition. The recent study by Subramanian and Deaton (1996) is based on information about rural households in Maharashtra state in India and is methodologically very meticulous, obtaining elasticities which support the previous conclusions. Their elasticity for food expenditures is around 0.75, which is then about equally divided between the elasticity for the quantity of calories and that of their price. The elasticity of calorie consumption with respect to total expenditures is in the range of 0.30 to 0.50.

The many empirical studies of the effect of prices on food demand and nutrient consumption lead to several general conclusions. The price elasticities for most foods are substantial; indeed, the absolute value may be greater than one. Typically, the households which have the lowest income have a stronger response to price changes. In other words, the absolute value of the price elasticities is greater for poorer households. With the poorest households devoting 60–80 per cent of their income to food, they tend to switch among foods in response to price changes (Alderman, 1986; Behrman *et al.*, 1988; Senauer, 1990).

Price increases for preferred staple foods have been found to have positive effects on nutrient intakes in several studies (Behrman *et al.* 1988). This can occur when poor households substitute foods that are a cheaper source of nutrients for a more expensive preferred food in response to its increased price. Senauer and Garcia (1991) found, for example, that the weight in relation to height (a measure of short-run nutritional status or wasting) of pre-school children in poor Philippine households improved in response to increases in the price of rice. However, the pre-schoolers' height for age (a measure of long-run nutritional status or stunting) declined. The households presumably substituted inferior staples, such as maize, for rice in response to its price increase. The inferior staples are a cheaper source of calories, but children's growth (height) suffers because they provide less protein and other nutrients.

Price increases can also positively affect the demand for a food and nutrient consumption when the household produces, as well as consumes, the commodity. This point is important because a significant portion of the poor and food-insecure in developing countries reside in semi-subsistence farm households. Agricultural household models encompass both the household's production and consumption decisions in a single unified theoretical framework. When a farm household produces a food commodity partly for sale and partly for consumption, a price increase affects farm profits and household income. Empirical research with this model for a number of countries shows that the profit effect can completely offset the traditional negative price effect, so that a price increase results in an increased consumption of the product by farm households (Singh *et al.*, 1986).

INTRA-HOUSEHOLD ISSUES

Intra-household allocation has been the subject of substantial research efforts by economists over the last dozen years. For a comprehensive review and appraisal, see Haddad *et al.* (1993). The household has traditionally been treated as a unitary entity with one set of preferences that can be represented by a household utility function. The recent alternative collective models allow for different preferences among individuals in the household. The empirical research has raised questions about the unitary model's ability to explain adequately the observed behaviour. However, it can be said that no one collective model clearly dominates the various alternatives. Economic changes and public policies and programmes can affect intra-household distributions under both unitary and collective models. With the latter, the intra-household allocation rules or decision-making process may also be affected.

Household-level information is frequently used to determine food consumption and nutritional status. However, the ultimate issue is the nutrition of individuals, particularly those who are considered 'at risk' nutritionally. A practical issue is this: if a household-level indicator is used, how many poorly nourished individuals reside in seemingly adequately nourished households and, conversely, how many adequately nourished individuals are there in poorly nourished households? This question can be likened to the statistical concept of type I and type II errors.

Tables 1 and 2 use data collected in conjunction with a pilot food subsidy programme in three provinces in the Philippines in 1983–4 (Senauer and Garcia, 1996). The material is discussed in detail in Garcia and Pinstrup-Andersen (1987). The survey covered 840 households and individual-level food consumption data were collected in 134 of those households. A 24-hour

TABLE 1   *The relation between household indicators and individual calorie adequacy (percentages)*

A.   Percentage of household members (ages 2–60) with individual calorie adequacy greater than :[1]

	70	75	80	85	90
If household calorie adequacy was less than:[2]					
70	29.9	22.4	16.3	11.5	8.3
	(18.2)	(12.2)	(8.0)	(5.1)	(3.6)
75	...	26.3	19.8	14.7	10.9
	...	(14.5)	(9.9)	(6.7)	(4.7)
80	...	...	22.8	17.2	12.9
	...	...	(11.3)	(7.9)	(5.5)
85	...	...	...	19.0	14.7
	...	...	...	(9.2)	(6.5)

B.   Percentage of household members (ages 2–60) with individual calorie adequacy less than:

	65	70	75	80	85
If household calorie adequacy was greater than:					
70	26.2	32.9	...	...	...
	(37.5)	(48.9)	...	...	...
75	19.3	26.2	32.1	...	...
	(29.1)	(40.3)	(49.9)	...	...
80	14.8	21.6	27.7	35.5	...
	(22.6)	(32.8)	(41.6)	(52.4)	...
85	11.4	18.6	24.8	31.9	38.7
	(18.0)	(29.1)	(38.4)	(49.5)	(61.3)

Notes: [1]The first row relates to unadjusted calorie adequacy and the second row (with the figures in parentheses) to calorie adequacy adjusted for activity level, as discussed earlier.
[2]Household calorie adequacy is not adjusted for activity level.

TABLE 2   *The relation between household indicators and individual calorie adequacy by age and gender*

Age (years)	Female	Male
A. If household calorie adequacy was less than 75 per cent of household members (by age and gender) with individual calorie adequacy greater than 85 per cent:[1]		
2–6	8.3	9.9
	(12.4)	(11.1)
7–15	6.9	7.3
	(6.1)	(7.7)
16–60	22.5	22.7
	(3.9)	(2.2)
B. If household calorie adequacy was greater than 85 per cent of household members (by age and gender) with individual calorie adequacy less than 75 per cent:		
2–6	37.8	35.6
	(21.6)	(33.9)
7–15	40.0	21.1
	(40.0)	(21.1)
16–60	18.1	11.3
	(48.2)	(47.9)

Note: [1]The first row relates to unadjusted calorie adequacy and the second row (with figures in parentheses) to calorie adequacy adjusted for activity level.

food-weighing method was employed in both the household and individual food consumption surveys. For the latter, interviewers were present at meals and weighed the food served to each person and any leftovers. Snacks and food eaten between meals were also accounted for. The adjustments in calorie requirements for physical activity and body weight are based on Haddad *et al.* (1992). Although from a different survey, their data were also drawn from rural Philippine households, in 1984–5. Using information on individual weights and time allocation for several categories of activity, they estimated energy expended per kilogram of body weight per hour for various activities. These were used to adjust the age–gender calorie requirements. The major adjustments were for men and women, ages 16–60. Their calorie requirements each increased by approximately one-third.

In Table 1 and 2, specific household calorie adequacy levels were chosen, and the pattern of calorie adequacy of individual members was analysed. In the first row of Table 1 (Part A), if the household calorie adequacy ratio was less than 70 per cent, 16.3 per cent of family members (ages 2–60) had unadjusted individual calorie adequacy ratios over 80 per cent; only 8.0 per cent had adequacy ratios over 80 per cent after adjustment for activity level. Conversely, in the last row of Part B, if household calorie adequacy was greater then 85 per cent, 18.6 per cent of those family members had unadjusted individual adequacy ratios below 70 per cent, and 29.1 per cent after adjustment for activity.

These results provide compelling evidence that, because of intra-household allocations, substantial numbers of food-insecure individuals are members of apparently food-secure households, but only limited numbers of food-secure individuals are in food-insecure households. Part A of Table 1 generally suggests that, if households below a certain calorie adequacy level were selected for a food subsidy, or other nutrition assistance, relatively few of the benefits would 'leak' to individuals with substantially higher adequacy levels, particularly after adjusting for activity level. In Part B, if households above a certain adequacy level were excluded, a considerable number of individuals with lower adequacy ratios would be excluded.

Table 2 examines age and gender differences with respect to better-nourished individuals in poorly-nourished households (Part A) and poorly-nourished individuals in relatively better-nourished households (Part B). In Part A, there appear to be no substantial gender differences. The differences between adults and children reverse when adjusted for activity level. Before adjusting for activity, 22.7 per cent of men aged 16–60 have adequacy levels over 85 per cent; after adjusting for activity, only 2.2 per cent do.

In Part B, there are a higher proportion of girls than boys and women than men with unadjusted adequacy ratios under 75 per cent in relatively better-nourished households. The gender difference for adults disappears after adjusting for activity level, though. Before adjusting for activity, there are substantially fewer adults whose calorie adequacy is less than 75 per cent of their requirements. However, after adjusting for activity, a considerably higher proportion of adults (ages 16–60) receive less than 75 per cent of their calorie requirements than do children (ages 2–15). Approximately 48 per cent of the adults in households with calorie adequacy ratios over 85 per cent have adjusted individual adequacy ratios under 75 per cent.

If confirmed by data from other locations, in which intra-household distribution patterns might differ, these findings have important implications for the design and allocation of food and nutrition programmes and policies. Conventional household allocation criteria may lead to substantial undercoverage of malnourished individuals. This might justify more generous or lenient household eligibility standards that would result in only relatively small leakages to relatively well-nourished household members.

NUTRITIONAL STATUS (HEALTH) PRODUCTION

Much has been learned about the determinants of individual nutritional status. Nutritional (health) status is typically measured by anthropometric indicators, for example weight and height in comparison to a reference group. Many prefer to use the more general term 'health status' for such indicators. Behrman and Deolalikar (1988) provide an excellent review of this research area.

Gary Becker's household model serves as the theoretical foundation, with health status viewed as a household-production good. The major inputs in an individual's health production function include food consumption (nutrient intake); health care; other goods and service which contribute to health; the time inputs of the individual and other family members which affect health, such as the childcare time of parents; demographic characteristics of the individual, such as age and education; community and environmental factors which affect health, such as sanitation conditions; and the person's genetic endowment.

Two issues have influenced the empirical estimation of this relationship. First, several of these explanatory factors are endogenous variables that result from individual or household choices. These variables may be simultaneously determined and themselves influenced by health status. Much of the empirical work, therefore, has estimated reduced-form health demand equations which contain only exogenous variables as explanatory factors. The second issue is that several of the explanatory factors may be unobserved, because of limits on data collection or, in fact, unobservable, such as genetic endowment. Longitudinal data with multiple observations for the same individuals over time allow the use of fixed-effects models which factor out the impact of time-invariant unobserved effects (Senauer and Garcia, 1996).

The results of this work have some important policy implications. Nutrient intake is only one determinant of a person's nutritional (health) status. Other factors may be of equal importance and the most crucial limiting factor may be something else. Adequately fed individuals may be malnourished because of parasitic diseases caused by unsanitary environmental conditions. More likely, they will aggravate the effects of an inadequate diet. Alleviating malnutrition and improving health is not just a matter of increasing food consumption.

Much of this research has focused on the health status of pre-school children, a group at high nutritional risk. The importance of the parents', particularly the mother's, education on child health has been confirmed by many of these studies. For example, Kassouf and Senauer (1996) examined the impact of parental education on heights and weights of pre-school children in Brazil. Education levels in Brazil are low; the average mother had only four years of schooling in the 1989 survey. Over 24 per cent of the pre-school children of mothers with less than four years of school suffered from stunting: at least moderate malnutrition in terms of height for age. If these mothers were all educated at least to the eleventh grade, this figure would fall to only 2.8 per cent. The mother's education has a strong positive direct effect on nutrition, a negative indirect effect through her wage and the increased value of time, and a very large, indirect positive effect via household full income. The father's education also has a positive effect, although not as impressive as the mother's.

OTHER FACTORS AND RECENT RESEARCH

Space limitations do not allow for more than a brief mention of three other factors that bear on household food security on which there are recent research

contributions. The factors are the impact of nutritional status on labour productivity, housing coping mechanisms and food subsidy programmes. As shown in
Figure 1, nutritional status has a feedback loop through an effect on labour
productivity, and hence the ability of the household to obtain food. Empirical
studies have shown that nutritional status positively affects wages and own-
farm output (Strauss, 1986; Sahn and Alderman, 1988; Haddad and Bouis,
1991). Child malnutrition can affect lifetime earnings because of stunting,
consequent poor health and the impact on human capital development.

Poor households have a number of coping mechanisms to cushion the impact from shocks due to agricultural shortfalls and market shortages or other
uncertainties (von Braun *et al.*, 1992). The household, extended family and
community can provide a safety net. The stages of household coping involve,
first, risk management and loss prevention and, then, loss containment and
disposal of assets. Under extreme conditions such as famine, the household
may collapse (von Braun *et al.*, 1992). Finally, food subsidies are a topic
which, although important, cannot be covered here, but Pinstrup-Andersen
(1988) provides an excellent review.

THE WORLD'S POOR

Most of the food-insecure are the world's poor. The World Bank has calculated
that 1.2 billion people live on $1.00 a day or less. The calculations are based on
country-level average per capita income figures and use the Bank's Atlas
method to convert national currencies to US dollars. There are two basic
problems. Purchasing power parity (PPP) for currency exchange is preferable
to the Atlas method. More crucially, the estimates do not account for the
possible skewed distribution of income in countries. Work at Minnesota and
the Economic Research Service of the US Department of Agriculture seeks to
remedy these problems (Gopinath *et al.* 1997).

In this research an income distribution profile is derived for each country in
the world for which data are available by fitting a gamma distribution to the
country's material. For countries in which information is not available, the
other results, just mentioned, are used to estimate the parameters of the distribution based on each country's characteristics. This is done so that the estimated
distribution exactly yields the country's observed average per capita income.
The results are shown in Table 3, for major regions and the world.

Given the World Bank's work on poverty and that of others, a reasonable
definition of the world's poor might be those living on $2.00 a day or less.
Some one billion people are in this category, representing 19 per cent of the
world's population. This figure agrees quite well with the widely used number
of approximately 800 million hungry people in the world (Bread for the World,
1994). Of the world's one billion poor, 10 per cent live in Latin America and
the Caribbean, 24 per cent in sub-Saharan Africa, 41 per cent in South Asia, 2
per cent in the Middle East and North Africa, 17 per cent in China and Korea,
less than 1 per cent in Eastern Europe, 4 per cent in the former Soviet Union
and 1 per cent in the OECD countries. When reading down each column in
Table 3, the figures are cumulative.

TABLE 3 *Population living on X dollars per day or less (in millions of people)*

$/day in PPP	Latin Am. & Carib.	Sub-Sah. Africa	South Asia	Mid. East & N. Africa	China, Korea, Hong Kong	East Europe	Former Sov. Un.	OECD	World
0.5	46.482	68.101	44.954	5.999	21.606	0.371	10.856	3.545	201.914
1	69.000	139.363	145.359	11.884	63.931	0.826	20.525	6.677	457.564
2	103.356	244.169	414.431	24.794	176.811	2.027	40.524	12.682	1 018.794
4	154.460	345.457	911.592	52.835	427.853	6.560	84.793	24.676	2 008.225
8	225.052	418.914	1 381.424	105.445	820.125	26.136	166.385	51.035	3 194.516
16	308.993	453.439	1 584.190	171.941	1 137.437	72.287	244.538	117.800	4 090.624
32	386.899	465.397	1 642.307	213.162	1 223.536	102.684	280.298	289.713	4 603.996
64	435.846	470.177	1 657.488	225.659	1 237.061	107.472	291.877	596.391	5 021.971
128	451.526	471.414	1 661.675	229.165	1 242.842	107.600	293.088	829.732	5 287.042
256	453.078	471.500	1 662.174	229.892	1 243.866	107.600	293.100	877.254	5 338.464
512	453.100	471.500	1 662.200	229.997	1 243.900	107.600	293.100	878.699	5 340.095
1 024	453.100	471.500	1 662.200	230.000	1 243.900	107.600	293.100	878.700	5 340.100

Source: Gopinath, Roe and Shane (1997).

Additional calculations were made of the amount of income realized by people living at each level of income per day by region and for the world. The key point is that the one billion poor receive only 1.3 per cent of the world's total income, $397 million out of $30.47 trillion total per year. The implication is that a very small transfer in relation to world income could have a very large impact on the incomes and welfare of the world's poor and food-insecure.

SPECIAL FOOD DRAWING RIGHTS

Large food price increases can have a devastating impact on the world's one billion poor, putting them at greater nutritional risk. They typically spend 70 per cent or more of their income on food, hence there is a large real income effect on people already at the subsistence level. Their existing inadequate diets can deteriorate even further, with subsequent increases in morbidity and mortality and declines in human capital.

Real food prices have declined over the last several decades. Evidence seems to be growing, however, that the rate of increase in agricultural production may be slowing. Future increases in demand, assuming a 1.7 per cent per year growth in world population and a 1.2 per cent annual growth in world GNP per capita, are likely to cause real prices to rise slightly, but not to an extent likely to cause a food crisis. The upward pressure on prices will be greater if world population grows more rapidly than assumed or populous countries, such as China and India, experience faster economic growth (Roe and Gopinath, 1996; and Gopinath *et al.* 1997).

However, it is the variance of world supplies and stocks that lead to price spikes which can have a devastating impact on the world's one billion poor. Even during the previous era of declining real food prices, the variability of prices, as measured by the coefficient of variation, increased (Gopinath *et al.* 1997). There are reasons to believe that, with greater variations in yields and smaller stocks due to less government intervention, price variability may be greater in the future. The world needs to devise a way to protect the one billion poor from the kind of transitory shock to world markets and prices that occurred in the early 1970s. As shown in the previous section, the size of the necessary transfer in relation to world income is relatively small.

One possibility is to establish a special food drawing right fund akin to the exchange rate drawing rights managed by the International Monetary Fund, which countries can use to protect their currencies. When there was a spike in world food prices, low-income countries could use the food drawing rights to make purchases on world commodity markets as needed to protect their poor and sustain their food consumption through the transitory shock. The drawing rights fund would be managed by an international agency and the conditions of withdrawal and repayment after the shock would be established.

REFERENCES

Alderman, H. (1986), *The Effect of Food Price and Income Changes on the Acquisition of Food by Low-Income Households*, Washington, DC.: International Food Policy Research Institute.

Behrman, J.R. and Deolalikar, A.B. (1987), 'Will Developing Country Nutrition Improve with Income? A Case Study for Rural South India', *Journal of Political Economy*, 95, 492–507.

Behrman, J.R. and Deolalikar, A.B. (1988), 'Health and Nutrition', in H. Chenery and T.N. Srinivasan (eds), *Handbook of Development Economics*, New York: North-Holland.

Behrman, J.R., Deolalikar, A.B. and Wolfe, B.L. (1988), 'Nutrients: Impacts and Determinants', *The World Bank Economic Review*, 2, 299–320.

Bouis, H.E. (1994), 'The Effect of Income on Demand for Food in Poor Countries: Are Our Food Consumption Databases Giving Us Reliable Estimates?', *Journal of Development Economics*, 44, 199–226.

Bouis, H.E. and Haddad, L.J. (1992), 'Are Estimates of Calorie-Income Elasticities Too High? A Recalibration of the Plausible Range', *Journal of Development Economics*, 39, 333–64.

Bread for the World (1994), *Hunger 1995: Causes of Hunger*, Silver Spring, Maryland: Bread for the World.

Garcia, M. and Pinstrup-Andersen, P. (1987), *The Pilot Food Subsidy Scheme in the Philippines: Its Impact on Income, Food Consumption and Nutritional Status*, Research Report 61, Washington DC: International Food Policy Research Institute.

Gopinath, M., Roe, T. and Shane, M. (1997), 'World Food Insecurity: Causes, Options, Affordability', mimeo, University of Minnesota, Department of Applied Economics, St. Paul.

Haddad, L. and Bouis, H. (1991), 'The Impact of Nutritional Status on Agricultural Productivity: Wage Evidence from the Philippines', *Oxford Bulletin of Economics and Statistics*, 53, 45–68.

Haddad, L., Hoddinott, J. and Alderman, H. (1993), 'Intrahousehold Research Allocation in Developing Countries: Methods, Models and Policy', mimeo, Washington, DC: International Food Policy Research Institute.

Haddad, L., Kanbur, R. and Bouis, H. (1992), 'Intrahousehold Inequality and Average Household Well-Being: Evidence on Calorie Intakes and Energy Expenditures from the Philippines', mimeo, Washington, DC: International Food Policy Research Institute.

Kassouf, A. and Senauer, B. (1996), 'The Direct and Indirect Effects of Parental Education on Malnutrition Among Children in Brazil: A Full Income Approach', *Economic Development and Cultural Change*, 44, 817–38.

Pinstrup-Andersen, P. (1981), *Nutritional Consequences of Agricultural Projects*, Staff Working Paper No 456, Washington DC.: World Bank.

Pinstrup-Andersen, P. (1988), *Food Subsidies in Developing Countries: Costs, Benefits and Policy Options*, Baltimore: John Hopkins University Press.

Roe, T. and Gopinath, M. (1996), *World Trade and Food Security*, Working Paper WP96-2, St. Paul: University of Minnesota, Center for International Food and Agricultural Policy.

Sahn, D. and Alderman, H. (1988), 'The Effects of Human Capital on Wages and the Determinants of Labor Supply in a Developing Country', *Journal of Development Economics*, 29, 157–83.

Senauer, B. (1990), 'Household Behaviour and Nutrition in Developing Countries', *Food Policy*, 15, 406–17.

Senauer, B. and Garcia, M. (1991), 'Determinants of the Nutrition and Health Status of Preschool Children: An Analysis with Longitudinal Data', *Economic Development and Cultural Change*, 39, 371–89.

Senauer, B. and Garcia, M. (1996), 'An Intrahoushold Analysis of a Philippine Food Subsidy Program', mimeo, University of Minnesota, Department of Applied Economics, St. Paul.

Singh, I., Squire, L. and Strauss, J. (eds) (1986), *Agricultural Household Models: Extension, Applications and Policy*, Baltimore: Johns Hopkins University Press.

Strauss, J. (1986), 'Does Better Nutrition Raise Farm Productivity?', *Journal of Political Economy*, 94(2), 297–320.

Subramanian, S. and Deaton, A. (1996), 'The Demand for Food and Calories', *Journal of Political Economy*, 104, pp. 133–162.

von Braun, J., Bouis, H., Kumar, S. and Pandya-Lorch, R. (1992), *Improving Food Security of the Poor: Concept, Policy and Programs*, Washington, DC: International Food Policy Research Institute.

DISCUSSION REPORT SECTION I

Eugenia Muchnik (Chile)[1] began the discussions with comments on the paper by Pinstrup-Andersen and Pandya-Lorch. She noted that IFPRI is not alone in studying the outlook for global food security, or indeed in coming to the broad conclusion that, for the next decade or so, global demand will be met, but that regional deficits will continue to take place in sub-Saharan Africa and in South Asia, where food imports are likely to increase substantially. For the longer run, there is a wider range of views due to different appreciations of the constraints of resource availability, though, on balance, most views present rather positive prospects. She fully supported these judgments about food availability.

That does not mean, however, that the problem of food insecurity will disappear. There are still problems on the demand side: that is, with access to food. Insecurity is obviously highly correlated with poverty, so that achieving improvement will necessitate policies for direct alleviation. The recommendations from the IFPRI work, in fact, include several features of good policy choice which look beyond the agricultural sector. But it is essential to acknowledge that there is controversy about whether or not the answer lies mostly with agricultural and rural development, and there are still issues to settle relating to the management of farming itself. A checklist has been developed at ECLAC which points to queries about the following:

- interventionism versus a subsidiary role of government;
- self-sufficiency versus agroindustrial export development;
- centrality of peasants or commercial farming in food production;
- pricing to encourage production or to favour consumers;
- acceptance or rejection of food aid; and
- the possible conflict between increasing productivity and sustainability.

As to whether food security in low-income food deficit countries should be achieved through agricultural policies seeking to increase food production or by means of general policies for economic development, which would be neutral with respect to economic sectors, there are differing views. For example, the 1990 *World Development Report* of The World Bank, which dealt with poverty, suggested encouraging both rural development and urban employment, as well as implementing specific policies to improve the participation of the poor in growth. But, in the case of resource-poor regions, the recommendation was to follow a different approach; given their low potential for agricultural development it suggested that policy should facilitate out-migration. That might

[1]United Nations, Economic Commission for Latin America and the Caribbean (ECLAC), Santiago.

provide some escape for areas like sub-Saharan Africa and part of South Asia, the regions with the largest number of food-insecure people still, it has to be faced, heavily dependent on the agricultural economy. Although rigid geographical determinism should be avoided, physical geography does matter in many tropical countries; food production is itself the key issue and it is facile to repeat the empty slogan that it is 'poverty' rather than 'food' which is the problem.

Finally, there was strong emphasis on the need for research to explore the lessons from other countries, for example in East Asia and Latin America, that have been successful in escaping from the poverty trap during the last 15 years. What was the sequence of policies followed; what were the key elements of economic policy; what would be a minimum critical effort for success; and what was the role played by the agricultural sector?

Anthony Ikpi (Nigeria)[2] discussed the paper by Rao and Radhakrishna, noting that India, with an estimated 1994 population of 909 million people, is at present nearly self-sufficient in food production. This has been attained as a result of a successful launch of a 'green revolution' in the early 1960s, during which there were large public investments in irrigation and agricultural research, large factor productivity gains especially in land, and a shift from cereal to non-cereal food consumption due to a deliberate change in consumer tastes and preferences. This has drastically reduced food grain imports. Backing this up, the Indian government uses a public procurement and distribution system (PDS) for foodgrains to overcome the country's transient food insecurity. All of that is still not enough for, despite a significant reduction in the incidence of poverty, chronic food insecurity persists in a large proportion of the population. Hence further efforts have included the setting up of several poverty alleviation programmes, employment guarantee schemes and nutrition programmes to try to place adequate purchasing power in the hands of those suffering from chronic food insecurity.

Ikpi expressed some concern about future prospects for India, but he did note that improvement there had been taking place in what could be regarded, given the relationship between population and land, as a classic 'food deficit' region. He then argued that this is not the situation of the 558 million people of sub-Saharan Africa, taken as a whole, where he estimated that there is a food surplus, in grain equivalents, of almost 500 million tonnes. Nevertheless, there is difficulty at a sub-regional level, notably in eastern and southern Africa, with a combined population of 276 million. The sub-regional focus is often forgotten. Much of the problem is caused by a (small) decline in production between 1979 and 1993, allied to growth in numbers, and it is very much concentrated on shortage of foodgrains.

His most important point related to strategy. He was impressed by India's record, but he was not convinced that her policy emphasis on overcoming food insecurity by subsidization of production and public food distribution is suitable for the rather different situation in those parts of sub-Saharan Africa which are in difficulty. The future policy perspective needs to be more on

[2]International Institute of Tropical Agriculture, Ibadan.

building specific human, institutional and infrastructural capacities to remedy past poor performance in food production and distribution. Efforts should be concentrated on promoting sustainable agriculture in sometimes difficult environments; on market development, deregulation and liberalization; and on international trade, regional cooperation and sub-regional integration. It would also be useful to foster diversification to give alternative means of income generation. A comprehensive framework for addressing the various identified capacity-building needs has to be articulated by sub-Saharan Africans themselves, developed and validated by all stakeholders, widely disseminated to all interested parties and meaningfully implemented in a systematic manner with the support of the international community.

Discussing the Senauer and Roe paper, *Luciano Venturini (Italy)*[3] considered their four themes of empirical evidence about elasticities, intra-household distribution, determinants of nutritional status and the resources necessary to relieve poverty, notably in the face of transitory shocks. In his opinion, the paper provided an excellent review of the current state of knowledge, though he called attention, in particular, to the fact that the evidence on some of the issues is still accumulating quite rapidly and that it does present somewhat mixed results rather than being in any way conclusive. For example, there is still substantial debate about the response of anthropometric measures of nutritional status to individual or household income. It is a very complex area, especially in relation to children, since age can be a powerful influence which is hard to disentangle from other factors in survey evidence. There are also considerable difficulties in the analysis of elasticities and in tackling the issue of whether higher food prices have a detrimental impact on the nutritional status of the poor, when they are farmers. The 'income effect' is the key issue and the results are equivocal.

Venturini drew particular attention to the problems of the 'billion poor', or some 19 per cent of the world population. The view that only a very small fraction of world income is needed to meet basic human needs is a matter on which there is far less doubt. It is probably only about one-quarter of the combined cost of debt servicing and the military budget of developing countries. Unfortunately, the situation is not being helped by reductions in official development assistance. These are relatively small in themselves, but they *are* reductions which represent a drop in the proportion of donor countries' gross national product being allocated to aid. Management of the *political economy* of aid remains problematic. This has direct relevance to the final suggestion in the paper for the creation of a drawing rights fund to tide countries over food price 'spikes' which are likely to become more pronounced in future. It could be attractive, in that it is meant to be a loan scheme – it is not seen as a transfer scheme. Donor countries, who appear to find it so difficult to devote higher proportions of their income to transfers, might be more easily persuaded to accept a loan system.

[3]Universita Cattolicà di Piacenza.

SECTION II

Agricultural Diversification and New Technology

ALEX F. McCALLA AND ALBERTO VALDÉS*

Diversification and International Trade

INTRODUCTION

We have struggled mightily with trying to understand the deeper meaning of our assigned title. What are the critical issues linking diversification of agriculture and international trade? Are they competitive, or even antagonistic, concepts in the broader context of food security and agricultural development? Are they complementary and synergistic and, if so, how? Or are they two ships passing in the night which have little if any linkage? We share our problem in searching for a conceptual framework for the paper with you because we are still not sure we have got it right.

We begin with a stylized review of conventional wisdom regarding diversification as a desirable strategy for agricultural development. We then note that much of the agricultural development literature assumes, implicitly or explicitly, a closed or at least closely managed economy. We then ask the question, what happens if you open the economy? Here we use a simple three-good trade model to explore the consequences for the agricultural sector of an open economy setting. We look at the effects on production, consumption and trade as well as the implications for price and income variability and overall economic performance. We then return to the two supposed advantages of a policy of diversification – expanded sources of growth and employment and use as a risk management tool – and ask a basic question: in a world of economy-wide reforms, including trade liberalization, deregulation and privatization, is agricultural diversification a relevant policy objective? To anticipate our answer, we conclude that diversification as a policy goal is not relevant. Those of you who came only for the bottom line can now leave; those who want to know why are invited to stay!

DIVERSIFICATION IN THE LITERATURE OF AGRICULTURAL DEVELOPMENT

Significant strands of the literature of agriculture development argue that agricultural diversification is a desirable outcome either of the dynamics of the development process or as a result of deliberate policy choice (Millikan and

*The World Bank, Washington, DC, USA. The views expressed are those of the authors and do not necessarily represent the views of the management or executive directors of the World Bank. The comments of Alain de Janvry are gratefully acknowledged.

Hapgood, 1967; Bainard and Cooper, 1968; Jabara and Thompson, 1980; Jaffee, 1992; Delgado, 1995). In many developing countries, agricultural production is seen as excessively specialized because of a limited natural resource base or deliberate policy choices or distortions. In the latter case, three examples come to mind.

(1)   A strong focus on specialized primary tropical exports for export tax revenue – coffee, tea and cocoa in Africa, rubber and tea in Sri Lanka, among others.
(2)   Centrally planned economies where regional agricultural specialization was mandated (FSU and Eastern Europe).
(3)   Mandated staple food production for food security; for example, rice in Indonesia, rice and wheat in India and China, rice in Japan.

Diversification, then, is seen as having two highly desirable properties: it expands the production possibility set, thereby expanding opportunities for income generation and employment creation, and it reduces the risk of having all of one's eggs in a basket with a few commodities with potentially high covariance risk. Two common characteristics of this literature are an implicit or explicit assumption of a closed economy (often as a component of an import substitution, inward-looking development strategy) or, to use Hla Myint's term (1975), a 'semi-open economy', where there is a pervasive, proactive role for the government in the rural sector. Government policies with respect to border control and taxation, internal movement regulation, import subsidization, price control, extensive enterprise regulation, parastatal marketing and supply organizations and direct government operation and ownership of infrastructure and marketing firms were, and still are, frequently encountered (Krueger, 1992). Clearly the semi-closed economy, import substitution model, with extensive government control, dominated in Africa, Latin America, FSU and Asia through the 1960s, 1970s and most of the 1980s. It still persists in a considerable number of countries in Africa and South Asia today.

Open economy, export-oriented policies in the NICs (newly industrialized countries), or what are now called the 'Asian Tigers', beginning in the 1970s foreshadowed a fundamental shift of development paradigms towards more open economy policies featuring export orientation, macroeconomic stabilization, deregulation and privatization. This was an economy-wide strategy. These economic reforms have become the order of the day in most of Latin America (after the Chile model) and in all of East Asia, and are at various stages of evolution in the former Soviet Union and Eastern Europe and pockets are even emerging in sub-Saharan Africa and South Asia. This process of general economic liberalization is opening traditionally closed agricultural sectors to trade for the first time,[1] and is raising many concerns about agricultural development and trade linkages.

Why should the issue of trade liberalization be a concern? Perhaps it is because the following scenario is often encountered. The potential for trade is based on comparative advantage and therefore opening to trade should lead countries to *specialize* in things they are good at producing (exportables) and to contract, or cease producing, import-substituting goods (importables). Further, trade would clearly reduce the range of non-traded goods. A useful indicator of the changes in openness is the ratio of $(X+M)$/GDP which, although this is usually measured for the economy as a whole, also applies to a large tradable sector such as agriculture. The countries which have liberalized trade have, almost without exception, experienced a sharp rise in this ratio (for example in Colombia, from 36 per cent until 1990 to 58 per cent after the reforms). If the agricultural/rural sector does not have significant comparative advantage in a wide range of agricultural products, trade could lead to reduced diversity of production and, perhaps, to sectoral contraction. In addition, opening the economy by removing border controls – often quantitative restrictions and/or export taxes – allows international market price variability to enter a previously sheltered, but distorted, domestic sector, increasing price variability and therefore income uncertainty. Hence the potential conclusion that trade is antithetical to a desired policy of diversification.

THE CONSEQUENCES OF OPENING THE ECONOMY

To address the impacts of trade on diversification we first use a simple three sub-sector model to explore the comparative static consequences of opening the economy. We then turn to a more detailed consideration of diversification – trade linkages with respect to the consequences for growth and risk management.

Assume the agricultural sector in a semi-closed economy produces three types of goods (import substitutes or 'importables', non-traded goods or 'home goods' and potential exports or 'exportables') on a continuum from comparative disadvantage to comparative advantage (see Figure 1). The shape of the function is arbitrary. It is simply a descending array of commodity production costs. Whether it is linear, concave or convex would depend on the particular resource endowment of the country. Given import protection and export taxation, as a typical policy set (Schiff and Valdés, 1992), the regime is depicted in Figure 1(a) showing small imports and exports and a large home goods sector. Protection, by tariffs and/or quantitative restrictions, is positive for importables and, from implicit or explicit export taxes, negative for exportables. With the removal of protection and the opening to trade, production of import substitutes contracts (imports increase), the home good sector contracts to contain only those goods whose domestic costs of production fall between c.i.f. (cost, insurance and freight) and f.o.b. (free on board) prices and the export sector expands.[2] Consumer prices of exportables will rise and prices of imports will fall. The basket of consumer goods should be more diversified, now defined by the global rather than the domestic production possibility set, and the basket should be cheaper given that the countries' resources are now more efficiently allocated, with lower average costs of production. The consequences for the degree of diversification in the agricultural sector are potentially ambiguous. The number of importables will decline, as will the number of home goods. However, the diversification of the export sector will increase, as will the volume of exports. The net impact, in a static sense, would appear to be to reduce diversification, but if trade is an engine of growth leading to the

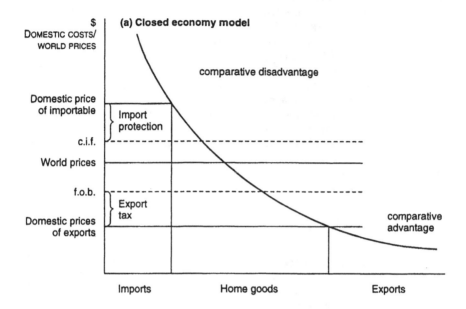

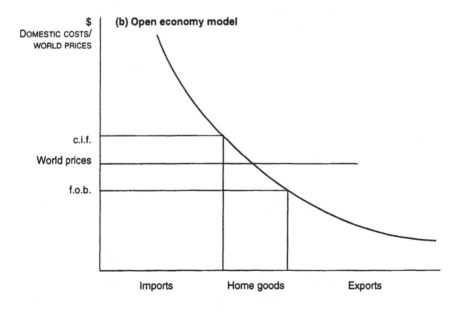

FIGURE 1   *Continuum of comparative advantage in the agriculture sector*

commercialization of the sector then diversification should increase at the economy-wide level and the sector level. However, there could be increased specialization at the firm or production unit level. We return to this point later.

We now need to explore further the impacts of opening the economy on (1) price variability, (2) farmer income, (3) the agricultural sector, (4) consumers, (5) government revenue and (6) the economy as a whole.

Price variability

The movement from a small closed economy to a small open economy fundamentally alters the sources of price variability. In a closed economy, price variability is a function of domestic supply variability. Its amplitude is determined by the elasticities of domestic supply and demand, increasing the greater the inelasticity of either or both. Policies of course could attempt to moderate price variability through storage, subsidies or price guarantees, but fundamentally market price variability is driven by domestic weather.

When the economy is opened, the source of domestic price variability is now world price variability, though it could, of course, be modified by border measures such as quotas, surcharges or variable levies. Whether induced domestic price variability in the semi-closed economy case is greater or less than world price variability cannot be determined *a priori*. Variability will be a function of production and trade composition of a country, of the elasticities of domestic supply and demand, plus the probabilities and magnitude of domestic supply shocks versus world supply and demand elasticities and the magnitude of global shocks. The normal presumption would be that, in a world of open markets, with large numbers of producers and consumers adjusting to shocks, the amplitude of price variation in international markets would be less than in domestic markets.

However, although the presumption is that a more open economy would probably increase the volatility of farm prices, this was not the result observed in Ghana during the economic reforms in the 1980s (Shively, 1996). Shively concludes that, in years subsequent to Ghana's adoption of reforms, a reduction in price volatility occurred in the important northern markets. While the immediate effect was higher and more volatile prices, these were followed by lower and less volatile prices in the longer run.

Farmer income

In the case of farmer income, there are also substantial differences between the closed and open cases for both stability and level. Given supply shocks, in the closed economy case, income is a function of the domestic demand elasticity. If demand was inelastic, farmer incomes would rise with supply shortfalls (fall with big crops), would be stable if the elasticity of demand was unitary and would fall (with shortfalls) if the demand was elastic.

However, in the open economy case farm income fluctuates directly with the magnitude of the supply shock because world prices are given. Short crops lead to a contraction of income; big crops lead to gains. This is the exact opposite of the traditional closed economy outcome with inelastic domestic demand. It seems clear that farm income from a particular commodity in the open economy case would be more unstable. Thus for the individual farmer, if opening to trade led to increased farm-level specialization, farmer income would be more unstable.

So far in this analysis we have not recognized the effect of fluctuations in the exchange rate on domestic price and income fluctuations. Under the open economy model we expect to observe frequent and relatively small adjustments in the nominal rate, in contrast to a regime of fixed rates which could be subject to large and less frequent devaluations under the semi-closed model. Thus it is hard to make the case for a general case of more or less instability in domestic prices induced by nominal exchange rate fluctuations under these two trade options. What the literature seldom recognizes, though, is the significant impact of fluctuations in the 'real' exchange rate (RER) on the variability of domestic 'real' farm prices (Valdés, 1996). A simple comparison of RER fluctuations between developed and developing countries indicates that these are much more pronounced in developing countries; this reinforces the perception that more emphasis should be given to the influence of RER on agricultural price stabilization policy for developing countries.

The agricultural sector

There is less that can be said *a priori* about the impact on the agricultural sector of opening the economy to trade. If the sector price to liberalization was heavily taxed, both directly and indirectly (Schiff and Valdés, 1992) liberalization would lead to expanding production of those commodities where the country has comparative advantage, which, coupled with higher prices, clearly should increase sector income. What can be said about the variability of income is less clear, as this would depend on domestic shocks and the degree of covariance risk among commodities compared to the variability of world prices.

Consumers

Consumers would experience access to a more diverse bundle of goods, prices of importables would fall, as would prices of home goods, while prices of exportables should rise. Overall, the real incomes of consumers, and real costs of intermediate producers, should become far less dependent on domestic supply shocks which, together with diversification in consumption, should make their incomes more stable and, on the average, higher.

Government revenue

If governments were directly protecting imports with high tariffs or were selling import quotas, revenue from previously imported goods would fall. If, however, after liberalization all imports were subject to a lower uniform tariff, revenue could rise if the range and quantities of imports increased. Clearly, export tax revenue would be lost. It is likely on balance that the government could lose revenue. Perhaps this is an explanation for governments being less than enthusiastic about liberalizing agriculture if trade taxes are a significant source of revenue.

The economy as a whole

The empirical evidence of gains in overall economy performance from policy reform and trade liberalization is overwhelming. Clearly, in the process there are losers as well as winners, but overall the economy is better off.

Summary

To sum up, the presumption is that, as part of the endogenous response to economic reform and trade liberalization, the new policy framework encourages the development of additional production alternatives and the economy becomes more diversified at the sectoral and economy-wide level, while becoming more specialized at the firm/farm level.

DIVERSIFICATION AND AGRICULTURAL DEVELOPMENT

On the basis of this general analysis, we can now return to the main theme. Basically, commercialization and diversification are part of an endogenous process determined largely by market forces. Commercialization of agricultural systems is an irreversible phenomenon, triggered by economic growth. It is not a frictionless process, as there will be some losers, although the majority should be winners. How government policies might alleviate many of the possible adverse transitional consequences was the theme of a special issue of *Food Policy* (Pingali and Rosegrant, 1995). Their analysis concludes that the key elements of a long-term strategy to facilitate commercialization and economy-wide diversification are (1) research and extension, (2) economic liberalization, including trade liberalization and deregulation of agriculture, (3) development of rural capital markets, (4) development of land markets, and (5) infrastructure investment. We agree with the key elements, but they seem to be applicable to a long-term rural development strategy which encourages growth, the result of which leads to commercialization and diversification. In other words, diversification becomes an inherent and desirable outcome of a growth strategy, rather than an objective *per se*.

The main components of economic liberalization and structural adjustment are a reduction in trade barriers on both imports and exports, an alignment of macroeconomic policies, and deregulation of internal factor and product markets in general. An outcome of this reform process is to accelerate the development of new production possibilities; that is, more diversification at both the sectoral and economy-wide level. This is an endogenous process and thus does not require a specific government policy.

At both the producer and the sectoral level, the scope for diversification as a risk management strategy in response to trade liberalization is limited by the co-movements of world prices of agricultural commodities. As reported in Quiroz and Valdés (1995), the evidence for 1970–91 shows that 22 of 28 correlations in world prices are positive, and the negative correlations are small and restricted to a couple of commodities (bananas and rice). There are substantial positive correlations in world prices for important commodities, including the combinations of wheat–maize, rice–wheat, cotton–maize, cocoa–coffee, among others. Thus one should not be overly optimistic regarding the returns in terms of export price risk reduction by diversification, at least within this range of commodities. The situation regarding horticultural products is less clear, requiring further analysis.

It is reasonable to expect that, over time, these correlations should increase, owing to factors both on the demand and on the supply side, and also to the dramatic improvements in transport and communications. On the demand side, with income growth and factors associated with it (urbanization, increase in the value of time, technological developments which increase the shelf-time duration of products), food consumption patterns are becoming more flexible and diversified. For example, regions which traditionally had a diet concentrated on rice or legumes have experienced a rise in the consumption of wheat and livestock products. The opening to trade reinforces this trend, by reducing the price of substitutes for the traditional staples. Thus, over time, one expects a rise in substitution possibilities, which in turn induce a higher correlation on world prices.

On the supply side, the impact of new technology and new investment in irrigation, roads and storage facilities makes a more diversified output increasingly possible. Parallel to the case with consumption patterns, the opening of trade reinforces this trend towards substitution possibilities in production and thus diversification of production and trade. Thus, as more and more countries stop taxing agricultural exports, adopt a more flexible diet and enter into a more diversified output mix on a global scale, the more positive should be the correlation between prices and the lower the returns to diversification (in terms of price risk reduction).

But this is not the whole story. In addition to the higher substitution possibilities in consumption and production through time and improvements in transport and communications, world prices of commodities (agricultural and non-agricultural) are also positively correlated because they have a common reaction to macroeconomic conditions (interest rates and so on). Thus one would expect an increase in correlations in world prices between the prices of imports and exports of developing countries. In a very real sense, these correlations tend to provide substantial price insurance for developing countries. Specifically regarding food-deficit countries, what this analysis suggests is that, when the food insecurity problem of food-deficit countries is analysed within the context of their foreign exchange position, fluctuations in their food import bill may coincide with fluctuations of their export revenues, and thus their food insecurity problem may be much less severe than when one looks at food imports alone. This relationship was analysed empirically by Valdés and Konandreas (1981) for 24 developing countries for the 1961–76 period. They found that the magnitude of the fluctuations in the food import bill shortfall is reduced considerably when adjusted for fluctuations in export revenues. Thus, while the higher positive correlation may not benefit a particular set of farmers, it would clearly help the economy as a whole.

TRADE POLICY AND DIVERSIFICATION

At the farm level diversification is a natural reaction to instability. It is well known that diversification of the production mix can be an efficient mechanism for diminishing the impact of risk on producers's welfare. Adding new products to the mix should contribute to reducing the variance of the value of production at the farm level; by how much will depend on the correlation between different prices. If this correlation is −1.0, the variance of the portfolio is brought down to zero; if it is + 1.0, the variance of the total is unaffected. For all cases in between some reduction in variance will be achieved (Newbery and Stiglitz, 1981).[3]

In a sophisticated market economy there are institutions that enable economic agents to manage risk to stabilize their consumption over time; thus diversification is less of a policy issue in developed economies. However, in agriculture in most developing countries, where these risk markets do not exist, farmers bear the full brunt of price and production risks. If they are risk-averse, they will undertake action – more diversification – that sacrifices mean income for a reduced degree of fluctuations; that is, risk will lead to underinvestment in risk-prone sectors. At the same time, there may be agents willing to accept increased fluctuations if they are given a higher mean income. Owing to a missing market for risk, they have the potential to buy insurance, but they cannot engage in this exchange which would increase their welfare. Thus the agricultural sector is somewhat 'trapped' in a lower risk/lower income situation.

But this is not the whole story. Three groups other than producers could be affected by increased exposure to agricultural price risk. There are the consumers of farm products, the producers of intermediate goods (based on farm products) and the government whose revenue fluctuates with the prices. Thus the spillover from fluctuations in farm prices can cause real income of consumers to fluctuate, as well as having multiplier effects on the costs and demand for intermediate goods (typically non-traded) and affecting government and foreign exchange accounts.[4]

In spite of the general conclusion of the theoretical economic literature arguing that the welfare cost from price risk in agriculture would be relatively small (ibid.), one observes that, historically, agricultural price interventions have been used to reduce domestic price instability vis-à-vis a counterfactual of no intervention. That is, this predicted low welfare cost is not consistent with the systematic effort by governments (revealed preferences) to smooth the transmission of border prices to domestic prices. This issue was analysed for 18 developing countries for the 1960–85 period in the Schiff and Valdés study (1992), where they found that price variability of domestic agricultural prices was consistently lower than that of border prices for the same commodities. Using a different analytical approach, Mundlak and Larson (1992) subsequently published results which suggest that the transmission elasticity from world prices to domestic prices is close to one, which is at variance with Schiff and Valdés (1992). However, the methodology used by Mundlak and Larson has been challenged by Quiroz and Soto (1993), whose results confirm the great importance that policy makers attribute to the minimization of between-years price fluctuations. However, the real issue for this paper is the change in domestic price instability from before to after the reform. Except for the paper on Ghana by Shively (1996), who finds price variability is less after an initial period of greater instability, we do not have new evidence on the post-reform scenario.[5]

It is a common presumption that a more open economy is more specialized and therefore riskier. Precisely because of price risk and the lack of risk-diffusing mechanisms in developing countries, the endogenous response of the farm sector (which is risk-averse) is to underinvest in risk-prone activities, closing more of the economy to trade. If, on the one hand, the assumption that farmers are relatively risk-averse and the government is risk-neutral is reversed, the argument could be made that farmers overexpose the economy to risk. Such a proposition was advanced several years ago by Bainard and Cooper (1968) and Jabara and Thompson (1980), suggesting that corrective action by the government was called for. We question whether such corrective action is appropriate. What should not be done, in our opinion, is to implement a policy of diversification by means of trade and price policy. In practice, this would involve diversifying domestic production by means of supporting the production of import-competing products and a resulting (implicit) taxation of the production of exportables, narrowing the export base. This would be going back to the inward-oriented policy of the past, which failed in terms of growth and thus made the whole economy more exposed to risk (for example, risk hurts more if the economy grows at a slower pace).

CONCLUDING COMMENTS

Our conclusion is that there is no general rationale for an active policy of diversification, with the exception of the case of export promotion which we discuss below. In both the static and dynamic cases, the two traditional arguments for diversification, risk reduction and contributing to growth, are not strong arguments that warrant a proactive government policy of diversification. There is no evidence that opening the economy to trade will have a significant impact on increasing risk for agriculture. Diversification is a natural process of growth and in fact opening of the agricultural economy will probably contribute to accelerating the process of production and trade diversification. Trade and diversification are complementary, therefore, rather than conflicting.

It is revealing that the topic of diversification as such simply does not appear in such a well recognized book on the normative theory of trade policy as *Trade Policy and Economic Welfare* by Max Corden (1997). There are, however, three themes in this body of literature which have direct relevance for the analysis in this paper. One is the literature on the optimal subsidy or tax to adjust for domestic divergence between market prices and social costs. This theme, in our opinion, is neutral regarding diversification of production or trade. The second is the topic of industrial policy (which Corden refers as the 'picking winners' approach) for the case of industries generating significant externalities and/or industries believed to have high growth potential, for which the infant industry argument applies. The third, often associated with agricultural exports in developing countries, concerns some dynamic aspects of trade policy and in particular refers to the case of fluctuations in export earnings and risk avoidance. More frequently in the past than today, the argument stated that there were conditions under which countries should reduce their dependence on trade and also diversify the pattern of their exports because of fluctuations in export earnings, which would filter through the economy to farmers, suppliers of inputs, government revenues and to consumers.

Whether or not the outcome of trade policy interventions to deal with any of these three policy issues will necessarily lead to more or less diversification is undetermined. Initial conditions vary from country to country and thus whether the outcome will lead to more specialization or diversification will vary accordingly. However, some analysts have argued that, at least for sub-Saharan Africa, a commodity (or commodity group)-specific agricultural diversification policy is a necessary component of adjustment, export promotion and employment promotion strategies (Delgado, 1995). There are three arguments: (1) Africa's dependence on agricultural exports, in a context of falling world prices for them, is inducing a significant diversification out of agricultural exports, but with little diversification within agriculture; (2) a large sector of non-tradable production exists as a result of high transactions costs (transport and others), so a large segment remains underdeveloped even if price policy distortions are removed; and (3) externalities and market failures provide governments with considerable latitude to influence the factor intensity of the long-run growth path. In a real sense, such a strategy favours an active pro-diversification policy as a way to improve competitiveness on a widespread basis. Delgado's analysis suggests a strategy focused on (1) promoting agricultural food production exports as a way to lower the risk of food insecurity, (2) trade-creating policies between low- and high-potential zones, and (3) the promotion of non-traditional agricultural exports, although these cannot be made the main component of agricultural development strategy in Africa.

What such an approach does not elucidate is whether the government should do this for the sake of diversification itself, or because these are initiatives which have a high payoff regardless of a diversification objective. The declining terms of trade argument seems to us to be an uninsurable risk; furthermore, if producers remain in these declining activities they must be obtaining higher returns than their alternatives, net of the cost of migration. Should the government step in to help declining industries? That would best be done through a social safety net, but not through commodity programmes. The cost of adjustment for unskilled farmers and farm workers with few alternatives is undoubtedly one of the most complex problems of adjustment; public policies should focus on retraining and labour mobility programmes, rather than on protecting particular sub-sectors for the sake of diversification.

We do find, however, that one can make the case for a proactive role of government towards promoting export diversification *per se*. This is through the partial funding of the cost of searching for new markets, including foreign ones. In the case of agricultural commodities, unlike industrial goods, the private sector will underinvest in the search for new markets, particularly as they would become open to other producers and exporters. The fixed costs of search could be high and there is a 'free-rider' situation. Thus there is, we submit, a public good element in favour of a government subsidy and/or direct assistance from export promotion agencies for the search for new markets. This is the only specialized case we can find that supports an explicit policy to support diversification in an open economy setting.

NOTES

[1]In Latin America, for the first time since the Second World War. These economies were very open to trade between approximately the mid-1800s and first third of the 1900s.
[2]Under an open economy scenario, we envisage a trade regime based on a fairly uniform and low tariff on all imports (say between 10 and 20 per cent) with no quantitative restrictions, and no export taxes or other restrictions on exports.
[3]This is under the assumption that the expected return of the new products is the same as for the old.
[4]There may be special cases of countries where a particular export sector is also a relatively large economic sector (for example, cocoa in Ivory Coast) and thus where per capita income would be correlated with fluctuations in the world price of that commodity. However, the evidence for Africa indicates that, while dependence on a few export commodities remains high, agricultural exports as a percentage of GDP have declined (Delgado, 1995).
[5]The issue of price risk is also becoming more important now in the context of trade and price policy reform aimed at aligning international prices more closely with domestic prices, particularly under the 'tariffication' rule agreed under the Uruguay Round Agreement.

REFERENCES

Bainard, W.C. and Cooper, R.N. (1968), 'Uncertainty and Diversification in International Trade', *Food Research Institute Studies*, 8, 257–85.
Corden, M.W. (1997), *Trade Policy and Economic Welfare*, Oxford: Oxford University Press.
Delgado, C.L. (1995), 'Agricultural diversification and export promotion in sub-Saharan Africa', *Food Policy*, 20, 225–43.
Jabara, C.L. and Thompson, R.L. (1980), 'Agricultural comparative advantage under international price uncertainty: The case of Senegal', *American Journal of Agricultural Economics*, 62, 188–98.
Jaffee, S. (1992), 'Enhancing agricultural growth through diversification in sub-Saharan Africa', in S. Barghouti, S. Garbus and D. Umali (eds), *Trends in Agricultural Diversification: Regional perspectives*, Technical Paper No. 180, Washington, DC: World Bank.
Krueger, A.O. (1992), *A Synthesis of the Political Economy in Developing Countries: A World Bank Comparative Study*, Vol. 5, Baltimore: Johns Hopkins University Press.
Millikan, M.F. and Hapgood, D. (1967), *No Easy Harvest. The Dilemma of Agriculture in Underdeveloped Countries*, Boston: Little, Brown and Company.
Mundlak, Y. and Larson, D.F. (1992), 'On the Transmission of World Agricultural Prices', *World Bank Economic Review*, 6, 399–422.
Myint, H. (1975), 'Agriculture and Economic Development in the Open Economy', in L.G. Reynolds (ed.), *Agriculture in Development Theory*, New Haven: Yale University Press.

Newbery, D.M.G. and Stiglitz, J.E. (1981), *The Theory of Commodity Price Stabilization. A Study in the Economics of Risk*, Oxford: Clarendon Press.

Pingali, P.L. and Rosegrant, M.W. (1995), 'Agricultural commercialization and diversification: processes and policies', *Food Policy*, **20**, 171–85.

Quiroz, J.A. and Soto, R. (1993), *International Transmission of Agricultural Price Movements: Do Governments Care?*, LATAD Working Paper, Washington, DC: World Bank.

Quiroz, J.A. and Valdés, A. (1995), 'Agricultural diversification and policy reform', *Food Policy*, **20**, 245–55.

Schiff, M. and Valdés, A. (1992), *A Synthesis of the Economics in Developing Countries*, Vol. 4 of *The Political Economy of Agricultural Pricing Policy*, ed. A. Krueger, Baltimore: Johns Hopkins University Press for the World Bank.

Shively, G.E. (1996), 'Food Price Variability and Economic Reform: An ARCH Approach for Ghana', *American Journal of Agricultural Economics*, **78**, 126–36.

Valdés, A. (1996), *Surveillance of Agricultural Price and Trade Policy in Latin America during Major Policy Reforms*, Discussion Paper No. 349, Washington, DC: World Bank.

Valdés, A. and Konandreas, P. (1981), 'Assessing Food Insecurity Based on National Aggregates in Developing Countries', in A. Valdés (ed.), *Food Security for Developing Countries*, Boulder: Westview Press.

CHRISTOPHER L. DELGADO AND AMMAR SIAMWALLA*

Rural Economy and Farm Income Diversification in Developing Countries

Farm-level diversification involves adding income-generating activities at the farm household level, including livestock, local non-farm and off-farm pursuits undertaken by farm people. The objective of this paper is to consider questions arising from an apparent inconsistency. In this respect, policy makers seem to consider farm diversification a major 'economic' issue, thus as an *objective*, while economists typically neglect it, seeing farm diversification as an *outcome* from pursuing another objective. This lack of a consensus is further reflected by disagreement over the extent to which national policies should proactively seek to promote diversification of the farm-level output mix in specific directions.

THE AMBIGUOUS MEANING OF 'FARM DIVERSIFICATION' FOR ECONOMISTS

Governments in developing countries have an intense interest in promoting increased output diversification at both the farm and national levels (Petit and Barghouti, 1992; Siamwalla *et al.*, 1992). Cited benefits of farm diversification are high and more stable farm incomes and employment, greater long-term prospects for farm income growth and more environmentally sustainable farming systems. Economists, on the other hand, often change the subject at the first mention of the topic.[1]

The simplest interpretation of farm diversification as an objective is that farmers seek to generate a portfolio of income from activities with different degrees of risk, expected returns, liquidity and seasonality, and adjust their output mix accordingly. Thus farm diversification would be the allocation of household productive assets among different income-generating activities. Farm diversification may be distinguished from village-level diversification, where households become more specialized over time, but village economies offer a wider array of goods and services for sale, reflecting the typical path of rural economic development under commercialization (Timmer, 1988; von Braun and Kennedy, 1994). Similarly, farm diversification as an objective involves a different set of issues than export diversification, out of a few agricultural commodities, as a means to stabilize foreign exchange receipts (Bautista, 1992).

*International Food Policy Research Institute, Washington, DC, USA, and Thailand Development Research Institute Foundation, Bangkok, Thailand, respectively.

Most economists in the Western tradition tend to see farm diversification as the endogenous outcome of economy-wide policies or secular trends affecting relative incentives. These policies can be primarily on the output or factor price side (for example, Schiff and Valdés, 1992) or on the input price or non-price sides, such as 'free' water supplies to farmers that encourage the overproduction of rice, or public investment choices for agricultural research priorities, or the creation of infrastructure that favours one product over another (World Bank, 1990; Hayami, 1991). Thus farm diversification is perceived as a process of adjustment to major changes in relative costs, benefits, risks and uncertainties of different household income generation strategies.

Without disagreeing, we argue that in some cases – but only in some cases – it makes sense for both economists and governments to approach farm diversification as a specific objective, even to the point of concentrating analysis and interventions on favoured sub-sectors or outputs. The key lies in the degree of market development, the degree of prior agricultural transformation and the relative importance of agriculture in the case concerned. Cases where agricultural input, factor and output markets work reasonably well – typically, where agriculture has evolved to a point where it has become a commercial sector just like any other – are very different from those where the commercialization of family agriculture is still at a very early stage and many markets are missing.

Where markets work well, relative price changes are transmitted throughout the economy (in the absence of distortions) and all actors face a common set of prices (adjusted for distance and so on). If agriculture is a relatively well-developed sector, most farmers will be able to respond to these signals. Since agriculture is only a small share of economic activity, situations deviating from the ideal are more an issue for equity than for growth, and can be dealt with through measures other than output mix diversification.

Where markets do not work well, other events will need to occur before adjustment to relative price changes in the macroeconomy can be transmitted to the farm level. If agriculture accounts for a large share of employment and exports as well, such adjustment in output mixes is crucial to growth as well as equity. If agriculture is also pre-commercial, shifting into a new set of commercial activities will require a host of major rural changes in addition to alterations in outputs. Under these circumstances, it will be argued, a commodity-specific approach may be needed to commercialize agriculture, to speed up the transmission of incentives to the farm level and to promote adjustment of output mixes in ways favourable for both growth and equity.

KEY ISSUES IN THE ECONOMIC ANALYSIS OF FARM DIVERSIFICATION FOR DIFFERENT TYPES OF ECONOMIES

Farm diversification in countries with developed markets

In well-functioning market economies, which in addition to the OECD countries probably include much of Southeast Asia and Latin America, the need for policies specifically to promote change in farm-level output mixes arises primarily because of the existence of prior distortions, such as differential protection of specific crops. These policies have led to overspecialization, and the subsidization of certain crop-specific inputs, such as water, in the case of rice. The barrier to adjustment to new relative prices is typically a policy distortion which drives a wedge between social prices and those affecting farmers. The likely policy recommendation is to remove the distortion.

Relevant research is not really a separate category of research from that dealing with market liberalization generally. In fact, farm diversification would be an endogenous outcome of pursuing a liberalization objective, not a target in itself. Indeed, most economists addressing diversification issues today in the context of functioning markets for inputs and outputs, and factors, go out of their way to insist that they are *not trying to pick the winners*.

In sum, in economies with strong markets, where agricultural transformation has largely occurred, and agriculture is a relatively small part of the overall economy, farm diversification as an objective is probably not a very important economic issue in its own right, even though the outcome of other policies for farm diversification is important. The relevant economic issues concern how to overcome distortions – usually policy-mediated – that drive a wedge between socially and privately optimal production and sales strategies. Solutions are likely to be found in policy changes addressing the source of the problem (such as free irrigation water) and farm diversification (or specialization) will be an endogenous result of those changes.

Farm diversification in the presence of missing major markets at early stages of agricultural transformation

In many parts of the world, while some markets for factors, inputs and outputs may work well, some key markets for agriculture (such as land and credit, for example) may not exist. Markets may be missing for a variety of reasons, and we will solely be concerned here with the case of market failure from incomplete transformation and commercialization of subsistence agriculture.

In countries at early stages of agricultural transformation, small and large farm households in rural areas typically do not have access to the same technology, information, asset base, input supplies and market outlets. The same is true for farm households in different locations. Under these conditions different farm households are likely to be subject to significantly different levels of *transactions costs* for producing and selling the same output mix (Akerlof, 1970; Lopez, 1984; de Janvry *et al.*, 1991). Broadly defined, transactions costs are the full costs of carrying out exchange, presumably including marketing costs (Coase, 1960).[2] They include intangibles such as search, monitoring and enforcement, and vary by product, type of agent in the marketing chain and individual agent within a category of agents.

Most high value-added products in agriculture are characterized by a high ratio of transactions costs to final value, because of the high degree of processing embodied in such items (Binswanger and Rosenzweig, 1986; Jaffee and Morton, 1995). Examples would be animal proteins and horticulture, which are prime candidates for farm diversification. Production of these items tends to increase returns to family resources. They also tend to be products with high income elasticities, which offer prospects for long-term growth. Rural households with different bases are likely to face different levels of transaction costs. Poorer households may have more difficulty diversifying into new activities than more wealthy ones.

Lowering and reducing disparities of transaction costs across rural households is therefore central in economies at early stages of agricultural transformation to promoting farm-level adjustment of agricultural output mixes to major changes in relative prices. Moving the shadow decision prices individual farmers face (market prices plus transactions costs) closer to a common new social optimum is central to growth; making sure that poorer farmers also adjust is central to equity and poverty alleviation. The key issue is the extent to which addressing high transactions cost barriers separating households from markets requires a commodity-specific, or at least a commodity group-specific, approach.

Policies for growth and poverty alleviation will probably involve increasing access of farm households – and especially the poor – to information and assets for adjustment, primarily through infrastructure provision and institutional development for collective action. Sectoral policies of governments play a key role here, and they typically have important commodity-specific attributes, particularly when dealing with high-value added commodities that typically have high transactions costs associated with processing, such as milk and meat in the tropics.

PRESENT PATTERNS AND DRIVING FORCES OF FARM INCOME DIVERSIFICATION

A snapshot of the process of diversification of the world's agriculture out of cereals over the last decade can be gleaned from Table 1, which shows relative growth rates for major farm outputs, excluding non-farm and off-farm income. For the world as a whole, aggregate production of fruits, vegetables and tree nuts grew faster from the mid-1970s to the mid-1990s than did cereals or other crops. Livestock output grew faster than crop output. In developing regions, cereals output grew at slower rates than other crops or livestock, with the notable exception of Africa. In Africa, cereals production grew at a higher rate than other crops over the period, which included some major droughts.[3] However, Africa is the only region of the world where a large share (up to half) of starchy staples comes from roots and tubers (Alexandratos, 1995). It seems likely that cereals are gradually replacing these crops, given the typically greater labour intensity of the latter.

Table 1 also illustrates the rapid rise in livestock production in Asia over the last two decades, where it is the key diversification activity (with fisheries, not shown) at the farm and national levels. Generally, the relatively strong showing for output growth of livestock and horticultural products over the last decade illustrates a broader pattern throughout the world of substitution of horticultural products and animal products for starchy staples in human diets over time, due to preferences for these items as incomes go up. Although Table 1

TABLE 1   *Compound annual growth in production of major agricultural items by major regions and selected countries, 1973–96 (per cent per annum)*

Region	All crops	Cereals	Vegetables and fruits/treenuts	Livestock
Africa	**1.84**	**2.64**	**2.14**	**2.65**
Burkina-Faso	4.38	4.65	3.14	4.85
Uganda	0.94	1.32	<u>0.64</u>	2.40
Zambia	2.07	<u>−0.20</u>	2.44	1.77
Asia	**2.88**	**2.74**	**4.41**	**6.36**
Bangladesh	1.68	2.30	1.03	2.01
Indonesia	4.02	4.15	3.62	7.00
Thailand	3.89	1.84	1.45	3.67
South America	**2.21**	**1.86**	**3.19**	**3.23**
Chile	3.81	3.45	4.14	4.62
Europe	**−0.05**	**1.01**	**0.22**	**1.20**
1984–96	−1.86	<u>−0.69</u>	−0.52	0.25
USA	**0.60**	**1.03**	**1.21**	**1.95**
World	**1.42**	**1.76**	**2.67**	**2.87**

Notes: Compound annual growth rate of annual output in metric tons. Underlined values not significantly different from zero at 10 per cent.

Source: Annual production data from FAO (1997).

does not contain figures for non-farm income, it seems reasonable to suppose that agricultural income continued to shrink around the world as a share of total farm household income and employment, as found for a selection of developing countries from 1965 to 1988 by Petit and Barghouti (1992).

In looking at specific country cases, we limit our analysis to the virtually polar opposites of Asian rice economies and African food/export crop economies. The former represent cases where markets work relatively well, agriculture has largely gone through a prior transformation into a commercialized sector, and it is a shrinking part of the overall economy. The latter tend to represent cases where some markets do not work well, agriculture is largely uncommercialized, and it still accounts for the largest share of economic activity.

Economies with functioning markets, where agricultural transformation has occurred, and agriculture accounts for a shrinking share of employment: examples from Asian rice areas

Agricultural diversification has mostly been a hot policy issue in Asian rice-growing countries. Indonesia, for example, went from being the world's largest importer of rice to being self-sufficient in the decade ending in the mid-1980s

(Hayami and Otsuka, 1994). This pattern was not unusual in the region during the 'green revolution' period, and typically involved substantial policy support for cereals production, through research and infrastructure investment, and even outright protection (Pingali and Rosegrant, 1995). Pressure to diversify resulted from the abrupt fall in world rice prices during the mid-1980s (World Bank, 1990).

Besides short-run price movements, the long-run outlook for many rice producers in Asia suggests a need for diversification. Under post-'green revolution' conditions, further growth of cereals production would lead to sharply falling producer incomes as cereals – being more costly to produce than world prices and having low price and income elasticities – encountered a domestic demand constraint.[4] Thus there are many pressures to diversify farm resources into high-income elasticity of demand items, preferably having broad export markets for outlets (Hayami and Ruttan, 1985).

The quickest form of market adjustment might result from letting abrupt price declines push small farmers and landless labourers off the land into cities. While sharp declines in rice prices would presumably provide an impetus to diversify, few governments would be able to ignore the welfare implications for millions of small producers, even if the short-run consequences for poor net consumers of rice were favourable (Timmer, 1988; Taylor, 1994).

Given that subsidized provision of irrigation water is one of the main incentive factors of the 'green revolution', diversification out of rice may be hard to achieve in the absence of tradable property rights in water that match social and private costs in water use (Rosegrant *et al.*, 1995). Now that irrigation infrastructure has been put in, passing on its maintenance cost will require substantial institutional change (Siamwalla *et al.*, 1992). We therefore need to be careful about assuming that markets alone will ensure a smooth adjustment out of overreliance on cereals.

Equity issues in farm diversification are hinted at by Table 2, which shows the share of farm household income across the household income distribution coming from various sectors, for selected cases. The first two, from Pakistan and the Philippines, arguably represent cases where local markets work fairly well. The latter two, from Guangdong, China in 1989 and Vietnam more recently, represent the case of substantially transformed agricultures in the early stages of privatization. In the first two, the share of crop profits increases with income, whereas in the latter it declines. Private ownership of land is critical to wealth in the first two, whereas access to non-farm opportunities is more important for income in the latter two.

The detailed data by income class available for Pakistan and the Philippines show that prime farm diversification activities, especially livestock but also fruits and vegetables, account for a large share of the income of the poorest households, and the share of these activities declines with increasing income. Hossein (1988) also shows that livestock, backyard crops and fisheries play a special role in the income of the poor in Bangladesh, in both 'green revolution' areas and areas that have not undergone this transformation. David and Otsuka (1994), in a comprehensive study of the impact of high-yielding rice varieties on income distribution in eight Asian countries, show that the relatively

TABLE 2 Asian farm household income sources by income quintile (percentage of household income, quintile 1 the poorest)

Country	Quintile	Crop profits	Livestock profits	Agricultural wages	Non-farm activities	Rents	Transfers
Pakistan 1986/7–1988/9, 3 province rural survey[a]	1	6	25	1	50	5	14
	2	9	24	0	48	5	13
	3	12	18	2	44	9	15
	4	20	16	1	43	8	13
	5	37	9	0	17	21	17
Philippines 1984/5 Mindanao[b]	1	29	23	31	17	(included in 'non-farm activities')	—
	2	25	18	39	19		—
	3	35	18	28	20		—
	4	36	18	20	27		—
	5	54	10	2	35		—
Vietnam 1992/3, national[c]	1	59	(included with crops and forestry profits)	23	15		3
	2	57		20	20		4
	3	48	—	19	28		4
	4	40	—	22	35		3
	5	18	—	23	52		3
China 1989, Guangdong[d]	1	74	(included with crops and forestry profits)	(included with non-farm activities)	22		4
	2	64			32		4
	3	60	—	—	34		7
	4	48	—	—	47		4

Sources: [a]IFPRI Rural Survey of Pakistan (Alderman and Garcia, 1993; Adams and He, 1995); [b]IFPRI/Institute for Mindanao Culture Survey (Bouis, 1991), 'Livestock' includes fruits and vegetables; [c]Vietnam, State Planning Committee, 1992/93 Vietnam Living Standards Survey (1994); 'Agricultural wages' includes non-farm wages; [d]1990 Qingyuan County Farm Household Survey (Hare, 1994), data are for quartiles', 'Agricultural wages' includes non-farm wages.

adverse impact of the 'green revolution' on rice in high-potential areas on incomes in lower-potential areas was largely mitigated by migration and diversification of the low-potential areas into non-rice activities.

Choices involved in fostering technological progress and providing rural infrastructure are likely to remain critical for providing the incentives for successful diversification of farmers faced by a structural need to adjust their output patterns away from exclusive reliance on cereals. Efforts in Southeast Asia to promote diversification while maintaining cereals production incentives have only had success where technological advances have increased the profitability of alternatives (Hayami and Otsuka, 1994; Siamwalla *et al.*, 1992).

Where technology is available, the constraints become infrastructure and institutions. Detailed work in Indonesia by Hayami and Kawagoe (1993) shows that, in countries with good infrastructure and a trade class, private marketing initiatives can do much to promote the shift of producer resources into diversification activities. Similar results have been reported for Thailand by Siamwalla *et al.* (1992).

Yet much of the agricultural infrastructure built in the 1970s and 1980s in Asia was built around the objective of cereals production, and in some cases is fairly specific to that objective by virtue of location or function. Furthermore, not all areas have the institutional capacity afforded by traditional Chinese traders in Indonesia. The 19th-century experience in Denmark (butter) and Japan (sericulture) suggests that the combination of technological innovation in the diversification activity (the cream separator and cold storage of cocoons, respectively) and non-monopolistic institutions of collective action, such as creamery cooperatives, was critical to historical diversification trends out of cereals (Hayami and Ruttan, 1985; Hayami, 1991). The need for institutional innovation for farm diversification will be greatest in economies that have not gone through agricultural transformation and where agricultural markets do not work well.

Economies at the early stages of agricultural transformation: farm income diversification in sub-Saharan Africa

By definition, agricultural transformation has not occurred in these cases and agriculture tends to remain the predominant sector for employment. Many markets are missing or severely restricted, especially for credit and land. Not all African economies fit this definition, and not all economies that fit the definition are in Africa.[5] Smallholders in Africa generate significant income from activities other than growing crops and tending livestock.

The results from 28 household case studies of farm household income generation across sub-Saharan Africa are summarized in Table 3. Farm income includes both income in kind and income from net sales of crops and livestock. Local non-farm income includes income earned by farm people working for wages (including work on someone else's farm) and local sales of goods and services. External non-farm income consists of remittances and transfers and does not depend upon buyers in local markets. These three types of income have different risk profiles for smallholders, who tend to diversify their income

TABLE 3   *Income sources for 28 samples of farming households across sub-Saharan Africa, various years (percentage of total household income)*

Share of farm income	Farm income[1]	Local non-farm income[2]	External non-farm income[3]
Maximum[4]	86	8	4
Mean[5]	63	28	8
Median[6]	63	20	16
Minimum[7]	37	51	11

Notes: [1]Income from net sales of raw crops and livestock plus subsistence consumption.
[2]Income from local wages (even on other farms) and local sales of non-farm goods and services, including processed foods.
[3]Income from migration, remittances and transfers.
[4]Gambia, uplands areas, 1985/6.
[5]Means for each income source separately, across the sample.
[6]Zimbabwe, natural region IV, 1988/9.
[7]Senegal, Sahelian zone, 1988/90.

Source: Compiled from data and independent studies listed in Table 1 of Delgado (1997). The survey data were mostly collected for a single harvest year, within the 1985/6 to 1988/9 period.

portfolios across different combinations of these three sources, depending on local circumstances. Non-farm income in the farm surveys in Table 3 ranges from 12 to 62 per cent of total household income, with a median value of 36 per cent.

The relationship between local and external non-farm income is highly variable across cases studied. The *raisons d'être* for the two are in fact distinct. Local non-farm income is largely a result of the development of the local farm economy for other reasons, such as cash crop development. Spending by households of cash crop income on non-tradable rural products creates employment for any underemployed local resources (Bell and Hazell, 1980). External non-farm income is largely the result of a deliberate effort by households to diversify into income sources that are not highly covariate with local cropping outcomes (Reardon *et al.*, 1988; von Braun and Pandya-Lorch, 1991). Not surprisingly, the correlation coefficient between the two forms of non-farm income across the 28 cases was low (0.17) and insignificant.

There are significant regional differences in farm income sources within Africa. Anecdotal evidence suggests that smallholder agriculture in Southern Africa tends to involve a much smaller number of secondary crops than in inland West Africa. In the Sahel, 20 to 25 crops per small farm, often intercropped in several different combinations, is the norm rather than the exception, whereas in the highlands of Eastern and Southern Africa, a dozen crops might be grown with a much lower incidence of intercropping (Ruthenberg, 1976). Farm income as a whole tends to account for a significantly higher share of total farm household income in Southern Africa than in West Africa, with the exception of the countries within the old Southern African Customs Union, which are heavily influenced by migration (Delgado, 1997).

In semi-arid and savanna West Africa, the relationship between income distribution and diversification out of agriculture appears to be monotonically increasing (Reardon *et al.*, 1994). At very low income levels, people are almost entirely occupied with subsistence agriculture. As commercialization increases, people diversify into non-farm income sources that provide some liquidity outside the harvest period and insurance against risky agricultural incomes. This appears to be the joint result of stagnant agriculture, risky returns in agriculture, urban bias that boosted returns to capital in non-agricultural pursuits such as commerce, and the fact that people principally involved in non-farm activities in rural areas of the Sahel often still reside on farms, not in market towns.

Diversification into non-farm activities in Africa occurs through different institutional forms from those in Asia. In Africa, the same households tend to be involved in both farm and non-farm activities; in South Asia, households tend to specialize, even though different households in the same village may have different economic functions (ibid.). In the savanna and Sahelian parts of West Africa, the term 'household' itself is misleading. In these zones, non-nuclear household compounds of more than 100 people can be observed, although there is considerable variation among households in the number of nuclear units and people.

The high degree of diversification of smallholder farmers in Africa, both within agriculture and outside it, appears to be closely related to risk management strategies devised to cope with risky agricultural returns (Reardon *et al.*, 1988; Eicher and Baker, 1992; von Braun, 1989). Furthermore, for those involved in single-season agriculture susceptible to climatic risk, diversification into non-farm activities may be the most appropriate solution. Yet it seems likely that such high diversification out of agriculture occurs at the cost of agricultural intensification strategies, which generally require concentration of farm investment and labour resources in farm production.

Farm diversification as a target seeks to promote a diversity of commercially marketed commodities, which is different both from a diversity of production activities and from actual experience in many African countries, where major cash-earning activities on the farm may be limited to one or two crops out of the many grown. The solution often addressed for this is to promote farm-level diversification in 'non-traditional exports', or at least into farm tradables that are different from the agricultural commodity exports. Thus 'farm diversification' as an objective in African smallholder agriculture should refer primarily to the part of farm household output undertaken specifically for cash generation, which may be significantly less than half the value of total output (Eicher and Baker, 1992).[6]

Experience with diversification into non-traditional commodities at the small farm level in East Africa through contract farming and coops

The impetus for farm diversification in these cases stems from the need to adjust to fundamental changes in price relationships: 60 per cent relative price declines for traditional export crops during the 1980s, and phasing out of many traditional agricultural subsidies at the farm level during the Structural Adjustment era, offset by substantial devaluation of real exchange rates (Hussain, 1994; Delgado, 1995).

It is often thought that the sum of these forces on Africa's small, relatively open economies has tended to increase the relative incentive for smallholders to engage in production of non-traditional agricultural exports, such as fruits, vegetables and spices. However, the anecdotal evidence suggests that the main production response of moving into non-traditional agricultural exportables, in those countries that have in fact gone forward with macroeconomic adjustment measures, probably concerns less than 15 per cent of small farmers (Little and Watts, 1994; Jaffee and Morton, 1995).

This raises the question of why other farmers have been slow to adjust their production patterns and what can be done about it. Part of the explanation is undoubtedly that proximity to infrastructure or physical access to other non-price incentives is crucial for participation, and this is not possible for everyone in the early stages of agricultural transformation (Lele *et al.*, 1989). However, it is hard to rule out the intriguing hypothesis that wealthier segments of the rural population in terms of control of factors of production and access are the first respondents to new opportunities. The issues then are how soon the rest of the population will follow, and what can speed the process up.

Clearly rural production and marketing institutions are of key importance in this environment (ibid.; Lele and Christiansen, 1989). Compare what is required for farmers to diversify into non-traditional tradable activities to what is available in economies at early stages of agricultural transformation. The eight requirements are (1) transfer, adaptation and extension of technology for producing the item cost-effectively; (2) investment at farm level, often with some lag before payback; (3) availability of specialized inputs; (4) heavy investment at the processing level, often in fairly activity-specific facilities; (5) availability of infrastructure (cold storage, roads, airports and so on) (6) a conducive regulatory environment for commercial risk taking; (7) thorough knowledge of OECD export markets; and (8) having an established reputation (trust) in export markets.

These items by and large are not much in evidence in most African countries. Furthermore, they all tend to be somewhat activity-specific. Even in the case of roads where transport infrastructure is lacking, policy makers have to decide whether to build the road to a cotton area or to a tea area, for example, and the two are not good substitutes. Commodity specialization is required to accumulate the knowledge necessary for success in marketing many of these items, raising the transactions costs for diversifying into any one of them.

The institutions that have been brought to bear in East Asia for reducing these transactions costs are vertical integration of production and marketing, contract farming and various forms of producer cooperatives or village self-help groups. Vertical integration through plantation agriculture tends to work well for capital-intensive items where rural population density is low (easy access to land) and quality is fairly uniform, as with palm oil in West Africa. However, it is not a tool to diversify smallholder agriculture. Contract farming tends to offer a more attractive option for processors – and a viable means of facilitating adjustment by smallholders to new structural incentives – where quality of the item in question is intrinsically heterogeneous and highly critical to success, where land is scarce and labour intensity is high, as with horticulture in Kenya and cotton in the Sahel (Minot, 1986; Watts *et al.*, 1988; Lele *et al.*, 1989; Jaffee, 1992; Little and Watts, 1994).

For smallholder producers, contract farming reduces risks and, most importantly, provides substantial access to specialized information and assets. For processing companies, it reduces costs and risks of labour supervision, matches incentives to quality control objectives and provides access to land, and may provide some political cover against arbitrary government actions. The key point for present purposes is that contract farming under the above structural conditions tends to be successful where it succeeds in reducing farm-level transactions costs for adjustment to viable commercial opportunities at an aggregate level. It does this by focusing in an integrated fashion on commodity-specific sub-sectors.

Producer cooperatives under some conditions might provide an alternative to vertical integration of processors or contract farming. An example would be the relatively recent explosion of private small-scale smallholder dairy cooperatives in Kenya and Uganda (Jaffee and Morton, 1995; Staal *et al.*, 1997). Since 1990, devaluation of real exchange rates and an end to dumping of milk powder by the developed countries has radically increased the potential profitability of domestic dairy farming in Africa (Staal *et al.*, 1997). The issue is whether smallholders in zones that can support cattle will diversify their market-oriented activity out of formerly subsidized items (such as maize in Zambia or peanuts in Senegal) into the new dairy opportunity or not.

Requiring specialized assets (semi-exotic breeds of dairy cows), the end product being highly perishable, and having a high share of retail value added coming from processing, dairy production for market is full of transactions cost barriers for smallholders. Vertically integrated companies might be an alternative near major consumption centres. While providing domestic milk in the short run, such schemes throw away one of the few viable opportunities for integrating smallholders into economic growth, made possible by rapid urbanization and macroeconomic reform.

Furthermore, East African experience suggests that vertically-integrated milk farmers/processors typically run afoul of the high labour intensity of dairy farming and the problem of feed costs; smallholders tend to do better on both through more intensive use of family resources at a lower reservation wage. However, allowing smallholders to benefit from the new commercial opportunity made available by economic reforms at home and abroad will require promotion of institutions of collective action. To date, small-scale producer coops have played this role in Kenya and Uganda, often with a lot of top-down involvement by NGOs, government and foreign aid agencies. Over time, agricultural cooperatives in Africa will need a certain amount of state intervention to provide support for complex technological, financial and managerial functions. Yet they cannot work unless they are run with substantial participatory involvement of local people and good local government (Lele and Christiansen, 1989).

SUMMARY AND CONCLUSIONS

Whether farm diversification should be considered a distinct objective – rather than an associated outcome – of good economic policy depends primarily on the economic structure of the economy in question. In places such as the Southeast Asian rice areas, where agricultural transformation has largely occurred, markets for goods and factors generally work well, and the role of agriculture in supporting overall growth and equity is waning, farm diversification is an important issue. The analytical issues for economists, however, are more in the area of market liberalization or property rights than in promoting diversification *per se*.

In such areas, there is a concern to see farmers diversify into items less likely to be subject to abrupt price falls in the future than are foodgrains, given the low price and income elasticities of demand for the latter. The main concern for diversification policies, however, is probably equity, not growth, and governments probably do not need to be – indeed should not be – involved in commodity-specific institutional innovation or other direct interventions on the marketing or pricing side.

Farm diversification acquires a more strategic aspect as an economic issue in areas where agriculture is still a large share of the economy, farming is only partially commercialized, some major agricultural markets for goods or factors do not work well for structural reasons and the level of technical progress is low. It is strategic because overall economic development depends on finding a viable way to commercialize agriculture, and a coordinated policy approach to sub-sector development will probably be necessary. In many countries of sub-Saharan Africa, farm household income is already highly diversified, although the number and quantity of agricultural items produced explicitly for sale from any one farm tend to be low.

While smallholder-led agricultural growth is critical for such economies, intensification paths for such farms are less clear than in the historical case of the Asian 'green revolution' in rice. Increasing farm value-added through high-yield cereals cultivation will not be extended as easily as it was in Asia, because of the much greater diversity of the agricultural resource base. Promotion of a variety of high-value agricultural tradables will be necessary to provide viable incomes in rural areas and to provide the rural income base for non-agricultural spending.

These high-value products tend to be subject to very high transactions costs for market entry by smallholder producers. These high transactions costs vary across rural households, as they are based on differential access to assets and information. To some extent this is true outside Africa as well, except that the institutional base for reducing these transactions costs is especially weak in economies at early stages of agricultural transformation. In this context, the poor and the less well informed in rural areas in Africa run a higher risk of being left behind in the adjustment of farming to a radically new set of relative incentives in the post-Structural Adjustment period. For these reasons, farm diversification in the sense of identifying promising candidates among tradable agricultural outputs seems a necessity for both growth and equity, through agricultural research, infrastructure investment and through appropriate institutional development.

Contract farming is an institution that has worked well in some African situations, although the total number of farmers involved to date is still low compared to the number who are not participating. Producer cooperatives have also had some success in some sectors, such as dairy farming. However, there have also been many failures in government attempts to pick winners and become involved in their marketing in Africa. It is clear that monopolistic approaches to institutions of collective action are not desirable. Actions taken need to encourage the use of markets, not replace them. On the other hand, failing to consider the probable need for a commodity-specific focus in promoting smallholder agriculture under these conditions is not helpful either.

Farmers and traders have usually been more successful than economists or governments at identifying lucrative opportunities, and Africa is no exception in this regard. However, the role of government in acquiring and sharing information and making assets available to small farmers is still very large in Africa. Identifying the appropriate rural institutions to mobilize participation and to incorporate the asset- and information-poor in post-Structural Adjustment economic growth is clearly a major priority for relevant policy research in Africa today. The right institutional forms to promote diversification of marketed output in Africa undoubtedly will involve a mix of public and private, and will need to associate the skills of better-off farmers with problem solving for the smaller farmers. Such research could begin by looking at existing forms of contract farming and cooperatives to access their economic viability, overall impact and extendability to large numbers of people. Research should attempt to quantify the barriers to participation in high-value markets by the poor, and their determinants. It should also develop quantified scenarios for different investment options to move forward and the overall impact of these investments on regional economies. The latter would take into account spinoff effects of commercialization through high-value commodities on local regions where underemployed resources can be brought into economic activity through the spending of increased farm incomes.

The second set of policy research priorities concerns the links between the incentives driving farm diversification, on the one hand, and the incentives for sustainable intensification of farming system, on the other. To the extent that intensification will probably require moving farming systems in Africa towards less diversity in total output (even if there is more diversity in commercial output), the present strong risk management incentives for diversification are likely to prevent such intensification, at least until market development can make food supplies on the market more reliable.

A third set of economic research priorities concerns ways and means of better using growth in dynamic areas – say rice-driven growth in the Mekong delta – to stimulate growth in remote areas without a comparative advantage in rice production, except perhaps for local consumption (say the central high-lands of Vietnam). Experience shows that farm diversification can be a critical component of strategies to promote national economic integration, and re-search is needed to identify the degree to which coordinated government intervention is necessary on the non-price front (directed research, roads, ex-tension, credit and so on) to allow the non-'green revolution' areas to profit from growth elsewhere.

Finally, environmental concerns have become especially important in the motivation of governments to promote diversification in Asian rice zones away from repeated sole cropping of rice. While such concerns are a cost factor pushing for farm diversification, the economic externality concerns how to share social costs with private producers. This points to the urgent need for policy research on water pricing. While resolution of these issues is of un-doubted relevance to farm diversification as an outcome, we have chosen not to attempt to deal with it as an objective, as this is best done within the general set of issues on property rights and the environment.

NOTES

[1]The definitive literature review, *Agriculture in Economic Development: 1940s to 1990s*, Vol. 4 in the massive *Survey of Agricultural Economics Literature* (Martin, 1992), contains over 1037 pages. Yet none of its 440 sub-titles and only a very small handful of the nearly 5000 titles of references surveyed mention 'diversification', much less 'farm diversification'.

[2]A non-exhaustive list of relevant transactions costs affecting the exchange of agricultural and livestock products in developing countries is (1) spoilage, (2) quality differences depending on processing, (3) lumpiness of initial investments, (4) lags in production, (5) seasonal variability, (6) search costs, (7) screening trade partners, (8) bargaining, (9) monitoring and (10) contract enforcement (Hoff *et al.*, 1993; Jaffee and Morton, 1995). In addition, locational issues such as (11) transport, (12) handling and (13) packaging, and temporal costs such as (14) storage, should be included.

[3]These are rates of absolute increase. Africa's very high population growth rate makes per capita growth seem paltry or negative.

[4]Vietnam and Thailand may be exceptions, but it is hard to see Bangladesh, Indonesia and China as major rice exporters in the future.

[5]For convenience, 'Africa' will be used as shorthand for the part of the continent south of the Sahara and north of the Limpopo River.

[6]This is different from the selling of occasional surpluses of grains grown primarily for household use.

REFERENCES

Adams, R. and He, J. (1995), *Sources of Income Inequality and Poverty in Rural Pakistan*, Research Report 102, Washington, DC: International Food Policy Research Institute.
Akerlof, G. (1970), 'The Market for Lemons: Qualitative Uncertainty and the Market Mecha-nism', *Quarterly Journal of Economics*, 84, 488–500.
Alderman, H. and Garcia, M. (1993), *Poverty, Household Food Security and Nutrition in Rural Pakistan*, Research Report 96, Washington, DC: International Food Policy Research Institute.
Alexandratos, N. (1995), *World Agriculture towards 2010: An FAO Study*, New York: John Wiley and Sons and the Food and Agriculture Organization.
Bautista, R. (1992), 'Rural Diversification in the Philippines: Effects of Agricultural Growth and

the Macroeconomic Environment', *Southeast Asian Journal of Agricultural Economics*, **1**, 25–44.

Bell, C. and Hazell, P. (1980), 'Measuring the Indirect Effects of an Agricultural Investment Project on its Surrounding Region', *American Journal of Agricultural Economics*, **62**, 75–86.

Binswanger, H.P. and Rosenzweig, M.R. (1986), 'Behavioral and Material Determinants of Production Relations in Agriculture', *Journal of Development Studies*, **22**, 503–39.

Bouis, H. (1991), 'The Relationship between Nutrition and Income Sources for the Rural Poor in a Southern Philippine Province', in J. von Braun and R. Pandya-Lorch (eds), *Income Sources of Malnourished People in Rural Areas: Microlevel Information and Policy Implications*, Working Papers on Commercialization of Agriculture and Nutrition No. 5, Washington, DC: International Food Policy Research Institute.

Coase, R. (1960), 'The Problem of Social Cost', *Journal of Law and Economics*, **1**, 1–44.

David, C. and Otsuka, K. (1994), *Modern Rice Technology and Income Distribution in Asia*, London: Lynne Rienner Publishers and Manila: International Rice Research Institute.

Delgado, C. (1995), 'Agricultural Diversification and Export Promotion in Sub-Saharan Africa', in M. Rosegrant and P. Pingali (eds), *Special Issue: Agricultural Commercialization and Diversification, Food Policy*, **20**, 225–44.

Delgado, C. (1997), 'The Role of Smallholder Income Generation from Agriculture in Sub-Saharan Africa', Final Report to the Land and Agricultural Policy Centre, Johannesburg, South Africa, Track I of the IFPRI/LAPC Project on Promoting Employment Growth in Smallholder Farming Through Agricultural Diversification, mimeo.

Eicher, C.K. and Baker, D.C. (1992), 'Research on Agricultural Development in Sub-Saharan Africa: A Critical Survey', in L. Martin (ed.), *Agriculture in Economic Development: 1940s to 1990s. Survey of Agricultural Economics Literature*, Vol. 4, Minneapolis: University of Minnesota Press.

Food and Agricultural Organization of the United Nations (FAO) (1996), *Production Yearbook 1995*, Rome: FAO.

Hare, D. (1994), 'Rural Nonagricultural Activities and their Impact on the Distribution of Income: Evidence from Farm Households in Southern China', *China Economic Review*, **4**, 59–82.

Hayami, Y. (1991), 'Conditions of Agricultural Diversification: A Historical perspective', in *Agricultural Diversification: Report of a Study Meeting* (17–27 October 1989), Tokyo: Asian Productivity Organization.

Hayami, Y. and Kawagoe, T. (1993), *The Agrarian Origins of Commerce and Industry: A Study of Peasant Marketing in Indonesia*, London: Macmillan.

Hayami, Y. and Otsuka, K. (1994), 'Beyond the Green Revolution: Agricultural Development Strategy into the New Century', in J. Anderson (ed.), *Agricultural Technology: Policy Issues for the International Community*, Wallingford, UK: CAB International with the World Bank.

Hayami, Y. and Ruttan, V. (1985), *Agricultural Development: An International Perspective*, Baltimore: Johns Hopkins University Press.

Hoff, K., Braverman, A. and Stiglitz, J. (eds) (1993), *The Economics of Rural Organizations: Theory, Practice and Policy*, Oxford: Oxford University Press for the World Bank.

Hossain, M. (1988), *Nature and Impact of the Green Revolution in Bangladesh*, Research Report 67, Washington, DC: International Food Policy Research Institute.

Hussain, I. (1994), *The Evolving Role of the World Bank: The Challenges of Africa*, Fiftieth Anniversary Paper Series, Washington, DC: World Bank.

Jaffee, S. (1992), 'Enhancing Agricultural Growth through Diversification in Sub-Saharan Africa', in S. Barghouti, L. Garbus and D. Umali (eds), *Trends in Agricultural Diversification: Regional Perspectives*, World Bank Technical Paper Number 180, Washington, DC: World Bank.

Jaffee, S. and Morton, J. (eds) (1995), *Marketing Africa's High-Value Foods: Comparative Experiences of an Emergent Private Sector*, Dubuque, Iowa: Kendall/Hunt Publishing Company.

Janvry, A. de, Fafchamps, M. and Sadoulet, E. (1991), 'Peasant Household Behaviour: Some paradoxes explained', *The Economic Journal*, **101**, 1400–17.

Lele, U. and Christiansen, R. (1989), *Markets, Marketing Boards and Cooperatives in Africa: Issues in Adjustment Policy*, Managing Agricultural Development in Africa Project, Discussion Paper No. 11, Washington, DC: World Bank.

142   *Christopher L. Delgado and Ammar Siamwalla*

Lele, U., Van de Walle, N. and Gbetibouo, M. (1989), *Cotton in Africa: An Analysis of Differences in Performance*, Managing Agricultural Development in Africa Project, Discussion Paper No. 7, Washington, DC: World Bank.

Little, P. and Watts, M. (1994), *Living under Contract: Contract Farming and Agrarian Transformation in Sub-Saharan Africa*, Madison: University of Wisconsin Press.

Lopez, R. (1984), 'Estimating Labour Supply and Production Decisions of Self-employed Farm Producers', *European Economic Review*, **24**, 61–82.

Martin, L. (ed.) (1992), Agriculture in Economic Development: 1940s to 1990s. *Survey of Agricultural Economics Literature*, Vol. 4, Minneapolis: University of Minnesota Press.

Minot, N. (1986), *Contract Farming and its Effect on Small Farmers in Less Developed Countries*, International Development Papers, Working Paper 31, East Lansing: Michigan State University.

Petit, M. and Barghouti, S. (1992), 'Diversification: Challenges and Opportunities', in S. Barghouti, L. Garbus and D. Umali (eds), *Trends in Agricultural Diversification: Regional Perspectives*, Technical Paper Number 180, Washington, DC: World Bank.

Pingali, P. and Rosegrant, M. (1995), 'Agricultural Commercialization and Diversification: Processes and Policies', in M. Rosegrant and P. Pingali (eds), *Special Issue: Agricultural Commercialization and Diversification, Food Policy*, **20**, 171–86.

Reardon, T., Matlon, P. and Delgado, C. (1988), 'Coping with Household-Level Food Insecurity in the Drought-Affected Areas of Burkina Faso', *World Development*, **16**, 1065–74.

Reardon, T., Fall, A.A., Kelly, V., Delgado, C., Matlon, P., Hopkins, J. and Badiane, O. (1994), 'Is Income Diversification Agriculture-led in the West African Semi-Arid Tropics? The Nature, Causes, Effects, Distribution and Production of Off-Farm Activities', in A. Atsain, S. Wangwe and A.G. Drabek (eds), *Economic Policy Experience in Africa: What Have We Learned?*, Nairobi: African Economic Research Consortium.

Rosegrant, M., Schleyer, R. and Yadav, S. (1995), 'Water Policy for Efficient Agricultural Diversification: Market-based approaches', in M. Rosegrant and P. Pingali (eds), *Special Issue: Agricultural Commercialization and Diversification, Food Policy*, **20**, 203–24.

Ruthenberg, H. (1976), *Farming Systems in the Tropics*, 2nd edn, Oxford: Clarendon Press.

Schiff, M. and Valdés, A. (1992), *A Synthesis of the Economics in Developing Countries*, Vol. 4 of *The Political Economy of Agricultural Pricing Policy*, ed. A. Kruger, Baltimore: Johns Hopkins University Press for the World Bank.

Siamwalla, A., Patamasiriwat, D. and Setboonsarng, S. (1992), 'Public Policies toward Agricultural Diversification in Thailand', in S. Barghouti, L. Garbus and D. Umali (eds), *Trends in Agricultural Diversification: Regional Perspectives*, Technical Paper Number 180, Washington, DC: World Bank.

Staal, S., Delgado, C. and Nicholson, C. (1997), 'Smallholder Dairying under Transaction Costs in East Africa', *World Development*, **25**, May, 779–94.

Taylor, D. (1994), 'Agricultural Diversification: An Overview of Challenges in ASEAN in the 1990s', *ASEAN Economic Bulletin*, March, 264–79.

Timmer, C.P. (1988), 'Crop Diversification in Rice-Based Agricultural Economies: Conceptual and Policy Issues', in R.A. Goldberg (ed.), *Research in Domestic and International Agribusiness Management: A Research Annual*, Greenwich, Connecticut: JAI Press.

Vietnam (1994), *Vietnam Living Standards Survey 1992–1993*, Hanoi: State Planning Committee and General Statistical Office.

von Braun, J. (1989), *The Importance of Non-Agricultural Income Sources for the Rural Poor in Africa and Implications for Food and Nutrition Policy*, PEW/Cornell Lecture Series on Food and Nutrition Policy, Ithaca: Cornell Food and Nutrition Policy Program.

von Braun, J. and Kennedy, E. (eds) (1994), *Agricultural Commercialization, Economic Development and Nutrition*, Baltimore: Johns Hopkins University Press for the International Food Policy Research Institute.

von Braun, J. and Pandya-Lorch, R. (eds) (1991), *Income Sources of Malnourished People in Rural Areas: Microlevel Information and Policy Implications*, Working Papers on Commercialization of Agriculture and Nutrition No. 5, Washington, DC: International Food Policy Research Institute.

Watts, M., Little, P., Mock, C., Billings, M. and Jaffee, S. (1988), *Contract Farming in Africa*, Vol. 1, *Comparative Analysis*; Vol. 2, *Case Studies*, Binghamton, NY: Institute for Development Anthropology.

World Bank (1990), *Agricultural Diversification Policies and Issues from East Asian Experience*, Agriculture and Rural Development Department, Policy and Research Series Occasional Paper, Washington, DC: World Bank.

DAVID ZILBERMAN, CHERISA YARKIN AND AMIR HEIMAN*

Agricultural Biotechnology: Economic and International Implications

INTRODUCTION

Over the last 150 years, agriculture has been subject to several waves of innovation which have significantly altered its institutional structures, its products and the way it is practised. Mechanical, biological and chemical innovations have, in turn, reduced labour requirements, increased yields and reduced the impact of agricultural pests. More recently, computer and remote sensing technologies have improved input precision. Agricultural biotechnology is now emerging as a wellspring of innovations that will reshape agriculture as profoundly as any previous innovation paradigm.[1] This new technology has unique features which economists need to understand in order to formulate appropriate policy advice.

This paper has two main purposes. First, we provide an overview of agricultural biotechnology. There are lessons from medical biotechnology which can be applied to agriculture. In addition, there are new institutions, including technology transfer offices and arrangements for intellectual property rights, which will be introduced and discussed. The second purpose is to introduce some basic analytical considerations and methodological issues which will be important in the study of biotechnology. In particular, these methodologies will relate to the issues in industrial organization associated with the process of product research, development and introduction; issues associated with adoption of biotechnology; and issues associated with pricing. Thus far, commercial biotechnology has been concentrated in the United States, but this technology has important global implications. This paper will examine and project what the American experience implies for the rest of the world and show how biotechnology and its evolution fit within the context of the relationship between developed and developing nations.

LESSONS OF MEDICAL BIOTECHNOLOGY

While agricultural biotechnology is relatively underdeveloped, medical biotechnology has become a successful business in which United States companies generate revenues of over $4 billion annually. The evolution and structure of

*University of California, Berkeley, USA (Zilberman and Yarkin) and Hebrew University of Jerusalem, Rehovot, Israel (Heiman).

medical biotechnology have some lessons for agricultural biotechnology, although the two also have some distinguishing features.

Similarities

Importance of university research, technology transfer and start-up companies
The formal process of technology transfer from universities to private companies has been crucial for the evolution of medical biotechnology. Research conducted at the University of California (UC) at San Francisco and Stanford provided the discoveries that have formed the foundation of commercial biotechnology, and university research discoveries continue to be an important source of medical biotechnology innovations. Universities' offices of technology transfer have registered patents to protect a number of these innovations and sold the right to private companies to develop and utilize them. In the United States, expansion in the number and size of university offices of technology transfer has been highly correlated with the evolution of medical biotechnology, and biotechnology licences provide the majority of licensing revenues received by the universities (Parker *et al.*, 1998).

Formal technology transfer provides incentives to researchers to invest resources in projects likely to lead to biotechnology innovations, since patent royalties are shared between the university, the inventor(s) and, sometimes, the department. Patent royalties may be substantial when linked to successful products and have been crucial for support of certain lines of research, although, even at the most successful universities, these revenues represent less than 5 per cent of the annual research budget.

Licensing arrangements vary. Exclusive licences are appropriate for discoveries which require significant investment in development before they enter the market-place, or which have narrow applications, since companies need the monopoly profit that exclusivity provides during the life of a patent to ensure that their commercialization costs will be recouped. For fundamental innovations that are essential for many applications, and which do not require much development effort in themselves, such as the Cohen-Boyer procedure of genetic manipulation, non-exclusive licences with low fees are necessary to facilitate broad diffusion.

Often, established companies are not interested in purchasing the rights to a discovery, but the innovations are developed through start-up companies established by the inventors and backed by venture capitalists. Two of the leading biotechnology companies in the United States (Genentech and Chiron) were established in this way. Once the companies became successful, major pharmaceutical firms bought majority ownership stakes.

Some of these patterns can be seen in agricultural biotechnology. University research discoveries have been crucial in the evolution of the technologies, and start-up companies have emerged through collaboration between researchers and venture capitalists. Large seed and agrochemical companies have bought control of some of these firms (for example, Monsanto recently acquired Calgene, a leading agriculture company). This pattern is likely to continue. Start-up companies will develop new discoveries, but marketing and production of most final products will be undertaken by the large agrochemical, seed and food-processing companies.

The importance of intellectual property rights   Intellectual property rights (IPR) have been of exceptional importance in the development of commercial biotechnology. Firms pay fees for use of patented processes (for example, manipulation of genetic material) and patented genetic knowledge (genes linked to specific traits). The incentive for violating IPR agreements is likely to increase significantly as the price of knowledge increases, so enforcement considerations set an upper bound on intellectual property fees. The relatively small numbers of entities that engage in medical biotechnology activities and their geographic concentration have probably facilitated enforcement of IPR arrangements to date. As biotechnology diffuses more widely, international policies regarding IPR will become more important.

The implications for pricing of IPR in developing countries require further study. Political pressure to respect IPR, unless accompanied by lower prices for the use of biotechnological knowledge in developing countries (at least for a transition period), is unlikely to result in broad adherence to these laws. Vigorous pursuit of IPR protection may inhibit the expansion of free trade, with adverse consequences for global welfare.

The geographic profile of production   Commercial biotechnology is heavily dependent on human capital formation, requiring a scientific and managerial workforce that is highly skilled and knowledgeable. The biotechnology industry has become concentrated in a small number of regions that are anchored by the high-quality research institutions which are the main sources of these skills and knowledge. The San Francisco Bay area is a prime example: both Genentech and Chiron are located in this region, benefiting from proximity to Stanford, UC San Francisco and UC Berkeley. Similarly, the area around UC Davis has become a hub for biotechnology firms, as have other regions anchored by leading agricultural research institutions. Other regions wishing to establish the capacity to discover, develop and produce biotechnology products will need to establish a critical mass of research and commercialization infrastructure and, in most cases, public (national and international) support of research and development activities will be needed.

Differences

Revenue-generating potential of products   Many medical biotechnology products have high revenue-generating potential because affluent populations have a substantial willingness to pay for medical advances. In contrast, demand for most agricultural products has a low income elasticity and, while expenditures on medical care have increased faster than the overall rate of inflation, the income share of food expenditures has declined over the last 50 years.

Differences in knowledge and complexity   Medical biotechnology has primarily focused on the human species, which has historically received most of the attention and research funds expended on biological research. Contrast this with agricultural application, which requires the knowledge of a vast variety of organisms and ecosystems but has enjoyed neither the funding levels nor the academic interest that have characterized medical research. While the agricultural biotechnology products currently on the market have been based on single gene changes, the development of new varieties which contain a complete bundle of desired characteristics may require complex manipulations.

Environmental regulation   Society is more tolerant of taking risks in search of cures for human diseases than in developing new agricultural products. In part this difference arises because disease is more of a threat than famine in most of the world. In addition, agricultural innovations are deployed in fields, not hospitals, so the monitoring of them is more complex than for their medical counterparts.

In the United States, public perceptions of relative risks, and historical differences in the mandate and purview of regulatory bodies governing the two areas of biotechnology, have resulted in a divergence in the costs and outcomes of regulation. Pharmaceutical products developed using biotechnology are regulated by a single agency, the Food and Drug Administration (FDA), and have been subject to virtually the same safety and efficacy requirements as conventionally derived drugs. In contrast, three agencies have purview over various facets of agbiotech research, development and product introduction (FDA, the Environmental Protection Agency and the United States Department of Agriculture). The regulations governing these activities have been much more rigorous than for equivalent products developed using non-molecular techniques. Unduly stringent regulation has reduced investor interest and, while agricultural and medical biotechnology investments were roughly equivalent in the first decade following the emergence of these technologies, they diverged significantly as regulatory hurdles became more daunting in agriculture (Huttner *et al.*, 1995).

Need for geographic adaptation   Most medical biotechnology products do not need to be adjusted for differences in the geographical location of the consumer. In agriculture, however, products have to be incorporated into farm production systems and so must be modified according to varying ecological conditions. This can involve high adaptation costs and products may not enjoy the large markets of some medical biotechnology items.

The differences between agricultural and medical biotechnology suggest that some of the forces that helped to establish medical biotechnology would not work as effectively in favour of agriculture. One would not expect as much private-sector investment; therefore innovation is likely to depend more on the continuing support for public research of relevant disciplines. Marketing, also, may not be as easy as for medical biotechnology products, and in many cases experiment station and extension efforts will be needed in order to facilitate adoption of biotechnology products.

STRUCTURE OF AGRICULTURAL BIOTECHNOLOGY

A few stylized facts will facilitate a conceptual analysis of agricultural bio-technology. In simplified form, its products can be thought of as the result of a linear five-stage process: (1) research, (2) development, (3) testing and regis-tration, (4) production, and (5) marketing. These stages result in three major outputs. Research produces new knowledge about genetic manipulation tech-niques or the properties of a genetic sequence. By obtaining a patent, intellectual property rights are established, and users must acquire the rights to use the discovery. Development leads to a product or process that has clear commer-cial potential, which is then retained in-house or licensed to a third party for testing and regulatory approval before moving finally into commercialization.

The interaction among five economic agents determines the outcomes of biotechnology discoveries. First is the university which conducts research that leads to important discoveries. Second are small biotechnology firms made up of researchers and supported by venture capitalists, which tend to concentrate on developing biotechnology products, often combining efforts and resource through alliances with pharmaceuticals, other biotech firms and academic re-searchers. The third group are large companies which, in addition to internal R&D capabilities and alliances with biotechnology firms, have strong market-ing networks in place and enough financial resources to bear the costs of product registration. The fourth element is government, which supports re-search at the universities, and regulates biotechnology-related activities. Finally, there are the buyers who, in the case of pharmaceuticals, are physicians and, for agriculture, are farmers.

Patterns of the division of responsibilities between entities for the introduc-tion and production of biotechnology products are presented in Table 1. As Parker and Zilberman (1993) argue, university research tends to produce fun-damental new knowledge which results in dramatically different ways of conducting research and entirely new products. University research receives support from three sources: government funding, technology transfer revenues

TABLE 1   *Division of responsibility for various stages of product development*

Patterns	Discovery	Development	Registration	Production	Marketing
1	U	B	B	B	B
2	U	B	B	M	M
3	U	B	M	M	M
4	U	M	M	M	M
5	B	B	M	M	M
6	M	M	M	M	M

Notes: M = major corporations with established market presence in pharmaceuti-cals, chemicals, seeds or food processing; B = biotechnology firm; U = university.

and grants or support for collaborative research activities from industry. Currently, government funding dominates other sources and supports the basic research which results in breakthrough discoveries. Translation of these discoveries to the market place is shown on rows 1–3, wherein university discoveries are licensed to biotechnology companies for development, with subsequent activities handled either by the firm or by multinationals.

The fourth pattern, in which university research discoveries are licensed by major corporations which then conduct the development, registration, production and marketing, is also common. Sometimes biotechnology companies make discoveries and then sell the developed product to multinationals (row 5). Pattern 6 is typical of the chemical industry, wherein large companies are involved in all stages, from research to production. As products become more complex, these patterns will become more complicated, but the framework in Table 1 is useful for thinking about the effects of alternative public policies.

Reduction of government support for academic research will stifle patterns 1 to 3, causing a significant reduction in the number and rate of technological advances. The rate at which discoveries reach the market-place is also affected by the conditions facing venture capitalists who finance start-up companies which develop the most novel innovations. Major corporations have often been unwilling to undertake development of path-breaking academic discoveries so, without the risk-taking behaviour of the start-up companies, these innovations might not have been developed. Private profit-maximization considerations may deter large firms from pursuing a socially desirable rate of technological change. Even if production and marketing are handled by a small number of large companies, university research and development funded by venture capitalists keep the industry competitive, facilitating a higher rate of technological change.

The government can also affect the structure of the biotechnology industry through registration requirements. Some of the most important biotechnology products have emerged through patterns 1 and 2 in Table 1, in which university discoveries are developed and registered by biotechnology companies. Strict registration requirements impose costs on registrants, reducing the expected profitability of a given product. Extra costs impede start-up companies' ability to proceed independently and reduce the incentive for venture capitalists to invest in these firms. In this way, registration requirements can serve as barriers to entry, giving relative advantage to large corporations that have the institutional infrastructure and financial wherewithal to meet intensive registration requirements, and which can then take advantage of their market power. Some have suggested that this phenomenon is occurring in agricultural biotechnology, with major corporations shaping the regulatory environment in a manner that disadvantages start-up businesses.

MODELLING BIOTECHNOLOGY

Agricultural biotechnology is an extension of traditional breeding techniques that increases precision (allowing for selection of individual traits) and versatility (permitting genes to be obtained from virtually any organism). There are several distinct types of products, each with different technical and economic implications, four of which are mentioned below.

Supply-enhancing products

Supply-enhancing biotechnology will generally improve consumer welfare, but may disproportionately benefit certain groups of producers. The beneficiaries will be determined by the characteristics of the technology and the distribution of producers across regions and sub-groups. These technologies can be conceptualized as improvements in the technological relationship linking inputs to outputs. Suppose a firm faces a choice among m varieties. The optimal variety choice for a given location is a two-stage process involving discrete and continuous choices. First, the optimal input levels for each variety are determined at a level where the value of marginal product of each variable input is equal to its price. Then the profit per acre under each variety is calculated at optimal input levels, and the optimal variety is the one with the highest non-negative profits per acre. Suppose per acre profits can be represented by the equation:

$$\max_{i,x} pf(x) - \sum_{j=1}^{m} w_j x_j - V_i$$

where p denotes output price, $f(x)$ is the production function, x is a vector of variable inputs, w_j denotes price of input j, and v_i denotes price per acre of payment for access to genetic inputs i. Then the optimal input level for technology i is determined at a level x_i^* where $pf'(x_i^*,i) = W$. Profit per acre of technology i,

$$\pi_i = pf(x_i^*,i) - Wx_i^* - v_i,$$

is calculated and the optimal variety i^* is the one with the highest non-negative profits per acre.

Economic conditions and policies will determine the likelihood of adoption of new varieties. In cases of two varieties, when $i = 1$ is the traditional and $i = 2$ is the biotechnological variety, it is likely that variety 2 increases yield and is input-saving for most users. It will be relatively more attractive in situations with high input prices, but, if it is costlier than existing varieties, it will be adopted only if the increases in variable profits, from yield increases and reduced variable input costs, exceed the extra seed cost.[2] Thus variety 2 will be adopted if

$$\underset{\substack{\text{yield-increasing}\\\text{effect}}}{p(y_2^* - y_1^*)} + \underset{\substack{\text{input-saving}\\\text{effect}}}{w(x_2^* - x_1^*)} > \underset{\substack{\text{extra genetic}\\\text{material cost}}}{v_2 - v_1}$$

In the case of innovations which conserve a variable input, especially at locations of low quality, crop acreage may increase owing to entry of land previously fallow or in other crops. Differences in land quality will become less important, so that regional disparities in profitability may decline as the new technology is introduced. A related set of technologies would allow utilization of saline water or mitigate the effects of ecological conditions such as frost. These varieties may expand the range of locations where high-value crops can be grown, reducing the rents for locations with special amenities.

The likelihood of adoption will also depend on exogenous market conditions and on other policies affecting agriculture. Reduction of input subsidies or increased input taxes will enhance adoption of varieties that increase input use efficiency. Induced innovation models suggest these changes will also prompt development of varieties that can substitute for affected inputs. Note that the introduction of variable-input-saving technology may increase resource use if demand is relatively elastic or market prices rise because of increased demand resulting from, say, increased income. Consumers gain if demand is not infinitely elastic, and high-quality locations may lose and producers on marginal lands may gain.

In contrast to the foregoing, a new technology which increases output per acre proportionally across locations will especially benefit locations with higher land quality, so differences in returns between locations with high and low qualities will widen, and supply will increase mostly through adoption of the technology on lands with higher quality. Increased supply will led to lower output prices when final product demand is inelastic, and thus some land of lower quality may not be utilized as a result of the introduction of the innovation. The main effects may be gains to consumers.

The adoption of such technologies may be enhanced by government programmes such as price supports, although their diffusion may actually reduce welfare (at least in the short run). Movement to a less distorted agricultural sector will reduce the likelihood that such innovations will be introduced in situations where they do not enhance welfare. If a period of excessive supply ensues, however, there may be political pressure to reinstitute price supports and similar policies that are now being eliminated. Under situations of competitive markets and inelastic demands, these proportional productivity-enhancing biotechnologies may help to achieve environment goals; for example, bovine growth hormone may reduce the animal waste problem and save on water currently allocated to alfalfa and pasture.

Pest control products

This line consists of varieties which can tolerate, repel or kill pests, or withstand applications of herbicides and genetically engineered microorganisms. As Ollinger and Pope (1995) have shown, most of the experimentation has concentrated on the first two categories, and their commercial use in the last two or three years has been significant. The commercial success of this line of products is due to the relative simplicity of the genetic manipulation that they entail and the fact that they seem to meet a need cost-effectively.

The relationship between new pest-controlling biotechnology innovations and chemical pesticide regulation is complementary and, to a large extent, these innovations are induced by pesticide policies. Whenever chemicals are banned or restricted, an unmet need arises, creating a market opportunity for substitutes. Conversely, if regulators are aware that a new alternative is likely to become available, they may take a stricter approach to a problematic chemical pesticide.

The finite life of patents provides another reason for development of pest control biotechnology. As their pesticide patents expire, companies may invest in development of biotechnology-based controls for the pest problem addressed by that pesticide, because their marketing network provides them with an edge in introducing and promoting a substitute product. Some pesticide companies may not have the scientific infrastructure to produce biotechnology solutions. One way to acquire this capacity is to buy start-up companies possessing new products as well as research and development capacity. Another is to develop internal research capacity and to buy rights to university innovations to jump-start their knowledge base. The biotechnology giant, Monsanto, has taken both approaches.

Pest control biotechnology offers new market opportunities to seed companies that generally have a relative advantage in biological processes. In the past, seed companies did not play a major role in pest control that mostly emphasized chemical solutions. These companies have a significant marketing capacity in the field and are likely to take advantage of their biological research and productive capacity to develop new products in pest control biotechnology. Indeed, some of the major seed companies (Pioneer, for example) are expanding their capacity in pest control, and the boundaries between pest control companies and those in seed are gradually eroding.

At the same time, some companies are reducing their involvement and may leave the pesticide market altogether. Stricter regulation of chemical pesticides, as well as the lack of an internal infrastructure for biotechnology, make it unprofitable for them to continue their operations. Another group of companies that may be disadvantaged are manufacturers specializing in production of chemical pesticides after the patent life has expired. Such manufacturers are especially important in developing nations, and they enable local farmers to buy cheaper pest control products. These companies generally lack the capacity to undertake biotechnology research or production.

The impact of agricultural biotechnology depends on the progress that is made in research and development and the pricing policies of producers. If the pest-controlling products currently under development reach the market at reasonable prices, these new varieties will diffuse widely. The supply of some major commodities may increase, both through reduction in crop damage and through expansion of utilized land. Naturally, price feedbacks will moderate these changes. These patterns will first be observable in cotton and soybeans, where new varieties are being intensively introduced. It is possible that trends in recent years (decline in acreage and agricultural productivity) will be reversed, and both land utilization and productivity rates will increase.

Quality-modifying biotechnology innovations

Biotechnology techniques allow modification of agricultural products to enhance desirable characteristics. As Ollinger and Pope (1995) observed, there has been less research and investment in biotechnology to modify quality than to address pest control attributes. Furthermore, while pest control biotechnology is being pursued by established companies, experimentation with quality-augmenting biotechnology is often done by start-up companies and university researchers.

Shelf life is a key quality attribute for highly perishable products and was the target of the first product to reach consumers, a type of tomato. The unexceptional market performance of this product was due in part to vocal opposition by anti-technology groups, but also to the fact that consumers were unimpressed by other quality attributes, such as flavour. A related quality dimension is the extension of the harvest period for desirable crop varieties. As Parker and Zilberman (1993) show, there is a significant price premium for high-quality, early or late-season varieties of fresh fruits and vegetables. A new variety with an altered harvest period may be valuable, although the market potential is limited because the affected crops have relatively small acreages and limited markets and, as supply expands, prices may fall.

Modifications that make a product more attractive or sweeter, or introduce desirable health characteristics, may be quite profitable if consumers' willingness to pay for the attributes exceeds innovation and extra production costs. The genetic manipulations required for development are relatively complex, however, and the risk associated with research is high, hence most of it has been done by universities. As promising innovations are discovered, the process of technology transfer will determine how commercial products are developed. As suggested earlier, even if the initial development is done by start-up companies, the final marketing and production may eventually end up in the hands of major agribusiness firms.

If a small group of companies gains control, through IPR, over significant portions of genetic knowledge about major agricultural products, they will be able to establish monopolistic power and capture rents which would otherwise have gone to agricultural producers. Furthermore, although many of the major companies are concentrated in developed countries, by controlling the rights for biotechnologies that enhance food quality, they may capture much of the value added by production that occurs in developing countries.

One implication of this scenario is that agricultural cooperatives and other farmers' organizations should organize to put themselves in a better position to secure rents by obtaining ownership of genetic material and the product that it may generate in the future. An important question for future research is to what extent farmers' organizations should be engaged in purchasing rights to new technologies that directly affect their industries, as a means to counter possible monopoly power by agribusiness firms and other entities outside their industry. As the cost of biotechnology research declines and the certainty associated with it increases, there is likely to be more involvement by agricultural producer organizations and large food packers and distributors in support of research on improving product quality.

Another effect of falling costs in biotechnology research and development will be to intensify the growing tendency towards product differentiation and monopolistic competitive behaviour in agriculture, particularly in speciality crops but also in poultry and other livestock products. It will become possible for producer groups and agricultural wholesalers to develop their own genetic varieties, as has already occurred with food processing companies such as Frito-Lay.

One development that may become important in the evolution of quality improvements is the interest of large biotechnology firms in support for university research for which they retain the right of first refusal to resulting patents. It has been argued that the rate of return to such complementary support of public research may be particularly high, especially when it allows companies to affect the way that the research capacity of the university is directed. Reduction of support for university research from public sources will probably increase the value and purchasing power of complementary support for university work by private companies. In the long run, it may have significant implications for market structure and income distribution in agriculture and the food sector.

New products

If we define farming as cultivation and production of commercial output using living organisms, biotechnology is likely to expand the range of agricultural activity significantly. Note that breweries, bakeries and similar activities are specifically excluded from our definition. There are already signs that, with biotechnology, one can expand the range of species that are 'farmed', as in production of fine chemicals (beta carotene) from algae, for example. Another important application is 'pharming', in which animals and plants are modified to produce pharmaceutical products. As we have seen in horticultural crops for which the market value of the product is sensitive to the level of effort and skill applied all along the value chain, farms raising these new products are likely to have contractual relationships with companies that provide the genetic materials and process and market the products, or may be subsumed into a vertically integrated entity that will also handle processing, marketing and some research and development activities. For example, pharmaceutical companies may establish farming operations to produce medical substances, or contract with independent growers. In this way, biotechnology will contribute to the industrialization of agriculture.

For new, land-intensive, grain or oilseed varieties, biotechnology companies may make their money through the sale of seeds to existing farmers, retaining or reinforcing a competitive structure in farming. Canola is a recent example of a new crop that was integrated within the traditional competitive farm production system. For reasons discussed above, however, few new biotechnology products will provide opportunities for the expansion of the competitive farm structure, but instead most will provide new farming opportunities within vertically integrated or contractual arrangements.

BIOTECHNOLOGY AND PRECISION AGRICULTURE

An intriguing question is the complementarity and substitution relationship between biotechnology and precision agriculture. Precision agriculture uses advanced information technologies to optimize the use of inputs. For example, it facilitates planting of different plant varieties, in a single field, to adjust for heterogeneity in land conditions and similar variation in pest control needs.

The possibilities which precision farming offers for increasing productivity through optimization of finely tailored seed varieties may generate an expanded market for biotechnology products, especially in areas with sufficient local variation in ecological conditions. In this respect, biotechnology and precision agriculture are complementary, and the diffusion of one will help push forward that of the other. Seed companies and agrochemical suppliers promoting precision farming in the United States may in the future promote biotechnology products as well.

The introduction of precision farming has been accompanied by the emergence of agricultural consultants, some of them independent and others employed by agricultural chemical and seed dealers. Furthermore, there are companies which provide custom services in the use of precision farming. All these professional infrastructures, which increase the capacity of agriculture to utilize scientific data effectively, will be increasingly important with the introduction and expansion of biotechnology products. The range of available plant varieties may expand greatly if agricultural consultants are able to identify conditions under which diversity can yield sufficient extra profits. One may also expect continuing development of software that will enable farmers and consultants to optimize their choice of varieties and equipment in farming activities. Thus the integration of biotechnology and precision farming may be the cornerstone of a more science-based agriculture.

An additional benefit of precision farming is that tailored applications of inputs reduce the residues which are the main cause of ground and surface water contamination. Increased precision may also provide better control of certain pest problems, though that may reduce the potential market for certain biotechnology products. Overall, it seems that the complementarity between biotechnology and precision agriculture will be much greater than the substitution, and the two technologies will build on one another.

INTERNATIONAL CONSIDERATIONS AND INTELLECTUAL PROPERTY RIGHTS

Within a partial equilibrium model, the main results supporting free trade are derived from a framework that maximizes the global aggregate net surplus. The classical model ignores the possibility of increasing returns to scale and the existence of public goods. These assumptions are especially important in crafting international arrangements concerning development of biotechnology products and processes. Using a standard public goods argument, the optimal level of research in a global context occurs where the marginal cost is equal to the sum of the marginal benefit across all users. However, when nations make research investments, they maximize the net benefits for their own citizens, not all users. If industry controls research, investment levels will be determined by even more limited criteria. Currently, research levels are largely determined by the developed nations, which implies that there is underinvestment in biotechnology research, resulting in sub-optimally high-priced intellectual property.

Developing nations may feel that, because this key element of international resource allocation is biased against them, they are justified in ignoring international property rights. Dissatisfaction may be further exacerbated by the fact that, although the genetic material is integral to many agricultural crops originating in developing countries, farmers in those countries may, in the end, be required to pay for use of the materials.

Another source of concern for developing countries is product registration requirements. The rules governing agricultural biotechnology in the United States are considered unduly strict, thus providing existing companies with protection from the entry of competitors. Developing countries may aim to have a biotechnology infrastructure to produce goods for export markets, but strict registration requirements in the United States, and sometimes in Europe, may deter investment. Thus an objective assessment is required of the value of the registration policies and regulations since they can be barriers to the introduction of alternative biotechnology products outside the United States.

The establishment and enforcement of less restrictive biotechnology safety regulations and intellectual property rules in developing countries make economic and political sense. This perspective is contrary to that of American environmental groups, as well as some agribusiness and farmers, supporting the imposition of strict global biotechnology safety regulations. American biotechnology firms and agribusinesses have lobbied for strict and broad intellectual property right rules, backed up with strong enforcement. These policies may not be sound economics or sound politics. Countries differ in their willingness to take certain risks and in the trade-offs associated with particular policy choices. In many cases, the perceived environmental safety of strict limits on biotechnology is, in effect, a luxury good, and willingness to accept possible environment risk in exchange for reduced hunger, increased income and other benefits may be higher in developing countries than in developed ones. Indeed, it is quite possible that environmental risks from biotechnology are dwarfed by the risks associated with constraining this line of innovation. Therefore the key policy question for the United States concerns the size of global externalities from biotechnology risk rather than the local externalities. The aim should be to institute and enforce standards offering the locally desired level of safety, rather than setting maximum levels which may be counterproductive.

Pressure to broadly define IPR on biotechnology knowledge and to enforce those rights aggressively may also backfire. From a global efficiency perspective, broad dissemination of knowledge in most cases is optimal, especially when research capabilities are also widely distributed. On the basis of both efficiency criteria and political common sense, it is preferable that corporations obtain returns to their investments in scientific infrastructures from the direct sales of seeds and services, rather than from broadly enforced IPR. There is a strong case for relatively low prices for use of knowledge, especially in developing countries, and narrowly defined property rights are inconsistent with that goal. The emphasis in trade negotiations should be on vigorously preventing non-market barriers of trade rather than emphasizing protection of strict IPR that are perceived to be discriminatory, and using trade barriers as a tool to enforce them.

Clearly, economic research on biotechnology and IPR is in its infancy. This research must better understand how the markets work and incorporate elements of political economy and international trade theory to be rigorous. However, on the basis of our knowledge from other areas of economics, there are some hypotheses to be further investigated. We would like to use them for starting intellectual debates on serious research agenda.

One issue that occupies much of the debate on IPR is the value of biodiversity in genetic material. The notion of option value, and some theories of pricing options under uncertainty (Dixit and Pindyck, 1994), may suggest that biodiversity is underpriced and that, if the price is corrected, many of the problems associated with the use of natural resources in developing countries will be solved. Similar arguments have been raised to justify establishing restrictions on the use of genetic material that is stored in gene banks throughout the world, as well as for raising the price of genetic materials that have been collected in developing countries.

Unfortunately, the 'option value' perspective has raised inflated expectations among scientists and governments in developing countries regarding their potential for making money from biodiversity and genetic material. First, as the Dixit and Pindyck model suggests, correct recognition of uncertainty may actually lead to delays in investment and, most importantly, will reduce the value of uncertain assets. These theories imply that the high uncertainty associated with biodiversity makes it less, not more, valuable. Obviously, preserved biodiversity has some value; therefore incentives should be developed to preserve biodiversity in a way that reflects option value and other values (Randall, 1990). Further, developing countries should not expect to get rich from licensing rights to prospect the genetic materials of their forests and natural environments because the experience of university technology transfer has been that the earning capacity is quite low for basic knowledge or genetic material that requires much downstream investment.

Some new schemes are being considered to preserve biodiversity and to alleviate the inadequacies of biotechnology research from a global perspective. For example, the concept of farmers' rights has been used in proposals to pay farmers in developing countries for the rights to continue use of certain traditional practices and varieties, and to justify transfer payments that recognize the contribution gene pools preserved by traditional farmers have made towards improving genetic material that is available globally. Much work is needed to design such programmes effectively. The experience of the Conservation Reserve in the United States suggests that, with the right target selection criteria, modest funds can preserve significant amounts of environmental quality (Babcock *et al.*, 1996).

PRICING AND BIOTECHNOLOGY

In order to understand the economic and policy implications of biotechnology, we need to develop an understanding of the pricing of IPR. A full-blown model of price and quantity determination in biotechnology has not been developed, but some basic principles can be sketched to point out one direction that modelling could take. Conceptually, the key distinction is between two types of goods: market products, that are the result of biotechnology, that embody the results of research, and components of knowledge, which are required to produce products, and are covered by IPR arrangements. This may be knowledge about genes or about processes. For simplicity, we also distinguish between two separate types of production units or organizations that produce and sell marketable goods and others selling knowledge and owning property rights.

In the case of agricultural biotechnology, varieties are obvious examples of market products, with biotechnology processes and genetic information as the components. The production of varieties in the future will rely heavily on biotechnological techniques. Over time, the available tools of genetic manipulation and the library of genetic knowledge will increase, and it is plausible that biotechnology companies will be able to 'assemble' a range of finely tailored varieties. As in the case of the computer industry, there could be significant competition in the assembling of varieties. Much of the monopolistic power will accrue to firms owning proprietary rights to the components. Companies such as Monsanto and Pioneer will accumulate IPR for processes and important genetic sequences, set prices for these components and will be paid whenever they are used (it has been said that Monsanto desires to be both the Microsoft and Intel of agricultural biotechnology). To model this situation, assume that there are K distinct components required in order to produce a crop cultivar, with k being a component index, allowing i to assume values from 1 to I.

Let U_k be the price of component k which may be the fee paid to IPR holders. Let δ_{ik} be an indicator equal to 1 if component k is integrated into variety i and 0 otherwise. The price of variety i is

$$V_i = c_i + \sum_{k=1}^{0} \delta_{ik} U_k$$

where c_i is the per-unit assembly cost.

In an ideal system, growers would have choices among many varieties and could make choices about each genetic component. Under such circumstances, a grower would purchase a genetic product if its price (U_k) was lower than the added benefits it generated. In reality, the product choice facing many growers is likely to be quite limited because of production and marketing costs and profitability considerations of variety producers. In this case, the decision whether or not to select a variety with a specific genetic component will depend less on the benefits of the component itself and more on the merits of complementary genetic products packaged in the varieties where it is included. Certain desirable components may not be purchased if they are not available in the most profitable variety.

Under these conditions, major corporations will design pricing policies for both products they make, and access to IPR they control, to maximize their profits. Profit will include revenues minus payments for IPR minus the cost of production and registration. Standard industrial organization theory implies that the value of IPR will be smaller when there is less purchased, as when there is an oligarchic pharmaceutical or agribusiness sector making the final product. High registration costs reduce the value of IPR directly and by contributing to reducing competition, as argued above. An interesting area for future research is the gaming situations that may occur under different IPR and industrial organization structures.

Further research will be needed to analyse the effects on resource allocation of monopolistic power that producers may have with respect to genetic material and the cost of assembly and distribution. It is clear, however, that the welfare of end users will be diminished in situations where a small number of firms have the ability to control the set of varieties available on the market. In such cases it will be important for government policies to be enacted to ensure competition in the assembly production of biotechnology items and to prevent the use of monopolistic power to limit choice and increase prices.

CONCLUSIONS

It has been suggested that the emergence of biotechnology will profoundly affect the future of agriculture, altering its institutional structures, its products and the way it is practised. Ten major points summarize our conclusions.

(1) Biotechnology is very research-intensive, and successful utilization of new technology will require continuous improvements in our knowledge about the properties of genetic materials and the function of biological systems. Some of the research will be done by private companies, but public sector-supported research will continue to provide breakthrough innovations and fundamental new knowledge. The process of technology transfer will provide some support for the universities, but it will not be enough to cover the research costs.

(2) Public research and extension activities are essential to foster competition and facilitate broad access to genetic materials, gene modification techniques and new varieties. Reduction in public investments in agricultural biotechnology may lead to underprovision of innovations, high prices for essential genetic materials and techniques, and a decrease in the rate of technological advance.

(3) Currently, biotechnology is being used to develop varieties which expand pest-control options, have better storage and handling attributes, and express more intensely traits important to food processors. These types of innovations are likely to continue to be developed and controlled by existing agrochemical, seed and food-processing companies. In the long run, biotechnology will be used to develop new varieties tailored to specific production conditions or consumer preferences, promoting product differentiation in agriculture. Biotechnology will

permit development of value-added products that will allow substitution of agricultural for industrial processes in the manufacture of pharmaceuticals and fine chemicals. Biotechnology techniques may be used to ameliorate adverse consequences of agricultural production through microbial waste management technologies. These fundamentally different types of biotechnology may be associated with the establishment of new firms, the entrance of consumer goods firms into agricultural production, and expansion of contracting and vertical integration in agriculture.

(4)   It is difficult to generalize about the distributional effects of biotechnology. Some innovations, such as Canola, engineered to replace tropical oils, will shift production from developing to developed regions. Other modifications, such as disease resistance and salinity tolerance, may provide new opportunities for marginal producers.

(5)   Clearly defined and enforceable intellectual property rights are essential for private-sector research and development of new biotechnology products. However, overly broad patents may grant excessive market power to patent holders, reducing their incentives to provide socially desirable levels of production or investment in innovation. Unduly broad patents and/or overly restrictive licensing of academic inventions will diminish the capacity for new entrants to compete.

(6)   Biotechnological processes and products must be monitored for safety and efficacy. However, registration and safety regulations that are unduly restrictive will lead to concentrations of research and production capacity, which may stifle the growth of agricultural biotechnology and in some cases result in less desirable health and safety outcomes.

(7)   Biotechnology provides a means to address many needs specific to developing countries; but to realize these opportunities, nations will have to develop their own research capacity to handle it. Additional investments in information and extension services will be needed to support adoption of new varieties.

(8)   Developed countries should not be overzealous in their enforcement of intellectual property rights in developing countries. First, excessive fees will encourage cheating and, second, undue emphasis on IPR protection may conflict with other goals, such as promotion of free trade. Consideration should be given to establishing two-tiered pricing systems for intellectual property rights, with developing countries paying lower prices.

(9)   Revenues from the sale of options to develop indigenous genetic resources will not be sufficient to protect natural areas that are reservoirs of biodiversity. Other mechanisms must be developed to protect these resources at globally desirable levels.

(10) Biotechnology provides new research challenges and opportunities for agricultural economists. New methodologies are needed to understand the welfare implications of alternative intellectual property rights policies under different industry structures and technology attributes, with attention to the role of universities' technology transfer practices. Welfare economics should be extended to questions regarding patent breadth, enforcement policy, and investment in public versus private research.

Furthermore, it is also very important that we understand the economics of biotechnology within a development and international context.

NOTES

[1]We define biotechnology as the application of the tools of molecular biology, primarily recombinant DNA and related techniques, to modify organisms in order to increase productivity, improve quality or introduce novel characteristics.

[2]Just and Hueth (1993) expanded this line of reasoning and argued that, in many cases, biotechnology varieties can be viewed as complementary or substitutes of variable inputs. Their adoption is likely to increase as the price of substitutes increases and price of complements declines.

REFERENCES

Babcock, B.A., Lakshminarayan, P.G., Wu, J. and Zilberman, D. (1996), 'The Economics of a Public Fund for Environmental Amenities: A Study of CRP Contracts', *American Journal of Agricultural Economics*, 78, 961–71.

Dixit, A. and Pindyck, R. (1994), *Investment Under Uncertainty*, New Haven and Princeton: Princeton University Press.

Huttner, S.L., Miller, H.I. and Lemaux, P.G. (1995), 'US. Agricultural Biotechnology: Status and Prospects', *Technological Forecasting and Social Change, (Special Issue on Biotechnology and the Future of Agriculture and Natural Resources)*, 50, 25–39.

Just, R.J. and Hueth, D.L. (1993), 'Multimarket Exploitation: The Case of Biotechnology and Chemicals', *American Journal of Agricultural Economics*, 75, 936–45.

Ollinger, M. and Pope, L. (1995), 'Strategic Research Interests, Organizational Behavior, and the Emerging Markets for the Products of Plant Biotechnology', *Technological Forecasting and Social Change, (Special Issue on Biotechnology and the Future of Agriculture and National Resources)*, 50, 55–68.

Parker, D. and Zilberman, D. (1993), 'University Technology Transfers: Impacts on Local and U.S. Economies', *Contemporary Policy Issues*, 11, 87–99.

Parker, D., Zilberman, D. and Castillo, F. (1998), 'Office of Technology Transfer, Privatizing University Innovations, and Agriculture', *Choices, Magazine of the American Agricultural Economics Association*, first quarter.

Randall, A. (1990), *Thinking About the Value of Biodiversity*, Columbus: Ohio State University, Department of Agricultural Economics and Rural Societies.

DISCUSSION REPORT SECTION II

Hassan Serghini (Morocco)[1] said that he had much enjoyed listening to McCalla and Valdés as they carefully sifted through the semantics involved in deciding whether 'diversification' can be regarded as a 'policy' or as a market 'response', with particular reference to agricultural trade. It did appear to him, however, that the subject is difficult to discuss in isolation and that much depended on circumstances in specific countries. From his viewpoint, the Maghreb has great advantages of climate, which helps in the production of numerous seasonally differentiated high-value crops which are potentially exportable, but the export opportunities are constrained by the nature of the agricultural policies followed in the European Union, which is the obvious market. The nature of the import restrictions, as well as the manner in which they have changed (or are changing) as a result of the completion of the Uruguay Round, for fruit and vegetables in particular, is extremely complex. It appeared to him that there does have to be a measure of guidance, stemming from the official level, if producers and traders are to be able to benefit from any marketing opportunities which do exist.

This type of issue also became evident in the comments of *Bradford Barham and Michael Carter (United States)*[2] as joint openers of discussion on the paper by Delgado and Siamwalla. They had experience of watching the development of agroexports in Latin America where, in examples such as that of Guatemala, something of a boom was occurring. The case in point was growth of winter vegetable supply, notably to North America, based on producer marketing cooperatives involving thousands of small-scale farmers (most having under two hectares). Here the issue was not so much one of entering export markets or organizing supply, where the cooperation structure appeared to offer considerable advantages. The important concern lay in the difficulty of encouraging poor farm households to engage in high-value activities. There remains a preference for subsistence crops – this is a type of implicit insurance as a risk-reducing measure – despite there being a much lower rate of return to their land and other factors. As scale increases, indeed as expected, the willingness to adopt agroexport crops also rises. It was then emphasized, however, that Latin America has a highly inegalitarian agrarian structure, which makes it difficult for the mass of poorer farmers to participate in new types of activity. They are hampered by their own low adoption rates, but there are good reasons why adoption should be tempered with caution.

[1]University of Hassan II, Rabat.
[2]University of Wisconsin-Madison.

Given their experience, the discussants felt a large measure of agreement with the authors. The latter, after all, did stress the need to make markets work well for smaller farmers. Cooperatives, contract farming and other institutional innovations can reduce the transaction costs that create competitiveness problems for smaller-scale operators. But they see a conceptual flaw in the Delgado/ Siamwalla paper. The authors stress 'diversification' of income sources as a helpful step. Part of the process, according to the discussants, is obviously 'commercialization', though even that could imply more 'specialization', or 'intensification', rather than seeking yet more potential income sources. It could well be apposite for sub-Saharan Africa, which they quoted as a region of considerable 'diversification'. But no matter how the semantics is approached, it is never going to be easy to overcome the barriers which lie in the way of adoption of new opportunities. It is even more difficult, according to the discussants, to promote 'equitable growth'.

Agricultural biotechnology was commented on by *Rafael Posada (Colombia)*[3]. He was impressed by the clarity of the paper by David Zilberman and his colleagues, commending special study of the complex roles and motivations involved in making final use of a biotechnology product. The worry must be that inequitable development will occur, partly because the property rights involved are rather tightly drawn and could isolate many countries from innovative technology, but mainly owing to the sheer lack of the capacity in the Third World to carry out research in the early discovery and development phases. To overcome this, special efforts are needed to promote arguments that will convince current and potential donors that investment in biotechnology in the Third World has positive benefits for the whole of global society, and also convince commercial firms that location of research facilities in developing countries could be privately beneficial. In short, there appears to be no inherent reason why they should not participate at all stages in the discovery and application process. This is important because a biotechnology output could be the source of an advantage in agricultural production for a developing country, while lack of anything could signal a serious loss of competitiveness. The most desirable situation is obviously one in which the outcomes of research, taken overall and bearing in mind that numerous potential products are involved, will be as neutral as possible in terms of interregional competitiveness.

[3]Centro Internacional de Agricultura Tropical (CIAT).

SECTION III

Resource Management in Agriculture:
Water and Land, Biodiversity, Agriculture and Climate

MARK W. ROSEGRANT, CLAUDIA RINGLER AND ROBERTA V.
GERPACIO*

Water and Land Resources and Global Food Supply

INTRODUCTION

The world population is expected to grow to 7.7 billion in 2020, from 5.3 billion in 1993 (UN, 1996). Although the latest population projections represent a slowdown from past estimates, the large absolute increase in population raises serious concerns about how food demand will be met in the next decades, especially in the context of a possibly stagnant or even decreasing stock of natural resources. These concerns have escalated sharply in recent years, in the face of dramatic increases in world cereal prices in 1996, combined with declining cereal stocks, and the simultaneous appearance of several widely read publications presenting the possibility of a starving world in the next century, unable to meet growing food demands from a deteriorating natural resource base (Brown, 1995; Tyler, 1995; Brown and Kane, 1994).

In this paper, we examine the prospects for global food supply and demand for the year 2020, in the light of the two most often identified natural resource constraints, land and water. We first briefly summarize recent trends in area, yield and production for cereal crops, the key staple crops for most of the world, describe the IMPACT global food projections model and present an overview of food demand and supply projections. We then ask whether land and water constraints will pose serious threats to long-term cereal production growth. In particular, we assess the effects of land degradation and land conversion to urban uses on agricultural production and the effect of increasing water scarcity on future global food supply. For the latter assessment, we develop projections of global water demand until 2020 that are consistent with the underlying assumptions in the global food projections. We conclude with implications for land and water policy.

GLOBAL FOOD DEMAND AND SUPPLY

Table 1 summarizes recent trends in area, production and yield for cereals for the periods 1967–82 and 1982–94, which roughly divide the period 1967–94

*Mark W. Rosegrant, International Food Policy Research Institute, Washington, DC, USA and International Irrigation Management Institute, Colombo, Sri Lanka; Claudia Ringler and Roberta V. Gerpacio, International Food Policy Research Institute, Washington, DC, USA.

TABLE 1   *Crop area, production and yield growth rates, 1967–94 (per cent per year)*[1]

	1967–82			1982–94		
	Area	Prod.	Yield	Area	Prod.	Yield
Wheat						
Developing	1.45	5.39	3.88	0.42	2.94	2.52
Developed	–0.12	1.73	1.87	–1.38	–0.03	1.35 USA
World	0.48	2.88	2.40	–0.59	1.20	1.80
Maize						
Developing	0.65	3.46	2.80	1.36	3.66	2.27
Developed	0.64	3.05	2.33	–0.26	0.69	1.01 USA
World	0.64	3.20	2.52	0.77	1.93	1.16
Rice						
Developing	0.81	3.21	2.38	0.21	2.03	1.81
Developed	–0.23	–0.14	0.09	–0.28	0.34	0.61 USA
World	0.78	2.96	2.17	0.20	1.94	1.74
Other grains						
Developing	–0.87	1.20	2.08	0.12	0.03	–0.09
Developed	0.52	1.32	0.79	–1.63	–0.78	0.85 USA
World	–0.15	1.28	1.43	–0.79	–0.52	0.26
All cereals						
Developing	0.48	3.36	2.87	0.46	2.34	1.87
Developed	0.23	1.92	1.69	–1.27	0.01	1.30 USA
World	0.37	2.61	2.24	–0.24	1.27	1.51

Note: [1] Based on three-year moving averages.

Source: Basic data, FAO (1997).

into a peak 'green revolution' period and a post 'green revolution' period. Global growth rates of cereal production declined substantially, from 2.6 per cent per year in 1967–82 to 1.3 per cent per year after 1982, mainly owing to a contraction of area harvested in the developed world and to a slowdown in growth of crop yields in both developing and developed countries. The pattern of global cereal yield growth also shows a significant slowdown, from 2.2 per cent per year in 1967–82 to 1.5 per cent per year in 1982–94. In the developed countries, the slowdown in crop area, yield and production growth was primarily policy-induced, with European and North American governments scaling back farm-price support programmes and cutting down on cereal stocks. In addition, the economic collapse and subsequent struggles with economic reform in the former Soviet Union and Eastern Europe further depressed production during the 1990s. In the developing countries, declining cereal prices have led to a direct shift of land out of cereals into more profitable crops and to a slowdown in growth in input use and in investment in research and irrigation infrastructure, with consequent detrimental effects on yield growth (Rosegrant and Pingali, 1994). At the same time, the achievement of relatively high cereal yields in parts of Asia, high input levels and increased land intensity slowed further increases in yields (ibid.; Byerlee, 1994).

The global food projections model

Projections of global food supply and demand have been made using an updated model of IFPRI's International Model for Policy Analysis of Commodities and Trade (IMPACT) (see Rosegrant *et al.*, 1995, for details of the original work). The model covers 37 countries and regions, and 17 commodities, including all cereals, roots and tubers, soybeans and meats. The model is specified as a set of country-level supply and demand equations, where each country model is linked to the rest of the world through trade. Demand depends on prices, elasticities, income and population growth, and incorporates the dynamic adjustment of income elasticities with respect to income growth. Prices and the rate of productivity growth determine growth in commodity production in each country, while it is also influenced by advances in public and private agricultural research and development, extension and education, markets, infrastructure and irrigation. The crop supply side now incorporates the effect of irrigation expansion as a separate variable that directly affects area harvested and yields. In this model, we have updated population data with the most recent United Nations projections (UN, 1996) and the baseline production and consumption data, on which projections are being made, have been updated to 1993.

Projected world food prices

The baseline results of IMPACT suggest that world prices of cereals will fall, but at a slower rate than in recent years. Cereal prices on average are projected to drop by 11 per cent by 2020. The slow decline in prices will be accompanied by rapidly increasing world trade in cereals, with the developing countries as a group increasing imports from the developing countries. Net cereal imports of developing countries will more than double by 2020, reaching 228 million metric tons (mt.).

Projected demand for cereals

Changing patterns of demand are apparent in the projected growth rates in food and feed demand shown in Table 2. In many developing countries, strong income growth, rapid urbanization and changing tastes and preferences will cause a shift to more diversified diets, with higher per capita consumption of meat, dairy products, fruits and vegetables. Growth rates in total cereal

TABLE 2   *Increase in total demand for cereals, by region, 1993–2020 (million metric tonnes)*

	Wheat	Maize	Rice	Other grains	All cereals
China	40.3	79.3	21.0	5.1	145.7
India	39.2	3.2	35.4	6.8	84.6
Other East Asia	3.4	11.0	1.2	0.7	16.3
Other South Asia	27.4	2.1	15.8	0.8	46.2
Southeast Asia	7.5	18.0	28.2	0.5	54.2
Latin America	12.8	40.5	7.8	9.4	70.5
WANA	51.2	9.9	6.5	20.9	88.4
Sub-Saharan Africa	10.3	28.1	11.9	34.2	84.5
USA	7.8	43.0	1.1	5.8	57.7
Western Europe	5.2	3.9	0.3	7.3	16.7
Eastern Europe & CIS	10.8	3.9	0.1	17.9	32.7
Other developed	6.7	5.3	–0.04	7.6	19.6
Developing	192.4	192.3	128.0	78.3	591.1
Developed	30.5	56.1	1.5	38.6	126.7
World	222.9	248.4	129.5	116.9	717.8

Source: IFPRI, IMPACT simulations.

demand will decline, owing to both changes in the diet structure and a continued gradual slowdown in population growth. Global per capita consumption will be virtually constant, with declining consumption of cereals at higher income levels balancing the increasing demands of lower-income countries. Total cereal demand will increase by about 718 million mt., from 1773 million mt. in 1993 to 2491 million mt. in 2020. More than 80 per cent of this change will come from the developing world, where increases in population and income will be more pronounced than in the developed world. China and India together will account for more than 30 per cent of the increase in global food demand. Additional demand for meat will lead to a strong expansion in the use of maize and other cereals for animal feeds, especially in the more rapidly growing developing economies, which will experience rapid growth of their livestock industries.

Projected area and yield growth for cereals

How will the expanding cereal demand be met? Expansion in area will almost cease to contribute to future production growth, with a total increase in cereal area of only 39 million hectares (ha) by 2020, from 700 million ha in 1993 (Table 3). Of this growth, 88 per cent will originate in developing countries, in particular sub-Saharan Africa, which accounts for almost 60 per cent of expan-

TABLE 3   *Crop area harvested, cereal crops, by region, 1993–2020 (million hectares)*

	1993	2020	Increase, 1993–2020
China	88.6	89.1	0.5
India	99.4	101.2	1.8
Other East Asia	3.7	3.3	−0.4
Other South Asia	26.7	27.5	0.8
Southeast Asia	47.2	48.2	1.0
Latin America	47.9	54.0	6.1
WANA	55.6	57.4	1.8
Sub-Saharan Africa	62.4	85.4	23.0
USA	63.3	65.3	2.0
Western Europe	36.8	37.2	0.4
Eastern Europe & CIS	127.3	129.0	1.7
Other developed	41.0	41.6	0.6
Developing	431.6	466.2	34.6
Developed	268.5	273.1	4.6
World	700.0	739.3	39.2

Source: IFPRI, IMPACT simulations.

sion in area harvested. The projected slow growth in area places the burden of meeting future cereal demand on crop yield growth. Although that will vary considerably by commodity and country, a further decline is projected compared with the already reduced rates of the 1982–94 period. The global yield growth rate for all cereals is expected to decline from 1.5 per cent annually in 1982–94 to 1.1 per cent in 1993–2020. For developing countries, wheat yield growth will drop from 2.5 per cent to 1.3 per cent per year, maize yield growth will decrease from 2.3 per cent to 1.4 per cent, and rice yield growth will decline from 1.8 per cent to 1.1 per cent per year. In developed countries, average crop yield growth is projected to slow from 1.3 per cent to 0.9 per cent per year (Table 4).

Can the crop area, yield and production growth rates projected here be attained? To what extent will land and water quality and availability limit the ability to attain the necessary production to meet the demands of rising populations and incomes? The following sections of the paper examine these possible constraints and discuss their implications for global food supply and land and water policy.

TABLE 4   *Projected annual cereal yield growth rate, 1993–2020 (per cent per year)*

	Wheat	Maize	Rice	Other grains	All cereals
China	0.88	1.40	0.69	0.39	0.98
India	1.53	1.75	1.43	0.80	1.42
Other East Asia	1.38	1.88	0.47	0.51	0.84
Other South Asia	1.45	1.84	1.50	0.62	1.50
Southeast Asia	0.29	1.79	1.19	0.50	1.30
Latin America	1.64	1.25	1.94	0.98	1.37
WANA	1.70	1.39	1.81	2.20	1.85
Sub-Saharan Africa	1.29	1.80	1.88	1.52	1.67
USA	1.24	0.87	1.13	0.75	0.96
Western Europe	0.35	0.67	0.94	0.40	0.42
Eastern Europe & CIS	1.24	1.22	0.45	0.99	0.75
Other developed	1.60	0.98	0.06	0.74	1.37
Developing	1.30	1.36	1.08	1.24	1.20
Developed	1.06	0.84	0.53	0.78	0.94
World	1.17	1.03	1.05	0.85	1.06

Source: IFPRI, IMPACT simulations.

LAND AND WATER AS LIMITING FACTORS TO GLOBAL FOOD SUPPLY

Cropland potential and land loss to urbanization

Total crop area harvested was 1593 million ha in 1993, of which 1077 million ha were in the developing world, and 516 million ha in developed countries (FAO, 1997). Cereal crop area harvested was 700 million ha in 1993: 269 million ha in the developed world, and 432 million ha in the developing world. It is expected to increase by 39 million ha by 2020, almost all of which will be accounted for by developing countries (see Table 3). Can the existing land base support this increase in cereal crop area harvested?

In order to estimate cropland potential, the entire land area that could be converted to agricultural uses must be taken into account. According to FAO (1997), in 1994, total land resources were 13 044 million ha, of which 1353 million ha were classified as arable land, 114 million ha as having permanent crops, 3399 million ha as pasture, 4172 million ha as forest and woodland and 4003 million ha as other land, including built-on areas, roads and barren land. Out of this area, Buringh and Dudal (1987) identified 700 million ha as prime agricultural land and 2600 million ha with low or medium capability for crop production. This would yield a potential land area suitable for crop production of at least 3300 million ha, and an additional crop area potential of 1833 million ha.

As most of the currently cultivated land is relatively good or prime agricultural land, the productivity of other land forms converted into cropland is expected to be lower than the existing land stock. Conversion may also eliminate forest and rangelands with important functions in their present uses. According to Kendall and Pimentel (1994), the world's arable land might be expanded at most by 500 million ha, at a productivity below present levels. Most of the potential cropland (about 87 per cent) is located in developing countries, mainly in sub-Saharan Africa and Latin America. In Asia, on the other hand, nearly 80 per cent of the potentially arable land is already under cultivation, and local cases of land scarcity for agricultural production have been reported from China, Indonesia and elsewhere in Asia (Plucknett, 1995). Although global per capita arable land has been decreasing steadily, from 0.35 ha in 1970 to 0.24 ha in 1994, per capita area harvested has declined much more slowly, from 0.23 ha to 0.20 ha in the same period. It is rarely noticed that the ratio of crop area harvested to arable land, which represents an aggregate cropping intensity index, has improved steadily over the past three decades, from 1.05 in 1970 to 1.20 in 1994 for the world, and from 1.28 to 1.56 for developing countries during the same period, making it less necessary to bring new land under cultivation (computed from FAO, 1997).

The world's urban population is expected to be more than 5 million by 2025, implying an overall urban growth rate of 2.3 per cent from 1995, and 61 per cent of the population in urban areas, up from 38 per cent in 1975. With the urban population being nearly stable in Europe and North America, about 90 per cent of the urban population growth will occur in developing countries, where roughly 200 000 people will be added to the urban population every day between 1995 and 2025. In China, the share of urban population is expected to triple between 1995 and 2025 and, in much of the rest of Asia, it is projected to double. Sub-Saharan Africa is expected to have more than half of its population living in urban areas by 2025, Latin America 85 per cent, and West Asia and North Africa (WANA) 75 per cent (WRI, 1996).

There is no doubt that this rapid urbanization will remove some agricultural land from production. Indeed, the conversion of land from agricultural uses to higher-value uses on the fringes of urban areas is part of the process of economic development, generating in most cases significant economic benefits (Crosson, 1986; Moya *et al.*, 1994). Biased urban and industrial growth strategies, together with the neglect of the agricultural sector, have also led to significant damage to prime agricultural land (Bhadra and Brandão, 1993). However, there is little evidence that the process of land conversion to urban uses poses a serious threat to future global food production. For developing countries, urbanization is expected to lead to the conversion of 476 000 ha of arable land annually, amounting to a loss of 14 million ha between 1990 and 2020 (USAID, 1988).

The projected increase in crop area of 39 million ha necessary to meet global food demand by 2020 is much lower than both the theoretical maximum additional potential crop area of 1833 million ha and the more realistic potential for economically feasible conversion of land resources to agricultural uses of 500 million ha. A possible loss of 14 million ha of agricultural land to urban uses in the developing countries appears small compared to potential expansions in crop area, and the continued increases in cropping intensity on existing cultivated area. Thus the lack of potential crop area *per se* cannot be considered a major constraint to future agricultural production growth.

Physical limits to crop productivity

Global food production can be increased through expansion of areas and increases in cropping intensity (extensification), or through increases in agricultural productivity (intensification). Crop area harvested, as projected in IMPACT simulations, is expected to grow only slowly. Thus increases in agricultural productivity will have to come from improved yields. Will agricultural productivity as the main engine of agricultural production growth be able to keep up with global food requirements in the face of current and future challenges? Are the projected 1993–2020 yield growth rates biologically achievable?

The earth's biophysical limit of food production is reached when all agricultural land is cultivated and irrigated, maximum potential yields are attained and the remaining suitable grazing land is grazed. The specific upper limit to crop yield is determined by soil type, climate, crop properties and available irrigation water; it is reached when the farmer selects the optimal combination of crop species and management practices (Penning de Vries *et al.*, 1995). Maximum theoretical yields are calculated for specific crops as the highest limit of biological potential for a given location on the basis of photosynthetic potential, land quality, length of the growing season and water availability. Maximum theoretical yields in grain equivalents have been calculated by Linneman *et al.* (1979) and Luyten (1995), and range from about 7.6 mt. per hectare per season in the former Soviet Union to just over 8 mt. per hectare per season for China, India and the rest of South Asia, and in excess of 9 mt. per hectare per season in Southeast Asia, sub-Saharan Africa, North America and Western Europe. Yield levels simulated by IMPACT for 2020 are all well below the maximum theoretical yields. Thus, despite the slowdown in yield growth over the past 15 years, overall trends by country and region indicate ample room for yield improvement for most crops and regions (Plucknett, 1995). However, continuing investment in agricultural research will be essential for maintaining current trends in yield growth and to further increase the yield potential.

Land degradation

The most comprehensive assessment of global land degradation, Oldeman *et al.* (1990), classifies the main types of land degradation as soil erosion from wind and water, chemical degradation (loss of nutrients, soil salinization, urban–industrial pollution and acidification) and physical degradation (compaction, waterlogging and subsidence of organic soils). Out of the total land resource base, Oldeman *et al.* estimated that 1964 million ha suffered from some degree of degradation. Water erosion accounted for 56 per cent of land degradation, wind erosion for 28 per cent, chemical degradation for 12 per cent and physical degradation for 4 per cent. However, for the estimated 562 million ha of degraded agricultural land, chemical degradation was much more important, accounting for 40 per cent of degraded land. Degradation leads to reductions in crop yields, may reduce total factor productivity by requiring the use of higher input levels to maintain yields, may lead to the conversion of land to lower-value uses and may cause temporary or permanent abandonment of plots.

Estimates of the crop production impacts of land degradation are rare. Comprehensive country-level studies have only been undertaken for the United States (Alt *et al.*, 1989; Crosson, 1986). These studies found very small long-term yield effects due to soil erosion: if erosion rates continued at the same rate as in 1982 for 100 years, national average yields in the United States would be 3–10 per cent lower than in the absence of erosion (Crosson and Anderson, 1992).

Crosson (1995), based on the Oldeman *et al.* analysis, estimated the 1945–90 cumulative crop productivity loss due to land degradation to be about 5 per cent, which is equivalent to a decline of 0.11 per cent per year. While this is not an insignificant loss, the impact of degradation was dwarfed by crop yield growth of 1.9 per cent annually during 1967–94. Crop yield losses due to past erosion show cumulative crop yield reductions that range from 2 per cent to 40 per cent across African countries, with a mean of 8.2 per cent for the continent and 6.2 per cent for sub-Saharan Africa (Lal, 1995, as cited in Scherr and Yadav, 1996). These national-level estimates confirm that land degradation can be devastating in some countries, especially in fragile environments within sub-regions of countries. However, estimated rates of land degradation and estimations of subsequent yield losses are relatively small and do not in general imply a threat to global food production. Furthermore, even these relatively small losses may considerably overstate the net impact of soil erosion, as eroded soil is often not lost to agricultural production, but rather deposited elsewhere on productive cropland or pasture (Crosson and Anderson, 1992). Thus, in many cases, soil erosion is a redistribution of crop production rather than a production loss.

Policies to counteract degradation should be aimed towards the zones of high risk and could include public investments in research, technology development, extension services and rural infrastructure, in order to stabilize or reverse degradation. Land degradation can also be mitigated through broader policy reforms, such as the establishment of property rights to land, market and price reforms, and the elimination of subsidies to agricultural inputs.

Water as a constraint to global food supply

In the following sections we examine whether water scarcity could limit the needed expansion in food production. The available annual renewable freshwater supply is estimated to be 9000–14 000 billion cubic metres (BCM)

(Rosegrant, 1997). Given the current global use of water of around 3700 BCM, the freshwater supply would be adequate to meet growth in demand for the foreseeable future, if supplies were distributed equally across the world's population. Freshwater, however, is distributed unevenly across the globe. While per capita water availability is highest in Latin America and North America, and lower in Africa, Asia and Europe, these regional figures also hide the huge variability in water availability. Freshwater is poorly distributed across countries (Canada has 120 000 cubic metres per capita per year of renewable water resources; Kenya has 600 cubic metres; and Jordan, 300 cubic metres), within countries (although India has adequate average water availability of 2500 cubic metres per capita, the state of Rajasthan has access to only 550 cubic metres per person annually), and across seasons (Bangladesh suffers from monsoon flooding followed by severe dry season water shortages) (ibid.). Moreover, with a fixed amount of renewable water resources supplying an increasing population, per capita water availability has declined steadily. Between 1950 and 1980, per capita water availability declined from 9600 cubic metres to 5100 cubic metres in Asia, and from 20 000 cubic metres to 9400 cubic metres in Africa (Ayibotele, 1992).

Water demand

Tightening water supplies have been accompanied by rapid growth in demand for water. Between 1950 and 1990, water use increased by more than 100 per cent in North and Latin America, by more than 300 per cent in Africa and by almost 500 per cent in Europe (Clarke, 1993). Global demand for water has grown by 2.4 per cent per year since 1970. Some key characteristics of water demand are presented in Table 5. Annual per capita domestic withdrawals in 1995 ranged from a high of 240 cubic metres in the United States to only 11 cubic metres in sub-Saharan Africa, a level that is just over one-half of the 20 cubic metres per capita estimated by Gleick (1996) to be required to meet the most basic human needs. China, India and other South Asian countries are all at or just above this basic human needs level. Southeast Asia, Latin America and WANA cluster at 56 cubic metres to 65 cubic metres per capita. For developing countries as a group, per capita water demand was 33 cubic metres in 1995, less than one-fourth the amount in developed countries.

The industrial water use (or withdrawal) intensity is defined as the amount of water used per one thousand US dollars of total GDP (cubic metres per US$1000). Intensity is affected by the share of industry within the economy, the proportion of different types of activity in industrial production and the efficiency of water use in individual industries. Among the developing countries, in general, the higher the per capita income, the lower the industrial water use intensity. Developed countries averaged 27 cubic metres per US$1000, compared to developing countries at 40 cubic metres per US$1000 (Table 5).

TABLE 5   *Irrigated area, per capita domestic water withdrawal, income elasticity for domestic withdrawal, and industrial water withdrawal intensity, 1995 and projected 2020*

Country/region	Irrigated area (million ha)		Income elasticity for domestic withdrawal	Industrial withdrawal intensity (m³ per US$1000)		Per capita domestic withdrawal (m³ per capita)	
	1995	2020		1995	2020	1995	2020
China	50.1	53.1	0.8	74	71	25	71
India	51.3	68.6	1.0	88	86	20	54
Other East Asia	2.9	2.9	0.2	25	23	77	98
Other South Asia	25.0	29.3	1.0	64	64	21	41
Southeast Asia	14.4	16.2	*a*	60	49	56	87
Latin America	17.3	18.7	0.6	23	23	65	82
WANA	24.3	31.2	0.6	28	27	56	70
Sub-Saharan Africa	5.0	7.4	1.2	38	38	11	15
USA	21.5	22.4	0.0	34	27	240	240
Western Europe	11.9	12.3	0.0	17	15	94	94
Eastern Europe & CIS	24.8	26.3	*b*	177	170	89	103
Other developed	7.4	7.6	*c*	12	10	169	180
Developing	190.2	227.4		40	43	33	59
Developed	65.6	68.6		27	22	135	147
World	255.8	296.0		29	28	56	75

Notes: *a* Malaysia: 0.1, Indonesia, Philippines, Thailand: 0.4, Vietnam: 0.5, Myanmar, Others: 0.8.
b Eastern Europe: 0.2, former Soviet Union: 0.4.
c Japan: 0.0, others: 0.1.

Sources: 1995 estimates of per capita domestic withdrawal, WRI (1994) and Raskin *et al.* (1997); income elasticity for domestic water withdrawal, IFPRI estimates; industrial water withdrawal intensity, WRI (1994) and Raskin *et al.* (1997); irrigated area, 1995 value interpolated from FAO (1997).

Projections of water demand to 2020

To understand the critical importance of water as a possible constraint to future agricultural growth, this section examines the future growth in water demand, and presents projections of water demand to 2020 that are consistent with the 2020 food supply and demand projections from IMPACT. Key underlying assumptions on growth in population, income and irrigated area are taken directly from the food supply and demand projections. Although water demand would ideally be defined as consumptive use of water, it is approximated here by water withdrawals, owing to a lack of consistent data on consumptive use at the national or regional level.

Irrigated area growth is based on recent past trends, including rates of changes in these trends, and on our assessment of planned investment in irrigation. Projected growth rates in irrigated area are significantly lower than in the recent past. Irrigated area in developed countries is projected to increase by only 3 million ha between 1995 and 2020, at an annual growth rate of only 0.2 per cent, compared with one of 0.8 per cent between 1982 and 1993. In developing countries, an additional 37.2 million ha of irrigated area is projected by 2020, at an annual rate of increase of 0.7 per cent, compared to 1.7 per cent per year from 1982 to 1993. For the world as a whole, irrigated area is projected to grow at 0.6 per cent per year, compared with 1.5 per cent during 1982–93. The largest increase is expected in India, with 17.3 million ha, as public investment in irrigation has remained relatively strong and public investment in tubewells has been very rapid. However, even in India, the projected 1995 to 2020 rate of growth in irrigated area of 1.2 per cent per year is well below the rate of 2.0 per cent per year during 1982–93 (Table 5).

Per capita demand for domestic water is a function of income growth and the income elasticity. The elasticities (Table 5) are synthesized from available information, which is sparse both at the aggregate, cross-country level (see Rock, 1996) and within countries. The available evidence indicates that water demand is highly elastic at low income and low water use levels, and that the elasticities for domestic water decline gradually as income and water use rise (see Table 5). Particularly strong growth in per capita domestic demand is projected for China and India, spurred by high income growth and supported by strong income elasticities: demand will nearly triple in China, to 71 cubic metres, while in India a 270 per cent increase will bring demand to 54 cubic metres per capita. In other South Asian countries, per capita domestic demand will almost double to 42 cubic metres. Sub-Saharan Africa, on the other hand, will experience the smallest increase in per capita domestic water demand in the developing world, as GDP growth will barely outpace population growth, resulting in slow growth in per capita income. For developing countries as a group, per capita domestic water demand is projected to increase by 79 per cent, to 59 cubic metres. The increase is much lower in developed countries, from 135 cubic metres to 147 cubic metres per capita (Table 5).

To project industrial water needs to 2020, it was assumed that the United States and other developed countries (except Japan) will reduce intensities by 20 per cent by 2020, reflecting continued long-term improvements in efficiency of industrial water use. Western Europe and Japan, which have already reached low industrial water use intensities, are assumed to achieve an additional 10 per cent reduction. Water use intensities for Eastern Europe, the former Soviet Union and the developing countries are projected using a 'convergence' algorithm developed by Raskin *et al.* (1995). Intensities in these countries converge towards the 2020 levels of the OECD countries in proportion to the rate at which their 2020 per capita GDP approaches the 1990 per capita GDP of the OECD countries. By postulating convergence towards the 2020 OECD water use intensities, rather than 1990 levels, the algorithm allows for 'leapfrogging'; that is, the developing countries can take advantage of improved water use and industrial processing technologies that were not available to OECD countries during their earlier development stages (ibid.).

As can be seen in Table 5, the actual degree of convergence achieved during the 1995–2020 period is limited. Because of the very low 1995 income levels in most of the developing countries, only a relatively small portion of the income gap is closed by 2020, even with fast growth rates in income. The biggest improvement (and degree of convergence) in industrial withdrawal intensity will be in Southeast Asia, where the initial per capita income level is fairly high, and per capita income growth is fast: industrial water withdrawal intensity is expected to improve by 18 per cent, from 60 cubic metres to 49 cubic metres per US$1000. Even though all of the developing countries and regions will have equal, or improved, intensities by 2020, the figure for developing countries as a whole will be increasing from 40 to 43 cubic metres per US$1000, because the most rapid growth in industrial demand occurs in countries with high water use intensities, in particular China and India.

Global average water withdrawal for irrigation (computed by dividing agricultural withdrawal by irrigated area) was estimated to be 10 259 cubic metres per hectare, with slightly higher figures in developing than in developed countries. Although there is a fairly wide range of experience across regions, it is difficult to know whether such cross-country variation corresponds to differences in irrigation practices, or technology, or the cropping pattern used on irrigated areas. The domestic and industrial water withdrawals shown in Table 5 conform broadly to the expected cross-country pattern relative to levels of economic and technological development. However, it is not even clear what the expected cross-country pattern of irrigation withdrawals should be, since cross-section and time-series data are virtually non-existent.

There is technological potential for improved irrigation practices that would reduce water withdrawals per irrigated area, but there is little evidence that this is actually occurring. In the United States, where data are available, water withdrawals per hectare of irrigated area increased by 35 per cent between 1960 and 1975, declined by about 15 per cent from 1975 to 1980, increased again, and in 1990 was still higher than the 1975 level (Raskin *et al.*, 1995). Given limited and mixed evidence, irrigation withdrawals were assumed constant for the projections period. Globally, water withdrawals are projected to increase by 35 per cent by 2020, to 5060 billion cubic metres (BCM) (Table 6), with growth in developing countries much faster than in developed countries. Developed countries as a group will increase water demand by 22 per cent to 1710 BCM, more than 80 per cent of which will be for industrial uses. The serious pressure on water resources, however, will be in the developing world, where withdrawals are projected to increase dramatically, by 43 per cent, from 2347 BCM in 1995 to 3350 BCM in 2020. In sharp contrast to past growth patterns in developing countries, the absolute increase in domestic and industrial water demand will be greater than the increase in agricultural water demand, projected at 589 BCM and 415 BCM, respectively, from 1995 to 2020 (Table 6). The combined share of domestic and industrial use in total demand in developing countries will hence more than double, from 13 per cent to 27 per cent, representing a significant structural change in their patterns of water use.

China and Southeast Asia show the most dramatic transformation in water demand structure, driven by rapid economic growth and slower growth in

TABLE 6   *Global water withdrawals for domestic, industrial and agricultural uses, 1995 and projected 2020 (billion cubic metres)*

Country/region	1995				2020			
	Dom.	Ind.	Agr.	Tot.	Dom.	Ind.	Agr.	Tot.
China	30	35	439	504	101	146	465	712
India	18	24	564	607	69	91	755	916
Other East Asia	8	13	26	47	12	28	26	66
Other South Asia	6	6	308	321	20	21	364	405
Southeast Asia	27	29	169	225	57	112	189	358
Latin America	31	33	193	257	54	67	209	330
WANA	22	22	266	309	45	52	341	438
Sub-Saharan Africa	6	6	65	77	16	15	95	126
USA	64	221	207	492	78	305	215	598
Western Europe	36	125	95	256	36	195	98	329
Eastern Europe & CIS	37	146	270	453	43	208	284	535
Other developed	38	67	92	197	47	105	95	248
Developing	147	170	2 030	2 347	375	531	2 445	3 350
Developed	174	560	664	1 398	204	813	693	1 710
World	322	730	2 694	3 745	579	1 344	3 138	5 060

Sources: 1995 estimates from Raskin *et al.* (1997) and WRI (1994).

irrigated agriculture. China is projected to more than triple domestic use, and to increase industrial withdrawals fourfold. As a result, the combined share of domestic and industrial water demand in total demand will increase from 13 per cent in 1995 to 35 per cent in 2020 (Table 7). In Southeast Asia, a doubling of domestic water withdrawals and a 290 per cent increase in industrial demand will boost the combined share of these sectors in total water demand from 25 per cent in 1995 to 47 per cent in 2020. India is projected to have the largest absolute increase in water withdrawals in the world, at 309 BCM (virtually the same demand increment as for the developed world), owing to a combination of strong growth in domestic and industrial demand and relatively rapid expansion of use for irrigation. Total withdrawals in India will be up by 50 per cent from the 1995 levels, including a 34 per cent increase in those for agriculture, and a 280 per cent increase in the domestic and industrial sectors.

Meeting future water demands

Can the rapid growth in water demand, particularly in the domestic and industrial sectors, be met without massive transfers of water out of agriculture that could derail the projected growth in crop yield and area described? Development

TABLE 7   *Sectoral water withdrawals as a percentage of total withdrawals, 1995 and projected to 2020*

Country/region	1995			2020		
	Dom.	Ind.	Agr.	Dom.	Ind.	Agr.
China	6	7	87	14	21	65
India	3	4	93	8	10	82
Other East Asia	16	28	56	8	42	40
Other South Asia	2	2	96	5	5	90
Southeast Asia	12	13	75	16	31	53
Latin America	12	13	75	16	20	63
WANA	7	7	86	10	12	78
Sub-Saharan Africa	8	8	84	13	11	76
USA	13	45	42	13	51	36
Western Europe	14	49	37	11	59	30
Eastern Europe & CIS	8	32	60	8	39	53
Other developed	21	35	44	19	43	38
Developing	6	7	87	11	16	73
Developed	13	40	47	12	48	40
World	9	19	72	11	27	62

Source: 1995 estimates from WRI (1994).

of irrigation and water supplies has become increasingly expensive. In India and Indonesia, for example, the real costs of new irrigation have more than doubled since the late 1960s and early 1970s; costs have increased by more than 50 per cent in the Philippines; they have tripled in Sri Lanka and increased by 40 per cent in Thailand (Rosegrant and Svendsen, 1993). The cost of supplying water for household and industrial uses is also increasing rapidly. In Amman, Jordan, the average incremental cost of water from groundwater has been US$0.41 per cubic metre. However, with shortages of groundwater, the city has begun to rely on surface water, pumped with a lift of 1200 metres from a site 40km from the city, at an average incremental cost of US$1.33 per cubic metre. In Shenyang, China, the cost of new water supplies will nearly triple, from US$0.04 to US$0.11 per cubic metre between 1988 and 2000, because pollution of the current groundwater source will require a shift to water conveyed by gravity from a surface source 51km from the city. In Mexico City, water is currently being pumped over an elevation of 1000 metres into the Mexico Valley from the Cutzamala River through a pipeline about 180km long, at an average incremental water cost of US$0.82 per cubic metre. That is almost 55 per cent more than the previous source, the Mexico Valley aquifer (World Bank, 1993). Non-traditional sources of water are unlikely to be a major component of new water supplies. Desalination offers an infinite supply of freshwater, but at a high price, and will not be a significant factor in most regions. The reuse of waste water will similarly make an important contribution only in arid regions such as the Middle East, where the cost of new supplies is very high. Water harvesting (the capture and diversion of rainfall or floodwater to fields to irrigate crops) will be important in some local and regional ecosystems, but will not have a significant impact on global food production and water scarcity (Rosegrant, 1997).

If high costs of development choke off new sources of water, the rapidly growing household and industrial demand will need to be met increasingly from water savings from irrigated agriculture. A particularly difficult challenge will be to improve the efficiency of agricultural water use to maintain crop yields and output growth, while at the same time allowing reallocation of water from agriculture to rapidly growing urban and industrial uses. How this will be managed could determine the world's ability to feed itself.

To meet this enormous challenge, it will be necessary to generate physical savings of water and economic savings by increasing crop output per unit of evaporative loss, by increasing the utilization before it is lost to water 'sinks' and by reducing salinization and other pollution that diminishes crop yield per unit of water. It is unclear how large each of these potential water savings might be. Water use efficiency in irrigation in much of the developing world is typically in the range of 25 to 40 per cent, while in urban supply systems 'water unaccounted for' (much of which is direct loss to the oceans) is often 50 per cent or more in major metropolitan areas in developing countries (Rosegrant, 1997). These inefficiencies seem to imply the potential for huge savings from existing uses of water. However, the potential savings in many river basins are not as dramatic, nor as easy to achieve, as implied by these efficiency figures, because much of the water 'lost' from irrigation systems is reused elsewhere (Seckler, 1996). In these basins, efficiency gains from existing systems may prove to be limited, because whole-basin water use efficiencies are quite high as a result of recycling of drainage water, even though individual users are inefficient. For example, estimates of overall water use efficiencies for individual irrigation systems in the Nile Basin are as low as 30 per cent, but the overall efficiency for the entire Nile river basin is estimated at 80 per cent (Keller, 1992).

Important research remains to be done on the issue of physical and economic water savings. Definitive estimates of the potential for improving crop yields per unit of water applied, and the potential for maintaining crop productivity growth while transferring water out of agriculture, require basin-specific analysis, with aggregation to the global level to assess the likely effects on food security. Can significant real water savings be achieved through improved water management policies? What would be the impact on food production and food security of transfers of saved water out of agriculture?

Implications for water policy

Although important questions must still be answered, a clear place to start in seeking water savings, improving water use efficiency and boosting crop output per unit of water is the reforming of existing water policies that have contributed to the current predicament: both urban and rural water users are provided with massive subsidies on water use; irrigation water is essentially unpriced; in urban areas the price of water does not cover the cost of delivery; and capital investment decisions in all sectors are divorced from management of the resource. These water-wasting policies can be attacked through comprehensive reforms to improve the incentives at each level of the allocation process. Institutional and legal environment reforms must empower water users to make their own decisions regarding resource use, while at the same time providing a structure that reveals the real scarcity value of water. Key elements for reform include establishment of secure water rights to uses; decentralization and privatization of water management functions; and utilization of incentives including markets in tradable property rights, pricing reform and reduction in subsidies, and effluent or pollution charges. Non-market instruments, such as licensing and regulation, and direct interventions, such as conservation programmes, can also play an important role. Failure to address the increasing demand for water could significantly slow the growth in crop production in developing countries.

CONCLUSIONS

In this paper, projections of future global food demand and supply were confronted by possible future limitations on land and water resources. Cropland availability is not a significant impediment to future global food supply. The primary constraint to further crop area expansion is not a physical limit, but the anticipated continued decline of real cereal prices, which makes further expansion of cropland unprofitable. On a global basis, the impact of land degradation on yields is small compared to projections of crop yield growth due to technological change and increased efficiency of input use. Degradation should be attacked by correcting policy and institutional failures, especially the failure to establish secure rights to land, which leads to overuse or overextraction, and the lack of investment in efficient use and conservation of the resource; market and pricing failures, including inappropriate subsidies that fail to account for the external costs of different activities and decisions; and government failures, in terms of poorly managed bureaucracies, excessively extractive policies and inability to regulate environmental damage.

The rapid growth in water demand, particularly for domestic and industrial purposes, coupled with the escalating cost of development of new water sources, could be a more serious threat to future growth in food production. If high costs of new water resources require household and industrial demand to be met primarily through water savings from irrigated agriculture, projected growth in agricultural production could be threatened. Policy reforms will be urgently required to improve water use efficiency to maintain crop yields and output growth with less water. Key elements of these reforms closely parallel the necessary changes in land policy, such as the establishment of secure water rights to users; decentralization and privatization of water management functions; and utilization of incentives for water conservation, including markets in tradable water rights, pricing reform and reduction in subsidies, and effluent or pollution charges.

184   *Mark W. Rosegrant, Claudia Ringler and Roberta V. Gerpacio*

REFERENCES

Alt, K., Osborn, C. and Colaccio, D. (1989), *Soil Erosion: What Effect on Agricultural Productivity?*, Agriculture Information Bulletin No. 556, Economic Research Service, Washington, DC: United States Department of Agriculture.

Ayibotele, N.B. (1992), 'The World's Water: Assessing the Resource', Keynote Paper at the International Conference on Water and the Environment: Development Issues for the 21st Century, 26–31 January, Dublin.

Bhadra, D. and Brandão, A.S.P. (1993), *Urbanization, Agricultural Development and Land Allocation*, World Bank Discussion Paper No. 201, Washington, DC: World Bank.

Brown, L.R. (1995), *Who Will Feed China?: Wake-up Call for a Small Planet*, New York: W.W. Norton.

Brown, L.R. and Kane, H. (1994), *Full House: Reassessing the Earth's Population Carrying Capacity*, New York: W.W. Norton.

Buringh, P. and Dudal, R. (1987), 'Agricultural Land Use in Space and Time', in M.G. Wolman and F.G.A. Fournier (eds), *Land Transformation in Agriculture*, New York: John Wiley.

Byerlee, D. (1994), 'Technology Transfer Systems for Improved Crop Management: Lessons for the Future', in J.R. Anderson (ed.), *Agricultural Technology: Policy Issues for the International Community*, Wallingford: CAB International.

Clarke, R. (1993), *Water: The International Crisis*, Cambridge, MA: MIT Press.

Crosson, P. (1986), 'Sustainable Food Production: Interactions among Natural Resources, Technology and Institutions', *Food Policy*, **11**, 143–56.

Crosson, P. (1995), *Soil Erosion and its On-farm Productivity Consequences: What Do We Know?*, Discussion Paper 95–29, Washington, DC: Resources for the Future.

Crosson, P. and Anderson, J.R. (1992), *Resources and Global Food Prospects: Supply and Demand for Cereals to 2030*, Technical Paper 184, Washington, DC: World Bank.

FAO (Food and Agriculture Organization of the United Nations) (1997), 'FAOSTAT database. Production Domain, Land Use Domain', <http://apps.fao.org/default.htm>, Rome: FAO.

Gleick, P.H. (1996), 'Basic Water Requirements for Human Activities: Meeting Basic Needs', *Water International*, **21**, 83–92.

Keller, J. (1992), 'Implications of Improving Agricultural Water use Efficiency on Egypt's Water and Salinity Balances', in M. Abu-Zeid and D. Seckler (eds), *Roundtable on Egyptian Water Policy*, Proceedings of a seminar on Egyptian water policy, sponsored by the Water Research Center, the Ford Foundation and Winrock International, at the Hotel Helnan International Palestine in Alexandria, 11–13 April, Cairo: Water Research Centre, Ministry of Public Works and Water Resources.

Kendall, H.W. and Pimentel, D. (1994), 'Constraints on the Expansion of the Global Food Supply', *Ambio*, **23**, 198–205.

Lal, R. (1995), 'Erosion–Crop Productivity Relationships for Soils in Africa', *American Journal of Soil Science Society*, **59**, (3).

Linneman, H., De Hoogh, J., Keyser, M.A. and Van Heemst, H.D.J. (1979), 'Potential world food production', in *MOIRA. Model of International Relations in Agriculture. Report of the Project Group on Food for a Doubling World Population*, Amsterdam: North-Holland.

Luyten, J.C. (1995), *Sustainable World Food Production and Environment*, Rapport 37, Agricultural Research Department, Research Institute for Agrobiology and Soil Fertility, Wageningen: Agricultural University.

Moya, P.F., Pingali, P.L., Pabale, D.L., Gerpacio, R.V. and Masicat, P.B. (1994), 'Conversion of Agricultural Land to Urban Uses: Who Gains and Who Loses?', Social Sciences Division, International Rice Research Institute, Los Baños.

Oldeman, L.R., Hakkeling, R.T.A. and Sombroek, W.G. (1990), *World Map of the Status of Human-induced Soil Degradation: An Explanatory Note*, Wageningen: International Soil Reference and Information Centre and Nairobi: United Nations Environment Programme.

Penning de Vries, F.W.T., Van Keulen, H., Rabbinge, R. and Luyten, J.C. (1995), *Biophysical Limits to Global Food Production*, 2020 Vision Brief No. 18, Washington, DC: International Food Policy Research Institute.

Plucknett, D.L. (1995), 'Prospects of Meeting Future Foods Needs through New Technology', in Nurul Islam (ed.), *Population and Food in the Early Twenty-first Century: Meeting Future*

Food Demand of an Increasing Population, Washington, DC: International Food Policy Research Institute.

Raskin, P., Hansen, E. and Margolis, R. (1995), *Water and Sustainability: A Global Outlook*, PoleStar Series Report No. 4, Boston: Stockholm Environment Institute.

Raskin, P., Gleick, P., Kirshen, P., Pontius, G. and Strzepek, K. (1997), 'Water Futures: Assessment of Long-range Patterns and Problems', Background Document for Chapter 3 of *Comprehensive Assessment of the Freshwater Resources of the World*, Boston: Stockholm Environment Institute.

Rock, M. (1996), 'Water Use, Water Scarcity, Economic Development and Trade Policy', mimeo, Winrock International Institute for Agricultural Development, Morrilton.

Rosegrant, M.W. (1997), *Water Resources in the 21st-Century: Challenges and Implications for Action*, 2020 Vision for Food, Agriculture and the Environment Discussion Paper No. 20, Washington, DC: International Food Policy Research Institute.

Rosegrant, M.W. and Pingali, P.L. (1994), 'Policy and Technology for Rice Productivity Growth in Asia', *Journal of International Development*, **6**, 665–88.

Rosegrant, M.W. and Svendsen, M. (1993), 'Asian Food Production in the 1990s: Irrigation Investment and Management Policy', *Food Policy*, **18** (2), 13–32.

Rosegrant, M.W., Agcaoili-Sombilla, M. and Perez, N.D. (1995), *Global Food Projections to 2020: Implications for Investment*, 2020 Vision for Food, Agriculture and the Environment Discussion Paper No. 5, Washington, DC: International Food Policy Research Institute.

Scherr, S. and Yadav, S. (1996), *Land Degradation in the Developing World: Implications for Food, Agriculture and the Environment to 2020*, 2020 Vision for Food, Agriculture and the Environment Discussion Paper No. 14, Washington, DC: International Food Policy Research Institute.

Seckler, D. (1996), *The New Era of Water Resource Management: From 'Dry' to 'Wet' Water Savings*, Research Report No. 1, Colombo: International Irrigation Management Institute.

Tyler, P.E. (1995), 'On the Farms, China Could Be Sowing Disaster', *The New York Times*, 10 April.

UN (United Nations) (1996), *World Population Prospects: The 1996 Revision*, Population Division, Department for Economic and Social Information and Policy Analysis, New York: United Nations.

USAID (1988), *Urbanization in the Developing Countries*, Interim report to Congress, Washington, DC: U.S. Aid.

World Bank (1993), *Water resources management*, World Bank Policy Study, Washington, DC: World Bank.

WRI (World Resources Institute) (1994), *World Resources 1994–95*, New York: Oxford University Press.

WRI (World Resources Institute) (1996), *World Resources 1996–97*, New York: Oxford University Press.

DARWIN C. HALL*

Impacts of Global Warming on Agriculture

The full and proper name for us is *Homo sapiens sapiens*, a kind of taxonomic stutter meaning 'double-wise man'. (James Shreeve, *The Neandertal Enigma*, p. 8)

INTRODUCTION

As Shreeve (1995) goes on to point out, our genus *Homo* includes several species that coexisted in pre-history 'carry[ing] no wisdom at all in their names' (p. 9). Are we now wise enough to recognize the bounds of our knowledge, our ignorance? There is the story of the drunk looking for car keys under the street lamp, rather than back in the alley where he heard them drop in the dark. When asked why he was looking in the wrong place, he replied that he could only look where he could see.

The best work done to date to illuminate future patterns of warming couples ocean and air general circulation models (GCMs) of the globe to project regional climates, based upon the assumption that the ambient concentration of CO_2 equivalent gases will double from the level before the Industrial Revolution, causing the radiative forcing of the atmosphere to increase (IPCC, 1996). Using their output from the GCMs as input for crop simulation models (CSMs), Rosenzweig and Parry (1994) and Adams *et al.* (1988, 1990, 1995a, 1995b) have projected the changes in regional potential yield and product; Adams *et al.* (1995b) include wheat, corn, soybeans, oranges, tomatoes, pasture, range land and livestock. Using output from CSMs as input to non-linear programming models of the United States and models of international agricultural trade, they have estimated changes in the net producer and consumer surpluses from a doubling of CO_2 equivalent gases. But there is no reason to expect that the ambient concentration of gases will double from our economic activities. A doubling will simply be a transitory state during a rapid expansion to well beyond that level.

Less compelling is the work by Mendelsohn *et al.* (1994), Williams *et al.* (1996), and Mendelsohn and Nordhaus (1996), who use a quadratic function to regress about 300 cross-section county land values (land and buildings per acre) on 30-year weighted (by location of weather station) county averages for temperature and precipitation (January, April, July and October), and on county averages for soil type (sand, clay, moisture capacity, permeability), physical

*California State University, Long Beach, USA. Jane V. Hall is thanked for her assistance.

186

characteristics of the land (solar flux – latitude, altitude, salinity, flood-prone, wetland, soil erosion, slope length), income per capita and population density. The regressors are in deviations from the mean. They use weighted least squares, so their model is given by

$$Y_i / w_i = \alpha / w_i + \beta X_i / w_i + \varepsilon_i / w_i \qquad (1)$$

They propose two sets of weights, based on cropland or on revenue. The cropland weights are county agricultural land as a percentage of total land in the county. The crop-revenue weights are county agricultural revenue as a percentage of total US agricultural revenue. Mendelsohn *et al.* (1994) then forecast land values, given an increase in temperature of 2.78°C and rainfall of 8 per cent, uniformly across the United States and uniformly across the seasons. The change in land values is their estimate of the impact on land rent from a doubling of CO_2 equivalent gases. Williams *et al.* (1996) extend this analysis by forecasting the change in land values based upon temperature and precipitation data forecasts that vary by region and season, where the weather data are forecasts from 16 GCMs calibrated for a doubling of CO_2 equivalent gases. Among other problems with this general approach, a doubling will simply be a transitory state during a rapid expansion to well beyond that level.

Figure 1 presents three projections of atmospheric CO_2 concentrations (in ppmv). Each one is a combination of one of three models of the economy (Nordhaus and Yohe, 1983; Reilly *et al.*, 1987; Manne and Richels, 1990); one of three assumptions about the amount of economically available coal (from

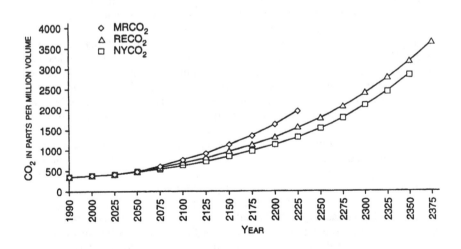

FIGURE 1   *Ambient CO_2 for three scenarios without policy intervention*

Edmonds and Reilly, 1985); and one of three assumptions relating to the sensitivity of climate to a doubling of emissions. The high, mid-range and low projections assume that the economically available coal reserves, respectively, are 20 000, 15 000 and 9500 gigatons (gt.). The computations follow those of Cline (1992). The ambient concentration of CO_2 is projected to rise from that of about 350ppmv in 1990, to a range of values: for the three projections, 1925, 2830 and 3635ppmv, increases of 550, 800 and over 1000 per cent. This is why analysis based upon a doubling of gas concentrations is like the drunk looking for his keys under the street lamp.

The IPCC (1990) report concluded that a doubling of emissions would increase the mean global temperature in the range of 1.5 to 4.5°C, with a mid-range value of 3.0 to 3.5°C. Lags between emissions and changes in equilibrium global temperature and the effects of aerosols, which are emitted when coal is burned (among other sources), help to explain discrepancies between actual temperature today and GCM projections of what should have occurred as a result of the emission of gases since the Industrial Revolution. The IPCC (1996, WG I, p. 39; WG III, p. 188) report suggests that there may be a transient effect which has lowered the sensitivity of warming to the range of 1.0 to 3.5°C, with a mid-range of 2.0°C. In their reply to Cline (1996), Mendelsohn and Nordhaus (1996) justify having used too low a temperature increase (2.78°C) relative to the mid-range values of 3.0 to 3.5°C as a downward adjustment of the warming to account for aerosols, although this adjustment is transient because the aerosols are not long-lived like CO_2. With a downward adjustment of Cline's (1992) computations, the warming for the three scenarios is projected in Figure 2 (Hall, 1996a). Since the transient nature of aerosols is ignored, downward adjustment makes these projections too low.

Figure 3 juxtaposes the mean global temperature of the last quarter-million years with a conditional prediction of the next two to four hundred years. The basis for the prediction is that we continue to use the economically available fossil fuels, rather than fashioning policies to bear the expense of research, development and substitution of alternative energy technologies for fossil fuels. Figure 3 shows the bounds of our ignorance. During the last quarter-million years, *Homo sapiens* evolved into *Homo sapiens sapiens*. Our species has experienced neither the abruptness nor the magnitude of the warming to come.

Over the last 5 million years, the ecosystem in Africa shifted from woodlands to grasslands, and the first hominids emerged, including *Australopithecus*, branching into *Homo*. Looking back in time even that far, the earth did not experience a climate as warm as the mid-range projection in Figures 2 and 3. The 'geo-economic time frame' (Hall, 1996a), when the earth was as warm as projected in Figure 2, extends back 50 to 100 million years to the Cretaceous period, the age of dinosaurs (Crowley, 1996). It is in this context that I will risk illuminating the impact of global warming on agriculture.

The pathways through which global warming is expected to affect agriculture, and adaptations expected to mitigate the impacts, are discussed in the next section. It is followed by a summary of the results of a few of the better known estimates of the impact on agriculture from a doubling of CO_2 equivalent gases. These are the comparative static analyses noted above. The approach by Mendelsohn and Nordhaus cannot be extended to a comparative dynamic

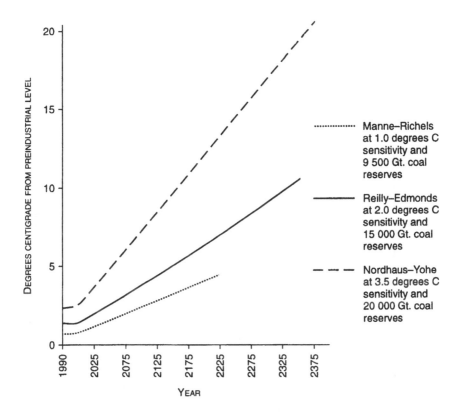

FIGURE 2   *Mean global temperature increase*

Note: Based upon the IPCC sensitivity of 1.5°C to 4.5°C, Cline (1992) extended
three models (Manne and Richels, 1990; Nordhaus and Yohe, 1983; Reilly
et al., 1987) to the next 375 years. This figure adjusts down Cline's analysis
to account for the lower sensitivity of an increase between 1.0°C and 3.5°C
for a doubling of warming gases in the atmosphere. The computations
follow those of Cline (1992).

analysis, but the approach by Rosenzweig and Adams can. Later the work of
Adams *et al.* (1995b) is extended to regimes beyond a doubling, presenting the
comparative dynamics in the form of time paths projecting the impact on
agriculture from anthropogenic increases in greenhouse gases. Possible outcomes are illustrated, though it is next argued that the outcomes are optimistic.

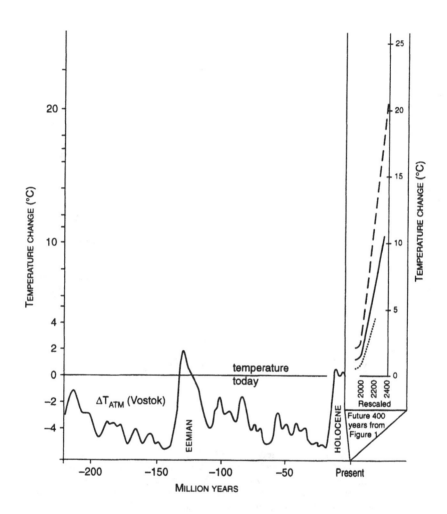

FIGURE 3   *Past and future mean global temperature*

Source: Adapted from IPCC (1996) and Figure 1.

PATHWAYS OF EFFECTS AND ADAPTIVE RESPONSES

The impact of global warming on agriculture stems from effects on the process
of photosynthesis (Rich, 1996; Rosenzweig and Hillel, 1995). In very broad
outline, the Calvin cycle is one in which plants draw moisture and nutrients from
the soil. Atmospheric CO_2 passes through stomata in the leaves and combines

with water to produce carbohydrates (sugar, starches and cellulose). The green colour in plants comes from chlorophyll molecules, similar to haemoglobin that gives blood its red colour, which are made of proteins. Amino acids are the primary units of proteins. Each amino acid has at least one carboxyl (COOH) group, which is basic, and the acid, or amine, is derived from ammonia, NH_3. Chlorophyll molecules are arranged in chloroplasts (organelles inside plant cells), which contain manganese, sulphur, iron, copper and phosphorus, in combination with other essential elements necessary for photosynthesis. Within chlorophyll molecules, light is altered to produce an electric charge. In the presence of CO_2, H_2O is broken down by electrolysis, and the result is sucrose, starches and oxygen. An oversimplified model is given by $6CO_2 + 6H_2O = C_6H_{12}O_6 + 6O_2$. Oxygen and water are transpired through the stomata.

The opposite of photosynthesis is respiration. For energy, animals burn sugar; oxygen is combined with hydrocarbons, releasing energy and CO_2. Plants use energy to draw water and nutrients from the soil, to grow and reproduce, to store energy, and in the process of photosynthesis. Photorespiration decreases the efficiency of photosynthesis, particularly at high temperatures, or when a plant is water-stressed and the stomates close to avoid loss of water by transpiration. Nutrients from the soil include nitrogen, phosphorus and potassium. When plants die, some of the carbon originating from the atmosphere is sequestered underground in the form of hydrocarbons. Fossil fuels contain atmospheric CO_2 from billions of years of photosynthesis; the atmosphere now has significantly more oxygen and less CO_2 than it once had.

Within the next 200 to 400 years, we can release billions of years' worth of stored carbon by burning coal. As atmospheric CO_2 rises, the stomata do not have to open as wide for plants to obtain it for photosynthesis. Consequently, less water is transpired. Soil moisture is used more efficiently, with less lost to the atmosphere from transpiration. So there is a beneficial interaction in the productivity of water and ambient CO_2. If nutrients and soil moisture are available, photosynthesis should increase, with a higher concentration, which is the CO_2 'fertilization effect' that is expected to accompany global warming. However, increased cloud cover would be expected to reflect and reduce the solar radiation, reducing the amount of light available for photosynthesis.

Plants, which have adapted the process of photosynthesis to different climates, are categorized by the number of carbon atoms that are fixed in the first stage of photosynthesis. C3 crops include wheat, rice, soybeans, fine grains, legumes, root crops and most trees. They should benefit most from CO_2 fertilization. Many tropical and subtropical plants in the C4 category (corn, sorghum, sugarcane, millet) have adapted to the heat by fixing carbon at night, and closing the stomata during the day.

As the global temperature increases, the growing season will increase in mid- and high-latitude regions, which should increase yields for small increases in temperature. At the same time, plant growth cycles will speed up, with an adverse effect on yield. At higher temperatures, photorespiration will reduce yields. Depending on the ability of soil types to hold and retain moisture, moderate increases in precipitation will improve yield. Even under optimal conditions, at some level further precipitation decreases yield, owing to root rot and interference with nutrient uptake.

Farmers have learned to adapt crops to different regional climates with pesticides, fertilizers and irrigation. We can expect that, as climate changes, regional and international trade will allow shifts of crop production to those regions where they are best suited. Regions now not suitable for growing crops will become major centres of production, and crop migration will occur to the extent that soils and terrain are suitable. Over time, countries with significant research infrastructure will develop crop varieties to take advantage of higher CO_2 concentration, to withstand higher temperatures and better fit changes in the growing season, and to adapt to water stress in regions with less precipitation.

UNDER THE STREET LAMP

It is believed that a doubling of emitted gases may be beneficial for the United States and other mid-latitude countries, but horrific for some developing poor countries. In their excellent article, Rosenzweig and Parry (1994) estimate the worldwide number of people at risk of hunger, accounting for food prices and income relative to nutritional requirements, as a result of global warming from a doubling of CO_2 equivalent gases. Their estimates are based on crop simulation models applied and calibrated for 18 countries and regions worldwide. The CSMs account for increased rates of photosynthesis and reduction in stomata reported from laboratory experiments, where plants are provided with ideal combinations of water and nutrients to maximize the benefit, as well as for temperature increases that can alter the period of the growing season, shorten the time during crop development stages and cause heat and water stress. The CSMs also incorporate the impact of precipitation on yields and deal with the impact of seasonal and geographic changes in temperature and precipitation, as well as looking at the effects of increasing ambient CO_2, based upon forecasts from three GCMs. Farm-level adaptations appear which involve altering planting and harvesting dates, crop and variety switching, and applications of fertilizer and irrigation in response to changes in precipitation. World trade is incorporated using a linked set of 34 economic models in a general equilibrium system, linking trade, prices and financial flows. In order to compare situations 'with' and 'without' global warming, growth rates for population, GDP and crop yield are used to estimate a base case for the year 2060, when a CO_2 equivalent doubling is forecast to occur. The mean global temperature increases from the GCMs are 4.2, 4.0, and 5.2°C, with growth in average global precipitation of 11, 8 and 15 per cent, respectively.

Depending on the GCM forecast, world cereal production falls between 11 and 20 per cent, but most of these losses are made up through CO_2 fertilization, and a small additional mitigation is achieved through adaptation. The distribution of effects, however, adversely affects 60 to 360 million additional people who are at risk of hunger. Even so, the predictions are optimistic in several respects, which Rosenzweig and Parry carefully acknowledge. A review of the logic underpinning the economic calculus reveals the nature of the optimism.

Mendelsohn *et al.* (1994) use cross-section data and regress farm land value on temperature and rainfall, using a quadratic function to capture the possibility that, beyond some temperature and rainfall, the third stage of production may be reached, with detrimental effects. Using the least squares technique shown in equation (1), they estimate that global warming will increase land rent when the analysis is based on crop revenue weights. These are claimed to be superior to the cropland weights, use of which suggests that global warming will decrease land rent. The estimated rent is taken to be the present value of future producer surplus, in what is termed a 'Ricardian approach'.

Cline (1996) criticizes Mendelsohn *et al.* (1994) for 'seriously understating greenhouse damage for three main reasons': the conceptual framework, infinitely elastic supply of water at today's prices and the assumption that mean global warming and precipitation is uniform across the United States at only 2.78°C for a doubling. Cline expands the 'conceptual framework' criticism by suggesting that (1) the Ricardian approach is 'a partial equilibrium analysis that assumes relative prices are unchanged' and food demand is inelastic, and (2) the Ricardian model implicitly assumes that, as US grain production declines, somewhere else in the world there is an equivalent increase.

Mendelsohn and Nordhaus (1996) respond first by calculating the percentage of bias introduced by ignoring demand and supply elasticity, showing that only if demand is highly elastic and supply highly inelastic will the bias be large. For inelastic demand, the bias is less than 2.3 per cent for a 25 per cent reduction in yield. They ignore the criticism that grain production needs to come from somewhere. In their second riposte, Mendelsohn and Nordhaus claim that Cline is wrong about the infinitely elastic supply of irrigation water. The Ricardian approach implicitly assumes that land value reflects cross-sectional water availability conditioned on existing precipitation and temperature across countries. So a hotter, drier climate produces water availability that mirrors the amounts available in the hotter, drier western United States today. This is a weak response. When El Niño sends warm storms to California, the snow melt can double or even triple the water flow, so that reservoirs cannot be kept filled to provide summer irrigation because a reserve capacity must be maintained for flood control. Since the snow is melted by the storms, it turns to storm run-off, losing that means of storing water on the mountain tops. The marginal cost of water is steep in the southwestern United States (Hall, 1996b) and clearly shifts upward with warming.

Mendelsohn and Nordhaus then cite Williams *et al.* (1996) in response to Cline's third criticism. Williams *et al.* re-estimate quadratic equations using cross-section data in the same manner as Mendelsohn *et al.* (1994). They regress county land values on weather, soil and socioeconomic variables, using weighted regression as given in equation (1) above, with quadratic forms. Then they estimate the impact of global warming on land rent, using the seasonal and regional dispersed temperature and precipitation changes from 16 GCMs. The average of those results differs slightly from the original results in Mendelsohn *et al.* (1994). There is an increase in revenue-weighed results over their original values, with a decrease in cropland-weighted results. In their reply to Cline, Mendelsohn and Nordhaus (1996) claim, 'the average results from the GCMs are consistent with a uniform change scenario of 4.5°C, which is the average predicted temperature change from these global climate models' (p. 1313). This is a misleading claim: the mean global temperature increase in the 16 GCMs averages less than 3.5°C, according to my calculation from the Appendix of Williams *et al.* (1996). Perhaps Mendelsohn and Nordhaus (1996) are referring to the average increase in the United States, a mid-latitude country which is expected to warm by more than the global average.

Mendelsohn and Nordhaus (1996) also point out that their favourable results could be even better because of the moderating influence of aerosols on temperature, and the benefits of CO_2 fertilization. While it is true that aerosols will moderate temperature in regions that burn coal and have high levels of tropospheric air pollution, it is also true that sulphur compounds and ozone reduce agricultural yields (Adams, 1986). Moreover, the effect of aerosols on cloud formation and precipitation affects solar flux and soil moisture, with impacts on photosynthesis. It is not clear that, on the balance of effects, aerosols will increase yields. Most importantly, the 'Ricardian approach' they use cannot be adjusted to capture the important effects of soil moisture, solar flux and CO_2 fertilization. This weakness is critical, since Rosenzweig and Parry (1994) have shown that fertilization is more important than adaptation, the sole claim of superiority of the 'Ricardian approach'.

Finally, Mendelsohn and Nordhaus (1996) cite Reilly's (1996) survey which argues that, compared with earlier estimates from CSMs, the later results based on CSMs with adaptation have results closer to those of Mendelsohn and Nordhaus. They cite Adams *et al.* (1995b) as an example. The logic behind the Ricardian approach is that farmers adapt their methods and techniques to different local climate conditions, just as farmers will adapt to future climate change. I agree that farmers will adapt to future climate change, but not in the ways that farmers adapt to local climate conditions. For example, if the grainbelt becomes hot and dry, the models of Mendelsohn *et al.* predict that the central portion of the United States will have land values like portions of Arizona and Texas, where cotton is produced. We will have plenty to wear and houses in which to retire, but nothing to eat. Mendelsohn *et al.* (1994) do not account for demand, our preference for a varied diet. According to these comparative static, Ricardian models, we will also be able costlessly to build irrigation systems in the grainbelt and operate them as we do in Arizona and California today. For example, when the ambient concentration of CO_2 equivalent gases quintuples, as opposed to doubling, land values will plummet to levels now prevailing in Central America, but Mendelsohn *et al.* omit that possibility. Williams *et al.* (1996) complain that regression coefficients show that land values are sensitive to August precipitation rates, particularly in the grainbelt, so aggregation of economic impacts using acreage as weights gives large damages for some GCM climate forecasts. But GCMs do not project the frequency of droughts or monsoons as a function of global warming. 'Ricardian models' forecast minimal damage from global warming, while failing to consider the essential elements that will determine the outcome.

There are three further criticisms of the work done by Mendelsohn and Nordhaus. One is that the weights chosen for equation (1) must not be correlated with the dependent variable, or they will introduce bias in the estimates. Indeed, crop revenue is correlated with land rent. Only expensive items like strawberries are grown near urban centres, while the last bit of speculative value is wrung from the land. The crop revenue weights introduce bias in the estimation. Interestingly, the results from the crop revenue approach are consistently different from the coefficients estimated using cropland weights. In fact, the estimated impact from global warming is negative using the latter weights, and positive using the former.

The second criticism is that land rents capture producer surplus. Global warming can reduce yield, increasing producer surplus, but reducing total surplus, a well known and well studied phenomenon in agriculture. The third and most important criticism is that the Ricardian approach has nothing to say about dynamics. What we want to know is the impact of global warming on agriculture. A comparative static analysis could answer the hypothetical, 'What if global warming were imposed on agriculture today and the agricultural industry were able to respond instantaneously and move to a new equilibrium?'

It is not enough to say that research and development will allow us to adapt to warming. Presumably, without warming, research and development would continue to improve yields. We want to estimate the impact of warming, not compare agriculture today with a warmer future. A second comparative static analysis could answer the hypothetical, 'What if global warming were imposed on agriculture between now and the year 2060 and the agricultural industry were over time able to respond and move to a new equilibrium?' That is what Rosenzweig and Parry (1994) do. Their counterfactual requires the construction of an estimate of agricultural surplus without warming, to compare it with agricultural surplus with warming.

In summary, the only advantage of the Ricardian approach is that it captures the effect of adaptation. It does not account for international trade, CO_2 fertilization or dynamics. In comparison, Mendelsohn and Nordhaus (1996) acknowledge that the alternative approach of linking CSMs with models of the agricultural economy has now captured adaptation and has results comparable to their own. They cite Adams *et al.* (1995b) as an example. This latter approach can account for international trade and CO_2 fertilization, and can be extended to comparative dynamics.

A comparative dynamic analysis can answer the question we are really interested in, without straining reason by ignoring global warming after the year 2060. The Ricardian approach forces the analyst to forget that a doubling of CO_2 equivalent gases will simply be a transitory state during a rapid expansion to well beyond that level. Intoxicated with analytical and computational prowess, the analyst ignores the fundamental feature of global warming, which is a continual, though potentially discontinuous, change. A Ricardian analysis, based upon a doubling of CO_2 equivalent gases, is like the drunk looking for his keys under the street lamp.

IN THE DARK ALLEY WITH ROSE-COLOURED GLASSES

In this section, I use data generated by Adams *et al.* (1995b) to study the comparative dynamics of the impact of global warming on US agriculture. I first discuss the work by Adams *et al.* and how they generated the data. Then I estimate a dynamic representation of agricultural surplus that depends on the time path for climate change. I previously adjusted Cline's (1992) analysis, lowering the projected mean global temperature to account for aerosols (Hall, 1996a). Using these projections of climate, I calculate time paths for agricultural surplus, with and without climate change.

The Adams *et al.* (1995b) report is the culmination to date of their previous work (Rosenzweig and Parry, 1994; Adams *et al.*, 1988, 1990, 1995a). Their approach is to combine GCMs with dynamic growth CSMs, and introduce changes in crop yields into an economic quadratic programming model. They compare regional climate predictions from different GCMs, to consider the possibilities of a milder, wetter climate compared to a drier, hotter climate. The CSMs were originally for soybeans, corn and wheat (Adams *et al.*, 1990), but later (Adams *et al.*, 1995b) cotton, potatoes, tomatoes and citrus fruit, forage and livestock were added. The CSMs account for solar radiation, precipitation, temperature, soil properties that capture moisture, and the enhanced yield 'fertilizing effect' of increased carbon dioxide in the atmosphere. The results from the CSMs are extrapolated to other crops in the economic model.

In their update, Adams *et al.* (1995a) correct their previous analysis to account for the difference between ambient CO_2 and a CO_2 equivalent doubling, a correction discussed in Cline (1992). They clarify that the convention of a doubling is from the pre-Industrial Revolution level of 280ppmv. The GCM studies vary in the level of CO_2 equivalent increases, from 600ppmv to 640ppmv. They perform a sensitivity analysis of the CO_2 fertilization effect, considering no increase in ambient CO_2, an increase to 440ppmv, and an increase to 555ppmv. For reference, in 1990 the level was 353ppmv.

Adams *et al.* (1995b) consider 64 climate configurations: precipitation changes (−10, 0, 7 and 15 per cent), temperature changes (0, 1.5, 2.5 and 5.0°C) and ambient CO_2 fertilization (355, 440, 530 and 600ppmv). Each configuration is assumed to spread uniformly across the United States. For each region, they change present climate data by these amounts and run the crop simulation models. In addition, they run the CSMs for regional climate changes predicted by two GCMs.

The CSMs project the impact of warming, depending on the agricultural product (Adams *et al.*, 1995b). The speed of wheat, corn and soybean crop development increases with temperature, causing yield decreases and higher water demand. Increases in ambient CO_2 decrease water demand by increasing the efficiency of water use. Cotton has decreased yield from temperature, since it reaches maturity in fewer days, but increased yield from precipitation. For irrigated areas, no change in cotton yield is expected from changing precipitation. Similarly, potatoes, tomatoes and citrus fruits are modelled to have no effect from precipitation since they are irrigated. Increases in citrus yield were assumed, although the reason is 'poorly substantiated in the present literature' (ibid., p. 10). Temperature decreases citrus yield in the south and increases yield in the north because of the loss of a suitable dormant period, but the sandy soils do not exist in the north, constraining potential migration. Potato yields fall with temperature, and rise with CO_2. Tomato yields increase with CO_2 and with temperature up to +1.5 to 2.5 degrees, then fall.

Adams *et al.* use two CSMs for forage production and livestock, one for the more arid west of the United States and another for the east. These were calibrated for various locations, using existing weather data to get a baseline prediction and then modifying the amounts of precipitation and temperature. For example, changes in precipitation were 'applied uniformly to each monthly value' (ibid., p. 16). The impacts varied by location, generally with increases in precipitation and CO_2 fertilization raising yields, but with mixed effects for temperature, depending on the existing level and the size of the increase. On balance, increases in yields are predicted; where there were reductions they were small reductions (ibid., p. 15), but in other locations rather large increases are projected, depending on the climate configuration. Direct effects on livestock include appetite-suppressing temperature increases, and decreased energy needed in the winter to stay warm. On balance, livestock production falls.

Adams *et al.* allow for changes in technology and adaptation. There will be adjustments to warming. Research will develop heat and drought-tolerant varieties, while farmers will adjust inputs and the timing of planting and harvesting. Crop migration may occur unless constrained by soil barriers that cause significant yield losses. Adams *et al.* rely on time-series regression to relate improvements in yields over time and with crop migration, with cross-section regression accounting for adjustments and adaptation of farmers to regional differences. The crop simulation results are compared with the regression of county yield on temperature and precipitation. Yields do not fall as much with increases in temperature (but that could be due to correlation with solar radiation). For some regions, wheat yields rise and then fall with temperature. Regressions show yields rising with precipitation, but not by as much as projected by CSMs. Yields fall with April precipitation, reflecting the monsoon effect. Intense precipitation damages crops. On the basis of their examination of these results, Adams *et al.* assume that at least 50 per cent of the damage from 2.5°C mean global warming can be mitigated through soil amendments, irrigation, crop migration and technological change. For 5°C, they assume 25 per cent mitigation of yield losses.

The economic model accounts for differences in crop demand, precipitation, costs of surface and ground water, crop selection to maximize consumer and producer surplus, costs of feed for livestock as a secondary industry, plus regional and international trade. It allows for future trends of basic variables, based upon those over the past 40 years, to account for increase in demand through population growth, quantities of inputs, and import levels and supplies. Inputs are adjusted to account for changes in yields over time. Forecasts are developed for the years 1990 and 2060, with and without the effects of climate change discussed next.

The authors then calculate net consumer and producer surplus for each region of the United States, as given in the economic model, and sum the impacts to obtain an aggregate for the United States (including foreign consumer surplus for exports). The exercise is repeated for each of the 64 climate combinations. For each year, 1990 and 2060, they then regress the economic value against precipitation, temperature and ambient CO_2, using a quadratic form, and also a simple analysis of variance. The result is a climate change response function. For each climate combination, they compare the predicted net surplus with the prediction conditioned on 353 ppmv of CO_2 (today's ambient concentration), with no change in precipitation or in temperature. The 1990 regression results amount to a comparative static experiment similar to that of Mendelsohn and Nordhaus (1996), predicting the impact of climate change if it were imposed on agriculture today, and the agricultural industry could instantaneously respond. The 2060 regression results are equivalent to the comparative static experiment of imposing climate change over time, with research and development to adapt, and comparing agricultural surplus in 2060 to the 2060 surplus if there were no warming, but with research and development continuing to improve yields.

The comparative static results for 1990 conditions are smaller relative to those for the year 2060. The impact of global warming is larger given the adjustments for technology and economic conditions. Whether the impact is positive or negative depends on the climate configuration. Overall, it is suggested that the impact is positive, but there are some cases in which the opposite result is obtained.

I use the data generated by Adams *et al.* (1995b) from both years simultaneously, 1990 and 2060, to estimate a generalized power function (GPF), which is of the form:

$$Y = \beta_0 X_1^{\beta X} X_2^{\beta X} \dots X_N^{\beta X} \exp(\phi X + \varepsilon) \tag{2}$$

where β and ϕ are vectors. This function is quite general (de Janvry, 1972). A simple version is given by:

$$Y = \beta_0 X^{\beta 1 + \beta 2 X} \exp(\beta_3 X + \varepsilon) \tag{3}$$

If $\beta_2 = 0$, this function has the desirable property that the marginal surplus of the climate input variable can take on 15 shapes (see Table 1), only four of which are consistent with theory. For each case in Table 1, the results are shown in Figure 4. The hypotheses to be tested allow for rejection of the functional form.

The alternative shapes of the functions are consistent with the hypothesized impacts of precipitation, temperature and ambient CO_2 on agricultural surplus. Moreover, it is possible to specify interaction terms, for example, accounting for increased efficiency in water use as emissions increase. Finally, technical change can be both embodied and disembodied, affecting all inputs equally, or having an influence through one or more of the inputs.

TABLE 1   *Correspondence among coefficients in equation (3) and 15 cases in Figure 4 ($\beta_2 = 0$)*

	$\beta_3 < 0$	$\beta_3 = 0$	$\beta_3 > 0$
$\beta_1 < 0$	11	12	13
$\beta_1 = 0$	21	22	23
$0 < \beta_1 < 1$	31	32	33
$\beta_1 = 1$	41	43	43
$\beta_1 > 1$	51	52	53

Since a power function cannot include zero values for the explanatory variables, the Adams *et al.* data cannot be used directly and base case values for
surplus, temperature and precipitation must be added. These were 15°C and 50
inches, respectively. (The mean global temperature is now estimated at about

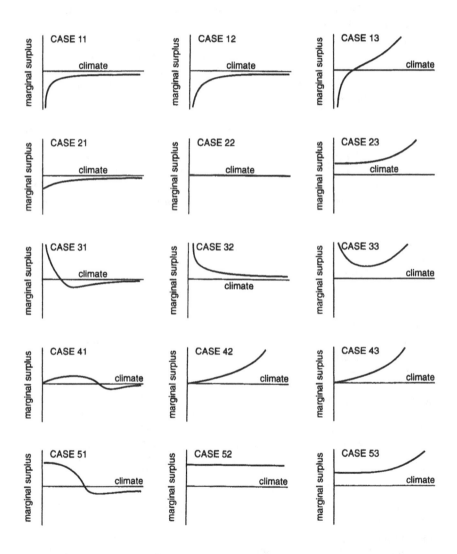

FIGURE 4   *Shapes of the GPF marginal surplus curves*

Note: Each case corresponds to values of the parameters given in Table 1.

200 *Darwin C. Hall*

15°C: IPCC, 1990, p. xxxvii). Adams *et al.* use a linear-dummy variable specification to estimate the impact of temperature, precipitation and CO_2 fertilization effect on total surplus (consumer, producer, foreign) for the United States. The intercept coefficient in Adams *et al.* (1995b, Appendix Table 3) is 1239.412, which I take to be the value of surplus for US agriculture, measured in dollars of 1990 purchasing power. Similarly, the intercept coefficient in year 2060 is 1750.594 in Hall (1996a, Appendix Table 4), which I take to be the total surplus in the base case for the year 2060 in similar units.

After considering alternative specifications, I chose the model with the best fit that also conserves parsimony and in which all terms are statistically signifi-cant. In this specification, there is an interaction term between CO_2 fertilization and precipitation, and there is both technical change embodied in CO_2 and disembodied technical change:

$$S = \beta_0 P^{\beta_1} T^{\beta_2} C^{\beta_3} \exp(\beta_4 P \cdot C + \beta_5 T + \beta_6 C \cdot Y + \beta_7 Y + \varepsilon) \quad (4)$$

where S = producer plus consumer plus foreign surplus, P = precipitation, T = temperature in °C, C = ambient CO_2 in ppmv of carbon, and Y = number of years (set to zero for 1990, increasing by one for each five-year period of the analysis). After taking logs of both sides, equation (4) is estimated, with the results presented in Table 2.

After estimating the parameters, the predicted values for the surplus are generated for the base case with no global warming, and for the three global warming scenarios computed in Hall (1996a), based on the work of Cline (1992): MR, RE and NY. The MR scenario couples the Manne–Richels (1990)

TABLE 2 *Regression results*

Variable	Coefficient	Std Error	t-Statistic	Prob.
C	3.252285	0.599388	5.426006	0.0000
LNP	0.260045	0.049319	5.272713	0.0000
P*CO$_2$	−6.57E-06	1.94E-06	−3.384783	0.0010
LNT	0.975737	0.221270	4.409707	0.0000
T	−0.063395	0.012682	−4.999005	0.0000
LNCO$_2$	0.216033	0.046847	4.611487	0.0000
Y*CO$_2$	3.32E-06	1.66E-06	2.006004	0.0471
Y	0.023649	0.000813	29.09319	0.0000

R-squared	0.995771	Mean dependent var.	7.299164
Adjusted R-squared	0.995522	S.D. dependent var.	0.179658
S.E. of regression	0.012022	Akaike info. criterion	−8.781129
Sum squared resid.	0.017199	Schwarz criterion	−8.601968
Log likelihood	385.3965	F-statistic	4002.918
Durbin–Watson stat.	1.650496	Prob. (F-statistic)	0.000000

Note: Dependent variable is LNS; number of observations: 127.

macromodel with a low climate sensitivity to greenhouse gases of a 1.0°C mean global temperature increase for a doubling of CO_2 equivalent gases, and a low estimate of 9500gt. of economically available coal. The RE scenario couples the macromodel of Reilly *et al.* (1987) with a climate sensitivity of 2.0°C and a mid-range estimate of 15 000gt. of coal. The NY scenario couples the Nordhaus–Yohe (1983) macromodel with a 3.5°C climate sensitivity and 20 000gt. of coal. The temperature increases and ambient CO_2 levels are in the Appendix of Hall (1996a) for the years 1990, 2000, 2025 and so on, in 25-year intervals, until the coal runs out. The coal is exhausted between the years 2250 and 2375, depending on the macromodel and the assumed amount of coal.

To predict the time path of the economic surplus, some adjustments in the forecast temperature data and the amount of precipitation that corresponds to each temperature must be specified. The ambient concentration of CO_2 is set equal to 353ppmv in 1990. The value grows for the three scenarios as given in the Appendix in Hall (1996a). The change in temperature is calculated as the mean global temperature increase for the three global warming scenarios: MR, RE and NY. Note that the values for 1990 are 0.6, 1.3 and 2.2°C. The temperature for 1990 was set equal to 15°C, so the future temperatures for each scenario are calculated by adding the change to the previous time period temperature. This procedure follows that of the accepted norm in the GCM literature. GCMs are used to predict the present temperature and the temperature for an equivalent doubling of CO_2. The difference in temperature is calculated, and this difference is added to current temperature to get the predicted temperature.

The predicted temperature requires an additional upward adjustment to account for the hotter climate in higher latitudes across the United States, relative to the global mean. On p. xxiv of IPCC (1990), for a mean global warming of 1.8°C, the projected warming varies from 2 to 4°C in winter and 2 to 3°C in summer. Thus, the ratios of average United States warming to the global mean is 3/1.8 = 1.67. This ratio is high compared to the figures in Table 3, which average 1.12. Aerosols are expected to moderate more in the region affected. Thus, aerosols moderate the mean global temperature, but moderate the temperature in the United States by more than the global mean; hence the ratio should be adjusted downward. In the analysis that follows, in fact, no adjustment is made. It is just one reason why this section has the title it does.

In IPCC (1990), United States precipitation is projected to increase by up to 15 per cent in winter and decrease by 5 to 10 per cent in summer. This does not easily compare with the three GCMs in Table 3. Consequently, results are presented that include a sensitivity analysis to precipitation.

In a review of 16 GCMs, Williams, Shaw, and Mendelsohn (1996) present mean global temperature increases and precipitation. The temperature increase averaged across GCMs is about 3.5°C, with an increase in precipitation equal to 7 per cent. But there are duplicate numbers for mean global temperature and precipitation increases, presumably because some of the 'models' are closely related in their construction to one another. Mendelsohn, Nordhaus and Shaw (1994) state they are following the IPCC with an 8 per cent increase in precipitation corresponding to a 3°C warming for a doubling of CO_2 equivalent gases. Since I am using 50 inches annually as the base case, precipitation will be proportionately increased by 8 per cent per increase of 3°C. I set the amount

TABLE 3   *Comparison of GCMs*

General circulation model (GCM)	Δ°C global mean[1]	%Δ precipitation global mean[1]	Δ°C US average (winter, summer)[2]	%Δ precipitation US average (winter, summer)[2]
Goddard Institute for Space Studies (GISS)	4.20	11.0	4.32 (5.46, 3.50)	20 (13, 24)
Geophysical Fluid Dynamics Laboratory (GFDL)	4.00	8.3	5.09 (5.25, 4.95)	9 (19, −8)
Oregon State University (OSU)	2.84	7.8	2.95 (2.95, 3.10)	17 (24, 11)

Notes: [1]From Williams *et al.* (1996).
           [2]From Adams *et al.* (1988).

of precipitation equal to, for example in the MR scenario, mrrain=50* (1 + 0.08* (mrt–15) /3).

For the base case and the three scenarios MR, RE and NY, the predicted surplus is given by:

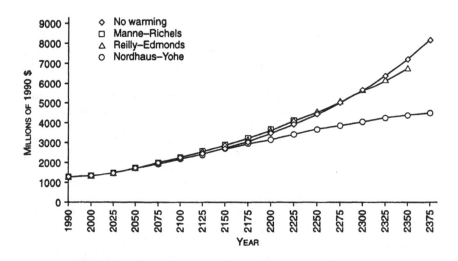

FIGURE 5   *Total agricultural consumer, producer, foreign surplus for four scenarios: no warming and three rose-coloured scenarios*

$$\text{shtbase} = \exp(c(1) + c(2)*\log(50) + c(3)*50*353 + c(4)*\log(15) \\ +c(5)*15 + c(6)*\log(353) + c(7)*\text{yr}*353 + c(8)*\text{yr}) \quad (5)$$

$$\text{mrsurplus} = \exp(c(1) + c(2)*\log(\text{mrrain}) + c(3)*\text{mrrain}*\text{mrco2} + c(4) \\ *\log(\text{mrt}) +c(5)*\text{mrt} + c(6)*\log(\text{mrco2}) + c(7)*\text{yr}*\text{mrco2} + c(8)*\text{yr}) \quad (6)$$

$$\text{resurplus} = \exp(c(1) + c(2)*\log(\text{rerain}) + c(3)*\text{rerain}*\text{reco2} + c(4) \\ *\log(\text{ret}) + c(5)*\text{ret} + c(6)*\log(\text{reco2}) + c(7)*\text{yr}*\text{reco2} + c(8)*\text{yr}) \quad (7)$$

$$\text{nysurplus} = \exp(c(1) +c(2)*\log(\text{nyrain}) + c(3)*\text{nyrain}*\text{nyco2} + c(4) \\ *\log(\text{nyt}) + c(5)*\text{nyt} + c(6)*\log(\text{nyco2}) + c(7)*\text{yr}*\text{nyco2} + c(8)*\text{yr}) \quad (8)$$

Figure 5 shows the projected impacts of global warming on economic surplus for the base case of no warming and the three scenarios. The MR scenario ends in year 2225 and is indistinguishable from the RE scenario. Figure 6 shows the difference between the three cases with warming and the case without warming. For the NY scenario, the agricultural sector fails. The present value of the three scenarios are illustrated in Figure 7 for two social discount rates: 1 per cent and 5 per cent. At 5 per cent, even though the NY scenario is a

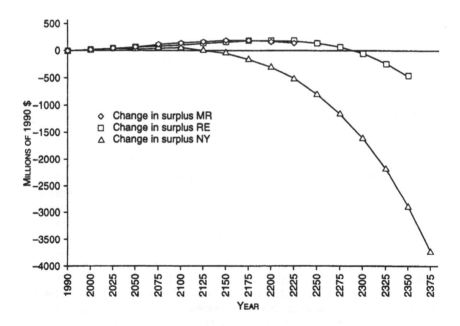

FIGURE 6   *Changes in surplus for three rose-coloured scenarios*

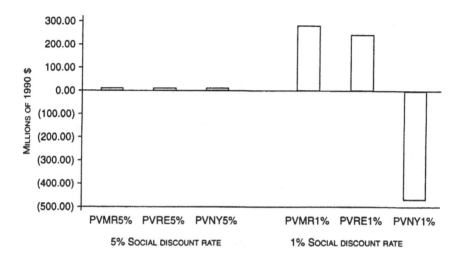

FIGURE 7   *Present value of three rose-coloured scenarios*

disaster, the present values of the three scenarios are almost identical. Only for a 1 per cent social discount rate is the present value of the NY scenario negative.

NOT JUST A QUESTION OF VALUES, THE OSTRICH EFFECT AND POLICY

After looking at these results it is tempting to terminate the analysis and ask, 'How much time do we have and what actions do we have to initiate now?' The apparent answer is that we have an entire century, even if the worst of the rose-coloured scenarios occurs. Those are the tinted glasses through which most economists are looking. Hoping for reliable, steady rain is a bit like relying on rain dances. Possibly the interior of the United States will become hot and dry, according to the IPCC (1990). Rather than the 2°C warming for the mid-case scenario above, assume that climate warms at 3.5°C for a doubling, the mean of the GCMs examined by Williams *et al.* (1996). This is in line with the mid-range scenario of Cline (1992), so assume his mid-range case of 10 000gt. of economically available coal, which he obtained from Edmonds and Reilly (1985). Now consider two possible cases. In case I, assume that precipitation falls by 25 per cent for a doubling. In case II, assume that precipitation increases by 35 per cent (rather than 8 per cent) for a doubling.

$$\text{Dry Case I:} \quad \text{nyrainI} = 50*(1 - 0.25*(\text{nyt}-15)/3.5) \qquad (9)$$

$$\text{Wet Case II:} \quad \text{nyrainII} = 50*(1 + 0.35*(\text{nyt}-15)/3.5) \qquad (10)$$

The surplus is predicted with the following equations:

$$\text{nysuri} = \exp(c(1) + c(2)*\log(\text{nyraini}) + c(3)*\text{nyraini}*\text{nyco2} + c(4) \\ *\log(\text{nyt}) + c(5)*\text{nyt} + c(6)*\log(\text{nyco2}) + c(7)*\text{yr}*\text{nyco2} + c(8)*\text{yr}) \qquad (11)$$

$$\text{nysurii} = \exp(c(1) + c(2)*\log(\text{nyrainii}) + c(3)*\text{nyrainii}*\text{nyco2} + c(4) \\ *\log(\text{nyt})+c(5)*\text{nyt} + c(6)*\log(\text{nyco2}) + c(7)*\text{yr}*\text{nyco2} + c(8)*\text{yr}) \qquad (12)$$

If it is either wetter, and particularly if it is drier, than the beneficial 8 per cent increase in precipitation I assumed in the previous section, for a CO_2 equivalent doubling, disaster strikes US agriculture, as shown in Figure 8. Return to the question, 'How much time do we have and what actions do we have to initiate now?' In answer, consider the next 150 years, where the change in economic surplus is shown in Figure 9. If it is drier, adverse affects could begin as soon as 25 years from now. Even so, if the discount rate is 5 per cent, Figure 10 shows that we are better off with minuscule gains over the next 25 years since they more than compensate for the complete collapse of agriculture shown in Figure 9 for the −25 per cent rain scenario. If the social discount rate is 1 per cent, as favoured by Khanna and Chapman (1996) and Arrow *et al.*

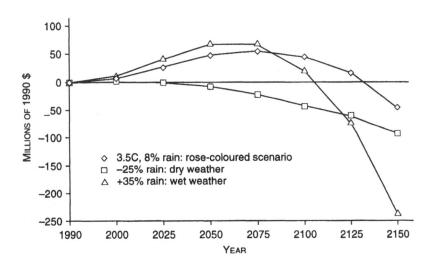

FIGURE 8 *Change in agricultural surplus with wetter and drier weather*

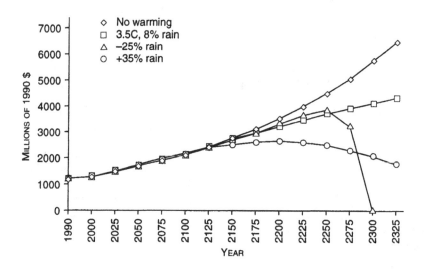

FIGURE 9   *Agricultural surplus with wetter and drier weather*

(1996), agriculture would be better off without global warming relative to all three of these scenarios. Does this mean that it is merely a question of values, whether we care about the future generations? If we use a 5 per cent discount rate, disaster seems bearable. Or is it that policy to alter the future would require government intervention in the economy, a change incompatible with our world view?

These assumptions do not capture the impact of a long-term drought, which would be harsh, turning the interior Great Plains of the United States to desert. These assumptions do not capture the impact of torrential rains, stripping the land of topsoil. Nor do they capture the possibility that the fluctuation between floods and droughts that we have experienced in the last 15 years could amplify, both washing away the topsoil and baking into laterite (McNeil, 1964) what soil remains. Erickson (1993) has a more complete set of reasons to be concerned.

Adams *et al.* (1990) acknowledge several critical omissions in their work and caution that their main contribution is 'highlighting uncertainties' (ibid., p. 219). The GCMs do not 'include changes in the space and time distributions of climate events. Therefore many significant climate and biophysical features are ignored'. They further caution (ibid., p. 220) that they do not account for changes in climate variability, such as frequency of droughts, 'mesoscale convection complex' rainfall and hail damage. The crop simulation models assume no limits to soil nutrients, and no pests that limit crop growth.

Adams *et al.* (1995b) explain that the CSMs allow amounts of fertilizer to vary for optimal results. For water supply, as long as the annual constraint is

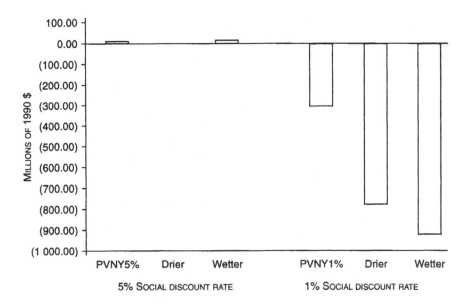

FIGURE 10   *Present value with wetter and drier weather*

not exceeded, the amounts needed over the growing season were allowed to optimize crop growth. The CSMs for corn, soybeans and wheat assume optimal pest management, and no nutritional limits in the soil that could limit CO_2 fertilization.

The results presented above are rosy indeed when comparisons are made between the impacts of global warming on US agriculture and on the developing countries. There are two important reasons. The first is that the United States has a greater ability to adapt. All the adaptation expected in the United States presumes that the present government policy of subsidizing research and development continues. The world view held by many economists is antagonistic to government intervention in the economy. Yet agriculture in the United States has the best possibility to adapt because of the Agricultural Experiment Stations and Extension Service. The institutional structure for adaptation in most of the developing parts of the world is minimal to non-existent.

In Africa, various studies cited in Reilly *et al.* (1996) predict near disaster for agriculture as the result of a mere doubling of greenhouse gases. Sivakumar (1993) compared the warmer period of 1965–88 with the cooler period of 1945–64 and found the growing season reduced by 5 to 20 days in Niger and West Africa. Akong'a *et al.* (1988) found significant reductions in maize and livestock productivity in Kenya owing to increased frequency of droughts. Downing (1992) estimated substantial decreases in yields of maize and millet in Zimbabwe, Senegal and lower elevations of Kenya owing to a warming of 2–4°C, but if precipitation increases Kenya at least comes out better nationally by shifting production to higher elevations. Schulze *et al.* (1993) and Muchena (1994) find substantial yield losses in South Africa and Zimbabwe, after fertilizer and irrigation adaptations, owing to a doubling of greenhouse gases. Eid (1994) finds substantial wheat and maize yield losses in Egypt as a result of a doubling.

In most of Latin America, the studies cited in Reilly *et al.* (1996) predict substantial losses for agriculture from a mere doubling of greenhouse gases. Baethgen (1994) estimates barley and wheat losses between 15 to 25 per cent in Uruguay, with adaptation. Baethgen (1994), Siquera *et al.* (1994), Liverman and O'Brien (1991) and Liverman *et al.* (1994) uniformly find wheat and maize yield losses, after adaptation, in Brazil and Mexico, although soybean yields increase. Downing (1992) has mixed results for Norte Chico, Chile, an area with a wide range of climates due to altitude changes, which makes assessment difficult. Sala and Paruel (1994) find maize yield losses in Argentina, after adaptation.

In China, the studies predict minor to substantial losses for agriculture resulting from mean global temperature increases of 1–1.5°C. While these are large temperature changes relative to the last 10 000 years, they are small temperature changes relative to the next 200 to 400 years. Tao (1993) finds wheat, rice, cotton, fruits, oil crops, potatoes and corn yield losses, with agricultural productivity losses greater than 5 per cent for a 1°C increase. Zhang (1993) and Jin *et al.* (1994) find substantial losses for rainfed rice in Southern China, but the possibility of increases in rice production for irrigated areas.

All of this work suffers the defect of considering a mere doubling, or less, of greenhouse gases. Reilly *et al.* (1996) report upper temperature bounds for wheat (C3) at 30–35°C, rice (C3) at 35–38°C, potatoes (C3) at 25°C, soybeans (C3) at 35°C and maize (C4) at 32–37°C, with optimum temperatures considerably below the upper ranges. For comparison, in the three scenarios considered in this paper, mean global temperature reaches a maximum at 19.4°C (Manne-Richels), 25.6°C (Reilly-Edmonds *et al.*) and 35.5°C (Nordhaus-Yohe). Of course, the mean global temperature will be considerably lower than the average temperature in the tropics, which are 10–15°C warmer. So the mid-range scenario results in tropical temperatures at or above the upper ranges for agricultural production. In this sense, the results presented here for the United States are rosy indeed, relative to worldwide prospects.

We can deny these possibilities, or simply use a 5 per cent discount rate and claim it is rational to ignore disaster, as long as it is far enough away. Or we can believe that we have enough time to make changes later, if we find out that climate change is not benign.

Consider the path dependence of technological change (Goodstein, 1995). It took 10 to 20 years for infant industries in solar and wind energy to emerge, and as long for institutions to learn how to develop policies which nurture them cost-effectively, rather than wastefully (Hall, 1996a). Power plants last for 30 to 50 years, and they will not be easily replaced, as long as variable costs of existing plants are less than long-run marginal costs of replacement plants. The electric car was scheduled to help replace the use of oil for transport, but that policy initiative has been delayed. We have considerable institutional, physical and economic barriers to clear before the market will replace coal and other fossil fuels, barriers that will delay any meaningful replacement for decades.

Reality exists independently of our world view. Like an ostrich, if reality is inconsistent with that view, we can bury our heads in the sand, refuse to believe the physical science, just consider the next 100 years, discount the future or believe we can always avoid disaster by waiting until later to invent and substitute alternatives to fossil fuel technologies. If we persist in ignoring reality because it requires actions inconsistent with our world view, we run the risk of condemning future *Homo sapiens sapiens* to the miseries of forced migration and malnutrition.

REFERENCES

Adams, R.M. (1986), 'Agriculture, Forestry and Related Benefits of Air Pollution Control: A Review and Some Observations', *American Journal of Agricultural Economics*, 68, 464–72.

Adams, R.M., McCarl, B.A., Dudek, K.J. and Glyer, J.D. (1988), 'Implications of Global Climate for Western Agriculture', *Western Journal of Agricultural Economics*, 13, 348–56.

Adams, R.M., Fleming, R.A., Chang, C-C., McCarl, B.A. and Rosenzweig, C. (1995a), 'A Reassessment of the Economic Effects of Global Climate Change on U.S. Agriculture', *Climate Change*, 30, 147–67.

Adams, R.M., McCarl, B.A., Segerson, K., Rosenzweig, C., Bryant, K.J., Dixon, B.L., Conner, R., Evenson, R.E. and Ojima, D. (1995b), *The Economic Effects of Climate Change on U.S. Agriculture*, Palo Alto: Electric Power Research Institute.

Adams, R.M., Rosenzweig, C., Peart, R.M., Ritchie, J.T., McCarl, B.A., Glyer, J.D., Curry, R.B., Jones, J.W., Boote, K.J. and Allen, L. Hartewell Jr. (1990), 'Global Climate Change and US Agriculture', *Nature*, 345, 17 May, 219–24.

Akong'a, J., Downing, T.E., Konijn, N.T., Mungai, D.N., Muturi, H.R. and Potter, H.L. (1988), 'The Effects of Climatic Variations on Agriculture in Central and Eastern Kenya', in M.L. Parry, T.R. Carter and N.T. Konijn (eds), *The Impact of Climatic Variations on Agriculture, Vol. 2, Assessments in Semi-Arid Regions*, Dordrecht: Kluwer Academic Press.

Arrow, K.J., Cline, W.R., Maler, K-G., Munasinghe, M., Squitieri, R. and Stiglitz, J.E. (1996), 'Intertemporal Equity, Discounting and Economic Efficiency', in IPCC, *Climate Change 1995: Economic and Social Dimensions of Climate Change, Contribution of Working Group III to the Second Assessment Report of the Intergovernmental Panel on Climate Change*, Cambridge: Cambridge University Press.

Baethgen, W.E. (1994), 'Impact of Climate Change on Barley in Uruguay: Yield Changes and Analysis of Nitrogen Management Systems', in C. Rosenzweig and A. Iglesias (eds), *Implications of Climate Change for International Agriculture: Crop Modeling Study*, Washington, DC: U.S. Environmental Protection Agency.

Cline, W.R. (1992), *Global Warming: The Economic Stakes*, Washington, DC: Institute for International Economics.

Cline, W.R. (1996), 'The Impact of Global Warming on Agriculture: Comment', *American Economic Review*, 86, 1309–11.

Crowley, T.J. (1996), 'Remembrance of Things Past: Greenhouse Lessons from the Geologic Record', *Consequences: The Nature and Implications of Environmental Change*, 2, 2–12.

Downing, T.E. (1992), *Climate Change and Vulnerable Places: Global Food Security and Country Studies in Zimbabwe, Kenya, Senegal and Chile*, Research Report No. 1, Environmental Change Unit, University of Oxford.

Edmonds, J. and Reilly, J. (1985), *Global Energy: Assessing the Future*, New York: Oxford University Press.

Eid, H.M. (1994), 'Impact of Climate Change on Simulated Wheat and Maize Yields in Egypt', in

C. Rosenzweig and A. Iglesias (eds), *Implications of Climate Change for International Agriculture: Crop Modeling Study*, Washington, DC: U.S. Environmental Protection Agency.

Erickson, J.D. (1993), 'From Ecology to Economics: the Case Against CO_2 Fertilization', *Ecological Economics*, **8**, 157–75.

Goodstein, E. (1995), 'The Economic Roots of Environmental Decline: Property Rights or Path Dependence', *Journal of Economic Issues*, **24**, 1029–43.

Hall, Darwin C. (1996a), 'Geoeconomic Time and Global Warming: Limits to Economic Analysis', *International Journal of Social Economics*, **23**, 64–87.

Hall, Darwin C. (1996b), *Advances in the Economics of Environmental Resources: Marginal Cost Rate Design and Wholesale Water Markets*, Vol. 1, Greenwich, Connecticut: JAI Press.

Intergovernmental Panel on Climate Change (1990), *IPCC First Assessment Report, Volume I: Overview and Summaries, Scientific Assessment of Climate Change*, New York: World Meteorological Organization and United Nations Environment Programme.

Intergovernmental Panel on Climate Change (1996), *Climate Change 1995: The Science of Climate Change*, Cambridge: Cambridge University Press.

de Janvry, A. (1972), 'The Class of Generalized Power Production Functions', *American Journal of Agricultural Economics*, **54**, 234–7.

Jin, Z., Daokou, Ge, H.C. and Fang, J. (1994), 'Effects of Climate Change on Rice Production and Strategies for Adaptation in Southern China', in C. Rosenzweig and A. Iglesias (eds), *Implications of Climate Change for International Agriculture; Crop Modeling Study*, Washington, DC: U.S. Environmental Protection Agency.

Khanna, N. and Chapman, D. (1996), 'Time Preference, Abatement Costs and International Climate Policy: An Appraisal of IPCC 1995', *Contemporary Economic Policy*, **14**, 56–66.

Liverman, D. and O'Brien, K. (1991), 'Global Warming and Climate Change in Mexico', *Global Environmental Change*, **1** (4), 351–64.

Liverman, D., Dilley, M., O'Brien, K. and Menchaca, L. (1994), 'Possible Impacts of Climate Change on Maize Yields in Mexico', in C. Rosenzweig and A. Iglesias (eds), *Implications of Climate Change for International Agriculture: Crop Modeling Study*, Washington, DC: U.S. Environmental Protection Agency.

Manne, A. and Richels, R. (1990), 'CO_2 Emission Limits: An Economic Cost Analysis for the USA', *The Energy Journal*, **11**, 51–74.

McNeil, M. (1964), 'Lateritic Soils', *Scientific American*, **211**, 96–117.

Mendelsohn, Robert and Nordhaus, William (1996), 'The Impact of Global Warming on Agriculture: Reply', *American Economic Review*, **86**, 1312–15.

Mendelsohn, R., Nordhaus, W. and Shaw, D. (1994), 'The Impact of Global Warming on Agriculture: A Ricardian Analysis', *American Economic Review*, **84**, 753–71.

Muchena, P. (1994), 'Implications of Climate Change for Maize Yields in Zimbabwe', in C. Rosenzweig and A. Iglesias (eds), *Implications of Climate Change for International Agriculture: Crop Modeling Study*, Washington, DC: U.S. Environmental Protection Agency.

Nordhaus, W. and Yohe, G. (1983), 'Future Carbon Dioxide Emissions from Fossil Fuels', *Changing Climate*, Washington, DC: National Research Council, National Academy Press.

Reilly, J. (1996), 'Climate Change, Global Agriculture and Regional Vulnerability', in N. Nakićenović, W.D. Nordhaus, R. Richels and F.L. Toth (eds), *Climate Change: Integrating Science, Economics and Policy*, Laxenburg, Austria: International Institute for Applied Systems Analysis.

Reilly, J., Edmonds, J., Gardner, R. and Brenkert, A. (1987), 'Uncertainty Analysis of the IEA/ORAU CO_2 Emissions Model', *The Energy Journal*, **8**, 1–29.

Reilly, J. *et al.* (1996), 'Agriculture in a Changing Climate: Impacts and Adaptation', in IPPC, *Climate Change 1995: Impacts, Adaptations and Mitigation of Climate Change: Scientific-Technical Analyses, Contribution of Working Group II to the Second Assessment Report of the Intergovernmental Panel on Climate Change*, Cambridge: Cambridge University Press.

Rich, P. (1996), 'Photosynthesis', *Grolier's Multimedia Encyclopedia*, Danbury, Connecticut: Grolier Interactive.

Rosenzweig, C. and Hillel, D. (1995), 'Potential Impacts of Climate Change on Agriculture and Food Supply', *Consequences: The Nature and Implications of Environmental Change*, **1**, 22–32.

Rosenzweig, C. and Parry, M.L. (1994), 'Potential Impact of Climate Change on World Food Supply', *Nature*, **367**, 13 January, 33–138.

Sala, O.E. and Paruel, J.M. (1994), 'Impacts of Global Climate Change on Maize Production in Argentina', in C. Rosenzweig and A. Iglesias (eds), *Implications of Climate Change for International Agriculture: Crop Modeling Study*, Washington, DC: U.S. Environmental Protection Agency.

Schulze, R.E., Kiker, G.A. and Kunz, R.P. (1993), 'Global Climate Change and Agricultural Productivity in Southern Africa', *Global Environmental Change*, 4, 329–49.

Shreeve, J. (1995), *The Neandertal Enigma*, New York: Avon Books.

de Siquera, O.E., Boucas Farias, J.R. and Aguiar Sans, L.M. (1994), 'Potential Effects of Global Climate Change for Brazilian Agriculture: Applied Simulation Studies for Wheat, Maize and Soybeans', in C. Rosenzweig and A. Iglesias (eds), *Implications of Climate Change for International Agriculture: Crop Modeling Study*, Washington, DC: U.S. Environmental Protection Agency.

Sivakumar, M.V.K. (1993), 'Global Climate Change and Crop Production in the Sundano-Sahelian Zone of West Africa', in Crop Science Society of America (ed.), *International Crop Science, Vol. I*, Madison: Crop Science Society of America.

Tao, Z. (1993), 'Influences of Global Climate Change on Agriculture of China', in R.G. Zepp (ed.), *Climate Biosphere Interactions*, New York: John Wiley and Sons.

Williams, L.J., Shaw, D. and Mendelsohn, R. (1996), *Evaluating GCM Output with Impact Models*, Palo Alto: Electric Power Research Institute.

Zhang, H. (1993), 'The Impact of Greenhouse Effect on Double Rice in China', *Climate Change and Its Impact*, Beijing: Meteorology Press.

TIMOTHY SWANSON*

The Management of Genetic Resources for Agriculture:
Ecology and Information, Externalities and Policies

EVOLUTION, INFORMATION, EXTERNALITIES AND POLICIES

This paper surveys the work in several fields relating to the economics of managing genetic resources for agriculture. Most fundamentally, this is a problem relating to inherent ecological dynamics in agriculture. Ever since agriculture was first developed, there has been a race implicit within it, with pests and pathogens eroding the resistance of the crop varieties currently in use and new varieties being devised to replace them. This contest can never be won with finality by agriculturalists, and the correct formulation of the question concerning agricultural sustainability must be whether it is possible to remain a player in the race indefinitely. As inputs into agriculture, genetic resources play a prominent role in the continuation of the contest, and their optimal conservation – in order to ensure an optimal supply of resistance into the indefinite future – is at present a necessary condition for the continuance of agriculture. This paper examines what is meant by the optimal management of genetic resources, as important inputs into both the improvement of productivity and the maintenance of agricultural sustainability. The four facets of the problem cover ecology, information, externalities and public policy.

The ecological facet concerns the definition of the dynamic processes inherent within the agricultural system. This requires the identification of the forces within the natural world which produce the changes in the pathogens and pests that result in the erosion of crop resistance. To counterbalance these forces, agriculture has devised a system for introducing particular traits and characteristics into crop species that resist evolutionary forces. The contest is to maintain a steady state of relative balance between the two. The first task is to describe the contest and derive the ecological constraint within which agriculture must exist.

The informational facet of the problem concerns the nature of the industry which works on the solution to the underlying ecological constraint. This is a classic research and development (R&D) problem, namely the need to generate solution concepts in anticipation of predictable, but non-deterministic,

*Faculty of Economics, University of Cambridge and Biodiversity Programme, Centre for Social and Economic Research on the Global Environment (CSERGE), University College, London. Timo Goeschl is acknowledged as the co-author of much of this material. We would both like to thank the International Plant Genetic Resources Institute for financial support and Pablo Eyzaguirre for comments and encouragement.

problems. Crop genetic resources act as information in this process, both as stocks (in the form of accumulated traits of known usefulness) and as generators of current flows. The plant breeding sector works to generate, use and appropriate the value of this information.

The externalities in the management problem concern the values of genetic resources which will not be taken into consideration when decisions are made concerning the conservation of genetic resources. Plant breeders will clearly wish to invest in the provision of supplies of crop genetic resources for purposes of their R&D work, but there are also resource values falling outside their decision-making framework. These involve the longer-term, and somewhat diffusive, insurance and informational values of crop genetic resources. Private plant breeders have the incentive to invest optimally in the supply and use of genetically based information, but only to the extent that values are appropriable on a timescale relevant to them. The gaps within this objective identify the public good nature of genetic resources and define the reason for which the public sector must be involved in supplying the socially optimal amount of genetic resources for agriculture. These externalities are defined later.

The existence of externalities implies that there is a clear public interest in the provision of optimal supplies of genetic resources for agriculture which are not being met by private-sector efforts alone. Once this is accepted, there are two fundamentally different approaches to the solution of the problem, namely *ex situ* and *in situ* conservation. These are fundamentally different both in their impacts on land use and in their implications for genetic resource conservation. One is focused on the conservation of existing stocks of useful crop genetic resources, while the other is focused on the appropriation of incoming flows of useful information. Both forms of conservation are essential for the distinctive role each plays, but it is important to analyse both in terms of the informational outputs which they generate. The optimal policy for resource conservation will be discussed.

The optimal management of genetic resources for agriculture is an important public function, because it has long-lasting implications for the sustainability of farming and because it is clear that there are impacts which are unmanaged otherwise. Any discussion of sustainability in agriculture must include an analysis of the optimal methods of management relating to the resources required to maintain an equilibrium within it. Currently, there is no substitute for the informational stocks and flows inherent within genetic resources for the solution of the continuing problem of instability (that is, erosion of resistance) in agriculture. Therefore the optimal management of genetic resources must be carefully considered in order to identify the precise nature of the tasks that must be undertaken to sustain global agriculture. This paper attempts to make a contribution to this area by outlining the fundamentally ecological and informational nature of the problem that must be resolved.

THE ECOLOGICAL PROBLEM: EVOLUTION AND AGRICULTURE

What does agroecology have to say about the stability of the modern system of agriculture? Biologists would ask how it is possible that pathogens and their hosts could coexist for hundreds of thousands of years without temporary advantages in one of the species leading to the natural extinction of the other. Increasingly, the answer given has been that pathogen and hosts coevolve by changing their genetic structure, and thereby their phenotypical traits, and that, while we observe fairly stable *ecological* relationships, there are races of 'genetic innovation' going on underneath this apparent equilibrium (Hofbauer and Sigmund, 1989). It is the underlying race to innovate that sustains the balance between predator and prey, and maintains the stability of the system.

In ecological terms, the stable dynamics witnessed in agriculture are known as a 'Red Queen' race (from *Alice in Wonderland*). It is necessary to continue to make moves in order to stand still. In coevolutionary settings of predator–prey models, it is possible to show that the populations of hosts and pathogens will reach an ecological steady rate where virulence, or its mirror image, susceptibility, do not change. In other words, the system converges to a long-run equilibrium of host off-take and stable population levels. This does not imply that the underlying dynamics have stopped, in fact, both pathogen and host populations continuously update their strategies in order to cope with the constant increase in the opponents' ability to improve its growth parameters.

How has the development of agriculture affected these evolutionary contests within the biosphere? The choices formerly made by evolution have been supplanted by human choice in certain spheres of activity, but the general nature of the contest remains. Humans have selected the crops and crop varieties most easily appropriated by themselves (and hence denied to competing pathogens), but this simple act of selection introduces genetic drift within the competing population pathogens that renders them increasingly competitive. This harvest's appropriation generates the next harvest's competition, and the race is on. Ever since human societies interjected themselves into the role as selector, the innovation contest between them and the pathogens affecting their crops has been going on.

The process is apparent in the studies of declining resistance in agriculture. There has been steady erosion of the productivity of the best performing and most widely used crop varieties owing to evolutionary pressures from pathogens. This has been addressed by means of the periodic interjection of new varieties into agriculture, and their consequent decline. A cycle of introduction and subsequent decline is documented for a range of crops and crop varieties (Evans, 1993; Smale, 1996; Rejesus *et al.*, 1996). A recent empirical analysis has even estimated the impact of 'age' of a variety (that is, years in agricultural use) on its productivity, and found that it is significantly negative (Hartell *et al.*, 1997). Though human choice has constantly altered the setting for the evolutionary contest, the basic nature of the problem remains unchanged. In the management of crops and crop varieties, we continue in a contest of appropriation and innovation with natural predators and pathogens.

The essence of the contest can be captured within a simple model of coevolution by adopting some formal techniques from evolutionary biology.

Let us denote by r the relative fitness of a particular pathogen of a particular crop. For the purpose at hand, 'fitness' is defined as the pathogen's ability to consume host tissue, measured against some fixed point in time. To say that 'r has increased' therefore means that the pathogen would be able to consume more host material per unit of time than before.

In terms of intertemporal methods of decision making, r may be regarded as a stock variable of a 'bad', which could be called 'virulence', or a 'good' which could be called 'resistance' (Hueth and Regev, 1974; Cornes *et al.*, 1995). The dynamic processes which govern the behaviour of r over time are attributable to changes in various characteristics in both the host and the pathogen, changes which alter the biotic potential of either organism, with r indicating the relative standing of each in this contest. Each may be seen as being engaged in an intricate exchange of moves to counter the change in strategies of the other, and this can lead over time to the development of the ecological interrelationships as well as the genetic structures of host and pathogen populations (Allard, 1990).

For simplicity, we will assume a one-to-one relationship between parasite and host (that is, a parasite only feeds on one variety of host plants and this host plant variety only has one parasite).[1] The expected increase of relative fitness of pathogen i equals the product of the natural mutation rate μ, a discrete change in fitness of size Δ occasioned by a 'beneficial' mutation in the genetic structure, and the probability (k) that a mutation of this size will become established in the pathogen population.

Basically, the *pathogen specific factors* determining changes in virulence/ resistance can be expressed as:

$$E(\dot{r}_i) = \mu \cdot \Delta \cdot k_i.$$

In considering the impact of human agriculture on the dynamics of pathogen evolution, the first characteristic in the equation (that is, the rate of mutation) is relatively exogenous, but the others are not. As summarized in Table 1, the impact of agriculture on pathogen dynamics has operated by determining the relative rates of availability of particular hosts and by generating greater discrete changes in pathogen fitness. In essence, the impact of agriculture has been to reward those pathogens which are adapted to the now widely cultivated modern varieties, while encouraging large gains in fitness (severe selection pressure) on those which are not.

To analyse the dynamics of host evolution within this hostile environment, it is important to note, first, that responsive evolutionary forces must exist in nature, in order to counterbalance the dynamics inherent within the pathogen populations. Otherwise, aggregate production by host populations will always be in a state of decline, as pathogens seek out and exploit these opportunities. The previously noted long-term stability within the overall system indicates that hosts possess the scope for evolutionary development in order to counter pathogen evolution and restore equilibrium (Allard, 1990).

The *host specific factors* determining changes in resistance/virulence are given as:

$$E(\dot{r}_i) = \pi \cdot \Gamma_i \cdot v.$$

This formulation of host dynamics is analogous to the representation of the pathogen dynamics set out previously. We will define π as the natural mutation rate of the host (which is presumably lower than that of pathogens) and Γ as the discrete change in the host's ability to produce in the face of pathogen infestation. Finally, we have the likelihood that this random change will become dominant within the host population, which we denote by v (Burdon *et al.*, 1990, p. 238).

TABLE 1 *Impact of agriculture on pathogen dynamics*

Ecological part affected	Symbol	Nature of impact
Pathogen	μ: mutation rate	no impact, exogenously given
	Δ: size of relative change in fitness	more competitive environment (lower general level of fitness) generates greater relative changes in fitness by successful mutants
	k: probability of successful mutation => host availability	enhanced likelihood of success for pathogens adapted to 'intensely cultivated' crops

Even in the absence of human intervention, host species have the inbuilt capacity for change that is necessary for survival within a dynamic environment. Natural selection within crops would select a *flow* of traits and characteristics capable of surviving in the then prevailing pathogen environment. In effect, the inherent stability evidenced by evolutionary processes represents a flow of responses to the problematic strategies thrown out by pathogens.

What, then, is the role of the agriculturalist in this context between hosts and pathogens? That is, how has agricultural selection performed a role in this contest of strategic response and reaction? The agriculturalist has contributed by means of observation of the results of the natural contest (observing which traits carry 'winning' strategies) allied with discriminatory transport and resource allocation of the varieties carrying those traits (accelerating the rate of their dispersal to lands made available for their introduction). In essence, the agriculturalist has aided the successful trait signalled by natural selection, through non-natural forms of diffusion and land allocation. Table 2 summarizes these impacts on agriculture.

The net effect of agriculture on these ecological contests within nature has not affected the stability of the system, but the nature of the contest has been altered. Agriculture has marked a shift from a natural form of competition to a

TABLE 2   *Impact of agriculture on dynamics of host evolution*

Ecological part affected	Symbol	Nature of impact
Host	π: mutation rate	no impact: exogenously given
	Γ: change in host resistance (potential for response to pest virulence)	greater changes in fitness through human observation of natural selection and human selection of the most successful from that set
	v: likelihood of successful mutation	enhanced likelihood of success by means of human transport and resource (land) allocation

human-made contest of innovation. Once human societies began taking production decisions regarding which species and varieties would grow where and at which intensity, important parameters of the ecological relationship between plants and pathogens started to become societal choice variables rather than purely natural processes. This is confirmed by a glance at Tables 1 and 2.

Not only did agriculture introduce a new form of contest between human society and nature, but it has been a steadily accelerating competition since that time. The rate of evolutionary change of pathogens of cultivated crops can be expected to be higher under agriculture than the average which prevailed prior to agriculture, since the previous pests faced a less competitive environment. As humans continue to appropriate an ever-higher share of photosynthetic product, they generate an ever more selective environment and, as a consequence, a more rapidly paced contest. Our previous conquests generate ever-greater challenges.[2]

How has the agriculturalist managed to keep pace in this environment? It is apparent that farming systems have been characterized by relative ecological sustainability, both under traditional agriculture and under modern intensive methods. The compensation for the increased speed of pest evolution must, therefore, originate from the ingenious use of the instruments available to the agriculturalist to 'manage' host evolution. Sometimes this has involved the selection of varieties with a high intrinsic propensity to develop resistance, but it has more commonly been associated with the observation and rapid dissemination of traits revealed as being successful in current pathogen environments (Evans, 1993). Hence the agriculturalist has contributed to the maintenance of stability in this contest by means of observation (of natural selection), own selection and biased resource allocation.

It is possible to view the maintenance of ecological stability as a sort of constraint that should be imposed when maximizing static productivity in agriculture. That is, if the short-term objective of maximum agricultural productivity is being pursued, this ecological constraint should also be observed in order to ensure that an unsustainable agricultural production path is not chosen.[3] Keeping up in this contest of innovation should be seen as a primary and fundamental goal of agriculture; otherwise, short-term gains may be pursued at the risk of long-term instability. Hence the following stability condition (1) might be viewed as the fundamental condition for maintaining agricultural sustainability (in the context of otherwise unconstrained agricultural production).[4] The *stability condition* in the dynamics of virulence/resistance is:

$$E(\dot{r}_i) = \mu \cdot \Delta \cdot k_i - \pi \cdot \Gamma_i \cdot v = 0. \tag{1}$$

The core of the issue that we are concerned with in the management of genetic resources for agriculture is whether it is possible to sustain this equilibrium indefinitely. Genetic resources constitute the 'strategies' that are available to human society in contesting this natural race of innovation. Genetic resources are, in effect, the *information* base on which we must rely in our continuing quest to retain agricultural stability. Of course, much of this contest is undertaken by a very successful private activity – the research and development sector of the plant-breeding industry – but the interesting issue for public economists remains. Is there an important or necessary role for the public sector in the management of the contest?

THE PUBLIC GOOD NATURE OF THE PROBLEM: EXTERNALITIES AND AGRICULTURE[5]

To what extent does the agriculture industry itself make the best use of genetic resources? The previous discussion indicates that the plant-breeding industry is addressing this fundamental problem, as well as supplying and using genetic resources in order to do so. Stability has been maintained for thousands of years of agriculture, without the need for intervention from the public sector; why would it be necessary now? This section sets out a broad framework for the conceptualization of all values of genetic resources, and then compares the private sector's management objectives with those of society generally.

There are two broad forms of values which best describe the role of genetic resources in agriculture: *insurance* and *information*. Insurance refers to the value of genetic diversity in providing a broad base of independent assets on which to build production. It was the motivation to which the individual isolated farmer responded when planting a wider range of varieties to insure against crop failure. In the past, if that happened, society also faced collapse. Investing in diversity provided the portfolio of different assets which insured against complete crop failure. Information refers to the uncertainty that exists about the future, which will only be revealed with the passage of time. In the context of agriculture, information arrives whenever the nature of the next invading pest or disease is revealed, or when the nature of the best strategy for resistance is identified. Diversity is useful in this context because it acts as a receiver, capturing information on the nature of successful resistance strategies through the process of selection. A greater diversity of plant varieties increases the prospects for the survival of at least one variety when a pest or disease passes through, thus providing the necessary information for the development of a successful strategy against the prevalent pest. It signals the traits and characteristics that are successful in the new environment. When these signals are used, or accumulated, they provide the basis for continuing stability in agriculture.

To look at the way in which the agricultural industry addresses these fundamental values in their broadest sense, and how well it manages genetic resources, requires some outline of the nature of a number of key concepts. A basic assumption is that the supply of genetic resources in agriculture corresponds directly to the objective function of agricultural producers. We can then look to the individual decisions which determine the production choices in agriculture, and attempt to identify which, if any, of the values of genetic resources are external to the process. These external values (covered below) determine the public interest in conserving biological diversity for agriculture.

Expected agricultural yield

Expected (average) yield is the fundamental criterion used in the determination of the vast majority of crop choice and land use decisions. The beneficial effect of this criterion is unquestionable. One example of the aggregate impact has been the 'green revolution', the increase in worldwide grain yields at a rate of nearly 3 per cent per annum over a period of 30 years. What has been the impact on genetic resource supplies? Empirical studies indicate that there is an opportunity cost implicit in the retention of a diversity of genetic resources in production (Heisey, 1990). Nevertheless, it is very often the case that local demands of consumer and producers lead to the retention of some amount of diversity (Altieri and Merrick, 1987). In summary, with the dissipation of the need for diversity as an individual insurance good, there has been an increasing focus of production choices and land use decisions on a small set of the highest yielding varieties across the globe.

Portfolio value

This is the static value (available in a single growing season) derived from the retention of a relatively wider range of assets within the agricultural production system. It is the value which individual farmers formerly pursued when they had few other assets to rely upon. Now that individual farmers rely upon other features for their insurance needs (access to markets, crop insurance programmes and so on), the public sector must consider the cumulative impact on yield variability deriving from individual farmers' land use decisions. As long as society is averse to risk and has, therefore, a distaste for yield variability, it will have a greater desire to invest in more diversity of production methods than would any individual farmer. Yield variability is smoothed by reason of non-conversion because this implies (1) a broader portfolio of assets (varieties) within the species, (2) a wider portfolio of assets (agricultural commodities) within the country and (3) a wider portfolio of assets (available methods of production) across the globe.

A topical example of a harmful 'portfolio effect' is the current BSE problem in the United Kingdom. Disease within the food chain is a problem in any event, but when an outbreak becomes endemic within an activity in which a country is heavily invested, the costs of the pathogen become extremely heavy. 'Mad cow disease' is a portfolio problem because it is the United Kingdom's investment strategy that has made it possible for this single pathogen to have such a substantial impact on such a large proportion of the agricultural industry. The country is so heavily invested in beef and dairy breeds that it is difficult for it alone to absorb the cost of the eradication campaign that is probably necessary to restore consumer confidence.

The most important level at which this externality operates is the global one. Any given country has the same incentives as the individual farmer to rely upon other national assets for insurance in times of crop failure. This obviously does not work on a global scale; if all countries plant common varieties, expecting to rely upon one another's harvests in the event of a national crop failure, the fallacy of their reasoning would be revealed only in the context of a global crop problem. This would occur, for example, if the four primary carbohydrate crops (rice, wheat, potatoes and maize), which now provide the majority of the world's diet were subject to severe pest invasions in the same year. The continued narrowing of the range of production methods, crops and crop varieties in use across the globe continues to enhance the cumulative probability of such an occurrence.

There is another more fundamental level at which this portfolio value operates. One of the ecological functions of diverse genetic resources is to act as 'fire breaks' in the event of pest and pathogen epidemics. As agriculture intensifies, these breaks are removed, enhancing the risks of the mutation of virulent strains of pest. The ecological portfolio value of genetic resources is positive by reason of the manner in which it reduces the contagion effect.

There is empirical evidence to demonstrate that modern intensive agriculture has had a systematic impact on correlated yields across the globe. The studies of yields have indicated that there has been a corresponding increase in variability going hand-in-hand with the increased average yield. The coefficient of variation in global grain yields has nearly doubled when the experience of the 1960s is compared with that of the 1970s (Hazell, 1984; 1989). The larger part of this enhanced variability is traceable to the reduced portfolio effect across space (international and intranational) rather than within species; that is, it is the adoption of a smaller number of crops and methods (rather than genetic uniformity itself) which is contributing most to the increase in variability. This is indicative of the externality that exists across countries when they are making their land use decisions.

Quasi-option value

This is the value of retaining a wider portfolio of assets across time, given that the environment is constantly changing and rendering known characteristics far more valuable than they are currently considered to be (Conrad, 1980; Hanneman, 1989). For example, this is the value of the retention of certain varieties of cultivated species (not known to be of any substantial expected value) but which are found to be of enhanced usefulness when a particular form of pest or disease becomes more prevalent. It is the change in the value of a known characteristic by reason of an unforeseeable change in the environment. Clearly, this is a value that is not addressed by means of expected (mean) yield forms of decision making.

There is also an ecological quasi-option value. It is the value of the retention of some manner of evolutionary process intact, in the event that some trait for resistance might be identified via natural selection. That is, it is the basis for a distinct value to *in situ* conservation. For example, the continued cultivation of a wide range of varieties of wheat within a natural environment would allow natural selection to signal which variety has the resistance to a newly invading pest. *In situ* conservation allows nature to signal this information and identify the important trait in the most direct fashion.

Although individual farmers utilizing the expected yield form of decision making do not consider these values, there are other parts of the agricultural industry which do. It was argued earlier that quasi-option values are one of the driving forces within the plant-breeding industry. Plant breeders retain genetic resources and continue to breed them into their lines of high-yielding varieties, for the express purpose of addressing the recurring problem of declining resistance. Are there any externalities at work within this process? One thing is certain: society would supply a much wider range of genetic resources than those which would be perceived as imminently profitable by a plant breeder. This is indicative of the difference in the discount rates in use in evaluating supply decisions. Clearly, a business firm will use its financial rate of return (usually in the range of 10 to 20 per cent) in order to evaluate investment options. Most economists agree that a social investment decision should be evaluated at a rate nearer to 2 to 5 per cent (Pearce and Ulph, 1995) while there is an argument to be made that the social discount rate should be even lower (or possibly zero) when the survival of future generations is at stake. This difference in discount rate will make a huge difference in the amount of genetic resources that would be supplied by the public sector, but would not be supplied by the private. It means that a business firm would be considering a time horizon of not more than five to ten years in making its decisions, while the public sector should be considering possible problems arising well beyond that length of time.

It is also important to note that private firms are less likely to focus on a range of information-generating mechanisms than would an idealized public sector. This is both on account of the need to have the information in immediately appropriable form (since appropriation after ten years would be discounted to zero) and because investments in information production must be relatively secure from the standpoint of the private investors concerned (that is, they are as concerned about the distribution of any informational gains as about production). Such considerations weigh in favour of conservative forms of investments. Information is difficult enough to generate and appropriate without making investments which are relatively insecure. A public sector less concerned with issues of distribution and appropriation would probably invest in very different methods. This is one reason (explored further below) for the investment in storage methods of supply rather than the usage-based methods of supply of information.

There is no doubt that change will occur over time (in the environment and in technology) and one of the values of genetic diversity is the flexibility it allows for response to future changes in circumstances. The agricultural industry definitely recognizes this value and provides against many eventualities, but there are clear instances in which there is a difference between what the private and the public sector would supply in terms of the quasi-option value of genetic resources. These differences identify one of the most important public interests in their conservation.

Exploration value

This is the value of retaining a wider portfolio of assets across time, given that the exploration and use of little-known assets will generate discoveries of currently unknown traits and characteristics. It is a 'Bayesian' sort of value, where information derives from the process of converging expectations. Long analysed resources will no longer divulge as much information as will those which are little analysed, even though the former might have much higher expected yields. For example, this can be conceived as the value of the retention of a given land area in an 'unused' state, because it is possible that certain wild relatives of cultivated varieties will be found which may generate new and valuable characteristics if investigated. The same idea may also be applied at the field level and the species level. Any non-modern production method or crop will be relatively unknown, compared to the heavily researched crops and crop varieties. It is important to continue to retain some of these little-known wildernesses, crops and crop varieties, if only because we must admit that these have received little exploration, while other paths have been much pursued.

Once again there are good reasons to expect that private industry will take some of this value into account in its approach to conserving genetic diversity, but there are also good reasons why the private approach will be inadequate. As with individuals, private industries (even those focusing upon informational values) will be using a criterion based on expected profitability, yet an argument could be made that the appropriate objective should be to maximize the amount of information derived per unit of expenditure (Weitzman, 1993). The public sector has a much wider range of social objectives which it may consider than the private sector, and one focused on the informational rather than the current production value of the resource would favour a much greater supply of genetic resources.

Another reason is based more on national externalities. Even if private companies should wish to invest in the conservation of particular land areas in certain countries, they might find it very difficult to obtain any return from doing so across political boundaries. The absence of universally recognized property rights in informational values renders investments across borders highly dubious. Most plant breeders mention 'insecurity of investment' as the primary reason why more investments in *in situ* conservation do not occur; it is one of the primary reasons why private firms put relatively little effort into it (Swanson, 1996b). This property right failure implies the necessity of public-sector intervention.

The public interest in genetic resource conservation for agriculture

This section has demonstrated the values of genetic resources which the private sector may, or may not, take into account systematically in making conservation and use decisions. It is then the role of the public sector to intervene to conserve genetic resources for agriculture to retain those values which are underappreciated by the private sector.

This framework helps to identify the values of genetic diversity which should be the subject of public interest and investment in order to ensure the future of modern agriculture. The nurturing and advancement of the 'green revolution' has been an important event in human history, but it is equally important that a scientific basis for conservation is developed in order to ensure the sustainability of this advance. The next section outlines an approach to analysing the optimal methods of conserving genetic resources for this purpose.

THE POLICY PROBLEM:
PUBLIC MANAGEMENT OF GENETIC RESOURCES

How should the public sector intervene in order to address externalities? There are two basic technologies for managing crop genetic resources, *in situ* and *ex situ* (Orians *et al.*, 1990). The fundamental difference between them lies in the quantities of land implicit in the conservation approach; one requires large quantities of land dedicated to conservation, while the other requires virtually none at all. The technologies of conservation also represent fundamentally different approaches to problem solving. In this section we will define how these strategies differ in their approach to the conservation problem in the context of the dynamic environment outlined earlier. In essence, *in situ* conservation may be defined as an approach to decision making that is focused on the *optimal appropriation of information* arriving over time, whereas *ex situ* conservation may be defined as the *optimal utilization of a given set of germ plasm* at a given point in time. The relative values of the two approaches are dependent upon the expected value of the flow of information in the decision-making context. When a flow of information across time is important, *in situ* conservation will afford additional values to those supplied by *ex situ* methods.

It will be necessary to evaluate each of the available approaches to conservation against a given societal objective. The objective here will be taken to be the

maximization of agricultural productivity subject to the pathogen/host dynamics set out earlier; this gives the following expression for *maximum sustainable
social welfare*:

$$Max \int_0^\infty e^{-\rho t} Y_t dt = Max \int_0^\infty e^{-\rho t} \left(f(\Omega_t)^{\bar{a}-\bar{r}} \right) \bar{p}_t dt \qquad (1)$$

where

$$\bar{r} = \mu \cdot \Delta \cdot k_i - \pi \cdot \Gamma_i \cdot v$$

Agricultural output Y_t is here represented as a function of the expected yield of
utilized crops (where the choice of utilized crops is dependent on the information in hand, which is denoted by the matrix Ω), an aggregate productivity
parameter vector $\bar{a}$, an aggregate of the virulence/resistance parameter r and
valued according to the price vector $\bar{p}$.

This objective function states that production across time is a function of
crop variety choice, which determines both productivity and resistance within
the system. In turn, crop variety choice is a function of the information which
the system produces across time (on the contribution of various crops to both
productivity and stability). Hence information drives the model; crop selec-
tions influence its generation and depend upon its existence. The dynamics of
the system are, however, both informational and ecological: crop selection
determines the resistance level of the current and future systems.[6] Despite the
added complexity, this remains a highly simplified version of the societal
objective function regarding global agricultural production, which places emphasis on the maximization of the stable values of global yields. This abstracts
from other issues such as distribution,[7] variability[8] and desirability,[9] and focuses on the single issue of how genetic resources should be managed in order
to provide for maximum *sustainable* global yields in agriculture.[10] This is the
question to which we now turn.

In situ conservation as a closed-loop strategy

In situ conservation (as used here) implies the existence of a group of individuals who continue to dedicate some amount of land use to a broad set of
crop genetic resources under very flexible technologies. In the past, individuals in less developed countries did precisely this as optimizing agents, using
crop genetic resources as a hedge against financial risks. As markets mature,
individuals have access to more efficient methods of hedging risk and replace *in situ* conservation with these other financial instruments. The object
of *in situ* conservation is to have some set of farmers engage in traditional
farming practices in continuing fashion. This requires the creation of a system of incentives which will induce a group of farmers to act so as to
maximize their risk-adjusted income by making use of the naturally sourced
information available at every point in time when carrying out their cultivation decisions.[11]

Let us assume that it is possible to institute a programme of *in situ* conservation on some set of lands. This means that there is a sub-set of farmers whose choice of crop germ plasm is made in response to the shifting environment; they are using broader portfolios of germ plasm to hedge against environmental risks, rather than other sorts of risk-hedging instruments. The germ plasm which results from this method of operation then incorporates a flow of information; that is, the crop varieties in use by this set of farmers will contain traits and characteristics that are effective under currently prevailing environmental conditions. These favoured traits and characteristics represent a flow of information from nature to the farmers in the *in situ* conservation areas. Then the modern agricultural sector is able to utilize this information to inform its choices of crop varieties throughout agriculture.

The solution of the problem of maximum sustainable production by *in situ* conservation represents a well-known approach to the use of information in making. This formulation of the decision process is generally known as a *closed-loop* or *feedback* rule under which the values of the choice variables depend upon the current performance of the system under control (Holly and Hughes Hallett, 1989).[12] The solution to a problem stated within the closed-loop format is normally a function (rather than an explicit set of values).[13] That is, the solution is a process of information acquisition and utilization rather than a specific set of choices taken by reference to the information available at one point in time. *In situ* conservation therefore accords with the idea of a closed loop method of decision making; it contemplates basing the decision in each period on the best information available *in the period in which that decision is taken*.

There is no doubt that there is information arriving in each period that is potentially valuable in decision making regarding the control of modern agriculture; the object of the earlier section on evolution and agriculture was to describe the systems that continue in motion across time and how they might contribute information to agriculture. The information from nature in each period is being provided by the existence of *in situ* conservation and the fact that relative performance of various plant varieties is directly observable by the decision maker in each period. On the other hand, the amount of information is necessarily limited by the size of the set of genetic resources in continued interaction with the environment.

The cost associated with this information-generating process is equal to the opportunity costs of the land dedicated to *in situ* conservation, since the cultivation of sub-optimally performing varieties under sub-optimal technologies will reduce the expected present values of these operations.

To illustrate the nature of closed-loop decision making, consider the following simple example. Under an *in situ* conservation programme, there will be a set of farmers who will devote a fixed proportion of the available land (c) to the cultivation of a diverse set of variables (y_d) of a single crop. The quantities c and y_d are exogenously determined by the system of incentives established under the *in situ* conservation system. Meanwhile, by focusing only on yield information, the lands in the modern agricultural sector will be invested in the currently best performing crop. Assuming that there is a relatively low level of output on the lands invested in conservation, *aggregate agricultural output with in situ conservation costs* in period t is therefore:

$$Y_t = (1-c) \cdot \left[E\left(y_{e_t}\right)^{\alpha_e - r_e} \right] \cdot \overline{p}_t$$

The decision rule in each period reduces to assigning the soil resources $(1 - c)$ to the asset e which maximizes output. A closed-loop decision-making process does this in a manner that makes maximum use of the information that is expected to flow into the system. Here we will focus on the use of the information flowing from nature, as derived from the land used for conservation (c). Therefore, looking forward one period, output in $t + dt$ with closed-loop decision making will be:

$$Y_{t+dt} = (1-c) \cdot \max\left\{ (\hat{y}_e)^{\alpha_e - r_e}; (\hat{y}_e + \Delta)^{\alpha_e - r_e}; (\hat{y}_f)^{\alpha_f - r_f}; (\hat{y}_f + \Delta)^{\alpha_f - r_f} \right\} \quad (2)$$

where $\hat{y}_f = \max_t \{y_d\}$.

Equation (2) just states that output in the modern agricultural sector will be produced by using the best available option from either the previous input variety e, potentially changed by depreciation or adaptation, or the best variety f available from the set of diverse resources in period t; or a variety from that set has recently been adapted to existing environmental conditions. This means that modern agriculture is able to rely upon the genetic resources within that sector so long as they produce the best yields, but that there are other sectors available if that is not the case. More importantly, the alternative sectors are simultaneously producing the information on the important traits and characteristics for adaptation while the environment continues to change.

For example, the usual pattern of use regarding a particular plant variety indicates that pest resistance will erode to render that variety economically non-resistant within four or five years; this rate of environmentally induced depreciation is represented by the third term in equation (2) above. On account of this predictable rate of depreciation (and the unlikelihood of economically significant adaptations in a monocultural system), the alternative varieties in use in the conservation system begin to become relatively more attractive; this is represented by the fourth term in equation (2). The conservation system operates as a 'bank' of previously existing but inferior varieties. However, the single most important function performed by the conservation system is the capture of a flow of adaptations within that system; this is represented in the final term in that maximand. It states that the *in situ* system will observe and make use of any important adaptation signalled within that environment. All that is required is the land use decision providing for the dedication of some amount of land to the cultivation of a wide range of diverse varieties. Then the desirable traits and characteristics identified within the diverse *in situ* system may be cycled into the more uniform modern agricultural sector on a systematic basis.

Therefore *in situ* conservation is an approach that maintains a set of farming systems for the information that such systems will generate for the decision-making process. In each period, decisions must be made concerning the maintenance of agriculture, and each and every farm practising traditional and diversity-based agriculture acts as a receptor of information on the shifting of the natural environment. The greater the number of receptors in existence, the greater the likelihood that the information on the solution to the problems inherent in the current shifts in the environment will be available. *In situ* conservation represents an approach dedicated to the capture of this incoming information.[14]

Ex situ conservation as an open-loop strategy

Ex situ conservation may be conceptualized as a very different form of approach to the problems arising in modern agriculture. It is based on the idea that the solution to future problems is probably to be found in the set of currently existing genetic resources. Rather than base decision making on the capture and use of a flow of future information, the *ex situ* approach attempts to make optimal use of an already existing stock of information (represented by the already existing closely related varieties). In short, the two approaches are distinct approaches to the same problem, and both are necessary components of a complete solution to agricultural problems.

We will conceptualize *ex situ* conservation as a process in which the decision maker selects the set of genetic resources to be used in the maintenance of modern agriculture at a single point in time (t_0). The decision maker does this by selecting the optimal set of assets from the available genetic pool at this time and storing them, for future use, as inputs into the agricultural production process. The decision-making process is distinct from the previous one because it is based on the optimal use of the set of information already existing rather than the optimal appropriation of a flow of incoming information. The decision-making rule in the open-loop case can be stated at:

$$\bar{u}_t = g_{t,t_0}\left(\Omega_{t_0}\right)$$

This is the usual formulation of an open-loop decision rule. In it the decision maker is committed to a specific decision-making process across time based on a calculation procedure $g(\cdot)$ applied to a given set of information available at some particular point in time (t_0) (Holly and Hughes Hallett, 1989). In this context the given set of information consists of the stock of genetic resources available for banking at a particular point in time. The irreversibility of genetic erosion imposes the restriction of a non-increasing set of genetic resources in storage over time (Frankel *et al.*, 1995).

Decision making of open-loop form is used when the supply of genetic resources is restricted to the use of gene banks. From the set of already existing varieties, a set is selected for conservation within the gene bank. This information set is then 'frozen' at the time of collection.[15] The remaining unbanked stocks of genetic resources are increasingly lost through displacement by modern agriculture. The flows of future information are lost by reason of the loss of the 'receptor sites' (that previously diverse agriculture represented) as traditional agricultural land uses are replaced by modern agriculture. In short, *ex situ* conservation represents a decision-making process concerning the optimal use of the already existing stocks of information inherent in landraces and other stocks of genetic resources, and nothing more.

Optimal conservation: combined strategies

Optimal genetic resource conservation for food security in agriculture is a general problem composed of two parts: the first concerns the optimal use of existing stocks of information (primarily for immediate yield improvements) and the second deals with the optimal appropriation and use of future flows of information (primarily for the maintenance of current yield levels). For the dynamic aspects of the problems of agriculture, it is best to use a dynamic approach to decision making; this implies the use of *in situ* conservation for addressing the optimal appropriation of flows of information, while *ex situ* conservation is used to optimize the use of existing stocks of information. In essence, there are two parts to this problem and therefore two instruments (*ex situ* and *in situ*) are necessary to reach the optimal solution.[16]

CONCLUSION

This paper has attempted to demonstrate the ecological and informational nature of the plant-breeding problem and the externalities that recommend public intervention within the plant-breeding industry. This has the responsibility for maintaining stability within the modern agricultural system by continually and perpetually introducing new resistance into the prevalent commercial strains. This requires a continual flow of information on successful resistance strategies available into the indefinite future.

Where is that supply of information to come from? It arrives as both a stock (of previously used crop varieties and the resistance they retain) and as a flow (of newly found successful traits within competitive environments). Both forms of information are important in the optimal management of agricultural stability, and different forms of conservation strategies are required to yield each. *Ex situ* conservation focuses on the former, while *in situ* conservation acts as the primary supplier of the latter.

NOTES

[1]It is also possible to reformulate this discussion in terms of pathogens and 'traits' or something similar which would focus the analysis on crop varieties rather than crops, but this version is retained for simplicity and clarity.

[2]Agriculture has some of the characteristics of an arms race. Escalation generates re-escalation. This indicates that there are only two bases upon which the considered adoption of agriculture would have originally occurred: (1) unceasing technological optimism regarding the innovative capacity of the species to outperform the evolutionary capacity of the pests and pathogens; or (2) discounting the impact of agriculture on future production choices. It makes no difference which was the original basis for the initiation of the contest; now that it is started, all that matters is keeping it going.

[3]This might be viewed as a practical example of the so-called 'strong sustainability' criterion (Tisdell, 1996). This is the criterion that states that a certain level of natural capital must be maintained for production to continue (Pearce, 1993). In this context, it could be argued that, at least at present, there is no substitute for natural selection as a mechanism for providing information on the optimal strategies for continuing within this contest, and therefore a constraint on maintaining the natural capital stock (of resistance) intact is required.

[4]A later section of the paper introduces a more general version of this model which includes condition (1) as a dynamic constraint rather than a static one.

[5]This section reprises Swanson (1996a). There is relevant discussion in Swanson (1996b).

[6]In this dynamic representation, the ecological constraint translates into the state variable in this programme. This is because in a static world the best way to think of this condition is as a constraint on the otherwise unconstrained maximization of static agricultural productivity. In a dynamic world, the level of virulence/resistance in the system is one very important factor contributing to the overall productivity of the system, and the generation of information (within agriculture and for use in agriculture) relating to resistance is one of the objectives of agriculture.

[7]We plead the standard excuse given by economists: redistribution is most efficiently accomplished through the most neutral taxation mechanisms available.

[8]So long as the vast majority of yields are susceptible to storage over at least one period, the problems raised by variability around a given yield level may be addressed through insurance mechanisms based upon consumption smoothing through storage. The problem that we address here is more concerned with the difficulty of ensuring that such variability does not result in continually declining levels of production, with declining consumption levels over the long term.

[9]It is of course debatable whether maximum food production is a desirable social objective, since food production for human use implies other opportunities forgone, such as the provision of habitats for other species.

[10]The issue of how to aggregate value across time is an important one in this context. Given that the issue concerns the provision of the resources for the survival of society (no reason for pure time preference) and there is little reason to expect that the demand for food will decline in the foreseeable future (elasticity of demand with income growth is probably changing no faster than are global populations), there are good reasons to believe that the relevant discount rate in this context is very near to zero.

[11]*In situ* conservation might be provided, for example, by paying farmers to dedicate certain designated lands to the use of only those plant genetic resources acquired from the previous year's harvest. There are other issues that must be considered, however. For example, it is also important for farmers to be provided with an incentive structure that causes them to consider using plant genetic resources in order to hedge risk in their agricultural decisions, so that they will retain diversity. Also there are other issues concerning the determination of the initial set of plant genetic resources available to the 'traditional farmer' and the forms of exchange (for example, between traditional farmers) that might be available between harvests. Finally, the technology utilized by the traditional farmers must be flexible enough to allow natural selection to play an important role in farmers' choice of crop varieties. In short, the essence of *in situ* conservation must be the maintenance of a set of farmers making their own decisions based on a restricted set of germ plasm choice but utilizing much of the natural information generated by the changing environment.

[12]The special case of a stationary function is normally described as a *stationary Markov strategy* (Cornes *et al.*, 1995) which takes as its arguments the currently observed results from recent choices.

[13]In other words, the vector of weights a farmer i attaches to his set of crop varieties at time t, that is, his control variable vector $\bar{u}_i$, is the outcome of a time-invariant decision rule ϕ, applied to the full set of currently available crop performance information which is a composite matrix of the mean yield vector $\bar{y}_t$ and the variance–covariance matrix of the yields $\prod_t$:

$$\bar{u}_t = \phi_i\left(\bar{y}_t;\prod_t\right) - \phi_i(\Omega_t)$$

[14]This conception of *in situ* conservation renders it analogous to an observation mechanism used within any context of stochastic control. It is a mechanism installed for the purpose of acquiring information on the current state of the system.

[15]'The genetic resources [of crop plants] that are preserved in genetic resources centres are maintained "frozen", which in many cases is literally true' (Frankel *et al.*, 1995, p. 5).

[16]A fuller treatment of this problem is provided in a paper by Swanson and Goeschl, titled 'Optimal conservation strategies: *In situ* and *ex situ*', which will appear in a volume to be edited by Stephen Brush.

BIBLIOGRAPHY

Allard, R.W. (1990), 'The Genetics of Host–Pathogen Coevolution: Implications for Genetic Resource Conservation', *Journal of Heredity*, **91**, 1–6.

Altieri, M. and Merrick, L. (1987), '*In situ* conservation of crop genetic resources through maintenance of traditional farming systems', *Economic Botany*, **41**, 86–96.

Burdon, J.J., Brown, A.H.D. and Jarosz, A.M. (1990), 'The Spatial Scale of Genetic Interactions in Host–Pathogen Coevolved Systems', in J.J. Burdon and S.R. Leather (eds), *Pests, Pathogens and Plant Communities*, Oxford: Basil Blackwell.

Conrad, J. (1980), 'Quasi-option value and the expected value of information', *Quarterly Journal of Economics*, **94**, 813–20.

Cornes, R., Long, Ngo Van and Shimomura, K. (1995), 'Drugs and Pests: Negative Intertemporal Productivity Externalities', mimeo, McGill University, Montreal.

Evans, L.T. (1993), *Crop Evolution, Adaption and Yield*, Cambridge: Cambridge University Press.

Frankel, O., Brown, A. and Burdon, J. (1995), *The Conservation of Plant Biodiversity*, Cambridge: Cambridge University Press.

Goeschl, T. and Swanson, T. (1997), *On the Relationship between Crop Genetic Diversity and Economic Development*, working paper, Rome: International Plant Genetic Resource Institute.

Hanneman, M. (1989), 'Information and the Concept of Option Value', *Journal of Environmental Economics and Resource Management*, **16**, 23–37.

Hartell, J., Smale, M., Heisey, P. and Senauer, B. (1997), *The Contribution of Genetic Resources and Diversity to Wheat Productivity: A Case from the Punjab of Pakistan*, Economics Working Paper 97-01, Mexico, DF:CIMMYT.

Hazell, P. (1984), 'Sources of Increased Instability in Indian and U.S. Cereal Production', *American Journal of Agricultural Economics*, **66**, 302–11.

Hazell, P. (1989), 'Changing Patterns of Variability in World Cereal Production', in J.R. Anderson and P. Hazell (eds), *Variability in grain yields: Implications for agricultural research and policy in developing countries*, Baltimore and London: Johns Hopkins University Press for the International Food Policy Research Institute.

Heisey, P. (ed.) (1990), *Accelerating the Transfer of Wheat Breeding Gains to Farmers: A Study of the Dynamics of Varietal Replacement in Pakistan*, Research Report No. 1, Mexico, DF:CIMMYT.

Hofbauer, J. and Sigmund, K. (1989), *The Theory of Evolution and Dynamical Systems*, Cambridge: Cambridge University Press.

Holly, S. and Hughes Hallett, A. (1989), *Optimal Control, Expectations and Uncertainty*, Cambridge: Cambridge University Press.

Hueth, D. and Regev, U. (1974), 'Optimal Pest Management with Increasing Resistance', *American Journal of Agricultural Economics*, **56**, 543–52.

National Academy of Sciences (1972), *Genetic Vulnerability of Major Crops*, Washington, DC: National Academy of Sciences.

Orians, G., Brown, G., Kunin, W. and Swierzbinski, J. (eds) (1990), *The Preservation and Valuation of Biological Resources*, Seattle: University of Washington Press.

Pearce, D. (1993), *Blueprint 3: Measuring Sustainable Development*, London: Earthscan.

Pearce, D. and Ulph, D. (1995), 'The Choice of the Social Discount Rate', CSERGE Discussion Paper, University College London.

Plucknett, D. and Smith, N. (1986), 'Sustaining Agricultural Yields', *Bioscience*, **36**, 40–45.

Rejesus, R., Smale, M. and Van Ginkel, M. (1996), 'Wheat Breeders' Perspectives on Genetic Diversity and Germplasm Use', *Plant Varieties and Seeds*, **9**, 129–47.

Smale, M. (1996), *Understanding Global Trends in the Use of Wheat Diversity and International Flows of Wheat Genetic Resources*, Economics Working Paper 96-02, Mexico, DF:CIMMYT.

Smale, M. and McBride, T. (1996), 'Understanding global trends in use of wheat diversity and international flows of wheat genetic resources', in CIMMYT, *World Wheat Facts and Trends 1995/96*, Mexico, DF:CIMMYT.

Srivastava, J., Smith, N.J.H. and Forno, D. (1996), *Biodiversity and Agriculture – Implications for Conservation and Development*, Technical Paper, 321, Washington, DC: World Bank.

Swanson, T. (1994), *The International Regulation of Extinction*, Basingstoke: Macmillan.

Swanson, T. (ed.) (1995), *The Economics and Ecology of Biodiversity Decline*, Cambridge: Cambridge University Press.

Swanson, T. (1996a), 'The Reliance of Northern Economics on Southern Biodiversity: Biodiversity as Information', *Ecological Economics*, **19**, 1–8.

Swanson, T. (1996b), 'Global Values of Biological Diversity', *FAO Plant Genetic Resources Newsletter*, **105**, 1–7.

Swanson, T., Cervigni, R. and Pearce, D. (1994), *The Appropriation of the Benefits of Plant Genetic Resources for Agriculture*, Rome: FAO Commission on Plant Genetic Resources.

Tisdell, C. (1996), *Agricultural Sustainability and Conservation of Biodiversity*, Working Paper No. 33, Brisbane: University of Queensland.

Weitzman, M. (1993), 'What to Preserve? An Application of Diversity Theory to Crane Conservation', *Quarterly Journal of Economics*, **111**, 157–83.

World Conservation Monitoring Centre and Faculty of Economics, Cambridge University (1996), *Industrial Reliance Upon Biodiversity*, Cambridge: WCMC.

DISCUSSION REPORT SECTION III

Anthony Chisholm (Australia)[1], opening the discussions, said that the report on water and land resources in relation to global food supply by Rosegrant, Ringler and Gerpacio (hereafter the IFPRI study) had a succinct central message: world cereal prices will continue to decline, in real terms, and land degradation does not pose a threat to global food production. However, water scarcity could threaten projected growth in agricultural production. He noted that two important assumptions are underlying the IFPRI model. First, the global yield growth rate for all cereals will decline from 1.5 per cent per year in 1982–94 to 1.1 per cent in 1993–2020 and, second, that China's GDP grows at 6 per cent per year, a lower rate than China has achieved over the past 15 years. Other things being equal, he said that the first assumption would tend to raise world prices, the second to lower them. All exercises of this type are sensitive to assumptions and highlighting them clearly is important. The other feature of the work is that it does not appear to reflect the implications of the final Uruguay Round agreement. That is likely to raise international food prices; it may only be a modest 2–4 per cent higher in a decade's time, though it is a factor that should enter the picture. It is also worth noting that there is no real consideration of the impact of climate change, where the vulnerability could mainly be with developing countries.

On land degradation, Chisholm argued that the authors make a good point, often ignored, when they indicate that existing soil erosion estimates usually do not account for soil eroded from one site sometimes being deposited elsewhere on productive agricultural land. However, on the other side, he did feel that there are a number of reasons why existing estimates of productivity loss, based on crop yield data, may understate the impact of soil erosion. For example, few studies appropriately account for costly use of inputs to substitute for loss of soil endowment, or the conversion of land to lower-valued uses due to soil erosion. It is possible that the negative rates of growth in total factor productivity (TFP) estimated for a number of developing countries in recent studies may be partly attributable to unmeasured loss of soil endowment. The picture is further complicated since non-linearities in the underlying relationships may cause there to be considerable lags between decline of some forms of soil endowment and the realization of productivity effects. To obtain a better understanding of the role of land degradation in global food production, we clearly require more detailed research linking physical/chemical measures of land degradation with soil productivity changes.

The IFPRI study identifies potential water constraints as a more serious threat to future food production than land degradation. In Chisholm's opinion,

[1]La Trobe University.

this stems from inadequate policies and institutions rather than a lack of availability of efficient technologies and management systems. Drop irrigation, a technology that has been available since the mid-1960s, conserves water and reduces drainage, but farmers will only adopt such technologies when policies and institutions provide incentive structures for socially efficient behaviour. He hoped that the highlighting of the 'water constraint' by IFPRI would result in far more thought being given to the regulation of its use, and stressed the fundamental importance of the issue.

Prabhu Pingali[2] discussed Darwin Hall's climate change paper. He felt that the paper had many interesting and informative features relating to the adaptation that might ultimately be needed in agriculture, but in more critical vein he was extremely sceptical about using regression methods to model the possible effects of climate change variables on agriculture. It appeared to him that simulation models were methodologically better fitted to the task than regression. Even in simulation the basic parameters had to be drawn from a few experiments conducted in controlled, rather than natural, conditions and not pursued over long time periods. He was also worried about the lack of reliable climate data for large parts of the world. The uncertainties of the modelling process, and the fact that we cannot put much trust in the results, do not, however, justify taking a 'head-in-the-sand', ostrich-like view. If there are effects of the size which Hall inferred, it is important to improve modelling rather than to abandon it. The urgency may not appear extreme, though the issue is potentially serious enough for people now being born to experience food security effects towards the end of the 21st century.

P.S. Ramarkrishna (India)[3] expressed the opinion that Timothy Swanson was taking a very narrow view of the biodiversity issue. In his opinion, 'state'-level actions had sometimes increased resource scarcity and had undermined the conservation of natural resources. He was much more hopeful about successful initiatives being taken at lower levels of government, or indeed at the communal level. This, he felt, needed to be brought into the discussion since there was a danger of regarding 'the government' as the locus of all solutions.

Clem Tisdell (Australia)[4], who had organized the section, summarized briefly by linking the three papers. The IFPRI work, as reported in the section and in the paper of Pinstrup-Andersen and Pandya-Lorch, was guardedly optimistic about food supplies over the short term to 2020 (decades are important in that context). The time bombs (climate change and the continuous need to replenish germ plasm) are set for later, over our ability to maintain food supplies of an adequate level *throughout* the next century.

[2]CIMMYT, Mexico.
[3]Jawaharlal Nehru University, New Delhi.
[4]University of Queensland, Brisbane.

SECTION IV

Economics of Policy and Institutional Change

P. MICHAEL SCHMITZ AND CORNELIA NOETH*

Institutional and Organizational Forces Shaping the Agricultural Transformation Process: Experiences, Causes and Implications

INTRODUCTION

In the light of about eight years of transition experience in the Central and Eastern European countries (CEECs), it remains a challenging task to look back to their original situation prior to the beginning of the agricultural transformation process, to compare targets and expectations with the outcome and to seek a fuller understanding of what has happened. At the beginning of the transition period and during the process itself, a great deal of advice was being given, though it was quite clear that there was no prior theory of transition that could help in the formulation of commonly accepted guidelines. Examples of successful radical transformation of distorted economies in the past were also rare. Even now most published papers in the mainstream literature treat the development of the economies in individual countries in a somewhat descriptive way, although certain aspects, like reform strategies, macroeconomic stabilization or alternative ways of privatization, have been discussed theoretically.

The intention of this paper is to provide an overview of the main problems that occurred during the transition period and to discuss their causes and attempted solutions. A key aspect for the progress of transition is the institutional change that provides the organizational infrastructure for the formation of a market economy. Hence the focus of this paper is on institutional aspects affecting the agricultural sector which will take centre stage after a preliminary discussion of the macroeconomic situation. The crucial question will concern the optimal form of farm organization, which will be discussed with the help of two models which incorporate essential elements of the new institutional economics, namely the problem of moral hazard and the principal–agent conflict.

The starting point of the paper is the objectives of the transformation process. In that respect, there is some agreement on the nature of the desired results, but how to get there is a matter of controversy, since the main pitfalls are not well understood. A central issue in the discussion which follows is the role of institutional design both as a determinant of past failures and as a key element shaping the future. It is a subject which can only be discussed with the help of conclusions derived from economic theory and particularly from the new institutional economics. The messages which emerge should be

*University of Giessen, Germany.

understood to be somewhat stylized in the sense that they abstract from the particular circumstances of individual CEE countries. However, the conclusions drawn will be confronted with the experiences of East Germany in order to provide some deeper insights into the complex interactions involved in real situations.

Last, but not least, a careful examination of the agricultural transition process in East Europe and East Germany is not only useful for further developing an efficient policy and institutional framework in former socialist countries but could also be useful in transforming farm policies in Western countries. Although some experience with agricultural transition programmes has already been obtained (in New Zealand and the United States) most countries still heavily rely on numerous command and control elements in their policies. In addition, reform and transition programmes to date have concentrated largely on the operational level (Hartmann *et al.*, 1991) and often exclude institutional and organizational adjustments in the agrifood sector. This accounts for the failure of some reforms, such as the European Union changes of 1992, to make domestic agriculture competitive in a world context.

In the paper, 'institutions' are defined as rules of the game in a society where personal behaviour and human interaction are rule-bound, not rule-determined (North, 1990, p. 3). Hence institutions reduce uncertainty by providing a cost-minimizing structure for transactions. A structure for human interaction can also be provided by 'organizations', which are groups of individuals bound by some common purpose to achieve objectives. They are players in the game. Against that background 'transition' or 'transformation' implies a more or less time-consuming and cost-intensive move to a new set of institutions and organizations.

TRANSITION IN CEECS: EXPERIENCE AND FIRST IMPRESSIONS

The main objectives of a successful transformation from a centrally planned system to a market economy can be summarized under a number of broad headings (Dewatripont and Roland, 1996; World Bank, 1996): (1) allocative efficiency, (2) competitive markets, (3) stabilized macroeconomy, (4) privatization and (5) institutional change. These features are closely related. For instance, without the necessary institutional background the protection and legal certainty of property rights will not be guaranteed, hence private investment as the engine for economic development is likely to be slowed down. The targets also have to be reached in a process that may take time and give rise to problems. In that respect, it was always anticipated that an economic recession could result during the shift from central planning towards a democratic market system, though in the event the duration of the recession has been much longer than expected and the economic and social costs of the transition have therefore been much higher. The agricultural sector, in particular, was adversely affected by the set of macroeconomic and sectoral problems which are listed below.

Substantial decline in the gross domestic product

Decline was a feature of all post-socialist countries, at least in the first two years of transition. To provide examples, Figure 1 shows the change in gross domestic product (GDP) from 1989 to 1996 for Bulgaria, the Czech Republic, Hungary and Poland. In each case, the worst years of dramatic decline were 1990 and 1991, though from 1992 deterioration became less marked in three cases, and had already given way to positive growth in Poland, through the emergence of new enterprises. Recovery eventually began to occur in Hungary, Bulgaria and the Czech Republic, although their GDP is still below the pre-transformation level. Rosati (1994) described the behaviour of output during the first stages of transition as an L-shaped, rather than a U-shaped, pattern in terms of the cumulative change in GDP from 1989 to 1993. The situation looks far worse for the CIS (Commonwealth of Independent States) and some Baltic countries. The largest countries in the CIS (Russia and Ukraine) still await the initial appearance of positive growth, whereas eight of the smaller CIS countries realized increases in industrial output in the first half of 1996 (Bartholdy, 1996).

That, however, is less promising than it might appear, since it is important to consider the current account of the balance of payments as well. In the Czech

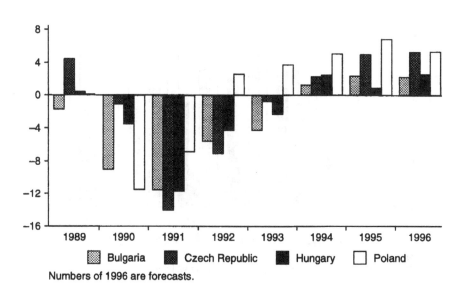

Numbers of 1996 are forecasts.

FIGURE 1   *Changes in gross domestic product in selected CEE countries (%)*

Source: OECD (1996, p. 167).

Republic, Poland, Romania, the Slovak Republic, Slovenia and the three Baltic countries, there was a sharp deterioration in the current account in 1995 and 1996. This indicates that strong expansion of domestic demand has tended to favour foreign producers, not least those in agriculture.

High levels of unemployment

Unemployment has risen substantially. From the figures in Figure 2 (again for the four illustrative cases) it can be seen that the percentage rates of unemployment have become larger than the percentage decreases in GDP. Furthermore, while the worst year for total production was 1991, unemployment continued to rise into 1993. This was very obvious in Poland and Bulgaria, which both reached a rate of 16 per cent. However, there is some variability; Poland has remained the unemployment black spot, Bulgaria and Hungary have experienced some recovery, while in the Czech Republic the unemployment rate rose only by small amounts and tended to hover around the very low level of 3 per cent. A recovery in the employment situation is especially important for rural and agricultural development.

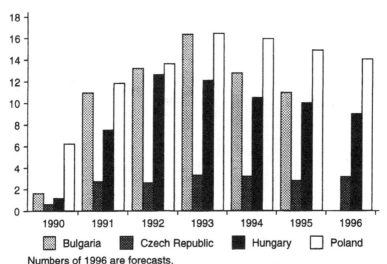

Numbers of 1996 are forecasts.
The unemployment rate of Bulgaria 1996 is not available.

FIGURE 2   *The development of unemployment in selected CEE countries (%)*

Source: OECD (1996, p. 167).

Inflation/hyperinflation

The rate of inflation has varied considerably in individual CEE countries since the beginning of the transformation process (Figure 3). In Poland, an enormous increase, to more than 500 per cent, was experienced in 1990, though after successful stabilization programmes the rate was driven back to 20–30 per cent. Experience has been similar in Bulgaria, with a time lag of one year. Other than in the Czech Republic, the inflation rate in CEE countries is still very high compared with the Western economies and thus contributes to a deterioration of the commodity terms of trade for agriculture. For Russia, the largest country of the CIS, inflation has declined gradually over the last five years, from over 800 per cent in 1993 to 50 per cent in 1996 (Bartholdy, 1996).

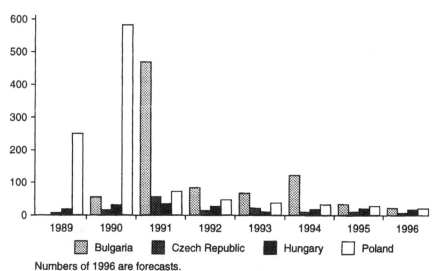

Numbers of 1996 are forecasts.
The inflation rate of Bulgaria 1989 is not available.

FIGURE 3   *The development of the annual average inflation rate in selected CEE countries (%)*

Source: OECD (1996, p. 167).

Reductions in the volume of agricultural output

Agriculture is far more important in the economies of the CEE countries than it is on average in the EU member states; in 1993, the shares in GDP were 7.8 per cent and 2.5 per cent, respectively. With regard to the share of employees in agriculture the difference, 26.7 per cent in the CEE countries and 5.7 per cent in the EU in 1993, is even more significant (Wissenschaftlicher Beirat, 1997, pp. 4–11).

Figure 4 demonstrates that, in comparison with the decline of GDP, the fall in agricultural gross product is less strong in the first two years. The massive breakdowns appear in 1992 and 1993 which, at 10 to 20 per cent, are even more dramatic than the highest reductions of GDP in 1991. Poland is the exception. After a decline of more than 10 per cent in 1992, there was a very sharp recovery in 1993, when a positive growth rate of 8 per cent was reached; it is true that there was a drop in 1994, though the rate then exceeded 10 per cent in 1995. A similar quick recovery in growth from minus 18 per cent in 1993 to plus 2.5 per cent took place in Bulgaria one year later.

In Poland, Hungary and the Czech Republic, there was success in establishing convertibility, which allowed some transmission of world prices to domestic producers and consumers. The starting level of distortions in these countries was therefore lower than in the former Soviet Union (FSU), and they were supported by being allowed some market access to Western Europe (Brooks, 1993).

As in the case of GDP, the agricultural situation in the FSU and the Baltic countries is not promising. In all of them agricultural gross output is still decreasing, although less then in the first years. An important reason for these

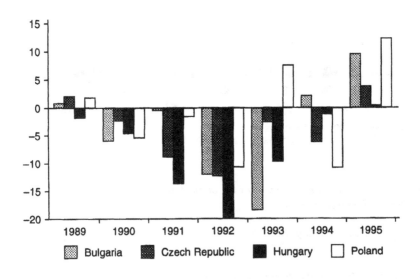

FIGURE 4   *The development of total gross agricultural output in selected CEE countries (%)*

Source: OECD (1996, p. 171).

differences lies in the slower progress in privatization, which will be discussed in more detail later, and in the problems of the Russian food sector (von Braun *et al.*, 1996).

Explanations of the problems

The reasons underlying transition problems have obviously been widely discussed (Schmieding, 1993; Rosati, 1994; Horn, 1996). Theoretically derived suggestions can be based on neoclassical explanations involving lack of resource mobility and factor price rigidities which result in lack of response to new opportunities and particularly those due to currency devaluation. Some authors mention the uncertainties caused by less than sufficient macroeconomic stabilization policies, while others focus on the tightening of credit conditions in underdeveloped and distorted financial markets, which lead into Keynesian approaches based on demand deficiency. Institutional factors have also been stressed. For example, by using regression analysis, Köhne (1997) was able to show that the importance of economic variables, such as price distortions and sector-specific taxes, is matched by that of political indicators, notably lack of political stability, in accounting for reductions in economic growth.

Most economists agree that the combination of various factors, rather than a single cause, is responsible for the problems which have been observed. However, there is one very common view which appears as an ingredient in most of the attempts at explanation; this is the 'lack of market argument'. Many of the problems occurring during the transformation process can be put down, to some extent, to the institutional vacuum in which the first reforms have been attempted. There are serious problems in creating new institutions in countries in transition (Koester, 1995). Though the implementation of the liberalization policies was quite straightforward, any institutional restructuring is a far more complicated process. This can now be discussed, though without too much country-specific detail, by considering the restructuring of the agricultural sector in order to show how the 'new institutional economics' can help to formulate guidelines for organizational design.

EXPLAINING THE AGRICULTURAL TRANSFORMATION CRISIS

Institutional deficits for restructuring

The main hypothesis is that the institutional vacuum which follows the collapse of socialism represents an essential cause of the transformation crisis. Following the neoclassical explanation, it can be argued that the structure of production had previously been distorted and resources had not been allocated according to their marginal value. Instead, overindustrialization was emphasized and infrastructure neglected. Consequently, the original GDP was far below the level it could have been. Why then has there been a further worsening in the position after an apparent correction has taken place, and is it the result of difficulties in adaption? Rigidities could consist of insufficient mobility of factors or inflexible factor prices, and could be exacerbated by the fact that structural adjustment needs time. Our view is that this is not the way in which to approach the issue and that there is more promise in an institutional approach, based on a belief that 'the economy' consists of more than the 'market mechanism'. With the growth of specialization in production, and the increasing complexity of the division of labour, it is not the market directly, but the organizational structure, that effectively allocates resources and reduces transaction costs. The institutions in what are now transition economies were designed to meet the needs of the socialist system. That did not stress decentralized decision making and the coordination of demand and supply through market prices. Far from it! Production decisions, and hence the allocation of resources, were centrally planned and consequently the design of the institutions was aligned to reducing the costs of central control and the prevention of incentives for individual actions. The main way to achieve these objectives was through state ownership of the means of production. The collapse of the socialist system brought the need for creation of a completely new institutional design, or at least one which was new to the countries concerned (Schmieding, 1993, p. 235, Wissenschaftlicher Beirat, 1997, pp. 72–5). That system had to

- introduce, define and protect private property rights to accompany the privatization process and create the environment for competitive incentives and structures;
- establish new information systems to report on prices and market developments;
- install a functioning banking and finance sector;
- facilitate risk dispersion and thus encourage private initiative; and
- create a social security system.

However, the conception and establishment of new institutions takes time. The attempt to stabilize the post-socialist economies with market-oriented macroeconomic measures could hardly be expected to be successful in the absence of a properly functioning market mechanism. Policies leading towards liberalization and stabilization could be introduced quite quickly, but new behaviour patterns emerge only gradually. The slowest part of the process is the development of trust, among economic agents, in all new institutional forms, as well as the accumulation of the necessary institution-specific human capital. The additional transaction costs of the establishment and acceptance of the new institutions have been larger than the positive effects of the switch from a planned to a market economy. Until the new institutions are functioning, information uncertainty hinders the coordination of economic activity. In fact, Schmieding (1993) argues that, even if new institutions could have been created quickly, unfamiliarity with new laws and arrangements would still have prompted investors to wait until institutional uncertainty had diminished over the course of time, and only to conclude immediate contracts on a costly, private and self-enforcing, basis.

The formation, as well as the use, of new institutions requires a certain mental attitude, incorporating a set of accepted norms of business behaviour, which can only be acquired with experience (Koester, 1993). The central plan is replaced by a cluster of contractual relations. This demands, on the one hand, experience in the formulation of contracts, and on the other the willingness to be bound by them. The development of such an attitude is a time-intensive process that is not completed, or even induced, by the declaration of market-oriented principles. Indeed, non-compliance with contracts has been a common feature in the CEECs. For example, 81 per cent of contracts in coal production and in the chemical industry, as well as 19 per cent in the food sector, were broken in 1990/91 (ibid., p. 432). Part of this was due to failures on the production side, though the major reason was opportunistic behaviour leading to the acceptance of more attractive alternatives. Thus, while a suitable institutional environment is in the process of being built up, it is possible for production to fall below the pre-transition level as this is being done.

Obstacles to successful privatization

In shaping an optimal organizational structure, privatization and the reform of property rights are a central element in the transformation process which are especially relevant for agriculture since land plays such a key role. The motivation for privatization can be summarized in three categories (Van Brabant, 1991, pp. 29–39): (1) improvement of the use of scarce resources through their efficient allocation within competitive structures; (2) obtaining fiscal receipts to reduce budgetary deficits; and (3) representing an essential element of an ideology associating freedom and liberty with private ownership. The reorganization of ownership and the creation of certainty in property rights has been the urgent precondition for the transformation of agriculture.

When transformation commenced in 1989, agriculture in the CEE countries was characterized by large-scale farms under state control, except in a few countries, such as Poland and Slovenia, where individual family farming had persisted throughout the communist period. During the transformation, state ownership has been transferred, posing questions about how to develop a market-oriented and competitive agricultural structure. Decisions have to be made concerning the distribution of the ownership of land, the form of reorganization of farms, the optimal firm size and the integration of the farming sector into the whole agribusiness sector (Ellman, 1991). Western experience appears to demonstrate the superiority of family farms, so is family work also a suitable model for CEE countries, and should land privatization be aiming to lead in that direction?

The starting point for privatization differed between the FSU, which had so much large-scale farming in state ownership, and the CEE countries, where land was never nationalized and collective farms dominated (Csaki and Lerman, 1997). The decollectivization of farms in the CEECs has been a far more straightforward task than the privatization of state farms. One reason for this is that most of the land used by collective farms remained privately owned during the socialist period and only had to be transferred to its owners (OECD, 1996, pp. 11–12). The process is far more complicated for state farms, where the privatization procedure is a two-stage process, transferring ownership from the state to the collective and then promoting individual ownership by distribution of land share certificates.

In both the CEE countries and the FSU, large-scale units are not necessarily divided into small family farms as a result of privatization. The new landowners frequently prefer to stay within the collective structure. Hence successor organizations to the state farms remained as large-scale farms, although the state property had been transferred in private shares to the former employees or owners. Figure 5 shows the division of agricultural land in the collective and private sector in 1995 for some CEE countries. It is striking that there is so much diversity. Agriculture in Albania, Latvia and Poland is characterized by highly fragmented structure, but large-scale farming dominates the picture in the Czech and the Slovak Republics. In Albania, nearly all agricultural land is managed by farms smaller than five hectares in size, whereas more than 90 per cent in the Czech and Slovak Republics is occupied by farms with more than 100 hectares (OECD, 1996, p. 11). The structures in the latter countries, however, are more characteristic of the situation in Central and Eastern Europe and in the FSU where, although 85 per cent of land had been privatized by 1996,

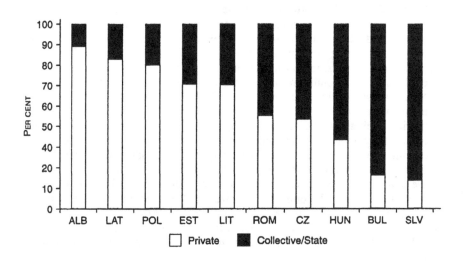

FIGURE 5   *Agricultural land in the collective and private sector in CEE countries in 1995*

Source: Csaki and Lerman (1997).

cultivation tends to be done by collectives rather than by individual farmers (Csaki and Lerman, 1997).

It remains important to underline that the new collectives are not a reprint of the old ones (Csaki and Lerman, 1994). One reason why the number of collective farms might even increase stems from the division of large-scale enterprises into smaller farm units that are, however, still collectively organized. Moreover, the internal structure in these new collectives has changed and private farmers associate voluntarily in order to improve efficiency. This retention of relatively large-scale farms also characterizes the agrarian restructuring in the former East Germany, even though the privatization preceding ownership was handled differently. Features of the East German case are picked up in more detail later.

These empirical facts alone do not necessarily lead to the conclusion that large-scale farm enterprises are more efficient. Another reason for their apparent popularity might be the lack of appropriate supportive conditions for small private farms, such as insufficient opportunity to obtain credit markets and the underdeveloped distribution system for farm inputs. In the case of Russia, the interregional trade opportunities are still badly developed, while the tendency to regionalize agricultural policy causes additional high transaction costs and leads to a further segmentation of the marketing system (von Braun *et al.*, 1996).

There is also another, more general, problem. Although state ownership has now been transformed to private ownership, many important rights are still restricted. Often it is difficult or impossible:

- to buy and to sell land,
- to lease land in and out,
- to choose freely the size of holdings,
- to exchange land,
- to use land in different ways,
- to find a reasonable price without any state control or intervention.

Restrictions on the property rights of owners clearly erode their ownership position and imply serious obstacles to the shaping of an efficient economic structure. This might even adversely affect the internal organizational restructuring of farms (that is, the division of labour, profits and risks among owners and management), which is discussed in more detail in the following section.

THE THEORY OF OPTIMAL FARM ORGANIZATION

Models of organizational structure in agriculture

A crucial point concerning the land privatization process is setting the optimal scale of ownership. One could argue that market forces will resolve this question automatically over time, so that after a period of structural adaption an equilibrium structure will be stabilized. But this process could take several years and involve large transaction costs. Moreover, many imperfections in the market, due to institutional failures already mentioned, would hamper the achievement of a satisfactory result.

Experiences of transformation in developing countries offer only limited insight into the particular issue of farm reorganization in Eastern and Central Europe because only a few countries have operated large-scale farm enterprises (Braverman and Guasch, 1990). In addition the role and size of the public sector in most developing countries are not comparable with those of Eastern and Central Europe. The often quoted example of China is a useful means of comparison between different forms of transformation and privatization strategies. This is the key question of the slogan, 'gradualism versus the big bang', which is often discussed, in various ways, in the theoretical literature. Roland (1994) formalizes the two alternatives by considering expected gains and losses in decision tree models; Xu (1996) simulates alternative reform proposals with a computable general equilibrium (CGE) model for China; Rausser and Simon (1993) present a game-theoretical approach that models the process of transition from centrally planned to market economies in a general conceptual perspective.

Generalization, here, will have to be limited, since there are many avenues of approach. Several alternative organizational forms, such as family farming, large-scale farms with hired workers or agricultural cooperatives, are imaginable. To give recommendations for the optimal size and organizational structure of an enterprise, the standard model derives the optimal size as the minimum of the long-run average cost function. This is generally assumed to be U-shaped, since it contains components which rise and some which decrease with additional scale of output. Typical decreasing cost elements consist of economies of scale in production, whereas internal coordination and control costs rise.

The theory of the new institutional economics goes one step further. Firms are no longer regarded as homogeneous units with no need for further exploration, while the production decision is not reduced to being a matter of technology. Instead, the new institutional economics focuses on transaction costs, human behaviour and the shaping of contract and coordination relations within and between firms. According to these new perspectives, farm structures can be analysed with the help of the transaction cost approach, the principal–agent issue and the theory of property rights. Pollak (1985) extends these considerations from the firm to families and households.

The next step will be to discuss the most efficient type of farm organization from the perspective of the new institutional economics and to take up the controversy of large-scale versus family farming. The common arguments can be listed prior to considering two stylized simple models.

Pollak (ibid., p. 585) groups the advantages of family farming into the categories relating to incentives, monitoring, altruism and loyalty. The advantages of family farming can then be summarized as:

- cost reduction, if the costs of organization and coordination rise progressively with an increase in size;
- reduction of internal transaction costs;

- avoidance of a principal–agent conflict, so that costs of control and supervision are avoided;
- improvement in the use of social capital (mutual trust, common values, social and political engagement, motivation) that is necessary for a competitive economy.

The advantages of large-scale farming are to be found in:

- economies of scale and the resulting reduction in costs;
- saving in labour, since with given equipment an increase in production can lower the average total costs if capacity is not fully exhausted;
- better choices of methods of production, with easier switches to those which offer lower costs per unit of output;
- economies of learning, with specialization allowing comparative advantages to be developed;
- enhanced bargaining power with regard to downstream and upstream firms;
- ability to finance and construct infrastructure projects;
- privileges of normal employees such as regular working hours, regular holidays, social security and fixed income.

Among the types of large-scale farming, two different forms, which are both highly relevant in the transformation process, can be distinguished: hierarchically structured farms with hired labour or cooperatives. In a hierarchically organized enterprise, the entrepreneur makes the decisions and gets the surplus. It is the farmer, in this context, who negotiates contracts with workers, in such a way as to maximize the farmer's gains by ensuring that any incentives for shirking on the part of workers are minimized. In a cooperative, decisions are made by voting, with the surplus being divided between the owners. In this case there will be costs of control, necessary to prevent 'free-riding'. The types can be modelled, in order to get deeper insights, a start being made with the overview in Figure 6. At the most basic level it can be said that family management is preferred in those farms where cost degression is very low, especially if control and supervision are difficult.

Schmitt (1992) proclaims the superiority of family farms, using the argument that the internal transaction costs, for coordination and control, are larger than the cost savings, stemming from the more effective employment of resources, associated with an increase in farm size. He bases this result on the fact that the family farm is the dominating and persistent form in agriculture in the Western economies. In addition, he emphasizes the problem of decision making in cooperatives and their difficulties in avoiding 'free-riding' by weakly motivated individuals. In a newly formed cooperative, emerging through the transfer of shares to former employees, there is the additional problem of overcoming their wish to preserve the structure of the enterprise. Even if a reduction in the labour force could increase efficiency, employees, understandably, would have no interest in dismissing themselves. However, the introduction of freely tradable shares could reduce the severity of the problem.

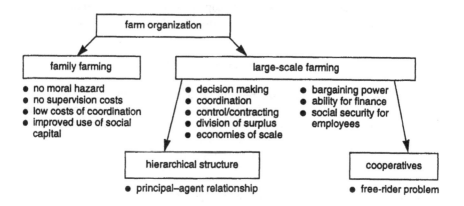

FIGURE 6   *Patterns of farm organization*

It can be argued, strongly, that the dominance of family farming is no proof, in itself, of the comparative advantages of this organizational form. For example, Peter and Weikard (1993) argue that the structure of the sector has evolved historically and appear to side with Brandes (1995) who regards path dependence as an important explanatory approach for handling the issue of agricultural structure. Even if a change in the economic environment, or technical progress, made an alteration in farm organization desirable on efficiency grounds, adjustment could still be slowed down, or even prevented, owing to adaptation costs and delays. Hence the conclusion that the status quo in the Western industrial countries represents an optimal structure is not soundly based. Indeed, there is currently major change taking place in Western farm organization, the end of which has yet to be seen.

Analysis of efficiency in organizational form will now be done using two models. The first is a simple household model which looks at the expansion from a family-managed farm to one using hired workers. The second step is analysis of incentive structures, comparing a hierarchically and a cooperatively organized farm.

Family farming versus labour hiring

De Janvry and Sadoulet (1995, pp. 259–71) formulate a model of household behaviour, based on work by Eswaran and Kotwal (1986), which incorporates two universal problems: entrepreneurs are confronted by limited access to credit, while any hired workers are susceptible to moral hazard and therefore require supervision. The start is with a stochastic production function of the form:

$$q = \varepsilon f(L, A) \text{ with } E(\varepsilon) = 1.$$

There is no definite relation between the input of labour L and the output q. Consequently, there is a moral hazard problem in hiring labour (h), whereas family labour has no incentive to shirk, but needs to supervise hired labour. The time spent in supervising hired labour ($s(h)$) is assumed to increase more than proportionately ($s' > 0$, $s'' > 0$). The family workers have the options to work on their own farm (li), to hire labour out (lo) or to spend time supervising hired labour ($s(h)$). The household is equipped with a certain amount of land, $\overline{A}$, but can rent land in and out (A) at the rental rate r. Under these conditions, the household decision problem is to maximize its utility function $u(y, le)$, which is assumed to be separable in income y and leisure le, under a time and an asset constraint. This can be summarized as follows:

$Max\ pf(L, A) + w(lo - h) - r(A - \overline{A}) - \overline{K} + u(le)$

Time constraint: $li + lo + s(h) + le = 1$
assets constraint: $rA + w(h - lo) + \overline{K} \le r\overline{A} + B(\overline{A}) = B'$

where p is producer price, w is wage, $\overline{K}$ is fixed starting costs, other than land and labour, and B is quantity of credit proportional to land owned.

The solution of the maximization problem shows that the optimum type of farm organization depends on the initial asset endowment and the level of fixed costs. Following de Janvry and Sadoulet (1995, p. 260) it becomes:

Initial assets position B'	Hire out lo	Own-farm work li	Supervision $s(h)$	Farm organization
$B' < \overline{K}$	+	0	0	employed worker
$\overline{K} \le B' \le B_1'$	+	+	0	worker–peasant
$B_1' \le B' \le B_2'$	0	+	0	family farmer
$B_2' \le B' \le B_3'$	0	+	+	family farmer + hired workers
$B' \ge B_3'$	0	0	+	large-scale farmer

With respect to the restructuring of state farms in CEE countries, the results of this simple model imply that credit and financial institutions play a crucial role in the farmer's production decision. Improved access to credit has also been a major policy instrument to accelerate development in the rural areas of developing countries (Braverman and Guasch, 1990). In the socialist system, loans for capital formation were distributed by state banks, with the result that severe constraints were imposed on the savings and investment behaviour of individuals and enterprises. Criteria for the allocation of credit were designed to meet the planned production targets, even when there was frequent support of loss-making operations. Therefore the creation of financial institutions, tailored to the needs of a market economy, is essential for the development of an efficient and competitive agriculture.

Cooperatively versus hierarchically organized farms

As mentioned above, there exist two different patterns of privatization. In the Eastern European states, the land was often transferred to its former owners, whereas in the FSU the state farms were divided among the employees. According to the distribution of property rights, two fundamental types of farm management in large-scale farms can be distinguished: the cooperative and the hierarchical style. These carry different implications for the decision-making processes of coordination and internal control. The following model examines whether, under certain conditions, the superiority of one form can be determined. The model used was developed by Kreps (1990) and has been further elaborated by Peter and Weikard (1993). The optimal amount of labour input and the maximally attainable utility for (1) a one-person enterprise, (2) the principal and the agent in a hierarchically organized farm and (3) the partners in a cooperative, are derived and compared in three steps.

1. The one-person enterprise   The one-person enterprise is characterised by a situation where the expected payoff π is uncertain, here assumed as 1 in the case of success or 0 in the case of failure. The probability p of success can be influenced by the amount of labour input L (in the model, L is expressed in units of utility loss and standardized between 0 and 1). The parameter α defines the relation between the input L and the probability of success, p. It is further assumed that the entrepreneur is risk-neutral and maximizes utility.

$$u = \pi - L \qquad \text{utility function}$$
$$\pi = 1p + 0(1 - p) \quad \text{expected payoff}$$
$$p = L^{\alpha} \qquad \text{probability of success}$$
$$\text{with } L \in [0,1], \alpha \in (0,1)$$

$$\underset{L}{Max}\, u = L^{\alpha} - L \quad \text{maximization problem}$$

$$\Rightarrow L^{*} = \alpha^{\frac{1}{1-\alpha}} \text{ and } u^{*} = \frac{1-\alpha}{\alpha}\alpha^{\frac{1}{1-\alpha}}$$

In the following, economies of scale are assumed. With the switch to a two-person enterprise, a new technology can be applied so that the outcome can be 3 instead of 1 in (1) in the case of success. Consequently, an incentive for an expansion is present. In (2) a principal offers a contract to an agent. In (3) two entrepreneurs join in a cooperative.

2.   *The principal–agent case*   The principal has to offer a contract which guarantees a level of utility for the agent which is higher than the agent could obtain alone (calculated in (1)). Under this restriction, given the knowledge that the agent works according to his own utility-maximizing function, the criterion for the wage w which the principal pays to the agent is the maximization of the principal's utility function. From the equations below it can be seen that there has to be a wage differentiation between the wage w_1 in the case of success and w_0 in the case of failure. Otherwise, if $w_1 = w_0 = w$, the agent maximizes his utility with $L_A = 0$.

$u_A = pw_1 + (1-p)w_0 - L_A$ utility function, agent

$u_p = p(3-w_1) + (1-p)(0-w_0) - L_p$ utility function, principal

$$p = L^\alpha = \left(\frac{L_A + L_p}{2}\right)^\alpha$$ probability of sucess

with $L_A, L_p \in [0,1], \alpha \in (0,1)$

According to the first order condition $\left(\dfrac{du_A}{dL_A}\right)$, the optimal labour input

for the agent is

$$L_A^* = 2\left(\frac{\alpha}{2}(w_1 - w_0)\right)^{\frac{1}{1-\alpha}} - L_p.$$

The principal maximizes his utility function u_p under the restriction:

$$u_A = pw_1 + (1-p)w_0 - L_A \geq \frac{1-\alpha}{\alpha}\alpha^{\frac{1}{1-\alpha}} = u^* \text{ from (1).}$$

With the help of the Lagrange function, the following solution can be derived:

$w_0^* = 0, L_p^* = 0$

$$w_1^* = \begin{cases} 2^\alpha & \text{for} \quad 0 \leq \alpha \leq \alpha' \\ 3\alpha & \text{for} \quad \alpha' \leq \alpha \leq \alpha'' \\ 2^\alpha \alpha^{-1} & \text{for} \quad \alpha'' \leq \alpha \leq 1 \end{cases}$$

$$L_A^* = \begin{cases} \alpha^{\frac{1}{1-\alpha}} & \text{for} \quad 0 \leq \alpha \leq \alpha' \\ 2\left(\frac{3}{2}\alpha^2\right)^{\frac{1}{1-\alpha}} & \text{for} \quad \alpha' \leq \alpha \leq \alpha'' \\ 1 & \text{for} \quad \alpha'' \leq \alpha < 1 \end{cases}$$

with $\alpha' = 0.458$ and $\alpha'' = 0.748$.

3. The cooperative The same preconditions as in (2) (the principal–agent case) are assumed. Because of the assumption that no-one knows the labour input of the partner, the expected outcome is shared equally between the two partners i and j (=3/2 for each in the case of success) and cannot be dependent on the individual labour input.

$$u_i = \frac{3}{2}p - L_i \quad \text{utility function for partner } i$$

$$u_j = \frac{3}{2}p - L_j \quad \text{utility function for partner } j$$

$$p = L^\alpha = \left(\frac{L_i + L_j}{2}\right)^\alpha.$$

The first order condition leads to:

$$L_u = 2\left(\frac{3}{4}\alpha\right)^{\frac{1}{1-\alpha}} - L_j$$

Therefore the sum of the maximal utility of i and j is:

$$u_i + u_j = 3\left(\frac{3}{4}\alpha\right)^{\frac{\alpha}{1-\alpha}} - 2\left(\frac{3}{4}\alpha\right)^{\frac{1}{1-\alpha}}$$

and the utility of each partner is half of the sum.

The results in (2) and (3) show that the optimal labour input and the maximum utility for each agent are both functions of α and hence can be compared. The utilities achieved, in the principal–agent case the sum of $u_p + u_A$, in the cooperative case the sum of $u_i + u_j$, as dependent on the parameter α, are graphed in Figure 7, which shows that for small α it is the cooperative which achieves a higher utility (the point of intersection is exactly at $\alpha = 0.5$). For large α the model of a hierarchical organization implies a higher utility, although the division of this total between the principal and the agent is not equal. Figure 7 demonstrates that the utility of the principal is always higher than that of the agent. The higher the α, the greater is the free-rider effect in the cooperative case. Although the model is very simple and stylized, it reveals that a definite superiority of any of the organizational forms cannot be provided. But, with increasing investments in human capital, the relation between labour input and output becomes less susceptible to interference. Thus a higher α is more likely, so that the principal–agent organized enterprise implies a higher gross utility.

EXPERIENCE FROM EAST GERMANY

In comparison with the conditions of transformation elsewhere, the process in the former German Democratic Republic was very special. The integration into the Federal Republic took place at high speed and was heavily supported

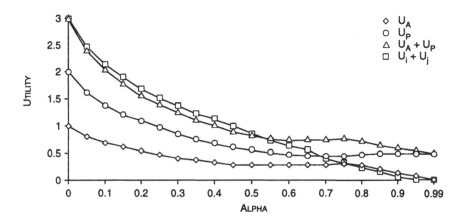

FIGURE 7   *The levels of utility according to the organizational form*

Source: Peter and Weikard (1993, pp. 320–21).

by financial and technical aid. Nearly 700 billion dollars have been provided to finance investments and social transfers (World Bank, 1996, p. 12). The institutional design, based on the existing institutions of West Germany, was already well defined, and there was a broad acceptance of the political, social and economic principles of the FRG (Mehl, 1997, p. 2). Although the preconditions for a successful transformation were almost ideal, many problems have occurred, the most serious being that of unemployment.

The agricultural sector in the unified Germany is a unique example of coexistence of two different types of organizational form. Family farming dominates in the former western part of Germany, where the farm family is the owner and operator of the farm. Principal and agent coincide. The average farm size was about 23 hectares in 1996 (Table 1). In the east before 1989, farming was characterized by large-scale enterprises, with an average size of 1300 hectares. During the transformation process these state-owned enterprises have been transformed into cooperatives and privately organized farms, linked with the complete reorganization of property rights. Table 1 shows the structural changes with regard to the number of farms, the average size and the number of workers.

Table 1 only contains information about average farm size, though it is important to realize that a characteristic feature in West Germany is the bimodal structure. Some 45 per cent of the 509 100 farms in West Germany are between one and ten hectares in size. A second peak can then be observed in the 50–100 ha interval (50 000 farms or 10 per cent of the total). The trend here

TABLE 1   *Key values of agricultural farm development from 1989 to 1996 in East and West Germany*

	1989		1991		1993		1995		1996	
	West	East	West	East	West	East	West	East	West	East
Numbers of farms (1000s)	648.0	4.7	598.7	18.6	567.7	25.4	524.8	30.2	509.1	30.8
Average size (hectares)	18.2	1305.0	19.6	284.0	20.7	208.6	22.2	182.8	23.0	181.8
Labour units per farm	2.75	179.36	2.53	19.49	2.46	7.06	2.35	5.2	2.35	5.18
Labour units per hectare	0.16	0.14	0.13	0.07	0.12	0.03	0.11	0.03	0.10	0.03

Source: *Agrarbericht der Bundesregierung*, different years; *Statistisches Jahrbuch über Ernährung, Landwirtschaft und Forsten*, different years.

256

is towards the 50–100 class, with declining numbers among the 1–10 ha size group. In the east, a similar dual structure has evolved; the number of small farms (1–10 ha) increased rapidly between 1989 and 1996, representing 44 per cent of 30 800 farms in 1996, along with around 26 per cent which remained large, at more than 100 ha. In the east, the decrease of the working population was particularly marked after 1989. After five years of transformation, the number of workers in agriculture declined from 850 000 to 160 000, or a reduction of more than 80 per cent. Labour force reduction was far more than predicted.

One important reason for the structural change is differing price relations. The producer prices for agricultural goods have declined dramatically, whereas factor prices, notably for labour, increased sharply after unification. In particular, the animal breeding and fattening sector was confronted by higher adjustment pressures (see Thiele, 1996). With the conversion of the currency (the DDR-Mark and the D-Mark) on a scale of 1:1, in the east the gross income per working hour increased from the fixed 39 per cent of the western level to 73 per cent in 1992. Productivity increased only from 22.7 per cent to 45 per cent of that in the west over the same period (Brücker, 1995). In effect, the factor costs for labour doubled while producer prices, on average, decreased by about 40 per cent.

Further distortions in factor prices have arisen through capital subsidies, which provided incentives to invest in grain production, and through discriminatory policies against successor enterprises of the large-scale farms of the east. The successors did not receive the same level of subsidies to labour, as well as being saddled with the burden of old debts (Thiele, 1996). A further problem is that the share of rented land is relatively high. Since owned land serves as collateral, East German farms have limited access to credit.

Workers dismissed from agriculture have great difficulty in being absorbed elsewhere. Figure 8 shows that only about 20 per cent of the 850 000 people involved found an occupation outside agriculture in 1991. By that time, of the 300 000 persons who stayed in agriculture, less than half were fully employed. Currently, in large parts of East Germany, the level of unemployment is higher than 17 per cent, or even above 20 per cent in some peripheral areas. Lack of purchasing power is obvious.

The rapid integration of East German agriculture into the European Union market has demonstrated its lack of competitiveness. It has neglected infrastructure and machines, outdated technologies, insufficient capital and underdeveloped marketing strategies. The situation is even worse in food processing and marketing (Tangermann, 1993). Moreover, the former 'internal' East European trade is no longer available. Consequently, the market for East German products has broken down on both the supply and the demand sides. Hence, even with financial and technical support, in addition to well-defined institutional patterns, the adjustment process is painful. It takes time to gain competitiveness and to rebuild trust into a new system. For the CEE countries, this is an even bigger problem, which will require even more Western help to overcome.

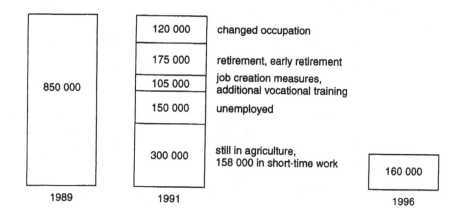

FIGURE 8   *Development of the working population in agriculture in the eastern part of Germany*

Source: *Agrarbericht der Bundesregierung*, different years; Mehl (1997).

CONCLUSIONS

Modern and efficient farming is successfully integrated into upstream and downstream activities within the domestic food chain and into international agricultural and food markets. The macroeconomic, agribusiness and trade environment, therefore, plays an important role in agricultural development. Much has already been done in transition countries, including macroeconomic stabilization, trade liberalization and domestic deregulation. Nevertheless, many obstacles remain which are responsible for the sluggish improvement of the agricultural situation. These include the problem of state monopolies in the food sector having been replaced by private monopolies, as well as the trade barriers of other countries discriminating against transition countries' exports. Limited GDP growth rates do not help.

However, the most important causes of the current transformation crisis in agriculture appear to lie in institutional, organizational and behavioural issues. Even in Western countries, despite numerous reform efforts, there is great resistance to adjustment and hence a lack of flexibility and competitiveness. Stiglitz (1993) notes the irony in Western economists' advice to rely on the market; it is a question of the motto, 'Do as we say, not as we do'.

Internal and external farm restructuring is slowed down or distorted owing to the following:

● the transfer of ownership to collective rather than to private owners;

- restrictions on ownership rights, which are becoming even more popular in Western countries' environmental policies;
- malfunction of land, labour and credit markets;
- state or cartel intervention in price formation on those markets (also a phenomenon in Western countries);
- the assumption that one, and only one, organizational structure or size of a farm is optimal and should be pursued as a political objective.

The need for orientation during the transition process is acute if a costly, long-lasting, trial-and-error process is to be prevented. Transformation of a system actually provides the chance to shape basic conditions in a conscious way and to improve them. The theoretical analysis has made clear that the initial asset situation, access to credits and the managerial skills to run a farm are important in determining the optimal farm size and farm organization. Since all of these factors can differ among individuals, so farm size and structures may differ accordingly. At each point in time one therefore finds an optimal distribution of sizes and structures which moves from some bimodal form to another. Any choices of farmers in terms of exit and entry, of growing and contracting and division of labour between management and owners, as well as the contract design for workers, should be as free as possible. This guarantees a flexible and efficient response to a changing environment and is the only way to strengthen the competitiveness of agriculture.

REFERENCES

Bartholdy, K. (1996), 'Statistical review', *Economics of Transition*, 4, 527–50.
Brandes, W. (1995), 'Pfadabhängigkeit: Ein auch für die Agrarökonomik fruchtbares Forschungsprogramm?', *Agrarwirtschaft*, 44, 277–9.
Braverman, A. and Guasch, J.L. (1990), 'Agricultural Reform in Developing Countries: Reflections for Eastern Europe', *American Journal of Agricultural Economics*, 72, 1243–51.
Brooks, K.M. (1993), 'Challenges of Trade and Agricultural Development for East/Central Europe and States of the former USSR', *Agricultural Economics*, 8, 401–20.
Brücker, H. (1995), *Privatisierung in Ostdeutschland. Eine institutionenökonomische Analyse*, Frankfurt: University of Frankfurt.
Bundesministerium für Ernährung (different years), *Landwirtschaft und Forsten*, Bonn: Agrarbericht der Bundesregierung.
Csaki, C. and Lerman, Z. (1994), 'Land Reform and Farm Sector Restructuring in the Former Socialist Countries in Europe', *European Review of Agricultural Economics*, 21, 553–76.
Csaki, C. and Lerman, Z. (1997), 'Land Reform and Farm Restructuring in the East Central Europe and the CIS in the 1990s: Expectations and achievements after the first five years', *European Review of Agricultural Economics*, 24, 428–52.
Dewatripont, M. and Roland, G. (1996), 'Transition as a process of large-scale institutional change', *Economics of Transition*, 4, 1–30.
Ellman, M. (1991), 'The contradictions of Perestroika: The case of Agriculture', *European Review of Agricultural Economics*, 18, 1–18.
Eswaran, M. and Kotwal, A. (1986), 'Access to Capital and Agrarian Production Organization', *Economic Journal*, 96, 482–98.
Hartmann, M., Henrichsmeyer, W. and Schmitz, P.M. (1991), 'Political Economy of the Common Agricultural Policy in the European Community', in P. Dasgupta (ed.), *Issues in Contemporary Economics. Vol. 3, Policy and Development*, London: Macmillan.
Horn, G.A. (1996), 'Some Theoretical and Policy Aspects of Transition', in H. Flassbeck and G.A. Horn (eds), *German Unification – An Example for Korea?*, Aldershot: Dartmouth.

260   *P. Michael Schmitz and Cornelia Noeth*

de Janvry, A. and Sadoulet, E. (1995), *Quantitative Development Policy Analysis*, Baltimore and London: Johns Hopkins University Press.
Koester, U. (1993), 'Potential und Hemmnisse des Agrarhandels osteuropäischer Länder. Herausforderungen für die landwirtschaftliche Marktforschung', *Agrarwirtschaft*, **42**, 429–36.
Koester, U. (1995), 'Pitfalls in Building Institutions in Countries in Transition', in Gesellschaft für Agrarprojekte (ed.), *Transforming Agriculture and Agro-Industry. Policies, Concepts and Cases from Central and Eastern Europe*, Kiel: University of Kiel.
Köhne, J. (1997), 'Die Bedeutung von Preisverzerrungen für das Wirtschaftswachstum ausgewählter mittel- und osteuropäischer Transformationsstaaten', dissertation, University of Frankfurt.
Kreps, D.M. (1990), *A Course in Microeconomic Theory*, New York: Harvester Wheatsheaf.
Mehl, P. (1997), 'Transformation of the Social Security System in Agriculture in East Germany. Lessons for Central and Eastern European Countries?', in K. Frohberg and P. Weingarten (eds), *The Significance of Politics and Institutions for the Design and Formation of Agricultural Policy*, Kiel: University of Kiel.
North, D.C. (1990), *Institutions, Institutional Change and Economic Performance*, Cambridge: Cambridge University Press.
OECD (1996), *Agricultural Policies, Markets and Trade in Transition Economies. Monitoring and Evaluation 1996*, Paris: OECD.
Peter, G. and Weikard, H.-P. (1993), 'Betriebsgröße und Organisationsform für die landwirtschaftliche Produktion', *Agrarwirtschaft*, **42**, 313–23.
Pollak, R.A. (1985), 'A Transaction Cost Approach to Families and Households', *Journal of Economic Literature*, **23**, 581–608.
Rausser, G.C. and Simon, L.K. (1993), 'The Political Economy of Transition in Eastern Europe: Packaging Enterprises for Privatization', in C. Clague and G.C. Rausser (eds), *The Emergence of Market Economies in Eastern Europe*, 2nd edn, Oxford: Blackwell.
Roland, G. (1994), 'The role of political constraints in transition strategies', *Economics of Transition*, **2**, 27–41.
Rosati, D.K. (1994), 'Output decline during transition from plan to market: a reconsideration', *Economics of Transition*, **2**, 419–41.
Schmieding, H. (1993), 'From Plan to Market: On the Nature of the Transformation Crisis', *Weltwirtschaftliches Archiv*, **129**, 216–53.
Schmitt, G. (1992), 'Der Zusammenhang zwischen Organisation und Betriebsgröße in der Landwirtschaft: Eine institutionenökonomische Erklärung und deren agrarökonomische und agrarpolitische Implikationen', *Berichte über Landwirtschaft*, **70**, 505–28.
Stiglitz, J.E. (1993), 'Incentives, Organizational Structures and Contractual Choice in the Reform of Socialist Agriculture', in A. Braverman, K. Brooks and C. Csaki (eds), *The Agricultural Transition in Central and Eastern Europe and the Former U.S.S.R.*, Washington, DC: World Bank.
Tangermann, S. (1993), 'United Western Europe and the Agriculture of Central and Eastern Europe and the USSR', in A. Braverman, K. Brooks and C. Csaki (eds), *The Agricultural Transition in Central and Eastern Europe and the Former U.S.S.R.*, Washington, DC: World Bank.
Thiele, H. (1996), *The Transition of Agriculture: Lessons to be learned from East Germany*, Discussion Paper No. 17. Siena: Universita degli studi di Siena.
Van Brabant, J.M. (1991), 'Property Rights Reform, Macroeconomic Performance and Welfare', in OECD (ed.), *Transformation of Planned Economies. Property Rights Reform and Macroeconomic Stability*, Paris: OECD.
Von Braun, J., Serova, E., tho Seeth, H. and Melyukhina, O. (1996), *Russia's Food Economy in Transition: Current Policy Issues and the Long-Term Outlook*, Food, Agriculture and Environment Discussion Paper 18, Washington, DC: IFPRI.
Wissenschaftlicher Beirat beim Bundesministerium für Ernährung, Landwirtschaft und Forsten (1997), *Die Entwicklung der Landwirtschaft in Mitteleuropa und mögliche Folgen für die Agrarpolitik in der EU*, Heft 458, Bonn: Schriftenreihe des Bundesministeriums für Ernährung, Landwirtschaft und Forsten.
World Bank (1996), *World Development Report 1996: From plan to market*, New York: Oxford University Press.
Xu, D. (1996), 'The Chasm in the Transition: A CGE Analysis of Chinese Economic Reform', *Journal of Policy Modelling*, **18**, 117–39.

KE BINGSHENG*

*Policy and Institutional Change for Agriculture in China:
Production, Consumption and Trade Implications*

INTRODUCTION

China's agricultural policy changes have attracted worldwide attention in recent years. During the first half of the 1980s, fundamental reforms were introduced which turned a rigid, inefficient, collective-based production system into one based on farmers' households and brought unprecedented production growth. In just a few years, the face of China's agriculture changed completely and much was accomplished. One of the greatest symbolic achievements of the reform policy was that for the first time in New China's history a surplus supply of agricultural products was achieved by the mid-1980s. At the same time, farming income and living conditions improved remarkably. As the world witnessed this agricultural transformation, many were interested in observing and analysing changes in China's agriculture, mainly in search of success stories and experiences for other planned economies and developing countries, but not because these changes had any significant direct implications for the world agricultural market. The focus of the interest was China's domestic production and policy, but not external trade policy.

More recently, China has attracted attention and concern for a different reason. The issue relates to the actual and potential future impact of China's agricultural development on the world food market. As a direct result of the reform and opening-up policy, along with the strengthening of overall economic development, China's agriculture has increasingly been integrated into the world market. The fact that China has grown to a position, physically and financially, to export or import large quantities of agricultural products has been explicitly shown in the grain trade in recent years. China registered a net grain export of 8 million tonnes in 1993 and then imported a net amount of more than 18 million tonnes in 1995. Though there is still much controversy over the question of who will feed China, there is no longer much doubt that the country has become a very influential player in world agricultural markets.

Putting China into the context of an increasingly integrated world, this paper first provides an overview of the recent institutional and policy changes affecting agriculture. The reasons behind these changes and their impacts on the domestic market and implications in the world market are discussed. Finally,

*China Agricultural University, Beijing, PR China. Helpful comments and editorial assistance from An Xiji, Zhong Funing and Henry Kinnucan are gratefully acknowledged.

the possible future trends of agricultural development and policy reform are considered.

DOMESTIC POLICY: DECENTRALIZATION AND REGIONALIZATION

Market liberalization and regionalization characterized the agricultural policy changes in China during the past decade. The liberalization process had begun much earlier with non-grain products, including vegetables, fruits, aquatic and livestock products, rather than with grain. Markets for almost all of these products had been liberalized by the early 1990s. Even oilseeds, one of the three mostly regulated product groups (with grain and cotton), had been virtually released from the system of quota procurement owing to the sluggish market price. However, the marketing reform process for grain and cotton did not proceed at the same pace, though a departure from the old regulations had already occurred in the mid-1980s when a two-tier system was introduced. These two products, especially grain, are given particular attention in China's agricultural development and policy reform.

The marketing reform process accelerated during the early 1990s, especially from 1992, when China explicitly declared that a socialist market economy system was to be the ultimate goal of the economic reform. More market-oriented reform steps, which will be discussed in turn, have been taken since then.

The grain ration system

Grain ration prices were raised twice, in 1991 and 1992, each time by an average of 50 per cent. This was a very bold and significant step for further reforms in the following years. Its most important effect was that it broke up a fixed price system, under which the grain rationing price had been frozen for 25 years (Ke, 1995). It dispelled an emotional taboo that grain ration prices should not be lifted and removed the fear that any changes would cause social instability. The calm acceptance of the change by consumers encouraged policy makers to take the step of abolishing the whole grain-rationing coupon system, which was finally eliminated nationwide in early 1994 (Chen, 1995). As a result of the later price increases, some kinds of coupons were reintroduced in some big cities, but the system no longer has its previous significance and is used mostly to assist the lower-income group. Even the author did not expect such a painless advance when he gave his contributed paper presentation six years ago at the XXI Conference of the IAAE (Ke, 1992).

Extension of land tenure

The Household Responsibility System is the most important reform element and has a symbolic meaning. Initiated at the end of the 1970s, and continuing to the early 1980s, it involved the abolition of the commune system and the contracting of publicly owned land to individual farmers. This greatly strengthened their incentives to increase production and allowed more efficient use of the land resource. Agricultural output, across all products, grew rapidly. However, owing to the short contract term, which was originally set at 15 years, and distrust about the stability of the reform policy, farmers tended to pursue short-term production gains at the potential cost of long-term productiveness. Since the original land tenure arrangement was approaching expiry in the mid-1990s, the Chinese government decided in 1994 to address the problem by extending the contract system for another 30 years. This applies to crop and pasture land, and also includes 'wasteland', especially barren hills (MOA, 1996). A tenure term of 50 years, or even longer, is allowed. In some regions, where similar practices were initiated several years ago, significant results have been achieved and young trees are growing on once barren slopes. The contract system for wasteland is of special significance in the ecologically weak regions, such as the Loess Plateau and the southwestern mountainous provinces. The policy is welcomed by farmers and their confidence in the long-term stability of the Household Responsibility System and reform policy is strengthened.

Marketing reform

Though the surprising price increase which occurred in late 1993 and 1994 disturbed and impeded the marketing reform plan for the remaining state-controlled products, including grain and cotton, other changes were made. In the first place, the state procurement prices increased substantially in line with the market price changes. For grain and cotton, this is illustrated in Table 1. As a result, the gap between the state set quota procurement price and the market price for grain has narrowed substantially. By early 1997, there was actually no significant gap between the two prices for wheat and corn, with the quota price for the latter being marginally higher. In major producing areas, such as in the northeastern province of Jilin, the market price for corn has fallen substantially below the quota price.

Generally speaking, the adjustment of the quota price is passive, usually following the trend in the free market. Nevertheless, the increase has been important, for two reasons. First, it has helped ease the difficulties of the procurement system and reduce the complaints of farmers about the effects of the quota system, thus contributing to the stability of rural society (Du, 1996). Second, though the subject provokes heated debate between academics, higher quota prices do appear to provide additional incentives for grain production.

Since the mid-1980s, open market trading of grain has been allowed after fulfilment of the state procurement quota measured on a county basis. However, the state grain marketing agencies have continued to maintain a dominant market share of 90 million tonnes in the total purchase, or about 35 per cent of production (MIT, 1995). Half of it is quota procurement and the remainder consists of 'negotiated purchasing', in effect purchase at the local prevailing market price. The amount entering the market through other channels is around 30–40 million tonnes, mostly for local feed and food-processing sectors, the

TABLE 1   *Grain and cotton prices in China (Yuan/tonne)*

	Wheat		Corn		Cotton
	Quota	Market	Quota	Market	
1985	430	466	310	370	3 400
1986	440	517	320	450	3 600
1987	440	576	330	500	3 800
1988	470	705	340	570	4 800
1989	510	979	370	780	6 100
1990	510	896	380	690	6 300
1991	510	795	380	600	6 200
1992	590	776	420	630	6 000
1993	660	810	460	730	6 600
1994	890	1 140	690	1 010	10 600
1995	1 080	1 690	860	1 580	14 000
1996	1 460	1 740	1 220	1 490	14 000
1997*	1 470	1 630	1 230	1 170	14 000

Note: * First quarter.

Sources: Ministry of Agriculture, China Agricultural Development report 1996;
Information Centre of the Ministry of Agriculture, unpublished report.

stress being on the predominantly local nature of trade. Owing to various constraints, most traders and institutions are not in a position to undertake interregional, especially interprovincial, grain marketing. The problems lie in storage capacities, transport for interprovincial movement in particular, and a marked lack of finance. As a consequence, the subsidized state grain marketing agencies take advantage of their monopoly position to make large profits in interprovincial grain trade, which causes an unreasonable price disparity between surplus and deficit provinces. For example, in July 1996, the market price for corn in the northeast and north was about 1200yuan per tonne, while in the south and the southwest it was 1800yuan. The regional disparity is more than the necessary transport cost, which is about 150yuan per tonne by rail from the northeast to the southwest provinces, and about 200yuan per tonne by sea from the northeast to the southern areas of Guangdong and Fujian. This lack of market integration within China has significant implications for the internationalization of agricultural markets, since the domestic price spread is markedly larger than the price gap between the domestic market and the world market.

As a result of these problems, a new policy measure has very recently been suggested and accepted by the administration. Five sectors are allowed to enter the interprovincial grain marketing and are eligible for preferential treatment in transport arrangements and subsidized loans. These five are the feed, food processing, brewery and pharmaceutical industries and the state land reclamation sector. There are still many issues relating to policy implementation which have to be settled, but the most important implication of the change is that it signals the disintegration of the virtual monopoly of state grain marketing agencies in interregional trade. Thus it paves the way for further marketing reforms.

The Governor Responsibility System

The 'Governor Responsibility System', introduced in 1995, gives the provincial leadership final responsibility for securing food, especially grain, in their area. This policy is intended to exert more pressure on the provincial leaders to pay greater attention to the development of agriculture and food production. The policy has already had some positive results, as investment in agriculture has been strengthened and the decline in areas sown to grain, especially in coastal locations, has been reversed. But it has also caused some adverse effects, since regional protectionism also tends to rise (Tang, 1995). Overemphasis on self-sufficiency in grain within each province impedes efficient resource allocation. It also worsens the problem of overreporting of production. For example, reported meat production figures show an annual growth rate of 13 per cent for the first half of the 1990s. The annual growth rate of beef for the same period is even more extraordinary, as high as 27 per cent, with a simultaneous inventory growth rate of 5 per cent (SSB, 1996), which is technically impossible. The overreporting of cattle numbers is as high as 15 million head (Ke, 1997). Furthermore, the system worsens the problem of market segmentation. Every province strives for internal market stabilization, often at the expense of other provinces. During a time of short supply, major production provinces often prohibit outflow of grain. An example is the case of corn in 1995, when Jilin Province, the most important producer in China, banned exports to other provinces and offered rewards to anyone prepared to report illegal trade.

Evaluation of the policy changes

The reform measures in the first half of 1990s are characterized by decentralization of policy making. More and more power was granted to local governments at the provincial and municipal levels. Provincial governments were granted the authority to decide when to eliminate the grain rationing system, how much price premium could be added to the centrally set quota price or support price, how much buffer stock of grain should be kept and how to time its release. The most important reason for decentralization is that the central government is not able to bear sole financial responsibility for desired policy actions. Owing to uneven economic development between the south and the north, and between the east and the west, there are noticeable regional differences in local governmental revenue and hence in actual policy practice. For example, while the state quota procurement is still practised in all the other provinces, it is virtually eliminated in Guangdong. A further example is that the quota procurement price for corn in Jiangsu was 40 per cent higher than that in Liaoning in 1995, owing to the difference in the local price premium.

The decentralization in policy making inevitably leads to regional market fragmentation, as in the case of corn, which was mentioned earlier. The unfamiliarity of policy makers with the functioning of the market, the conservative attitude towards the market mechanism in some cases, and inevitable complications and constraints in the transitional process are the three major reasons for the deficiencies in the domestic policy changes. The government did make a major effort to redefine its functions to conform to the market by shifting from direct control to indirect market support and stabilization, but the well-intended policy reforms were not properly designed and did not function well.

An example is the so-called 'Special Stock' system, established in 1990 to stabilize the grain market by functioning as a buffer stock mechanism. However, owing to underfunding of the programme, the government just sets the stock level and provides the necessary subsidies to the state marketing agencies to cover loan and storage costs, now standing at around 0.12yuan/kg (Wang, 1996). The local state marketing agencies have to buy the required amount of grain and put it into storage as 'Special Stock', while the government decides when and at what price to release the stocks. Such a system does not provide adequate incentives for enterprises to maintain 'Special Stocks'. In practice, it is rather difficult to distinguish physically between the grain in the 'Special Stock' and other grain held by a local enterprise, for both types belong to the enterprise, making it very difficult to operate effective control (Tang, 1996). Local state grain marketing agencies may just 'report' but not 'keep' the stocks, and there is no way to know what the exact position is, since commercial stocks can easily be taken to be 'Special Stocks'.

To make matters worse, the system is practised at two administrative levels, by central and by provincial governments. Each sets separate stock targets for the same local state grain marketing agencies. Hence it is possible for the local agency to report the same commercial stock twice, separately, to central and provincial governments as the amount of 'Special Stock', leading to the aggregated national total being greatly overreported. In fact, no-one knows for certain what the real level is. During the grain price increase of 1994, local state grain marketing agencies were ordered to release grain, though it was hard to know how much was actually marketed. The failure of the system was believed to be one of the major reasons why the price increase of 1994 was not brought under control in an effective and timely way (MOA, 1995).

An inconsistency between policy making and implementation is another problem, which is well illustrated with another recent example. In principle, the government-determined support price for grain is meant to protect producers (it is the same as the quota price) but the policy is seldom implemented. Since the end of 1996, farmers in the northeastern provinces have not been able to market corn from the bumper harvest and have been forced to stockpile on their own small premises, while many state marketing agencies have had empty storehouses. Local state grain marketing agencies in producing areas have been instructed to buy corn at the quota price, which is 1.00yuan/kg, while the market price has fallen to 0.80yuan/kg. Though the government provides subsidized loans to the marketing agencies, these are not sufficient to cover the market risk, and the agencies have chosen to wait rather than to buy. As a result, the free market corn price dropped by half within a few months.

The failure to prevent grain market instability in recent years has had significant impacts on overall agricultural and general economic development. It is believed that the grain price increase caused the soaring food prices and general inflation of 1994 and 1995. Consequently, in recognition of the deficiencies and constraints of a closed economy, policy makers in China have increasingly recognized the importance of using the world market to balance the domestic market.

TRADE POLICY: DESUBSIDIZATION AND LIBERALIZATION

Agricultural trade in China used to be perceived as an important means to earn hard currency to support industrial development. This policy goal has changed gradually because overall trade is growing very rapidly, resulting in a continued decline in the share of food and agriculture within the total. As shown in Table 2, food exports increased from US$ 3 billion in 1980 to US$ 10 billion in 1995, while food imports fluctuated at around US$ 2–4 billion, but with a peak of over US$ 6 billion in 1995. The food share in total exports declined substantially from 16.5 per cent to 7 per cent during the 15 years. The import share fell more dramatically. Given these features, plus the fact that stockpiling of foreign exchange reserves had taken them to over US$ 100 billion by the end of 1996, the major goals of agricultural trade policy are shifting more towards profit making and domestic market stabilization.

It can also be seen from Table 2 that China has enjoyed a food trade surplus since the mid-1980s, even in 1995, when there were greatly increased grain imports and little export. It seems that China is not only feeding China itself, but also some others in the world! Major export items other than grains include live pigs and poultry, pork and chicken, vegetables, fruits and aquatic products. Major import commodities include grain, and particularly wheat, chicken wings, sugar, edible oil and cotton.

Policy changes in agricultural trade have taken place against a background of general trade policy reforms. The elimination of export subsidies and the merging of the two-tier foreign exchange system are among the most important measures in recent years. These changes have provided the preliminary conditions paving the way towards a more market-oriented trade policy. In addition, import tariffs have been reduced for major agriculture-related products. For cotton and fertilizer, the range is no higher than 3 per cent to 8 per cent, while grains (wheat, corn and rice) and breeding animals are exempted from import charges. For animal products the tariffs have been reduced from over 50 per cent to around 15 per cent since 1996. As in the domestic market, trade of agricultural products, other than grain, is largely released from central control. But grain importing and exporting is still under strict central government control owing to the high significance attached to it. Though reform has been undertaken, the current situation is still being widely criticized in China. Recognizable shortcomings of the system include the very complicated and

TABLE 2   *Food trade development in China*

	Export			Import		
	Total (US$ billion)	Food (US$ billion)	Food share (%)	Total (US$ billion)	Food (US$ billion)	Food share (%)
1980	18.12	2.99	16.5	20.02	2.93	14.6
1981	22.01	2.92	13.3	20.02	3.62	16.4
1982	22.32	2.91	13.0	19.29	4.20	21.8
1983	22.23	2.85	12.8	21.39	3.12	14.6
1984	26.14	3.23	12.4	27.41	2.33	8.5
1985	27.35	3.80	13.9	42.25	1.55	3.7
1986	30.94	4.45	14.4	42.91	1.63	3.8
1987	39.44	4.78	12.1	43.21	2.44	5.7
1988	47.52	5.89	12.4	55.27	3.48	6.3
1989	52.54	6.15	11.7	59.14	4.19	7.1
1990	62.09	6.61	10.6	53.35	3.34	6.3
1991	71.84	7.23	10.1	63.79	2.80	4.4
1992	84.94	8.31	9.8	80.59	3.15	3.9
1993	91.74	8.40	9.2	103.96	2.21	2.1
1994	121.01	10.02	8.3	115.61	3.14	2.7
1995	148.77	9.95	6.7	132.08	6.13	4.6
1996	151.07	10.23	6.8	138.84	5.67	4.1

Source: SSB, *Statistical Yearbook of China*, various years.

slow decision-making process, low efficiency of institutional arrangements and irrational marketing links (Tang, 1996).

A national grain trade plan is usually made at the beginning of the year, based on estimation and judgment of the domestic and world market situation and the demand of individual provinces. Several ministries are involved in the decision-making process, including the Ministry of Internal Trade, the Ministry of Foreign Trade and Economic Cooperation, the State Planning Commission and, to a much lesser extent, the Ministry of Agriculture. The final decision has to be approved by the top government leaders. The set plan, with its import and export quotas, is then disaggregated to individual provinces. This rigid system runs counter to the flexibility required in an ever-changing domestic and world market. A recent example can be drawn from the events of the early summer of 1996, when there was a price surge in the world corn market but some decline in the domestic market. Price relationships became favourable for Northeast China to export corn. It then took two months before all involved ministries and agencies reached a consensus to change the export plan, by which time the world market price had already fallen again to far below the domestic market price. Another problem is the separation of the domestic marketing agencies from the trade agencies. International trade in grain is arranged by specialized state trade agencies, which do not undertake domestic trade. They obtain grain from domestic state marketing agencies for export, and deliver any imported grain to the domestic marketing agencies for internal sale. The business relationship is centrally regulated. This arrangement places a wedge between the domestic and world market, removing any possibility of beneficial interactions.

To make the situation worse, a substantial portion of the grain provided to the state trade companies was 'quota grain', purchased from farmers at the low quota price. As a result, the trading companies continued exporting even when the domestic price was already well above the world price. There was a similar episode with corn in 1994, when China exported nearly 9 million tonnes despite the world price being less than the average domestic market price. In the second half of 1994, corn was priced at around US\$85/tonne in the world market, US\$120/tonne in China's domestic market and US\$65/tonne for quota procurement.

Owing to this inconsistency between domestic and foreign trade policy, there has been considerable instability in the trade of some major agricultural commodities. As indicated in Table 3, clear trends in the trade situation for grain, edible oil and sugar are hard to find over the past decade. Some fluctuations in trade were caused by variability in domestic production, but there were years in which the imperfections in the domestic and foreign trade system were responsible for swings in trade, especially for grain and edible oils. For example, it could be argued that the direction of trade was such as to exacerbate supply variability due to fluctuations in production, rather than to reduce it. This appears to have occurred in 1994, when grain exports remained high despite the decline in production, and in 1995, when imports surged despite the production recovery. Many suggestions have been made for overcoming such difficulties, including merging the state trade agencies and domestic marketing agencies. However, this seems unlikely to happen without the related ministries being merged.

FOOD SECURITY OUTLOOK AND FUTURE POLICY PERSPECTIVES

Food security is a long-standing concern for Chinese policy makers. Through various adjustments, including reforms in the production management system, the phasing out of state marketing controls and other measures, farmers have more incentive to increase output. Great advances have, in fact, been made in the past two decades. The Chinese people have never before faced such an abundant and diversified food market, spread nationwide.

For the future, however, there are still great challenges for the further development of the food and agricultural sector. Factors which pose pressing challenges include continued population growth, rising income and aspirations, plus resource depletion and degradation. The price increase for agricultural products, with the associated high inflation since the end of 1993, has dispelled the overoptimistic atmosphere characteristic of the easier times of only a few years earlier. Great concern about future domestic food supply potential has re-emerged among agricultural administrators and the general public, and there has been much heated discussion about a number of gloomy predictions for the first quarter of the next century.

TABLE 3   *Instability of trade in China (million tonnes)*

	Grain			Edible oil			Sugar		
	Export	Import	Production	Export	Import	Production	Export	Import	Production
1985	9.32	6.00	379.1	0.16	0.03	4.01	0.18	1.91	4.51
1986	9.42	7.73	391.5	0.17	0.20	4.41	0.27	1.18	5.25
1987	7.37	16.28	403.0	0.06	0.51	4.78	0.45	1.83	5.06
1988	7.17	15.33	394.1	0.03	0.21	4.80	0.25	3.71	4.61
1989	6.56	16.58	407.6	0.06	1.06	4.96	0.43	1.58	5.01
1990	5.83	13.72	446.2	0.14	1.12	5.44	0.57	1.13	5.82
1991	10.86	13.45	435.3	0.10	0.61	6.44	0.34	1.01	6.40
1992	13.64	11.75	442.7	0.07	0.42	6.61	1.67	1.10	8.29
1993	15.35	7.52	456.5	0.14	0.24	9.65	1.85	0.45	7.71
1994	13.46	9.20	445.1	0.27	1.63	7.23	0.95	1.55	5.92
1995	2.14	20.81	466.6	0.50	2.13	11.45	0.48	2.95	5.59
1996	1.24	10.83	490.0	0.47	2.64		0.66	1.25	

Source: SSB, *State Statistical Yearbook of China*, various years.

Most of these have concentrated on the grain sector, since it is of such decisive concern in China. Projections of demand, production potential and import needs in the coming decades do, however, vary considerably because of differences in assumptions, data and estimation methods (Fan *et al.*, 1996). For example, the projected grain import demand for 2030 ranges from the pessimistic view of over 200 million tonnes to the far more optimistic figure of around 40 million tonnes. Nevertheless, consensus does exist on the following: (1) demand will increase continuously over the next three decades; (2) supply cannot keep pace with demand, and thus (3) there will be an ever-rising import demand.

In response to such worries, the government issued a white paper on 'Grain Issues in China' in October 1996, just before the World Food Summit. The seven-part document provided an overview of the progress in food supply during the past four decades and then estimated future demand and production growth potential for the coming three decades. Strategies for achieving the goal of self-sufficiency included increasing investment levels in agriculture, enhancing application of advanced technology, promoting more efficient and sustainable utilization of natural resources and furthering reforms to provide a better institutional and policy environment. Generally speaking, the authoritative views expressed in the document are optimistic. It foresees a moderate growth in grain demand, estimating that 400kg of grain per capita (in the Chinese definition including paddy rice, tubers and beans) will be sufficient to support food demand by 2030. This is based on the assumptions that the Chinese diet, with its dependence on plant products for major energy and nourishment, will not change significantly and that feed/livestock conversion ratios will increase and hence reduce feedgrain needs. The white paper also assumes that the elimination of subsidies in housing and medical care will have an income effect which will reduce food demand. On the supply side, potential is seen first in further yield improvement. The demand of 400kg/per capita can be met if yields increase annually at 1 per cent from 1996 to 2010 and at 0.7 per cent in the period 2011–30. Both of the assumed rates are substantially lower than the average rate of over 3 per cent for the past four decades. Farmland protection, raising the cropping index and reclaiming 0.3 million hectares of land (from a total of reclaimable area which is as large as 14.7 million hectares) will be able to stop the decline in farmed area and stabilize the area sown to grain. Further potential exists to increase productivity in grassland, fishery cultivation and forestry. Reduction by half in post-harvest grain loss, estimated at over 10 per cent at present, will also save 20 million tonnes.

The white paper also recognizes the great challenges ahead. The first is the general resource constraint, caused by a low per capita availability of land and water resources which requires alleviation through increasing agricultural inputs and investment. Infrastructure remains underdeveloped, while agriculture is almost defenceless against unfavourable changes in natural conditions. Small farmers (around half a hectare per farm is the national average) often make blind production and marketing decisions because of the lack of an efficient information system in the transition process from a planned economy to a market-oriented one, thus tending to exaggerate supply fluctuations. Finally, the growth of industry will inevitably place the agricultural sector at a disadvantage in competing for all types of resources with other sectors of the economy.

A set of policies has been mapped out to combat the constraints to increasing production. The first is to increase agricultural investment to improve the condition of the land. Irrigation systems will be further expanded to raise the irrigated area from the current 49.3 million hectares to 53.3 million by 2000, 56.7 million by 2010 and 66.7 million by 2030. These are increases on the 52 per cent of the currently irrigated cropland area, to raise it to 56, 60 and 70 per cent, respectively. Efficiency in the use of water will also be improved as the irrigated land with water-saving technology will increase from the current 13 million hectares to over 40 million. The rate of effective utilization of rainwater will also improve, to reach 30 per cent. These will be some of the factors which will help to upgrade an existing 60 million hectares of land with low and medium levels of yield.

Ambitious plans are also being made to promote the supply of fertilizers, pesticides, agricultural plastics, farm machinery and rural electricity. By the year 2000, the share of agricultural investment in the total infrastructure investment of the central government will be raised from the current 17 per cent to 20 per cent. The growth of agriculture expenditure should be higher than that of the government revenue, and the growth of agricultural loans should be more than the average growth rate of other loans. Extension of existing and new technologies is seen as another key agricultural policy. Efforts will be made to improve the breeding, extension and marketing of new and high-yield varieties. Seed coating will be spread to cover 50 per cent of the total marketed seeds by the year 2000. Major new technologies will include dry-breeding and cast-planting of paddy rice, plastic coverage, precise seeding, integrated pesticide management, appropriate utilization of fertilizer, water-saving irrigation and dryland farming. Professional training of farmers will be pursued through reform in the agricultural education system, and the research system will be enhanced to enable better technical support to be provided. The strategies to address the food problem will extend beyond the grain sector to include animal husbandry, horticulture and aquaculture. The government plans to improve the productivity of grassland, to increase industrial feed production, which only processes one-fourth of the feedgrain in China, and to tap the potential of nonconventional feed, such as straw treated with ammonia. Aquaculture, using sea water close to the coast and fresh water in inland areas, is seen as the major way to increase fishery production. Reforestation programmes will be further implemented to curb the problem of soil and water erosion, to improve biological and environmental protection and to enlarge fruit and nut harvests.

Further institutional changes and marketing reforms have been announced. First, the Household Responsibility System will remain as a long-term institutional arrangement. For existing farmers, as indicated above, the right to use contracted land will be extended for an additional 30 years after the original 15-year contract term expires. Furthermore, rights of use can be inherited or transferred to others against payment, provided that the land remains in farming. Second, further grain marketing reform measures will be taken. The regulated pricing system will give way to pricing determined by market forces.

Elimination of the two-tier pricing system is currently under discussion. Inter-provincial grain trading, which is currently heavily regulated, will be replaced by free trade between surplus and deficit regions according to their need. The government will use indirect means to achieve a market stabilization goal, while the state grain marketing agencies will be further reformed to separate the functions of government and business. Development of intermediate marketing organizations, to improve the links between small farmers and the market, will be encouraged. Third, waste in food consumption will be reduced. Alcohol production, which at present consumes over 20 million tonnes of grain a year, will be reduced and replaced by more soft drinks and fruit wines. Fourth, the current market stabilization system will be improved to increase food security against natural calamities.

China is determined to make every effort to rely on domestic resources in order to ensure basic long-term food security for the growing population. However, international cooperation and trade will not be ignored. Agricultural policy makers recognize the need to open up the domestic market to meet the requirements for entering the World Trade Organization, to become more integrated into the global market and to benefit from international cooperation (Wan, 1996). Even for its most important product, grain, China does not pursue a policy of complete self-sufficiency. For the first time, a target has been declared and set at 95 per cent (State Council, 1996). In normal years, holding net imports of grain to less than 5 per cent of domestic consumption will translate to a net import of 25 million tonnes currently and 32 million tonnes by 2030, when total domestic consumption is estimated at 640 million tonnes.

It is, however, possible that grain imports larger than the 5 per cent target in any individual year in the coming three decades will be allowed. Indeed, the most important implication of the self-sufficiency statement is perhaps not the figure itself, but the message that China is willing to keep its grain market open and might possibly adjust the policy goal. In a global environment of increasing international cooperation, with the improvement in mutual understanding and build-up of trust between China and other countries, there is increasing awareness of the benefits of trade for optimizing domestic resource use. The deepening of domestic market reform and further liberalization of agriculture are also important. Against such a background, the acceptable self-sufficiency rate for grain may be further lowered, perhaps to 90 per cent. Under a more reasonable trade policy, China will export labour-intensive products, such as vegetables and other horticultural items, and import additional land-intensive products such as grain. This is a point much stressed by Chinese and oversees scholars.

Nevertheless, there are two constraints which make it unlikely that China's grain imports will become very large. First, real income improvement will slow down as the trend of recent years continues. The reduction of subsidies for housing, transport, medical care, education and other social welfare provisions for the urban population will substantially offset the income growth effects on food consumption, slowing the consumption growth of livestock products in particular. The large rural population, on the other hand, faces increasing difficulty in raising income through expanding farm production. Long-standing

underemployment and unemployment in both urban and rural areas have become more and more critical and cast a shadow over the prospects for future
improvement in incomes. In general, China, as a country, will have no financial problem in buying a large volume of grain from the world market, but the
individual Chinese, especially the rural dwellers who make up the majority of
the population, will not be able to afford a high level of expensive food
consumption.

Transport capacity is a second constraint. This relates not only to harbour
unloading capacity, but also to inland movement. For the vast inland and
mountainous areas, limited capacity and very high transport costs currently
hamper large-scale trade in food. In the next two to three decades, this situation cannot be completely changed. Hence it seems unlikely that China will
import more than 10 per cent of her food or grain needs in the near and distant
future.

CONCLUSIONS

To sum up, the agricultural policy changes in China during the past decade
were characterized by market liberalization and regionalization. Markets for
almost all non-grain products had been liberalized by the early 1990s. Even for
grain, the most strictly regulated farm product, significant market reforms have
been accomplished, though the reform process has not been very smooth.

Agricultural policy decision making and implementation has been substantially decentralized. This reduces the budget burden of the central government,
but also leads to undesirable consequences such as regionalism and market
fragmentation. The most difficult challenge ahead is to reform the state grain
and cotton marketing sectors. The mixture of functions of government and
business in those enterprises makes every step in the reform process complicated. Many state grain marketing enterprises will not be able to survive under
free market competition, and the resulting losses from bankruptcy have to be
borne by the government. This poses a dilemma for the government in making
reform decisions.

The many inconsistencies arising from the transition process, coupled with
market fluctuations, may weaken the determination of the policy makers towards further reforms. Bold market-liberating measures are usually taken in
times of market surpluses. Policy makers are much more cautious and conservative during periods of supply shortages.

Food and agricultural sectors have become increasingly linked with the
world market and China has become an influential force in world agricultural
markets, as both an exporter and an importer. As a result, domestic market
policy will have an increasingly significant impact on the world market. A
more liberalized and integrated domestic market will provide a good foundation for promoting the internationalization process.

The goals of food and agricultural trade have shifted from earning hard
currency to matters concerning food security and economic efficiency. Technically, China might be able to feed her increasing population. However, with
improved international cooperation and greater emphasis on the principle of

comparative advantage, China can be fed better and more efficiently. More and more people involved in agricultural policy formulation have recognized this and it is the basic reason for being optimistic about the future of marketing policy reform through the coming years.

It is vital, therefore, to strengthen the understanding and confidence of policy makers in market mechanisms and to build up more reliance on major food partners for long-term and stable cooperation. China will have a sounder agricultural policy given better comprehension and trust of policy makers in market forces. She will open her door for food and agricultural trade much more widely so long as she feels that food security and national sovereignty are not threatened by world food powers. Both Chinese and overseas agricultural economists can make great contributions towards this goal.

REFERENCES

Chen, Xiwen (1995), 'On the current grain supply, demand and prices in China', *Chinese Rural Economy*, **11**, 3–8.

Du, Yin (1996), 'Reforming and improving grain production and marketing systems in China', paper presented at an international conference on 'Food and Agriculture in China: Perspectives and Policies', 7–9 October, Beijing.

Fan, Shenggen *et al.* (1996), 'Why projections on China's future food supply and demand differ?', paper presented at an international conference on 'Food and Agriculture in China: Perspectives and Policies', 7–9 October, Beijing.

Ke, Bingsheng (1992), 'Price subsidy policy for grain in China: Performance, problems and prospects for reform', in M. Bellamy and B. Greenshields (eds), *Issues in Agricultural Development*, IAAE Occasional Paper No. 6, Aldershot: Dartmouth.

Ke, Bingsheng (1995), *Grain market and policy in China*, Beijing: Agricultural Publishing House of China.

Ke, Bingsheng (1997), 'Recent developments in the livestock sector in China and the livestock/feed relationship', report prepared for FAO.

MIT (Ministry of Internal Trade) (1995), unpublished report.

MOA (Ministry of Agriculture) (1995, 1996), *China agricultural development report*, Beijing: Agricultural Publishing House of China.

SSB (State Statistical Bureau) (various years) *Statistical Yearbook of China*, Beijing: State Statistical Bureau.

State Council (1996), *Grain Issues in China*, Beijing: Press Office of the State Council.

Tang, Renjian (1995), 'Reform of grain policy: difficulties and scenarios', *Chinese Rural Economy*, **11**, 11–14.

Tang, Renjian (1996), 'The reform of the grain circulation system in China: Present situation, targets and ways', paper presented at an international conference on 'Food and Agriculture in China: Perspectives and Policies', 7–9 October, Beijing.

Wan, Baorui (1996), 'Perspectives and policies of China's agricultural development', keynote speech at an international conference on 'Food and Agriculture in China: Perspectives and Policies', 7–9 October, Beijing.

Wang, Lingui (1996), 'Improving the grain stock regulating system to enhance food security', paper presented at an international conference on 'Food and Agriculture in China: Perspectives and Policies', 7–9 October, Beijing.

THOMAS W. HERTEL, WILLIAM A. MASTERS AND MARK J. GEHLHAR*

Regionalism in World Food Markets: Implications for Trade and Welfare

INTRODUCTION

This paper surveys the role of regional trading groups in food and agricultural markets. It begins with a review of economic regionalism in general and then considers historical experience in food markets. After that it presents several estimates of the magnitude of regionalism's effects on world welfare, trade and the shape of the global food system in the coming decade. The aim is to address two of the most dramatic changes in agricultural markets likely to occur over the coming years: eastward expansion of the European Union and deepening of integration in the Asia–Pacific region.

It will be suggested that world food trade will become concentrated increasingly within regional zones and that trading patterns are likely to be heavily influenced by the formation of regional trade agreements (RTAs). Furthermore, changes in food trade caused by RTAs may well have large economy wide welfare effects, dominating the RTA's impact on other sectors. The key role played by food trade arises mainly from the high degree of government involvement in the sector. Changes in food trade alter the costs of intervention, which in turn changes the incentives for governments to undertake particular policies.

When RTAs are formed among countries seeking to protect a particular sector (such as agriculture in Western Europe), they tend, for a variety of reasons, to facilitate higher levels of protection than each country might have instituted individually. However, this process can also work in reverse. For example, eastward expansion of the European Union is likely to reduce Europe's level of farm protection by increasing the variety of its members, thereby making the current Common Agricultural Policy (CAP) much more costly. Similarly, negotiations of an Asia–Pacific agreement are likely to avoid regional protection because of the diversity among participants. Only if a sub-group of similar countries were to initiate separate talks might they be affected by what can be termed the 'CAP trap', or a regional decision-making structure which facilitates rent seeking by some groups while muting the countervailing power of others.

*Purdue University, Indiana, USA (Hertel and Masters) and Economic Research Service, United States Department of Agriculture, Washington, DC, USA (Gehlhar).

REGIONALISM IN THE WORLD ECONOMY

Since ancient times, alliances and conquests have led to regional integration. The resulting economic growth has then helped to motivate and finance political expansion and to promote worldwide growth. However, rivalry among competing regions can be costly. The issue has spawned a vast literature in both economics and political science, to which we cannot possibly do justice. Excellent surveys of theory and experience from an economics perspective can be found in Anderson and Blackhurst (1993), de Melo and Panagariya (1993), Baldwin and Venables (1995) and Winters (1996).

Regionalism versus globalism in trade negotiations

It can be argued that the 1947 General Agreement on Tariffs and Trade (GATT) was the first serious attempt to pursue truly 'global' liberalization, defined in Article I as the application of common trading rules to all member countries on a most-favoured-nation (MFN) basis. Through Article I, signatories pledge to extend agreements made with one partner to all other partners, so that each receives the same treatment as the most favoured nation.

From its inception, GATT recognized exceptions to the MFN principle. Article XXIV permits the formation of RTAs among members, subject to certain restrictions which have not always been strongly enforced (Snape, 1993, p. 285). The largest and most economically important example, formed within the GATT, was the European Economic Community, created in 1957 through the Treaty of Rome. Expansion of the European Community in the 1980s, followed by deeper integration to form the European Union in 1992, helped spur trade policy changes throughout the world. Fearing a protectionist 'fortress Europe', other regions responded with their own agreements, notably in North America (NAFTA), South America (MERCOSUR) and Asia (APEC). In all, the number of regional agreements under Article XXIV has more than doubled since 1990 and there were 76 which were active in 1996 (*The Economist*, 1996). There has also been an attempt to limit European protectionism through expanding the scope of GATT in the Uruguay Round to include agriculture, services and other areas of policy not formerly included, as well as establishing a more visible global institution through the World Trade Organization (WTO).

Regionalism and world welfare

The development of RTAs may or may not be in conflict with global welfare. Many studies have addressed this issue, building on Viner (1950). Perhaps the most important point from this literature for the purposes of this paper is that, while a great deal can be said about the likely impact of an RTA on its member countries, it is much harder to formalize the question of what impact it will have on the global trading system (Baldwin and Venables, 1995). The outcome is inherently ambiguous and depends on the conditions under which it operates: using terms coined by Bhagwati (1991), RTAs can be either 'building blocks' or 'stumbling blocks' towards global liberalization.

The consensus view of trade economists is that most regional agreements formed to the present time have had largely positive effects on world welfare, with the major exception of European integration in food markets through the Common Agricultural Policy (Harmsen and Leidy, 1994). In that case, regional integration had a decisively protectionist quality from the beginning, with the CAP permitting European countries to achieve higher levels of protection from the rest of the world than would probably have been possible for each country acting alone (Winters, 1994).

The operation of Europe's CAP has imposed significant welfare costs on the rest of the world as well as on Europe itself (Kreinin and Plummer, 1992; Winters, 1995). It can be argued that the CAP's high degree of protectionism has been due to its particular decision-making structure rather than regional integration itself. Decisions are made largely by a Council of Ministers of Agriculture, with limited checks and balances from other interest groups. This situation, likened to a committee of foxes joining together to guard a common henhouse, is not a necessary feature of RTAs. Nevertheless, they may often facilitate protectionist rent-seeking, either by insulating policy makers from competing interests or by offering the pro-trade cover of regional integration.

Europe's experience suggests that treatment of agriculture and food markets is important to the overall impact of regional agreements, and also that the specific institutional structure of a regional agreement is important to its outcome. The fear that other RTAs have the potential to be highly protectionist has been highlighted by *The Economist*. In a memorable image, its cover during the week of the WTO's first Ministerial meeting on 9 December 1996 portrayed the WTO amidst 13 major RTAs as so many chefs, under the headline 'Spoiling world trade' (*The Economist*, 1996).

Although RTAs can have important effects, empirical assessments suggest that the magnitude of their impact remains far less than that of global agreements under the GATT/WTO, simply because the size and number of partners is smaller. This emerges from a comparison of Uruguay Round studies (Francois *et al.*, 1996) and those of RTAs (Srinivasan *et al.*, 1993). The relatively modest economic importance of RTAs in relation to global agreements does not, however, correspond to their relative political importance.

In practice, RTAs seem to attract a disproportionate degree of public interest, perhaps because the issues they raise are clearer to the public. This is most evident when comparing the treatment of NAFTA and the Uruguay Round in the United States. One direct measure of NAFTA's relatively greater public profile is its dominance of the 1991 congressional debate over giving 'fast-track' authority to negotiate the two agreements. Destler (1995) has suggested that that this debate focused on NAFTA, and 'with everyone's attention on Mexico, the Uruguay Round got almost a free ride'. Another measure of relative importance would be press coverage, whose attention to NAFTA is probably far greater than its economic importance alone might warrant.

Regionalism and trading patterns

The formation of regional groupings is not simply a matter of trade agreements, since they can appear for a variety of reasons, independently of RTAs. To evaluate the role of regionalism in world markets we need to review the historical evidence on regional patterns of trade (as in Lloyd, 1992, or Anderson and Norheim, 1993) and then examine alternative models of what might be causing the observed patterns.

To compare regions over a long time period, Anderson and Norheim (1993) take continents as their basic unit of observation, and focus on *extra*regional trade in order to control for differences in intraregional trade owing to differing numbers of countries on each continent. They also control for differences in continent size by considering extraregional trade as a share of world imports from that region, and adjust for openness using the region's overall trade/GDP ratio. The main finding from the resulting 'propensity-to-trade' indexes is that extraregional trade has risen along with intraregional trade, even as a share of

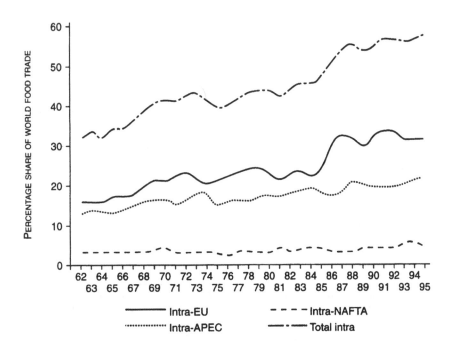

FIGURE 1   *Intraregional food trade in EU, NAFTA and APEC, 1962–95*

Note: Intra-APEC excludes intra-NAFTA.

GDP. Anderson and Norheim argue that, while 'this does not constitute proof that regional agreements benefit outsiders ... it at least throws doubt on the opposite conclusion' (ibid., p. 91).

The Anderson and Norheim propensity-to-trade indices cannot be applied to specific sectors, so to examine trends in food trade we focus on simple trade shares. We also differ from Anderson and Norheim in defining our regions in terms of RTAs (such as NAFTA) rather than continents. The focus, also, is on basic food commodities whose value-added occurs primarily on the farm (grains, oilseeds, fruits and vegetables, sugar and livestock products). This is important since 'food trade' is often defined to include processed intermediates (such as flour) and consumer-ready items (pasta), though we take the view that these items are more appropriately included in studies of industrial-product trade.

Figure 1 reports the shares of world trade in food accounted for by intraregional flows in the world's three major trading regions: EU12 (including 12 countries over the entire sample period), NAFTA (Canada, Mexico and the United States) and APEC (intra-APEC trade excludes intra-NAFTA trade). The total for these three regions now accounts for more than half of world agricul-

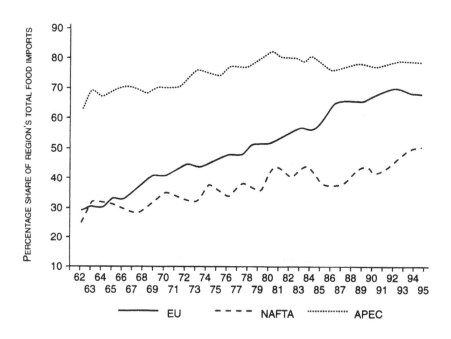

FIGURE 2   *Intraregional food imports in the EU, NAFTA and APEC, 1962–95*

tural trade, up from a third in the early 1960s. But the bulk of this increase derives from growth in intra-EU trade, which grew particularly quickly in the mid-1980s with the accession of Spain, Portugal and Greece.

A more detailed view is given in Figures 2 and 3, showing the share of each group's total imports and exports occurring within the region. On the import side (Figure 2), all three obtained an increasing share intraregionally until 1980, but Europe's increase was much greater and continued longer than the increases in APEC and NAFTA. North America's share was unchanged in the 1980s, but grew sharply in the early 1990s with the signing of the Canada–United States agreement and then NAFTA. APEC's share has remained unchanged since the late 1970s.

On the export side (Figure 3), the share staying within the region has been roughly constant for the EU, but has risen steadily for APEC since 1975 as APEC's food exporters have shifted their sales to fast-growing countries within the region. NAFTA experienced a similar increase over the same period, but from a much lower level. The sudden dip in 1995 is likely to be a transient effect of the devaluation of the Mexican peso.

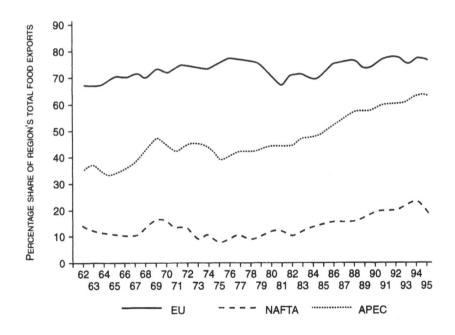

FIGURE 3   *Intraregional food exports from the EU, NAFTA and APEC, 1962–95*

Some of the variation in regional trade shares can be explained by disaggregating the regions and examining each country's trade patterns. Table 1 displays intraregional shares and the ratio of exports to imports for each region's members, using 1992 as the base year. The EU12 covers a highly diverse set of countries, including heavy food exporters (such as Ireland and Denmark) as well as importers (such as Portugal), whose trade with each other gives the region a strong *inward* orientation. In contrast, NAFTA is dominated by two heavy food exporters who sell mainly to overseas markets, resulting in a strong *outward* orientation for food trade. APEC is similar to the EU, in that it includes both positive and negative net food traders, and on average has an inward orientation. But while APEC's higher-income importers (Taiwan, South Korea and Japan) trade almost exclusively with other members, several of APEC's major exporters (such as Australia, New Zealand and Thailand) send significant shares of their produce to other regions; Chile could be considered an 'outsider', having low food trade-dependency with APEC.

Although each region's average level and trend in intraregional trade can be partly explained in terms of its members' domestic resources and policies, regional trade policies are also important. We can begin to see the impact of

TABLE 1   *Regional and total food trade by country, 1992*

Country	Import share from EU12	Export share to EU12	Exports/ imports	Country	Import share from APEC	Export share to APEC	Exports/ imports
Ireland	85	82	4.87	Australia	69	62	24.20
Denmark	73	62	4.62	New Zealand	69	50	21.60
France	69	75	1.54	Thailand	71	49	5.59
Netherlands	67	83	1.50	Chile	32	40	4.95
Spain	55	81	1.45	USA	58	57	3.16
Belgium–Lux.	78	89	0.97	Canada	81	59	2.08
Greece	82	77	0.63	China	79	65	2.07
Germany	69	74	0.47	Philippines	77	87	1.17
Italy	72	71	0.42	Taiwan	90	96	0.79
UK	66	75	0.40	Papua N.G.	94	74	0.51
Portugal	72	67	0.18	Malaysia	78	74	0.50
Total EU	70	77	0.90	Indonesia	73	41	0.40
				Mexico	83	92	0.40

Country	Import share from NAFTA	Export share to NAFTA	Exports/ imports				
				Singapore	84	55	0.30
				Hong Kong	79	70	0.08
				South Korea	88	90	0.06
				Japan	87	86	0.01
				Brunei	94	100	0.00
Canada	67	21	2.08	Total APEC	79	60	1.32
Mexico	77	86	0.40				
USA	28	17	3.16				
Total NAFTA	47	20	2.31				

RTAs by looking at the timing of trade-share changes, notably the rise in the share of European and North American imports sourced from within after integration episodes in each of those regions. Even more telling is the comparison between regional products, shown in Figure 4 for imports into the EU12 and APEC over the period 1975–95. Figure 4 indicates that Europe's intra-EU food imports rose sharply, while its non-food intraregional import share stayed roughly constant, whereas intra-APEC shares stayed constant for food and rose steadily for non-food. This difference is largely due to the trade policies adopted in each region. The EU's CAP offers very high barriers against non-members and preferences for members, reducing extraregional imports. The CAP effect is most graphically illustrated by the case of wheat (Figure 5): in 1975, European wheat imports were bought in roughly equal proportions from within and outside the EU12, but the extra-EU share had been almost completely eliminated by 1994. In the case of APEC, no such intraregional preferences were granted and the sourcing of agricultural imports has remained largely unchanged. In contrast, non-food imports were increasingly obtained from within APEC, as a result of increased trade in

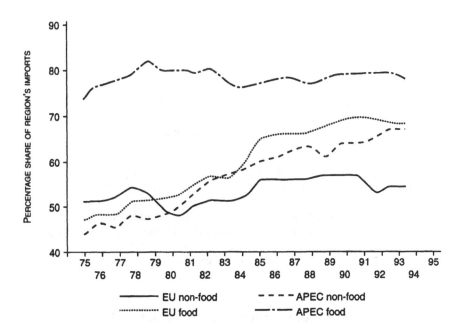

FIGURE 4 *Intraregional food and non-food imports in the EU and APEC, 1975–95*

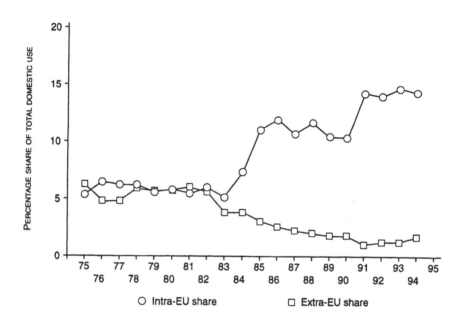

FIGURE 5   *Sources of imported wheat for use in EU, 1975–94*

Note: Domestic use = production + imports – exports.

capital goods (machinery and equipment) and consumer products (clothing, footwear and electronics) between industrialized and newly industrialized countries.

How can we systematically isolate the impact of trade policies from all of the other developments under way in the world economy? How would alternative trade policies affect trade and welfare? To address these questions formally, we turn to approaches which involve the explicit modelling of international trade.

MODELLING REGIONAL INTEGRATION

In order to assess the consequences of an RTA, it is necessary to consider what would be likely to happen in its absence: the counterfactual scenario, or what Winters (1996) calls the 'anti-monde'. To be realistic, this alternative must be based on an appropriate analytical model, including specification of the policies that would be used in place of the RTA. There are now quite a number of excellent surveys of alternative approaches for analysing RTAs, notably Francois and Shiells (1994) and Srinivasan *et al.* (1993). Rather than replicate these surveys we will summarize their key conclusions, to provide a foundation for the empirical case studies which follow later.

Alternative modelling approaches

In surveying NAFTA models, Francois and Shiells (1994) highlight three groups: sectoral econometric studies, applied general equilibrium models and linked macroeconometric models. They note (ibid., p. 13) that:

> In principle, it would be best to employ models that incorporate all three approaches. One would ideally like to specify a complete general equilibrium system based on microeconomic theory, collect time-series data on all pertinent variables in a way that satisfied all relevant accounting identities, and econometrically estimate the complete structural equation system utilizing all of the constraints and other information implied by economic theory. Relevant macroeconomic features (such as investment dynamics and the formation of expectations) should also be incorporated into the overall model structure.

Needless to say, this is not likely to be an attainable goal and researchers are forced to adopt only one of the three approaches.

At the one extreme lie the detailed econometric sectoral studies which justifiably have the greatest credibility with individual industries. As Francois and Shiells point out, the NAFTA debate stimulated a tremendous demand for this type of study and the level of detail desired by industry surpasses that which is attainable in most applied general equilibrium (AGE) models. The problem comes when one tries to add it all up to evaluate an RTA's impact on national income or factor returns. Even if similar methods are used, not all sectors will be covered and no economy-wide constraints are imposed to enforce consistency in the aggregate. Thus a survey of sectoral studies could well conclude that all sectors will contract, even though this is impossible for a region with reasonably fixed endowments and full employment. Typically, the concentrated losses in vulnerable sectors are exaggerated, while the widespread gains from access to lower-cost imports tend to be ignored.

AGE models are explicitly designed to address resource allocation across sectors, and hence capture the gains from trade which lie at the heart of most regional trade agreements. By accounting for all alternative uses of factors in the economy, they capture the essence of *comparative* advantage. Furthermore, with the addition of endogenous product differentiation, imperfect competition and scale economies, AGE models also offer some scope for capturing the impact of RTAs on intraindustry trade and the rationalization of global production within any given industry. The drawback of AGE models is that they are rarely amenable to empirical validation (for an exception, see Gehlhar, 1997), so their credibility hinges on the quality of the base data, parameters used and model structure. There is room for dispute on each count, and the economics profession is divided as to AGEs' value in policy analysis. Their continued use is largely due to the absence of practical alternatives.

In principle, macroeconomic models could play an important role by assessing an RTA's impact on investor expectations, capital flows and, hence, exchange rates. As noted by Francois and Shiells (1994, p. 14), however, these models 'were designed for very different purposes than the analysis of multisector trade liberalization' and 'the (macroeconometric) models employed have been in use for many years, in some cases reflecting over 20 year of poorly documented, *ad hoc* evolution of their original structure'. It is possible that new global, multi-sector macroeconometric models will change this assessment, but as macro models introduce sectoral detail and multi-region AGE models introduce capital mobility, the distinction between these two approaches is likely to blur.

Srinivasan *et al.* (1993) highlight a different methodological dimension of the problem, namely whether the analysis is undertaken *ex post* or *ex ante*. All of the AGE studies done to date provide ex ante evaluations beginning in a pre-RTA world, simulating the impact of implementing the RTA in that context. Furthermore, most of these comparative static analyses are based on a state of the world economy which considerably predates the RTA itself. For example, Roland-Holst *et al.* (1994) examine the impact of NAFTA as if it had been implemented in 1988. When the key features of the database change slowly, the implementation date may not matter very much. But, as shown by Bach *et al.* (1996), structural change, combined with the presence of non-tariff barriers, can make the base year quite important. In assessing the impact of the Uruguay Round agreement, they note that there has been rapid growth in Asia, allied with increases in quota premia on restricted textiles and apparel products. The result is that a historical approach can significantly understate the gains from the agreement relative to an assessment based on projections for the world economy at the end of the Uruguay Round's ten-year implementation period.

In contrast to these *ex ante* studies, Srinivasan *et al.* (1993) refer to a number of *ex post* assessments of the quantitative effects of RTAs. They cite several econometric studies from the 1960s and 1970s which sought to assess the degree of trade diversion/creation due to RTA formation in Europe and Latin America. Unfortunately, none of these studies lent themselves to welfare analysis owing to the absence of firm microeconomic foundations. It would be very interesting to attempt similar *ex post* analysis of NAFTA, using an explicit AGE model to evaluate the accuracy of model predictions relative to observed changes. However, this type of exercise requires a very large amount of data since it is necessary to specify a fairly complete set of changes over the relevant period. This includes actual policy reforms as well as key exogenous shocks to endowments and technology. A lone attempt at *ex post* evaluation of an AGE model is offered by Kehoe *et al.* (1991) for the case of Spanish tax reform.

Decomposition of welfare effects

To ascertain what is driving welfare changes in AGE models, it is very useful to disaggregate them into their component parts. Baldwin and Venables (1995) offer a clear decomposition, grouping the possible mechanisms causing welfare to alter into a total of seven categories.

(a) In perfectly competitive world markets, an RTA may affect welfare through:
    (i)   trade volumes, and hence changes in tariff revenue or quota rents;
    (ii)   trade costs, and hence changes in import/export margins;
    (iii) the terms of trade, through large-country effects.
(b) In imperfectly competitive markets, the RTA may affect welfare through:
    (iv) output effects, and hence changes in producer rents;
    (v)   scale effects, and hence changes in production costs;
    (vi) variety effects, where consumers value diversity itself.
(c) In the long run, an RTA may affect welfare through:
    (vii) accumulation effects, which arise from changes in the rate of investment in those cases where the social rate of return diverges from the social discount rate.

The first group of effects (trade volume, trade costs and terms of trade) are the most commonly discussed in the empirical literature and are present in virtually all AGE work on regional integration. Unfortunately, until recently no convenient mechanism existed for quantifying the changes when shocks are non-marginal, and traded goods are differentiated. The decomposition approach of Huff and Hertel (1996) provides a solution. In addition, it accounts for the impact of domestic distortions on changing welfare. The approach is particularly useful for agriculture, where domestic distortions due to tax/subsidy or regulatory policies are widespread. As a result, changes in farm output can have large effects on other sectors and on aggregate welfare. Indeed, it is the existence of domestic distortions which has caused agriculture to be such a stumbling block in the expansion of the European Union and NAFTA (Burfisher *et al.* 1994; Levy and Wijnbergen, 1994). As we will see from the empirical results, ignoring this aspect of regional integration also means missing a large part of the story on the efficiency consequences of the major prospective RTAs now under consideration.

Of the remaining welfare components the variety (vi) and scale (v) effects are the most frequently featured in RTA studies, as they appear in AGE models with monopolistic competition (Francois and Shiells, 1994). The remaining two terms are rarely mentioned, since they hinge on the analyst's assessment of pure industry profits (iv) and the divergence between the social discount rate and the return to investment (vii), which are notably difficult to measure.

EMPIRICAL CASE STUDIES

The methods surveyed above highlight the need for data-intensive analysis of the specific policy changes associated with RTAs. Here we bring these tools to bear in studies of two prospective RTAs which are expected to play an important role in shaping future food trade: eastward enlargement of the EU, and free trade in the Asia–Pacific region.

EU enlargement

In order to assess the likely impact of EU expansion on world trade and welfare, we draw primarily on recent studies by Frandsen *et al*. (1998), Hertel *et al*. (1997) and Swaminathan (1997). Each of these examines the impact of enlarging the EU to incorporate six of the Central and Eastern European Countries (CEECs): Poland, Hungary, Czech Republic, Slovak Republic, Romania and Bulgaria. The analysis is conducted in a post-Uruguay Round (UR) environment, eliminating barriers on intra-European trade and harmonizing external barriers at post-UR, EU levels. Harmonization involves lowering CEEC tariffs on non-farm goods, while raising import tariffs and export subsidies for farm products. This results in a massive shift of resources from the non-farm to the farm sectors in the CEECs.

The main interest is in the consequences of CEEC accession for trade within the region, extraregional trade and welfare. We consider first the changes in aggregated, bilateral trade volumes reported by Hertel *et al*. By far the largest percentage increase is in CEEC–EU15 trade, which rises by about 39 per cent in the base case. All other trade flows shrink, with the exception of CEEC gross exports to non-EU regions, which rise in the wake of massive agricultural export subsidies. This suggests the possibility of trade diversion and a decline in world welfare, but in fact those authors report a worldwide welfare gain of 4.2 billion European currency units (ECUs) from integration. How does this welfare gain arise?

In contrast to the Baldwin–Venables decomposition, Hertel *et al*. take account of the presence of the distortions caused by domestic farm policies. As a result, they find that, although allocative efficiency will deteriorate in the CEECs as it becomes subject to EU levels of agricultural protection, the rest of the EU and other OECD countries benefit from replacing subsidized domestic output with imports from the CEEC. As a result, worldwide allocative efficiency and welfare improves. This highlights the critical importance of pre-existing distortions in the analysis of the global welfare effects of regional integration. This is clearly a problem of the second-best; hence simple statements about trade diversion and creation are incomplete when it comes to assessing the impact of regional agreements on global welfare.

Swaminathan uses the same basic approach to the analysis of integration, but at a more disaggregate level and with greater attention to the role of scale and varietal effects. Of greatest interest here is her decomposition of the trade volume effects of integration, as summarized in Table 2. This table is organized around bilateral trade volume changes, with rows corresponding to source regions and columns corresponding to destinations. Each cell contains entries relating to the percentage change in trade volume (Vol, with numbers reported in parentheses) and the welfare change on the exporter side (Exp) as well as the importer side (Imp) of the transaction and the sum of these two terms (Total), reported in millions of 1992 ECU.

By way of explanation, consider the entries in the cell corresponding to the CEEC7 food row and the rest of world (ROW) columns of Table 2. Here is can be seen that, as a result of integration (and subsequent adoption by the CEEC7 of EU export subsidies), the volume of food and agricultural exports from the CEEC7 to ROW rises by 164 per cent. This causes an efficiency loss of 576 million ECU in the CEEC7, since these exports are subsidized and would be more valuable in domestic uses. However, since the rest of the world taxes food imports, the volume effect at the other end of this transaction is positive. Indeed, since the latter exceeds the former, world efficiency increases as a result of this isolated transaction. In other words, CEEC farmers may not be the lowest-cost suppliers of these food exports, but they appear to be lower-cost (on average) than the domestic producers they are displacing in countries such as Japan or Korea.

This general result – a marginal increase in the efficiency of food and agricultural trade – applies across the entire first row in Table 2, with the negative CEEC export entry dominated by the positive import entry. The last group of columns reports the World total for a given row. In the case of CEEC7 food exports, the large expansion in subsidized sales reduces efficiency in that region by 752 million ECU, but the associated imports raise world welfare by almost 5 billion ECU, resulting in an overall welfare gain of over 4 billion ECU. Clearly, this is a second-best effect, illustrating the difficulty of predicting the consequences of regional integration in the absence of careful quantitative evidence.

Next, turn to the EU15 food exports row of Table 2. Sales to the CEEC7 jump by 74 per cent as a result of eliminating bilateral trade barriers. This generates a significant welfare gain on the CEEC7 side. However, there is a small loss in the EU15, since these exports were previously subsidized. Intra-EU15 barriers are zero, so there is no trade volume effect here. Finally, the efficiency gain from reducing subsidized EU exports to ROW is offset by the loss from reduced imports in ROW.

The last group of rows in Table 2 corresponds to exports from the ROW region. For food and agriculture, trade volumes fall in all three market groupings, with the largest percentage drop occurring in CEEC7. Very substantial efficiency losses follow, particularly in the case of European imports displaced by intra-EU trade. Table 2 also reports the volume changes and welfare effects for all commodities (food plus non-food manufactures and services). Comparing these entries with those for food, it is clear that the latter dominate the total efficiency effect. In the final analysis, efficiency in world trade rises by 2.4 billion ECU.

Swaminathan also finds important interactions between regional integration and domestic agricultural subsidies. Both Hertel *et al.* and Swaminathan assume that 'compensation payments' in the EU15 will not be extended to the CEECs so that expansion of lightly subsidized output in the east displaces more heavily subsidized farm output in Western Europe, thereby generating substantial efficiency gains. This outcome depends critically on the degree to which internal policies permit the adjustment called for by regional integration. It is ultimately a question of how agricultural policy is implemented. Frandsen *et al.* (1998) explore this issue in greater depth, going well beyond

TABLE 2 Trade volume effects on world welfare due to EU enlargement, millions of 1992 ECU (% change in trade volume in parentheses)

	CEEC7				EU15				ROW				WORLD			
	Vol.	Exp.	Imp.	Total	Vol.	Exp.	Imp.	Total	Vol.	Exp.	Imp.	Total	Vol.	Exp.	Imp.	Total
CEEC7																
Food	(10.3)	−4	7	3	(415.2)	−172	3 514	3 342	(164.2)	−576	1 394	818	(27.7)	−752	4 915	4 163
All	(−3.6)	−4	−25	−29	(42.0)	−135	3 743	3 607	(4.3)	−576	1 042	466	(0.7)	−715	4 760	4 044
EU15																
Food	(74.1)	−10	238	228	(−1.9)	0	−2	−2	(−2.1)	325	−305	20	(−1.7)	315	−70	246
All	(35.7)	−4	606	602	(−0.1)	0	−2	−2	(−0.2)	319	−286	34	(−0.0)	314	318	634
ROW																
Food	(−22.1)	−10	−138	−148	(−4.0)	−25	−1 463	−1 488	(−0.3)	32	−421	−389	(−0.3)	−4	−2 021	−2 025
All	(0.7)	−8	−130	−138	(−0.4)	−2	−1 625	−1 627	(−0.0)	49	−405	−355	(−0.0)	39	−2 160	−2 120
Total	−17	−17	451	434		−137	2 115	1 978		−208	351	145		−362	2 918	2 556

Source: Swaminathan (1997).

the simple *ad valorem* representation used by others. In particular, they introduce export restrictions on grains, in line with the UR agreement, along with production quotas for dairying. As a result, EU15 agriculture is less flexible in its adjustment to a post-integration environment and there is less potential for efficiency gains to occur. Furthermore, the compensatory payments currently made to EU15 farmers are extended to the CEECs. The effect is to make integration even more distorting for the new eastern members of an enlarged Union and there could be a small decline in world welfare.

Asia–Pacific economic cooperation (APEC)

Apart from Europe, the largest regional integration effort on the horizon is the proposal for free trade in the Asia–Pacific region (APEC), initiated in Bogor, Indonesia, in November 1994. The specific proposal was to eliminate all trade barriers in the APEC region on an MFN basis. The timetable is more rapid for the advanced economies (2010) with a longer period of adjustment for the developing countries (2020).

While the principle of 'open regionalism', or non-preferential trade liberalization, has been reaffirmed from time to time, the fact remains that, as a large region, APEC has the potential to extract sizeable terms of trade gains from the rest of the world if members chose to proceed on a preferential basis. An early comparison between these two approaches to APEC liberalization is offered by Young and Huff (1997). They find that the world welfare gain would jump by 31 per cent under MFN liberalization and that, while APEC gains would be higher under preferential free trade, the non-APEC region would then suffer a substantial welfare decline. A third alternative would be global liberalization, which could yield even larger gains to APEC members (Lewis *et al.*, 1994).

The potential terms of trade gains from preferential liberalization have not been lost on participants in the negotiations. Indeed, Adams *et al.* (1997) note that Australia, recently a strong advocate of universal free trade, has now itself indicated it is prepared to consider membership of an APEC free trade area with external barriers. The authors rework the Young–Huff study at a far greater level of commodity disaggregation (37 sectors rather than 3) and show that the measured gains from preferential free trade in APEC generally increase with sectoral detail. However, the main contribution of their study is to explore the possible impact of APEC on long-run GDP, through increased investment. They find that this effect is quite dramatic in the case of the smaller APEC economies owing to the tendency for current trade policy to levy relatively high tariffs on imported capital goods. Under free trade, their price would fall, thereby raising the expected return on new investment and luring additional capital into the region. For Thailand and the Philippines, real GDP increases by nearly 40 per cent under the long-run APEC scenario.

Anderson *et al.* (1997) explore the impact of MFN liberalization by APEC countries in a post-Uruguay Round setting. Their focal point is 2005, the year when the UR agreement is due to be fully implemented. From that base, they assume that APEC liberalization would not fully eliminate the remaining barriers, but only reduce their level by 50 per cent. Of particular interest are their findings with regard to regionalization, summarized in Table 3. The first scenario presented there refers to the base year for their study (1992), in which 64.7 per cent of APEC trade was intraregional. The comparable figure for East Asia alone was 38.5 per cent. The authors then project their model forward to the year 2005 – first without the UR reforms and then with them, including accession of China and Taiwan in the UR system. The rise in intraregional trade purely as a consequence of rapid economic growth in the APEC region is quite striking. Indeed, in East Asia the projected share of intraregional trade jumps from 38.5 per cent in 1992 to 46.1 per cent in 2005, with no change in trade policies (that is, the absence of the UR). However, this growth in the share of intraregional trade does not mean that trade with the rest of the world is declining. Indeed, as seen from the latter two columns of this table, even the share of extraregional trade in GDP is rising over this period. Economic growth and structural change are simply forcing the region to become more reliant on trade. This general tendency is further reinforced by the Uruguay Round.

TABLE 3   *Regional trade shares for Asia in 1992 and projections for 2005*

	Percentage share of total trade that is intraregional		Extraregional (intraregional) trade percentage of regional GDP	
	East Asia	APEC	East Asia	APEC
1992	38.5	64.7	11.1 (7.0)	5.0 (9.2)
2005 no UR	46.1	67.8	11.7 (10.0)	5.3 (11.2)
2005 UR	46.5	67.5	13.5 (11.7)	6.1 (12.6)
2005 UR/APEC	47.6	69.1	14.5 (13.1)	6.3 (14.1)

Source: Anderson *et al.* (1997).

Table 3 also shows that the 50 per cent MFN cut in post-UR protection in the APEC region boosts the share of intraregional trade in total trade by about 1.5 percentage points. However, it also increases extraregional trade – particularly in the case of East Asia. In sum, the work of Anderson *et al.* suggests that the share of total trade that is intraregional will continue to rise in the APEC region. As a result of increased openness, the importance of extraregional trade – relative to GDP – will also rise, unless the region reverts to preferential trade liberalization. In addition, the study highlights the key role of food and agricultural liberalization in an overall APEC scenario. Including agriculture as an equal partner in post-UR cuts boosts the global trade gain by one-fifth and causes farm and food trade to be 18 per cent higher in 2005 than would be the case without further liberalization.

CONCLUSIONS

International trade is becoming more regionalized. Our review of recent history indicates that the share claimed by intraregional trade in the EU, NAFTA and APEC has been increasing for food and non-food products alike. However, this does not mean that the global trading system is failing. As shown by Anderson and Norheim (1993), extraregional trade has, by and large, weathered the formation of regional trading blocks. Increased openness to trade in general has resulted in increases in extraregional trade as a share of GDP. The one notable exception has been in the EU, where the Common Agricultural Policy has created a strong tendency to substitute intraregional imports for extraregional ones – in some cases nearly eliminating the latter altogether.

But what does the future hold? In an effort to say something about this, we review several *ex ante* studies of two important current regional integration initiatives. We begin with the question of EU enlargement to include six of the Central and Eastern European economies (CEECs). Here a key question is how domestic agricultural policies will be extended to the new entrants. This is an area which authors writing on regional integration have largely ignored. In their excellent survey of the economic effects of RTAs, Baldwin and Venables (1995) abstracted from domestic policies altogether, yet, in the case of agriculture, these programmes are often at the centre of the debate over integration.

If EU15 producer subsidies are not extended to the CEECs, it appears that the potential for integration to lead to global welfare gains is quite good. This is because one of the primary effects of integration is to substitute low-cost CEEC agricultural output for higher-cost EU15 produce. In addition, the subsidized CEEC food exports displace relatively higher cost domestic production in East Asia and, together, these two positive forces dominate the negative trade diversion caused by displacing low-cost supplies of food from the rest of the world (Hertel *et al.*, 1997; Swaminathan, 1997).

If the CAP were to be fully extended to the CEECs and if EU15 producers were to avoid full adjustment to the new entrants' comparative advantage in agriculture, the CAP would become much more expensive. Indeed, it seems unlikely that such a scenario would be sustainable, particularly in light of UR commitments made by the CEECs. In this case, we believe that enlargement will require reform of the CAP itself. When viewed as a package, EU enlargement coupled with CAP reform is expected to be beneficial for global trade and welfare.

What about APEC? Clearly, there is less of a political mandate for establishing an RTA in the Pacific Rim. Indeed, we find that the region has become increasingly integrated in the absence of any formal agreement, and projections to 2005 indicate that this trend is likely to continue over the next decade, with increases in the share of intraregional trade as a consequence of economic growth and structural change. This is also the region making the deepest cuts in protection under the Uruguay Round, which adds to the general trade expansion. However, this increasing intraregional trade share does not appear to come at the expense of extraregional trade, which is also projected to rise relative to GDP over the coming decade.

If APEC liberalization does become more than a talking point in the region, two key issues will arise from the perspective of global trade and welfare. First, will liberalization be on an MFN or a preferential basis? The former will be supportive of the trend towards increasing extraregional trade, while the latter would threaten to reverse this. Second, will agriculture be included on an equal basis in the liberalization agreement? Or will it be relegated to a slower timetable, or left out altogether? In the latter case, the global benefits from APEC liberalization would be greatly diluted (Anderson *et al.*, 1997).

A remote but dangerous possibility would be for a sub-set of APEC governments to seek agricultural protection through a CAP-type structure of their own. Experience with the CAP suggests that, should regional protection instruments be developed, the resulting protection levels could well be quite high. The likely candidates to join a farm-trade block would be the higher-income or rapidly growing countries where agricultural adjustment is most painful, beginning with Japan, Korea and Taiwan and possibly extending to Malaysia, Indonesia and elsewhere. Ultimately, it would be up to foreigners and non-farm interests within these countries to oppose such a move, in the name of further growth. So far the prospects for APEC avoiding the 'CAP trap' remain good, but increasingly persuasive global AGE models will be needed to ensure that RTAs remain beneficial building blocks of the global economy, rather than costly stumbling blocks.

REFERENCES

Adams, P., Huff, K., McDougall, R., Pearson, K.R. and Powell, A. (1997), 'Medium- and Long-Run Consequences for Australia of an APEC Free-Trade Area: CGE Analyses Using the GTAP and Monash Models', mimeo, Centre of Policy Studies, Monash University.

Anderson, K. and Blackhurst, R. (eds) (1993), *Regional Integration and the Global Trading System*, New York: St Martin's Press.

Anderson, K. and Norheim, H. (1993), 'Is World Trade Becoming more Regionalized?', *Review of International Economics*, 1, 91–109.

Anderson, K., Dimaranan, B., Hertel, T.W. and Martin, W. (1997), 'Economic Growth and Policy Reform in the Asia–Pacific: Trade and Welfare Implications by 2005', *Asia–Pacific Economic Review*, 3, 1–18.

Bach, C.F., Dimaranan, B., Hertel, T.W. and Martin, W. (1996), *Growth, Globalization and the Gains from the Uruguay Round*, Policy Research Working Paper 0–1170, Washington, DC: World Bank.

Baldwin, R.E. and Venables, A.J. (1995), 'Regional Economic Integration', in G. Grossman and K. Rogoff (eds), *Handbook of International Economics, Vol. III*, Amsterdam: Elsevier.

Bhagwati, J.N. (1991), *The World Trading System at Risk*, Hemel Hempstead: Harvester Wheatsheaf.

Burfisher, M.E., Robinson, S. and Thierfelder, K.E. (1994), 'Wage Changes in a US–Mexico Free Trade Area: Migration vs. Stolper-Samuelson Effects', in J.F. Francois and C.R. Shiells (eds), *Modeling Trade Policy: Applied General Equilibrium Assessments of North American Free Trade*, New York: Cambridge University Press.

de Melo, J. and Panagariya, A. (1993), *New Dimensions in Regional Integration*, Cambridge: Cambridge University Press.

Destler, I.M. (1995), *American Trade Politics*, 3rd edn, Washington, DC: Institute for International Economics and New York: The Twentieth Century Fund.

The Economist (1996), 'Spoiling World Trade' and '*All* free traders now', 7 December, 15–16 and 21–3.

Francois, J.F. and Shiells, C.R. (1994), 'AGE Models of North American Free Trade', in J.F.

Francois and C.R. Shiells (eds), *Modeling Trade Policy: Applied General Equilibrium Assessments of North American Free Trade*, New York: Cambridge University Press.

Francois, J.F., McDonald, B. and Nordstrom, H. (1996), *A User's Guide to Uruguay Round Assessments*, Staff Working Paper RD-96-003, Geneva: World Trade Organization.

Frandsen, E.F., Bach, C.F. and Stephensen, P. (1998), 'European Integration and the Common Agricultural Policy', in M. Brockmeier, J.F. Francois, T.W. Hertel and P.M. Schmitz (eds), *Economic Transition and the Greening of Politics: Modelling New Challenges for Agriculture and Agribusiness in Europe*, Kiel: Vauk.

Gehlhar, M. (1997), 'An Evaluation of Growth and Trade Patterns in the Pacific Rim: An Evaluation of the GTAP Framework', in T.W. Hertel (ed.), *Global Trade Analysis: Modeling and Applications*, New York: Cambridge University Press.

Harmsen, R. and Leidy, M. (1994), 'Regional Trading Arrangements', in IMF (ed.), *International Trade Policies: The Uruguay Round and Beyond, Volume II: Background Papers*, Washington, DC: International Monetary Fund.

Hertel, T.W., Brockmeier, M. and Swaminathan, P. (1997), 'Sectoral and Economywide Analysis of Integrating Central and East European Countries (CEE) into the European Union (EU): Implications of Alternative Strategies', *European Review of Agricultural Economics*, 24, 359–86.

Huff, K. and Hertel, T.W. (1996), 'Decomposing Welfare Changes in the GTAP Model', Technical Paper No. 5, Purdue University, Centre for Global Trade Analysis, West Lafayette.

Kehoe, T.J., Polo, C. and Sanchez, F. (1991), *An Evaluation of the Performance of an Applied General Equilibrium Model of the Spanish Economy*, Working Paper 480, Minneapolis: Federal Reserve Bank of Minneapolis.

Kreinin, M. and Plummer, M. (1992), 'Effects of Economic Integration in Industrial Countries on ASEAN and the Asian NIEs', *World Development*, 20, 1345–66.

Levy, S. and S. Wijnbergen (1994), 'Agriculture in the Mexico–US Free Trade Agreement: A General Equilibrium Analysis', in J.F. Francois and C.R. Shiells (eds), *Modeling Trade Policy: Applied General Equilibrium Assessments of North American Free Trade*, New York: Cambridge University Press.

Lewis, J.D., Robinson, S. and Wang, Z. (1994), 'Beyond the Uruguay Round: The Implications of an Asian Free Trade Area', *China Economic Review*, 6, 35–50.

Lloyd, P.J. (1992), 'Regionalization and World Trade', *OECD Economic Studies*, 18, 7–43.

Roland-Holst, D.W., Reinert, K.A. and Shiells, C.R. (1994), 'A General Equilibrium Assessment of North American Economic Integration', in J.F. Francois and C.R. Shiells (eds), *Modeling Trade Policy: Applied General Equilibrium Assessments of North American Free Trade*, New York: Cambridge University Press.

Snape, R.H. (1993), 'History and Economics of GATT's Article XXIV', in K. Anderson and R. Blackhurst (eds), *Regional Integration and the Global Trading System*, New York: St Martin's Press.

Srinivasan, T.N., Whalley, J. and Wooton, I. (1993), 'Measuring the Effects of Regionalism on Trade and Welfare', in K. Anderson and R. Blackhurst (eds), *Regional Integration and the Global Trading System*, New York: St Martin's Press.

Swaminathan, P.V. (1997), 'Regional Integration in the Presence of Monopolistic Competition: Implications for Enlarging the European Union', PhD dissertation, Department of Agricultural Economics, Purdue University, West Lafayette.

Viner, J. (1950), *The Customs Union Issue*, New York: Carnegie Endowment for International Peace.

Winters, L.A. (1994), 'The EC and Protection: The Political Economy', *European Economic Review*, 38, 596–603.

Winters, L.A. (1995), 'Regionalism and the Rest of the World: Theory and Estimates of the Effects of European Integration', mimeo, Washington, DC: World Bank.

Winters, L.A. (1996), *Regionalism versus Multilateralism*, Policy Research Working Paper No. 1687, Washington, DC: World Bank.

Young, L. and Huff, K. (1997), 'Free Trade in the Pacific Rim: On What Basis?', in T.W. Hertel (ed.), *Global Trade Analysis: Modeling and Applications*, New York: Cambridge University Press.

DISCUSSION REPORT SECTION IV

Ewa Rabinowicz (Sweden)[1] expressed her belief that most economists now take the view that 'institutions matter', though this has to be coupled with serious questions about exactly *how* they matter and whether it is possible to choose between alternative sets of arrangement. The subject can quickly become something of a mystery. In the light of this, she wanted to make it clear that the discussion of 'institutions' as a leading part of the conference programme was something that she greatly welcomed. The really difficult issues need more discussion rather than less, even when the results might be rather unsatisfactory.

That brought her to the paper on transformation by Schmitz and Noeth. She could hardly differ from them in their view that institutions matter. Furthermore, she also believes that the institutional vacuum has, most probably, contributed to the economic problems experienced during transition in Central and Eastern Europe and in the former Soviet Union. However, she was worried about the precise components that make up the 'vacuum' (if it can be put in that way). It is well known, from the various writings of Douglass North, that 'institutions' consist of formal rules, informal constraints (norms of behaviour, conventions and self-imposed codes of conduct) and the enforcement characteristics of both. Institutions are not organizations, which is a point about which the authors are very well aware.

The difficulties are then obvious. For example, what is the state of contract law and are firms still as bad in complying with contracts as they were in 1990/91? Schmitz and Noeth provide little evidence. Furthermore, on a slightly different tack, Rabinowicz pointed out that several CEECs, most notably Hungary, made attempts to introduce partial market-oriented economic reforms during the late stages of the socialist period. The institutional vacuum was perhaps far from being uniform between the countries. The obvious question, therefore, is whether the countries which have performed better are also those where the vacuum was less prominent. Without controlling for the influence of other factors, and without an attempt to link directly some measures of the degree of institutional deficiency to performance, the issue of how much institutions matter cannot be explored. She realized that this was a highly critical remark, but it was being made to emphasize the complexities involved in institutional analysis.

Rabinowicz also expressed disappointment with the second part of the paper. It is easy to show that the evolution of agrarian structures has been profoundly different in different countries, for instance in the Czech Republic and Albania. The development has also varied between sub-sectors in agricul-

[1]Swedish University of Agricultural Sciences, Uppsala.

ture. It is a challenge to understand why. Yet the authors make no attempt to use the models presented to predict or to explain what actually is happening in the agricultural sectors mentioned. This lack of linkage between the models and the actual development constitutes a major weakness of the paper. Moreover, only a comparative static exercise is provided. In the simple models used, there is not much which can evolve during the process of transition! Thus the models are not well suited to analysis of the *process* of transformation in agriculture. The paper does not offer us much understanding of fundamental questions such as why agriculture is still organized in collective forms, whether it will continue to be so in the future and, in particular, why the degree of decollectivization differs so dramatically between the countries. This is linked to 'politics' or 'political economy', which have affected the design and the outcome of the process of privatization. Explanation of restructuring is almost incomprehensible without taking into account the political forces which have shaped the process. There is a borderline here between *institutional economics* and *political economy* which needs much more clarification and investigation.

Mahabub Hossain (Bangladesh)[2] was impressed by Ke's excellent account and qualitative evaluation of recent agricultural policies and institutional change in China and of the prospects for sustaining food security in the early 21st century. There is no doubt that many of the reforms introduced qualify as *institutional* innovations. That is particularly true of the Household Responsibility System, which triggered rapid growth in agricultural productivity in the early 1980s. It is now proceeding further since the government has extended tenure of the contracted-out public land to individual farmers for another 30 years. All of that has been accompanied by many other changes which are strengthening the operation of markets and reducing the role of the central government. International trade in grains is still under strict control (which may be sensible, given the recent fluctuations in the world market) though there is a problem since it is subject to lack of coordination among different ministries and state trading agencies involved in the decision-making process.

According to Mahabub Hossain, China has earned the world's acclamation for its ability to feed over one-fifth of the global population with only one-fifteenth of the arable land. The question is whether that can be sustained into the 21st century. Reverting to the food security theme, he offered a number of comments to suggest that China might become less outward looking in agricultural trade issues than others have inferred. As in the cases of Japan and South Korea, China might keep strict control over its domestic market and in its international trade in grain in order to manipulate the key relationship between prices in general and agricultural prices. That has great political significance. It may only provide food surplus countries with the minimum access to its grain market agreed in trade negotiations, to keep its important trade partners happy.

The third paper in the section (Hertel, Masters and Gehlhar) dealt with the major trade policy issue of the growth of regional blocks through regional

[2]International Rice Research Institute, Manilla, Philippines.

trade arrangements (RTAs). *Dieter Kirschke (Germany)*[3] opened the discussion on the work of colleagues whom he described as 'masters of the art' of equilibrium modelling, always capable of producing competent analysis and comment. Having said that, however, he added that the whole arena is one which is becoming stylized and far from exciting. This could be arising because we know so much about trade liberalization, in the broadest sense, and fully appreciate that it can be welfare enhancing. Any move towards regional integration is likely, therefore, to have similar effects, since it is usually a further step along the path of liberalization (trade creation dominates over trade diversion). If transition countries come to share in such moves, through expansion of the European Union, they are almost certainly going to benefit. As for global welfare, that, too, might increase if the pressure of budget costs cuts down average protection of agriculture in an enlarged Union. Kirschke's comment was 'hopefully the authors are right', though he then noted that work on applied general equilibrium models must be understood to be appreciated. A conditional assumption can be fed in and results emerge. The danger lies in looking at the results and forgetting the assumption.

From what he described as his somewhat cynical stance, he then went on to plead for greater realism in modelling. For example, the drift of EU agricultural policy is now towards sharp reductions in policy-determined prices towards compensatory factor-tied subsidies. This is an adjustment which does not necessarily amount to liberalization, yet it is one which needs thorough analysis.

Kirschke also made comments about methodology. General equilibrium models are powerful, but other techniques of analysis can be equally useful. There was a discussion of the point by Hertel, Masters and Gehlhar, though they seemed dismissive of anything else. In their conclusions they appeared to be positively euphoric in selling their technique as the means of ensuring beneficial progress in trade organization. That is surely an overoptimistic view of the persuasive powers of applied general equilibrium models – they are simply models, they are not policies.

[3]Humboldt University, Berlin.

CONTRIBUTED PAPERS

Households, Diets and Credit

AWUDU ABDULAI AND CHRISTOPHER L. DELGADO*

Determinants of Time Spent in Non-farm Employment by Farmers in Northern Ghana

INTRODUCTION

Absorbing the large and rapidly increasing rural labour force in productive employment is one of the principal challenges of development, especially in sub-Saharan Africa. Many farm families have responded to increasing population densities, declining farm sizes and environmental stress by increasing the extent of their participation in non-farm pursuits to generate additional income for family needs, despite the impact of Structural Adjustment reforms in the 1980s that were largely designed to restore the profitability of agriculture relative to non-farm activities. Farm household surveys have shown that the rural non-farm economy accounts, on average, for 10–30 per cent of all full-time employment and 25–40 per cent of rural income in rural sub-Saharan Africa (Haggblade *et al.*, 1989).

One of the curious findings of research in this area in West Africa is that the share of non-farm income in total rural household income tends to increase over the income distribution, with higher-income rural households being more heavily involved, both absolutely and relatively, in on-farm activities (Reardon *et al.*, 1992; 1994). This is the opposite of what has been observed in Latin America and South Asia, where the rural rich tend to be landed gentry, or at least heavily involved in high-yield agriculture (von Braun and Pandya-Lorch, 1991; Adams and He, 1994).

A considerable amount of research on the rural non-farm economy in Africa has been carried out in recent years. Previous studies have concentrated on the characteristics of microenterprises in rural areas (Liedholm *et al.*, 1994), quantifying the share of non-farm in total income and employment to show the range of roles played by non-farm activities in the household economy (Eicher and Baker, 1992) or simulating farm–non-farm growth linkages through calculation of growth multipliers, where rural enterprise growth is typically a demand-driven spinoff of agricultural growth (Haggblade *et al.*, 1989; Delgado *et al.*, 1994). Very few studies have considered empirically the factors that influence the decisions of rural farm households in sub-Saharan Africa to participate in non-farm production and labour supply off-farm (see, for example, Reardon *et al.*, 1992).

*Awudu Abdulai (Ghana), Swiss Federal Institute of Technology, Zurich, Switzerland; Christopher Delgado (USA), International Food Policy Research Institute, Washington, DC, USA.

The hypotheses to explain the higher share of non-farm income for richer households which emerge from this work are that (1) agriculture is a less viable investment for most West Africans than for the better-off in South Asia, (2) wealth is less correlated with land ownership in West Africa than Asia, where land is also correlated with agricultural income, and (3) households in West Africa are faced by imperfect land and credit markets that allow some to participate in lucrative opportunities more easily than others. To the extent that non-farm activity requires capital, for example, households with higher agricultural income are relatively more likely to be able to overcome asset barriers to entry into non-farm activity where credit markets do not function.

The third hypothesis is the key for the present paper. Certain household characteristics are thought to be good proxies for the ability to overcome transactions costs of market participation for smallholder farmers in West Africa (de Janvry *et al.*, 1991). The contribution of the present paper is to investigate empirically the link between household characteristics, on the one hand, and on the other, the amount of time spent in income-oriented non-farm work, for a sample of farm households in Northern Ghana.

A HOUSEHOLD MODEL

The determinants of labour allocation by rural households is analysed using the conceptual framework of Huffman (1991). It is assumed that the decision unit is a risk-neutral single-family farm household with one utility function and that the husband and wife time are heterogeneous. The optimal allocation of time by husbands and wives between leisure, non-farm work and farm work is obtained by solving the following optimization problem

$$U = u(Q, L_1, L_2; \mathbf{Z}^c, \Omega); \qquad (1)$$

$$T = T_{i1} + T_{i2} + L_i; T_{i2} \geq 0 \text{ for } i = 1, 2; \qquad (2)$$

$$Y = Y(T_{11}, T_{21}, H_{11}, H_{21}, X; \mathbf{Z}^p, \mathbf{M}, \Omega); \qquad (3)$$

$$PQ = W_{12}T_{12} + W_{22}T_{22} + P_y Y - P_x X - W_{11}H_{11} - W_{21}H_{21} + R \qquad (4)$$

where U in equation (1) is the household's utility function, assumed to be monotonic, twice differentiable and strictly concave; Q and P denote the quantity and price of the consumption good purchased in the market; T is the total time available to the husband and wife; T_{i1} and T_{i2} are, respectively, time allocated by husbands ($i = 1$) and wives ($i = 2$), to farm and non-farm production; L_i is the leisure time of the husband or wife; H_{11} and H_{21} represent hired male and female labour; and X denotes purchased non-labour inputs. P_y and P_x are prices of farm output and non-labour inputs, respectively; R is non-labour income; $\mathbf{M}$ is a vector of fixed factors such as land; while $\mathbf{Z}^c$ and $\mathbf{Z}^p$ are vectors representing household characteristics affecting production decisions; and Ω is a vector of location-specific effects, such as population density and infrastructure.

Assuming interior solutions, the first-order conditions for utility maximization, subject to the specified constraints, gives the reduced-form time allocation equations for both husbands and wives to non-farm work, which are of the form:

$$T_{i2} = T_{i2}(W_{12}, W_{22}, W_{11}, W_{21}, P_y, P_x, P, R; \mathbf{Z}^c, \mathbf{Z}^p, \Omega). \tag{5}$$

The first stage of the analysis involves an examination of the probability of participation in non-farm work, using a Probit model, while a second stage deals with the extent of participation, using a Tobit model (Maddala, 1983). The probability of participation can be expressed as the probability that an individual's reservation wage is less than his (her) anticipated market wage. For the ith individual in the hth household, we can define:

$$D_h^i = \begin{cases} 1 \text{ if } i\text{th individual participates} \\ 0 \text{ otherwise} \end{cases}$$

where $l = 1, 2$. The probability of participation for the ith individual is then:

$$P_r\{D_h^i = 1\} = F[W_{ah}^i > W_{rh}^i]; \quad i = 1, 2, \tag{6}$$

where W_{ah}^i and W_{rh}^i are the anticipated and reservation wages of the ith individual, respectively. Expressed in terms of the predetermined variables in the reduced-form labour supply function derived in equation (5), equation (6) can be written as:

$$P_r\{D_h^i = 1\} = F[W_{12}, W_{22}, P_3, R, K, \mathbf{Z}^c, \mathbf{Z}^p, \Omega]; \quad i = 1, 2, \tag{7}$$

The function $F(\ )$ in equations (6) and (7) is a cumulative distribution function. A Probit model is used to examine the probability of participation, while a Tobit specification is employed to analyse the extent of participation in cash-oriented non-farm work.

DATA AND RESULTS

The data used in this study were obtained from a random survey of 256 farm households in 37 villages of four districts located in the Northern Region of Ghana. The data were collected between 1992 and 1993 through repeated visits. The dependent variable used to represent non-farm employment, separately for males and females, is time allocated to non-farm activities. Non-farm employment information collected for males and females includes non-farm self-employment off the compound, non-farm self-employment on the compound and off-farm employment for salaries and wages. Time spent at non-farm employment was recorded as hours per week and weeks per year.

Table 1 defines the variable labels and gives summary statistics. Table 2 presents the results of the estimates of the equations explaining the probability of participating in non-farm activities. The log-likelihood ratio test statistics for goodness of fit for the models for males and females are both significant at

TABLE 1   *Data definitions and descriptive statistics*

Variable	Variable description	Sample mean	Standard deviation
Dependent variables			
D^1	1 if husband participates in non-farm activities	0.59	0.56
D^2	1 if wife participates in non-farm activities	0.68	0.59
T^1	Total male hours allocated to non-farm activities*	886	740
T^2	Total female hours allocated to non-farm activities*	1403	1360
Independent variables			
AGE	Age in years	35.81	7.25
EDUCM	Number of years of schooling for husband	4.33	4.47
EDUCF	Number of years of schooling for wife	4.24	4.46
TTRADE	Terms of trade between farming and non-farming	1.02	0.39
CHILD	Number of children less than 6 years old	2.16	1.10
HHSIZE	Household size	7.25	2.89
AGWAGE	Village average wage rate for hired farm labour	15.27	6.38
INFRA	1 if individual is in a location with relatively adequate state of infrastructure	0.40	0.49
POPDEN	Population per square km	37.88	39.75
CREDIT	1 if the person is credit non-constrained	0.38	0.49

Note: *Calculated only for those who participated in non-farm employment; does not include search time or other transaction costs for finding non-farm work.

the 1 per cent level, and imply in each case that the independent variables taken together influence participation decisions. At young ages, a higher age increases the probability of labour supply to the non-farm sector. At older ages, the probability of participating in non-farm activities decreases as age increases.

A husband or wife who has relatively more schooling has a significantly higher probability of engaging in non-farm activities. This implies that additional schooling raises an individual's off-farm wage by more than it raises his or her reservation wage at farm and home activities. The marginal effect of a year of female schooling on the probability of participation is greater than that of male schooling, suggesting that a year of schooling raises the difference between a woman's reservation and market wage relatively more than for males.

TABLE 2   *Probit analysis of the off-farm labour participation decisions*

Variable	Males		Females	
	Coefficients	T-value	Coefficients	T-value
INTERCEPT	−0.762	−3.08	−0.651	−2.24
AGE	0.086	2.95	0.097	3.65
AGE²/100	−0.120	−2.16	−0.144	−1.38
TTRADE	−0.112	−1.48	−0.198	−1.56
EDUCM	0.244	3.27	−0.096	−1.28
EDUCF	−0.182	−2.34	0.258	2.63
CHILD	−0.114	−1.22	−0.069	−1.35
INFRA	0.975	7.36	0.928	6.94
HHSIZE	0.359	2.38	0.131	1.08
AGWAGE	0.288	2.23	−0.218	−1.66
POPDEN	0.056	1.91	0.103	2.06
CREDIT	0.384	2.47	0.465	2.92
Sample size	199		199	
Log-likelihood ratio	76.61		87.35	

Note: Coefficients with *t*-statistics greater than 1.96 (absolute value) are statistically significant at the 5% level; an absolute value greater than 1.64 indicates significance at the 10% level.

Access to institutional credit also tends to increase the probability of participation. A higher farm wage increases the probability of participation by males. For females the effect is negative, although not significant. *INFRA* and *POPDEN* both have positive and significant impacts on the probability of off-farm work, indicating that a well developed infrastructural network influences the non-farm participation decisions of rural farm households. These variables may also reflect lower search costs for securing non-farm work for households located in more populated areas and better infrastructure, since these costs are not reflected elsewhere in the data. The coefficients for terms of trade for males and females have negative signs, but are not significantly different from zero, suggesting that relative prices between the farm and non-farm output products do not significantly influence participation decisions of households. The presence of children appears to have no significant effect on the participation decision of women in the study area, while adding a person to a household increases the probability of participation for males.

The results of the determinants of the extent of participation are presented in Table 3. The male and female non-farm wage rates used in the labour supply functions are estimated using the instrumental variable approach, based on a wage-predicting equation, including experience, education, infrastructure, farm size and population density as explanatory variables. The wage rate for self-employment is calculated as net non-farm income divided by the total time allocated to non-farm work in hours. The log-likelihood ratio test statistics for

TABLE 3   *Tobit model for non-farm labour supply of farm households, 1992*

Variable	Males		Females	
	Coefficients	T-statistics	Coefficients	T-statistics
INTERCEPT	4.085	5.17	4.897	3.18
ln PWAGEM	1.226	2.86	−0.591	−3.29
ln PWAGEF	0.673	1.32	1.698	2.08
AGE	0.019	3.96	0.016	2.67
AGE^2/100	−0.009	−1.88	−0.008	−2.55
EDUCM	0.563	5.21	0.462	2.11
EDUCF	0.298	1.45	0.708	2.66
TTRADE	−0.382	−1.49	−0.135	−1.22
CHILD	−0.269	−1.25	−0.187	−1.57
HHSIZE	0.354	1.98	0.442	1.17
INFRA	2.782	7.36	3.481	6.26
POPDEN	0.915	2.63	0.718	1.96
CREDIT	0.585	2.98	0.738	2.77
Log-likelihood ratio	89.48		112.97	

Note: Coefficients with *t*-statistics greater than 1.96 (absolute value) are statistically significant at the 5% level; an absolute value greater than 1.64 indicates significance at the 10% level.

the Tobit model for males and females are also significant at the 1 per cent level and imply that the independent variables taken together influence labour supply to non-farm work.

Both male and female own-wage effects are positive and significant, suggesting that higher wages lead to substitution effects that are greater than the opposing income effects, leading to increased labour supply to non-farm employment – an upward sloping labour supply, supportive of the utility maximization hypothesis.

The estimated cross-effect of male wages on female labour supply is negative and significant. The cross-effect of female wages on male labour supply is positive, but not significant, indicating that males do not reduce their labour supply when their wives earn more from non-farm activities. Individual characteristics also show significant effects on the supply functions. Both male and female labour supply appear to exhibit a concave pattern in age, with older individuals working more, but at a decreasing rate. The male own-education has significant impacts on supply of male and female labour. Females' own-education seems to have impacts only on female labour supply, but not on male supply functions. The presence of children appears to have no significant effect on the labour supply to non-farm work of males and females in the study area. The coefficient for the household size variable is positive and significantly different from zero. This indicates that extra effort gained as a result of increases in household size is directed to cash-oriented non-farm work instead of work on the farm.

The coefficients of the credit variables are positive and significant for both males and females, supporting the notion that farm households that have access to formal credit are more liable to invest in non-farm activities. They are also more likely to reinvest non-farm profits in non-farm ventures. The coefficients of terms of trade variables are negative, but not significant for either males or females.

As expected, locational characteristics such as state of infrastructure and population density increase the labour supply for both males and females. The positive coefficients for the two variables support the view that well developed infrastructure and high population densities are associated with a high level of non-farm work, and consequently high demand and supply for labour in these activities.

CONCLUSIONS AND POLICY IMPLICATIONS

This paper has investigated the impacts of household and locational characteristics on the participation decisions of rural farm households in cash-oriented non-farm pursuits in Northern Ghana, where the latter include both non-farm production for cash sale and wage labour outside the household. The theoretical expectations of the model are broadly confirmed by the data analysis.

Results suggest that several factors beyond household characteristics and farm income condition the household's participation in non-farm work. Access to credit, education, population density and the state of infrastructure are found to influence positively and significantly the probability of participation, as well as supply of labour to the non-farm sector.

These findings suggest that public actions and investments have impacts on the participation of rural farm households in non-farm pursuits. If rural farm households are to be helped to divert more of their labour time to non-farm income-generating activities to help maintain rural residence, there must be sources of gainful employment within commuting distance. It follows that the design of rural development policies, in addition to providing the necessary support to increase agricultural productivity, should also address the needs of rural non-farm pursuits. Providing training programmes to meet the needs of less educated rural households may have a high pay-off, while streamlining the acquisition of credit for poor rural households may reduce the financial constraint serving as a barrier to entry into non-farm business.

Further research in this area needs to investigate the differential determinants of non-farm earnings levels for men and women and to improve the handling of jointly determined participation decisions by men and women. The marginal impacts of improving infrastructure on education and net farm income on labour supply to the non-farm sector also need to be investigated.

REFERENCES

Adams, R. and He, J. (1994), *Sources of Income Inequality and Poverty in Rural Pakistan*, Research Report No. 102, Washington, DC: International Food Policy Research Institute.

Delgado, C.L., Hazell, P., Hopkins, J. and Kelly, V. (1994), 'Promoting Intersectoral Growth Linkages in Rural Africa Through Agricultural Technology and Policy Reform', *American Journal of Agricultural Economics*, **76**, 1166–71.

Eicher, C. and Baker, D. (1992), 'Agricultural Development in Sub-Saharan Africa: A Critical Survey', in Lee, R. Martin (ed.), *A Survey of Agricultural Economics Literature*, Vol. 4, *Agriculture in Economic Development, 1940s to 1990s*, Minneapolis: University of Minnesota Press.

Haggblade, S., Hazell, P. and Brown, J. (1989), 'Farm and Nonfarm Linkages in Rural Sub-Saharan Africa', *World Development*, **17**, 1173–1201.

Huffman, W.E. (1991), 'Agricultural Household Models: Survey and Critique', in M.C. Hallberg, J.L. Findeis and D.A. Lass (eds), *Multiple Job Holding Among Farm Families*, Ames: Iowa State University Press.

Janvry, A. de, Fafchamps, M. and Sadoulet, E. (1991), 'Peasant Household Behaviour with Missing Markets: Some Paradoxes Explained', *The Economic Journal*, **101**, 1400–1417.

Liedholm, C., McPherson, M. and Chuta, E. (1994), 'Small Enterprise Employment Growth in Rural Africa', *American Journal of Agricultural Economics*, **76**, 1177–82.

Maddala, G.S. (1983), *Limited Dependent and Qualitative Variables in Econometrics*, Cambridge: Cambridge University Press.

Reardon, T., Crawford, E. and Kelly, V. (1994), 'Links Between Non-farm Income and Farm Investment in African Households: Adding the Capital Market Perspective', *American Journal of Agricultural Economics*, **76**, 1172–6.

Reardon, T., Delgado, C.L. and Matlon, P. (1992), 'Determinants and Effects of Income Diversification Amongst Farm Households in Burkina Faso', *Journal of Development Studies*, **28**, 264–96.

von Braun, J. and Pandya-Lorch, R. (eds) (1991), *Income Sources of Malnourished People in Rural Areas: Micro-Level Information and Policy Implications*, Working Papers on Commercialization of Agriculture and Nutrition, No. 5, Washington, DC: International Food Policy Research Institute.

CHERYL R. DOSS*

Intra-household Resource Allocation in Ghana:
The Impact of the Distribution of Asset Ownership within the Household

Economists have recently begun to examine household economic behaviour with the explicit recognition that individual preferences and access to resources within households may affect the outcomes of economic decisions. This approach contrasts with economic models of household behaviour which treat a household as a single economic actor and it is able to offer many policy relevant insights into their decision making (Alderman *et al.*, 1995). In addition, recent literature has stressed the importance of the ownership of property within the household (Agarwal, 1994; Udry, 1996), suggesting that the distribution of property rights may affect production and consumption decisions and the relative well-being of household members. The research presented in this paper explores how the distribution of asset ownership among household members affects household expenditure patterns. Using detailed household survey data from Ghana, the intention is to demonstrate that the share of assets owned by women has a significant impact on household expenditure decisions.

GHANAIAN HOUSEHOLDS: EXPENDITURES AND ASSETS

The analysis uses data from the 1991–2 Ghana Living Standards Survey (GLSS3). The income, consumption and expenditure data are quite detailed and much of the income and asset ownership data can be disaggregated to the level of individual household members.

For the purposes of the GLSS3, a household was defined as a group of people who had usually slept in the same dwelling and had taken their meals together for at least nine of the 12 months prior to the survey. Household size range from one to 30, with a mean of 4.5. Over half of the households reported having both a head of household and spouse present. Households reporting a female head of household and no spouse present comprised 32 per cent of the surveyed households, while 6 per cent of households were polygynous.

GLSS3 contains detailed information on expenditure and income. Data on frequent expenditures, both food and non-food, were collected at two-day intervals for rural households over a period of 14 days and at three-day intervals for urban households over a 30-day period. Annual expenditures were obtained for goods infrequently purchased. Imputed values were calculated for

*Williams College, Williamstown, MA, USA.

housing, where appropriate, and for consumer durable goods. In addition to cash expenses, data on the value of food and other home-produced goods were collected.

Data on individual ownership or control of saving accounts, land and business assets are also included. Each individual was asked the current value of their savings held in both formal and informal accounts. The identity of the owner and the value of the land are provided for each plot of land. Finally, details were collected on the assets for up to three businesses controlled by the household.

THEORETICAL FRAMEWORK

This section provides the theoretical framework to examine the impact of the distribution of asset ownership on household expenditures and to test whether a model that disaggregates asset ownership collapses to a unified model of the household.

In a unified household model, the utility function for the household can be specified:

$$U = U(\mathbf{X}, \mathbf{M}; \mathbf{Z}) \tag{1}$$

where $\mathbf{X}$ is a vector of market goods, $\mathbf{M}$ is a vector of non-market goods and $\mathbf{Z}$ is a vector of demographic characteristics that would be expected to influence household preferences. The household faces a budget constraint

$$P_x\mathbf{X} + P_m\mathbf{M} = \sum_{i=1}^{I} w^i l^i + \sum_{i=1}^{I} t^i (L^i - l^i), \tag{2}$$

where P_x is a vector of prices corresponding to $\mathbf{X}$; P_m is a vector of shadow prices corresponding to $\mathbf{M}$; w^i is the wage level of individual I in the household; l^i is the amount of time spent in the labour force; t^i is the shadow wage rate for person I producing outside the labour market; and L^i is the total amount of labour time available to person I. Maximizing equation (1) subject to (2) gives the reduced form demand equation:

$$\mathbf{X} = g(P_x, P_m, \sum_{i=1}^{I} w^i l^i, (L^i - l^i), \mathbf{Z}) \tag{3}$$

This standard demand framework examines household demand for a commodity based on prices, household full income and preference-shifting demographic factors.

In a cooperative bargaining framework, each household member has a utility function

$$U^i = U^i(\mathbf{X}^i, \mathbf{M}^i; \mathbf{Z}). \tag{4}$$

Households solve the Nash bargaining problem:

$$\max N = \prod_{i=1}^{I} [U^i(\mathbf{X}, \mathbf{M}; \mathbf{Z}) - V_0^i(P_x, P_m, w^i, \alpha^i)]$$

$$s.t. \; P_x \mathbf{X} + P_m \mathbf{M} = \sum_{i=1}^{I} w^i l^i + \sum_{i=1}^{I} t^i (L^i - l^i).$$

(5)

V_0^i represents the threat point of individual I; this is the amount of utility that individual I would receive if she or he were not a part of the household. It is based on prices, wage income and α, which are other factors that would affect individual welfare if the individual was no longer a household member. The reduced form demand equation that results is:

$$\sum_{i=1}^{I} \mathbf{X}^i = g(P_x, P_m, w^i, t^i, L^i, \alpha^i, \mathbf{Z}) \quad i = 1 \dots I$$

(6)

This equation includes α^i which is a parameter affecting the threat point of individual I. Previous work has suggested that α^i could include non-labour income or transfer payments that individual I would receive even if the household dissolved (Schultz, 1990; Thomas, 1993). In this analysis, this parameter is represented by the percentage of assets within the household held by women.

By estimating the reduced form equation, we can test whether the coefficient on α is zero. If so, the reduced form of the bargaining model collapses to that of the unified household model. However, if the coefficient on α is not zero, we reject the unified model of the household and conclude that the distribution of assets among household members is a determinant of household economic outcomes.

DOES THE DISTRIBUTION OF ASSET OWNERSHIP MATTER?

The influence of the distribution of property ownership was examined by regressing the percentage of assets held by women on budget shares for 14 categories of expenditures, where shares are the percentage of total expenditures, including the value of goods received as in-kind payments. Using budget shares, rather than spending levels, controls for differing standards of living among households and captures the trade-offs among commodities that households must make.

A number of other factors are expected to affect household expenditure patterns. The variables included are monthly household income, total household assets, a vector indicating the age and gender composition of the household (number of individuals in 12 age/gender categories), education levels of the head of household and his or her spouse, and dummy variables indicating the month of the interview, location in one of three agroecological zones, urban or rural location, and whether or not the household owned any assets.

Since rural and urban households might be expected to make different economic decisions for any specified distribution of assets among household members, dummy variables for urban and rural location are interacted with the

percentage of women's assets. Thus the effects of the influence of the ownership share of women's assets are estimated separately for urban and rural
households.

EFFECTS OF WOMEN'S ASSETS ON FOOD EXPENDITURE

OLS estimates are first obtained using the budget share for food, including
both cash expenditures and the value of food produced and consumed by the
household, as the dependent variable. The full results of this estimation are
presented in Table 1.

The estimated coefficient on the percentage of assets held by women is
significantly different from zero for urban households. The mean expenditure
on food for urban households is 33 409 cedis and the budget share for food is
47.7 per cent. For urban households which own some assets, a 1 per cent
increase in the share of assets held by women increases the budget share spent
on food to 50.3 per cent. For rural households, food is 60 per cent of the
household budget, with an average monthly expenditure of 35 321 cedis.
However, the percentage of assets held by women in rural households did not
have a statistically significant impact on the budget share spent on food.

The other coefficients in this estimation are consistent with previous findings and hypotheses. Total monthly expenditure has a negative effect on the
budget share of food, which is consistent with Engel's Law. The level of assets
and the dummy variable indicating whether the household has any assets also
have a negative effect.

Although education is included since it may shift preferences, economic
theory does not give us any *a priori* expectations about the direction of the
change in expenditures for food relative to other goods. Women's education is
often associated with increased nutritional status of children; however, it is not
necessarily associated with an increased share of the budget spent on food,
holding total income or expenditure constant. Educated women may be able to
provide better nutrition for their children with the same level of expenditure.
All of the coefficients on the variables indicating education levels are negative,
suggesting that in Ghana an increase in education shifts preferences in favour
of spending on non-food items more than it shifts preference in favour of
additional spending on food.

Many of the dummy variables that indicate the month of the interview are
significant, capturing the seasonal price variations and any relative price changes
over time.

EFFECTS OF WOMEN'S ASSETS ON
OTHER HOUSEHOLD EXPENDITURES

The effect of women's ownership of assets on the budget share of other
household expenditures is also tested (Table 2). For urban households, ten of
the 14 categories of goods are significantly affected by women's asset holdings
(at the 10 per cent significance level or better). Food, education and utilities

TABLE 1   *OLS estimates of the determinants of budget share on food, Ghana, 1991–2*

Variable	Estimated coefficient	t-statistic
Intercept	0.5071***	27.10
% assets owned by women* (urban)	0.0361***	3.93
% assets owned by women* (rural)	0.0109	1.48
Household income ($\times 10^8$)	−2.046***	−3.53
Household assets ($\times 10^{10}$)	−7.68*	−1.87
Dummy if owned assignable assets	−0.018696***	−3.25
# of male infants (age 0–4)	0.0058	1.48
# of male children (age 5–9)	0.0091***	2.68
# of male youth (age 10–14)	0.0026	0.68
# of male adults (age 15–49)	−0.0127***	−4.58
# of male older adults (age 50–64)	−0.0014	−0.21
# of male elders (age 65+)	0.0128	1.46
# of female infants (age 0–4)	0.0109***	2.84
# of female children (age 5–9)	0.0001	0.03
# of female youth (age 10–14)	0.0022	0.54
# of female adults (age 15–49)	−0.0098***	−3.32
# of female older adults (age 50–64)	0.0227***	3.91
# of female elders (age 65+)	0.0280***	3.66
Dummy if male and female head present	0.0176***	2.89
Female head: 4 years' primary education	−0.0153***	−2.60
Female head: attended secondary school	−0.0605***	−5.89
Female head: completed 'O' level	−0.0783***	−3.75
Male head: 4 years' primary education	−0.0415***	−5.35
Male head: attended secondary school	−0.0417***	−5.17
Male head: completed 'O' level	−0.0780***	−7.59
Interview 9/91	0.0187	0.82
Interview 10.91	0.0393**	2.08
Interview 11/91	0.0445**	2.40
Interview 12/91	0.0547***	2.95
Interview 1/92	0.053***	2.88
Interview 2/92	0.038**	2.10
Interview 3/92	0.0638***	3.45
Interview 4/92	0.0607***	3.28
Interview 5/92	0.0474**	2.56
Interview 6/92	0.0289	1.56
Interview 7/92	0.0187	1.01
Interview 8/92	0.0185	0.98
Location: rural	0.0961***	15.68
Location: forest	−0.0321***	−6.05
Location: savannah	0.0263***	3.95

Note: *, ** and *** denote significance at the 0.10, 0.05 and 0.01 levels, respectively; $N = 4,516$, $R^2 = 0.288$, $F = 46.4$.

TABLE 2   *Selected results from OLS estimations of the effect of the percentage of assets or land owned by women on budget shares*

Budget share	Assets, urban women	Assets, rural women	Land, urban women	Land, rural women
Food	0.036***	0.011	0.057**	0.026**
	(3.93)	(1.479)	(2.32)	(2.489)
Alcohol	−0.008***	−0.011***	−0.012**	−0.0193***
	(−3.13)	(−0.011)	(−1.770)	(−6.468)
Clothing	0.002	0.0001	0.0003	0.0001
	(0.671)	(0.261)	(0.034)	(0.029)
Education	0.004**	0.003**	0.0005	0.007***
	(2.079)	(1.965)	(0.091)	(3.013)
Household items	0.001	−0.001	−0.003	−0.002
	(0.594)	(−1.005)	(−0.558)	(−1.311)
Housing	−0.005**	0.002	−0.006*	0.001
	(−3.577)	(1.492)	(−1.844)	(0.728)
Consumer durables†	−0.008***	−0.001	0.0008	0.0008
	(0.002)	(−0.870)	(0.152)	(0.374)
Medical	0.003	−0.001	0.012**	0.0007
	(1.228)	(0.002)	(1.837)	(0.256)
Miscell.	−0.007**	0.004	−0.019**	−0.0005
	(−2.116)	(1.462)	(−2.281)	(−0.134)
Recreation	−0.006**	−0.007***	−0.008	−0.008***
	(−2.836)	(−4.030)	(−1.342)	(−3.148)
Remittances	−0.004*	−0.004**	−0.003	−0.0003
	(−1.98)	(−2.342)	(−0.513)	(−0.113)
Tobacco	−0.006***	−0.006***	−0.006*	−0.008***
	(−4.416)	(−5.279)	(1.674)	(−4.927)
Transport	−0.004	0.005*	0.001	0.003
	(−1.382)	(1.893)	(0.166)	(0.637)
Utilities	0.011***	−0.003	−0.008	−0.007***
	(5.170)	(1.485)	(−1.424)	(−2.799)

Note: *, ** and *** denote significance at the 0.10, 0.05 and 0.01 levels respectively;
† indicates imputed values; $N = 4,516$; *t*-statistics are in parentheses.

are positively related to the percentage of assets held by urban women, while alcohol, tobacco, housing (actual and imputed expenses), the imputed value of goods received in kind and use value of consumer durable goods, miscellaneous items (including personal care, jewelry, taxes, ceremonies and gifts), recreation and entertainment, and remittances are all negatively related to the percentage of assets held by urban women.

For rural households, six of these 14 categories of goods are influenced by women's asset holdings. Education expenses are again positively related to women's asset holdings along with transport expenses. Alcohol, recreation, remittances and tobacco are negatively related to women's asset holdings.

When asked who paid for their education expenses, 61 per cent of the respondents who had attended school in the past year said their father, while only 17 per cent said their mother. Thus it is interesting that, for both urban and rural households, women's asset ownership increases expenditures on education. This may reflect the fact that women use their increased influence from owning assets to encourage men to increase education expenses, rather than that women pay for education out of their earnings.

In Ghana, recreation, alcohol and tobacco are considered items that men purchase and consume, and thus we might expect that, as women have more influence in household decision making, the proportion spent on these categories would decrease. The results are consistent with this expectation. Clothing purchases cannot be broken down by type for men and women, so it is not possible to test whether differential control of assets affects the composition of clothing expenditures among items for men, women and children. The results might be significant for these different categories. Medical expenses (including visits to clinics, hospital or traditional healers and over-the-counter treatments) are not significantly affected by the distribution of asset ownership. Medical expenses are primarily for curative care, and, thus, increases in health expenditure due to women's increased bargaining power may be offset by increased preventive care which lessens the need for curative care.

CONCLUSION: ASSETS AND WOMEN'S INFLUENCE IN HOUSEHOLD DECISIONS

The evidence suggests that the distribution of assets among men and women within Ghanaian households affects expenditure decisions. Therefore, to understand household expenditure patterns, it is important not to treat the household as a single economic actor, but to incorporate individual preferences and access to resources into models. Policies that affect individual ownership of assets, such as land titling programmes and small business development programmes, may have an impact on household expenditures regardless of their effect on household income. Conversely, programmes that are simply aimed at the household may have unintended consequences, depending on how they affect the relative levels of assets among household members and how they affect intra-household bargaining power.

The results presented in this paper are consistent with other disaggregated models of the household (see Doss, 1996, for a description of the models, or Schultz, 1990, and Thomas, 1993, for background). In a collective framework (Chiappori, 1992) the results suggest that women's ownership of assets is one of the factors that affects the household's sharing rule. In a cooperative bargaining framework, such as the one presented in this paper (see also Lundberg and Pollak, 1993; McElroy, 1990), we would conclude from these results that ownership of assets increases women's 'threat point', or the amount of utility that they would receive if they no longer participated in sharing resources within the household. In a non-cooperative bargaining model (Woolley, 1993), women's ownership of assets would influence their ability to bargain for transfers of resources, including labour transfers, and the provision of household 'public' or shared goods by other household members.

REFERENCES

Agarwal, Bina (1994), *A Field of One's Own: Gender and Land Rights in South Asia*, New York: Cambridge University Press.

Alderman, H., Chiappori, P-A., Haddad, L., Hoddinott, J. and Kanbur, R. (1995), 'Unitary vs. collective models of the household: Is it time to shift the burden of proof?', *World Bank Research Observer*, **10**, 1–19.

Chiappori, P-A. (1992), 'Collective labour supply and welfare', *Journal of Political Economy*, **100**, 437–67.

Doss, Cheryl R. (1996), 'Testing among models of intrahousehold resource allocation', *World Development*, **24**, 1597–1609.

Lundberg, S.J. and Pollak, R.A. (1993), 'Separate spheres bargaining and the marriage market', *Journal of Political Economy*, **101**, 988–1010.

McElroy, Marjorie (1990), 'The empirical content of Nash-bargained household behavior', *Journal of Human Resources*, **25**, 559–83.

Schultz, T. Paul (1990), 'Testing the neoclassical model of family labour supply and fertility', *Journal of Human Resources*, **25**, 599–634.

Thomas, Duncan (1993), 'The distribution of income and expenditure within the household', *Annales d'Economie et de Statistique*, **29**, 109–36.

Udry, Christopher (1996), 'Gender, agricultural production and the theory of the household', *Journal of Political Economy*, **104**, 1010–6.

Woolley, Frances (1993), 'A Cournot–Nash model of family decision making', mimeo, Carleton University, Department of Economics, Ottawa.

D. BOUGHTON, T. REARDON AND J. WOOLDRIDGE*

*Determinants of Diversification of Urban Sahel Diets into Maize:
A Contingent Valuation Study of Processed Maize Demand in Mali*

INTRODUCTION

The shift in urban diets from the traditional coarse grain (millet and sorghum) to (mainly) imported rice has worried policy makers in Sahelian West Africa for two decades. This trend has hurt trade balances, as cities have grown rapidly, and has sapped potential gains of a growing urban food market to coarse grain farmers (Delgado and Reardon, 1987). Moreover, there has been limited substitutability between coarse grains and rice in urban consumption (Rogers and Lowdermilk, 1991), probably because rice is easier and less time-consuming to process, prepare and cook than the traditional coarse grains (millet and sorghum) and with maize, a relative newcomer to Sahel urban diets (Bricas and Sauvinet, 1989). Even the large devaluation of the CFA (Communauté financière d'Afrique) franc in 1994 did not lead to any substantial reversal of rice consumption in the Sahel (Reardon *et al.*, 1996). Stagnating millet and sorghum yields have also exacerbated the situation over the past three decades, reducing optimism concerning their price competitiveness.

By contrast, policy makers have recently been turning a hopeful eye towards maize as a promising candidate to win back urban diets to domestically produced coarse grains. Unlike millet and sorghum, increases in the output of which have come almost entirely through increases in area cultivated, maize has the potential for rapid yield growth through intensification with improved varieties, manure and chemical fertilizer. This will give maize an advantage as arable land constraints grow rapidly in the Sahel and fragile extensive margins degrade. There is already evidence of maize intensification and incipient commercialization in several Sahel countries, especially in cotton production areas where farm cash incomes and fertilizer availability contribute to the success of maize (Dione, 1989; Sanders *et al.*, 1996).

Nevertheless, there are important and unresolved questions about the potential of maize on the demand side. Without an expanding urban market, Sahelian maize producers will hesitate to expand production because of price risk in thin markets (Témé and Boughton, 1992). A particularly important question concerning potential urban demand for maize addresses the demand for *processed* maize, which may then compete with rice as a convenience food. The

*D. Boughton, ICRISAT/Malawi; T. Reardon and J. Wooldridge, Michigan State University, USA.

current 'conventional policy wisdom' is that, if maize were much more widely available in the market as flour of various grades of fineness of grind, thus appealing to different strata of consumers, demand would increase substantially. Maize consumption at present is nearly all in grain form, and represents less than 10 per cent of urban Malian cereal consumption (Rogers and Lowdermilk, 1991; Témé and Boughton, 1992).

This paper uses contingent valuation data from a survey undertaken in Bamako, Mali, in 1993, to examine the question of the potential (purchased) demand for various grades of processed maize, at various prices, and for different income groups. Moreover, a gender component is added to the analysis because, if these new products became available on the market, they would probably be perceived very differently by women who normally do the cooking and will, therefore, be most concerned with the allocations of time which most affect their time and utility.

The key issue will be addressed by analysing contingent valuation quantity responses as they vary by proposed prices, hence generating a demand curve. Here there are two points to note. First, contingent valuation has rarely been used in food policy analysis in developing countries. Recent exceptions in Africa have been in Zimbabwe and Kenya, where maize is the main staple and, hence, provides a very different context than the Sahel (for example, see Rubey, 1993; Jayne and Rubey, 1993). Second, it is rare for contingent valuation studies to generate a demand curve empirically; the only exception appears to be in the valuation of new water systems in India (Griffin *et al.*, 1995). This rarity is probably due to the bulk of applications of contingent valuation having dealt with public goods (such as a new irrigation project), where price differences and product differentiation are not major issues, as they are for maize products in urban Mali.

MODEL, ESTIMATION PROCEDURE AND DATA

The model seeks to explain the demand for maize flour (the monthly quantity of maize flour a household would purchase, in kilograms per adult equivalent), as a function of the following independent variables (with the expected signs of their coefficients):

(1) (hypothetical) maize flour price (–);
(2) household income (+);
(3) flour quality (+);
(4) gender-related variables:
     (a) respondent's gender (+ for females),
     (b) gender of household head (+ for females),
     (c) proxies for women's opportunity cost of time:
         (c.1) proportion of women in the household (–); (c.2) proportion of children in the household (–); (c.3) proportion of women working outside home (+); (c.4) household has a maid (–);
(5) demographic and qualitative variables:
     (a) household size (–),

    (b)   region of origin (+ for maize-growing area),
    (c)   currrent (actual) maize consumption (+),
    (d)   whether the household head works in the civil service or the military[1] (–),
    (e)   food preparer's evaluation of the quality of dishes prepared from flour samples (+).

As the contingent valuation dependent variable has a number of zero observations, but is essentially continuous over positive values, OLS estimators will be biased. Hence we use maximum likelihood estimation of a standard censored Tobit model which, subject to the assumption of constant variance of the error term, is well suited to the problem at hand (Amemiya, 1984).[2]

Information was obtained through consumer tests of refined maize flours (made from dehulled grain) and whole-grain maize flours (made from whole grain). The respondents (household heads and food preparers) belonged to a sub-sample of 115 Bamako households drawn from a current year-long (1993) study of cereal consumption (using a sample of 640 households) (Témé and Boughton, 1992). Using the sample flour, respondents prepared and tasted the principal coarse grain-based dishes ('bouillie', a thin porridge usually consumed at breakfast, and 'toh', a thick porridge for the evening meal). They also observed the 'keeping quality' of the dish. Respondents were then asked at how many meals during a week they would use the maize flour product. Responses were recorded first for the superior dehulled flour at flour prices (starting with the highest price) and then for the whole-grain flour over the same price range. The highest price corresponded to the current market price of import-quality rice, the lowest to the current market price of unprocessed maize.

REGRESSION RESULTS

Table 1 presents the Tobit regression results based on the contingent-valuation survey data.[3] In general, we find that the gender-related determinants of demand for flour are important, especially in interaction with other household characteristics (such as regional origin and income), and lower transaction costs of cereal acquisition (proxied by being in the military) increase demand for flour. Statistically significant results are discussed below.

As expected, an (hypothetical) increase in the maize flour price decreases the quantity demanded. Although the effect of income is not statistically significant, the effect of 'income squared' is, and is negative, as expected. The income effect is also expressed in interaction terms. The coefficient on 'income-by-flour-quality' is positive, indicating that there is a positive demand response to income for dehulled (superior-quality) flour.

The effect on maize flour demand of the household being headed by a woman is positive (note that only 25 per cent of the sample households are headed by women), and the effect of household size is negative, as expected. But the coefficient on the sole effect of the respondent being a woman is negative (recall that women respondents were surveyed in all households, not

TABLE 1   *Maize flour demand, Tobit regression results*

	Coefficient	T-ratio	Prblt|≥x
Constant	21.262	11.086	0
Price	−0.15111	−13.993	0
Gender	−6.8085	−3.993	0.00007
Flour quality	0.01277	0.011	0.99151
Gender–price	0.050095	3.942	0.00008
Gender–quality	1.6117	1.093	0.2746
Income–quality	0.2174	2.727	0.00639
Gender–income	0.28819	3.782	0.00016
Gender–income–quality	−0.213	−2.285	0.02231
Income per adult equivalent	−0.029061	−0.342	0.73272
Income per adult equivalent squared	−0.0035288	−3.005	0.00265
Household size	−0.20876	−2.272	0.02311
Household size squared	0.0029427	1.394	0.16332
Woman ratio	−8.7645	−4.503	0.00001
Child ratio	−0.7609	−0.528	0.59769
Women w/primary job	1.4419	3.857	0.00011
Women w/secondary job	−1.4445	−3.865	0.00011
Maize consumption	−0.097399	−5.796	0
Region of origin	−0.0021541	−1.723	0.08487
Gender–region	1.8279	2.541	0.01106
Gender–region–quality	0.28495	0.292	0.77022
Civil servant	−0.67493	−1.209	0.22684
Military	5.6055	1.113	0.26558
Military–quality	−2.0103	−0.963	0.33576
Military–income	1.218	2.125	0.03356
Military–income squared	−0.053206	−3.095	0.00197
Military–gender	−23.313	−6.147	0
Military–gender–income	0.60132	2.431	0.01507
Military–gender–quality	6.7565	1.798	0.07211
Military–gender–income–quality	−0.1158	−0.495	0.6207
Military–price	0.039659	2.355	0.01853
Household head = woman	2.0717	1.755	0.07927
Maid	0.00047612	0.188	0.85119
Toh quality	0.0038731	2.749	0.00598
Bouillie quality	0.00066136	−0.696	0.48653

just women-headed households), controlling for other important interaction effects of respondent gender–employment and gender–income. These interaction effects are interesting. The respondent gender–income interaction has a positive effect, which makes sense in that one expects women's opportunity cost of time to influence choice of convenience foods. Yet the interaction term gender–income–flour quality is negative. The two effects together imply that women have a higher maize flour demand response to income than do men for (less costly) whole-grain flour, but this response is not significantly affected by flour quality. The gender–price interaction term has a positive effect on flour demand, indicating that women's demand is less price-responsive than is that of men. Finally, the effect of the household being from a maize-growing area is negative, though numerically very small; yet women from those areas have stronger demand for maize flour than do men.

The proportion of women in the household has a strongly negative effect on maize flour demand, as expected (as household labour supply for grain processing and cooking is higher). The proportion of women with primary cash-earning activities has a strong positive effect on demand for maize flour, but the proportion of women with secondary cash-earning activities has a negative effect. A possible explanation for these apparently conflicting results is that coarse-grain processing tasks do not compete for time with secondary activities (such as petty commerce operated from the home) but do in the case of primary activities (such as marketing activities away from home).

The characteristics of household maize flour demand where the household head is in the military give rise to a substantially different demand pattern. They are interesting because the army's cereal credit provision provides a 'living experiment' of the effect of decreasing transaction costs for cereal acquisition, and the demands of the military profession put a premium on access to convenience foods. The interaction terms military–income, military–gender–income and military–gender–flour quality are all positive. The military–price interaction term's effect is positive. These results imply that flour demand by military households is more income-responsive and less price-responsive than that by civilians. Possible explanations for this are that the army provides interest-free credit for the purchase of cereals, and male household heads are often absent for long periods on military duties. In contrast to military households, the coefficient for households where the head is employed in the civil service is not significantly different from zero.

Moreover, the effect is positive, but small, for the perceived quality of 'toh' prepared from the flour. The coefficient on the quality of porridge prepared from flour is not significant, which suggests that most of the total variation in flour quality relevant to consumer demand has been captured by the flour quality and flour quality interaction terms. It does not imply that flour quality is unimportant.

PREDICTED DEMAND FOR MAIZE
FLOURS AND FOOD POLICY IMPLICATIONS

Predicted demand is first calculated for six sub-groups, then aggregated on the basis of the weight of each sub-group in the population of Bamako. The sub-groups are military and civilian, each comprising three income terciles.[4] For each of the six sub-groups, the quantity demanded is based on the responses of male respondents (that is, all gender interaction terms are restricted to zero) at the sub-group mean value of each independent variable. Evaluation of expected demand for male respondents reflects the prevailing household characteristic that its head is responsible for cereal purchases.

The contingent valuation data were collected prior to the 50 per cent devaluation of the CFA franc in January 1994. To estimate post-devaluation demand, we assume a 40 per cent decline in real income for civilian sub-groups, based on average price increases in the first quarter following devaluation, and a 33 per cent decline for the military (civil servants received a 10 per cent pay increase to compensate for the rise in cost of living). Average maize consumption by the sub-sample households over the one-year survey (excluding flour provided for the tests) was approximately 8kg. per adult equivalent, compared to 22kg. for millet, 55kg. for sorghum and 107kg. for rice. Aggregated for the population of Bamako, maize consumption amounts to approximately 4800 tons per year, or 400 tons per month. Before devaluation, assuming prices of 150 CFA F/kg. for dehulled and 115 CFA F/kg. for whole-grain flour, projected demand would be approximately 380 tons per month for dehulled and 815 tons per month for whole-grain flour. After devaluation, assuming a price of 175 CFA F/kg. for dehulled and 130 CFA F/kg. for whole-grain flour, projected demand falls sharply, to 70 tons per month for dehulled and 490 tons per month for whole-grain flour. Even for the cheaper whole-grain flour, this is only slightly higher than current levels of maize grain consumption. This result is consistent with Dibley et al. (1995), which shows that the cost of preparing coarse grain-based dishes with pre-processed flour in Bamako would actually be 13 per cent higher than home-processed grain at prevailing opportunity costs of women's time.

Before devaluation, own-price elasticities of demand at estimated retail flour prices, for civilian households and averaged across income terciles, are −7.4 for dehulled maize flour, and −4.8 for whole grain flour. Such high elasticities reflect the small quantities households would purchase at estimated retail prices. After devaluation, own-price elasticities increase to −11.5 and −6.14 for dehulled and whole grain flour, respectively, reflecting the still smaller quantities purchased at higher retail prices.

In sharp contrast to price elasticities, income elasticities of demand for maize flour are low. Prior to devaluation, income elasticities of demand were 0.8 for dehulled maize flour and −0.1 for whole-grain flour (and thus an inferior good for predominantly male household heads). Although we cannot calculate cross-price elasticities (to evaluate whether processed maize products can improve substitutability with rice), analysis of the meals at which maize flour would be used provides a preliminary indication. As the price of maize flour decreases, increased consumption occurs primarily at meals where coarse grains are already predominant (namely breakfast and dinner) and there is little increase in consumption of maize flour at lunch, where rice is more important.

CONCLUSIONS

The results point to the importance of the convenience characteristics of maize flour, especially to working women. The demand for this convenient flour rises as a function both of ability to afford it and of the opportunity cost of time (both of which rise with household income). Yet, as many urban households are poor, the overall effect on aggregate demand for the grain of the availability of new maize flour products is still relatively modest. This is consistent with budget analysis of the costs of preparing coarse grain-based dishes that show purchased flour to be uncompetitive with household processing owing to low average opportunity costs of women's time in Bamako.

NOTES

[1]The military and the civil service often provide interest-free credit for the purchase of cereals (sacks of cereal in the form of grain), either directly to the employee or through employee cooperatives.

[2]One possible concern with use of the Tobit is violation of the assumption of constant variance (heteroskedasticity), which would theoretically result in biased parameter estimates. A reason for suspecting that the violation might occur is that, when respondents are asked about behaviour in hypothetical situations, the further the situation is removed from their experience the harder it is for them to predict their own behaviour, leading to higher variance in the error term. The problem goes beyond one of biased parameter estimates, however. Heteroskedasticity in the latent model would imply different formulae for the calculation of partial effects and expected demands. These formulae would depend on the specific functional form of the heteroskedasticity. The cost of identifying its specific form, and deriving the partial effects and expected demands for the heteroskedasticity-robust case, would be high. Yet, since both the estimated coefficients and the formulae for deriving partial effects and expected demands change, the results obtained may not differ greatly from those generated by a model that ignored the violation. The question of the magnitude of error in predictions of the actual rather than latent dependent variable is one that requires further research.

[3]Given the non-linear estimation procedure, estimated coefficients cannot be interpreted directly as partial effects.

[4]We divide the sample into military and civilian to correct for the overrepresentation of military personnel in the sub-sample compared to the population.

REFERENCES

Amemiya, T. (1984), 'Tobit Models: A Survey', *Journal of Econometrics*, **24**, 3–61.

Bricas, N. and Sauvinet, R. (1989), 'The Trend Towards Diversification in Sahelian Food Habits', paper presented at seminar on Regional Cereals Markets in West Africa, Lome, CILSS/Club du Sahel.

Delgado, C. and Reardon, T. (1987), 'Policy issues raised by changing food patterns in the Sahel', in CILSS/Club du Sahel (ed.), *Cereals Policies in Sahel Countries: Acts of the Mindelo Conference*, Paris: CILSS/Club du Sahel/OECD.

Dibley, D., Boughton, D. and Reardon, T. (1995), 'Processing and preparation costs for rice and coarse grains in urban Mali: subjecting conventional wisdom to empirical scrutiny', *Food Policy*, **20**, 41–50.

Dione, J. (1989), 'Informing food security policy in Mali: interactions between technology, institutions and market reforms', PhD dissertation, East Lansing, Michigan State University.

Griffin, C.C., Briscoe, J., Singh, B., Ramasubban, R. and Bhatia, R. (1995), 'Contingent Valuation and Actual Behavior: Predicting Connections to New Water Systems in the State of Kerala, India', *The World Bank Economic Review*, **9**, 373–96.

Jayne, T.S. and Rubey, L. (1993), 'Maize Milling, Market Reform and Urban Food Security: The Case of Zimbabwe', *World Development*, **21**, 975–88.

Reardon, T., Dione, J., Adesina, A. and Tefft, J. (1996), 'Rice in West Africa before and after Franc CFA devaluation: focus on CILSS countries', paper presented at WARDA Conference, 25–9 March 1995, Ndiaye, Senegal.

Rogers, B.L. and Lowdermilk, M. (1991), 'Price policy and food consumption in urban Mali', *Food Policy*, **16**, 461–73.

Rubey, L. (1993), *Consumer Maize Meal Preferences in Zimbabwe: Survey Results and Policy Implications*, Report prepared for Ministry of Lands, Agriculture and Water Development and USAID/Harare.

Sanders, J., Shapiro, B. and Ramaswamy, S. (1996), *The Economics of Agricultural Technology in Semi-arid Sub-Saharan Africa*, Baltimore: Johns Hopkins University Press.

Témé, B. and Boughton, D. (1992), *Déroulement de l'Enquête sur les Caractéristiques et les Habitudes de Consommation des Unités Alimentaires du District de Bamako et Organisation du Suivi et des Tests de Produits à Base de Maïs*, Etude sur la Filière Maïs: Note d'Information No. 1, Bamako, Mali: IER/DPAER.

A. GRACIA, J.M. GIL AND A.M. ANGULO*

Will European Diets be Similar? A Cointegration Approach

INTRODUCTION

The European Union (EU) is experiencing an integration process, which has accelerated in the current decade. Any integration process has several effects on the countries involved, including trade liberalization, internationalization of industries, distribution channels and markets, harmonization of economic parameters and similar harmonization of public policies. These effects are responsible for the economic convergence that is taking place, which can be seen in various indicators (GDP, productivity, unemployment and so on) and which is also affecting habits, behaviour and attitudes. As regards food consumption, Blandford (1984) for OECD countries, and Wheelock and Frank (1989), for nine developed countries, suggested that convergence is taking place in dietary patterns. Grigg (1993) related the phenomenon to economic development and to concerns about health. Herrmann and Röeder (1995) and Gil *et al.* (1995) used different methodologies to measure food consumption convergence, though they reached similar conclusions. This work looks at food diet convergence in more depth for EU countries, plus Norway.

The first step is to define what convergence means. In general terms, it can be said to be the tendency towards the equalization of relevant variables among individuals in the various countries and regions. In the case of food consumption, however, it is important not to be too general but to adopt a rather more specific definition. Gil *et al.* (1995) used the proportions of different food products within the total, expecting to find that shares tend to equalize across European countries. In the present work, we are interested in analysing whether food consumer behaviour is similar across Europe; that is, whether the allocation of total calories in the different food products (the diversification of diets) is responding in a similar way in response to changes in total calorie intake. Therefore a measure of the total calorie response (total calorie elasticities) is needed in this kind of convergence analysis.

The paper is therefore organized as follows. First, we study the two steps in the food consumer decision process: (1) the relation between food consumption and income, which gives the maximum potential consumption level and the income elasticities, (2) the relation between consumption of specific food products and total calorie intake, which gives the total calorie intake elasticities.

*Unidad de Economia Agraria, Servicio de Investigación Agraria, Saragossa (Gracia and Gil); Facultad de Ciencias Económicas y Empresariales, Universidad de Zaragoza (Angulo), Spain.

Finally, a cointegration approach is used to measure the long-run convergence relationship among total calorie intake elasticities of different products across the European Union.

THE EVOLUTION OF FOOD CONSUMPTION ACROSS EU COUNTRIES

Total food consumption and income

Table 1 shows the evolution of total food consumption (daily per capita calories intake) and the real income (per capita GDP) in the EU countries and Norway from 1972 to 1992. The daily average per capita food consumption in EU countries was 3180 kilocalories in 1972, and this increased at an average annual rate of 0.5 per cent to 3475 in 1992. In the same period, average per capita GDP increased at an average rate of 2.1 per cent. Behaviour has been different across countries, depending on the initial GDP level. Food consumption in most countries has shown an upward trend, the exception being Finland, where it has declined slightly. Countries with the lowest per capita GDP and food consumption in 1972 (Spain, Greece and Portugal) have shown the largest increase. From 1982 to 1992, however, calorie intakes of animal products stabilized, or even declined, in most of the countries.

It can be seen that total calorie consumption and the relative animal calorie intake have reached a ceiling, while income is still increasing. To measure the response of total food consumption to income, as well as to calculate the maximum food consumption level, a functional form that relates total calories and per capita GDP is specified. The selected functional form has to hold two requirements: income elasticities must be decreasing (Engel's Law) and it must have an upper asymptote (maximum consumption level). The reciprocal functional form satisfies both requirements:

$$TCAL_t = \alpha + \beta \frac{1}{y_t} + U_t \quad t = 1965,......,1992 \tag{1}$$

In equation (1) *TCAL* is the total calorie intake (Kcal/per capita/day); y_t is the per capita GDP at constant 1985 prices; U_t is an error term; α is an upper asymptote (maximum potential consumption level); and β is the income parameter to calculate the elasticities. Annual material from 1965 to 1992 has been used. Total calorie intake data comes from the *Food Balance Sheets* gathered by the FAO, while GDP is taken from *Financial Statistics*, published by the IMF (International Monetary Fund). Model (1) was estimated by generalized least squares (GLS).

Table 2 presents the maximum potential food consumption levels and the food consumptions in 1992. Also it shows income elasticities at 1972, 1982, 1992 and mean values. Some significant positive relationship between total food consumption, in calorie terms, and income has been found in all countries, except for Finland. Owing to the chosen functional form, income

TABLE 1 *Evolution of average calorie intake and per capita GDP in European Union countries and Norway (Kcal/per capita/day and thousand dollars)*

	1972			1982			1992		
	Total calories	Animal calories (%)	Per capita GDP	Total calories	Animal calories (%)	Per capita GDP	Total calories	Animal calories (%)	Per capita GDP
Austria	3 253	34.8	6 363	3 410	36.8	8 128	3 497	35.6	10 023
Belg.-Lux.	3 198	36.7	6 503	3 467	36.8	7 994	3 680	35.3	9 991
Denmark	3 272	40.1	8 826	3 427	41.9	10 158	3 663	43.5	12 137
Finland	3 178	41.9	7 576	3 110	44.1	10 260	3 018	39.6	11 354
France	3 310	37.9	7 418	3 498	38.7	9 238	3 633	40.0	10 784
Germany	3 201	34.9	7 876	3 386	35.3	9 516	3 344	34.7	9 674
Greece	3 206	21.1	2 421	3 533	24.6	3 000	3 815	25.2	3 364
Ireland	3 438	37.8	3 915	3 639	37.0	5 076	3 847	33.4	7 041
Italy	3 462	19.6	5 194	3 395	24.9	7 045	3 560	25.4	8 865
Netherlands	3 063	33.3	7 288	3 059	38.2	8 184	3 222	31.7	9 815
Portugal	3 025	17.4	1 580	2 954	27.5	2 062	3 633	26.0	2 710
Spain	2 905	24.0	3 535	3 304	30.1	4 119	3 707	31.9	5 452
Sweden	2 891	34.0	9 632	3 005	39.0	11 051	2 971	37.6	12 365
Great Britain	3 204	41.2	6 510	3 159	40.0	7 470	3 317	32.4	9 001
Norway	3 099	39.8	11 691	3 134	40.0	12 139	3 219	33.4	15 594

Sources: FAO (1995) and IMF, *Financial Statistics* (several issues).

TABLE 2   *Maximum potential food consumption level and total food calories in 1992, estimated income elasticies at 1972, 1982, 1992 and mean values*

	α	tc1992[a]	1972	1982	1992	Mean

	α	tc1992[a]	E_{TCALY} 1972	1982	1992	Mean
Germany	2 877	2 551	0.13	0.11	0.11	0.12
France	3 127	2 978	0.13	0.10	0.08	0.12
Italy	3 341	3 075	0.19	0.13	0.10	0.16
Denmark	3 417	2 878	0.33	0.27	0.22	0.30
Spain	4 105	3 145	0.65	0.51	0.34	0.6
Portugal	3 232	2 996	0.031	0.023	0.017	0.027
Greece	3 705	3 294	0.25	0.19	0.17	0.24
Netherlands	2 384	2 374	0.007	0.006	0.005	0.006
Belg.–Lux.	3 696	2 991	0.48	0.36	0.27	0.44
Great Britain	3 075	2 621	0.28	0.24	0.19	0.25
Ireland	3 414	3 038	0.25	0.18	0.13	0.22
Austria	3 033	2 770	0.18	0.13	0.11	0.16
Sweden	2 710	2 380	0.18	0.15	0.13	0.16
Finland[b]	—	—	—	—	—	—
Norway	3 117	2 662	0.21	0.20	0.15	0.19

Notes: [a]Total food calorie intake in 1992.
[b]No significant relationship between total food calorie intake and per capita GDP.

elasticities decrease over time but at a higher rate in the first period (from 1972 to 1982). Differences between food consumption in 1992 and the maximum estimated consumption level are low, therefore a saturation level has been attained. The largest differences have been found in Spain, Belgium and Luxembourg, Denmark, Greece and Norway.

The diversification of food consumption

The allocation of food calorie intake to specific products has been changing during the period of study. However, some differences between Mediterranean and northern countries are still important. Mediterranean countries have a higher consumption of cereals and of fruit and vegetables than the other countries. On the other hand, the consumption of milk and dairy products is lower. Differences in meat consumption are not very large, though there is remarkably high consumption in Spain and Denmark.

Because of these similarities, countries are classified in homogeneous groups according to the food consumption dietary structure. A cluster analysis, where variables are the proportion of specific food products consumption in total calorie intake, is used. From the analysis, five homogeneous groups are found: (1) Denmark, France and Great Britain; (2) Finland, Norway and Ireland; (3) Sweden, Netherlands, Belgium-Luxembourg, Austria and Germany; (4) Portugal, Greece and Italy; and (5) Spain. We used the following food products: (1) cereals, (2) meat, (3) fish, (4) milk, dairy products and cheese, (5) fruits and vegetables and (6) fats and oils. The analysis of the allocation of total food calorie intake to different food products has been conducted for the five clusters using the AIDS model. Demand functions, in budget calorie terms, have the following form:

$$w_{it} = \alpha_i + \beta_i lnTCAL_t + \varepsilon_i^t \qquad (2)$$

where w_{it} is the calorie share of the ith good ($i=1,2...,n$) in period t ($t =1...T$); $TCAL_t$ is the total calories in period t ($t = 1...T$); and ε_t is the error term. The adding-up restriction implies that $\sum_i \alpha_i = 1$ and $\sum_i \beta_i = 0$.

Economic studies of food demand often show that consumers do not adjust instantaneously to changes in prices, income or other determinants of demand (the static approach); adjustment takes place gradually. Such dynamic behaviour has been incorporated in the AIDS model (2), using Anderson and Blundell's (1983) approach. This general dynamic specification assumes that changes in endogenous variables are responses to anticipated and unanticipated changes in exogenous variables. The general model, assuming a first-order autoregressive distributed lag, can be expressed in an error-correction form (error correction model, ECM):

$$\Delta w_{it} = \varphi_i \Delta lnTCAL_t - \sum_{j=1}^{n-1} \lambda_{ij}[w_{j,t-1} - a_j - \theta_j lnTCAL_{t-1}] + \varepsilon_t \qquad (3)$$

where φ_i are short-run total calorie effects, λ_{ij} are adjustment coefficients to the long-run equilibrium and θ_j are long-run total calorie effects.

Model (3) nests other dynamic specifications, such as first-order autoregressive (AR), partial adjustment (PA) and the static models, by imposing some parameter restrictions. If $\varphi_i = \theta_i$ is imposed on equation (3), we get the autoregressive model; if the restriction $\varphi_i = \sum \lambda_{ij}\theta_j$ is imposed, we get the partial adjustment model; and, finally, if $\lambda_{ij} = 1$ (if $i = j$), $\lambda_{ij} = 0$ (if $i \neq j$) and $\varphi_i = \theta_i$ are imposed, the result is the static model.

The different dynamic specifications are estimated for the five clusters using full information maximum likelihood (FIML) and some tests are carried out to determine which specification fits the data better. Because all alternatives are nested in equation (3), a likelihood ratio test has been used. In all clusters, the first-order autoregressive specification has not been rejected at the 1 per cent level of significance, which means that relative specific food products depend not only on present total calories but also on the previous total calorie intake (results are not included owing to space limitations). Finally, total calorie elasticities are calculated using the estimated parameters (Table 3).

All total calorie elasticities except fish are positive and significantly different from zero. The negative elasticities for fish are not significant. Positive values mean that, as total food calories increase, consumed calories from

TABLE 3   *Total calorie elasticities for different food products at mean values[a]*

	Cereals	Meat	Fish	Dairy	Fruits	Fats
Denmark	0.73**	0.77**	−0.43	1.83**	1.14**	1.11**
France	0.76**	0.75*	−1.5	1.70**	1.12**	1.14**
Great Britain	0.75**	0.72*	−1.95	1.70**	1.11**	1.12**
Finland	0.06	0.47**	0.11	3.13**	0.47**	1.09**
Ireland	0.15	0.32*	−1.08	3.25**	0.54**	1.08**
Norway	0.06	0.28	0.55	3.54**	0.53**	1.07**
Sweden	0.74**	0.05	1.67**	0.63*	3.04**	0.88**
Austria	0.76**	0.26	4.18**	0.49*	2.98**	0.89**
Netherlands	0.73**	0.17	3.15**	0.59*	2.74**	0.89**
Belg.–Lux.	0.75**	0.11	2.61**	0.40*	2.77**	0.91**
Germany	0.76**	0.30	2.14**	0.40*	2.73**	0.88**
Italy	1.12**	0.77*	−0.32	0.67**	1.12**	1.01**
Greece	1.13**	0.79*	−0.26	0.71**	1.09**	1.01**
Portugal	1.12**	0.79*	0.52	0.51*	1.09**	1.01**
Spain	0.71**	2.47**	1.78**	−0.93**	0.47*	1.66**

Note: [a]Two stars indicate that elasticity is significant at 1%; one star that it is significant at 5%.

different products also increase, more or less than proportionally depending on whether elasticities are greater or less than unity. In all countries, except for Italy, Greece and Portugal, cereals are losing relative importance in total food calorie consumption. Meat consumption is also losing weight in total consumption in all countries except for Spain. On the other hand, fruit and vegetables are increasing their relative importance, except for Finland, Ireland, Norway and Spain. It seems that consumers tend to replace products with high calorie contents (cereals, meat) with those with low calorie content (fruits and vegetables).

CONVERGENCE AND COINTEGRATION

The aim of this section is to ask whether food consumption behaviour is becoming standardized; or, in other words, to see if a convergence process is taking place as far as the reactions to changes in total calorie intake (elasticities) are concerned. There are different methods to measure convergence from which, in this paper, stochastic definitions for both convergence and fluctuations in long-term elasticities are used. These definitions are based on the recent developments in unit root tests and cointegration. Following Bernard and Durlauf (1995), it is possible to define convergence in elasticities as follows: if e_{ij} denotes total calorie elasticity for product i in country j and e_{iej} the average total calorie elasticity for all countries except for the cluster to which country j

belongs and for product i, then country j and the rest of the countries converge if the long-term forecast of elasticities for both groups become equal at a fixed time t. In the equation below, I_t is the information set at time t.

$$\lim_{h \to \infty} E(e_{ij,t+h} - e_{iej,t+h} / I_t) = 0 \qquad (4)$$

Following this definition, the natural way to test for convergence is to test for cointegration with cointegrating vector $[1, -1]$. If both elasticities are cointegrated, but with cointegrating vector different from $[1, -1]$, then it is said that both groups of countries' elasticities contain a common trend but do not converge.

Then, in order to test for convergence, first we have to test if the series of elasticities have unit roots and if they are integrated of the same order. The augmented Dickey–Fuller test (ADF) is used (Said and Dickey, 1984). The test has been sequentially implemented. First, for each series the presence of two unit roots (I(2)) is tested against I(1). If rejected, the null of a unit root is tested against stationarity. Owing to space limitations, only the results from the second step are included in Table 4, as the first test was rejected in all cases. In most cases, we fail to reject the null hypothesis of one unit root, so most series have to be differentiated to achieve stationarity. Only meats and fats elasticities in Great Britain, and cereals elasticities in Portugal and in the group of countries excluded from cluster 1, are stationary at the 5 per cent significance level. In cases where e_{ij} and e_{iej} are I(1) the next step is to test for cointegration. The maximum likelihood (ML) approach of Johansen (1988) and Johansen and Juselius (1990) has been used.

Johansen (1988) showed that a vector of p economic variables X_t may be represented as a VAR model:

$$X_t = \sum_{i=1}^{k} \pi_i X_{t-i} + u_t \quad t = 1, 2..., T$$

The number of cointegration vectors (r) is given by the rank of a $\prod$ matrix defined by $\prod = I - \pi_1 - \pi_2 - ... - \pi_k$, where I is an identity matrix of order p. When the rank of matrix $\prod$ is r with $r < p$, r stationary lineal relationships among the variables of the X_t vector exist. In this case, the matrix $\prod$ can be decomposed in the product of two matrices $\prod = \alpha\beta'$, where β is a matrix of the long-run parameters and α is a matrix of coefficients which indicates the speed of adjustment after a shock in the long-run equilibrium. The Johansen (1988) procedure starts with the estimation of the following autoregressive vectors:

$$\Delta X_t = \sum_{i=1}^{k-1} \Gamma_{0i} \Delta X_{t-i} + V_{0t}$$

$$\qquad (5)$$

$$X_{t-h} = \sum_{i=1}^{k-1} \Gamma_{1i} \Delta X_{t-i} + V_{1t}$$

TABLE 4   *Augmented Dickey–Fuller test on elasticities*

	CEREALS	MEAT	FISH	DAIRY	FRUITS	FATS
Excl. clus. 1	$\tau_c = -3.82\,(2)^*$	$\tau_\mu = -1.31\,(0)$	$\tau_\mu = -1.25\,(1)$	$\tau_\mu = -1.27\,(2)$	$\tau = -0.45\,(1)$	$\tau = -1.57\,(0)$
Denmark	$\tau = -0.11\,(0)$	$\tau_\mu = -0.48\,(0)$	$\tau = -0.62\,(1)$	$\tau_\mu = -0.77\,(0)$	$\tau_\mu = -2.9\,(0)$	$\tau_c = -2.61\,(1)$
France	$\tau = -1.71\,(0)$	$\tau_\mu = -1.47\,(1)$	$\tau = -1.08\,(3)$	$\tau = -0.77\,(0)$	$\tau_\mu = -1.21\,(2)$	$\tau_\mu = -1.02\,(1)$
G. Britain	$\tau_\mu = -2.69\,(0)$	$\tau_c = -4.1\,(3)^*$	$\tau = -0.40\,(0)$	$\tau_\mu = -0.3\,(0)$	$\tau = -0.71\,(1)$	$\tau_\mu = -3.5\,(0)^*$
Excl. clus. 2	$\tau_\mu = -1.87\,(0)$	$\tau_\mu = -1.81\,(0)$	$\tau_\mu = -1.18\,(0)$	$\tau_\mu = 1.74\,(0)$	$\tau = -0.42\,(1)$	$\tau = -1.59\,(0)$
Finland	$\tau_\mu = -2.35\,(0)$	$\tau_c = -3.07\,(2)$	$\tau_\mu = -2.23\,(2)$	$\tau_\mu = -1.12\,(3)$	$\tau_\mu = -0.78\,(0)$	$\tau_\mu = -0.66\,(0)$
Ireland	$\tau = -1.06\,(0)$	$\tau_\mu = -1.51\,(0)$	$\tau_c = -1.82\,(2)$	$\tau_\mu = -1.36\,(0)$	$\tau = 0.11\,(0)$	$\tau = -1.27\,(0)$
Norway	$\tau = -0.21\,(1)$	$\tau_\mu = -2.86\,(3)$	$\tau_\mu = -1.2\,(1)$	$\tau_c = -0.57\,(3)$	$\tau = -0.36\,(0)$	$\tau_\mu = -1.01\,(2)$
Excl. clus. 3	$\tau_\mu = -2.68\,(1)$	$\tau_\mu = -1.93\,(0)$	$\tau_\mu = -0.85\,(0)$	$\tau_\mu = -1.15\,(2)$	$\tau = -0.26\,(0)$	$\tau = -1.59\,(0)$
Sweden	$\tau = 0.03\,(0)$	$\tau = -0.84\,(0)$	$\tau = -0.09\,(2)$	$\tau = -0.06\,(3)$	$\tau = -0.02\,(0)$	$\tau = -1.11\,(0)$
Austria	$\tau_\mu = -1.71\,(0)$	$\tau_\mu = -2.85\,(0)$	$\tau_\mu = -0.04\,(2)$	$\tau = -0.14\,(0)$	$\tau = -0.22\,(1)$	$\tau_\mu = -2.55\,(1)$
Netherlands	$\tau_\mu = -1.33\,(0)$	$\tau_\mu = -2.13\,(1)$	$\tau = 0.11\,(0)$	$\tau = -0.07\,(0)$	$\tau = -0.91\,(1)$	$\tau = -0.59\,(0)$
Belg.–Lux.	$\tau = -1.65\,(2)$	$\tau_c = -2.87\,(3)$	$\tau = -0.85\,(1)$	$\tau = -0.41\,(2)$	$\tau = -0.34\,(0)$	$\tau_\mu = -1.19\,(0)$
Germany	$\tau = -1.05\,(2)$	$\tau_c = -2.67\,(1)$	$\tau_\mu = -1.29\,(0)$	$\tau_c = -1.32\,(0)$	$\tau_\mu = -1.95\,(1)$	$\tau = -1.01\,(2)$
Excl. clus. 4	$\tau_\mu = -2.51\,(1)$	$\tau_\mu = -1.44\,(0)$	$\tau_\mu = -0.29\,(1)$	$\tau_\mu = -1.12\,(2)$	$\tau = -0.35\,(1)$	$\tau = -1.57\,(0)$
Italy	$\tau_\mu = -0.46\,(0)$	$\tau_\mu = -1.71\,(1)$	$\tau = -0.84\,(0)$	$\tau_\mu = -1.91\,(0)$	$\tau_\mu = -2.05\,(1)$	$\tau_\mu = -1.43\,(1)$
Greece	$\tau_c = -1.47\,(1)$	$\tau_c = -1.78\,(5)$	$\tau = -0.63\,(0)$	$\tau_\mu = -2.24\,(0)$	$\tau = -0.23\,(0)$	$\tau = -1.19\,(0)$
Portugal	$\tau_c = -3.61\,(3)^*$	$\tau_\mu = -2.06\,(0)$	$\tau = -0.77\,(0)$	$\tau_\mu = -0.31\,(3)$	$\tau_\mu = -1.71\,(1)$	$\tau = -0.467\,(0)$
Excl. clus. 5	$\tau_c = -3.51\,(2)$	$\tau_c = -2.45\,(0)$	$\tau_\mu = -0.79\,(0)$	$\tau_c = -0.46\,(3)$	$\tau = -0.18\,(1)$	$\tau = -0.09\,(0)$
Spain	$\tau_\mu = -0.52\,(1)$	$\tau_\mu = -2.75\,(1)$	$\tau_\mu = -0.86\,(0)$	$\tau = 0.02\,(0)$	$\tau = -0.90\,(1)$	$\tau = -1.59\,(0)$

Note: Critical values are shown in Fuller (1976) and for 5% level are: $\tau_c = -3.60$, $\tau_\mu = -3.00$ and $\tau = -1.95$; one star means the null hypothesis is rejected at 5%; the number of lags of the endogenous variable are in parentheses.

332

The R_{0t} and R_{1t} vectors of residuals from the above-estimated models are used to perform a likelihood ratio test (the trace test) to calculate the number of cointegration vectors in X_t. The null hypothesis is that at least r cointegration vectors exist and it is defined as:

$$T_r = -T \sum_{i=r+1}^{p} ln(1 - \lambda_i)$$

where $\lambda_{r+1}, \ldots, \lambda_p$ are $p - r$ canonical correlations of R_{0t} with respect to R_{1t}. The distribution of this statistic is a multivariate version of the Dickey–Fuller distribution and depends on the number of $(p - r)$ non-stationary components under the null hypothesis. Critical values are provided in Johansen and Juselius (1990) and in Osterwald-Lenum (1992).

We apply this test to determine the number of cointegration relationships between the elasticity for each country and the average elasticity for the heterogeneous countries. Therefore the number of variables in our case is two. Then both variables will be cointegrated if we can accept that one cointegration vector ($r = 1$) exists. The number of lags included in equation (5) has been determined using the likelihood ratio test suggested by Tiao and Box (1981). The trace test results are shown in Table 5, where the values in parentheses are the number of lags. In most cases, the null hypothesis has not been rejected, which means that no cointegration relationship, and therefore no long-run equilibrium, exists. Only in the case of the meat elasticity can a cointegration relationship be accepted in all countries. However, the existence of a long-run equilibrium relationship is a necessary condition but not sufficient for convergence. As mentioned before, the cointegrating vector must be [1,–1].

Johansen and Juselius (1990) developed several methods to make specific hypothesis tests concerning the size and relative characteristics of the β and α coefficients. The hypothesis on the β takes the form: $\beta = H\phi$, where H is a design matrix with dimension $p \times s$ ($r \leq s \leq p$) and s is the number of β coefficients that are not restricted. The statistic test is $-2 \, ln \, (Q) = T \sum ln \, [(1 - \lambda_i^*)/(1 - \lambda_i)]$, where $i = 1, 2, \ldots, 5$, and λ_i^* and λ_i are eigenvalues generated by the model with and without restrictions, respectively. The test is distributed as $\chi^2_{r(p-s)}$.

Cereal elasticities for Austria and Spain have a long-run relationship with the rest of the countries. However, the null hypothesis that the cointegrating vector is [1,–1] is rejected, so both countries show a common trend but do not converge in elasticities. More cointegration relationships have been found among meat elasticities. However, only in the case of Denmark and Greece can we fail to reject the null of convergence at the 5 per cent level of significance. If the significance level was 1 per cent, Norway and Austria would also show a trend to convergence in meat elasticities with the rest of countries. It is important to mention again that convergence in this case means that meat consumers in all European countries will react in the same way to changes in total calorie intake. That does not mean that meat calorie shares will equalize across countries.

In the case of fruits and vegetables and fats, no long-run relationships have been found; that is, elasticities move independently. Finally, only Austria, in

TABLE 5 Cointegration (trace statistic) and convergence test on food elasticities

H_0:	Cereals r=0[a]	r≤1	[1,-1][b]	Meat r=0	r≤1	[1,-1]	Fish r=0	r≤1	[1,-1]	Dairy r=0	r≤1	[1,-1]	Fruits r=0	r≤1	[1,-1]	Fats r=0	r≤1	[1,-1]
Denmark	—	—	—	27.4(2)*	5.42	3.49	14.81(2)	5.26	—	15.66(2)	2.63	—	12.2(2)	1.29	—	12.2(2)	4.32	—
France	—	—	—	19.0(2)	7.20	—	37.10(4)*	3.58	28.67**	22.60(2)*	9.15	11.15**	14.63(2)	5.62	—	18.0(2)	5.82	—
G. Britain	—	—	—	—	—	—	15.76(2)	4.23	—	15.39(2)	2.7	—	9.35(2)	1.20	—	—	4.11	—
Ireland	15.4(2)	4.74	—	19.0(2)	3.45	—	9.51(2)	3.07	—	7.58(2)	1.09	—	18 (2)	0.42	—	11.5(2)	4.11	—
Finland	16.9(2)	4.29	—	25.3(2)*	4.81	6.07**	31.6(2)*	3.35	19.42**	13.08(2)	2.79	—	17.34(2)	2.73	—	12.7(2)	4.3	—
Norway	10.8(2)	2.98	—	28.0(2)*	8.72	5.13*	7.13(2)	2.01	—	12.36(4)	3.01	—	7.14(2)	0.58	—	12.9(2)	3.72	—
Sweden	15.0(2)	4.97	—	21.2(2)*	4.11	9.12**	10.72(2)	1.67	—	20.30(2)*	3.3	15.86**	8.88(2)	2.44	—	14.8(2)	4.11	—
Netherlands	12.3(2)	1.73	—	24.8(2)	5.59	8.27**	9.78(2)	2.71	—	19.00(2)	5.36	—	7.71(2)	1.15	—	9.6(2)	3.72	—
Belg.-Lux.	12.0(2)	1.02	—	30.1(2)	8.87	12.28**	11.99(2)	1.19	—	6.61(3)	2.39	—	9.49(2)	2.18	—	11.6(2)	3.34	—
Austria	31.8(2)	7.41	10.13*	22.7(2)	4.68	5.98*	21.9(3)	9.14	1.40	17.25(2)	3.13	—	7.91(2)	1.04	—	17.5(2)	4.23	—
Germany	17.1(2)	6.25	—	25.8(2)	7.16	8.66**	9.62(2)	1.36	—	19.00(2)	3.89	—	14.44(2)	5.95	—	14.9(2)	6.93	—
Greece	17.5(2)	3.81	—	20.0(2)	5.90	0.22	12.29(2)	5.42	—	23.80(2)	7.19	14.87**	11.3(2)	0.51	—	19.0(2)	7.02	—
Portugal	—	—	—	19.0(2)	4.40	—	8.49(2)	2.71	—	24.70(4)	3.62	1.40	12.79(2)	2.18	—	13.2(2)	5.22	—
Italy	19.0(2)	4.97	—	19.0(2)	8.10	—	10.32(2)	2.82	—	26.20(2)	6.34	18.57**	8.03(2)	0.75	—	16.5(2)	5.17	—
Spain	23.7(2)	7.64	11.24*	27.8(2)	5.38	10.43**	12.01(2)	2.55	—	17.43(2)	5.89	—	11.31(2)	3.44	—	10.4(2)	2.53	—

Notes: [a] Critical values for the trace test are on Osterwald-Lenum (1992); one star means that a hypothesis is rejected at 5%.
[b] The null hypothesis is that the cointegrating vector is [1,-1]. Critical value at the 5% is: $\chi^2(2) = 5.99$. One star means that restrictions are rejected at 5% and two stars means rejection at 1% level of significance.

334

the case of fish, and Portugal, in the case of milk and dairy products, show a convergence process in elasticities with respect to the rest of the countries and, in a few cases, the existence of a common trend (but not convergence) is not rejected.

CONCLUSIONS

Total food consumption, and its distribution among different food products, have been changing in the last few years. Some authors suggest that this evolution is leading to a standardization of food diets across European Union countries. Nevertheless, after testing whether the allocation of total food calorie intake among different products will converge in the long run, the conclusion is that, in general terms, this is not the case. In most cases, total calorie elasticities between specific products and the average do not show a long-run relationship.

We can conclude that, at this aggregate level covering broad food categories and countries taken as whole rather than being regionally differentiated, there are few convergence relationships. Those which have been detected are for animal products (meat, fish and dairy products). The same method should be applied at a more disaggregated level to discover whether results which challenge this broad conclusion could be obtained.

REFERENCES

Anderson, G. and Blundell, R. (1983), 'Testing restrictions in a flexible demand system: an application to consumers' expenditure in Canada', *Review of Economic Studies*, **50**, 397–410.

Bernard, A.B. and Durlauf, S. (1995), 'Convergence in International Output', *Journal of Applied Econometrics*, **10**, 97–108.

Blandford, D. (1984), 'Changes in food consumption patterns in the OECD area', *European Review of Agricultural Economics*, **11**, 43–65.

FAO (1995), *Computerized Information Series. Faostat PC. n° 6: Food Balance Sheets*, Rome: FAO.

Fuller, W.A. (1976), *Introduction to Statistical Time Series*, New York: Wiley.

Gil, J.M., Gracia, A. and Perez y Perez, L. (1995), 'Food Consumption and Economic Development in the European Union', *European Review of Agricultural Economics*, **22**, 385–99.

Grigg, D. (1993), 'The European diet: regional variations in food consumption in the 1980s', *Geoforum*, **24**, 279–89.

Herrmann, R. and Röeder, C. (1995), 'Does food consumption converge internationally? Measurement, empirical test and the influence of policy', *European Review of Agricultural Economics*, **22**, 400–414.

Johansen, S. (1988), 'Statistical analysis of cointegrating vectors', *Journal of Economic Dynamics and Control*, **12**, 231–54.

Johansen, S. and Juselius, K. (1990), 'Maximum likelihood estimation and inference on cointegration – with applications to the demand for money', *Oxford Bulletin of Economics and Statistics*, **52**, 169–210.

Osterwald-Lenum, M. (1992), 'A note with fractiles on the asymptotic distribution of the maximum likelihood cointegration rank test statistic: four cases', *Oxford Bulletin of Economics and Statistics*, **54**, 461–72.

Said, S. and Dickey, D. (1984), 'Testing for Unit Roots in Autoregressive-Moving Average Models of Unknown Order', *Biometrika*, **71**, 599–607.

Suriñach J., Artís M., López, E. and Sansó, A. (1995), *Análisis Económico Regional. Nociones básicas de la Teoría de la cointegración*, Barcelona: Antoni Bosch.

Tiao, G.C. and Bok, G.E.P. (1981), 'Modeling multiple time series with applications', *Journal of the American Statistical Association*, 75, 802–16.

Wheelock, J.V. and Frank, J.D. (1989), 'Food consumption patterns in developed countries', in B. Trail (ed.), *Prospects for the European Food System*, London: Elsevier Applied Science.

CYNTHIA DONOVAN, ROBERT MYERS, DAVID TSCHIRLEY AND
MICHAEL WEBER*

The Effects of Food Aid on Maize Prices in Mozambique

INTRODUCTION

Peace Accords signed in October 1992 ended a long period of civil war in
Mozambique, but the war had caused severe constraints on food production.
Furthermore, a devastating regional drought during 1991–2 put additional
pressure on the food system, so that by the beginning of 1992 a major famine
was threatening the country. The response was food aid, which during 1992–3
represented 60 per cent of the total cereals available to consumers (Tschirley *et
al.*, 1996). The country and its economy recovered slowly and food aid gradually declined. By 1994–5, the proportion of food aid in total cereal supply had
dropped to 15 per cent (ibid.).

The objective here is to evaluate the effects of commercial food aid, in the
form of yellow maize imports, on the domestic prices of white and yellow
maize in Maputo, the capital of Mozambique. Maputo is the main port for food
aid arrivals and distribution, as well as the main consumption market for
locally produced cereals. The analysis is undertaken using weekly data in order
to focus on some of the short-term dynamic responses to food aid that cannot
be captured in an annual or quarterly model (for example, Farzin, 1991; Stevens,
1979). Furthermore, the analysis is undertaken for two distinct periods: the
war/drought period of April 1990 to February 1993 and the recovery from
April 1993 to November 1995. The two periods are contrasted to illustrate
different effects that food aid can have in different situations.

In contrast to many previous structural analyses of the effects of food aid,
the approach here is to use a vector autoregression (VAR) model. The advantage of the approach is that the dynamics of the model are left unrestricted and
identification is based only on contemporaneous relationships between variables in the system (Sims, 1980; Fackler, 1988; Myers *et al.*, 1990). This is a
particular advantage in the case of food aid in Mozambique because there is
considerable uncertainty surrounding what types of traditional identification
restrictions should be imposed during periods of drought and war. In addition,
a traditional structural analysis using a large-scale econometric model would
require data that are either unavailable or questionable in the case of maize
markets in Mozambique. Using minimal identification restrictions, a VAR
approach provides a vehicle for summarizing historical correlations in food aid

*West African Rice Development Association, Saint-Louis, Senegal and Michigan State University.

arrivals and maize prices, and can be used to estimate the effects of food aid 'shocks' on market prices for white and yellow maize.

THE VAR MODEL

The VAR model is specified as a three-equation system in weekly food aid arrivals and weekly retail prices of white and yellow maize in Maputo. Food

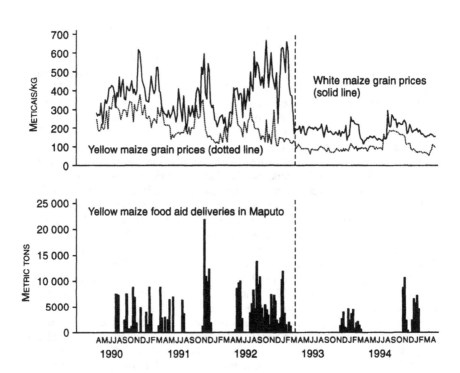

FIGURE 1   *Weekly real retail prices and food aid deliveries in Maputo, April 1990–April 1995*

Note: Prices are deflated to a 1989 base year with the CPI deflator. Food aid deliveries are the metric tons of yellow maize grain delivered to private agents in Maputo each week, from warehouses or the port of Maputo. Dashed vertical line indicates March 1993.

Source: MOA/MSU SIMA Database, 1995.

aid arrivals are commercial yellow maize food aid delivered into the hands of private agents each week, either directly at the port or from warehouses. The price data are weekly real retail prices in meticais per kilogram, deflated by the consumer price index with a base year of 1989.

Figure 1 plots the data used to estimate the VAR, with the dotted vertical line indicating March 1993, the transition month between the war/drought and recovery periods. Summary statistics for the data are also provided in Table 1. Mean prices are clearly higher in the war/drought periods and there are larger mean food aid deliveries. There is also much greater variability in all series during that war/drought period. A rapid decline in white maize prices occurred when the first post-drought harvest of white maize came onto the market and domestic traders were able to gain access to the production zones. This represents a structural shift and suggests estimating separate models for the two periods.

Preliminary testing was conducted on each variable in the system to determine its stationarity properties. The Augmented Dickey–Fuller, the Phillips–Perron and the Kwiatkowski–Phillips–Schmidt–Shin tests were applied (Hamilton, 1994; Banerjee *et al.*, 1993). The results generally support the conclusion that each of the series is stationary. Given this evidence, the VAR models for both time periods were each specified in the levels of the food aid and real price variables, with a linear trend included in all equations.

Lag lengths for the VAR were chosen on the basis of Akaike's Information Criterion (AIC), the Schwartz Criterion (SC), and sequential likelihood ratio (LR) tests (Hamilton, 1994). The AIC suggested seven lags, SC one lag and LR four lags. In view of the well-known tendency for AIC to overparameterize as the sample size increases, and for SC to underparameterize in small samples, a lag length of four was chosen for the VAR.

One of the most critical aspects of VAR modelling is the identification and interpretation of the structural error terms ('shocks') which drive the dynamics of the system. In this study we investigated a range of alternative identifications to determine the degree of sensitivity of the results to each one. Except for a few cases, in which the identification restrictions seemed implausible from an economic perspective, the outcomes turned out not to be very sensitive to the identification chosen. Hence results are reported for just one identification scheme per model.

For the war/drought period, a recursive identification was chosen with white maize prices (WP) ordered first, food aid deliveries (FA) ordered second, and yellow maize prices (YP) ordered last. The logic behind this specification is that, during this period, local white maize markets were somewhat isolated, sporadic and dominated by the large quantities of yellow maize appearing as food aid. However, white maize remained the preferred consumption good when it was available. Thus it is hypothesized that WP is not influenced contemporaneously (that is, within a week) by the availability of food aid or shifts in yellow maize prices. On the other hand, releases of food aid and yellow maize prices may be sensitive to contemporaneous changes in supply and demand conditions for white maize (that is, white maize price shocks). Similarly, food aid does not respond contemporaneously to yellow maize prices but food aid shocks can immediately (within a week) influence yellow maize prices through their supply effect.

TABLE 1 *Descriptive statistics*

Statistic	War/drought period (3 Apr. 1990 – 28 Feb. 1993)			Recovery period (4 Apr. 1993 – 28 Apr. 1995)		
	White maize price (meticais/kg)	Yellow maize price (meticais/kg)	Food aid (metric tonnes)	White maize price (meticais/kg)	Yellow maize price (meticais/kg)	Food aid (metric tonnes)
Mean	384.30	234.04	2 276.30	201.72	123.52	733.86
Standard deviation	102.08	66.38	3 738.17	32.99	31.21	1 867.42
Variance	10 420	4 406	13 973 915	1 088	974	3 487 257
Median	386.19	222.30	0.00	196.69	113.04	0.00
Maximum	658.71	413.92	21 660.00	306.70	204.46	10 414.35
Minimum	191.19	126.50	0.00	135.32	78.63	0.00
Skewness	0.48**	0.49**	2.02***	0.64***	1.48***	3.16***
Kurtosis	−0.21	−0.51	4.77***	0.18	1.17**	10.50***

Note: * indicates significance level of 10%; ** indicates significance level of 5%; *** indicates significance level of 1%.

Source: Banerjee *et al.* (1993) for significance level.

For the recovery period, a different recursive identification scheme was selected, based on changes taking place in the maize market. At that time white maize supply constraints were released by a combination of increased domestic and regional production, increased movement of traders, continued growth in informal markets and gradually reduced availability of yellow maize. As a result of these changes, food aid declined in importance and apparently became less responsive to contemporaneous changes in white maize prices. Indeed, with the increased importance and integration of white maize markets, it is logical to assume that white maize prices were now influenced contemporaneously by food aid arrivals and yellow maize prices. This leads to an ordering of FA, YP, WP.

Another important event occurred during the recovery period. In July 1994, some donors and non-governmental organizations (the World Food Programme in particular) announced a plan to purchase local white maize for their emergency programmes, rather than import yellow maize. As a result, maize prices experienced a sharp increase which cannot be explained by any other observed market phenomenon, either on the supply or the demand side. The change is incorporated as a one-time mean shift, following the work of Perron (1989). Seasonality also becomes a factor in the period because local white maize becomes available only in June, when the harvest begins. To adjust for this a seasonality indicator variable was added for the hungry season.

VAR ANALYSIS

Analysis of the VAR models was conducted using standard impulse response methods (Hamilton, 1994). Primary interest lies in the dynamic response of white and yellow maize prices to typical shocks to the amount of food aid being delivered. If there is no response, we can conclude that market prices are not influenced by food aid. If yellow maize prices respond, but white maize prices do not, we can conclude that yellow maize food aid influences domestic yellow maize prices, while white maize markets are isolated from food aid effects. On the other hand, if there is a significant response in both prices we would conclude that the markets are connected and yellow maize food aid significantly affects white maize prices.

Historical simulation of prices, obtained in the assumed absence of commercial food aid, can also be conducted using the VAR. In this case, the yellow maize and white maize price shocks are set at their historical values. The food aid shocks are then altered to ensure that the amount of food aid in each period becomes zero (see Myers *et al.*, 1990). The VAR is then simulated with the new shocks in order to estimate historical price paths in the absence of food aid. Price paths with and without the food aid can then be compared to isolate the effects of the food aid.

RESULTS AND DISCUSSION

There has been considerable previous research on the effects of food aid on developing economies (for example, Isenman and Singer, 1977). Previous research has also indicated that informal maize markets in Maputo are relatively competitive and responsive (Tschirley *et al.*, 1996; MOA/MSU, 1993). The results presented in this section support this view of responsive, connected markets leading to important food aid effects. We first examine the war/drought period and then turn to the recovery period.

The war/drought period

The results of the VAR analysis support the argument that informal market prices were responsive to food aid imports, even during the war/drought period. The responses of each variable to a one-standard deviation shock in each of the structural errors during the war/drought period are plotted in Figure 2. A one-standard deviation shock corresponds to 2600 metric tonnes for food aid, 65 meticais/kg. for white maize prices, and 34 meticais/kg. for yellow maize prices (in real 1989 meticais). The middle plot in Figure 2 shows the response of each series to a single food aid shock of 2600 metric tonnes, holding other shocks to zero. Yellow maize prices immediately decline about 0.4 s.d. (14 meticais/kg.) and then gradually return to their previous level by about the eighth week. White maize prices do not drop at all as an immediate response to a food aid increase because of the identification scheme. However, even when no contemporaneous response is allowed, white maize prices decline in later periods, although to a lesser degree than yellow maize prices. Thus food aid appears to have a strong depressing effect on white maize prices.

The historical simulation of maize prices, with and without food aid, in the war/drought period is shown in Figure 3. It is interesting that elimination of the food aid would have increased the level of both white and yellow maize prices substantially above their actual values, although other supply and demand shocks in these markets cause the direction and variability of price movements to be similar in the two cases. White maize prices would have been 33 per cent higher in January and February 1993, on average, without the food aid, and yellow maize prices an average of 150 per cent higher. Clearly, in this period, the food aid deliveries played a key role in ensuring the availability of maize at an accessible price for Maputo consumers. Furthermore, the scarcity of white maize, and its role as a preferred consumption good, meant that its price remained relatively high and volatile in spite of the yellow maize arrivals and price movements. Nevertheless, the food aid clearly kept white maize prices down as well, though not to the same extent as yellow maize prices.

The recovery period

The impulse responses for the recovery period are plotted in Figure 4. In this case a one-standard deviation shock corresponds to an innovation of 1250

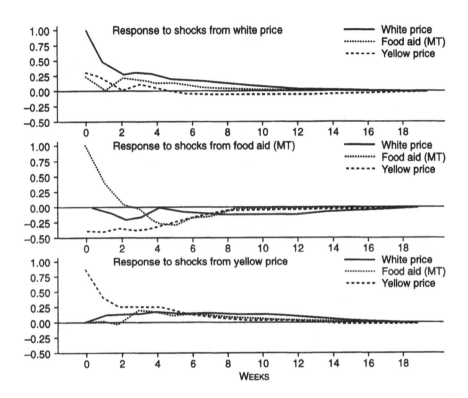

FIGURE 2   *Impulse responses for the war/drought period*

metric tonnes of food aid, 20 meticais/kg. for the price of white maize and 12 meticais/kg. for the price of yellow maize. Comparing these standard errors to those in the war/drought period (2600 metric tons, 65 meticais/kg. and 34 meticais/kg., respectively), it is clear that there was much less uncertainty during the recovery period.

The top plot in Figure 4 shows the responses to a typical food aid shock, holding all other shocks constant. The response of yellow maize prices follows a similar pattern to that in the war/drought period; food aid has a depressing effect on price that dies out after about eight weeks. However, the white maize prices responds differently. The initial (contemporaneous) response of white maize price remains zero but in the following week there is a WP *increase*. This may be a result of the unexpected increase in food aid being interpreted as a signal that white maize supplies are tighter than had been thought, resulting

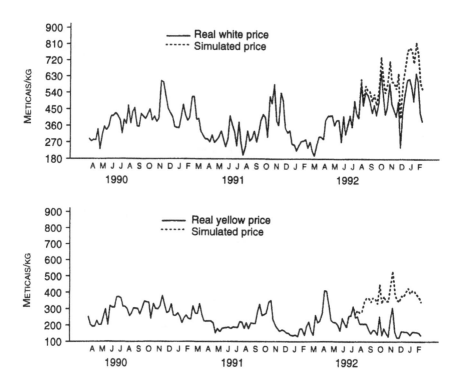

FIGURE 3 *Simulation for the war/drought period assuming no food aid after 31 July 1992*

in an increase in demand (and price) for the preferred white maize product. In subsequent weeks, however, the effect of the food aid shock on white maize prices becomes negative, since it would seem increasingly clear that supply and demand conditions for white maize have not changed (remember that other shocks besides food aid are set to zero) and the additional supply of yellow maize food aid begins to depress prices for both types of maize. Eventually (after about eight weeks), the food aid shock no longer has any significant price effects.

The simulations which show how prices would have evolved through the recovery period in the absence of food aid are shown in Figure 5. The removal of two large food aid shipments in the November 1994–January 1995 period (a total of 47 600 metric tons) would have led to generally higher yellow and white maize prices through the period. The simulated white maize price for February 1995 was 208 meticais/kg., 14 per cent higher than the actual real

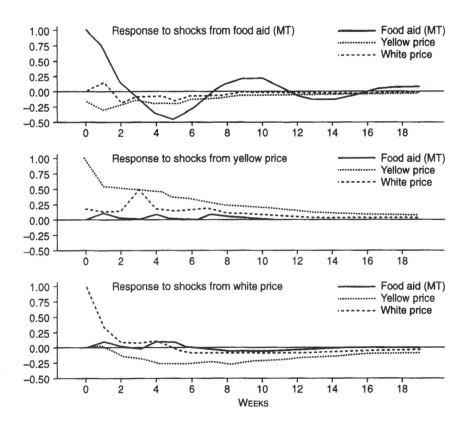

FIGURE 4   *Impulse responses for the recovery period*

price of 183 meticais/kg. For yellow maize, the simulated price was 76 per cent higher than the observed price (160 meticais/kg., compared with 91 meticais/kg.). In a period in which overall price fluctuations were relatively small and prices were low compared to earlier times, these represent important effects for traders.

CONCLUSIONS

In the war/drought period, consumers benefited from increased yellow maize supply and lower yellow maize prices that can be traced back to the arrivals of yellow maize food aid on the Maputo market in the 1990–93 period. However, the local white maize market was also influenced in very important ways as a

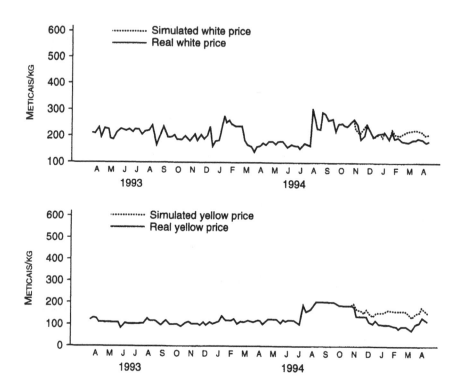

FIGURE 5   *Simulation for the recovery period assuming no food aid during November 1994–January 1995*

result of food aid. Indeed, the results in this paper show that the general level of white maize prices was considerably lower with the food aid than it would have been without it, but that the food aid did little to reduce the tremendous white maize price fluctuations and market uncertainty that characterized the war/drought period.

In the recovery, with agricultural production increasing and the economy beginning to benefit from the Peace Accords, yellow maize food aid arrivals continued to influence white maize prices, as well as their expected strong effect on yellow maize prices. The simulation results show that food aid arrivals just prior to and during the hungry season can lower white maize prices in a countercyclical fashion, long before the next harvest is due. This affects traders' margins and the ability to recover storage costs, and thus may be affecting storage and marketing investment in the domestic markets. Domestic consumers benefit in the short run, with lower prices for both yellow and white maize prices; however, a disincentive effect on domestic production and marketing cannot be ruled out in the longer run.

REFERENCES

Banerjee, A., Dolado, J.J., Galbraith, J.J. and Hendry, D.F. (1993), *Co-Integration, Error Correction and the Econometric Analysis of Non-Stationary Data*, Oxford: Oxford University Press.

Fackler, P. (1988), 'Vector Autoregressive Techniques for Structural Analysis', *Revista De Análisis Económico*, 3, 119–34.

Farzin, Y.H. (1991), 'Food Aid: Positive or Negative Effects in Somalia?', *Journal of Developing Areas*, 25, 261–82.

Hamilton, J. (1994), *Time Series Analysis*, Princeton: Princeton University Press.

Isenman, P.J. and Singer, H.W. (1977), 'Food Aid: Disincentive Effects and Their Policy Implications', *Economic Development and Cultural Change*, 25, 205–37.

MOA/MSU Research Team (1993), *The Organization, Behavior and Performance of the Informal Food Marketing System*, NDAE Working Paper 10, East Lansing: Michigan State University.

Myers, R.J., Piggott, R.R. and Tomek, W.G. (1990), 'Estimating Sources of Fluctuations in the Australian Wood Market: An Application of Var Methods', *Australian Journal of Agricultural Economics*, 34, 242–62.

Perron, P. (1989), 'The Great Crash, the Oil Price Shock and the Unit Root Hypothesis', *Econometrica*, 57, 1361–1401.

Sims, C. (1980), 'Macroeconomics and Reality', *Econometrica*, 48, 1–48.

Stevens, C. (1979), *Food Aid and the Developing World: Four African Case Studies*, New York: St Martin's Press.

Tschirley, D., Donovan, C. and Weber, M. (1996), 'Food Aid and Food Markets: Lessons from Mozambique', *Food Policy*, 21, 189–210.

MARK SCHREINER, DOUGLAS H. GRAHAM AND MARIO MIRANDA*

Choices by Poor Households when the Interest Rate for Deposits Differs from the Interest Rate for Loans

INTRODUCTION

A dynamic model of optimal decisions by a poor household, with an infinite horizon and rational expectations over uncertain future income, can be solved and simulated using the technique of orthogonal polynomial projection. The household faces a credit limit, and the interest rate on savings (deposits) differs from the interest rate for loans (borrowing). The change in the spread between the interest rate for deposits and for loans, and the effects of that spread on household decisions, suggest that attention should be paid to access to formal financial services and to the effects of decreasing the transaction costs associated with them.

The model to be used incorporates five basic features of a poor household and its financial contracts. First, poor households both borrow and save. They borrow from formal or informal lenders, and households save in financial deposits or in real goods. Second, poor households face a credit limit. Third, financial contracts take place through time. Resources are lent in the present for the promise to repay in the future, so saving/borrowing choices in the present affect consumption in the future. Fourth, poor households earn less for saving than they pay for borrowing. Fifth, income for poor households is variable and uncertain (Besley, 1995).

The model also omits at least 10 basic features of the financial contracts used by poor households. First, and most importantly, the possibility, prevention and punishment of default affect financial contracts. Second, households smooth both consumption and income, so production and consumption choices depend on each other (Morduch, 1995). Third, the transaction costs of small loans or deposits swamp the interest earned or paid. We model changes in transaction costs as changes in the spread between the interest rates for deposits and loans. This makes transaction costs vary with the size of the loan or deposit. In reality, most transaction costs are fixed, regardless of the size of the loan or deposit. Fourth, we model financial contracts as credit cards or passbook accounts. Real financial contracts often involve multi-period commitments such as instalment loans or certificates of deposit. Fifth, most loans require collateral. Sixth, both savings and borrowing may be non-zero at once. Seventh, households engage in non-financial saving and borrowing. Eighth, contracts may have non-divisibilities.

*Ohio State University, Columbus, Ohio, USA.

Ninth, households may save not only for precautionary motives but also for investment, speculation and convenience. Tenth, and finally, interest rates and institutions are determined endogenously in general equilibrium.

Because of algebraic complexity, no single analytic model has captured more than a couple of these features (for example, Mendelson and Amihud, 1982; Helpman, 1981). Many models omit credit limits, but without explicit restrictions on the utility function, the optimal decision is then to play a Ponzi game. Few analytic models recognize the fact that borrowing costs more than saving pays.

The results extend those of Deaton (1991; 1992). Simulations suggest that more favourable interest rates increase the mean of consumption and decrease its variance. Thus access to formal financial services and/or lower transaction costs for financial transactions can improve the welfare of poor households. This is necessary but not sufficient to justify interventions in financial markets designed to help households.

The remainder of the paper consists of a presentation of the model, with discussion of optimal decision rules, followed by examination of the long-run distribution of consumption.

THE MODEL

The decision problem of the poor household is formulated as a Bellman equation. Time is indexed by t. If the household lives 40 years and makes financial decisions weekly or monthly, the horizon is effectively infinite. The household has rational expectations over labour income $\tilde{y}_t$. Labour income is an independent identically distributed (iid) random variable realized at the start of each period. The per-period discount rate is δ. The time-separable, time-invariant, per-period utility function $U(\cdot)$ is defined over a single composite consumption good c_t whose price is unity. More consumption increases utility but at a decreasing rate, so the household is risk-averse.

The poor household chooses a level of net saving s_t. Borrowing is negative net saving. With formal financial contracts or with low transaction costs, deposits earn an interest rate of d_f and loans cost an interest rate of l_f. In contrast, the interest rates with informal contracts or with high transaction costs are d_i and l_i. Formal deposits earn more than informal savings, and formal loans cost less than informal loans:

$$r(s_t) = \begin{cases} d \text{ if } s_t > 0 \\ l \text{ if } s_t \leq 0 \end{cases}, \text{ where}$$

$$d = \begin{cases} d_f \text{ with formal savings or low transactions costs} \\ d_i \text{ with informal savings or high transactions costs} \end{cases},$$

$$l = \begin{cases} l_f \text{ with formal loans or low transactions costs} \\ l_i \text{ with informal loans or high transactions costs} \end{cases},$$

(1)

$$d_f > d_i, l_f < l_i \text{ and } d_k < l_k, k = i, f.$$

On the savings side, several forces make the rate of return to informal saving low and even negative: households usually lend informally to friends or relatives for low or no interest; stocks of grain or building materials depreciate; inflation erodes cash balances; and relatives seek gifts from liquid households (Binswanger and Rosenzweig, 1986). In contrast, formal deposits hide wealth from light-fingered relatives and provide safer, higher returns.

On the borrowing side, formal loans should be cheaper than informal ones. For example, moneylenders often charge astronomical rates. In addition, the reduced transaction costs implicit in loans from friends or relatives are more than overcome by the opportunity cost of maintaining the social ties required to get informal loans. The revealed preference of borrowers and savers in developed economies for formal financial contracts shows that, at least in deep financial markets, formal contracts offer more than informal contracts.

The household starts each period with wealth w_t, the sum of labour income, net saving from the past period and any interest from net saving in the past period:

$$w_t = y_t + s_{t-1} \cdot [1 + r(s_{t-1})]. \tag{2}$$

The household allocates wealth between consumption and savings:

$$w_t = c_t + s_t. \tag{3}$$

New households have no savings. Borrowing is less than the credit limit k, and saving is less than wealth:

$$k \leq s_t \leq w_t. \tag{4}$$

The value function $V(w_t)$ is the sum of current and discounted expected future utility, given current wealth and optimal decisions in all future periods. The Bellman equation for the household's maximization problem is:

$$V(w_t) = k \leq \overset{\max}{s_t} \leq w_t U(w_t - s_t) + \left(\frac{1}{1+\delta}\right) \cdot E_t V\{\tilde{y}_{t+1} + s_t \cdot [1 + r(s_t)]\}, \tag{5}$$
$$\tilde{y}_t \sim \text{iid},$$

with $r(s_t)$ defined as in (1).

Equation (5) is a functional equation in $V(\cdot)$. Since w_t is continuous, the solution function $V(\cdot)$ must make (5) hold at an infinite number of values of w_t. Savings is the function $f(w_t)$ that maximizes (5). Given assets and savings, (3) gives consumption.

The parameterization of (5) follows Deaton (1992). Utility is CARA(2). This assumption has some empirical support (Hildreth and Knowles, 1982; Kydland and Prescott 1982; Friend and Blume, 1975; Tobin and Dolde, 1971). What matters for the results is not the exact number used but rather the fact that the poor household is risk-averse.

With favourable interest rates, deposits earn 5 per cent and loans cost 25 per cent. When rates are unfavourable, savings earn −5 per cent and loans cost 50 per cent. The credit limit is 10. Again the result does not depend on the exact numbers but rather on the fact of the credit limit and the changes in the spread between the favourable and unfavourable cases. Income is normal with mean 100 and standard deviation 10. The discount rate δ is 10 per cent. These choices match those of Deaton (1992) and Dercon (1992). We cannot defend these choices as empirical facts – they are made to facilitate comparisons between the simple model of Deaton (1992) and the same model with a credit limit and a spread between the interest rate on savings and loans.

Miranda (1994) and Judd (1991) show why numerical solutions of (5) by orthogonal polynomial projection are more accurate, elegant and quick than the grid techniques of Deaton (1991; 1992). The value function is represented by a polynomial with nice approximation properties. Given an initial guess for $V(\cdot)$ at a few well-chosen levels of wealth, we use the first-order conditions of (5) to solve for the level of savings that maximizes $V(\cdot)$, taking the current approximation to $V(\cdot)$ as given when evaluating the right-hand side of (5). We approximate the distribution of the income shock with Gaussian quadrature. This process iterates until $V(\cdot)$ converges.

OPTIMAL DECISIONS

Figure 1 shows optimal savings as a function of wealth. Consumption is wealth less savings. The solid line stands for choices with favourable interest rates, and the dashed line stands for choices with unfavourable interest rates. The 'wiggles' reflect approximation error.

Four insights can be gleaned from Figure 1. First, low levels of wealth lead to borrowing and net saving is negative. In fact, a household may borrow so much that the credit limit binds, as at wealth levels below 75 units for poor households in the favourable case. The cheaper the loan, the higher the level of wealth at which a household will start to borrow. In practice, more poverty means a hungry household waits longer before it will borrow.

Second, households can sometimes consume all their assets and neither save nor borrow. That is, net saving is zero. This flat stretch of the net-savings function comes from the unequal interest rates for saving and borrowing. It disappears when the two rates are the same, as most analytical models assume (for example, Deaton, 1992; Dercon, 1992). This is how the flat stretch comes about. For some levels of wealth, one more unit of consumption in the present is worth more than the discounted expected value of one more unit plus interest in the next period, but less than the discounted expected value of not having to repay an extra unit plus interest in the next period. The range of disintermediation decreases as the spread between the interest rates for loans and deposits decreases. This flat stretch in the net savings function may be part of the answer to the puzzle of why so many poor households have no deposits or loans at all (Hubbard *et al.*, 1994). With a low reward for deposits and a high price for loans, a poor household might maximize utility by living hand-to-mouth.

Third, the household saves at high levels of wealth. Furthermore, the interest elasticity of saving increases as the return to saving increases. Not only does

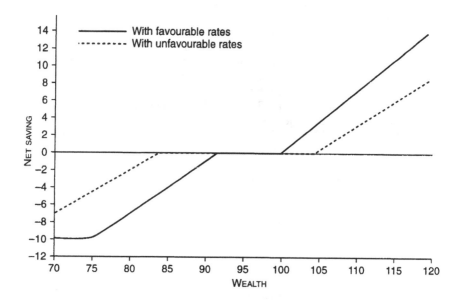

FIGURE 1   *Optimal decisions with different interest rate spreads*

the household begin saving at lower levels of wealth, but the rate at which the household increases savings as wealth increases also increases. This matches the stylized fact that, although rich and poor both save, the rich save a larger percentage of their income than the poor. For this parameterization, increasing the return to savings increases savings more than decreasing the cost of borrowing decreases savings, since cheaper loans reduce the need for a buffer of savings. In results not shown here, deposits decrease as loans get cheaper and the need to self-insure falls, all else constant.

Fourth, poor households will save even with negative returns and borrow even at exorbitant rates, since they want to avoid episodes of low consumption so much. The desire to borrow when consumption is low helps explain the high rates charged by loan sharks and moneylenders (Adams and Fitchett, 1992).

Figure 1 shows decision rules. Given wealth, it depicts the level of net savings that maximizes the sum of current and discounted expected future utility over an infinite horizon. The decision rules alone do not, however, reveal the particular levels of savings and consumption of a poor household using the optimal decision rule through time. Nor do they reveal how interest rates affect the way in which the household can smooth consumption.

THE LONG-RUN DISTRIBUTION OF CONSUMPTION

To approximate the long-run distribution of consumption for both the favourable and unfavourable scenarios, the behaviour of a poor household can be simulated using the decision rules in Figure 1 for 100,000,000 periods (Figure 2). In the unfavourable case (dashed line), the mean of consumption is 99.88 with a standard deviation of 8.34. In the favourable case (solid line), the mean is 100.14 with a standard deviation of 6.02.

More favourable interest rates smooth consumption in two ways. First, cheaper loans help to avoid low consumption. The extreme left tail of the distribution of consumption is thinner with favourable rates than with unfavourable rates. Second, more rewards for saving decreases episodes of high consumption. The extreme right tail of the distribution of consumption with favourable rates is inside the extreme right tail of the distribution with unfavourable rates. Increased savings and the higher interest earnings pad the buffer of the household against poor income draws.

Figure 2 highlights two other insights. First, savings and loans both buffer consumption, but not in the same way, skewing consumption to the left. The credit limit means the poor household can avoid gluts more easily than famines. In addition, loans cost more than savings earn. Second, the distribution of

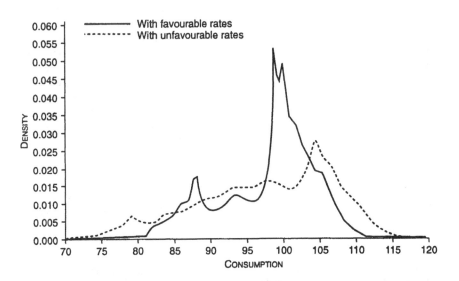

FIGURE 2   *Long-run distribution of consumption with different interest rates*

consumption has three modes. Roughly speaking, this happens because the overall distribution is a mixture of the distributions of current assets conditional on the levels of net savings in the past period. Only the tail modes require explanation, and the modes in the left tail (91 units with favourable rates and 82 units with unfavourable rates) are the most interesting. These peaks happen because, when wealth is near the range where borrowing starts, a wide range of wealth maps into a narrow range of consumption. For example, consumption is almost the same when wealth is just below the point where nothing is saved or borrowed as when wealth is just above that point. The need to repay old debt and interest means that the conditional mean of wealth is lower if the household borrowed in the past period. This increases the likelihood of wealth being in the range where nothing is borrowed or saved or just in the range where something is borrowed. The same argument holds for savings accounts for the modes in the right tail (103 with favourable rates and 109 with unfavourable rates).

CONCLUSION

An attempt has been made to solve and simulate a model of financial choices by a poor household with favourable and unfavourable interest rates. The model accounts for the uncertainty of income, the intertemporal nature of financial contracts and the reality of credit limits and of different interest rates for loans and deposits.

Incorporating the features often missed by analytic models makes a difference. In particular, the spread between the interest rates for deposits and loans means that it is sometimes optimal neither to save nor to borrow. This disintermediation creates extra modes in the long-run distribution of consumption. Simulations suggest that favourable interest rates help the household increase mean consumption and decrease its variability. These results strengthen the idea that formal finance and/or decreased transactions costs can improve the welfare of poor households. They do not, however, justify interventions in financial markets. All that is suggested is that benefits could be positive, though neither the level of benefits or that of costs has been measured.

REFERENCES

Adams, D.W. and Fitchett, D.A. (1994), *Informal Finance in Low-Income Countries*, Boulder: Westview Press.
Besley, T. (1995), 'Non-market Institutions for Credit and Risk-Sharing in Low-Income Countries', *Journal of Economic Perspectives*, 9, 115–27.
Binswanger, H.P. and Rosenzweig, M.R. (1986), 'Behavioral and Material Determinants of Production Relations in Agriculture', *Journal of Development Studies*, 22, 503–39.
Deaton, A. (1991), 'Savings and Liquidity Constraints', *Econometrica*, 59, 1221–48.
Deaton, A. (1992), 'Household Savings in LDCs: Credit Markets, Insurance and Welfare', *Scandinavian Journal of Economics*, 94, 253–73.
Dercon, S. (1992), *The Role of Assets in Coping with Household Income Fluctuations: Some Simulation Results*, Oxford: Centre for the Study of African Economies, University of Oxford.

Friend, I. and Blume, M.E. (1975), 'The demand for risky assets', *American Economic Review*, **65**, 900–22.

Helpman, E. (1981), 'Optimal Spending and Money Holdings in the Presence of Liquidity Constraints', *Econometrics*, **49**, 1559–70.

Hildreth, C. and Knowles, G.J. (1982), *Some estimates of farmers' utility functions*, Technical Bulletin 335, Agricultural Experiment Station, University of Minnesota.

Hubbard, R.G., Skinner, J. and Zeldes, S.P. (1994), 'Expanding the Life-Cycle Model: Precautionary Saving and Public Policy', *American Economic Review*, **84**, 174–9.

Judd, K.L. (1991), *Numerical Methods in Economics*, Stanford: Hoover Institution, Stanford University.

Kydland, F.E. and Prescott, E.C. (1982), 'Time to build and aggregate fluctuations', *Econometrica*, **50**, 1345–70.

Mendelson, H. and Amihud, Y. (1982), 'Optimal Consumption Policy Under Uncertain Income', *Management Science*, **28**, 683–97.

Miranda, M.J. (1994), *Lecture Notes on Dynamic Computational Economics*, Columbus: Department of Agricultural Economics, The Ohio State University.

Morduch, J. (1995), 'Income Smoothing and Consumption Smoothing', *Journal of Economic Perspectives*, **9**, 103–14.

Tobin, J. and Dolde, W. (1971), 'Wealth, liquidity and consumption', in Federal Reserve Bank of Boston (ed.), *Consumer spending and monetary policy: The linkage*, Boston: Federal Reserve Bank of Boston.

MANFRED E. KUHN AND MARK A.G. DARROCH*

*Factors Affecting Rural Medium-term Loan Repayment:
Evidence from a South African Development Finance Institution*

INTRODUCTION

Poor loan repayment performance experienced by many development finance institutions (DFIs) has placed an increasing financial burden on these agencies and governments, with default rates ranging from 27 to 60 per cent in African countries such as Ghana and Nigeria (Okorie, 1986). Lugemwa and Darroch (1995) reported a default rate of 40 per cent for small-scale seasonal credit borrowers at the Transkei Agricultural Bank. Without an adequate flow of funds, the capacity of the DFIs to provide more funds in the future is undermined, as financial success depends on a good loan recovery rate. Past African studies of loan repayment performance have focused on determinants of a binary loan outcome where loans were either current or in default. Loan repayment was positively related to factors such as timeliness of disbursement, enterprise profitability, additional sources of income, established previous loan history and lower client debt–asset ratios (Okorie, 1986; Vigano, 1993; Lugemwa and Darroch, 1995).

The above analyses ignore another dimension of the loan repayment problem, namely loans that are repaid in arrears. These can have considerable impacts on DFI liquidity management over time and hence should be considered when analysing loan repayment (Aguilera-Alfred and Gonzalez-Vega, 1993). To date, no research on loan performance in a DFI using multiple loan repayment categories has been done in South Africa. This study therefore aims to use a multiple category response model to estimate factors influencing medium-term loan repayment performance at a South African DFI (which for confidentiality purposes may not be named). This DFI is a parastatal organization financing small business, agricultural/rural development and housing predominantly in the former homeland areas of KwaZulu–Natal, South Africa. It obtains funds primarily from the Development Bank of Southern Africa at concessional interest rates, and has recently also begun actively to mobilize savings. Lenders often have limited information on borrowers and so may select clients who are more risky than they believe, leading to major repayment problems (the adverse selection problem) (Barry *et al.*, 1995). This study will

*University of Natal, Pietermaritzburg, South Africa. The financial assistance of the Centre for Science and Development (CSD) South Africa is gratefully acknowledged. Opinions expressed and conclusions reached are those of the authors and are not necessarily to be attributed to CSD.

therefore help the DFI to mitigate adverse selection by identifying characteristics of problem loans, and can also assist other DFIs in the region to improve selection procedures and reduce default rates. The lender–borrower relationship is first outlined, after which the model, results and policy implications are discussed.

THE PRINCIPAL–AGENT PROBLEM

Credit markets involve an exchange of money for a promise of repayment later. Consequently, there is a risk involved in such a transaction, with the risk being related to the level of information possessed by the two parties (Herath, 1994). An agency problem arises because the lender (principal) has insufficient information on borrower (agent) characteristics and the outcome of their investments. In addition, the principal is seldom able to monitor the actions of the agent perfectly and is therefore concerned with designing a contract which motivates the agent to act in the principal's interest. These contracts are seldom perfect since the principal has imperfect information on the agent's work effort and thus cannot ascertain whether poor performance on the part of the agent results from shirking or unfavourable external factors. Hence the agent is assumed to choose his action so as to maximize his expected utility given the structure of the reward function, while the principal selects a utility function that maximizes his own expected utility (Hayami and Otsuka, 1993).

The principal can limit divergencies from his objectives by establishing appropriate incentives (such as continued access to credit if the present loan is repaid) for the agent. The principal is also concerned with the ability of the agent to perform and successfully conclude the contract by timely repayment. To try to reduce adverse selection, the principal can devise a contract which will induce the desired self-selection by the agent (ibid.). Interest rates can be used to screen potential borrowers since they reflect the potential riskiness of the contract. Lenders may offer different loan contracts with different interest rates. Borrowers who are willing to pay higher interest rates may, on average, be worse risks because they perceive their probability of repayment to be low. However, increasing interest rates have a harmful effect on lenders' expected returns beyond some 'optimum' interest rate since the riskiness of the underlying pool of borrowers increases. Consequently, borrowers are rationed even if they are willing to pay higher interest rates to receive loans (Stiglitz and Weiss, 1981).

Development finance institutions face the additional problem of interest rate restrictions, whereby their interest rates are capped or subsidized below the optimum interest rate by governments wanting to make credit more accessible to the rural poor (Adams, 1984). This reduces the role of interest rates as a screening device and lenders have to resort to alternative means of screening borrowers. Loan contracts are thus adapted by many rural lenders to increase the indirect costs of lending by imposing more stringent collateral requirements and increasing the transaction costs through higher loan application fees and more frequent visits. Stricter collateral criteria have had limited success in development finance because many rural borrowers do not have sufficient collateral. Realization of the collateral in the event of default is also often very costly and politically not feasible, leading to the use of collateral substitutes such as third party guarantees and group lending (Nagarajan and Meyer, 1995). In addition to appropriate interest rates and collateral substitutes, lenders can limit adverse selection by improving client information using data on characteristics that they observe directly and independently of what applicants claim. The following section will discuss the empirical model used in the study to improve the information base for the local DFI.

EMPIRICAL ANALYSIS

Data sources

Two branches of the DFI, with major medium-term agricultural loan portfolios, were selected for the analysis as they could provide the most comprehensive information required for the study. Following Aguilera-Alfred and Gonzalez-Vega (1993), repayment performance over time was monitored to avoid distortions in delinquency measurement resulting from different loan maturities and portfolio growth rates. Primary information from 59 individual borrower dossiers was obtained for all medium-term agricultural loans disbursed in 1993 and 1994. The repayment status of these loans, at a selected cut-off date of 31 March 1996, was classified into three categories: (1) current or without repayment problems (all instalments paid within 30 days of the cut-off date); (2) paid with arrears (all instalments due paid within 30 to 90 days of the cut-off date); and (3) in default (with instalments still unpaid more than 90 days after the cut-off date). Of the 59 loans, 29 per cent were current, 17 per cent were in arrears and 54 per cent in default. A total of R1 408 000 was disbursed to the sample borrowers, with an average loan size at disbursal of R22 417, R38 116 and R20 179, respectively, for current, in arrears and default loans (1 Rand is currently equal to US$0.22). The main economic activities of the borrowers were chicken production, contract maize milling, contract timber and sugarcane harvesting and cartage, and contract ploughing and cartage. The nominal interest rates charged ranged from 14 per cent to 15 per cent, which is 4–5 per cent below the prime rate charged by commercial lending institutions.

Empirical model

The above empirical definition of loan repayment status implies that discrete regression models can be used to estimate determinants of the three loan categories. Both discriminant and logistic regression are well known techniques for analysing binary outcome data. Discriminant analysis can be extended to the multiple category case, but was not used because it requires that, within the groups, variables follow a multivariate normal distribution, with equal covariance matrices (Manly, 1986). Although the violation of this assumption will not necessarily lead to poor results, Press and Wilson (1978) recommended the logistic regression model because of its robustness in respect of the underlying distribution of the independent variables, which need not be multivariate normal. This is particularly useful if binary independent variables are used in the analysis. The maximum likelihood estimation of regression models with multiple category dependent variables is discussed by Madalla (1983). Given that P_j ($j = 1,....,3$) are the probabilities of each one of the three repayment categories occurring, the multinomial logit model can be expressed as:

$$ln\left(\frac{P_j}{P_1}\right) = \beta_{0j} + \beta_{1j}X_{1i} + ... + \beta_{kj}X_{ki} + \mu_{ji} \qquad (1)$$

for $j = 2,3$; and $i = 1, ... , n$, where P_1 is the probability of loans being current, P_2 of loans paid with arrears and P_3 of loans in default. The X_{ki} are vectors of explanatory variables, β_{kj} are estimated parameters, n is the number of observations and k is the number of explanatory variables. Loan repayment status was estimated as a function of the following loan, business and personal variables.

- Loan characteristics
  LSIZE = loan principal amount (Rands);
  OWNLN = borrower's direct equity contribution relative to loan size.
- Business characteristics
  CONTRACT = 1 if the borrower funded a chicken production or contract ploughing and cartage business venture, and 0 is the borrower funded a maize milling or timber/sugar-cane contract harvesting and transport business;
  LIQUID = present annual income relative to annual debt obligations.
- Personal characteristics
  PREVLN = 1 if the borrower has had previous loans with the DFI, and 0 if a first-time borrower;
  GENDER = 1 for male borrowers, and 0 for female borrowers.

A proxy variable for asset collateral relative to loan size was not included in the analysis because file information on asset values was not reliable (DFI staff constraints meant that asset value data were often not validated by visits to clients). As information on the monitoring activities of the lender, number of years the borrower had been in the business, borrower education and family size was often missing from borrower case files, the possible impact of these variables on loan performance could not be evaluated.

Lenders can reduce the risk of client default by spending more resources on loan evaluation and supervision, obviously increasing administration costs. Wealthier rural loan applicants with larger asset bases can reduce lender information collection costs by being able readily to pledge (verifiable) collateral. This could result in the concentration of loan portfolios amongst wealthy clients with larger loan sizes (Gonzalez-Vega, 1984). Lender behaviour could also be influenced by the applicant's resource allocation, risk management and product choices (Barry *et al.*, 1995). Consequently, more funds are available to investments having a better risk–return combination possibly due to better markets or higher product prices. Sample borrowers with larger loans had larger asset bases, were diversified, had investments with higher net returns and dealt in well established markets for their products. Wealthier borrowers may also be better able to withstand negative income shocks by drawing on their own assets and diverting fewer loan funds to personal consumption (Barham *et al.*, 1996). Loan size (LSIZE) as a proxy for larger, wealthier clients is expected to be negatively related to loan repayment problems.

Borrower's direct equity contribution relative to total loan (OWNLN) shows what the borrower has at stake in the proposed investment and reflects a risk-sharing agreement in which some of the risk of project outcome is borne by the borrower as an incentive to repay. This will not provide a first-best outcome since, as long as only part of the risk is borne by the borrower, he or she will equate his or her marginal cost of effort with his or her share and not the total marginal product of the investment (Hayami and Otsuka, 1993; Stiglitz and Weiss, 1981). If it partly motivates the borrower to try to ensure investment success, OWNLN could negatively affect loan repayment problems.

Data on the sector financed was included to account for the relative riskiness of different activities. Business ventures involving contract harvesting and carting of timber and sugar-cane had well established markets, while maize milling is a service in demand in the rural areas where maize is predominantly grown for consumption purposes. The more regular cash flows which result should improve the potential repayment ability of borrowers. Loans involving the purchase of tractors and implements, although offering attractive potential returns, were deemed more risky by loan staff because borrowers often failed to maintain equipment used for contracting services. Experience also shows that contractors involved in land preparation, such as ploughing, had liquidity problems because they seldom had enough work throughout the year (Ross, 1996). Chicken production enterprises, though they need relatively low capital outlay, faced intense competition, while increased feed costs and Newcastle disease have led to large losses and repayment difficulties. The CONTRACT variable should, therefore, be positively related to loan repayment problems.

Gross annual income relative to annual debt obligations (LIQUID) indicates borrowers' liquidity (ability to service the debt). The higher is LIQUID, the greater is the ability to repay loans on time. The previous use of DFI loans by the borrower (PREVLN) is used as a proxy for the extent of the lender–borrower relationship. The lender is likely to have more reliable information on established borrowers, while the borrower has a better knowledge of the lending procedures and late payment penalties imposed by the DFI (where the DFI does not refinance clients who default on previous loans). Clients having an established track record with the DFI are more likely to repay loans than new borrowers. The GENDER variable is also a potentially important dis-criminator. A general research finding about rural borrowers is that women have better repayment records (Christen *et al.*, 1994), so that GENDER (with a value of 1 for males) is likely to be positively related to loan repayment problems.

RESULTS

The multinominal logit parameter estimates are presented in Table 1. The residual deviance of 86.89 has a chi-squared distribution with 46 degrees of freedom, showing moderate lack of fit. However, the residual deviance is an unreliable indicator of goodness of fit where continuous variables are included in the logistic regression model (Collett, 1991). Logistic regression diagnostics, which included statistics to assess the influence of individual observations on the overall regression and individual parameter estimates (Hosmer and Lemeshow, 1989; Collett, 1991), showed no apparent lack of fit. An overall classification rate of 74 per cent was achieved, with 59 per cent of current loans, 50 per cent of arrears loans and 90 per cent of defaulters being predicted correctly.

The signs of the estimated coefficients mostly agree with *a priori* reasoning. For DFI lending policy purposes, larger loans and ploughing contractor businesses and broiler ventures are the key factors associated with payment in arrears $(ln(P_2/P_1)$. Although *a priori* expectations were that borrowers with larger loans would have fewer loan repayment problems, this result is mainly due to a few borrowers in the arrears category having bought expensive tractors and implements and not having enough contract work to fund loan repayment on time. The log odds of defaulting relative to being current $(ln(P_3/P_1)$ are greater for clients who are first-time borrowers, have modest loans, smaller own direct equity contributions, and manage contract ploughing or broiler ventures.

CONCLUSIONS

More stringent client monitoring and enforcement of loan contract provisions could reduce loan arrears and default at the institution studied. Business type is another factor for loan officers to consider, as ploughing contractors and broiler producers tended to repay in arrears and default. The contractors probably needed closer monitoring to ensure that equipment is properly maintained and sufficient income can be obtained to enable loan repayment, or they could be encouraged to diversify into contract transport (for example, sugar-cane, timber or inputs) to improve liquidity. Given increased competition and periodic disease outbreak, the lender should exercise caution when financing broiler production. Borrowers need to be made aware of the management requirements and should be encouraged to diversify to reduce price risk.

Results specific to this study sample suggest that clients with larger loans are less likely to default. Such loans tended to be associated with more (verifiable) collateral, lower administration costs per unit of credit and probably better quality information on potential investment returns. Increasing the owner's equity stake in the business increases the share of the risk borne by the client and provides a stronger incentive for loan repayment. Although this measure is a second-best option, it can be an alternative when collateral is an ineffective means of enforcing loan contracts. Borrowers having an established record with the bank tended to repay their loans, highlighting the importance

TABLE 1 *Parameter estimates of the multinomial logit model*

Variable	CONSTANT	LSIZE	OWNLN	CONTRACT	LIQUID	PREVLN	GENDER
$ln(P_2/P_1)$	34.93474	0.00009*	-1.15182	4.33428*	0.091111	-1.93530	-1.64722
	(0.74)	(1.78)	(-0.88)	(1.77)	(1.48)	(-1.33)	(-1.10)
$ln(P_3/P_1)$	67.04195	-0.00005*	-9.29282**	1.84108*	-0.02078	-2.08309**	-1.58103
	(1.53)	(-1.58)	(-2.09)	(1.74)	(-0.41)	(-1.95)	(-1.21)

Notes: t-statistics in parentheses; * and ** indicate significance at 10% and 5% levels, respectively; Madalla's pseudo $R^2 = 0.4307$; McFadden's pseudo $R^2 = 0.2805$

362

of reputation in a borrower–lender relationship. Local DFIs need to be flexible in designing suitable contracts and criteria for client selection to promote viability and continued outreach into rural areas. Finally, the study identifies key extra information such as asset value and education level which must be captured, and verified, in borrower case files to assess how these factors affect loan repayment performance.

REFERENCES

Adams, D.W. (1984), 'Are the arguments for cheap agricultural credit sound?', in D.W. Adams, D.H. Graham and J.D. von Pischke (eds), *Undermining Rural Development with Cheap Credit*, Colorado: Westview Press.

Aguilera-Alfred, N. and Gonzalez-Vega, C. (1993), 'A multinominal logit analysis of loan targeting and repayment at the Agricultural Development Bank of the Dominican Republic', *Agricultural Finance Review*, 53, 55–64.

Barham, B.L., Boucher, S. and Carter, M.R. (1996), 'Credit constraints, credit unions and small scale producers in Guatemala', *World Development*, 24, 793–806.

Barry, P.J., Ellinger, P.N., Hopkin, J.A. and Baker, C.B. (1995), *Financial Management in Agriculture*, Chicago, Illinois: Interstate Publishers.

Christen, R.P., Rhyne, E. and Vogel, R.C. (1994), 'Maximising the outreach of microenterprise finance: The emerging lessons of successful programmes', IMCC Paper No. 6860.

Collett, D. (1991), *Modelling Binary Data*, London: Chapman and Hall.

Gonzalez-Vega, C. (1984), 'Credit rationing behaviour of agricultural lenders', in D.W. Adams, D.H. Graham and J.D. von Pischke (eds), *Undermining Rural Development with Cheap Credit*, Colorado: Westview Press.

Hayami, Y. and Otsuka, K. (1993), *The Economics of Contract Choice: An Agrarian Perspective*, New York: Oxford University Press.

Herath, G. (1994), 'Rural credit markets and institutional reform in developing countries: Potential and problems', *Savings and Development*, 18, 169–91.

Hosmer, D.W. and Lemeshow, S. (1989), *Applied Logistic Regression*, New York: John Wiley & Sons.

Lugemwa, W.H. and Darroch, M.A.G. (1995), 'Discriminant analysis of seasonal agricultural loan repayment by small-scale farmers in Transkei', *Agrekon*, 34, 231–4.

Madalla, G.S. (1983), *Limited-dependent and Qualitative Variables*, New York: Cambridge University Press.

Manly, B.J.F. (1986), *Multivariate Statistical Methods: A Primer*, Bristol: J.W. Arrowsmith.

Nagarajan, G. and Meyer, R.L. (1995), *Collateral for loans: When does it matter?*, Economics and Sociology Paper No. 2207, Department of Agricultural Economics and Rural Sociology, Ohio State University.

Okorie, A. (1986), 'Major determinants of agricultural smallholder loan repayment in a developing economy: Empirical evidence from Ondo State, Nigeria', *Savings and Development*, 10, 89–99.

Press, S.J. and Wilson, S. (1978), 'Choosing between logistic regression and discriminant analysis', *Journal of the American Statistical Association*, 73, 699–705.

Ross, K. (1996), 'Personal communication', head of rural development for branch of study, Development Finance Institution.

Stiglitz, J.E. and Weiss, A., (1981), 'Credit rationing in markets with imperfect information', *American Economic Review*, 71, 393–410.

Vigano, L. (1993), 'A credit scoring model for development banks: An African case study', *Savings and Development*, 17, 441–79.

CONTRIBUTED PAPERS

Methodology

HANS LÖFGREN AND SHERMAN ROBINSON*

The Mixed-complementarity Approach to Specifying Agricultural Supply in Computable General Equilibrium Models

INTRODUCTION

In computable general equilibrium (CGE) models, it is typically assumed that agricultural resources are smoothly substitutable in neoclassical production or cost functions, with flexible wages, rents and prices generating market equilibrium in a setting with full resource employment.[1] Although this specification is often adequate, it is also often inadequate, especially when the analysis focuses on resource allocation and production technology issues. With more disaggregation, which is becoming common in CGE models with an agricultural focus, the use of smooth, twice-differentiable, production or cost functions to specify agricultural technology is increasingly unrealistic. The purpose of this paper is to show how CGE models formulated as non-linear mixed-complementarity (MC) problems can incorporate alternative, more realistic, specifications of agricultural technology and supply, drawing on the extensive literature on mathematical programming models applied to agriculture.[2]

First, we present a stylized standard neoclassical CGE model, which is then extended to a CGE–MC format to include Leontief (activity analysis) technology, endogenous determination of the market regime for agricultural factors (unemployment or full employment) and inequality constraints on agricultural factor use. In an analysis of reduced agricultural water supplies in Egypt, it is then shown how such a model can generate realistic results concerning water use and productivity that cannot be captured in a standard CGE model. The main conclusion is that, in analyses focused on agricultural supply issues, CGE–MC models that selectively incorporate features from the mathematical programming literature offer a powerful alternative to standard models. The underlying producer optimization problems for the different situations are presented in an Appendix.

THE STANDARD CGE APPROACH TO TECHNOLOGY AND FACTORS

Table 1 presents a stylized neoclassical CGE model which, like most of those in the literature, is formulated as a system of simultaneous equations, all of

*International Food Policy Research Institute, Washington, DC, USA.

TABLE 1   *A stylized CGE model*

Equation

1    $q_s^s = NC(q_{fs}^f) \quad s \in S$

2    $q_{s's}^{int} = \alpha_{s's}^s q_s^s \quad s' \in S, s \in S$

3    $p_s^{va} = p_s^s - \sum_s p_s^s \alpha_{s's}^s \quad s \in S$

4    $w_{fs}^s = \dfrac{\partial q_s^s}{\partial q_{fs}^f} p_s^{va} \quad f \in F, s \in S$

5    $w_{fs}^s = \overline{w}_{fs}^{dist} w_f \quad f \in F, s \in S$

6    $q_s^h = NC\left(\sum_s p_s^{va} q_s^s, p_s^s \right) \quad s \in S$

7    $q_s^s = q_s^h + \sum_{s'} q_{ss'}^{int} \quad s \in S$

8    $\overline{q}_f^f = \sum_s q_{fs}^f \quad f \in F$

9    $\overline{p} = \prod_s \Omega_s p_s^s$

Notation

Sets

$s, s' \in S$ sectors (commodities)

$f, f' \in F$ factors

Variables

p_s^s price for sector s

p_s^{va} value-added price for sector s

q_s^h quantity of household demand for output of sector s

q_s^s quantity of output for sector s

q_{fs}^f quantity of demand for factor f from sector s

$q_{s's}^{int}$ quantity of intermediate demand for commodity s' from sector s

w_f wage of factor f

w_{fs}^s wage of factor f in sector s

Note: The letters in the column #Eq. refer to the number of elements in the corresponding sets. The domains of some equations (and related variables) are smaller than indicated if each sector does not use all factors or intermediate input commodities. The producer problem is presented in optimization form in the Appendix.

Description	#Eq.	Var.
Sectoral production	S	q_s^s
Intermediate input demand	$S \cdot S$	$q_{s's}^{int}$
Value-added price	S	p_s^{va}
Factor demand	$F \cdot S$	q_{fs}^f
Sectoral factor prices	$F \cdot S$	w_{fs}^s
Household demand	S	q_s^h
Commodity market	S	p_s^s
Factor market	F	w_f
Cost-of-living index	1	—

Parameters

$\alpha_{s's}^s$	quantity of intermediate input s' per unit of output in sector s
Ω_s	household expenditure share for sector s
$\bar{p}$	cost of living index
$\bar{q}_f^f$	supply of factor f
w_{fs}^{fdist}	relative wage distortion for factor f in sector s

Functions

NC	neoclassical function

which are strict equalities. The model is highly simplified – government, foreign trade and savings-investment are omitted – to focus on producer technology and resources.

Producers in each sector maximize profits given their technology, specified by a nested neoclassical value-added function (with factor inputs as arguments) and fixed (Leontief) intermediate input coefficients (equations 1–4). (The underlying producer optimization problems for this and following models are presented in the Appendix.) The treatment of agriculture is the same as for other sectors. Exogenous relative gaps between sectoral factor rents (wages) are permitted (equation 5). Households receive all factor incomes and spend it on the basis of neoclassical demand functions, derived from utility maximization subject to an income constraint (equation 6). The markets for factors and commodities are in equilibrium 7–8) with flexible wages and prices as equilibrating variables. Production techniques are assumed to be sufficiently flexible to ensure that fixed aggregate factor supplies are always fully employed at positive prices. Equation 9 fixes a measure of the aggregate price level, the cost-of-living index, defining the *numéraire*. Given that the real side of the model is homogeneous of degree zero in prices, the model can only determine relative prices. In Table 1, the number of equations exceeds the number of variables by one — with the exception of the last equation, the last column of Table 1 pairs each equation with a variable of identical dimension. However, given Walras' law, one of the equations is functionally dependent. The model has an equal number of variables and independent equations, and a unique solution can almost invariably be found.

A model with this structure (or variations on the theme: for example, with neoclassical substitutability for intermediate inputs) has proved itself to be a dependable workhorse. It is well-behaved, can be implemented with a small data set, and is almost invariably solvable, generating a solution with strictly positive prices. In some contexts, however, it has serious drawbacks – in particular, if the analysis is focused on agricultural technology and resource questions. Neoclassical production functions exaggerate the smoothness of real-world input substitutability and preclude tests of the attractiveness of discontinuous technical alternatives, for example introducing new crop varieties. When viewed from a disaggregated perspective, land and water resources are often unemployed, with zero prices.

In many contexts, these shortcomings can be overcome, or mitigated, if the agricultural supply module of the CGE model incorporates features that are standard fare in agricultural mathematical programming models, such as Leontief technology and inequality constraints for resources and other production aspects. Pathbreaking work in this area is due to Keyzer, who developed a tailor-made algorithm for solving general equilibrium models with complementarity relationships used to capture regime shifts in foreign trade and storage policies (Fischer *et al.*, 1988; Keyzer *et al.*, 1992). Up to this point, such mixed complementarity (MC) CGE models have rarely been used to model the agricultural supply side. Recent advances in computational technology make it possible to solve CGE–MC models at reasonable cost. In the next section, we give a simple example of such a model, with a treatment of agricultural supply that draws on the agricultural mathematical programming literature.

AN AGRICULTURAL CGE–MC MODEL

An MC model consists of a set of simultaneous (linear or non-linear) equations that are a mix of strict equalities and inequalities, with each inequality linked to a bounded variable in a complementary-slackness condition (Rutherford, 1995). Such models are familiar to economists because the Kuhn–Tucker optimality conditions define a mixed-complementarity problem (which is necessary and sufficient for a global optimum for nearly all well-behaved economic linear and non-linear optimization models, including agricultural sector mathematical programming models). Indeed, all programming models can be written as MC problems. From the perspective of this paper, a CGE–MC model can incorporate features found in agricultural mathematical programming models, with inequalities, which cannot readily be captured in strict equality simultaneous equation systems. For example, it is easy to incorporate resource unemployment (with associated zero wages), crop rotations, self-sufficiency production targets, stocking targets and credit rationing.

Table 2 shows a simple CGE–MC model, which is an augmented version of the stylized model in Table 1.[3] Equations with the same number as in Table 1 are unchanged except for slight notational and domain adjustments. New equations are numbered with single or double asterisks. As opposed to the model of Table 1, each sector may generate more than one commodity, with the quantities determined by fixed yield coefficients (equation 1'). This extension is particularly useful when crop–livestock interactions matter.

The model distinguishes between sectors (or activities, the set S) and commodities (produced by sectors, the set C). Sector returns per unit activity are given by the sum of commodity prices times yield coefficients (equation 3'). The model also makes a distinction between (agricultural) sub-factors (the set $FSUB$, here land and water) and factors (the set F), one or more of which are aggregates of the sub-factors (here one of the factors is a land/water aggregate). Sub-factor demand is a Leontief function of the level of the aggregate land/water factor (equation 4'); that is, land and water are used in fixed proportions in the production of a given crop. For each sub-factor, there is an upper limit on the supply share that may be allocated to any single sector (equation 4''). In any applied model, the domain of this equation and associated variables should be constrained to relevant sub-factor–sector combinations. The price of the aggregate land/water factor is a linear function of the prices of the sub-factors and a penalty variable (equation 5'). The penalty variable (or scarcity price) takes on a positive value when needed to ensure that the sub-factor constraint is not violated. More specifically, it enters the complementary slackness condition linked to the sub-factor constraint (equation 4''): if the constraint is (not) binding, the penalty is positive (zero). The market equilibrium conditions of the sub-factors (equation 8') are inequalities linked to the corresponding prices in complementary slackness conditions: if the price is positive, the resource is fully employed; if it is zero, unemployment is permitted. (Cf. the note at the bottom of Table 2.) Accounting for one dependent equation, the model has an equal number of variables and independent equations.

TABLE 2   *A stylized CGE–MC model*

	Equation

1     $q_s^s = NC(q_{fs}^f) \quad s \in S$

1' $q_c^c \sum_s \gamma_{cs} q_s^s \quad c \in C$

2     $q_{cs}^{int} = \alpha_{cs}^s q_s^s \quad c \in C, s \in S$

3     $p_s^{va} = p_s^s - \sum_c p_c^c \alpha_{cs}^s \quad s \in S$

3' $p_s^s = \sum_c \gamma_{cs} p_c^c \quad s \in S$

4     $w_{fs}^s = \dfrac{\partial q_s^s}{\partial q_{fs}^f} p_s^{va} \quad f \in F, s \in S$

4' $q_{fs}^{fsub} = \alpha_{fs}^{fsub} q_{f's}^f \quad f \in FSUB; s \in S; f' = land / water$

4'' $\Psi_{fs}^{max} \bar{q}_f^{fsub} \geq q_{fs}^{fsub} \quad f \in FSUB, s \in S \quad [w_{fs}^{max} \geq 0]$

5     $w_{fs}^s = \bar{w}_{fs}^{dist} w_f \quad f \in FF, s \in S$

5' $w_{f's} = \sum_{f \in FSUB} \alpha_{fs}^{fsub} \left(w_f^{sub} + w_{fs}^{max} \right) \quad s \in S, f' = land / water$

6     $q_c^h = NC\left(\sum_s p_s^{va} q_s^s, p_c^c \right) \quad c \in C$

7     $q_c^c = q_c^h + \sum_s q_{cs}^{int} \quad c \in C$

8     $\bar{q}_f^f = \sum_s q_{fs}^s \quad f \in FF$

8' $\bar{q}_f^{fsub} \geq \sum_s q_{fs}^{fsub} \quad f \in FSUB \quad [w_f^{sub} \geq 0]$

9     $\bar{p} = \prod_s \Omega_s p_s^s$

1* $\sum_f w_{fs}^s \alpha_{fs}^f \geq p_s^{va} \quad s \in S \quad [q_s^s \geq 0]$

4* $q_{fs}^f = \alpha_{fs}^f q_s^s \quad f \in F, s \in S$

New notation

Sets

$c \in C$	commodities
$f, f' \in FF (\subset F)$	factors without sub-factors (all except land/water)
$f \in FSUB$	sub-factors (land, water; sub-factors to land/water aggregate)

Variables

p_c^c	price for commodity c
q_c^c	quantity (production level) for commodity c
q_{fs}^{fsub}	quantity of demand for sub-factor f in sector s
q_{cs}^{int}	quantity of intermediate demand for commodity c from sector s
w_f^{fsub}	wage of sub-factor f
w_{fs}^{max}	penalty on sub-factor f in sector s

Note: Equations with same number as in Table 1 are unchanged except for domain changes. Equations 1* and 4* replace 1 and 4 for a model with Leontief technology also for all factors. Variables entering the associated complementary slackness condition are provided in brackets after the inequalities; for example, the following complementary slackness condition is linked to equation 8' and the lower bound on

Description	#Eq.	Var.
Sectoral production	S	q_s^s
Commodity production	C	q_c^c
Intermediate demand	$C \cdot S$	q_{cs}^{int}
Value-added price	S	p_s^{va}
Sector price	S	p_s^s
Factor demand	$F \cdot S$	q_{fs}^f
Sub-factor demand	$FSUB \cdot S$	q_{fs}^{fsub}
Sub-factor constraint	$FSUB \cdot S$	w_{fs}^{Max}
Sectoral factor price	$FF \cdot S$	w_{fs}^s
Sectoral sub-factor price	S	$w_{lw,s}^s$
Household demand	C	q_s^h
Commodity market	C	p_c^c
Factor market	FF	w_f
Sub-factor market	$FSUB$	w_f^{sub}
Cost-of-living index	1	—
Leontief first-order condition for profit-max. (replacing 1)	S	q_s^s
Leontief factor demand (replacing 4)	$F \cdot S$	q_{fs}^f

Parameters

α_{fs}^f	quantity of factor f per activity unit in sector s
α_{fs}^{fsub}	quantity of sub-factor f per unit of factor f in sector s
α_{cs}^s	quantity of intermediate input c per unit of output in sector s
Ω_c	consumption expenditure share for commodity c
γ_{cs}	yield of commodity c per activity unit in sector s
ψ_{fa}^{Max}	maximum share of the supply of factor f used in sector s
$\bar{q}_f^{fsub}$	supply of sub-factor f

the sub-factor price:

$$w_f^{sub}\left(\bar{q}_f^{fsub} - \sum_s q_{fs}^{fsub}\right) = 0, f \in FSUB.$$ The two producer problems are presented in optimization form in the Appendix.

Alternatively, Leontief technology may be extended to all factors by substituting equations 1* and 4* for equations 1 and 4. The new profit-maximization condition, with the associated complementary slackness condition, states that marginal value-added product is less than or equal to the marginal factor cost and that, if the sector activity is positive, marginal value-added product and marginal cost are equal. This condition is written as an inequality to allow the specification of several activities for each 'crop' (combination of commodity outputs), some of which may not be operated. If the model is limited to one activity per crop, the range of input substitutability would typically be understated. While it is feasible to permit multiple outputs for sectors in a standard CGE model, allowing factor unemployment, constraints on factor use and the use of Leontief technology, all involving inequality constraints, requires an MC formulation.

AN APPLICATION TO EGYPT

In order to demonstrate the significance of the MC approach to CGE modelling, we here briefly present results from experiments using a dynamic (recursive) CGE–MC model of Egypt with a detailed treatment of agriculture.[4] The model is solved for 1990 (the base year), 1993 and 1995, and every five years thereafter until 2020. Apart from being dynamic, this model differs from the stylized model in Table 2 in that it portrays an open economy with a more complete set of domestic institutions (including government and enterprise sectors), as well as investment and savings.

The agricultural supply side of the model quite closely follows the basic version of Table 2 (that is, the one with activity analysis technology limited to sub-factors). One difference is that the land sub-factor is disaggregated by season (summer and winter). Hence crops may be classified according to whether they use water in summer, winter, or in both seasons (for perennials). Upper limits on sub-factor use are only imposed for cotton use of summer land: following Egypt's standard crop rotation, cotton is not permitted to occupy more than one-third of the land not covered by perennial crops. An additional equality constraint (with an associated penalty variable) makes sure that the areas for cotton and a short winter clover crop (typically preceding cotton) are equal. Outside agriculture, an MC formulation is used for labour to permit endogenous choice of market regime (unemployment or full employment). The model is solved in GAMS, using PATHS or MILES, two solvers for MC problems.[5]

One set of experiments explored the impact of a gradual reduction of agricultural water supplies, reflecting some combination of reduced supplies from the Nile or the transfer of increasing volumes to non-agricultural sectors. In the experiments, agricultural water supplies were reduced in steps of 10 per cent, with declines ranging from zero to 60 per cent, taking place gradually between 1990 and 2020. At the aggregate level, the impact is quite manageable. As the cut in water supplies changes from zero to 60 per cent, annual growth in real GDP at factor cost for 1990–2020 falls from 5.2 to 4.8 per cent. However, the impact on the agricultural sector is more severe: its annual growth rate falls

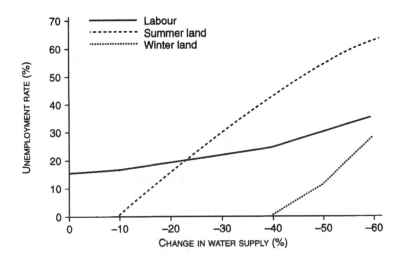

FIGURE 1 *Factor unemployment rates with reduced water supplies, tiger scenarios*

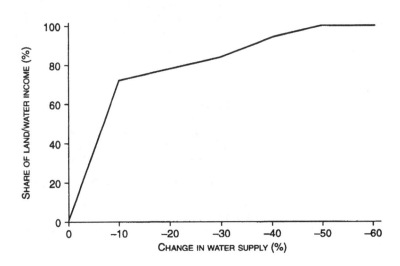

FIGURE 2 *Water share in total land/water income, tiger scenarios, 2020*

from 3.5 to 2.0 per cent. At the micro level, the mix between labour, capital and, for crop activities, a land/water aggregate is driven by profit maximization subject to a CES function. Given this flexibility, the marginal return to the land/water aggregate is always positive. It is allocated to the land/water sub-factors (water, winter land and summer land) some, but not all, of which may be slack.

Figure 1 shows that, with no cut in water supplies, both land types are fully employed in 2020 while the labour unemployment rate is 15 per cent. When the water supply cut has reached 10 per cent, summer land is taken out of production. Part of the winter land becomes idle when the cut exceeds 40 per cent. For labour, unemployment increases gradually from 15 per cent for no water cut to 34 per cent when the water cut reaches 60 per cent. Accordingly, Figure 2 shows that, as water becomes scarce and excess supplies emerge for both land types, the water share in total land/water income gradually moves from zero to 100 per cent: that is, while initially water has excess supply and a zero rent, it eventually becomes binding while both types of land become partly unemployed, with zero rent. In this model, endogenous determination of the factor market regime (unemployment or full employment) is highly significant. In the background, inequality constraints on the cropping pattern ensured that the production structure remained agronomically feasible.

CONCLUDING REMARKS

In analysis focused on agricultural supply issues, CGE–MC models, which selectively incorporate features from the mathematical programming literature, offer a powerful alternative to standard approaches. The strength of the CGE–MC formulation is that it can capture critical aspects of the institutional and technological structure of agricultural production. Moreover, this is one of the rare occasions when the lunch is free – there is no sacrifice of other features, including the treatment of foreign trade and policy tools, that have made CGE models attractive.

NOTES

[1]Early CGE models specified sectoral production functions and derived factor demand functions. Many models now start with cost or profit functions. Chambers (1988) discusses the use of cost functions in agriculture. Computationally, the approaches are essentially identical.

[2]See Agrawal and Heady (1972) and Hazell and Norton (1986).

[3]The model in Table 2 draws on formulations in Robinson and Gehlhar (1996) and Löfgren *et al*. (1996).

[4]For additional details, including discussion of the 'tiger' and 'turtle' scenarios (the former is mentioned in the figures), see Löfgren *et al*. (1996).

[5]For GAMS, see Brooke *et al*. (1988). Rutherford (1995) provides more information on PATH and MILES.

REFERENCES

Agrawal, R.C. and Heady, E.O. (1972), *Operations Research Methods for Agricultural Decisions*, Ames, Iowa: Iowa State University Press.

Brooke, A., Kendrick, D. and Meeraus, A. (1988), *GAMS: A User's Guide*, Redwood, California: The Scientific Press.

Chambers, R.G. (1988), *Applied Production Analysis*, Cambridge, Mass: Cambridge University Press.

Fischer, G., Frohberg, K., Keyzer, M.A. and Parikh, K.S. (1988), *Linked National Models: A Tool for International Food Policy Analysis*, International Institute for Applied Systems Analysis, Boston: Kluwer Academic Publishers.

Hazell, P.B.R. and Norton, R.D. (1986), *Mathematical Programming for Economic Analysis in Agriculture*, New York: Macmillan.

Keyzer, M., van Veen, W. and Tims, W. (1992), 'The SOW Applied General Equilibrium Model', in E. Thorbecke (ed.), *Adjustment and Equity in Indonesia*, Paris: OECD Development Centre.

Löfgren, H., Robinson, S. and Nygaard, D. (1996), *Tiger or Turtle? Exploring Alternative Futures for Egypt to 2020*, Discussion Paper 11, Trade and Macroeconomics Division, August, Washington, DC: International Food Policy Research Institute.

Robinson, S. and Gehlhar, C.G. (1996), Impacts of Macroeconomic and Trade Policies on a Market-Oriented Agriculture', in L.B. Fletcher (ed.), *Egypt's Agriculture in a Reform Era*, Ames, Iowa: Iowa State University Press.

Rutherford, T. (1995), 'Extensions of GAMS for Complementarity Problems Arising in Applied Economic Analysis', *Journal of Economic Dynamics and Control*, **19**, 1299–1324.

APPENDIX

In the CGE models in the main body of the paper, the equations relevant to producer behaviour are written in the form of first-order conditions. We will here present the underlying producer optimization problems using the same notation as in Tables 1 and 2. In the model of Table 1, the producer in sector S (agricultural or non-agricultural) is represented by equations 1–4. Producer technology is specified as a nested neoclassical value-added function and fixed (Leontief) intermediate input coefficients. In condensed form, the optimization problem for the producers in sector S is to select q_{fs}^f for $f \in F$ so as to maximize

$$\pi_s = p_s^s NC(q_{fs}^f) - \sum_{s' \in S} p^s \alpha_{s's}^s NC(q_{fs}^f) - \sum_f w_{fs}^s q_{fs} \qquad (A1)$$

where π_s is profit in sector S. In the process of embedding producer behaviour in the full CGE model, new equations defining $q_s^s, q_{s's}^{int}$, and p_s^{va} are added (equations 1–3 in Table 1) while the first-order condition (derivative of (A1) with respect to q_{fs}^f set to zero) is rearranged and simplified (equation 4).

In Table 2, two alternative CGE–MC model versions are presented. For the first, behaviour and technology for sector S is represented by equations 1, 2, 3, 3', 4, 4', 4'', 5'. The new elements in producer technology are (1) that one of the arguments in the value-added function is a land/water aggregate, made up of land and water in fixed proportions; and (2) a constraint on sectoral factor use that may reflect agronomic considerations or policy. The condensed version of the underlying profit-maximization problem for S is to select q_{fs}^f for $f \in F$ so as to maximize

$$\pi_s = \sum_{c\in C} p_c^c \gamma_{cs} NS(q_{fs}^f) - \sum_{c\in C} p_c^c \alpha_{cs}^s NC(q_{fs}^f) - \sum_{f\in F} w_{fs}^s q_{fs}$$

$$- \sum_{f\in FSUB} \sum_{f'=lw} w_f^{sub} \alpha_{fs}^{fsub} q_{f's}^f \tag{A2}$$

subject to

$$\sum_{f'=lw} \alpha_{fs}^{fsub} q_{f's}^f \le \Psi_{fs}^{max} \bar{q}_f^{fsub} \quad f\in FSUB$$

where

$$lw = \text{land/water}$$

In Table 2, the first-order conditions (derivatives of the Lagrangean with respect to q_{fs}^f and w_{fs}^{max}, the constraint function multiplier, both set to zero) are manipulated and simplified to yield equations 4 and 4″, drawing on definitions of $q_s^s, q_{cs}^{int}, p_s^{va}, p_s^s, q_{fs}^{fsub}$ and w_{fs}^s (the latter for f = land/water aggregate), represented by equations 1, 2, 3, 3′, 4′ and 5′.

In the second model version in Table 2, with Leontief technology for all inputs (factors and intermediates), equations 1* and 4* replace 1 and 4. The optimization problem for sector S producers is to select q_s^s so as to maximize

$$\pi_s = \sum_{c\in C} p_c^c \gamma_{cs} q_s^s - \sum_{c\in C} p_c^c \alpha_{cs}^s q_s^s - \sum_{f\in F} w_{fs}^s \alpha_{fs}^f q_{fs} - \sum_{f\in FSUB} \sum_{f'=lw} w_f^{sub} \alpha_{fs}^{fsub} \alpha_{f's}^f q_s^s$$

subject to equation (A2). The full CGE–MC representation of the producer problem is found by adding the same definitions as for the preceding problem, with the exception that an equation is needed for q_{fs}^f (4*) instead of q_s^s. After manipulation, the first-order conditions (derivatives of the Lagrangean with respect to q_s^s and w_{fs}^{max} set to zero) can be restated as 1* and 4″.

JESÚS ANTÓN*

Explaining Stocks and Export Subsidies in Agriculture

INTRODUCTION

In the agricultural markets of many developed countries, notably in the European Union (EU), governments finance, or have financed, very expensive policies of guaranteed prices for producers. The guarantee means that the government, normally acting through a specialized agency, isolates the national market with two types of interventions: those designed to deal with internal excess supply or demand, and those which involve imposition of a variable tax/subsidy on exports/imports. This type of government behaviour is the rule in several commodity regimes within the EU's Common Agricultural Policy (CAP) and it is also common in other developed countries.

The classical objective of government action is to stabilize farmers' incomes through action on prices, even if this effect is controversial (Anderson, 1996). In many markets the accumulation of stocks is also important. For this paper the interest lies in explaining government rationality when (1) the country concerned is an exporter, with the guaranteed national price being above the autarky price, (2) variable subsidies are provided for exporters, with the national price being above world price, and (3) the intervention agency has accumulated a high level of stocks, which may grow. One of the main objectives is to consider whether the presence of imperfect competition may add some rationality to the situation described in points (1), (2) and (3). Of course such a situation is not uncommon; it has been observed in some world agricultural markets during recent years, especially in the case of wheat (Antón, 1997). International trade theory does, in fact, suggest that there is a case for unilateral intervention in trade and that export subsidies may be rational (Brander and Spencer, 1985; Eaton and Grossman, 1986; Klette, 1994). This could occur if there is market power: if national exporters are behaving in a collusive manner, in the world market, export subsidies may force them into 'more aggressive' behaviour which may be beneficial. Export subsidies are explained here using similar reasoning. Government support of a high internal price works as a 'catalyser' for a cartel of many relatively small producers, who could not otherwise obtain a common 'high' price. Furthermore, if the government did not subsidize exports, output would be sold in the national market or to the government agency, and exports would be zero. Market power also gives

*Universidad Complutense, Madrid, Spain.

an explanation for stock changes which differ from what might be expected
with short-run price speculation (Blakeslee and Lone, 1995).

The first oligopoly models for the wheat market, due to McCalla (1966) and
Alaouze *et al.* (1978), did not link internal price decisions with those concerning export subsidies. Internal market decisions, now, are usually modelled
using a policy preference function (Sarris and Freebairn, 1983; Paarlberg and
Abbott, 1986; Johnson *et al.*, 1993), despite the identification problems involved in the methodology (von Cramon-Taubadel, 1992). Baffes (1993) points
out that the policy preference function approach requires that some conditions
are imposed on the group weights for the second-order condition to hold.

This paper develops a model in which there are links between the two
approaches appearing in the literature. Internal and external agricultural policy
decisions are modelled under the assumptions of a homogeneous product and
imperfect competition. The rational explanation of the behaviour of a government which subsidizes its export and stores part of its internal excess supply
requires both a bias in government preferences and price power in the world
market. The model is for a two-stage non-cooperative oligopoly. In Stage 1, the
most rigid decision is taken; it relates to the internal price. In Stage II, the most
flexible variable is decided; that is, the total for exports, which cannot exceed
the addition of excess supply plus stocks from the past. The solution will be a
sub-game perfect equilibrium obtained using backward induction. There may
be two kinds of links between the stages: the price decided in Stage I determines the maximum level of exports in Stage II; and earnings from exports in
Stage II may create an incentive for a high price and excess supply in Stage I.
The links do not necessarily exist.

STAGE II: THE WORLD MARKET

To develop the complete general model, a number of assumptions are needed
concerning government agricultural policy.

Assumption 1: national price policy

All intervention policy is determined by fixing a guaranteed price for national
producers. The government will defend this internal price using two kinds of
action. First, it will buy any internal excess supply at that price and will meet
any excess demand from stocks. Second, if the guaranteed price P_i is above the
world price P_w, the government may subsidize exports or tax imports, covering
the price difference. This mechanism isolates the national market from any
world market shock.

In Stage II, governments of different exporting countries compete in the
world market. Stage I decisions create a ceiling for the exports of each country
which is equal to the excess supply plus the carry-over stocks.

Assumption 2: world excess demand function

We assume that the rest of the net importer countries generate a world excess demand defined by:

$$P_w = f(X) \quad \text{with} \quad f'(X) < 0. \tag{1}$$

The inverse world excess demand function, including demand from all net importers, is decreasing.

Assumption 3: a seller's world market

World demand is competitive, while supply is represented by a constant conjectural variations oligopoly (Iwata, 1974). Total transport cost is a linear function of total exports:

$$CTX_i = c_i x_i. \tag{2}$$

Exporting to the world market in Stage II does not add any production costs to the exporting country, since government will purchase the excess supply anyway, from Assumption 1. The only relevant marginal exporting cost is for transport. Export decisions are made taking into account only two elements, namely, income from world market exports $(P_w x_i)$ and transport costs linked to exports $\{CTX_i (x_i)\}$. The government tries to maximize export earnings,[1] subject to exports being less than or equal to excess domestic supplies:

$$\frac{MaxEE_i}{x_i} = P_w \cdot x_i - CTX_i(x_i) \quad \text{s.t.} \quad x_i < ES_i^*. \tag{3}$$

Whenever the restriction is not binding, this market is just a standard oligopoly leading to an optimal export quantity x_i^*. The indirect objective function when the restriction is not binding can also be calculated. The complete indirect objective function depends on excess supply ES_i^* derived from Stage I:

$$EE_i^* = x_i \cdot (P_w - c_i) = \begin{cases} x_i^* \cdot [P_w - c_i] \text{ if } x_i^* \leq ES_i^* \\ ES_i^* \cdot [P_w - c_i] \text{ if } x_i^* > ES_i^* \end{cases} \tag{4}$$

The discrimination between these two alternative forms can be done using Proposition 1 (with $P_w^i = P_w - c_i$).

Proposition 1: necessary and sufficient condition for optimal storage Storing part of the crop would be optimal in Stage II $(0 < x_i^* < ES_i^*)$ if and only if government oligopolist market power (the capacity for changing world price) is high enough in terms of the absolute value of the elasticity:

$$\left| \varepsilon_{P_w^i, x_i}(ES_i^*) \right| > 1. \tag{5}$$

Proof:

$$Max(P_w^i \cdot x_i) \Rightarrow x_i^* = -\frac{P_w^i}{\delta P_w^i / \delta x_i}; \quad x_i^* < ES_i^* \Leftrightarrow \left| \varepsilon_{P_w^i, x_i}(ES_i^*) \right| > 1$$
$$x_i$$

Using this result, each net exporter can be classified by the value of the above elasticity, which represents the perceived power of each country over world prices. We can differentiate between two kinds of exporters.

Competitive fringe of exporters or 'fringe' with $\varepsilon_{P_w^i, x_i}(ES_i^*) \leq 1$. These countries are not able to modify world price substantially. Therefore they export all their excess supply and they take advantage of high prices without reducing their exports. The relevant excess demand function in Assumption 2 is calculated subtracting Fringe's supply from world importer's demand.

Oligopolist exporters or 'oligopoly' with $\varepsilon_{P_w^i, x_i}(ES_i^*) > 1$. In this group of sufficiently powerful exporters, each country reduces its exports and stores part of its crop. The group as a whole is able to determine the world price, given the residual excess demand function.

STAGE I: NATIONAL MARKET

In Stage I (national market), we assume general demand and supply functions representing the aggregation of the competitive behaviour of a large number of consumers and producers.

Assumption 4: demand function in each country

The quantity demanded in each country is a decreasing function of the national price.

$$q_i^d = q_i^d(p_i) \text{ with } \delta q_i^d(p_i)/\delta p_i < 0.$$

Assumption 5: supply function in each country

The quantity supplied in country is an increasing function of the national price.

$$q_i^s = q_i^s(p_i) \text{ with } \delta q_i^s(p_i)/\delta p_i > 0.$$

Assumption 6: government behaviour

Additionally, we define government behaviour using a political preference function (PPF) approach. Government internal price policy defined in Assumption 1 is based on the attempt to maximize the weighted sum of producer surplus, consumer surplus and taxpayer loss (budget costs):

$$\underset{p_i}{Max}\, PPF_i(p_i, x_i) = \alpha \cdot PS_i + \beta \cdot CS_i - \gamma \cdot BC_i. \tag{6}$$

Using Hotelling's Lemma, the derivative of the indirect profit function is just the Marshallian supply function; that is, $PS_i(p_i)$ is an increasing and convex function. Consumer surplus may be measured by the expenditure function; using Shephard's Lemma, it can be shown that its derivative is just minus one times the Marshallian demand and the function $CS_i(p_i)$ is decreasing and convex. The budget costs are $BC_i(p_i) \cdot ES_i(p_i) - EE_i^*$. Changes in budget costs are more difficult to sign and can be written as:

$$\frac{\delta BC_i}{\delta p_i} = p_i \cdot \left[\frac{\delta q_i^s}{\delta p_i} - \frac{\delta q_i^d}{\delta p_i} \right] + (q_i^s - q_i^d) - \frac{\delta EE_i^*}{\delta p_i}. \tag{7}$$

Using the results above we can derive the first-order condition for programme (6). This condition may be written (we assume second order conditions hold[2]) as:

$$\alpha \cdot q_i^s - \beta \cdot q_i^d - \gamma \cdot \left\{ (q_i^s - q_i^d) + \left[\frac{\delta q_i^s}{\delta p_i} - \frac{\delta q_i^d}{\delta p_i} \right] \cdot p_i \right\} = 0$$

if $x_i^* < ES_i^* \Leftrightarrow \left| \varepsilon_{P_w^i, x_i} \right| > 1$

$$\tag{8}$$

$$\alpha \cdot q_i^s - \beta \cdot q_i^d - \gamma \cdot \left\{ (q_i^s - q_i^d) + \left[\frac{\delta q_i^s}{\delta p_i} - \frac{\delta q_i^d}{\delta p_i} \right] \cdot \left[p_i - P_w^i - \frac{\delta P_w}{\delta x_i} \cdot (q_i^s - q_i^d) \right] \right\} = 0$$

if $x_i^* \ge ES_i^* \Leftrightarrow \left| \varepsilon_{P_w^i, x_i} \right| \le 1$.

It can be proved that both equations in (8) become identical whenever $\left| \varepsilon_{P_w^i, x_i} \right| = 1$.

CONDITIONS FOR OPTIMAL
STORAGE AND EXPORT SUBSIDIZING

Bias in government preferences

Proposition 2   In the context of an oligopoly defined in Assumptions 1 to 6, a government with no preference bias ($\alpha = \beta = \lambda$) will never have an optimal policy leading to a net exporter position involving an export subsidy, and/or the storage of part of the crop. The proof can easily be obtained assuming that the weights given to the three groups of agents are equal to unity, with α

= β = λ = 1, and analysing the first-order condition (8) for each net exporter case. The existence of a bias in the preferences of the government (for instance, a bias in favour of producers) is required in order to obtain an optimum with an export subsidy and/or with some storing. In this static framework of analysis, bias towards producers is a necessary condition to be an active oligopolist; power over price is not enough. The incompatibility between government group indifference and export subsidies is due to the fact that the national market is assumed to be competitive; Eaton and Grossman (1986) prove that export subsidies can be optimal only if the exporting firm is not competitive.

Market power

It is not possible to obtain an analogous proposition about the incompatibility between lack of market power and the same two properties of the optimum. But from Proposition 1 we know that lack of power is not compatible with optimal storing. However, export subsidies are compatible with lack of price power in the world market; this can be proved with an example (for instance, a linear model with rigid supply and $\beta_i = \gamma_i = 1$); this lack of market power by government is not understood by farmers, who are willing to sell their output at the guaranteed price.

BASIC COMPARATIVE STATICS

In order to obtain comparative statics results about the optimal internal price in each country the implicit function theorem is applied to the first-order condition (8). For any exogenous parameter k, we know that

$$\frac{\delta p_i^*}{\delta k} = \frac{\delta(8)/\delta k}{\delta(8)/\delta p_i} \Leftrightarrow sign(\frac{\delta p_i}{\delta k}) = sign(\delta(8)/\delta k),$$

since $\delta(8)/\delta p_i < 0$ is just the second-order condition. From the derivative of expression (8), we can easily sign the comparative statics. Table 1 presents some of these results for an exporting country. The columns headed with world price and internal supply refer to the particular cases of perfectly elastic world demand and rigid internal supply, respectively. The signs obtained all have an intuitive underlying explanation in terms of internal and external incentives. The main difference between a fringe exporter and an active oligopolist is the result of world price power, which has a negative effect on the internal price of a fringe exporter, but a zero effect on the internal price of an oligopolist. The last column shows that the optimal price increases when a rigid domestic supply expands; this is true whenever $\alpha > \gamma$ because additional supply creates additional incentives to increase price through the effect of the producer's surplus on the PPF. These incentives more than offset disincentives arising from budget costs. The results from Table 1 can be used to illustrate a number of points.

TABLE 1   *Comparative statics of an exporter's optimal price (sign of $\delta p_i^*/\delta k$)*

K=	World market		Government preferences			National market	
	$\left|\dfrac{\delta P_w}{\delta x_i}\right|$	$P_w = P_w^0$	α	β	γ	$\left|\dfrac{\delta q_i^s}{\delta p_i}\right|$	$q_i^s = q_i^0$
$\left|\varepsilon_{P_w^i,x_i}\right| \in (0,1)$ Subsidy	−	+	+	−	−	−	−/+
(Fringe) Tax	−	+	+	−	−/+	−/+	−/+
$\left|\varepsilon_{P_w^i,x_i}\right| \geq 1$ Subsidy	0¹		+	−	−	−	+²
(Oligopoly) Tax	0¹		+	−	−	−	+²

Notes: ¹There are no marginal changes in price incentives when exporting marginal conditions change since in this case export earnings are independent of internal prices.
²The price effect of an expansion in a rigid supply would be zero if $\alpha = \gamma$, but if $\alpha > \gamma$ as assumed, a higher price will increase the value of the PPF once supply has grown.

How does optimal storing begin?

An active participation in the oligopoly requires that a country store part of its production. Proposition 1 suggested that this storage will be optimal if and only if world price power is sufficiently high:

$$\left|\varepsilon_{P_w^i,x_i}(ES_i^*)\right| = \underbrace{\left[-\frac{\delta P_w}{\delta X}\cdot\frac{\delta X}{\delta x_i}\right]}_{=e(1+\lambda_i)>0}\cdot\frac{ES_i^*}{P_w - c_i} = e\cdot(1+\lambda_i)\frac{ES_i^*(p_i^*)}{P_w - c_i} > 1,$$

where $\lambda_i = \partial(X - x_i)/\partial x_i$ is the standard conjectural variation measure of the degree of collusion. Excess supply is a monotonically increasing function of the internal price, but the world price is not an increasing function of internal price. Therefore the elasticity shown above is a monotonically increasing function of internal price. Shifts in some parameters may lead to a fringe country having enough price power to be an 'active' oligopolist. There are four cases.

(1) Changes in the internal market, or in government preferences, which may increase the optimal internal price and excess supply. An example would be an increase in the government weighting preference for producers α, though it has to be borne in mind that α has a ceiling determined by the second-order condition.

(2)   Changes in the world market, including increases in the rigidity of demand or price power of a government, represented by parameters e and $1 + \lambda_i$.
(3)   Reductions in the degree of collusion, leading to a fall in world price. The competitive fringe members behave as 'free-riders': they can export at higher prices without contributing anything to achieve them. The lower the oligopoly price, the lower the incentive to free-ride.
(4)   Increases in the marginal costs of transport which reduce optimal exports: the countries with higher export costs have more incentive to participate in the oligopoly.

The two key variables in determining oligopoly participation are the power to change world price represented by $(1 + \lambda_i)$ and the preference towards producers. If these two parameters have high enough values, the country concerned will participate in the oligopoly. Figure 1 shows the values of these two parameters corresponding to 'oligopoly' and competitive 'fringe', assuming all other parameters remain constant. The decreasing line $\in = 1$ represents the values above which a country would be an active oligopolist. There are two necessary conditions in order to be an oligopolist, namely some government bias for producers' welfare ($\alpha > 1$) and some capacity to change world price ($e > 0$). However, these are not sufficient conditions; reduced values of both parameters will make the specified country a member of the competitive fringe. The line α_{Max} represents the second-order condition when demand and supply

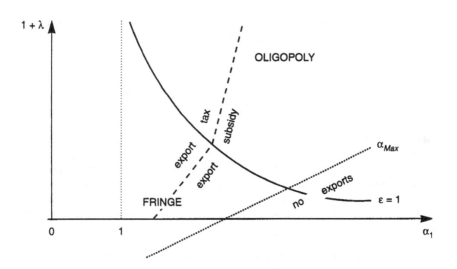

FIGURE 1   *Fringe v. oligopoly/tax v. subsidy*

are linear; all the values above the line guarantee that the second-order condition holds. Changing from the 'fringe' to the 'oligopoly' may happen when price power and/or government bias are high enough, or if one of the parameters increases enough to compensate for a reduction in the other.

When is an export subsidy optimal?

An export subsidy will be optimal whenever $p_i^* > p_w^i$. The minimum preference required for an export subsidy to be optimal is smaller, the smaller the market power; this positive relationship has a kink at $\varepsilon_{p_w^i, x_i} = 1$ (see Figure 1).[3] Changing from taxing exports to subsidizing them may happen when there is an increase in government bias or a fall in price power. Four different areas can be identified in Figure 1, combining oligopoly/fringe as well as tax/subsidy behaviour. Export subsidies and stocks will be simultaneously optimal whenever government bias α is high enough and world price power e is not too high or too low.

A SIMULATION EXAMPLE

In this section the results are illustrated briefly with a numerical simulation. It is assumed there is a world market, with four exporting countries actively participating in the oligopoly. The model is linear. The world residual demand function[4] is $P_w = 40 - X$; all four countries have identical internal demand and supply, $q_i^d = 50 - 3 \cdot p_i$ and $q_i^s = 30$; marginal export costs are constant and identical, so that $c_i = c = 1$ and all countries have Cournot behaviour $(1 + \lambda_i = 1)$. The focus is on changes of α_i and $(1 + \lambda_i)$ in a single country, assuming the other three remain participants of the oligopoly. The results appear in Table 2.

When there is no bias in government preferences ($\alpha_i = 1$), stocks and/or subsidies can never be optimal (Proposition 2); furthermore, storage cannot be an optimal choice if $\alpha_i \leq 1.67$; additionally, positive net exports are guaranteed when $\alpha_i > 1.67$. For values of α_i in the interval 1.67 to 1.84, stocks and subsidies can be optimal for appropriate market power, but never simultaneously; on the contrary, in the interval 1.84 to 1.98, stocks and subsidies can be optimal at the same time whenever the market power parameter $(1 + \lambda_i)$ belongs to a determined open interval. Finally, if $\alpha_i \geq 1.98$, subsidies are optimal for any value of market power, but there is still a lower bound which ensures stocks will also be optimal.

For instance, if $\alpha_i = 1.84$ and $1 + \lambda_i = 1.5$, this leads to exports exactly equal to the excess supply with no need of any subsidy. If $1 + \lambda_i = 4$ (collusive behaviour), stocks will become positive while exports will be taxed. For the intermediate value $\alpha_i = 1.9$, both stocks and subsidies can become optimal if market power also has an intermediate value such as $1 + \lambda_i = 1.59$; but stocks also become zero when market power fall to 1.14 and subsidies change into taxes for higher values such as $1 + \lambda_i = 4$. When the preference bias is high enough, as for $\alpha_i > 2$, subsidies are always optimal,

Jesús Antón

TABLE 2   *An Example*

Areas of optimal storage and subsidy

α_i	Stock	Subsidy	Comments
$\alpha_i = 1$	No	No	Never stock
$1 < \alpha_i \leq 1.67$	No	$1 + \lambda_i <$ upper bound	Never stock
$1.67 < \alpha_i \leq 1.84$	$1 + \lambda_i >$ lower bound	"	or subsidize
$1.84 < \alpha_i < 1.98$	$1 + \lambda_i >$ lower bound	$1 + \lambda_i <$ upper bound	Possibly both
$\alpha_i \geq 1.98$	"	Yes	Always subsidize

Calculating optimal stocks and subsidies

α_i	$1 + \lambda_i$	Stock	Subsidy
1.84	1.59	0	0
1.84	4	2.99	−0.75
1.9	1.14	0	1
1.9	1.59	1.71	0.57
1.9	4	4.71	−0.18
2	0.72	0	2.7
2	1	2.2	2.2

but optimal storage requires $\alpha_i > 0.72$, which is more competitive than the Cournot solution.

CONCLUSIONS

This paper underlines some interactions between internal and world market in the case of a homogeneous commodity with price intervention in national markets. In this context, persistent 'low' prices in the world market are compatible with the existence of market power. Under internal price isolation, in Assumption 1, production costs are opaque for international trade and they have no influence on export marginal costs, which are the only relevant costs. Therefore the world price can be low with respect to production costs in oligopoly countries.

There are two key determinants of the world market position for each country: the perceived price power and government preferences towards producers. The existence of market power is not sufficient to induce active participation in the world market oligopoly; perceived capacity to change world price should be high enough in elasticity terms ($|\varepsilon_{P_w^i, x_i}| > 1$). This condition implicitly requires some bias in government preferences. Biased preferences are also a necessary condition for storage to be optimal. A numerical simulation underlines the sensitivity of optimal policy to small changes in preferences bias parameter α.

Internal policies have great influence on the structure of international trade flows, not only in the determination of export shares, but also in determining which countries export and which import. Government preferences may be much more significant than production efficiency. Though the issue is one for empirical measurement, the potentially distorting effects of policy can be enormous.

NOTES

[1]We assume that storage costs are zero. Relaxing this assumption, with linear storing costs such as $SC = a \cdot (q_i^s - q_i^d - x_i)$ included in the expression for the budget costs, has no significant effects on the results. Optimal excess supply would be smaller and exports higher, but the signs of the comparative statics hold. Assuming non-linear storage costs may eliminate the possibility of indefinite building of stocks. Other policies, such as the EU's set-aside, may also prevent ever-growing stocks; these types of policy may be induced by international trade rules.

[2]Baffes (1993) studies the conditions under which the second-order conditions hold when markets are competitive. He considers two national policy instruments instead of just one, and he states conditions on the groups' weights for different concavity assumptions on demand and supply functions. Even under perfect competition it is difficult to ensure that the second-order conditions hold. However, we can find interesting cases for which they do; for instance: $\alpha > 1 = \beta = \gamma$. Additionally assuming rigidity of supply and linear demand ensures that this condition is satisfied. The government bias towards agricultural producers has usually been explained as a bias in favour of the inhabitants of rural areas.

[3]A 'Fringe' exporter will find that higher market power reduces the incentive for a higher internal price, leading to a lower excess supply and a higher world price; these effects may be compensated by a larger α, which increases optimal internal price and reduces P_w; an active oligopolist will find no effect of price power on internal price and no effect of α on P_w, but the sign of the relationship will be the same.

[4]The absolute value of the elasticity of residual demand is around 0.3 in all cases, not far from the estimate for wheat in Antón (1997).

REFERENCES

Alaouze, C.M., Watson, A.S. and Sturgess, S. (1978), 'Oligopoly Pricing in the World Wheat Market', *American Journal of Agricultural Economics*, **60**, 173–85.

Anderson, R.W. (1996), 'Trade and storage', in D. Martimort (ed.), *Agricultural Markets: Mechanisms, Failures and Regulations*, Amsterdam: Elsevier.

Antón, J. (1997), 'Oligopolio de Gobiernos en el Mercado Mundial de Trigo', *Investigación Agraria-Economía*, **12** (3).

Baffes, J. (1993), 'Optimal tax/subsidy intervention in commodity markets when the groups of interest are weighted unequally', *European Review of Agricultural Economics*, **20**, 365–78.

Blackeslee, L. and Lone, J.A. (1995), 'Modelling optimal grain marketing decisions when prices are generated autoregressively', *European Review of Agricultural Economics*, **22**, 87–102.

Brander, J.A. and Spencer, B.J. (1985), 'Export Subsidies and International Market Share Rivalry', *Journal of International Economics*, **18**, 83–100.

Cramon-Taubadel, S. von (1992), 'A Critical Assessment of the Political Preference Function Approach in Agricultural Economics', *Agricultural Economics*, **7**, 371–94.

Eaton, J. and Grossman, G.M. (1986), 'Optimal Trade and Industrial Policy under Oligopoly', *Quarterly Journal of Economics*, **101**, 383–406.

Iwata, G. (1974), 'Measurement of Conjectural Variations in Oligopoly', *Econometrica*, **42**, 947–66.

Johnson, M.A., Mahé, L. and Roe, T.L. (1993), 'Trade compromises between the European Community and the U.S.: an interest group–game theory approach', *Journal of Policy Modeling*, **15**, 199–222.

Klette, T.J. (1994), 'Strategic Trade Policy for Exporting Industries: More General Results in the Oligopolistic Case', *Oxford Economic Papers*, **46**, 296–310.

McCalla, A.F. (1966), 'A Duopoly Model of World Wheat Pricing', *Journal of Farm Economics*, **48**, 711–27.

Paarlberg, P.L. and Abbott, P.C. (1986), 'Oligopolistic Behavior of Public Agencies in International Trade: The World Wheat Market', *American Journal of Agricultural Economics*, **68**, 528–42.
Sarris, A.H. and Freebairn, J. (1983), 'Endogenous Price Policies and International Wheat Prices', *American Journal of Agricultural Economics*, **65**, 214–24.

BRADFORD L. BARHAM AND JEAN-PAUL CHAVAS*

Sunk Costs and Resource Mobility:
Implications for Economic and Policy Analysis

INTRODUCTION

Unfettered resource mobility is crucial in obtaining a Pareto-optimal allocation of resources in a Walrasian economy. Accordingly, government interventions in markets are often seen as distorting or restricting the fluid movement of resources, thereby limiting the effectiveness of competitive markets to achieve an efficient allocation. Recently, the inherent mobility of a broad class of resources, including many investments in physical and human capital, has been questioned by a large body of theoretical and empirical research on sunk costs and market performance (Baldwin and Krugman, 1989; Chavas, 1994; Dixit and Pindyck, 1994; Pindyck, 1991; Sutton, 1991; Tirole, 1989; Dixit, 1992). Sunk costs occur whenever investment expenditures cannot be fully recovered in the case of later disinvestment. The resulting immobility of capital raises questions about the efficiency of markets and the role of private and public institutions in mitigating the ill-effects of sunk costs.

The effects of sunk costs and imperfect resource mobility on the agricultural and food sector warrant more attention than they have received to date. While Johnson and Quance (1972) raised the issue in their seminal work on 'asset fixity', the implications of sunk costs for many key questions in agricultural economics remain unexplored. This paper focuses on agricultural markets and trade policy, showing how they can distort economic outcomes and how institutional and policy innovations might improve welfare outcomes when factor mobility is impeded.

Initially, the paper will review the causes of sunk costs, suggesting reasons why they may be more prevalent than is commonly perceived by economists. Discussion of a dynamic model of investment behaviour in the presence of sunk costs, giving different outcomes from those of a standard competitive model, will follow. The next section considers when sunk costs are, and are not, subject to management by private or public agents. The paper concludes with an exploration of the way sunk costs could affect agricultural market performance and trade policy.

*University of Wisconsin-Madison, USA.

THE MEANING AND ORIGINS OF SUNK COSTS

An investment cost is considered sunk when it cannot be fully recovered through transfer or sale once the investment has been undertaken. The extent of sunk costs, therefore, depends on the difference between the value of the original investment (minus any depreciation) and its salvage value – resale or transfer price. What factors increase original investment costs or reduce salvage values?

Physical characteristics of investment that make it specific to a given site, time, firm or industry are perhaps the most well known cause of sunk costs. An investment is site-specific when its physical features make it costly to install, remove or relocate, as in the case of structures and infrastructure. It is time-specific when its value deteriorates sharply after a given time period (as with perishables, or inputs with time-sensitive productivity). It is firm or industry-specific when its features make it costly to retrofit or transfer to other firms or industries. In many cases, even slight adjustments of the product or service produced by a given investment may require major adjustment costs that re-duce its salvage value.

Secondly, *transaction costs* are an important source of sunk costs, since they can increase original outlays and reduce salvage values. Examples are worker hiring, training and retention, negotiating transfers, transport costs, informa-tional asymmetries among buyers and sellers and accumulated experience or goodwill with suppliers or buyers.

Thirdly, *the 'investment package effect'* arises when a given investment is vital to the salvage value of other investments. Thus, even if it can be trans-ferred at a high salvage value, its mobility may be limited by its role in the salvage value of other investments.

Finally, *the 'same boat effect'* occurs when the simultaneous efforts of economic agents to sell off similar investments drive down salvage values, thereby increasing sunk costs. This effect is most likely when down-side risks in an industry or region are widely felt, and prompt agents to sell off what might otherwise be readily transferable investments.

The likely presence of positive gaps between the original value and salvage value of investments is a more common feature than is often recognized in economic analysis and needs to be explored.

THE ECONOMICS OF SUNK COSTS

Consider an agent involved in an economic activity requiring an investment decision. Let x_t be the amount of investment made by the agent at time t. This investment contributes to increasing the amount of capital controlled by the agent, as given by the following state equation:

$$y_t = (1-\delta)y_{t-1} + x_t \geq 0, \tag{1}$$

where y_t is the amount of capital at time t, and δ is the depreciation rate of capital. In the case where capital y_t is a necessary input for a given economic activity, $y_t > 0$ (= 0) means that the agent participates (does not participate). Then the agent enters at time t whenever $y_{t-1} = 0$ and $y_t = 1$. Alternatively, the agent exits at time t when $y_{t-1} > 0$ and $y_t = 0$. Understanding the agent's investment behaviour provides all the information needed to understand entry–exit behaviour.

At the time t, the agent generates profit $\pi_t = R(y_t, e_t) - C(x_t)$, where $R(y_t, e_t)$ denotes revenue, e_t is a random vector reflecting revenue uncertainty faced by the agent at time t and $C(x_t)$ denotes cost. Substituting equation (1) into the function yields $\pi_t = R(y_t, e_t) - C(y_t - (1 - \delta)y_{t-1})$. The agent's budget constraint is:

$$w_t = A(w_{t-1}) + R(y_t, e_t) - C(y_t - (1 - \delta_t)y_{t-1}) - z_t, \tag{2}$$

where w_t is the agent's monetary wealth at time t, $A(w_{t-1})$ is the return at time t on wealth w_{t-1}, and z_t is a consumption good assumed to have unit price.

Let the objective function of the agent be represented by the expected discounted utility $E\Sigma_{t-1}^{T}\beta^t U_t(z_t)$, where E is the expectation operator, T is the length of the planning horizon, β is the time-preference discount factor ($0 < \beta > 0$) and $U_t(z_t)$ is the agent's von Neumann–Morgenstern utility function at time t. This allows for risk neutrality (when $U_t(z_t)$ is linear) as well as risk aversion (when $U_t(z_t)$ is strictly concave). The agent's economic rationality is then represented by the maximization of $E\Sigma_{t-1}^{T}\beta^t U_t(z_t)$, subject to equations (1) and (2). Assuming learning over time, this can be expressed as the following dynamic programming problem:

$$V_t(w_{t-1}, y_{t-1}) = \max_{z_t, y_t}\{E_t U_t(z_t) + \beta E_t V_{t+1}(A(w_{t-1}) + R(y_t, e_t)$$

$$- C(y_t - (1 - \delta)y_{t-1}) - z_t, y_t)\}, \tag{3}$$

$t = T, T-1, \ldots, 2, 1$, where $V_t(w_{t-1}, y_{t-1})$ is the value function, and E_t is the expectation operator based on the information available to the agent at time t. Equation (3) is Bellman's equation defining $V_t(w_{t-1}, y_{t-1})$ recursively from backward induction.

Consider here the case where the investment decision x_t is unrestricted in sign: it can be positive ($x_t > 0$) when the agent invests, zero ($x_t = 0$) when the agent is inactive in the capital market, or negative ($-(1 - \delta)y_{t-1} \le x_t < 0$) when the agent disinvests at time t. The following assumption is made about the cost function $C(x, \cdot)$.

Sunk cost assumption: The cost function $C(x, \cdot)$ satisfies:

$$[\delta C / \delta x \text{ given any } x > 0] \text{ is greater than } [\delta C / \delta x) \text{ given any } x < 0] \quad \text{(A1)}$$

and

$$C(x, \cdot) > |C(-x, \cdot)| \ge 0 \text{ for any } x > 0. \tag{A2}$$

(A1) and (A2) simply state that the cost of acquiring capital is always larger than the value of its disposal. This difference represents *sunk costs*, and might stem from a transaction cost associated with the transfer of the capital. Our assumption implies that investment cost is (at least partially) sunk both in terms of marginal cost (as stated in (A1)) and in terms of total cost (as stated in (A2)). This is illustrated in Figure 1, where

$$C(x) \; = px \quad \text{if } x \geq 0,$$
$$= sx \quad \text{if } x < 0,$$

p being the unit purchase of price of x, s being the unit selling price (or salvage value) of x and $p > s$. Then $(p - s)$ is the *unit sunk cost of investment*, that is the unit cost of investment that cannot be recovered in the event of a later disinvestment.

The first-order conditions for an interior solution with respect to (z_t, y_t) in (3) are:

$$\delta E_t U_t / \delta z_t - \beta \partial E_t V_{t+1} / \partial w_t = 0, \text{ and} \qquad (4a)$$

$$\partial E_t V_{t+1} / \partial y_t - (\partial E_t V_{t+1} / \partial w_t)(\partial C / \partial x_t) = 0. \qquad (4b)$$

Assuming $(\partial E_t U_t / \partial z_t) > 0$, substituting (4a) into (4b) yields the following optimal investment rule:

$$\beta(\partial E_t V_{t+1} / \partial y_t)/(\partial E_t U_t / \partial z_t) = \partial C / \partial x_t. \qquad (5)$$

This is the *standard neoclassical result* stating that, at the optimum, the marginal present value product of capital, $\beta(\partial E_t V_{t+1} / \partial y_t)/(\partial E_t U_t / \partial z_t)$, must equal the marginal cost of investment, $\partial C / \partial x_t$.

What are the implications of this decision rule when investment is (at least partially) sunk? Assuming that the random variable e_t becomes observable at time t, its realized value e_t shifts $E_t V_{t+1}$. It follows that the marginal value of capital shifts in some unpredictable fashion over time. Equation (5) then generates four possible investment regimes at time t, depending on the level of marginal present value of capital, $\beta(\partial E_t V_{t+1} / \partial y_t)/(\partial E_t U_t / \partial z_t)$ and the gap between original investment cost and its salvage value. These are illustrated in Figure 1, where the investment marginal cost is equal to the unit purchase price p under investment $(x_t > 0)$ and to the salvage value s under disinvestment $(x_t < 0)$, with $p > s$.

In regime 1, the marginal value product of capital is high and cuts the investment marginal cost curve in the positive region, implying that it is optimal for the agent to invest $(x_t^1 > 0)$. In regime 2, the marginal value product of capital is at an intermediate level. The agent has no incentive to invest or disinvest $(x_t^2 > 0)$. In this zone of 'asset fixity', the agent's behaviour is unaffected by small changes in the economic environment because of the gap between the original cost and the salvage value of investing. In regime 3, the marginal value product of capital is low, and the agent disinvests $(-(1-\delta)y_{t-1} < x_t^3 < 0)$. Finally, regime 4 corresponds to a very low marginal product of capital, where total disinvestment leads to the agent's exit $(x_t^4 = -(1-\delta)y_{t-1})$.

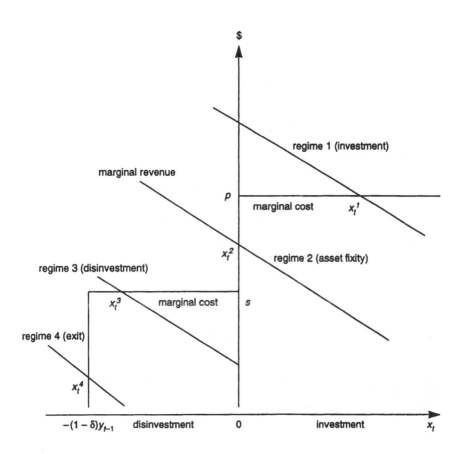

FIGURE 1   *Investment behaviour under sunk costs*

The first implication of this analysis is the existence of a 'zone of *asset fixity*' corresponding to regime 2 (Johnson and Quance, 1972), where it is optimal for the agent not to react to economic signals. Consequently, the agent has no economic incentive to participate in the capital market.

The second concerns the nature of dynamic adjustments. Sunk costs generate *irreversible behaviour* and *hysteresis*. Hysteresis is characterized by irreversible effects where particular changes are not reversed after their original cause is removed. To illustrate, consider an agent in regime 2 in period t, in regime 1 in period $t + 1$, and back in regime 2 in period $t + 2$. There would be an investment in period $t + 1$, but no disinvestment in period $t + 2$, even though the original signal generating the incentive to invest in $t + 1$ was reversed in $t + 2$.

The third implication relates to the *adverse effects of risk on investment* under sunk costs (see Dixit and Pindyck, 1994; Chavas, 1994). Consider a situation where an investor has a positive probability of exiting during the planning horizon. In the presence of sunk costs, this means that the investor also faces a positive probability of paying the sunk cost in the case of later disinvestment: the larger the sunk cost and the higher the probability of facing them, the stronger is the disincentive to invest. This implies the existence of key interactions between risk and sunk cost as adversely affecting investment incentives. Such effects can hold irrespective of the agent's risk preferences and across a wide range of economic environments (Chavas, 1994).

The fourth implication is a corollary to the third. To the extent that entry requires investment, it follows that sunk cost and risk interact with each other to provide *negative incentives to enter*. In other words, sunk cost and risk constitute entry barriers under very general conditions.

The fifth implication relates to the incentive to exit. Consider an agent who is disinvesting (exiting) and has a positive probability of reinvesting (re-entering) over the rest of the planning horizon. In the presence of sunk costs, the agent will have a positive probability of facing the sunk cost in the case of later reinvestment (re-entry): thus, the larger the sunk cost, the higher the probability of facing them, the less the incentive to disinvest (exit). This reveals another vital interaction between risk and sunk costs in that *they reduce the incentive to disinvest and to exit*.

Sunk costs and risk interact to *reduce resource mobility* since they adversely affect both the incentive to invest and/or enter and the incentive to disinvest and/or exit. In this sense, sunk cost and risk are sufficient conditions to invalidate the standard competitive market equilibrium. Since such conditions appear prevalent in the real world, this suggests a need to examine in more detail their implications for resource allocation, contract and institutional design, and policy prescription.

THE MANAGEMENT OF SUNK COSTS

The knowledge that interactions between sunk costs and risk adversely affect efficient resource allocation raises two issues, namely whether sunk costs and risks are subject to management and if so, how and by whom.

Firstly, sunk costs may be subject to private management. For example, private investment in education and training can reduce the specificity of human capital and thus improve the mobility of labour. Another example is provided by the use of private contractual arrangements which reduce the uncertainty associated with sunk assets. Examples in agriculture include production and marketing contracts or vertical integration schemes commonly found in the fruit and vegetable industry. In these cases, contracts appear to be a superior means of allocating resources, compared with reliance on typical produce markets, primarily because contracts are more effective in controlling quality and managing timing, especially for perishable items.

Secondly, sunk costs may be subject to public management. A simple example is the case of transport costs, which can be reduced by public investment in infrastructure. Another is public investment in education, training, research and market information. The case of sunk investments in research and information collection is especially interesting because efforts to acquire information can involve major sunk costs and uncertainty for private agents, especially those in developing countries. Government support for such investments, via coordination and assistance with inter-firm information sharing, can reduce the sunk costs and uncertainty involved, stimulating investment in learning and increasing resource mobility and productivity improvements (see Pack and Westphal, 1986, for discussion of the case of East Asia).

Thirdly, in some cases sunk costs may not be subject to direct public or private management, yet they may be made manageable indirectly by reducing the probability that agents will have to face them. In other words, one way of managing the adverse effects of resource immobility is to reduce the exposure to down-side risk problems faced by agents most affected by sunk costs. Examples include private insurance, social 'safety nets' (including food aid and welfare programmes), price support programmes (such as minimum wage legislation) and limited liability rules. Properly directed, such features reduce exposure to down-side risk and limit the adverse effects of sunk costs on resource allocation.

SUNK COSTS AND AGRICULTURAL ECONOMICS

Agriculture is greatly affected by potentially sunk costs. Investments in land, buildings and equipment, crops, animals or human capital are all affected, to varying degrees, and the implications for farm sector performance may be far-reaching. There are five such implications which can be considered briefly.

First, *new technology adoption* requires investments not only in physical equipment but also in learning, management and handling new relationships. All involve some irreversibility and uncertainty, the extent depending on inherent features of the new technology and the price–cost conditions of the activity to which it is applied. Saha *et al.* (1994) and Purvis *et al.* (1995) explore the discouraging effects on adoption of irreversibility and uncertainty. Arguably, some of the US agriculture's impressive productivity growth since the 1950s stems from investments in technologies which might not have been adopted were it not for the reduction in down-side risk afforded by commodity price floors.

Second, *the entry and exit behaviour of farmers* is likely to be affected since adjustment processes may be slow in agricultural activities where sunk costs and uncertainty are present. Thus, during the price and profitability declines suffered by US agriculture in the 1980s, existing farmers were probably less likely to leave the industry than they would have been in the absence of sunk costs. Alternatively, in more recent years, potential entrants may have been discouraged by the growing down-side risk associated with declining government price supports. Indeed, in the future, there could be periods of high prices and profits before entry and investments become sufficient to expand supply and bring prices down, unless other risk-reducing arrangements emerge as substitutes.

Third, *prices of goods whose production involves high sunk costs are likely to be more volatile* than those with low sunk costs. Structuralists have long argued that primary product prices are more volatile than other sectors because of their inelastic demand and supply. The microfoundations of investment behaviour, by incumbent firms and potential entrants, that underly supply inelasticity, and hence the likelihood of larger and longer price swings, have been discussed earlier.

Fourth, *free markets may not be optimal in agriculture under uncertainty*. For the reasons given above, price floors or better futures markets can provide Pareto-improving insurance against down-side risk that in turn encourages outcomes with less underinvestment. Indeed, a price floor that is non-binding 'on average' can offer significant insurance against down-side risk and stimulate additional entry and investment in a sector. As Dixit and Pindyck (1994) argue, government price support programmes could, in this manner, ironically give rise to a 'cheap food' outcome by increasing investment and lowering long-run prices.

Finally, *sunk costs help to explain the persistence of 'family farms'*. If agriculture is prone to high levels of sunk costs and uncertainty, family farms also suffer from them. Investments in land, buildings, equipment and business relations are obvious cases in which costs may be sunk. It is also important to remember, however, that the 'human capital' of the asset owners is very similar. Capital and labour are thus all tied up in the family farm, making easy adjustments to price signals unlikely. This feature may help to explain the persistence and resilience of family farms worldwide under varying economic conditions, both within a generation and across generations.

SUNK COSTS AND INTERNATIONAL TRADE

There are also a set of core issues in international economics where conventional wisdom may be challenged by incorporating imperfect resource mobility associated with sunk costs and uncertainty. Three brief examples can be mentioned.

First, *import protection can provide the basis for export promotion when sunk costs are present* (Brander and Spencer, 1985; Krugman, 1984). Preemptive commitments to a sector by one country can, in turn, lower the returns to sunk investments in that sector for other countries. This first-mover advantage can be especially valuable as a basis for export promotion if the sector has increasing returns to scale, either internal or external, to firms.

Second, *export promotion can induce overinvestment and adjustment problems when sunk costs are present*. Overinvestment can result from direct subsidy of sunk costs or the 'overinsuring' of investments in export-oriented activities. The prevailing enthusiasm in international development and trade circles for export-led growth strategies could lead countries to (over)encourage investments in sectors with high levels of sunk costs and uncertainty. This problem could be especially acute for small countries with a strong reliance on one or two sectors with high sunk costs (Barham and Coomes, forthcoming).

Third, *trade liberalization may shift returns in favour of capital and against labour because of labour's relative immobility*. If common arguments regarding capital's relative mobility are correct, one reason for recent declines in wage/rental rates in developed countries could be higher levels of sunk costs for labour (related to labour market skills and location commitments). If the origin of external economies (a core mechanism in endogenous growth models) is in the skills and training of labour, the investment-discouraging effects of labour immobility could be a cause for both growth and distributional concerns.

CONCLUSION

Using a highly general model of individual investment behaviour, three crucial points have been explored. Firstly, sunk costs and uncertainty generate investment outcomes that are distinct from those predicted by standard competitive models and thus call into question the efficiency of markets where the ill-effects of the imperfectly mobile resources are not managed in some way. Secondly, depending on the circumstances of a given investment decision, the problem of sunk costs may be subject to direct or indirect management by private or public agents. Thirdly, conventional wisdom in agricultural economics and trade policy may be shaken once the implications of sunk costs and uncertainty for investment behaviour, market performance and policy options are better understood. A similar statement could probably be made for almost any field in economics.

This paper only illustrates some of the many possibilities for further research. The issue of whether sunk costs can be managed, and by whom, is fundamental. In common with many other agnostics, we view public efforts to solve market problems as prone to information problems and institutional imperatives of their own. However, the degree to which sunk costs can, and do, shape economic performance in ways not predicted by standard competitive models should be the initial research priority, for it is only after we understand more about potential and observed outcomes that the fundamental issues of institutional and policy design can be carefully examined.

REFERENCES

Baldwin, B. and Coomes, O. (forthcoming), 'Sunk costs, extractive industries and development outcomes', in S. Bunker and T. Priest (eds), *Extractive Economies*, Durham: University of North Carolina Press.

Brander, J.A. and Spencer, B. (1985), 'Export subsidies and international market share rivalry', *Journal of International Economics*, 22, 81–100.

Chavas, J.P. (1994), 'On sunk cost and the economics of investment', *American Journal of Agricultural Economics*, 76, 114–27.

Dixit, A. (1992), 'Investment and hysteresis', *Journal of Economic Perspectives*, 6, 107–32.

Dixit, A.K. and Pindyck, R.S. (1994), *Investment under Uncertainty*, Princeton: Princeton University Press.

Johnson, G.L. and Quance, L.C. (1972), *The Overproduction Trap in U.S. Agriculture*, Baltimore: Johns Hopkins University Press.

Krugman, P. (1984), 'Import protection as export promotion', in H. Kierzkowski (ed.), *Monopolistic Competition in International Trade*, London: Oxford University Press.

Pack, H. and Westphal, L. (1986), 'Industrial strategy and technological change: theory versus reality', *Journal of Development Economics*, **22**, 87–128.

Pindyck, R.S. (1991), 'Irreversibility, uncertainty and investment', *Journal of Economic Literature*, **29**, 1110–52.

Purvis, A., Boggess, W.G., Moss, C.B. and Holt, J. (1995), 'Technology adoption under irreversibility and uncertainty', *American Journal of Agricultural Economics*, **77**, 541–551.

Saha, A., Love, H.A. and Schwart, R. (1994), 'Adoption of emerging technologies under output uncertainty', *American Journal of Agricultural Economics*, **76**, 836–46.

Sutton, J. (1991), *Sunk Cost and Market Structure*, Cambridge, Mass.: MIT Press.

Tirole, J. (1989), *The Theory of Industrial Organization*, Cambridge, Mass.: MIT Press.

JOAQUIM BENTO DE SOUZA FERREIRA FILHO*

External Adjustment, Production Subsidies and Agricultural Growth in Brazil

INTRODUCTION

At the beginning of the 1980s, the Brazilian economy experienced a drastic change in its pattern of development. The appearance of the external debt crisis, together with the continuing effects of the world oil crisis of the late 1970s, saw the end of the import substitution model, which had been financed by massive external capital inflows. The interruption of these financial flows, together with increased international interest rates, made it necessary for Brazil to rely increasingly on domestic saving to service the external debt and to meet growth targets.

For the farm sector, this saw the end of agricultural subsidies and the introduction of indexation on rural credit contracts. The drastic reduction in agricultural support, in a very short time period, lowered expectations about the growth possibilities of the agricultural sector. That fear was sustained by the fact that agricultural subsidies amounted, in 1980, to about 22 per cent of agricultural GDP, or about 2.4 per cent of total GDP. Corresponding figures were, respectively, 14.0 and 1.41 per cent in 1981, 16.0 and 1.4 per cent in 1982, 10.0 and 1.1 per cent in 1983, going down to 0.78 and 0.09 per cent in 1985 (Shirota, 1988). The effects of the reductions were even more drastic than they might appear since total GDP experienced a fall of 8 per cent between 1980 and 1984.

But the Brazilian agricultural sector, unexpectedly, grew in that period, despite the fall in agricultural subsidies. The real GDP contributed by agriculture expanded by about 10 per cent between 1981 and 1984, and by about 20 per cent between 1980 and 1985. In fact, Brazilian agriculture not only grew throughout the entire decade of the 1980s, but its rate of growth was faster than that of the industrial sector (Ferreira Filho, 1996a). This phenomenon is exactly contrary to what would be expected by looking at the issue in a partial equilibrium framework. In that case, the reduction of agricultural subsidies would cause a movement of the supply curve to the left, thus reducing agricultural output. It will be argued here that the problem is too complex to be analysed in partial equilibrium models. The amount of subsidies involved is large enough to have generated macroeconomic effects which could have been dampened the microeconomic ones. The purpose of this paper is to evaluate the problem in a general equilibrium framework, using a computable general

*Escola Superior de Agricultura Luiz de Queiroz, Universidade de São Paulo, Brazil.

401

equilibrium model (CGE) to perform counterfactual simulations in order to analyse the linkages and feedbacks relating to the fall in agricultural subsidies and the simultaneous agricultural growth.

THE CGE MODEL[1]

The CGE model used in this study is based on the structure of the RUNS model (Burniaux *et al.*, 1990). However, a number of important modifications were made to the model to make it match the Brazilian economy in the 1980s and to focus on the problem at hand. To avoid confusion, the model presented here is the 'Megabrás' version. In the following summary, the model presented is a static one, with the simulation for each year being linked to the others through exogenous growth rates attributed to factors and capital stocks.

The economy is divided into two distinct sectors: rural and urban. The rural sector has 11 activities, producing soybeans, sugarcane, corn, coffee, rice, cotton, wheat, other agricultural products, livestock, milk and poultry. Urban sector efforts are separated into seven typical activities (transport, engineering, fertilizers, chemicals, energy, services and others), but also covers 10 agroindustries dealing with the processing of coffee, sugar (including alcohol), rice, wheat, fibres, vegetable oils, meat (excluding poultry), poultry and milk, plus the feed-producing industries. There are, thus, 28 productive activities in the model, each dealing with only one 'product'.

There are four institutions in the economy – rural and urban families, enterprises (investment) and government – and three primary factors of production: labour, capital and land. Only the agricultural sector utilizes land. Owing to their great degree of homogeneity the domestically produced agricultural products are assumed to be perfect substitutes for imports. Note that this does not refer to processed goods. The 'small country hypothesis' is also used so that agricultural tradable prices are defined by the exogenous world prices and import or export tariffs, while agricultural non-tradable prices are defined by excess demand in each market. For the period considered in the analysis (which is the first half of the 1980s) there are only three agricultural tradables in the model: coffee, soybeans and wheat.

For processed agricultural products, as well as the non-agricultural products, on the other hand, there is imperfect substitution between domestic production and imports, which is modelled through a CES formulation which defines a composite good for those activities. The prices of urban domestic production are defined by costs of production, while import prices are dependent on exogenous external prices and tariffs. Urban export prices are 'made' internally, through domestic prices and taxes on exports. The demand for these goods is not perfectly elastic, though it can be high in some cases.

In the agricultural sector, the production structure is specific to vegetable and animal products, both experiencing decreasing returns relative to an aggregate input, made up of urban and rural products, land and labour. The model seeks to keep track of complementarity and substitution patterns in the way primary factors and intermediates combine in the production process. This is done through a CES-linked structure, specific to the types of production activity, with two levels of linkages and two substitution elasticities. This kind of structure divides the cost minimization problem into two sub-problems, separating inputs in each level of production from those in other levels.

Production in the urban sector displays constant returns, through a Leontief formulation for intermediate inputs and a value-added aggregate that is a CES combination of capital and labour. The nominal urban labour wage is considered rigid, parameterized to reproduce the trend of urban unemployment in the period under analysis. Agricultural wages are flexible and adjust to clear the rural labour market in each period.

The model has a neoclassical closure, in which total investment is given by saving. The nominal exchange rate is flexible and external capital flows are exogenous, so providing external sector closure. Imports, however, are subject to quantitative restrictions, in proportion to the desired imports. Government consumption is exogenous and public tax revenues endogenous, thus making the aggregate government current account endogenous. The closure of the government sector simulates an important mechanism used by the Brazilian government, in the relevant period, to finance its deficits, namely 'money creation'. The equilibrium between receipts and expenses is obtained through a type of 'seigniorage', that is, a variable that ensures the equilibrium in the government current account. This mechanism of transfer of funds between institutions is used to simulate the effects of a particular monetary phenomenon.

CALIBRATION AND THE BASE RUN

Having defined the theoretical model to be used the next step was its calibration. This was done through the construction of a social accounting matrix (SAM) for Brazil for 1980. There was a complication since the 1980 input–output matrix treated the agricultural sector as a single activity, although production was disaggregated. It was necessary, therefore, to split agriculture up into the 11 activities used in the study in a way described elsewhere (Ferreira Filho, 1996b). The resulting SAM for Brazil in 1980, evaluated at consumer prices, appears in Table 1 in a summarized form with products and activities aggregated to save space.[2] This provides a broad outline of the nature of the magnitudes involved within the economy and need not be discussed in more detail.

When the model was satisfactorily reproducing the observed pattern of the variables in the base year (1980) it was then run for the period 1981 to 1985, solving for the endogenous variables given the exogenous (observed) ones, so building the base run against which counterfactual analysis could be done. The model was solved as a non-linear optimization problem, using the General Algebraic Modelling System (GAMS) with MINOS5 (Brooke *et al.*, 1988). The price of urban value added is the *numéraire* of the model.

TABLE 1   *Social accounting matrix, Brazil, 1980 (millions of 1980 cruzeiros)*

	Activities				Products				Labour
	agritrad	agrinont	agroind	urbind	agritrad	agrinont	agroind	urbind	Rural
Activities									
agritrad	0	0	0	0	325 225	0	0	0	
agrinont	0	0	0	0	0	1 743 900	0	0	
agroind	0	0	0	0	0	0	1 896 170	0	
urbind	0	0	0	0	0	0	0	22 503 422	
Products									
agritrad	15 945	56 563	254 163	12 917	0	0	0	0	0
agrinont	1 101	185 146	572 729	261 758	0	0	0	0	0
agroind	1 921	126 356	360 497	457 983	0	0	0	0	0
urbind	137 845	449 735	586 367	12 640 564	0	0	0	0	0
Factors									
Rural labour	29 081	194 822	0	0	0	0	0	0	0
Urban labour	0	0	116 670	4 579 481	0	0	0	0	0
Rural capital	179 544	733 804	0	0	0	0	0	0	0
Urban capital	0	0	210 835	4 210 747	0	0	0	0	0
Institutions									
Rural families	0	0	0	0	0	0	0	0	224 031
Urban families	0	0	0	0	0	0	0	0	0
Government	−15 609	35 162	178 370	1 135 422	0	0	0	0	0
Capital account	0	0	0	0	0	0	0	0	0
Stocks	0	0	0	0	0	0	0	0	0
ROW	0	0	0	0	35 825	24 750	26 527	1 520 480	0
Total expenses	349 828	1 781 588	2 279 632	23 298 871	361 050	1 768 650	1 922 697	24 023 901	224 031

Notes: agritrad = agricultural tradables; agrinont = agricultural non-tradables; agroind = processed agricultural products; urbind = urban industry.

EMPIRICAL RESULTS

For the counterfactual analysis, the model was run again for the 1981–5 period, but the values of the agricultural subsidies were adjusted to fit the value observed in 1980, taken as 2.4 per cent of total GDP. The results were then compared with the base run. Table 2, for example, shows the results of the

TABLE 2   *Macroeconomic aggregates as relative variations from the base run*

Year	GDP	EXP	IMP	CONS	INV	RER1	RER2
81	−0.020	−0.027	−0.017	−0.003	−0.062	−0.009	−0.008
82	−0.025	−0.035	−0.021	0.000	−0.083	−0.012	−0.010
83	−0.021	−0.020	−0.019	−0.013	−0.046	−0.008	−0.006
84	−0.044	−0.037	−0.040	−0.027	−0.092	−0.015	−0.011
85	−0.039	−0.031	−0.037	−0.024	−0.086	−0.013	−0.009

Labour Urban	Capital Rural	Capital Urban	Rural families	Institutions Urban families	Government	Capital	Stocks	ROW	Total receipts
								24 615	349 840
								37 703	1 781 603
								383 591	2 279 761
								795 517	23 298 939
0	0	0	6 663	4 105	0	0	10 528	0	360 884
0	0	0	136 945	355 808	2	108 943	145 913	0	1 768 344
0	0	0	278 772	692 559	217	1 076	3 152	0	1 922 532
0	0	0	643 559	5 270 339	1 269 531	2 921 169	103 846	0	24 022 955
0	0	0	0	0	0	0	0	0	223 903
0	0	0	0	0	0	0	0	0	4 696 151
0	0	0	0	0	0	0	0	0	913 348
0	0	0	0	0	0	0	0	0	4 421 582
0	913 872	0	0	0	168 212	0	0	0	1 306 115
4 697 189	0	4 422 737	0	0	1 513 848	0	0	0	10 633 774
0	0	0	137 956	1 243 054	0	626 467	0	0	3 340 821
0	0	0	101 909	3 065 162	112 107	0	0	639 414	3 918 593
0	0	0	0	0	3 376	260 161	0	0	2 63 537
0	0	0	0	0	273 319	0	0	0	1 880 900
4 697 189	913 872	4 422 737	1 305 803	10 631 026	3 340 611	3 917 816	263 440	1 880 840	

experiment concerning some macroeconomic aggregates and the exchange rate. The values are shown in relation to the base run, being expressed in the form of relative variations (that is, multiplication by 100 provides percentage changes). Aggregates covered are GDP, exports (EXP), imports (IMP), consumption (CONS) and investment (INV), plus two concepts of real exchange rates. These are the nominal exchange rate (RER1), which can be seen as a real (deflated) exchange rate since the price of urban value added is the *numéraire*, while the other is deflated by an index price of domestic products (RER2). It can be seen that the volume of subsidies is large enough to cause macroeconomic effects in the model.

It is interesting that the maintenance of agricultural subsidies at the levels observed in 1980 causes a general fall in macroeconomic aggregates in the model. To give one example, GDP could have fallen by as much as 4.4 per cent in 1984 and by 3.9 per cent in 1985. The 'increase' in agricultural subsidies, for that is what is implied, is also associated with a larger drop in aggregate investment, meaning that aggregate saving would have fallen, since, by the neoclassical closure of the model, investment is determined by the amount of saving. This happens because the income transfer to agriculture is made, in the main, through a reduction in urban income. The transfer is financed by government through seigniorage, extracted from rural and urban sectors in proportion to the share of each in GDP. Thus the urban sector contributes the bulk of the agricultural subsidy. Since rural families have a greater marginal propensity to consume than urban families, the transfer affects consumption more than saving, thus reducing aggregate saving and investment.

The government deficit (which is not shown in Table 2) would have considerably worsened in the period. Seigniorage needs would have risen from 4.23 to 4.95 and 9.5 per cent, respectively, in 1983, 1984 and 1985 (in the base run), and from 5.87 to 8.44 and 12.9 per cent (in the simulations), for the corresponding years. This, of course, should be interpreted as an indication that government income, as determined in the model, would not be enough to meet its expenses.

The reduction in aggregate saving leads to a drop in investment, mainly because investment absorption is concentrated in some urban industries, notably manufacturing and services which have a high value-added coefficient in production. With the drop in investment, there is a fall in the demand for those composite products, reducing both domestic production and imports. As a consequence, the 'price' of domestic production falls and imports are reduced, resulting in the 'fall' in the equilibrium exchange rates (defined as Cr/US$, so that revaluation is involved). The changes in the composition of internal absorption, from high value-added activities to relatively low ones, is then associated with a fall in GDP (and then in imports).

Turning now to variables more closely related to agriculture, the evolution of agricultural production and prices appear in Tables 3 and 4. It can be seen that only wheat, soybean and corn show important increases in production in the 'high subsidies' experiment. These are three of the four agricultural tradables in the model, along with coffee. As regards the latter, however, production would have fallen. That would have been the result because the agricultural production function is defined in terms of the relative prices of products and

TABLE 3   *Changes in agricultural production as relative variations from the base run*

Year	81	82	83	84	85
Coffee	−0.002	−0.020	−0.002	−0.002	−0.001
Sugarcane	−0.006	−0.008	−0.005	−0.007	−0.003
Rice	0.004	0.005	0.004	0.010	0.011
Wheat	0.130	0.168	0.169	0.366	0.374
Soybean	0.033	0.043	0.044	0.107	0.113
Cotton	−0.004	−0.004	−0.002	0.003	0.009
Corn	0.017	0.030	0.012	0.024	0.033
Other agric.	−0.010	−0.014	−0.009	−0.019	−0.018
Poultry	0.005	0.009	0.002	0.003	0.004
Livestock	0.004	0.008	0.002	0.003	0.004
Milk	0.002	0.005	−0.004	−0.008	−0.006

TABLE 4   *Evolution of agricultural prices as relative variations from the base run*

Year	81	82	83	84	85
Coffee	-0.009	-0.012	-0.008	-0.015	-0.013
Sugarcane	-0.031	-0.040	-0.030	-0.063	-0.059
Rice	-0.074	-0.095	-0.095	-0.200	-0.205
Wheat	-0.009	-0.012	-0.080	-0.015	-0.013
Soybeans	-0.009	-0.012	-0.008	-0.015	-0.013
Cotton	-0.091	-0.114	-0.108	-0.220	-0.218
Corn	-0.171	-0.190	-0.236	-0.416	-0.403
Other agric.	0.009	0.012	0.025	0.050	0.046
Poultry	0.017	0.026	0.010	0.020	0.019
Livestock	0.019	0.029	0.013	0.026	0.024
Milk	0.016	0.026	0.004	0.008	0.009

inputs. For coffee, the fall in input prices, as a result of the subsidy, would not have compensated for the drop in its price caused by the revaluation in the exchange rate. So, despite the subsidy, the coffee/input relative price would have fallen, reducing production.

For soybeans and wheat, on the contrary, *relative* prices would have been greater with heavier subsidization. Although their market prices would have been affected in the same proportion as that of coffee owing to the exchange rate effect, the rate of subsidy in the cost of the composite input in those cases is considerably higher than for coffee. The rate was about 7 per cent for coffee, but 32, 30 and 25 per cent for wheat in 1981, 1982 and 1983, respectively, and 18, 17 and 14 per cent for soybeans. Similar influences would have affected corn, although it is not a tradable product in the model, with production rising as a result of high subsidies on input prices. Cotton and sugarcane, which are also non-tradable products in the model, have their prices reduced. Since they are mainly inputs to the export agroindustries, their prices are strongly linked to exchange rate movements, though they benefit less from input subsidies.

The three animal production activities, dealing with poultry, livestock and milk, would have experienced higher prices. This is a consequence of redistributive effects raising demand for those products, notably working through increasing rural disposable incomes, as shown in Table 5. In effect, the financing mechanism assumed to be adopted by government for the model (it mirrors what happened in the 1980s) is, in fact, a mechanism that redistributes income from the urban to the rural sector.

The rise in the production of soybeans and wheat would have had a marked impact on external trade. Soybean exports would have risen substantially in value, while wheat imports would have fallen. However, raw coffee exports would also have risen, though not as a consequence of any increase in production. There would have been a decline in urban consumption, not matched by

TABLE 5   *Changes in rural and urban disposable income as relative variations from the base run*

Disposable income	Years				
	81	82	83	84	85
Rural	0.067	0.099	0.083	0.194	0.186
Urban	−0.024	−0.024	−0.038	−0.089	−0.073

expansion in rural consumption, allied to a fall in processed coffee exports caused by the revaluation of the equilibrium exchange rate.

The maintenance of rural subsidies at levels observed in 1980 would have generated a strong rise in rural wages. As a result, their share in disposable income would have improved, with the positive variation reaching a maximum of 12 per cent, in 1984. This is shown in Table 6. In effect, rural wages would have appropriated a considerable share of the subsidies. It should be noted, however, that these results depend strongly on the hypothesis made about the evolution of the stock of agricultural machinery ('tractors'). Observed values for the 1980s showed a yearly rate of growth of 4 per cent, with that rate being used in the base run. But it has to be recognized that the size of the stock is not independent of the size of the subsidy programme. To explore the extent to which the results are affected, a rate of growth of 7 per cent, which was actually still below the growth rate of 10.3 per cent in the period 1975–80, was inserted to obtain a new solution. The results appear in Table 7.

TABLE 6   *Value added, real wages and labour shares relative to the base run*

Year	Value added		Real wages		Rural labour share in agricultural disposable income
	rural	urban	rural	urban	
81	0.000	−0.023	0.094	−0.024	0.025
82	0.000	−0.028	0.133	−0.031	0.031
83	0.000	−0.023	0.141	−0.026	0.054
84	0.001	−0.048	0.342	−0.053	0.124
85	0.005	−0.043	0.314	−0.048	0.108

The new results suggest that a higher rate of growth of mechanization would modify the earlier results. Although rural wages would still have risen in some years, the greater availability of tractors would have favoured substitution towards their use, generating a net fall in the rural wage share in total rural income.

TABLE 7 *Alternative scenario with tractor stock increasing at 7 per cent annually, variations from the base run*

Year	Value added		Real wages		Rural labour share in agricultural disposable income
	rural	urban	rural	urban	
81	0.0	–0.023	0.027	–0.025	–0.038
82	0.0	–0.026	0.014	–0.028	–0.074
83	0.0	–0.020	–0.023	–0.022	–0.095
84	0.0	–0.044	0.093	–0.048	–0.080
85	0.0	–0.038	–0.021	–0.042	–0.134

CONCLUSIONS

The CGE results provide interesting insights that would not have been obtained from partial equilibrium analysis. In a programme of agricultural subsidies, which is large enough to generate macroeconomic effects, the sources of funding are important. Though they are always dependent on the various hypotheses made about the structure of the economy, as well as on the parameter values chosen, CGE results make it possible to analyse the various links and feedbacks observed in a highly complex and interdependent economy. Perhaps of greater importance than the particular solution magnitudes for any of the variables is the demonstration of the possibility that a programme of agricultural subsidies can, in some circumstances, have unexpected results. Our results can help understand why the halting of the Brazilian agricultural subsidy programme in the 1980s, unexpectedly, did not have any significant impact on agricultural production. One popular explanation is that productivity gains would have offset the apparent fall in direct incentives in the relevant period. The results obtained with the Megabrás model, however, suggest that other forces, working through market mechanisms in a general equilibrium situation, could also have played their part.

NOTES

[1]The complete system of equations will be omitted, since it is too large. The interested reader should refer to Ferreira Filho (1995), for the complete system used, or consult Burniaux *et al.* (1990) for the basic structure of the RUNS model. Alternatively, the author can be contacted directly for additional information.
[2]The original disaggregated SAM can be obtained from the author upon request.

REFERENCES

Brooke, A., Kendrick, D. and Meeraus, A. (1988), *GAMS: A user's guide*, Washington, DC: The World Bank and The Scientific Press.

Burniaux, J.M., van der Mensbrugghe, D. and Waelbroek, J. (1990), 'The food gap in the developing world: a general equilibrium modelling approach', in I. Goldin and O. Knudsen (eds), *Agricultural Trade Liberalisation: Implications for Developing Countries*, Paris: OECD.

Ferreira Filho, J.B.S. (1995), *MEGABRÁS – Um modelo de equilíbrio general computável aplicado à análise da agricultura brasileira*, São Paulo: FEA/USP, Doutorado.

Ferreira Filho, J.B.S. (1996a), 'Ajustamento estrutural e crescimento agrícola na década dos oitenta: notas adicionais', working paper, Department of Agricultural Economics and Sociology, Escola Superior de Agricultura Luiz de Queiroz, Universidade de São Paulo.

Ferreira, Filho, J.B.S. (1996b), 'Um matriz de contabilidade social para o Brasil em 1980', working paper, Department of Agricultural Economics and Sociology, Escola Superior de Agricultura Luiz de Queiroz, Universidade de São Paulo.

Shirota, R. (1988), *Crédito rural no Brasil: subsídio, distribuição e fatores associados à oferta*, Piracicaba: Mestrado.

CONTRIBUTED PAPERS

Transition

ERIK MATHIJS AND JOHAN F.M. SWINNEN*

Agricultural Decollectivization in Central and Eastern Europe

INTRODUCTION

Under the communist regime, agricultural production, in most Central and Eastern European Countries (CEECs), used to be organized in large-scale collective and state farms. Economic reforms since 1989 include both the privatization of agricultural assets and the restructuring of state and collective farms. Quite remarkably, the break-up of large-scale agricultural production units into individually operated farms – a process we define as decollectivization – differs considerably in the various countries. We define decollectivization in a very strict sense, as the break-up of state and collective farms into individual farms. A common critique is that, defined in this way, the issue is one of 'fragmentation' rather than 'decollectivization'. While the two concepts coincide in some cases, such as Albania, this is not necessarily the case in general. In most of the CEECs we study, many individual farms cover 100 hectares and more.

Our calculations give an index of decollectivization (DI), based on the percentage of agricultural land used by individual farms but corrected for the initial situation, which varies between 5 and 95 per cent in the different countries of Central and Eastern Europe (Table 1). The value is low in countries where large-scale successor organizations to the former state and collective farms still dominate, such as Slovakia (5 per cent), Hungary (13 per cent) and the Czech Republic (20 per cent). The index is highest in Albania (95 per cent) and Latvia (80 per cent), where a massive break-up of the collective farms resulted in a domination of individual production units. Within the CEECs there is also wide variation in the decollectivization between different regions and agricultural sub-sectors.

Are these differences random? We argue that they are not, and discuss some of the factors affecting the decollectivization process. This paper presents the intuition behind the results derived and discussed more extensively in Mathijs and Swinnen (1998). The empirical analysis is based on data from nine countries and presents remarkable correlations between decollectivization and our explanatory variables. Specifically, it suggests the importance of relative productivity, factor intensity and privatization procedures in explaining differences in decollectivization between CEECs.

*Catholic University of Leuven, Louvain, Belgium.

TABLE 1   *Decollectivization index (DI), 1994*

Country	Decollectivization index (%)
Albania	95
Latvia	80
Lithuania	60
Romania	47
Estonia	38
Bulgaria	36
Czech Republic	20
Hungary	13
East Germany	11
Slovakia	5

Note: The DI is calculated by dividing the difference between the share of individual farms in total agricultural land in 1994 (IND94) and in 1989 (IND89) by 100 minus the share of individual farms in total agricultural land in 1989: DI = (IND94 − IND89)/(100 − IND89). Data on land use are derived from Swinnen *et al.* (1997).

THE PROCESS OF DECOLLECTIVIZATION

The whole process is driven by the decision of collective farm members to leave the collective production framework and start up individual farms. As suggested by Carter (1987) and Machnes and Schnytzer (1993), this decision, in principle, involves comparing the expected utility of being a member of a collective farm with that of leaving and starting up an individual farm, independent of the collective farm.

Their model of the collective farm is an extension of the Ward–Domar–Vanek approach to agricultural producer cooperatives and labour-managed firms (Bradley, 1971; Israelsen, 1980). We extend their standard model by relaxing assumptions about fixed membership, a homogeneous workforce with identical labour productivity and a perfectly democratic labour-managed firm. Furthermore, we explicitly take into account the costs of leaving the collective farm and analyse how exit costs (and, thus, the decollectivization process) are affected by exogenous factors, such as farm-specific labour productivity, factor intensity, technology, asset privatization procedures and government regulations.

This framework accounts for both advantages and disadvantages in collective production emphasized in the literature. Disadvantages include high transaction costs associated with the monitoring of labour and inefficiencies due to the right of codetermination (Lin, 1988; Schmitt, 1993). Advantages of collective farms include economies of scale in risk management, the provision of information and credit, input purchasing, marketing and production (Putterman, 1985; Carter, 1987; Pryor, 1992; Machnes and Schnytzer, 1993; Deininger, 1995). However, many of these advantages can also be captured by individual farms, for example by establishing a service cooperative (Deininger, 1995).

FACTORS AFFECTING DECOLLECTIVIZATION

A number of factors affect the decision of a member to leave, and hence the process of decollectivization. First, risk has a negative effect on decollectivization only if collective farms have an advantage of scale in dealing with risk. However, we argue that this advantage is to a great extent only temporary and conditional on the transition period, which is characterized by uncertainty and missing markets. With the development of markets, differences in risk management disappear and the adverse impact of risk on decollectivization is reduced.

Second, terms of trade improvements stimulate decollectivization, independent of risk, because the marginal income effects of an output price increase, for example, are larger for an individual producer than for a collective farm member, other things being equal. An important policy implication of this result is that government interventions to increase farm output prices, as might occur through general price support policies, would stimulate decollectivization.

Third, decollectivization is inversely related to the pre-reform average productivity of the collective farm. Members compare their productivity with the average productivity of the collective farm, and are more likely to leave if their productivity is high and/or the average collective farm productivity is low. High initial average collective farm productivity therefore reduces the incentives of members to leave.

Finally, exit costs are costs related to the withdrawal of productive assets and reduce the benefits of leaving the collective farm. Their size is influenced by the capital intensity of production and the property rights distribution of the collective farm. It is easier and less costly for a member to withdraw from a more labour-intensive collective farm than from one which is more capital-intensive. The privatization procedure affects the allocation of production factors in the presence of transaction costs and therefore influences the decollectivization process. As a result of high transaction costs for former owners who left agriculture under communism, so-called 'outsiders', restitution of land does not necessarily lead to a fragmentation of farm structures. The opposite may happen: restitution may lead to consolidation of large-scale farms as these outsiders prefer to lease their land to the collective farm. Transaction costs are lower for members, or 'insiders', who also have more incentives to start up an individual farm. Therefore we predict that distribution of assets to members stimulates decollectivization, while restitution to outsiders may hinder decollectivization. Privatization and decollectivization policies can decrease exit costs, by facilitating the withdrawal of assets from the collective farm, or increase exit costs if they have the opposite effect. The latter is most frequently observed in practice. Less productive members and management also try to increase exit costs (a) by influencing the regulations for privatization of property rights and factor allocation at the government decision-making level and (b) by slowing down and limiting the implementation of the registration at the farm level.

EMPIRICAL EVIDENCE

The quality and quantity of the available information, as well as the nature of the transition, do not, as yet, allow a sophisticated empirical analysis to be attempted. Therefore the empirical evidence has to be interpreted as being indicative, rather than conclusive. The reasons are listed below.

First, there are no consistent data to calculate the impact of *prices and risk* on decollectivization. We do observe that the adverse movement in the agricultural terms of trade in 1989–91 has stabilized throughout the CEECs, and that the situation has improved substantially for some commodities since 1991. We can also conclude that price variation has reduced substantially since 1992, and that agricultural producers generally have a better understanding of the emerging market economy (Jackson and Swinnen, 1995). Both developments are correlated with increased decollectivization in CEECs.

Second, to analyse the impact of *average collective farm productivity*, we considered the relationship between the decollectivization index (DI) and pre-reform value added per farm worker (as a proxy for average collective farm productivity). Figure 1 shows that CEECs with low productivity on collective farms, such as Albania, have a significantly higher degree of decollectivation than those where collective farm productivity was higher, such as Hungary. Figure 1 is based on 1993 data on gross agricultural product (GAP) per worker.

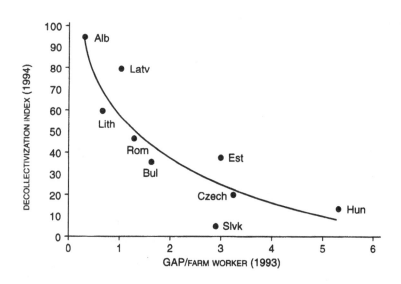

FIGURE 1   *Relationship between decollectivization in 1994 and gross agricultural product (GAP) in ECU per farm worker in 1993*

A better indicator would have been pre-reform GAP/collective farm worker data. However, necessary data for calculating this indicator were unavailable for several CEECs. A sensitivity analysis based on those CEECs for which necessary data were available suggests that there is no fundamental change in the relationship if pre-reform estimates of average productivity are used.

Third, to deal with the relationship between decollectivization and *factor intensity*, we used the share of agriculture in employment as a proxy for labour intensity: a high share implies a labour-intensive agriculture, generally characterized by a low degree of mechanization, making it easier to decollectivize. Figure 2 shows a positive relationship between decollectivization and the share of agriculture in employment, consistent with our expectations that decollectivization is more likely to occur where labour intensity is higher. Notice that the three Baltic countries are all above the curve in Figure 2. Latvia especially stands out. Its high rate of decollectivization has been further enhanced (a) by the egalitarian pre-1945 land distribution which implies that restitution of land returns land mostly to insiders, and (b) by the active restitution and decollectivization policy of the government. Latvia's active policy was inspired by nationalistic motivations, with land going to native Latvians in a country with a very high share (46 per cent) of ethnic non-Latvians in the population (see Rabinowicz, 1997, for extensive discussion and Swinnen, 1997, for an analysis of ethnic impacts on CEEC privatization choice). The Latvian

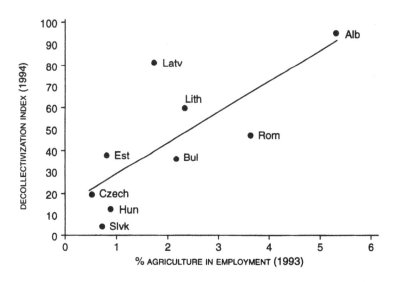

FIGURE 2   *Relationship between decollectivization in 1994 and the share of agriculture in total employment in 1993*

TABLE 2 *Various indicators of land reform and transformation regulations*

| | Decollectivization index 1994 | Share in total agricultural land (in %) | | | | Share of agriculture in total employment 1993 | Exit costs due to government regulations* |
		Individual farms 1989	Privatized land by restitution	Privatized land by distribution	State-owned land 1994		
Albania	95	4	—	93	3	53	1
Latvia	80	4	64	30	2	17	1
Lithuania	60	9	69	21	1	23	2
Romania	47	14	43–58	15–30	13	36	2
Estonia	38	4	74	22	—	8	2
Bulgaria	36	13	81	—	7	22	2
Czech Republic	20	—	79	—	13	5	2
Hungary	13	14	62	19	5	9	3
East Germany	11	10	82	—	8	na	2
Slovakia	5	—	74	—	20	7	3

Note: *Own estimate of exit costs induced by farm transformation regulations (1 = low, 2 = medium, 3 = high), based on case studies in Swinnen (1997) and Swinnen *et al.* (1997).

Source: Own calculations based on European Commission (1995), OECD (1996) and Swinnen *et al.* (1997).

reform regulations specify that individual farms are given the highest priority in land allocation. The lowest priority is given to reforming collective farms (quite unlike the case in many other CEECs, where collective farms receive preferential treatment).

Fourth, data on the impact of *land reform and transformation regulations* appear in Table 2 and suggest that decollectivization is more important where (a) more of the land was distributed to farm workers, (b) the share of agriculture in employment is high, and (c) exit costs are low. It is remarkable to see how the two countries at the extremes of the spectrum are exactly opposite in these three factors. Albania, where decollectivization is highest, distributed land to farm workers, has a high share of agriculture in employment and low policy-induced exit costs. Slovakia, where decollectivization is lowest, restituted land to former owners, has a low share of agriculture in employment and high policy-induced exit costs. These observations confirm the expectation that decollectivization is more likely when assets are distributed to insiders than to outsiders.

Finally, another factor which affects the relationship between land reform policies and decollectivization is the *pre-collectivization land ownership distribution*. A more fragmented pre-collectivization land distribution implies more transaction costs for potential farmers to set up a farm of a given size. This factor may also partly explain the difference in decollectivization between Slovakia and the Czech Republic. Inheritance rules were different in the two countries. In Slovakia, it was based on the Napoleonic code, which stipulates that all sons receive an equal piece of land upon their father's death. This resulted in a stronger fragmentation of land ownership than in the Czech Republic, where the eldest son inherited all the land. As a result, former owners received smaller plots in Slovakia than in the Czech Republic and faced more transaction costs to take out their land from the collective farm.

CONCLUSION

Important differences in decollectivization can be observed both between CEECs and between sectors and regions within these countries. This paper summarizes several factors that affect decollectivization. These include general economic factors, such as terms of trade and risk, and organizational factors that result in differences between collective and individual farms, such as differences in effective output prices, risk management and labour supply. We further show that productivity and the exit costs which a member faces when wishing to withdraw assets from the collective farm are important factors influencing the decision of collective farm members to stay or to leave and start up an individual farm.

Available data show empirical evidence consistent with our propositions. A relative improvement in terms of trade since the beginning of transition and gradual reduction of price variability and transition-related risk have induced an increase in decollectivization throughout CEECs. Our index of decollectivization is positively related with proxies for several of our explanatory variables. More specifically, the empirical analysis supports the conclusions

(a) that the average productivity of collective farms has a negative impact on decollectivization, (b) that decollectivization is less in capital- and land-intensive production activities, and (c) that privatization policies affect decollectivization.

REFERENCES

Bradley, M.E. (1971), 'Incentives and Labour Supply on Soviet Collective Farms', *Canadian Journal of Economics*, **IV**, 342–52.

Carter, M.R. (1987), 'Risk Sharing and Incentives in the Decollectivization of Agriculture', *Oxford Economic Papers*, **39**, 577–95.

Deininger, K. (1995), 'Collective Agricultural Production: A Solution For Transition Economies?', *World Development*, **23**, 1317–34.

European Commission (1995), 'Agricultural Situation and Prospects in the Central and Eastern European Countries', working document, Directorate-General for Agriculture, Brussels.

Israelsen, L.D. (1980), 'Collectives, Communes and Incentives', *Journal of Comparative Economics*, **4**, 99–124.

Jackson, M. and Swinnen, J.F.M. (1995), *A Statistical Analysis and Survey of the Current Situation of Agriculture in the Central and Eastern European Countries*, Report to DG I, EU Commission, Louvain: The Leuven Institute for Central and Eastern European Studies.

Lin, J.Y. (1988), 'The Household Responsibility System in China's Agricultural Reform: A Theoretical and Empirical Study', *Economic Development and Cultural Change*, **36**, S199–S224.

Machnes, Y. and Schnytzer, A. (1993), 'Risk and the Collective Farm in Transition', in C. Csaki and Y. Kislev (ed.), *Agricultural Cooperatives in Transition*, Boulder: Westview Press.

Mathijs, E. and Swinnen, J.F.M. (1998), 'The economies of agricultural decollectivization in East Central Europe and the Former Soviet Union', *Economic Development and Cultural Change*, **46**, 1–26.

OECD (1996), *Agricultural policies, markets and trade in transition economies: Monitoring and evaluation 1996*, Paris: OECD.

Pryor, F.L. (1992), *The Red and the Green. The Rise and Fall of Collectivized Agriculture in Marxist Regimes*, Princeton: Princeton University Press.

Putterman, L. (1985), 'Extrinsic versus Intrinsic Problems of Agricultural Cooperation: Anti-incentivism in Tanzania and China', *Journal of Development Studies*, **21**, 175–204.

Rabinowicz, E. (1997), 'Political Economy of Agrarian Reform in the Baltics', in J.F.M. Swinnen (ed.), *Political Economy of Agrarian Reform in Central and Eastern Europe*, Aldershot: Ashgate.

Schmitt, G. (1993), 'Why Collectivization of Agriculture in Socialist Countries Has Failed: A Transaction Cost Approach', in C. Csaki and Y. Kislev (eds), *Agricultural Cooperatives in Transition*, Boulder: Westview Press.

Swinnen, J.F.M. (ed.) (1997), *Political Economy of Agrarian Reform in Central and Eastern Europe*, Aldershot: Ashgate.

Swinnen, J.F.M., Buckwell, A. and Mathijs, E. (eds), *Agricultural Privatisation, Land Reform and Farm Restructuring in Central and Eastern Europe*, Aldershot: Ashgate.

JENS-PETER LOY AND PETER WEHRHEIM*

Spatial Food Market Integration in Russia

INTRODUCTION

This paper analyses the dynamics of food price relationships between several regions in the European part of Russia,[1] to determine whether the first sequence of reforms has led to better functioning and/or integrated regional food markets. The integration of markets is of particular importance in a country the size of Russia, with very different climatic conditions. Because of various comparative advantages, spatial trading is a prerequisite for balancing regional shortfalls in the supply of food items. Furthermore, well-functioning markets are necessary to enhance the allocative and distributive efficiency.

During the transition period, the Russian government first liberalized prices in January 1992, and later regulatory power was shifted to regional authorities. These reforms resulted in geographical price differences of significant magnitude for a wide range of food products. Koen and Phillips (1993, p. 10) expected that this regional dispersion of food prices in Russia would be 'largely dissipated after a few months'. Gardner and Brooks (1994) tested retail food prices by applying a modified Ravallion model for the period February 1992 to April 1993 and concluded that there was a lack of market integration in the Russian Federation during the first period of transition. In the meantime, the reform of food policies in Russia continued and further changed market conditions. The increasing independence of regional authorities contributed to a regionalization of food policies (Melyukhina and Wehrheim, 1996).

To address the question of regional food market integration in Russia, we proceed as follows. In the next section factors which are likely to have an important impact on the degree of spatial market integration (SMI) are considered. There is then a description of the link between regional market integration and spatial market efficiency. Use is then made of weekly price data for the period between January 1993 and December 1995, for 10 consumer products at five locations, in testing for integration, cointegration and causal relationships using bivariate and multivariate models. Finally, we draw some conclusions concerning the economic and political implications of the empirical results.

*Christian-Albrechts-University, Kiel, Germany. The financial support of the Deutsche Forschungsgemeinschaft and the Volkswagen Foundation is acknowledged.

FACTORS INFLUENCING SPATIAL MARKET
INTEGRATION IN THE TRANSITION PROCESS

Regional markets must be linked by well-functioning trade institutions and transport infrastructures in order to communicate with each other. Within the reform period, public investment in transport declined significantly as a result of budget deficits. The share of federal government expenditures for transport infrastructure declined to less than 1 per cent in 1995 (IMF, 1995), resulting in a sharp fall in the amount of railroad freight carried. This drop suggests that transport of foodstuffs between regions also declined. Another vacuum was created by the lack of marketing institutions which could level out supply and demand shocks between different regions. Many of the former food processing and wholesale firms were restructured or collapsed. A substantial diversification of trade channels and trade arrangements including barter trade and payment-in-kind, and give-and-take operations took place in the Russian food sector (Wehrheim, 1996). Hence the old nationwide network of marketing institutions vanished, while a new one is slowly evolving. Additionally, the marketing chain for various food products evolved very differently during the transition period.

By the presidential decree of December 1991, price controls on most retail goods were eliminated. In March 1992, another decree empowered local governments to reintroduce price control on a regional level. Furthermore, some basic food product prices were not liberalized in order to protect the most vulnerable part of the population. This was achieved through a minimum binding list by the federal government, which authorized the regional governments to set minimum prices for bread, milk and dairy products, sugar, vegetable oil and baby food. Regional governments adopted a wide range of measures to control retail prices, such as limiting their marketing margins. The enforced measures and the products under price control vary to a large extent between these regions. In Orel (Rostov, Pskov) county, retail prices were controlled for 23 (35, 27) food products in 1994. Hence it is expected that the market integration for these products under regional price control will be weaker than for other products. It must also be noted that the regional governments were only able to regulate retail prices for formal outlets, such as state shops. Other retail outlets, such as town markets, where officials have little or no control over food prices, became more important (Tho Seeth, 1997).

In perfect markets, changes in the relative availability of goods and scarcity of resources result in price changes which are signals for consumers and producers. In the process of reform, however, markets in Russia were distorted by many macroeconomic developments. With respect to market integration, accelerating inflation in the first period of the Russian transition process was very likely to have been one of the central factors influencing SMI. First, inflation distorts the transmission of price signals between markets. Second, inflation also increases price variability and, hence, insecurity, while uncertainty increases if high inflation rates prevail. Third, this may result in risk-reducing strategies by consumers, such as increased stockholding, which itself accelerates the price spiral again as supplies fall. A fourth argument claims that Russian firms are not familiar with market pricing and overestimate the required price increase to balance inflationary effects resulting in inventory accumulation. Fifth, inflation also has distributive effects. In Russia it has undermined the real income of pensioners and low-income groups, which also affects the allocative and distributive efficiency of markets.

All of this suggests that the macroeconomic environment for food markets in Russia was characterized by significant restructuring and uncertainty in 1993 and 1994. Only slight improvements in SMI are expected, given that the empirical analysis only covers the first three years of economic restructuring. Since market structures and policy interventions have evolved differently for various products, it is also likely that SMI will be rather different for various crops.

THE MEANING AND THE
MEASUREMENT OF SPATIAL MARKET INTEGRATION

SMI is based on arbitrage pricing theory. Efficient spatial price spreads should not allow for expected profits by applying any kind of trading rules. In the first place, efficient price spreads are not directly related to SMI, which is defined as a significant statistical relationship between spatial price series (Monke and Petzel, 1984). However, time-varying cost structures can lead to unrelated spatial prices that are efficient (Fackler, 1994). Thus only in the case of more or less constant cost structures and trading relationships can long-run statistical relationships be expected. Furthermore, the measurement of SMI is mainly based on linear or log-linear relationships between prices, which implies that absolute or relative price changes should be related across markets. The exact parameterization of these relationships is generally undetermined because adjustment costs might vary between markets and/or products. Even if constant cost structures and stable trading relationships can be assumed, the rejection of long-run relationships does not imply inefficiency because the observed price differences might be unimportant from an economic point of view, even though they are highly predictable. Thus the results of SMI studies have to be combined with the knowledge of market experts who can assess predicted profit opportunities or compare the results with those for other markets or time periods.

The measurement of SMI in recent years has been strongly influenced by the introduction of cointegration theory, since many price series show non-stationary behaviour. Numerous studies provide a detailed explanation of the statistical background on this issue (Alexander and Wyeth, 1994; Von Cramon-Taubadel *et al.*, 1995). The general methodological procedure in this study is based on the following steps.[2]

(1) The hypothesis of integration is tested against stationarity for all price series using the test procedure developed by Phillips and Perron (1988).
(2) If the hypothesis of integration cannot be rejected, the hypothesis of cointegration is tested for all bivariate combinations of regional prices, applying the procedure developed by Johansen (1988).

(3)   Bivariate error correction models (ECMs) are estimated for the cointegrated systems by ordinary least squares (OLS), and WALD tests are applied to test for exogeneity.

(4)   Multivariate tests to prove cointegration and exogeneity are applied to the regional systems of markets for each product to determine the multi-market linkages (Johansen, 1988).

DATA AND ESTIMATION
RESULTS FOR THE RUSSIAN FOOD MARKETS

The empirical evaluation of food market integration in Russia is based on weekly price data from January 1993 to December 1995 for beef, butter, milk, eggs, sausages, bread, potatoes, sugar, vegetable oil and wheat flour for five regional markets (Moscow, St Petersburg, Pskov, Orel and Rostov). Table 1 shows the distance matrix for these locations.

TABLE 1   *Distance matrix for the five spatial markets in Russia (km)*

	St Petersburg	Pskov	Orel	Rostov
Moscow	682	837	426	1262
St Petersburg		228	1065	1926
Pskov			1058	1972
Orel				1015

Source: Loy and Wehrheim (1996).

The analysed series relate to consumer prices, which were collected by regional branches of the Russian Statistical Office (Goskomstat, 1996). These were monitored for 'official' retail shops and town markets separately until December 1993. From January 1994, the price series reflect a weighted average of all registered market outlets. Because prices are significantly influenced by inflation, the series are deflated by a weekly food price index. Generally, the deflated price series still show significant movements in levels, which indicate non-stationary behaviour of the underlying data-generating processes (DGPs) (see Figure 1). The products under regulatory control, such as milk, bread and wheat flour, show the largest upward movements. This might be expected as regulation here often means cost-plus pricing which provides no incentives to reduce costs. The null hypothesis of non-stationarity (integrated of order one) cannot be rejected in most cases.[3] Except for some potato and vegetable oil prices, all series are integrated even if a trend is included. All first differences are stationary or more precisely integrated of order zero.[4]

In the second stage, cointegration is tested for all combinations of regional markets for all products. The existence of long-run linear price relationships is supported by testing for most of the bivariate regional market combinations of

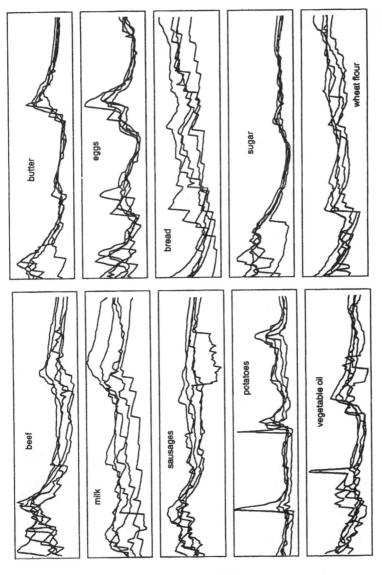

FIGURE 1   *Deflated weekly prices of food products for five regional markets in Russia, Jan. 1993 to Dec. 1995*

Source: Goskomstat (1996).

beef, butter, eggs, potatoes, sugar and vegetable oil prices. For milk, sausages, bread and wheat flour, no cointegration is indicated in most cases. Regional patterns could not be derived from the results.

In the next step for all bivariate combinations structural error correction models (ECMs) of the following type are estimated. In the notation used, i and j are indices for different spatial markets and p stands for the respective prices. In addition, α^* is the error correction coefficient (ECC), which indicates how deviations from the linear long-run relationship are reduced over time. β_0 is the parameter for the contemporaneous price adjustment, which describes the comovement of prices in the same period. As further difference lags are generally not found to be statistically significant, result documentation and discussion are focused on the ECC and contemporaneous adjustment parameters.[5]

$$\Delta p_t^i = \alpha_0 + \alpha^* p_{t-1}^i + \beta^* p_{t-1}^j + \beta_0 \Delta p_t^j + \sum_{k=1}^{p} \alpha_i \Delta p_{t-1}^i + \sum_{l=1}^{q} \beta_i \Delta p_{t-1}^j$$

Estimates for milk, sausage, bread and wheat flour prices reveal the lowest ECCs, potato prices the highest (see Table 2, column 3). But potato prices show a strong seasonal component that might have contributed to this result. As only three years of data are available, this problem could not be considered adequately, especially as the seasonal component does not seem to be constant in time (see Figure 1). The estimated contemporaneous adjustment coefficients are often not significant and, in addition, are relatively low in comparison to other results for the European Union, Poland or world agricultural markets (see Table 2, column 4, and Von Cramon-Taubadel *et al.*, 1995; Loy, 1995; Von Cramon-Taubadel and Loy, 1996).[6] The number of significant coefficients is relatively high for butter and potatoes compared with other products. Other lagged adjustments are generally not significant. For the products covered, it takes from eight weeks to a year for there to be reductions of price shocks by 90 per cent between spatial markets (Table 2, column 5). These results indicate very weak SMI, which is mainly driven by low ECCs. Furthermore, spatial price differences seem to be economically important. Average maximum differences between 40 and 250 per cent for the whole sample are observed. That means, for instance, that in the case of milk the highest spatial market price is 2.5 times higher than the lowest, on average.

The causal direction within the bivariate systems is determined by testing for weak exogeneity. If the null hypothesis cannot be rejected for both variables, it is not possible to identify the leading market. The hypothesis of weak exogeneity is rejected for most of the cointegrated price pairs. This implies, whenever a causal relationship is indicated, that it is based on a feedback relationship. Therefore the estimations of the ECM cannot be further interpreted with respect to the direction of information flows or price adjustment. Nonetheless, the magnitude of the estimated coefficients gives an idea of the way close spatial markets are linked.

In the last step, the maximum likelihood estimation method is used to determine the rank of the matrix of cointegrating vectors. In most cases the results with five lags are consistent with the results for 10 lags. For beef and sugar, four cointegrating vectors are revealed. Thus these markets show the

TABLE 2 *Estimation and test results for various deflated weekly food prices on five spatial markets in Russia from Jan. 1993 to Dec. 1995*

Product	Share of spatial cointegrated price series 1	Number of cointegrating vectors 2	Average error correction coefficient α^*(ECC) 3	Average contemporaneous adjustment β_0 4	Time for reduction of price deviations by 90% 5	Minimum, maximum of standard deviation 6	Average maximum spatial price difference 7
	(%)	(number)	(%/week)	(%)	(weeks)	$std(\Delta p_t^i / p_t^i)$	$\left(\dfrac{Max(p_t^i)}{Min(p_t^i)} - 1\right) *100$
Beef	90	4	11	17	20	3.0–8.3	58
Butter	90	2	10.5	19	20	4.2–11.7	50
Milk	70	1	7	4	33	4.0–39.2	248
Eggs	70	1	11	10	20	5.9–10.2	43
Sausage	30	2	5.5	1	43	3.0–55.1	140
Bread	20	1	4.8	7	47	8.2–19.2	183
Potatoes	90	1	24.5	35	8	24.7–75.3	174
Sugar	80	4	9	7	25	2.8–10.4	56
V. oil	80	1	13.5	18	16	6.3–12.2	57
W. flour	20	1	8	19	27	3.3–26.1	71

Notes: (1) Number of cointegrated bivariate price series divided by the number of all bivariate combinations of spatial markets. (2) Number of cointegrated vectors (Johansen procedure). (3) Average ECC for all bivariate combinations. (4) Average price transmission in the same week for all bivariate combinations. (5) Average time period for a reduction of a price shock by 90 per cent for all bivariate combinations. (6) Minimum and maximum of standard deviations of relative price changes on spatial markets. (7) Average of maximum relative spatial price differences for the respective period (in this case, Jan. 1993 to Dec. 1995).

Source: Own calculations; data from Goskomstat (1996).

highest degree of SMI. The lowest degree is for bread and wheat flour. Except for beef, sausages, butter and sugar, the number of cointegrating relationships is generally one. This means such market systems consist of four different non-stationary price movements; respectively, the system is driven by four different random walks. Systems with four cointegrating vectors are only driven by one common stochastic trend or random walk. To prove the causal directions within these systems, several restrictions on the weighting matrix have to be tested. The systems with four cointegrating vectors can indicate one market leader, or one weakly exogenous market. Those with one cointegrating vector can show four weak exogenous markets or one following market. None of the markets could be identified as a leader or follower. This supports results for the bivariate estimations because the hypothesis of weak exogeneity could not be rejected in most cases. The only exception is St Petersburg, which seems to be a leader in the beef market. Hence most multivariate estimations are not identified, and no information about impulse responses can be extracted.

Finally, an attempt is made to test whether SMI has improved over the reform period, by applying the methods outlined above to only the second half of the sample. Generally, it would be expected that SMI might improve after an adjustment period, because establishment of markets and traders would take considerable time, and gathering of information would increase and become faster over time. The results are summarized in Table 3. As for the whole sample, the hypothesis of integrated DGPs cannot be rejected for all price series. Cointegration is less observed even though one would expect markets to be linked more closely after an initial post-reform period. Also the speed of price adjustment processes between spatial markets has not increased, compared to the results for the whole sample, and spatial price differences are still rather important for most of the products. Thus SMI has not improved significantly in the second half of the observation period. This might be the result of a counterproductive influence of regional pricing policies, or the slow adjustment to more efficient spatial transaction arrangements which are taking place without yet leading to significant improvements.

CONCLUSIONS

Even though major economic reforms started in 1991 and 1992, the food marketing system in Russia seems to be restricted by the lack of well-functioning infrastructure and institutions. Additionally, the shift of policy decisions to the regional governments may have increased market segmentation. These hypotheses are tested by analysing weekly consumer prices for 10 food products for five locations in the European part of Russia, over the period from January 1993 to December 1995. Even though the material analysed covers a period of up to four years after the initial price liberalization, only low levels of regional market integration are revealed, which do not increase significantly in time. Long-run linear price relationships were found for nearly all bivariate regional market combinations of beef, butter, eggs, potatoes, sugar and vegetable oil. Contemporaneous adjustment is revealed for many bivariate market combinations for these products, even though levels of coefficients are mostly

TABLE 3 Estimation and test results for various deflated weekly food prices on five spatial markets in Russia from May 1994 to Dec. 1995

Product	Share of spatial cointegrated price series 1 (%)	Number of cointegrating vectors 2 (number)	Average error correction coefficient α^*(ECC) 3 (%/week)	Average contemporaneous adjustment β_0 4 (%)	Time for reduction of price deviations by 90% 5 (weeks)	Minimum, maximum of standard deviation 6 $std(\Delta p_i^t / p_i^t)$	Average maximum spatial price difference 7 $\left(\frac{Max(p_i^t)}{Min(p_i^t)} - 1\right)*100$
Beef	40	1	14	4	16	1.5–5.8	63
Butter	83	2	24	26	9	4.7–9.5	30
Milk	10	2	6	8	37	2.8–15.0	184
Eggs	41	2	13	4	18	5.9–6.8	31
Sausage	30	2	9	–5	26	1.8–72.3	204
Bread	15	1	7	6	33	2.6–12.9	117
Potatoes	88	3	27	7	9	8.3–100	155
Sugar	26	1	11	12	20	2.7–4.6	22
V. oil	41	1	14	9	16	3.5–13.4	54
W. flour	4	1	7	10	32	1.8–6.5	57

Notes and source as for Table 2.

very low compared to other market integration studies. Milk, sausages, bread and wheat flour are in many cases not cointegrated at all. This can be explained by specific product properties such as non-tradability (for example, milk), different qualities (for example, sausages) and different government price settings (for example, bread and wheat flour). For bread and wheat flour prices, extremely low levels of cointegration are obtained. As quality standards for this category of bread are still rather homogeneous across Russia, the impact of political interference seems to be high. Deviations from the long-run equilibrium are reduced significantly for some products, but the speed of adjustment is relatively low. For instance, 90 per cent reductions of price shocks take up to a year for some products (such as sausage and bread). Potato prices reveal cointegration more often and even the speed of comovement is relatively high in the whole sample. Product-specific differences in the degree of cointegration may suggest that the interregional trade network is more advanced for beef, butter, eggs, potatoes and vegetable oil. With the exception of potatoes, this might imply that spatial cointegration in Russia is more advanced for food products that are characterized by a relatively high value density and which, therefore, have somewhat lower transport costs. Hence these products can be traded more easily and provide more incentives to arbitrage. At the same time, regional price regulation seems to lower spatial market integration for certain products, such as bread, wheat flour and milk. Both facts highlight important conclusions. First, not surprisingly, regional price policies tend to increase market segmentation. The regionalization of food policy should be reversed whenever it is linked to increased barriers to spatial trading. As political interests of the 89 sub-national regions in Russia are often conflicting, the issue of food price liberalization should be decided at the national level to avoid market segmentation. Second, weak spatial market integration could be reduced by offering firms in the food marketing chain the legal security and the technical infrastructure to exchange food products in bulk over long distances.

NOTES

[1]Food markets in Moscow and St Petersburg, Russia's two largest urban centres, are compared with three Russian counties. All three counties (Pskov, Orel and Rostov) are located in the European part of Russia. Pskov is the most northern county, located adjacent to Estonia and Belarus. Orel is located in the central region south of Moscow, the so-called 'red belt'. In contrast to other regions, the population of this industry-dominated oblast maintains a rather anti-reform government. Rostov, located on the Don, has the most liberal food policy.

[2]We use here the procedures by Phillips and Perron (1988) and Johansen (1988) as these have improved properties, especially in the case of more complex data generating processes and in small samples, compared to classical procedures such as the augmented Dickey–Fuller test or the Engle–Granger two-step procedure (see Engle and Granger, 1987; Banerjee *et al.*, 1993).

[3]All results are based on the 95 per cent significance level. The robustness of results is tested by using two different lag structures (5 and 10 lags). The maximum lag length of 10 ensured the absence of residual autocorrelation in most cases, but the 'white noise' properties of the error terms in the regression to test stationarity as well as to estimate the ECM are often not fulfilled with respect to homoskedasticity and normality. Thus the estimation results can be biased and have to be interpreted with caution.

[4]More details about the calculations are given in Loy and Wehrheim (1996) and can be obtained from the authors upon request.

⁵These are only included to ensure uncorrelated error terms.
⁶In these studies, contemporaneous price adjustments are often considerably above 0.5 or 50 per cent.

REFERENCES

Alexander, C. and Wyeth, J. (1994), 'Cointegration and Market Integration: An Application to the Indonesian Rice Markets', *The Journal of Development Studies*, **30**, 303–28.

Banerjee, A., Dolado, J.J., Galbraith, J.W. and Hendry, D.F. (1993), *Co-Integration, Error Correction and the Econometric Analysis of Non-Stationary Data*, Oxford: Oxford University Press.

Engle, R.F. and Granger, C.W. (1987), 'Cointegration and Error Correction: Representation, Estimation and Testing', *Econometrica*, **55**, 251–76.

Fackler, P.L. (1994), 'Spatial Equilibrium and Tests of Market Efficiency and Integration', mimeo, North Carolina University.

Gardner, B. and Brooks, K. (1994), 'Food Prices and Market Integration in Russia: 1992–93', *American Journal of Agricultural Economics*, **76**, 641–6.

Goskomstat (Statistical Office of Russia) (1996), *Weekly Food Prices*, Moscow: Official Publication.

IMF (International Monetary Fund) (1995), *Russian Federation – Statistical Appendix*, Staff Country Report No. 95/107, Washington, DC: IMF.

Johansen, S. (1988), 'Statistical Analysis of Cointegration Vectors', *Journal of Economic Dynamics and Control*, **12**, 231–54.

Koen, V. and Phillips, S. (1993), *Price Liberalization in Russia*, Occasional Paper 104, Washington, DC: IMF.

Loy, J.-P. (1995), 'Möglichkeiten zur Beurteilung der Markteffizienz – Theorie, Methodik und eine erste Evaluierung für polnische Agrarmärkte in der Transformationsphase', dissertation, Institut für Agrarökonomie der Christian-Albrechts-Universität, Kiel.

Loy, J.-P. and Wehrheim, P. (1996), 'Spatial Food Market Integration in Russia', Discussion Paper No. 6, Series: The Russian Food Economy in Transition, University of Kiel.

Melyukhina, O. and Wehrheim, P. (1996), 'Russian Agricultural and Food Policies in the Transition Period: Federal and Regional Responsibilities in Flux', Discussion Paper No. 5, Series: The Russian Food Economy in Transition, University of Kiel.

Monke, E. and Petzel, T. (1984), 'Market Integration: An Application to International Trade in Cotton', *American Journal of Agricultural Economics*, **66**, 481–7.

Phillips, P. and Perron, P. (1988), 'Testing for Unit Root in Time Series Regression', *Biometrika*, **75**, 335–46.

Tho Seeth, H. (1997), *Rußlands Haushalte im Transformationsprozeß – Einkommens-, Armuts- und Versorgungsanalyse*, Frankfurt/Main: Europäische Hochschulschriften, Peter Lang.

Von Cramon-Taubadel, S. and Loy, J.-P. (1996), 'Price Asymmetry in the International Wheat Market: A Comment', *Canadian Journal of Agricultural Economics*, **44**, 311–17.

Von Cramon-Taubadel, S., Loy, J.-P. and Musfeldt, E. (1995), 'Empirische Methoden zur Analyse der Marktintegration am Beispiel des EU-Schweinefleischmarktes', *Schriften der Gesellschaft für Wirtschafts- und Sozialwissenschaften des Landbaues*, **31**, 119–37.

Wehrheim, P. (1996), 'Institutional Change in the Russian Food Marketing System', in *Proceedings of the 50th EAAE Seminar 'The Significance of Politics and Institutions for the Design and Formation of Agricultural Policy'*, Halle/Saale: IAMO.

JEAN-MARC BOUSSARD AND ANE KATHRINE CHRISTENSEN*

*The Place of Agriculture in the Development of Poland and Hungary:
Lessons from a Computable General Equilibrium Model with Risk
Considerations*

INTRODUCTION

The possibility of the Central and Eastern European countries (CEECs) entering the European Union (EU) prompts the need for us to investigate their
agricultural potential. Will they become importers or exporters of food products? Will their entry in the EU force a complete revision of the existing
common agricultural policy (CAP)? These are questions that anybody interested in European agricultural policies may ask. At the same time, since the
same kind of problem arises almost everywhere, the method used to find an
answer may be of interest to almost any agricultural economist.

A traditional approach in this field consists of the building of general equilibrium models, which allow calculations to be made of equilibrium prices and
quantities under different scenarios of trade liberalization. Such models, generally, are optimistic in suggesting that there are large benefits that the CEECs
can derive from membership of the European Union (see, for instance, Folmer
et al., 1995). At the same time, in view of the large agricultural potential
among the CEECs, there is concern both about the future of the EU farm sector
and about policy issues, since it is commonly thought that applying the present
CAP system to the CEECs would result in an enormous oversupply of agricultural products. As a consequence, recommendations often centre on the need
for a change in the CAP, which should rely on market efficiency, rather than on
price support, as the only possible way of capturing the potential benefits of an
enlargement.

It is normally the case that general equilibrium models, based on standard
theorems, lead to the conclusion that general welfare is superior when there is
a customs union, rather than without, because there are fewer obstacles to
exchange. Hence the typical suggestion that 'liberalization is good'. However,
this conclusion depends on the assumption that the future is known with
certainty, as usually hypothesized in the construction of such models. It is an
assumption which is far from being justified in reality, since, in practice,
decisions are taken under risk and uncertainty. As a consequence, the 'no
profit' hypothesis cannot be met, and production is normally less than it would
be if marginal cost equates demand. This is a case for state price intervention

*INRA, Paris, France and University of Aarhus, Denmark, respectively.

which, by reducing the cost of risk, would play the same role as productivity-increasing technical progress.

As a consequence of the above analysis, computable general equilibrium (CGE) models have to be modified, in order to take account of the effects of risk and uncertainty in production decisions. This is possible, but rarely done. In addition, it has been shown that to take uncertainty into consideration will, in general, modify the dynamic path of results. Uncertainty creates uncertainty, so that unregulated markets may end up in a situation less favourable, in respect of general welfare, than those which are regulated. This is particularly true of agricultural markets, where demand is rigid (Boussard, 1996).

For the present study, the classical general equilibrium model has therefore been modified, by explicitly introducing risk as a determinant of producers' decisions. It should be noted, at this stage, that the risk considered here is not the traditional technical risk (as exemplified, for instance, by meteorological variation), but rather the economic risk associated with price instability. The latter is not difficult to introduce into a CGE model, since the method follows from the basic equations of portfolio theory.

Such modified models have been applied to the present situation of two East European countries, Poland and Hungary.[1] To study the growth path of present economic systems the work was done in a dynamic perspective, by letting each fixed factor depend recursively on the equilibrium solution for the previous year, and making the estimates for the variability of prices on the basis of earlier fluctuations. In that way, the equilibrium path is calculated over a series of years. It is then possible to demonstrate that capital accumulation, growth and intersectoral transfers of resources can be affected, in a sensitive manner, by the nature of the trade regime and by price stabilization policies.

SCENARIOS AND METHODS

The general equilibrium models are based on social accounting matrices (SAMs) for each country. They are first solved under the standard conditions of the free market, on a 'no risk' basis, for comparison. This leads into the study of country growth, over a period of 10 years, by making the model recursive.

The next step is to establish a scenario under free market assumptions, but with decision makers having a relatively large degree of risk aversion. In that way 'all stable' scenarios are generated. Here prices are stable in the sense that foreign prices are kept constant, according to the tradition of CGE models, though they can alter in response to changes in the availability of fixed factors, as in the 'no risk' scenario. Now, however, decision makers are averse to such changes, and consider them detrimental.

In this context, the only source of variability is endogenous. It results from the adaptation of the economy to new conditions. But it was also necessary to examine the consequences of exogenous shocks affecting foreign agricultural prices, leading to the introduction of two additional scenarios. One, referred to as 'world prices random' is built with large shocks affecting both world and European agricultural prices (implying that the present EU price stabilization policy does not apply in the CEECs). The second, referred to as 'European prices stable' is made with the same shock only affecting world prices, but with EU agricultural prices remaining stable at the initial year level. It must be borne in mind that non-agricultural foreign prices are kept constant.

The CGE models used in this context are standard (de Janvry and Sadoulet, 1995), with CES production functions, and use of the 'Armington assumption', to make foreign trade dependent upon demand elasticity, and of the 'Fisher equation', to relate the general price index to the quantity of money. The models are particular, nevertheless, with respect to risk and recursivity assumptions.

INTRODUCING RISK

The central assumption here is that producers, instead of maximizing expected profits, maximize the certainty equivalent of these profits. In addition, according to the basic Markowitz model of portfolio selection, it is assumed that the certainty equivalent of the random profit z is given by $U = \bar{z} - A\sigma_z^2$, where σ_z^2 is the variance of z and $\bar{z}$ stands for the expected value of z, with A as a risk aversion coefficient.

Obviously, each of these assumptions is extremely contentious (though the notion of there being an aggregate risk aversion coefficient is perhaps the least audacious), since the 'mean variance model' has been the object of many criticisms. It is not possible to discuss these issues at length. Our only justification (which should be taken seriously) is that it is certainly better to take account of risk, even, in an imperfect way, than to neglect it completely. Once the two major assumptions above are admitted, the model modifications are straightforward. If one neglects covariances, with $z = pq - C(q)$, where p is the price, q the quantity, and C the cost (a function of q), one has $\sigma_z^2 = \sigma_p^2 q^2$, with σ_p^2 being the variance of prices, and $\bar{z} = \bar{p}q - C(q)$ if $\bar{p}$ and $\bar{z}$ are the expected values of p and z.

Reporting these expressions in U, and deriving with respect to $\bar{q}$, gives the producer's optimality condition:

$$C'(\bar{q}) = \bar{p} - 2A\sigma_p^2 q.$$

This expression is then used to compute the elements of the matrix of technical coefficients, instead of its traditional counterpart $C'(\bar{q}) = \bar{p}$, which is made use of when risk is neglected.

The production function now exhibits a profit, the magnitude of which is $2A\sigma_\pi^2\bar{q}^2$. This profit is the entrepreneurial reward for taking risk, which has to be accounted for in the construction of the SAM matrix. Additional rows and columns have been defined, called 'risk in xx', where xx stands for agriculture, industry, services and other production activities. An estimate of the quantity $A\sigma^2 q^2$ for each activity has been made, on a rather arbitrary basis, with A being defined as the inverse of the average wealth in the industry, and other parameters determined by the necessity of balancing the SAM under examination.

At the same time, the corresponding column activities must spend their incomes somewhere. It has been assumed that 'risk' columns of the SAM were spending their incomes exactly as 'capital' columns would do. In that way, it is recognized that risk benefits are the reward of profit, and minimal changes are involved in the original SAM.

THE DYNAMICS OF THE CGE MODEL

Because risk takes place in time, it is practically impossible to set up a risk model without dynamic considerations. In the present case, the source of price variability cannot be anything other than time. Thus we have to take account of time to set up our experiment 'with' and 'without' risk. In order to make the model dynamic, first, one must derive the level of fixed factors in year t from the results of year $t - 1$ and, second, specify how expectations are modified across time.

Factors are labour and capital. For labour, in Poland, the SAM allowed for a distinction between agricultural and non-agricultural labour. As a consequence, it was easy to define an elasticity of emigration from rural to urban occupations with respect to the price ratio of agricultural and urban wages. In Hungary, no such distinction between labour type was available. As a consequence, the total quantity of labour is kept constant, and the shift from agricultural and non-agricultural occupations is supposed to be instantaneous, and regulated by prices only. Actually, such an assumption is probably much more justified for Hungary than for Poland.

The basic recursive equation for capital is:

$$K_{it} = K_{it-1} - a_i K_{it-1} + I_{it-1},$$

where K_{it} is capital stock at date t for sector I; a_i the depreciation factor; I_{it} investment of sector I at date $t - 1$ (I_{it} is given by the level of capital account activity I, with i being 'agriculture' or 'other'). This equation was used in its basic form in the Polish model, with agricultural savings financing agricultural capital, and non-agricultural savings, non-agricultural capital. In the Hungarian case, a complication arose from the fact that the SAM did not indicate anything about the origins of savings. Thus it was necessary to allocate savings and investment between the stocks of capital in four production activities. This was done through a portfolio sub-model allocating investment according to each sector's profitability (as measured by the corresponding 'price') and riskiness (measured by the price variability).

With respect to expectations, first, it must be noticed that there is an almost complete lack of coverage of expectations pertaining to the *mean levels* of prices in this model.[2] Since prices are always equilibrium prices, one is permanently within the framework of rational expectations, where agents accurately forecast the outcome of the equilibrium and take decisions on that basis. However, this is in some sense contradictory with the existence of risk, as introduced above. Actually, it is probably not unreasonable to assume that average prices are more or less rationally expected, whereas, at the same time, expectations pertaining to *price variability* are revised each year.

In fact, it is easy to see that, given the risk aversion coefficient A (which can be held constant), a guess is necessary at σ_p^2, the variance of price for each producing activity. Here a 'naive' expectations scheme for variances has been defined which, with i as the activity index and t as time, is given as:

$$\sigma^2_{pi} = (P_{it-2} - P_{it-2})^2$$

RESULTS

Simulations were performed under various scenarios, as indicated above.[3] A summary of the numerous results thus obtained is presented in the figures below. In particular, there are a number of observation which can be made, which follow as brief comments on the figures.

The predicted growth path of consumption within the economy is considerably influenced by risk (Figures 1 and 2). In this respect, in both countries (although it is more visible for Poland than for Hungary), the 'no risk' solution is very much superior to the other three solutions. As in plain linear programming models, suppressing risk (should it be possible!) would play the same role as a huge dose of technical progress.

Risk considerations especially affect the quantity of agricultural production, through manpower availability, as suggested for Poland by Figures 3 and 4 (similar results apply to Hungary).

The consequences of risk for investment (and thus for future growth) are extremely important, as illustrated by Figures 5 and 6, which represent savings and investment in Hungary. One should note the high discrepancy between real investment and saving, as well as the fact that the discrepancy increases with

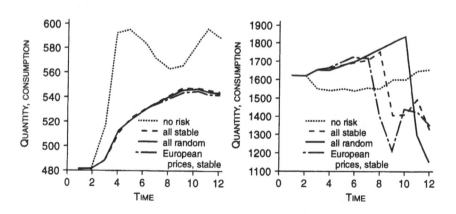

FIGURE 1   *Consumption in Poland*   **FIGURE 2**   *Consumption in Hungary*

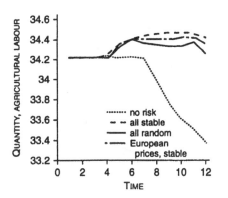

FIGURE 3 *Poland, agricultural labour*

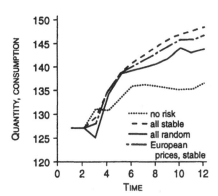

FIGURE 4 *Poland, agricultural production*

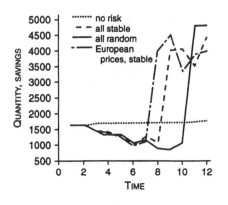

FIGURE 5 *Hungary, savings (volume)*

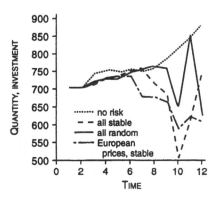

FIGURE 6 *Hungary, investment (volume)*

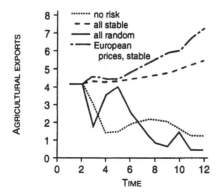

FIGURE 7 *Poland, agricultural exports to EU*

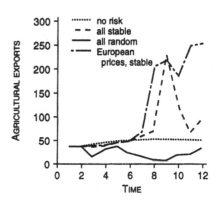

FIGURE 8 *Hungary, agricultural exports to EU*

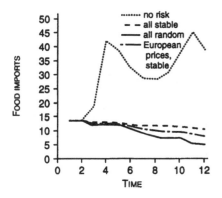

FIGURE 9 *Poland, food imports*

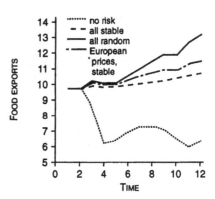

FIGURE 10 *Poland, food exports to EU*

risk. This is fully in accordance with the core of Keynesian theory (Shackle, 1965).

If we now turn our attention towards the various 'with risk' scenarios, the observed differences are smaller than expected. However, while this is true for growth in general, it is not the case when trade is considered. In particular, if the European Union remains as a buyer of agricultural products at fixed prices, while leaving the general level of world prices unstable, it could face an explosion of agricultural exports from Poland and Hungary, as shown in Figures 7 and 8. Note that, for different reasons, the same situation may occur if none of the foreign prices are fixed. In that case, the situation of the Polish and Hungarian economies is so bad that the resource transfer between agriculture and non-agriculture is difficult, resulting in an increase of agricultural production.

It must also be noted that what is true for agriculture is not necessarily true for food imports or exports, as shown in Figures 9 and 10, where Polish food imports and exports are displayed. Instability decreases food industry exports, and increases imports, in Poland, by comparison with 'no risk' situations. The same is true of Hungary, though that is not illustrated here. The precise mechanism in operation in these situations is not yet fully understood.

CONCLUSIONS

The results which have been obtained are only illustrative of what can be expected when risk considerations are explicitly introduced into general equilibrium models. They show that many optimistic statements about positive effects of trade liberalization may be far less justified than is commonly admitted. But they are only partial, and should be supported by additional experiments. In particular, the phenomena which have been observed here are much too dependent upon assumptions regarding foreign trade elasticities, which are obviously always disputable. A more general and comprehensive model at the world level, on roughly the OECD RUNS model format (as described, for instance, by Goldin and Knudsen, 1990), but modified along the lines described above, is now being considered.

NOTES

[1]The restriction to these two countries is caused more by data availability than anything else. It was extremely difficult to obtain social accounting matrices for countries such as Romania or Latvia. Many thanks are due to W. Orlowski (World Bank), who let us have access to Polish and Hungarian SAMs.

[2]The only exception is with the price ratio of agricultural labour against non-agricultural labour, as discussed above in the recursive definition of the population. Here, naive expectations ($^P_t = P_{t-1}$, with ^P_t standing for expectation in year t, and P_t, for the actually observed price in year t) are assumed, very naturally.

[3]Since results were thought to be sensitive to the elasticities of substitution used in the CES production functions, different sets of elasticities were investigated. Although slight differences were found in the results, they were not sufficiently significant to be presented. Only results with the 'high elasticities of substitution' set are mentioned.

REFERENCES

Boussard, J.M. (1996), 'When risk generates chaos', *Journal of Economic Behavior and Organi-sation*, **29**, 433–46.

de Janvry, A. and Sadoulet, E. (1995), *Quantitative Development Policy Analysis*, Baltimore: Johns Hopkins University Press.

Folmer, C., Keyzer, M., Merhis, M.D., Stolwijk, H.J.J. and Veenendaal, P.J.J. (1995), *The CAP beyond the McSharry Reform*, Amsterdam: North-Holland.

Goldin, I. and Knudsen, O. (1990), *Agricultural Trade Liberalisation: Implications for Develop-ing Countries*, Paris: OECD.

Shackle, G.L.S. (1965), *A Sketch of Economic Theory*, Cambridge: Cambridge University Press.

CONTRIBUTED PAPERS

Trade and Trade Effects

LUCA SALVATICI, COLIN A. CARTER AND DANIEL A. SUMNER*

The Trade Restrictiveness Index and its
Potential Contribution to Agricultural Policy Analysis

INTRODUCTION

Consider the following statements: 'Country A has reduced (increased) its trade distortions in recent years', 'Policies followed by country A are less (more) trade distortive than policies followed by country B', 'Trade negotiations should lead to a reduction of trade distortions'. All three can be seen to share the common assumption that 'trade distortion' is a concept that can both be properly defined and also be measured in such a way as to allow comparisons through time, between countries and across a range of policy mix.

The need to provide a consistent measure of aggregate trade distortion arises in the debate over the benefits of trade liberalization whenever efforts are made to measure its impact on welfare or growth. In addition, it is obvious that the process of trade negotiations provides an important application for this type of index. In the case of agriculture, for example, the Uruguay Round of GATT established commitments in terms of aggregate measures since, on the one hand, internal policies were combined into a single indicator (the aggregate measure of support) while, on the other hand, most non-tariff barriers were transformed into tariff equivalents ('tariffication'). There is clearly a demand for 'trade distortion indicators' which are consistent with economic theory and whose construction is feasible. Unfortunately, many of the traditional indicators have serious theoretical flaws and are difficult to interpret (for a stimulating survey, see Pritchett, 1996). The case of agriculture is usually even more difficult, since one of the principal characteristics of agricultural protectionism is the close link between domestic and border policies (De Benedictis *et al.*, 1991).

According to Anderson and Neary (1996), the elements that define a theoretically consistent policy index of trade restrictiveness include the following:

- a comprehensive policy coverage (tariffs, import quotas, border and domestic policies, and so on);
- a reference point for the 'equivalent-impact' in which there is interest (iso-welfare measures, iso-income measures, and so on);

*University of Rome 'La Sapienza', Italy (Salvatici) and University of California, Davis, USA (Carter and Sumner). Luca Salvatici acknowledges financial support from Consiglio Nazionale delle Ricerche.

- a scalar aggregate in the form of a policy instrument into which the measures considered under the policy coverage are translated (tariff-equivalent measures, subsidy-equivalent measures, quota-equivalent measures, and so on).

A general definition of such an index is as follows: 'depending on a prede-termined reference concept, any aggregate measure is a function mapping from a vector of independent variables – defined according to the policy coverage – into a scalar aggregate'. As soon as thought turns to the problem of finding a single number capable of summarizing a set of policies applied in different markets, it is apparent that there is a need to define the types of information which have to be summarized. This means that the process of aggregation should allow certain basic pieces of information to be preserved or, put in a different way, that the final single number is *equivalent* to the original multiple data in terms of the information in which there is interest.

One of the most interesting recent suggestions in the literature is repres-ented by the Trade Restrictiveness Index (TRI) proposed by Anderson and Neary (Anderson and Neary, 1994; Anderson, 1995; Anderson and Neary, 1996). This paper will examine the functioning and the properties of the index, arguing that the TRI can usefully enrich the arsenal of indicators usually applied by agricultural economists.[1] Nonetheless, it is important to note at the outset that it has nothing to do with trade (flow) restrictions. In point of fact, the TRI focuses on the domestic welfare impact of a given set of policies.

The paper is organized around the TRI and its theoretical background; it highlights some of its features and discusses the type of questions which can be addressed using the index. In terms of the notation, subscripts always indicate partial derivatives, with the exception of the letters i and j, which are used as indices.

THE TRADE RESTRICTIVENESS INDEX

The TRI represents a uniform tariff-equivalent, iso-welfare measure. Although the inclusion of import quotas introduces analytical complications – for exam-ple, in terms of how the quota rent is shared between the importing and exporting country (Anderson and Neary, 1992) – both price and quantity import restrictive policies can be handled by the TRI. For the sake of simplic-ity, the following presentation deals only with tariffs.

The TRI (Δ) is defined as the inverse of the uniform tariff factor (one plus the uniform tariff), which would compensate the representative consumer for the actual change in tariffs, holding constant the balance of trade. Economic efficiency is defined in terms of the welfare of the representative agent and distributive issues are ignored.

If new tariffs are equal to zero, $1/\Delta - 1$ is the uniform tariff which is equivalent in efficiency to the original trade policy. More generally, $1/\Delta$ is the scalar factor of proportionality by which period 1 prices would have to be adjusted to ensure balanced trade when utility is at period 0 level. It should be noted that this is not the same as raising tariffs by a uniform proportionate rate, except in the case of a full liberalization.

Formally,

$$\Delta(\pi^1, u^0; k^0) = [\Delta: B(\pi^1/\Delta, u^0; k^0) = 0], \tag{1}$$

where $B(\pi, u; k)$ is the balance-of-trade function. The $B(\cdot)$ function is equal to the net income transfer (equal to zero in equilibrium) required to reach a given level of aggregate national welfare (u) for an economy with a given vector of domestic prices (π) and a vector (k) which includes all the variables assumed exogenous (world prices, factor endowments and so on). The balance-of-trade function represents the external budget constraint of the economy, since it summarizes the three possible sources of funds for financing imports: earnings from exports, earnings from trade distortions or international transfers.

Since Δ deflates period 1 prices and quantities to attain period 0 utility, it is a compensating variation type of measure. The welfare cost of protection can be expressed as the integral over the scalar TRI inverse, in exactly the same way as the cost of protection with a single tariff equals an integral over the price of the tariff-restricted good. It is important to point out that standard welfare measures of the cost of protection give a correct indication of the shift in the relevant general equilibrium budget constraint, but they lack a scale (normalization) that would permit international and intertemporal comparisons.

The proportional change in the TRI is a weighted average of the proportional changes in domestic prices. Totally differentiating equation (1) we get

$$(B_\pi'/\Delta)d\pi - (B_\pi'/\Delta^2)d\Delta = 0, \tag{2}$$

then

$$d\Delta/\Delta = \sum_i (B_{\pi i}\pi_i/B_\pi'\pi)(d\pi_i/\pi_i). \tag{3}$$

The weights in (3) turn out to be the proportions of marginal deadweight loss due to each tariff, and they depend on the partial derivatives of the $B(\cdot)$ function with respect to prices. In order to have a more precise idea of the components of these derivatives, we use a standard model, based on the following assumptions:

- perfect competition,
- constant returns to scale technology,
- only tradable goods are produced (alternatively, the price of non-traded goods is determined competitively),
- small country,
- net revenues from trade distortions are returned to the representative agent,
- at least one untaxed good is used as the *numéraire* (it is assumed that it is the export good), and exogenous trade policy.

If there are no international transfers, the balance-of-trade constraint can be expressed as:

$$\pi' m - r = t' m, \tag{4}$$

where
π = domestic price vector of tariff-constrained goods,
m = vector of tariff-constrained imports,
r = vector of exports,
$t = \pi - \pi^* = $ tariff.

The left-hand side of equation (4) is the trade expenditure function $E(\pi, u)$, expressing the optimal behaviour of the representative agent. It is important to note that, even if the function $E(\cdot)$ is homogeneous of degree one in prices, the balance-of-trade function does not have this property because of the presence of trade restrictions and the fact that there is an implicit *numéraire*.

The function $E(\cdot)$ is obtained as the difference between the consumer's expenditure function, $e(\pi, u)$, and the gross domestic product (GDP) function, $g(\pi, k)$. The derivatives of $E(\cdot)$ with respect to prices are the compensated import demand functions.

As far as the GDP function is concerned, k represents the fixed endowment of factors of production. The derivatives of the $g(\cdot)$ function with respect to prices are the economy's general equilibrium net supply functions by Hotelling's Lemma. Accordingly, g_π is equal to the supply function of the tariff-constrained good if there is domestic production of a perfect substitute for the import; it is equal to minus the imported input demand function if the good is an intermediate input into production; and it is equal to zero if the import is for final consumption only and there is no domestic production (the 'Armington assumption').

Totally differentiating the external budget constraint (4) implies:

$$\pi' dm + m' d\pi - dr - t' dm - m' dt = 0. \tag{5}$$

Using the small country assumption ($d\pi = dt$), (5) can be rewritten as:

$$\pi' dm - dr = t' dm. \tag{6}$$

The left-hand side of equation (6) is the change in net trade expenditure at the initial prices ($B_u du$). It might arise, for example, if a gift of foreign exchange enabled more net expenditure at constant prices. The right-hand side of (6) is the net foreign exchange effect of the change in trade policy.

Holding utility constant,

$$dm = m_\pi dt. \tag{7}$$

Hence

$$t' m_\pi = -B'_\pi, \tag{8}$$

where the left-hand side of (8) represents the marginal cost of tariffs, while the right-hand side of (8) is the vector of transfers needed to compensate for increases in tariffs.

The sign of $(B'_\pi dt)$ is positive if tariff increases are inefficient. This appeals to intuition, but it should not be taken for granted, since cross-price effects can make it negative (this would be a typical 'second-best' result).

INTERPRETATION OF THE RESULTS

Figure 1 (adapted from Anderson, 1995 and Neary, 1995) provides a graphical illustration of the main results. U^0 is an iso-welfare contour in tariff factor space (T_1, T_2), where the tariff factor is defined as one plus the ad valorem tariff rate. In the convex region, for each level of utility the value of $B(\cdot)$ increases as tariffs rise. The regions with a positive slope are drawn in order to show a typical second-best 'perverse' result. In these regions, as a matter of fact, the marginal cost of the tariff is negative. This means that a reduction of T_2 from F, for example, would actually decrease the welfare level, while an increase of the tariff would imply a lower trade expenditure for the same level of utility.

The curve labelled τ illustrates the locus of tariff factors along which the import-weighted average remains constant. Its shape depends on the substitution properties within the economy, but it is necessarily downward-sloping in

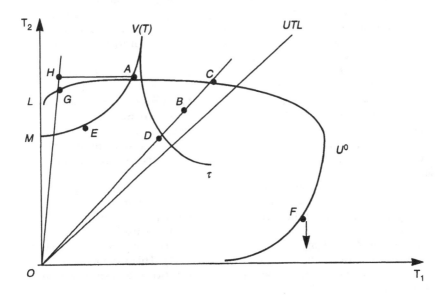

FIGURE 1   *Consistent and inconsistent measurements of trade reform*

this two-good case. $V(T)$ is an iso-variance contour. Since the partial derivative of the variance with respect to tariff factor i is equal to

$$dV(T)/dT_i = 2(t_i - \tau)/n, \tag{9}$$

the contour's slope is equal to

$$dT_2/dT_1 = -(t_1 - \tau)/(t_2 - \tau). \tag{10}$$

In this two-good case, the partial derivatives must have opposite signs, hence the slope is positive. The variance increases with distance from the uniform tariff locus (*UTL*).

The first result presented in Figure 1 is the comparison between the TRI and the moments of the traditional tariff indices. Let us assume that trade reform leads to a movement from A to B. The TRI is equal to *OB/OC* and shows a reduction of the index. On the contrary, the mean tariff index would register a rise in protection, while the coefficient of variation would show a reduction of dispersion (lower variance, higher mean). Area *ALM* represents a set of (possible) tariff reforms which are welfare-improving according to the TRI ($\Delta < 1$), but which the coefficient of variation would measure as welfare-inferior (lower mean, higher variance). The bottom line, then, is that purely statistical measures, such as the trade-weighted average tariff or the coefficient of variation of tariffs, bear no necessary relation to the welfare cost of trade policy.[2]

Secondly, points D and E show that (1) a mean-preserving tariff reform is efficient if it reduces the tariff's variance, and (2) an average tariff reduction with constant variance is efficiency improving. However, Anderson (1995) shows that these propositions hold only if the balance of trade function has a constant elasticity of substitution form.

Thirdly, Figure 1 can also be used to show how the TRI considerably enlarges the possibility of evaluating trade reforms. According to the standard results of the piecemeal trade reform literature (Foster and Sonnenschein, 1970; Hatta, 1977), it can only be said that welfare increases if there is a move along any ray towards the origin (the 'radial reduction' rule) or a move towards *UTL* (the 'concertina' rule). In the case of the TRI, on the other hand, any point within the iso-welfare contour shows a reduction of the uniform tariff equivalent.

Finally, it can be seen how even the TRI measure is not completely free from counterintuitive 'second-best' results. As a consequence of the theoretical ambiguity about the sign of the weights in (3), an increase in tariffs or a decrease in quotas may be associated with either a rise or a fall in the TRI.[3] For instance, moving from A to H simply implies a reduction of T_1; nonetheless, the TRI will signal an increase in the index ($\Delta = OH/OG > 1$). This means that it is not possible to be sure *a priori* about the relation between a change in Δ and a change in welfare.

So far, only import restrictions (namely tariffs) have been considered. The converse case of import subsidies does not seem to have a great practical relevance but, as far as exports are concerned, both restrictions and subsidies are widely adopted by national governments. The European Union's export refund policy and the United States' Export Enhancement Program are classic examples of export subsidy policies in the agricultural sector. In terms of export restrictions, quantitative restrictions have become increasingly common under the label of 'voluntary export restraints', while several developing countries traditionally use export taxes as a revenue source for the public budget.

Even if all the existing presentations of the TRI focus on import tariffs and quotas, it is important to note that the interpretation of the TRI differs according to the type of trade policy considered. Table 1 summarizes the impact of changes in the different types of policies in terms of changes in the TRI, the volume of trade and the welfare level.

Each of the rows in Table 1 represents a reduction in a trade-distortive policy, with different intensities across markets that are summarized through the TRI. Assuming that all goods are substitutes, welfare impacts are always positive. Import taxes and export subsidies fit our previous description: a reduction in a trade distortion implies that $\Delta < 1$ and is signalled by a reduction in the TRI.

TABLE 1   *Comparison of different border policies*

	Policy change	TRI change	Trade volume change	Welfare change
Import tax ($\Delta < 1$)	–	–	+	+
Export subsidy ($\Delta < 1$)	–	–	–	+
Import subsidy ($\Delta > 1$)	–	+	–	+
Export tax ($\Delta > 1$)	–	+	+	+

Each of the rows in Table 1 represents a reduction in a trade-distortive policy, with different intensities across markets that are summarized through the TRI. Assuming that all goods are substitutes, welfare impacts are always positive. Import taxes and export subsidies fit our previous description: a reduction in a trade distortion implies that $\Delta < 1$ and is signalled by a reduction in the TRI.

However, if there are import subsidies and export taxes, the results are reversed. In these cases world prices are higher than domestic prices and a reduction of the distortion leads to an increase of the latter. Trade liberalization, then, implies $\Delta > 1$ and an increase in the TRI. The message here is that great care should be used in interpreting the TRI results, especially if different types of border policies are taken into account.

In Table 1, the impact on trade flows is obviously of different sign in the cases of the reduction of taxes or the reduction of subsidies. Even if in each case the resulting volume of trade is closer to the one prevailing under free trade, it is important to realize that the concept of 'trade restrictiveness', assumed in the definition of the TRI, is a very precise (and limited) one. It is related to, but nonetheless very different from, the one that could be considered, for example, in the context of trade negotiations. In that case, the trade volume displacement due to a certain set of policies may very well be more relevant to cross-country comparisons than the effects on domestic welfare.

Figure 2 provides a graphical example of the differences in the implied trade volumes resulting from alternative definitions of trade restrictiveness. We consider a partially decoupled set of policies, which includes a tariff and a production quota fixed at exactly the same level of production that would have occurred under free trade.

In the quantity space of a two-good economy (y_1, y_2), A is the production bundle and FT is the consumption bundle under free trade. As a consequence of the introduction of the tariff-cum-quota set of policies, the consumption bundle shifts from FT to TQ, while the production quota y_2^q does not allow the production bundle to change. On the other hand, if there is replacement of the tariff-cum-quota with a tariff-equivalent in terms of welfare (that is, the type of counterfactual experiment used in the construction of the TRI), the economy will produce at D and consume at TE. Clearly, in the latter case both imports $(TE - C < TQ - B)$ and exports $(C - D < B - A)$ are lower than under the tariff-cum-quota case, although the economy is on the same indifference curve U^1.

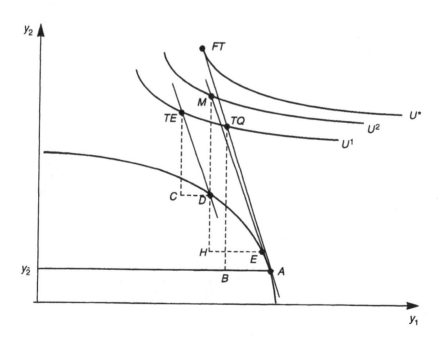

FIGURE 2   *Comparison between different tariff equivalents*

It is possible to draw the tariff equivalent in terms of the volume of trade for the tariff-cum-quota set of policies, obtaining the points E and M where, by construction, $M - H = TQ - B$ and $H - E = B - A$. In this case, however, the level of welfare achieved by the two policies is different, with $U^2 > U^1$.

CONCLUSIONS

This paper has pursued two goals. Firstly, the nature of the TRI and its theoretical background have been considered. Secondly, the meaning of the index has been discussed, with an explanation of possible ambiguities in its interpretation.

The TRI is a scalar representing the uniform tariff which is equivalent (in a welfare sense) to a given protective structure. It is a theoretically consistent answer to a precise question. To the contrary, for many alternative indices, like the average tariff, it is not possible to frame a meaningful question for which the index provides an answer.

Even if the TRI seems to provide an acceptable answer, it is by no means the only possible one. The impact of any economic policy is evident in several dimensions, which require a variety of quantifying measures. Hence different results do not necessarily indicate that one measure is more correct than another, but rather that each captures different aspects.[4]

The TRI focuses on a crucial dimension for economic analysis, namely the impact on domestic welfare. However, as far as trade policies are concerned, another traditional and relevant parameter is represented by the impact on flows of trade. In this respect, it was shown that 'trade restrictiveness' is a misnomer, which may lead to serious misunderstandings about the meaning of the index.

NOTES

[1]There have already been some applications dealing with agricultural policies by Anderson *et al.* (1995) and Draaisma and Fulponi (1996).

[2]In fact, all the existing empirical results show that the correlation between changes in the TRI and changes in the tariff moments is close to zero.

[3]It should be noted that, if the denominator of (3) changes sign, it is impossible to exclude multiple solutions or the possibility that Δ is not even defined in certain regions.

[4]A very popular index among agricultural economists is the Producer Subsidy Equivalent (PSE), which represents a first-order approximation of the change in producer surplus or, alternatively, can be considered an 'iso-revenue, subsidy equivalent'. The differences between the PSE and the TRI are analysed in Anderson *et al.* (1995).

REFERENCES

Anderson, J.E. (1995), 'Tariff Index Theory', *Review of International Economics*, 3, 156–73.
Anderson, J.E. and Neary, P.J. (1992), 'Trade Reform with Quotas, Partial Rent Retention and Tariffs', *Econometrica*, 60, 57–66.
Anderson, J.E. and Neary, P.J. (1994), 'Measuring the Restrictiveness of Trade Policy', *The World Bank Economic Review*, 8, 151–70.

Anderson, J.E. and Neary, P.J. (1996), 'A New Approach to Evaluating Trade Policy', *Review of Economic Studies*, **63**, 107–25.

Anderson, J.E., Bannister, G.J. and Neary, P.J. (1995), 'Domestic Distortions and International Trade', *International Economic Review*, **36**, 139–56.

De Benedictis, M., De Filippis, F. and Salvatici, L. (1991), 'Between Scylla and Charibdys: Agricultural economists' navigation around protectionism and free trade', *European Review of Agricultural Economics*, **18**, 311–37.

Draaisma, T. and Fulponi, L. (1996), 'Measuring the Aggregate Trade Effects of the Change in Domestic Policies: An Application of the Trade Restrictiveness Index', paper presented at the VIIth meeting of the European Agricultural Economists Association, September, Edinburgh.

Foster, E. and Sonnenschein, H. (1970), 'Price Distortion and Economic Welfare', *Econometrica*, **38**, 281–97.

Hatta, T. (1977), 'A Theory of Piecemeal Policy Recommendation', *Review of Economic Studies*, **44**, 1–21.

Neary, J.P. (1995), 'Trade Liberalisation and Shadow Prices in the Presence of Tariffs and Quotas', *International Economic Review*, **36**, 531–54.

Pritchett, L. (1996), 'Measuring outward orientation in LDCs: can it be done?', *Journal of Development Economics*, **49**, 307–35.

SUZANNE THORNSBURY, DONNA ROBERTS, KATE DeREMER AND
DAVID ORDEN*

A First Step in Understanding Technical Barriers to Agricultural Trade

INTRODUCTION

It is widely recognized that technical barriers to trade create many obstacles to the international exchange of agricultural goods. Such barriers exist in most industries, but are particularly important in the trade of primary and processed agricultural products. Agricultural exporters are often required to demonstrate that native species or human health are not endangered by their products, while simultaneously satisfying the nutrition, packaging and labelling standards of the importing country. Policy makers acknowledge that the recent prominence of technical barriers is due in part to growing demands in the developed world for enhanced food safety and for protection of the earth's resources. However, they also recognize that the disingenuous use of technical measures can be a non-transparent means of providing protection for domestic producers.

The proliferation of such measures in recent years was a catalyst for the negotiation of new disciplines on their use in the Uruguay Round Agreement on the Application of Sanitary and Phytosanitary Measures (SPS Agreement) and the Agreement on Technical Barriers to Trade (TBT Agreement). Both stipulate that technical measures should not constitute a disguised restriction on international trade, or be applied in an arbitrary or discriminatory manner. Additionally, a country should not enforce an SPS measure (related to protection of plant, animal and public health) without sufficient scientific evidence about the risks posed by an imported product and how the measure mitigates that identified risk (GATT Secretariat, 1994).

While having the new discipline on technical barriers in place is potentially constructive, their formal existence does not guarantee that greater discipline will be imposed on international use of technical trade barriers. When importing countries resist unilaterally bringing their measures into conformity with the SPS and TBT Agreements, legal scholars conclude that a strategy to encourage compliance may be to 'expose them to the light of day, on the premise that transparency and the attendant publicity will increase the costs of self-serving or scientifically dubious decision making and thus discourage it' (Sykes, 1995, p. 86).

*Virginia Polytechnic Institute and State University, Economic Research Service U.S. Department of Agriculture, Economic Research Service U.S. Department of Agriculture, and Virginia Polytechnic Institute and State University, respectively.

In this context, further study of technical barriers can clearly contribute to strengthening the disciplining role of the recent Uruguay Round agreements. Economic analysis can advance understanding on a wide breadth of issues including the net costs of technical trade barriers; sources of international regulatory heterogeneity; the benefits of harmonization of standards; least-trade restrictive measures; and distinctions between justifiable and unjustifiable technical barriers. However, this analysis has been slow to develop (Sumner and Lee, ch. 15 in Orden and Roberts, 1997).

One reason for the dearth of literature is that confusion over the basic definition of the term 'technical barrier to trade' has thwarted advancement towards the basic goal of identifying the characteristics that distinguish these measures from other non-tariff barriers. This absence of a *lingua franca* for technical barriers has been an important impediment to analysis, hampering development of conceptual foundations upon which further economic analysis can build. Furthermore, efforts to expand knowledge about technical barriers by means of empirical studies have been stymied by the lack of systematically collected data on the incidence of these measures (Ndayisenga and Kinsey, 1994). Therefore most of the empirical literature on technical barriers consists of case studies that together provide only fragmentary evidence of the costs to the international economy.

This paper represents a first step in advancing understanding of technical barriers as a distinct class of trade-restricting measures. It proposes an explicit definition of technical barriers followed by discussion of measures that would consequently be included or excluded from this sub-set of non-tariff barriers. Next the paper features a presentation and discussion of the results from a 1996 US Department of Agriculture (USDA) survey of technical barriers to US agricultural exports, one of the few institutional efforts to systematically collect information on the incidence and impact of these barriers. The final section proposes a general framework for taking the next steps in analysing technical barriers.

WHAT ARE TECHNICAL BARRIERS?

There are differing views on what constitutes a technical barrier. Earlier literature recognized sanitary and phytosanitary (SPS) measures, standards and an amorphous array of measures that delayed entry of products at the border, as technical barriers; more recently, technical barriers have been viewed as a subset of environmental regulations (Baldwin, 1970; Hillman, ch. 1 in Orden and Roberts, 1997). For this paper, technical barriers are defined as legally binding regulations and standards governing the sale of products in national markets, where the prima facie objective is the correction of market inefficiencies stemming from externalities associated with the production, distribution and consumption of the relevant products. This definition comprises regulations that have as their apparent primary objective the correction of information asymmetries (which includes standards of identity, standards of measurement and attribute or quality identification), or those aimed at correction of production externalities (which includes SPS measures and global commons measures), or ones aimed at correction of consumption externalities (which includes packaging measures). The words 'prima facie' in the definition acknowledge the existence of regulatory capture, which occurs when domestic groups with a vested interest in limiting competition successfully lobby for measures that potentially represent a net cost to society.

This view of technical barriers is both broader and narrower than others found in the literature. The above definition excludes incentive measures such as subsidies and taxes, even though they may have been established to address environmental externalities (Figure 1). It is broader than other definitions of technical barriers in two respects. Technical barriers (especially in recent years) have been regarded as nearly synonymous with SPS measures; the above definition includes attributes such as organic production standards or shelf-life restrictions designed to ensure product freshness. Secondly, the definition comprises more than just a small set of border measures, such as import bans, which often dominate discussion of agricultural technical barriers; it also includes measures that range from input standards to information remedies (Roberts *et al.*, forthcoming).

The previous discussion implicitly notes two features of technical barriers that distinguish them from other trade policy instruments. Unlike conventional

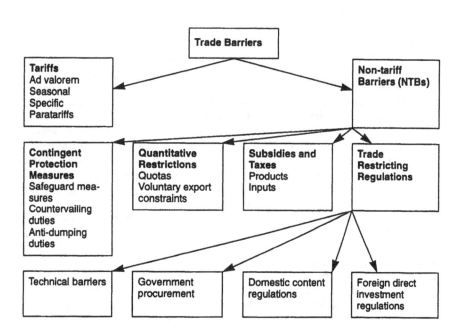

FIGURE 1   *Tariff and non-tariff barriers to trade*

trade measures, such as tariffs and quotas, the public goods dimension of technical barriers implies that these measures can sometimes be economically efficient. Also a large class of technical barriers, sanitary and phytosanitary regulations, are not most-favoured-nation policy instruments: that is, the conditions for entering the importing country's market are not identical for all trading partners. The bilateral nature of these measures can beget product differentiation and create market power in trading arrangements.

DATA SOURCES

USDA recognized the need for an assessment of technical barriers faced by US agricultural exporters as these barriers began to appear with increasing frequency at the centre of international commercial disputes. In lieu of a formal statistical survey, such as that used by the European Communities (Sykes, 1995), USDA began its assessment of technical barriers with a survey of experts from six economic and regulatory agencies within the Department, supplemented by a survey of representatives from selected producer groups. This assessment capitalized on the internal multidisciplinary expertise of the Department, and focused on foreign technical measures for which remedies were potentially available under the new Uruguay Round agreements (Roberts and DeRemer, 1997).

Field personnel from USDA's Foreign Agricultural Service (FAS), who collectively cover 132 countries representing 98 per cent of the 1996 US agricultural export market, as well as representatives from producer groups which co-sponsor overseas market development activities with FAS, were asked to identify foreign technical barriers to US exports. They were also asked to provide estimates of annual US export revenue losses caused by each identified measure (estimated trade impact). This information was reviewed by USDA's four regulatory agencies: the Animal and Plant Health Inspection Service (APHIS), the Food Safety and Inspection Service (FSIS), the Agricultural Marketing Service (AMS) and the Grain Inspection, Packers and Stockyards Administration (GIPSA). Scientists and regulatory officials in these agencies deleted measures that were judged to have potential scientific justification (for SPS measures) or that were otherwise in conformity with the new trade agreement disciplines (for other technical measures).

The survey results therefore represent a cross-section of *questionable* technical barriers that were recently proposed or enforced in June 1996 which decrease, or potentially decrease, US agricultural exports to the specified market. The barriers are considered questionable because they appear to violate one or more principles of the new GATT trade agreements. This survey design permitted sharp focus on foreign measures that affected US commercial agricultural interests and for which provisions of recent trade agreements potentially offered some prospect of resolution in favour of greater access to foreign markets.

SURVEY RESULTS

The 1996 USDA survey identifies 303 questionable technical barriers to US agricultural exports with a total estimated trade impact of $4907.89 million. Trade impact is estimated as the loss in producer revenue resulting from a restricted quantity at a fixed world price. The average estimated trade impact per barrier is $16.20 million. Table 1 shows a distribution of barriers by their estimated impact on trade. The survey identified very few individual barriers with large estimated trade impacts. There are only 18 barriers (6 per cent) with effects of at least $50 million per barrier. The majority of barriers have small estimated trade impacts. More than 38 per cent of them have an impact between $5 million and $49.99 million and 55 per cent have estimated effects of less than $5 million per barrier.

TABLE 1   *Estimated trade impact of barriers in the 1996 USDA survey*

Estimated trade impact per barrier	Number of barriers
at least $50 million	18
$25–$49.99 million	19
$10–$24.99 million	51
$5–$9.99 million	48
$1–$4.99 million	97
$0.5–$0.99 million	22
$0.1–$0.49 million	29
less than $0.1 million	19
Total	303

Over 85 per cent of the barriers identified by the survey are questionable SPS measures. Other technical barriers, disciplined under the TBT Agreement, were small in both number and average trade impact. The average trade impact per barrier is $17.02 and $9.00 million for SPS and TBT barriers, respectively (Table 2). The average trade impact of barriers in the Multiple or Other Provisions of GATT 1994, which, for example, includes some grading and standards issues that are disciplined by Article XI of the GATT Agreement, is $15.01 million.

Technical barriers are categorized by the type of market restriction being imposed (Table 3). Market access barriers are import bans denying any exports of a US product to a country. The estimated trade impact is the potential value of US exports that could be sold if the ban was rescinded and the product gained access. Market expansion barriers are measures that limit, but do not preclude, US exports of a certain product to a country. The estimated effect is again the value of increased trade that might result from their removal. Market retention barriers are those measures under consideration by a foreign government that may adversely affect US exports if enacted. The estimated trade

TABLE 2 *WTO legal classification and regulatory goals for barriers identified in the 1996 USDA survey*

WTO classification Regulatory goal	Number of barriers	Estimated trade impact	Average trade impact per barrier
		($ million)	
SPS Agreement*	260	4 424.73	17.02
Plant health		2 516.79	
Animal health		868.82	
Food safety		2 288.00	
Natural environment		0.51	
TBT Agreement*	27	243.06	9.00
Quality		202.72	
Compatibility		41.04	
Multiple or Other Provisions of GATT 1994	16	240.09	15.01
Totals	303	4 907.88	16.20

Note: *the sum of the estimated trade impact for the regulatory goals is greater than the estimated trade impact for the agreement because an issue may have multiple regulatory goals.

impact is the value of current export revenue that they threaten and could potentially be lost.

Of the 19 barriers with the largest impact, 12 are classified as market access or expansion barriers, while seven are classified as market retention barriers. The average trade impact per barrier in the 19 cases is approximately ten times larger than the average impact for all barriers in the survey. The 12 market access and expansion barriers, with effects of at least $50 million, account for 60 per cent of the $3732.21 million in estimated total impacts attributed to all barriers (calculated by summing rows 1 and 2 in Table 3). If these 12 barriers alone were absent, US agricultural exports might increase by 3.2 per cent from the 1996 level. The seven largest market retention barriers account for 70 per cent of the $1175.67 million in total impact attributed to all market retention barriers in the survey. If the seven largest market retention barriers are not resolved and the restrictions take effect, US exports could decrease by 1.2 per cent from 1996 levels.

Over half of the barriers with estimated trade impacts between $5 and $49.99 million and less than $5 million are classified as restricting market expansion. Barriers with $5–$49.99 million in estimated impact account for 33 per cent, while the smallest 174 barriers account for less than 3 per cent, of the total for all barriers in the survey.

When the individual countries identified as applying questionable barriers are divided into six geographic regions, by far the largest number of barriers (92) is identified in the Americas (Table 4). The largest estimated trade impact

TABLE 3 *Type of market restriction from barriers identified in the 1996 USDA survey*

Type of market restriction	Barriers with at least $50 million in estimated trade impact		Barriers with $5–$49.99 million in estimated trade impact		Barriers with less than $5 million in estimated trade impact	
	No.	Estimated trade impact ($ million)	No.	Estimated trade impact ($ million)	No.	Estimated trade impact ($ million)
Access	2	200.00	40	449.50	66	73.15
Expansion	10	2 049.60	64	848.13	90	111.83
Retention	7	828.61	17	316.39	18	30.67
Totals	19	3 078.21	121	1 614.02	174	215.65

Note: *the sum of the number of barriers is greater than the sum reported above as some barriers may impose more than one type of market restriction.

($2325.3 million) and average trade impact per barrier ($29.81 million) is found in the countries of East Asia. The Middle Eastern countries impose the smallest number of barriers (11) with the lowest total estimated trade impact ($39.6 million).

Of the 18 barriers with the largest estimated trade impact, eight are imposed by countries in East Asia, six are European, and four are imposed by countries in the Americas. There are no barriers in this category for Africa, Oceania or the Middle East. Barriers with the estimated trade impacts less than $50 million are found in all six of the regions. A similar number of barriers with estimated trade impacts from $5 million to $49.99 million are imposed by the countries of the Americas (32 barriers) and East Asia (34 barriers), but the questionable barriers in East Asia account for a higher proportion of the total estimated trade impact. Of the 167 barriers with estimated trade impacts less than $5 million, 34 per cent stem from the Americas, 23 per cent are European, while countries in East Asia account for a smaller proportion of the total impact.

When specific products are considered, six of the 18 barriers with the largest effect apply to broadly defined product categories: further processed foods (four barriers), all agricultural, fish and forestry products (one barrier), and all animal products (one barrier). In addition, five of the 18 barriers are applied to grains with three specifically focused on wheat. The most prevalent product categories facing questionable barriers with $5–$49.99 million in estimated trade impact are fruit (20 barriers), grains (19 barriers) and further processed foods (12 barriers). Of the 167 barriers where the effect is less than $5 million, many tend to be applied to very specific commodities, such as live crayfish or exotic meat. When grouped together by product category, the largest number of barriers in this group is applied to fruit (35 barriers), followed by further processed foods (22 barriers), vegetables (17 barriers) and poultry (14 barriers).

Table 5 shows a regional product cross-tabulation for those cases where more than 10 barriers or $50 million in estimated trade impact is identified within one of the regions. This will highlight examples where there are a smaller number of questionable barriers with larger estimated trade impacts and cases where there are many questionable barriers of little overall significance. The results show that the pattern of questionable trade barriers follows the broad pattern of trade flows for US agricultural products. Barriers in the grains group are distributed across all geographic regions. Those affecting fruit and vegetable groups are concentrated mainly in East Asia. Barriers against animal products are mainly among the European countries and barriers in seed products are concentrated in the Americas.

THE NEXT STEPS IN ANALYSIS OF TECHNICAL BARRIERS

The 1996 USDA survey provides the first step in an organized accounting of technical restrictions that constrain world agricultural trade. Identification of the 303 barriers confirms their wide scope across regions and products in international markets. The estimates which are provided for actual or potential

TABLE 4 *Regions imposing barriers identified in the 1996 USDA survey*

Region	Barriers with at least $50 million in estimated trade impact		Barriers with $5–$49.99 million in estimated trade impact		Barriers with less than $5 million in estimated trade impact	
	No.	Estimated trade impact ($ million)	No.	Estimated trade impact ($ million)	No.	Estimated trade impact ($ million)
Africa			9	166.40	10	13.30
Americas	4	761.00	32	398.26	56	74.55
East Asia	8	1 771.40	34	512.73	36	41.17
Europe	6	555.81	23	307.73	38	36.01
Middle East			3	30.00	8	9.60
Oceania			17	204.50	19	25.42
Totals	18	3 088.21	118	1 619.62	167	200.05

461

TABLE 5   *Barriers identified in the 1996 USDA survey, by product category and region*

Product	Region*			
	Africa	Americas	East Asia	Europe
		Estimated trade impact ($ million (number of barriers))		
All products	—	—	500.00 (1)	—
Fruits and vegetables				
Fruit	—	75.62 (26)	302.29 (24)	—
Vegetables	—	22.46 (11)	68.40 (14)	—
Citrus	—	—	87.50 (7)	—
Grains and feed				
Grains	62.00 (4)	705.00 (9)	140.00 (3)	108.81 (7)
Animal products				
Beef	—	58.00 (5)	—	157.80 (7)
Pork	—	—	—	68.50 (5)
Beef and pork	—	—	—	50.00 (1)
All animal products	—	—	—	201.00 (2)
Other products				
Further processed foods	—	—	1 059.06 (7)	112.91 (13)
Seed	—	162.75 (12)	—	—
Forestry	—	—	—	76.00 (4)
Fish	—	—	50.00 (1)	—
Totals	62.00 (4)	1 023.83 (63)	2 207.25 (57)	775.02 (39)

Note: *there are no product categories in the Oceania or Middle East regions with more than 10 barriers or $50 million in estimated trade impact identified; — less than 10 barriers or $50 million in estimated trade impact identified in the USDA survey.

US trade losses contribute to a greater understanding of the importance of questionable practices.

The design of the USDA survey limits the inferences that can be drawn directly from these preliminary results. The survey obviously does not provide a global assessment of the incidence and impact of technical barriers since only those affecting US exports are included. Although the estimated trade impacts can be viewed as an order-of-magnitude indication of the significance of the measures for US exporters, these values are consensus estimates supplied by FAS economists, not results derived from formal empirical trade models. The estimates reflect only the trade impact of the barriers, not associated welfare changes. Finally, the survey results provide very limited evidence about potential gains that could be realized from the much broader issue of regulatory reform. Sizeable trade and welfare gains would likely be realized by further alignment, unilateral modification, or even elimination of some measures that are viewed as legitimate under the provisions of the Uruguay Round Agreements.

Acknowledging these limitations, further investigation is still likely to yield useful insights. Simple categorization and cross-tabulation of the data represents the beginning of a systematic look at technical barriers that has not been possible previously. It is evident that there are many types of impediment faced by US agricultural exports, though the 18 largest barriers account for over 60 per cent of the total estimated trade impact. One approach to further analysis is to identify differences between the largest and smallest barriers under the hypothesis that there are certain characteristics that identify barriers where the estimated trade impact will be large. For example, there were only two large barriers identified where market access was restricted. There was a higher proportion of barriers with large estimated trade impacts when market retention was threatened, suggesting that the stakes tend to be higher where there is a possibility of removing or restricting access to a market that is already established.

Economists have used political economy models to explain the incidence of traditional tariff barriers and the approach can be extended to cover technical barriers. Theoretical and empirical models can be developed using an equilibrium framework where barriers result from a combination of market and political forces. One hypothesis is that certain kinds of restriction have characteristics that lend themselves to active public or government intervention in the policy determination process. Another is that the level of technical barriers simply reflects commodity trade levels between regions. A third hypothesis is that technical barriers are substitutes for (or complements to) other forms of trade protection. These, and many similar hypotheses, can be tested once an empirical model of the incidence and impact of technical barriers has been constructed.

REFERENCES

Baldwin, R.E. (1970), *Nontariff Distortions of International Trade*, Washington, DC: The Brookings Institution.

GATT Secretariat (1994), *The Results of the Uruguay Round of Multilateral Trade Negotiations: The Legal Texts*, Geneva: GATT.

Ndayisenga, F. and Kinsey, J. (1994), 'The Structure of Nontariff Measures on Agricultural Products in High Income Countries', *Agribusiness*, **10**, 275–92.

Orden, D. and Roberts, D. (eds) (1997), *Understanding Technical Barriers to Agricultural Trade*, St Paul, Minnesota: International Agricultural Trade Research Consortium, University of Minnesota Department of Applied Economics.

Roberts, D. and DeRemer, K. (1997), *An Overview of Technical Barriers to U.S. Agricultural Exports*, Staff Paper AGES-9705, March, Washington, DC: Economic Research Service, U.S. Department of Agriculture.

Roberts, D., Josling, T. and Orden, D. (forthcoming), *Technical Barriers to Agricultural Trade: An Analytic Framework*, Washington, DC: Economic Research Service, U.S. Department of Agriculture.

Sykes, A.O. (1995), *Product Standards for Internationally Integrated Goods Markets*, Washington, DC: The Brookings Institution.

KEVIN CHEN, JIANGUO HUI AND PETER CHEN*

Does China Discriminate Among Origins in the Pricing of its Wheat Imports?

INTRODUCTION

China, the world's largest wheat producer and consumer, has also emerged as the world's largest wheat importer during the 1990s. Fast economic growth and an increasing density of population relative to arable land will continue to make China the world's largest wheat importer in the coming decades (Rozelle *et al.*, 1996). Major wheat-exporting countries have seen great opportunities in China. However, the market is government-controlled and exclusively operated by a single giant buyer, the China National Cereals, Oil and Foodstuff Import and Export Corporation (COFCO), which manages all wheat imports and deals with both transnational private companies and wheat boards in exporting countries. Mercier (1993) hypothesized that China appears to be fairly efficient in taking advantage of its position as a major wheat importer by exercising market power and receives export subsidies or low prices for the wheat which it buys.

Do structural characteristics of the international wheat trade provide a giant buyer, such as China, with opportunities for non-competitive pricing in international wheat trade? The empirical evidence regarding the relevant degree of buyers' market power is limited and disputed (Love and Murniningtyas, 1992; Pick and Park, 1991), though a number of studies have suggested that large buyers may exercise market power (Carter and Schmitz, 1979; Mercier, 1993). For example, by jointly estimating market power with cost and demand parameters, Love and Murniningtyas found evidence that Japan exerted a high degree of monopsony power. However, by using the pricing to market model, Pick and Park concluded that this was not the case. In the same study, by contrast, the authors found evidence that China and the former Soviet Union had exerted a high degree of monopsony power in the international wheat trade. Nevertheless, Pick and Park's testing for monopsony power was rather indirect because their main focus was on the exporter's market power. They tested the shares of importing countries in the US wheat export (price) equation and interpreted the negative coefficient on the importing shares as evidence of monopsony power exercised by importing countries. Goodwin (1992) studied prices in international wheat markets and found that they are highly integrated in markets which are spatially separated markets. Given the limited and mixed evidence on buyers' market power, a direct test of monopsony power from the side of

*University of Alberta, AT&T, and Agriculture and Agri-food Canada, respectively.

buyers' pricing behaviour in the international wheat trade is obviously desirable.

The objective of this paper is to extend the pricing-to-market (PTM) framework first proposed by Krugman (1987) and implemented by Knetter (1989). Knetter's empirical model has been applied to investigate the notion of price discrimination across destination markets by major agricultural export countries (Pick and Park, 1991; Pick and Carter, 1994; Yumkellar *et al.*, 1994). As the PTM model was developed on the basis of pricing decisions by exporting firms across destinations, however, it might not be readily suitable for the examination of pricing behaviour by importers. In this paper it is modified for that purpose.

THE MODEL OF INVERSE PRICING TO MARKET

As in the case of an exporter, so an importer with market power can use exchange rate changes in order to 'price to market' (Krugman, 1987; Knetter, 1989). This can be called 'inverse pricing to market' (IPTM). Assume that an importer, say China, minimizes its total expenditure when buying wheat from n exporters $q_t = (q_{1t}, q_{2t}, \dots, q_{nt})$ at prices $p_t = (e_{1t}p_{1t}, e_{2t}p_{2t}, \dots, e_{nt}p_{nt})$ where p_{it} is the import price in terms of the importer's currency and e_{it} is the exchange rate measured in exporter's currency per unit of the importer's currency for $i = 1, 2, \dots n$. The importer can behave as a monopsonist, segmenting markets and adjusting import prices to bilateral exchange rate changes. Supply in each origin market is represented as $q_{it} = F(e_{it}p_{it})\phi_{it}$, where ϕ_{it} is a random variable that may shift supply in market i in period t.

Let the importer's given level of utility when it imports the predetermined quantity of wheat be $\overline{U} = U(q_{1t}, \dots, q_{nt})\mu_t$, where μ_{it} is a random variable that may shift the utility function in period t. The importer's decision problem therefore becomes

$$Min\left\{\sum_{i=1}^{n} p_{it}q_{it} \mid \overline{U} = U(q_{1t}, \dots, q_{nt})\mu_t, q_{it} = F(e_{it}, p_{it})\phi_{it}\right\} \quad (1)$$

Differentiating equation (1) with respect to prices and expressing in terms of elasticities, the first-order conditions are

$$p_{it} = b_t \frac{\varepsilon_{it}}{1+\varepsilon_{it}}; i = 1, \dots, n \text{ and } t = 1, \dots, t \quad (2)$$

where $b_t = \omega(\partial U_t / \partial q_{it})$ (ω is the Lagrangean multiplier) and is interpreted as the marginal benefit of wheat imports from origin i in period t, and ε_{it} is the supply elasticity for exports in exporting country i in period t. These conditions parallel the price discriminating monopoly case (Knetter, 1989). Equation (2) embodies the basic result of price discrimination: the price discriminating monopsonist will equate marginal cost in each market to the common marginal benefit. It states that price in the importer's currency is a mark-down determined by elasticity of supply in the various origin markets. In a competitive market with constant marginal benefit, exchange rate changes should be fully reflected in import prices. If an importer has market power, it can adjust origin-specific import prices as exchange rates change. The extent to which exchange rate changes are reflected in import prices is taken to indicate the possible existence of price discrimination in international trade and as one of the key explanations for prices of 'similar' goods possibly differing among origins.

In order to test for price discrimination and measure the mark-down following Knetter, a two-way fixed-effects regression model is considered

$$lnp_{it} = \theta_t + \lambda_i + \beta_i lne_{it} + \nu_{it} \tag{3}$$

where θ_t is a time effect, λ_i is a country of origin effect, β_i is the parameter, e_{it} is the exchange rate and ν_{it} is a regression disturbance. Equation (3) can be used to distinguish between three models of market structure. First, that $\lambda = 0$ and $\beta = 0$ imply the competitive market structure, in which import prices will be the same for all supplying origins. There will be country effects ($\lambda = 0$) and changes in the bilateral exchange rates will not affect bilateral import prices ($\beta = 0$). Note that the origin-specific variables (such as EEP export subsidies in the United States) may affect the unit values, but if markets are integrated these effects will be transmitted across sources and are thus accounted for by the time effects in the model. Thus, in a competitive market, the time effect measures factors affecting price for all origins.

Second, the conditions that $\lambda \neq 0$ and $\beta = 0$ imply price discrimination with constant elasticity of export supply. The country effect, λ, measures the component of the mark-down factor that differs across origins when a monopsonistic importer can segment markets. Such price discrimination will not vary in response to bilateral exchange rate changes if there is constant elasticity of supply in the exporting country, implying that they are not significantly different from zero. Although the mark-down is constant, it may vary over time and across regions, implying that the country effects are significantly different from zero ($\lambda \neq 0$).

Third, that $\lambda \neq 0$ and $\beta \neq 0$ implies price discrimination with varying elasticity of export supply. If supply elasticity varies with exchange rate changes, the optimal mark-down from the marginal benefit for a monopsonistic importer will vary with exchange rates. Import prices will depend on exchange rates and this implies that $\beta \neq 0$. The sign of the coefficients reveals the way in which the mark-down varies with changes in the exchange rate. A positive (negative) coefficient indicates that export supply is less (more) convex than the constant elasticity supply curve, and that exchange rate changes are not (more than) fully reflected in import prices. At the same time, the mark-down may vary over time and across sources, implying that the country effects are significantly different from zero. This case is referred to as 'inverse pricing to market' because the optimal mark-down by a price-discriminating monopsonist will vary across regions and with changes in bilateral exchange rates, implying that both $\lambda \neq 0$ and $\beta \neq 0$.

DATA, ESTIMATION AND EMPIRICAL RESULTS

The basic data set to be analysed consists of annual observations from 1981 to 1995 on the prices of wheat imports from the five suppliers, Argentina, Australia, Canada, EU and the United States, as well as relevant bilateral exchange rates. Though the annual nature of price information is not entirely suitable, there is no easily available material to use instead. The prices are unit values measured in importer's currency, calculated using annual observations on the landed quantities and values of China's wheat imports by origin. All the information used in the study was obtained from various issues of *Yearbook of Chinese Imports and Exports* published by China Customs. However, 1985 and 1992 prices for Argentina and the 1994 price for the European Union are not observable owing to the lack of shipments. These three missing prices were therefore fitted using an estimated regression line between prices and time in the respective country. The exchange rates are expressed in units of the exporter's currency per unit of the Chinese yuan and are based on annual average nominal exchange rates published in the 1996 *International Financial Statistics Yearbook*. Official exchange rates for Argentina and China are used since, although they are not determined in the free market, they are adjusted by the respective governments to reflect economic conditions. To obtain real exchange rates for the five origin markets, the nominal exchange rates are adjusted by the consumer price indexes (CPI) in each country given by the *International Financial Statistics Yearbook* for 1996. The exchange rates are normalized by dividing each observation by the value for the first observation. This allows comparison of the β coefficients across origins.

Equation (3) contains a regression constant, a set of time effects and a set of country of origin effects. The dummy variable for year 1995 and for Argentina are dropped, hence the fixed country effects which show higher or lower import prices are measured relative to Argentina. The model is estimated with both nominal and real exchange rate measures. As suggested by Knetter, the rationale is that the optimal import price should be neutral with respect to changes in the nominal rate that corresponds to inflation in the origin market. The variance of ε_{it} in equation (3) might well vary with t or i, or both. Moreover, the error terms v_{it} and v_{jt} might be correlated for some $i \neq j$ if random shocks affect several exporters at the same point of time. Similarly, the error terms v_{it} and v_{is} might be correlated for some $t \neq s$ if certain shocks affect the same exporter at more than one point in time. To avoid these problems, we estimated equation (3) with two versions of Kmenta's model (1986), namely the groupwise heteroscedastic and timewise autoregressive model (GHTAM) and the cross sectionally correlated and timewise autoregressive model (CSCTAM).

For the purpose of comparison, we also estimated equation (3) by OLS. Tables 1 and 2 report estimates of equation (3) by OLS, GHTAM and CSCTAM using nominal and real exchange rates, respectively. Using the nominal exchange rate, the GHTAM estimates appear to be unstable, while both OLS and CSCTAM estimates are remarkably similar. The CSCTAM estimates, however, have smaller standard errors. Using the real exchange rate, the three models are more different, though the OLS and CSCTAM estimates appear to be close

TABLE 1 Country effects and exchange rate coefficients for China wheat import price equation: nominal exchange rate

Source country	Fixed effect model		Groupwise heteroscedastic and timewise autoregressive model		Cross sectionally correlated and timewise autoregressive model	
	λ	β	λ	β	λ	β
Argentina		0.005 (0.397)		0.000 (0.004)		0.006 (0.997)
Australia	-0.432 (0.873)	0.094 (0.836)	-0.308 (1.051)	0.068 (1.017)	-0.454 (1.724)*	0.099 (1.630)
Canada	-0.608 (1.546)	0.153 (1.597)	-0.503 (1.970)*	0.129 (2.062)**	-0.625 (2.868)**	0.157 (2.905)**
EC	-0.161 (0.505)	0.041 (0.550)	-0.75 (0.253)	0.023 (0.313)	-0.180 (0.686)	0.045 (0.697)
USA	-0.836 (2.194)**	0.202 (2.161)**	-0.751 (3.184)**	0.183 (3.157)**	-0.877 (3.872)**	0.212 (3.707)**
Time	Yes		Yes		Yes	
	Adj. $R^2 = 0.786$		*Buse* $R^2 = 0.923$		*Adj.* $R^2 = 0.998$	
	$F^1_{4,51} = 2.008$		$F^1_{4,51} = 3.357$**		$F^1_{4,51} = 4.388$**	
	$F^2_{9,51} = 1.349$		$F^2_{9,51} = 2.924$**		$F^2_{9,51} = 3.495$**	

Note: Values in parentheses are *t*-statistics. The asterisks ** indicate that *t*-statistics and *F*-statistic are significant at the 0.05 level, while the asterisks * indicate that *t*-statistics and *F*-statistic are significant at the 0.10 level.

$F^1_{4,51}$ is the *F*-statistic for H_0:$\lambda_i = 0$ for all $i = 2, 3, 4, 5$;

$F^2_{9,51}$ is the *F*-statistic for H_0:$\lambda_i = 0$ for all $i = 2, 3, 4, 5$; $\beta_i = 0$, for all $i = 1, 2, 3, 4, 5$.

TABLE 2 *Country effects and exchange rate coefficients for China wheat import price equation: real exchange rate*

Source country	Fixed effect model		Groupwise heteroscedastic and timewise autoregressive model		Cross sectionally correlated and timewise autoregressive model	
	λ	β	λ	β	λ	β
Argentina		−0.002 (0.159)		−0.005 (0.637)		0.002 (0.316)
Australia	−0.081 (0.132)	0.021 (0.149)	0.054 (0.141)	−0.009 (0.104)	−0.279 (0.841)	0.064 (0.857)
Canada	−0.252 (−0.406)	0.076 (0.556)	−0.123 (0.326)	0.046 (0.530)	−0.442 (1.375)	0.119 (1.578)
EC	−0.038 (0.073)	−0.001 (0.013)	0.156 (0.429)	−0.027 (0.318)	−0.131 (0.407)	−0.035 (0.462)
USA	−0.446 (0.755)	0.117 (0.855)	−0.333 (0.895)	0.092 (1.072)	−0.663 (2.033)**	0.167 (2.182)**
Time	Yes		Yes		Yes	
	$Adj.\ R^2 = 0.786$		$Buse\ R^2 = 0.927$		$Adj.\ R^2 = 0.998$	
	$F^1_{4,51} = 0.1746$		$F^1_{4,51} = 2.898^{**}$		$F^1_{4,51} = 3.681^{**}$	
	$F^2_{9,51} = 1.367$		$F^2_{9,51} = 3.287^{**}$		$F^2_{9,51} = 4.308^{**}$	

Note: As for Table 1.

again. It is also interesting to note that the CSCTAM estimates using either nominal or real exchange rates appear similar, the CSCTAM estimates fitting data best among the three models. The following discussion is therefore based on CSCTAM estimates.

Using either nominal or real exchange rates, the country effects are significantly different from zero. The F-statistics, denoted as $F^1_{4,51}$ in Tables 1 and 2, indicate that the null hypothesis of identical values of λ_i across origins is rejected by the data at the 5 per cent level. Also the F-statistics, denoted as $F^2_{9,51}$, indicate that the null hypothesis of identical values of identical λ_i and β_i across origins is rejected. This indicates that China, as the largest importer of wheat, engages in price-discriminating behaviour in purchasing wheat from the international wheat market.

The regression results with nominal exchange rates suggest that Canada and the United States received lower import prices than Argentina, Australia and the EC during the period under study. Such lower prices could reflect either their inelastic supply compared to the other three sources or their sales effort to gain market share. In particular, imports from the United States may have been priced lower in a bid to gain market share. Since mid-1985, export subsidies (EEP) have contributed to an increase in US exports to China. Price discrimination against Canadian wheat could be attributed to monopsony power, in that China is the largest buyer, accounting for over 25 per cent of the total from 1980 to 1995. The regression with nominal exchange rates also indicates monopsonistic pricing in the form of imperfect exchange rate pass-through for imports from Canada and the United States. The positive β_i coefficients indicate that China, being capable of price discrimination, tries to offset relative price changes in the local currency induced by exchange rate fluctuations. The mark-downs are adjusted upwards by 1.6 per cent for a 10 per cent appreciation in the Chinese yuan for Canada and by 2 per cent for a 10 per cent appreciation in the Chinese yuan for the United States. Such pricing behaviour indicates inelastic supply of Canadian and US wheat exports to China. In such cases, the importer attempts to maintain stable prices by reducing the effect of the exporter's currency valuation in markets where there are other competing purchasers. Kraft *et al.* (1996) observed that, while Canada, the EU and the United States lowered their exporting prices as a result of trade war competition, Australia and Argentina appeared to be shifting out of wheat production.

The regression with real exchange rates indicates only one violation of invariance of import prices to origin and exchange rates. This is puzzling as nominal exchange rate changes frequently reflect inflation differentials across countries and therefore may not induce changes in the local currency relative to the price of an import. One would expect idiosyncratic adjustments in import prices to exhibit more correlation with nominal exchange rates than the price-level adjusted exchange rates. Similar results are observed in Knetter's study.

It is also interesting to compare the results with those of Pick and Park (1991) and Pick and Carter (1994). Pick and Park, using both nominal and real exchange rates, found that the United States receives a higher price from its wheat exports to China, but no evidence of imperfect exchange rate pass-through associated with China. Given the fact that the United States has the highest import demand elasticity in the Chinese market (Hui *et al.*, 1995), it is a surprising result. In contrast, Pick and Carter, using real exchange rates, found that the United States receives lower prices from its wheat exports to China and that there is strong evidence of imperfect exchange rate pass-through. Pick and Carter also estimated the PTM model for Canada, without finding that exports were lower-priced but having strong evidence of imperfect exchange rate pass-through associated with China. Obviously our results using real exchange rates are more consistent with Pick and Carter, except that no strong evidence of imperfect exchange rate pass-through associated with China is found in the case of Canada. The key difference rests on prior beliefs about whether the international wheat market could be characterized by either monopoly or monopsony.

CONCLUSIONS

This study extends the pricing-to-market (PTM) framework to ask whether China, as a large buyer, can engage in price discrimination among exporting origins in the international wheat market. Using price information about China's wheat imports from the five supply origins (Argentina, Australia, Canada, the EC and the United States), the evidence of price-discriminating behaviour on China's part is strong. In particular, China consistently paid lower prices for US wheat than it paid to Argentina, Australia, Canada and Europe. While quality differences could account for some of the price variations, structural characteristics in China's wheat import market provide opportunities for non-competitive pricing. Stronger evidence of non-competitive pricing is found in imperfect exchange rate pass-through observed for the United States. The result confirms Mercier's speculation that China appears to engage in strategic behaviour in an effort to extract additional benefits from the wheat exporters.

The ability of China to successfully practise price discrimination is likely to arise from a combination of (1) the structure and practice of single-desk state trading, (2) the difference in wheat export supply elasticities, (3) the excessive capacity in wheat-producing countries, and (4) the inherent characteristics of wheat production. To appreciate our results fully, three limitations are worth noting. First, no attempt is made to account for seller's market power, as identified in several studies in international trade. Second, no attempt is made to control for the prices of close substitutes in the import markets. Instead of the monopsonistic model, it would be interesting to assume oligopsony. Third, product and time aggregation could bias the coefficients. If there is heterogeneity within a wheat category used in this study, changes in the composition of imports may be correlated with exchange rates if the elasticity of supply for the varieties differs. The same argument applies to time aggregation. Further empirical work, when data permit, should investigate whether significant country effects reflect quality or time differences among wheat imports.

REFERENCES

Carter, C. and Schmitz, A. (1979), 'Import Tariffs and Price Formation in the World Wheat Market', *American Journal of Agricultural Economics*, **61**, 517–22.

Goodwin, B.K. (1992), 'Multivariate Cointegration Tests and the Law of One Price in International Wheat Markets', *Review of Agricultural Economics*, **14**, 117–24.

Hui, J., McLean-Meyinsse, P.E. and Couvillion, W.C. (1995), 'The Market Structure and Price Competition in China's Wheat Import Market: Implications for U.S. Wheat Exports', *Journal of International Food and Agribusiness Marketing*, **7**, 53–64.

Kmenta, J. (1986), *Elements of Econometrics*, New York: Macmillan.

Knetter, M.M. (1989), 'Price Discrimination by U.S. and German Exporters', *American Economic Review*, **79**, 198–210.

Kraft, D.F., Furtan, W.H. and Tyrchniewicz, E.W. (1996), *Performance Evaluation of the Canadian Wheat Board*, Ottowa: Canadian Wheat Board.

Krugman, P. (1987), 'Pricing to Market when Exchange Rates Change', in S.W. Arndt and J.D. Richardson (eds), *Real-Financial Linkages Among Open Economies*, Cambridge, Mass.: MIT Press.

Love, H.A. and Murniningtyas, E. (1992), 'Measuring the Degree of Market Power Exerted by Government Trade Agencies', *American Journal of Agricultural Economics*, **74**, 546–55.

Mercier, S.A. (1993), *The Role of Quality in Wheat Import Decision-making*, Agricultural Economic Report Number 670, Washington, DC: ERS-USDA.

Pick, D.H. and Carter, C.A. (1994), 'Pricing to Market with Transactions Denominated in a Common Currency', *American Journal of Agricultural Economics*, **76**, 55–60.

Pick, D.H. and Park, T. (1991), 'The Competitive Structure of U.S. Agricultural Exports', *American Journal of Agricultural Economics*, **73**, 133–41.

Rozelle, S., Huang, J. and Rosegrant, M. (1996), 'Would China Starve the World?', *Choices*, Spring.

Yumkellar, K.K., Unnevehr, L.J. and Garcia, P. (1994), 'Noncompetitive Pricing and Exchange Rate Pass-Through in Selected U.S. and Thai Rice Markets', *Journal of Agricultural and Applied Economics*, **26**, 406–16.

ROMEO M. BAUTISTA AND MARCELLE THOMAS*

Income Effects of Alternative Policy Trade Adjustments on Philippine Rural Households: A General Equilibrium Analysis

INTRODUCTION

Unsustainable current account deficits have been a common underlying factor in the unstable economic growth of many developing countries over the past few decades. The capital inflows that accommodate such deficits represent additional financial resources that can increase domestic investment in the short run. However, they can also lead to an overvalued exchange rate, distorting relative profitabilities, resource allocation and investment efficiency. In particular, exchange rate overvaluation acts as a tax on the production of tradable goods, which in many developing countries include their major agricultural products.

This paper examines quantitatively the economy-wide income and equity effects, focusing on lower-income rural households, of alternative trade policy adjustments to cope with an unsustainable current account deficit. The context is the Philippines, which in the 1970s and 1980s was buffeted by a succession of external shocks and associated macroeconomic imbalances, the latter also partly induced by inappropriate domestic policies (Power, 1983; Bautista, 1988). We use a computable general equilibrium (CGE) model of the Philippine economy in generating the comparative results of simulation experiments involving alternative trade policy adjustments.

The relative merits of alternative policy regimes need to be evaluated, at least in the Philippine case, in terms of their effects on both income growth and equity. This is important in view of the country's past development experience in which spurts of economic growth were not accompanied by a reduction in poverty and income inequality (Bautista, 1992). Indeed, the overall distribution of income in the Philippines has remained highly skewed, the incidence of poverty being the highest among landless agricultural workers and cultivators of small-sized farms (Balisacan, 1992). The induced changes in the relative incomes of small farmers and rural labourers therefore warrant particular attention.

The next section describes the nature of external shocks to the Philippine economy, the severity of current account deficits and the changes in trade policies adopted since the early 1970s. We then briefly discuss the structure of the CGE model for the Philippines used in the present study. A description of

*International Food Policy Research Institute, Washington, DC, USA.

the model simulations follows. These show the comparative results of alternative trade policy adjustments to deal with the current account imbalance.

EXTERNAL SHOCKS,
CURRENT ACCOUNT IMBALANCES AND TRADE POLICIES

Like many other oil-importing developing countries, the Philippines incurred large current account deficits arising from the marked deterioration of the external terms of trade that began in 1973–4 with the quadrupling of the world price of oil. The latter's adverse impact was clear and direct, the Philippines being dependent on imported oil for over 90 per cent of its energy requirements. At about the same time, the world commodity boom of 1972–4 ended, ushering in almost a decade-long period of declining prices for the country's principal exports (sugar, coconut products, logs and minerals). As a result, the external terms-of-trade index (1987 = 100) declined almost continuously, moving from 173.1 in 1973 to 113.6 in 1979 and 85.7 in 1982 (World Bank, 1993, pp. 490–91). The current account changed from a positive balance of US$337 million in 1973, to deficits of $362 million in 1974, $1621 million in 1979 and $3364 million in 1982 – the latter representing about one-third of Philippine 'trade' (average of import and export values) and 10 per cent of GDP.

Increased capital inflows accommodated the burgeoning current account deficits. There was a small net capital outflow of $49 million in 1973, which reversed to a substantial foreign borrowing of $642 million in 1974; this then increased continuously, to nearly $3 billion in 1982, just before the external debt-related foreign exchange crisis came to a head in the following year.

External financing effectively propped up the exchange rate, at least until the early 1980s. Although a flexible exchange rate policy was being followed, the massive capital inflows removed the immediate pressure for the domestic currency to depreciate. When foreign borrowing was sharply reduced, as happened in 1983 (following the assassination of the political opposition leader, Benigno Aquino), exchange rate adjustments could no longer be postponed. There was understandably a large depreciation of the Philippine peso (by about 30 per cent relative to the US dollar) in 1983.

With active support by the World Bank, the Philippine government initiated a 'structural adjustment' programme in 1981. It included measures to gradually liberalize the foreign trade regime through tariff reform and relaxation of import licensing. There was wide agreement by that time, within and outside government circles, that restrictive trade policies have excessively protected import-substituting industries at the expense of agriculture and export-oriented enterprises. Unfortunately, the programme was overtaken by the 1983 foreign exchange crisis, and some of its components were superseded by policy actions designed to deal with short-term contingencies.

Import rationing was implemented, reminiscent of the comprehensive system of direct controls on imports and foreign exchange installed by the government during the 1950s (see Power and Sicat, 1971). Additional trade taxes were also imposed, including a general 3–5 per cent import surtax. During 1983–4, the Philippine peso was devalued three times, before it was allowed to float in October 1984. Under an IMF standby agreement, the Central Bank reduced money supply growth from 19 per cent in 1983 to 7 per cent in 1984 and 10 per cent in 1985. Relatedly, government current expenditure was lower (in real terms) by 19 per cent and 11 per cent in 1984 and 1985, respectively, than in 1983. The current account improved dramatically, the deficit (after official transfers) decreasing from US$2771 million in 1983 to US$1294 million in 1984 and US$35 million in 1985. However, GDP declined during 1984–5 (down 7.3 per cent in each year), with the fall being widely believed to have contributed to the downfall of the Marcos regime in early 1986.

Under the new government of Corazon Aquino, who served as President from 1986 to 1992, macroeconomic policies became more expansionary. There was a resumption of large capital inflows, accommodating a current account deficit of US$2695 million by 1990. Trade liberalization was given increased emphasis as significant tariff reductions and relaxation of quantitative restrictions were implemented. Further tariff cuts and import liberalization measures were adopted under the administration of President Fidel Ramos, who took office in 1992. The average import-weighted tariff rate had been reduced to 14 per cent by mid-1995, and a target uniform tariff rate of 5 per cent by 2003 has been set.

In light of the foregoing discussion, the following types of trade policy adjustment to deal with an unsustainable current account imbalance appear relevant in the Philippine context: (1) import rationing; (2) a uniform surcharge on imports; and (3) trade liberalization. Each of these trade policy responses will be examined for their economy-wide income and equity effects, with focus on rural households, based on the simulation results from a CGE model of the Philippine economy. The model's underlying accounting framework and benchmark data derive from a balanced SAM (social accounting matrix) for 1979 constructed earlier (Thomas and Bautista, 1996).

THE CGE MODEL

The CGE model used in the present study follows closely what has become a standard theoretical specification of trade-focused general equilibrium models (Robinson, 1989). Markets for goods, factors and foreign exchange are assumed to respond to changing demand and supply conditions, which in turn are affected by government policies and the external environment. The model is Walrasian in that it determines only relative prices and other variables in the real sphere of the economy. The *numéraire* used is an aggregate consumer price. An appendix to this paper contains the CGE model specification and parameterization (available from the authors on request). A GAMS programme is used to implement the model.

There are five agricultural crop sectors ('palay' or unmilled rice, corn, coconut, sugarcane and other crops) among the 16 production sectors in the model. The other sectors are livestock, fishery, forestry, mining, rice and corn milling, other food processing, light manufacturing, other manufacturing, fertilizer, energy and services. Households are classified into three rural (large-farm, small-farm and other rural) and two urban (Metro Manila and other urban) categories. Households in Metro Manila had the highest average income (46.7 thousand pesos) in 1979 (the benchmark year), followed by the large-farm and other urban households (31.9 and 24.7 thousand pesos, respectively). Small-farm and other rural households were the poorest (with average incomes of 17.3 and 13.7 thousand pesos, respectively).

Four primary factors are distinguished in the model: skilled labour, unskilled labour, land and capital. Factor market distortions are allowed, differentiated by sector according to the extent to which the average return for a factor differs from the marginal revenue product of that factor.

The production technology is represented by a set of nested CES and Leontief functions. Domestic output in each sector is a CES function of value added and aggregate intermediate input use. Value added is a CES function of the primary factors, while intermediate input use is defined by fixed input–output coefficients. Each sector is assumed to produce differentiated goods for the domestic and export markets, sectoral output being a CET function of the amounts sold in the two markets. Subject to this transformation function, producers maximize revenue from sales. Similarly, imported and domestic products are differentiated at the sectoral level. The composite (consumption) good is a CES aggregate, and consumers minimize the cost of obtaining a given amount of composite good.

Based on the small-country assumption, the domestic price of sectoral imports is represented in terms of the foreign price, exchange rate and tariff rate. The country is also assumed small on the export side; the domestic price of sectoral exports is therefore determined by the world price, exchange rate and any applicable export tax. Positive externality is associated with sectoral export performance, total factor productivity in each sector being enhanced by increased exporting (de Melo and Robinson, 1992). The model assumes an exogenous current account deficit, which in the Philippine context of the late 1970s is determined by government policy on the foreign borrowing financing the deficit.

The four components of sectoral demand are intermediate, consumption, investment and government. Fixed input–output coefficients determine intermediate demand. Household consumption demand is based on the Cobb–Douglas utility function and associated fixed expenditure shares. Inventory investment is assumed proportional to sectoral output, while fixed investment is the difference between total investment and inventory demand. Government consumption expenditures are in fixed proportion to the exogenously determined total government consumption.

As well as the supply–demand balances in the product and factor markets, three macroeconomic balances are specified in the model: (1) the fiscal balance, showing that government saving is the difference between government revenue and spending; (2) the external balance, equating the supply and demand for foreign exchange; and (3) the specification that total investment is determined by total savings, which corresponds to the 'neoclassical' macroeconomic closure (Robinson, 1989).

The model makes use of the numerical SAM for 1979 as database, representing the initial conditions that are perturbed by the postulated exogenous shocks (changes in trade policy). The economy-wide effects of these shocks should be interpreted, therefore, in reference to the domestic price structure existing in 1979.

MODEL SIMULATIONS AND RESULTS

Three of the four policy options considered here for model simulation are subject to the macroeconomic constraint that the current account deficit is reduced to zero. This is obviously an extreme case that may arise only if the economy is in a financial crisis. Normally, some level of current account deficit is sustainable for developing countries during the early, capital-borrowing, stage of economic development. In the Philippine context, the external debt-related foreign exchange crisis that began in October 1983 was in fact accompanied by a drastic (involuntary) reduction of foreign borrowing until early 1986 and associated decline in the current account deficit to less than 0.1 per cent of GDP in 1985. Counterfactually simulating a movement towards a balanced current account serves to dramatize the comparative effects of alternative trade policy adjustments.

The first trade policy option (Simulation I) involves the imposition of direct import control, the quantity restrictions affecting all sectors equally in proportionate terms. An 8 per cent across-the-board reduction of base-year sectoral imports is applied that ensures a balanced current account. The resulting scarcity premium on imports (or quota rent), representing the difference between the implicit and legal tariffs, is reasonably assumed (reflecting political reality) to accrue to Metro Manila households.

In our second counterfactual experiment (Simulation II), the government is assumed to levy an additional tax on imports (beyond the existing tariffs), representing therefore a price disincentive. A general import surtax of 4 per cent is used, which is within the 3–5 per cent additional import tax actually charged in the aftermath of the 1983 foreign exchange crisis.

The third policy option (Simulation III) is trade liberalization. Specifically, it involves a shift from the highly restrictive import policy that existed in 1979 to adopting a uniform tariff rate of 5 per cent that, as already indicated, is the official target for year 2003. This represents a fundamental policy reform, in contrast to the first two options which are non-strategic trade policy adjustments, that can improve microeconomic efficiency and the economy's long-run growth prospects.

A fourth policy scenario (Simulation IV) that is also useful to consider is one in which the tariff reduction is accompanied by only a 50 per cent cut in the current account deficit. The latter serves as a 'carrot' that makes trade policy reform attractive, and approximates more closely the macroeconomic adjustment in many developing countries actively supported by the two Bretton Woods institutions.

The simulation results are presented in Table 1, including the effects on household and enterprise incomes, as well as those on some macroeconomic variables of major policy interest. We observe first that there are marked differences in the macroeconomic effects of the alternative trade policy

TABLE 1	*Simulation results (percentage changes from base-run values)*

	Simulation I	Simulation II	Simulation III	Simulation IV
Gross GDP (at factor costs)	−4.98	−0.56	4.52	5.93
Government Income	−3.94	2.61	−14.49	−14.14
Total exports	0.15	6.98	17.28	16.49
Total imports	−8.00	−2.82	5.60	9.03
Exchange rate	−2.26	−0.09	10.10	3.18
Household incomes				
Metro Manila	7.98	−3.47	−4.78	0.81
Other urban	−9.71	−3.23	−3.54	1.20
Large-farm	−8.60	−3.01	1.96	2.29
Small-farm	−6.34	−1.85	4.00	3.67
Other rural	−8.38	−2.58	−1.22	2.31
Enterprises				
Agricultural	−6.71	−2.39	8.21	4.15
Non-agricultural	−3.92	0.49	2.59	6.79

Notes:	Simulation I – sectoral imports reduced by 8 per cent across the board, balanced current account; Simulation II – import tax surcharge of 4 per cent across the board, balanced current account; Simulation III – tariffs reduced to a uniform rate of 5 per cent, balanced current account; Simulation IV – repeating Simulation III, except that the current account deficit is reduced by 50 per cent.

adjustments. GDP declines significantly as a result of import rationing (Simulation I), which is not surprising since it adds to the existing market distortions and rent seeking. By contrast, trade liberalization increases GDP; having to reduce the current account deficit by only 50 per cent (Simulation IV) leads to an additional GDP growth rate of about 1.4 per cent relative to the balanced current account scenario (Simulation III). Government income expected goes up with the imposition of an import surtax (Simulation II), but decreases with import rationing and, more drastically, with the tariff-reduction scenarios. The latter implies that the positive revenue effect of the expanded income tax base (due to the larger GDP) does not fully offset the direct impact of lowering the tariff rate to a uniform 5 per cent.

Trade liberalization under both Simulations III and IV is seen to result in a large increase in total imports and, to meet the requirement of a balanced current account, an even larger proportionate increase in total exports. As might be expected, Simulations I and II lead to import compression, and the worst export performance is associated with the import control regime. Relatedly, the increased import restrictions cause the exchange rate to appreciate, while the tariff reduction under Simulations III and IV leads to an exchange rate depreciation.

Turning to the income and equity effects, we find that Metro Manila households are the only beneficiary of import rationing, the other household groups suffering relatively large income losses (from 6.3 to 9.7 per cent of base-year incomes). Under Simulation II, incomes of all five household groups decline;

the heaviest burden of the import surtax falls on Metro Manila households, while incomes of small-farm and other rural households are the least unfavourably affected. Thus, in terms of both GDP and equity effects, the regime of quantitative import restrictions under Simulation I is inferior to the imposition of an across-the-board import surtax. Indeed, the income reduction for each household group, except Metro Manila, is seen to be lower under Simulation II in comparison to that under Simulation I.

Adjusting through trade liberalization apparently makes for a better income prospect for agricultural households, especially small-farm households. With liberalized trade and balanced current account (Simulation III), small-farm and large-farm households gain while the three other household groups lose. These results corroborate an earlier finding of the anti-agriculture bias of trade policy in the Philippines (Bautista, 1987). Trade liberalization does not appear to involve a tradeoff between the twin objectives of income growth and equity. Interestingly, the less stringent requirement on current account deficit reduction under Simulation IV leads to an income gain for each household group and the most favourable equity effect among the four trade policy options.

That foreign trade restrictions are likely to hurt agriculture more than the rest of the economy is again suggested by the more adverse impacts of import rationing and surtax on the income of agricultural enterprises relative to non-agricultural enterprises. Furthermore, larger income benefits for agricultural enterprises are shown under the trade liberalization scenarios compared to those under Simulations I and II.

Finally, it is notable that, moving from Simulation III to Simulation IV, non-agricultural households (including 'other rural') and enterprises benefit much more than their agricultural counterparts; that is, cutting the current account deficit by half, rather than in full, under a liberalized trade regime yields larger income gains for non-agriculture. This result would seem to imply that the capital inflows that accommodated the current account deficit tend to have a 'spending effect' and generate a demand stimulus favouring the non-agricultural sectors.

CONCLUSION

The comparative simulation results based on a CGE model of the Philippine economy presented in this paper indicate significant differences in the income effects of alternative trade policy adjustments to deal with an unsustainable current account imbalance. At the macro level, GDP decreases under a regime of quantitative import restrictions and, less markedly, with the imposition of a general import surtax. These are not unexpected results. It is also not surprising that adjustment through the reduction of tariffs to a low and uniform rate leads to a larger GDP. This favourable result, however, is counterbalanced by a substantial loss in government income. It suggests the need to implement an effective tax reform – if government revenue is to be protected – as the country's trade regime is being liberalized.

Our findings concerning the distribution of income gains (and losses) from trade policy adjustments are interesting, especially as the subject has been given much less attention in the development literature. The additional market distortions and rent seeking that accompany the implementation of import rationing heavily discriminate in favour of the already most affluent Metro Manila households. Moving to a general import surtax represents an improvement, in that non-Metro Manila households will be penalized less. However, these first two policy options are shown to be inferior to tariff liberalization, especially if the current account deficit is to be reduced by only half. In the latter case, reducing tariffs to a uniform 5 per cent (the official target for 2003) not only improves the average income of each household group but also raises the incomes of small-farm and 'other rural' households relative to those of the more affluent Metro Manila, other urban and large-farm households.

The anti-agriculture bias of restrictive trade policy is part of the explanation for the favourable income and equity effects of import liberalization. Past trade and exchange rate policies in the Philippines distorted production incentives to the benefit of urban-based, import-substituting industries at the expense of export producers, both agricultural and non-agricultural, as well as the small-scale, rural enterprises (Bautista, 1987). The broadly based rural income growth associated with a more open trade regime in turn will have strong labour-intensive linkages to the rest of the economy, reinforcing the income multiplier effects that cut across rural and urban sectors. It is not surprising, therefore, that the larger income increases accruing to small-farm and other rural households (relative to the three other household groups) from import liberalization are found to be accompanied also by a relatively large GDP increase.

These results from CGE analysis lead us to conclude that Philippine rural households, especially the lower-income ones, had been heavily penalized by the imposition of import rationing and general import surtax in response to past current account deficits that were unsustainable. Moreover, overall economic growth would also have been adversely affected. This 'lesson of experience' has relevance for the Philippines at the present time, in view of the large and growing current account deficits in recent years (averaging 4.4 per cent of GDP during 1993–5). Indeed, the latter problem confronts many contemporary developing countries that are still heavily agricultural (in the context of sub-Saharan Africa, see Sahn *et al.*, 1996). As shown in this paper, inappropriate trade policy adjustments can stand in the way of promoting a rapid and equitable growth of the national economy.

REFERENCES

Balisacan, A.M. (1992), 'Rural Poverty in the Philippines: Incidence, Determinants and Policies', *Asian Development Review*, **10**, 125–63.
Bautista, R.M. (1987), *Production Incentives in Philippine Agriculture: Effects of Trade and Exchange Rate Policies*, Research Report 59, Washington, DC: International Food Policy Research Institute.
Bautista, R.M. (1988), *Impediments to Trade Liberalization in the Philippines*, Thames Essay No. L 54, London: Gower Publishing Company for the Trade Policy Research Centre.
Bautista, R.M. (1992), *Development Policy in East Asia: Economic Growth and Poverty Alleviation*, Singapore: Institute of Southeast Asian Studies.

de Melo, J. and Robinson, S. (1992), 'Productivity and Externalities: Models of Export-led Growth', *Journal of International Trade and Economic Development*, 1, 41–68.

Power, J.H. (1983), 'Response to Balance of Payments Crisis in the 1970s: Korea and the Philippines', Staff Paper Series No. 83–105, Manila: Philippine Institute for Development Studies.

Power, J.H. and Sicat, G.P. (1971), *The Philippines: Industrialization and Trade Policies*, London: Oxford University Press.

Robinson, S. (1989), 'Multisectoral Models', in H. Chenery and T.N. Srinivasan (eds), *Handbook of Development Economics*, Vol. II, Amsterdam: Elsevier Science Publishers.

Sahn, D., Dorosh, P. and Younger, S. (1996), 'Exchange Rate, Fiscal and Agricultural Policies in Africa: Does Adjustment Hurt the Poor?', *World Development*, 24, 719–45.

Thomas, M. and Bautista, R.M. (1996), 'Constructing Social Accounting Matrices for Multiplier and CGE Analyses: The Philippines', mimeo, International Food Policy Research Institute, Trade and Macroeconomics Division.

World Bank (1993), *World Tables*, Baltimore: Johns Hopkins University Press.

ALEXANDER H. SARRIS*

*Post-GATT Agricultural Trade Liberalization and
Growth in Developing Countries: The Case of The Philippines*

INTRODUCTION

The agricultural trade policies of developing countries have not been much of an issue in international debates because the prevailing view is that most of them tax their agricultural sectors. Nevertheless, it is not clear what type of agricultural trade policy should be followed in the course of development. The purpose of this paper is to investigate the trade policy issue in the context of overall trade policy in a post-GATT economic environment, for countries that are characterized by a dual economic structure, a large agricultural sector and a large degree of poverty among the population. The arguments will be made for the case of the Philippines, an economy that fulfils the above criteria, and also a country that is currently attempting to increase its economic growth to match the pattern of other Southeast Asian newly industrializing economies. After looking at the country background, the paper describes an appropriate methodology, presents some empirical results and draws conclusions.

AGRICULTURE, TRADE POLICY AND THE PHILIPPINE ECONOMY

During the last few years, growth performance in the Philippines has lagged behind that of its most dynamic neighbours. One of the reasons suggested for the poor performance is the degree of protection afforded to the domestic economy. On the basis of this, senior policy officials have been calling for unilateral trade liberalization of the Philippine economy. The aim is to achieve a uniform tariff for all sectors by 2003 at a low 5 per cent rate.

The Philippine economy has been heavily protected in the past. The average effective rate of protection (ERP) of all sectors in 1988 was estimated at 33.1 per cent, which was lower than the 49.8 per cent of 1983 (Tan, 1994). The pattern of agricultural protection has been similar to that of the overall economy, with an average ERP on importables of 45.1 per cent and on exportables of –6.7 per cent,

*University of Athens, Greece. Part of the research for this paper was conducted in the context of a Food and Agriculture Organisation of the United Nations (FAO) policy project with the Philippine Department of Agriculture. Help from and discussions with Donato Antiporta, Marinela Castillo, Ramon Clarete, Beulah de la Pena and Preceles Manzo are gratefully acknowledged. The analysis and conclusions of the paper, however, are the sole responsibility of the author.

482

but with an overall ERP substantially lower than that of the overall economy at 3.7 per cent. In the 1990s, substantial trade liberalization took place. Balisacan *et al.* (1992) estimated that the weighted average book tariff rate on agricultural products by 1996, as a result of liberalization measures, would be 28.6 per cent compared with 16.6 per cent for non-agricultural products, down from 33.2 and 23.9 per cent, respectively, in 1991. Agricultural importables have been regulated by very strict quotas that have resulted in domestic prices that exceed the border prices by amounts much larger than the book rates of tariff (David, 1994; deDios, 1994; Sarris, 1994; 1995a). This implies that agriculture has in fact been protected at a higher level than non-agriculture.

Agriculture (including forestry and fisheries) constitutes 22.5 per cent of Philippine gross domestic product (GDP) on the basis of 1992 figures, and accounts for about 45 per cent of total employment and 20 per cent of export earnings. It is characterized by a dual production structure. Duality is also a characteristic of the non-agricultural sector. Poverty is considerable in the Philippines as a whole, and particularly in the agricultural sector.

Agricultural imports are considerable, accounting for about 15 per cent of total domestic demand for agricultural products. However, imports of so-called 'sensitive' products (such as rice, corn, sugar, all meats, live animals, potatoes and coffee) have been very small, and are heavily controlled by quotas. Importation of these sensitive agricultural products beyond the quotas is a big political issue and often requires approval by the Senate.

The major non-economic argument that applies to agricultural trade policy and protection is that of food security. In the Philippines, that has meant self-sufficiency to the fullest extent possible in rice and corn. A major issue that is very important from a macrodevelopment perspective, is how increases in the prices of agricultural products influence the general cost of food in the economy, and subsequently the cost of labour. Policies that increase the price of food drive the cost of living, and hence wages, upwards, with the result that the competitiveness of labour-intensive export-oriented sectors is adversely affected. Protection also leads to overvaluation of the exchange rate and also penalizes the export sectors.

METHODOLOGY

The methodology uses a computable general equilibrium model (CGE). While there have been some which have been built for the Philippine economy, such as those of Clarete (1989), Habito (1986) and the APEX model (Clarete and Warr, 1992), they remain largely 'neoclassical', without representing many of the relevant structural and institutional features of the Philippine economy. The structure of the current model is presented in detail in Sarris (1995b). It is based on a reduced and adapted version of the 1990 social accounting matrix (SAM) of the Philippines that has been constructed by the National Central Statistical Office (NCSO). In the model the economy in the aggregate consists of three producing sectors, namely formal agriculture, formal non-agriculture and the unincorporated (informal or small-scale) sector. The two formal sectors produce a composite product that, in turn, is allocated between domestic supply and exports. The informal sector also produces a composite product that is allocated between a domestic agricultural and a domestic non-agricultural product. These two products are identical to the domestic products produced by the formal sectors.

The key structural difference between the formal and informal sectors is in the labour employment and remuneration practices. The formal sector firms employ labour that is paid a wage which is influenced by the minimum wage policies of the government, and hence by the cost of living. The informal sector firms, on the other hand, employ the remaining labour at wages that are lower on average than formal sector wages, but that are also kept flexible, so as to balance the domestic labour market. This is a key structural feature of the Philippine economy that has not featured in previous CGE models.

Both the agricultural and the non-agricultural products are assumed to be imperfect substitutes with imports in the Armington fashion. Income in the economy is allocated to three classes of households (poor, middle-income and rich), to formal and unincorporated firms and to the government. The rest of the world is assumed exogenous. The formal sector firms obtain income from production in the two formal sectors (agriculture and non-agriculture), while the unincorporated firms obtain income from production of the unincorporated sector. Households obtain income both from wage employment in the three sectors, and from the distribution of profits from the two types of firms, as well as transfers. Households, after paying taxes to the government, utilize their income for private consumption, transfers to other households and savings. They are assumed to consume two products, food and non-food, according to a linear expenditure system. The non-food product is the composite non-agricultural product mentioned above. Food, however, is a combination of the composite agricultural product and the composite non-agricultural product. Private investment is savings-determined, while public investment is exogenously set as a policy variable.

The four balancing markets in the economy are the markets for the domestic agricultural and non-agricultural goods, the market for domestic labour and the market for foreign exchange. The model also incorporates the possibility of endogenous import quota rent generation, which accrues to rich households. The model assumes that the capital stock in the three producing sectors is fixed, and only labour can move between the sectors. Hence it can be considered a short-run model. The type of question that can be analysed with such an assumption concerns the different outcomes of the economy, given its current structure, if trade policy was different *in the base period*.

EMPIRICAL RESULTS

We first investigate the 'tariffication' of quotas. In that context 'equivalence' means application of a tariff providing the same level of protection as the original nomination tariff, together with the quotas. The equivalent tariff rate on the basis of equivalent protection is equal to $(1 + t)(1 + z) - 1$, where t is the base rate of tariff, and z is the unit quota rent. With the base figures, this gives a rate of equivalent tariff of 80.5 per cent.

Scenario 1 in Table 1 indicates the impact of tariffication of agricultural imports. The major effect is to transfer to the government rents that previously accrued directly as income to rich households. This has the effect of lowering the total income and savings of rich households and increasing the total revenue and current savings of the government. Rich households decrease their consumption as well as their savings. The increase in government savings, however, is larger than the decrease in rich households' savings. This is because quota rents accrue as income to rich households, and only a fraction of the income of the rich is saved, while tariff revenue accrues directly to the government, and in the absence of variations in government real spending it all goes towards augmenting government savings. The increase in total economy-wide savings is reflected in larger amounts of overall business investments of 1.56 per cent, which is a sizeable amount.

Scenario 2 in Table 1 exhibits the effect of a unilateral reduction of the tariffs on the agricultural and non-agricultural products to 5 per cent (after the tariffication of agricultural quotas). To understand the final impacts, it is instructive first to understand the immediate changes that occur if the tariffs on both products are reduced. Consider the immediate effect of a tariff reduction for both sectors to 5 per cent. The first effect will be a substantial reduction in the domestic prices of importables, and an attendant decline in the prices that domestic purchasers pay for the composite good that is available domestically. Given that producer prices initially stay unchanged, the reduction in the prices of composites results in an initial increase in the effective prices of value added, as the composites are purchased for intermediate consumption. The decreases in the prices of the composites also lead to a decrease in the price of the two domestic consumer goods, and hence via the wage adjustment equation to a decline in the wage of the formal sectors. Hence, at the initially unaltered producer prices, the tendency of all sectors will be to increase production and demand more labour. This will lead to increases in incomes of all institutions (except the government), even for rich households who lose the rents. Total demand for the domestically available composites thus increases considerably.

However, this increased demand results largely in an increased initial demand for the imported goods and a relative stagnation of the demand of the domestically produced good, because the elasticities of substitution between domestic and imported goods are assumed for both products larger than one. This results initially in excess supplies for the domestically produced goods, but in excess demands for labour. It also results in initial excess demands for foreign exchange, as the initial increased supply of exportable products resulting from the improved production incentives is counterbalanced by the large increase in the demand for imports that results from the tariff decline.

To balance these excess demands requires decreases in the producer prices of the two domestically produced goods, increases in the unincorporated wages and a devaluation. Of these tendencies, the price of the non-agricultural good cannot change as it is the *numéraire*. In its place there is a shift of the production of the formal non-agricultural sector towards exports, and this leads to a decline in the supply of the non-agricultural domestically produced product. The unincorporated sector also decreases its overall supply because the

TABLE 1 *Results of various liberalization scenarios*

	Base values (million 1990 pesos)	Scenario 1 Tariffication of quotas	Scenario 2 Unilateral uncompensated trade liberalization	Scenario 3	Scenario 4 Quota tariffication or unilateral trade liberalization compensated by domestic tax increases	Scenario 5	Scenario 6	Scenario 7	Scenario 8
			All tariffs at 5%	Agr. tariff 30% Non-agr. tariff at 5%	Tariffication of quotas	All tariffs at 5%	Agr. tariff 30% Non-agr. tariff at 5%	All tariffs at 10%	All tariffs at 0%
Real GDP at fc	986 385	-0.01	7.68	6.45	0.00	7.68	6.43	5.83	9.72
Production									
Form. agriculture	95 845	0.06	4.25	7.25	0.03	4.25	7.35	1.31	7.48
Form. non-agric.	1 317 261	-0.01	8.26	6.70	-0.01	8.26	6.68	6.45	10.23
Unincorporated	619 657	0.00	-3.47	-2.96	0.00	-3.47	-2.95	-2.58	-4.46
Prices*									
Formal wage	4	0.01	-0.87	-0.44	0.00	-0.87	-0.43	-0.84	-0.91
Uninc. wage	1	0.02	2.26	2.96	0.01	2.26	2.99	1.13	3.53
Exchange rate	1	0.00	15.48	14.25	0.00	15.48	14.25	11.19	20.15
Agricultural good	1	0.05	-1.95	0.88	0.03	-1.95	0.96	-2.82	-0.99
CPI	1	0.01	-1.09	-0.55	0.00	-1.09	-0.54	-1.05	-1.14
Real private investment total	208 943	1.56	-13.35	-12.60	-0.04	4.19	3.56	3.30	5.11
Rich households	78 474	-0.95	11.13	10.02	-0.26	3.63	3.07	2.81	4.48
Formal enterpr. agric.	4 103	3.23	-25.62	-19.21	0.17	8.10	14.00	2.88	13.71
Formal enterpr. non-agric	69 486	3.02	-15.64	-15.87	0.06	22.59	18.33	17.86	27.62
Uninc. enterprises	56 880	3.10	-43.44	-39.33	0.10	-17.80	-14.56	-13.79	-22.12
Household welfare**									
Poor	1	-0.14	5.99	5.34	0.05	3.91	3.43	2.99	4.88
Middle	1	-0.10	9.91	8.58	0.25	6.22	5.18	4.89	7.67
Rich	1	-0.95	11.82	10.05	-0.26	4.27	3.10	3.56	5.00

Government								
Current revenue	144 669	3.34	-36.50	-33.99	0.00	-0.27	-0.51	-0.07	-0.47
Current expenditure	108 843	0.00	-0.27	-0.51	0.00	-0.27	-0.51	-0.07	-0.47
Current savings	35 826	13.48	-146.57	-135.72	0.00	-0.27	-0.51	-0.07	-0.47
Exports in for. currency (total)	294 466	-0.01	11.66	10.02	-0.01	11.66	10.00	8.81	14.76
Agricultural products	16 523	0.05	7.06	9.45	0.03	7.06	9.54	3.56	10.90
Non-agricultural products	277 943	-0.01	11.94	10.05	-0.01	11.93	10.03	9.12	14.99
Imports in for. currency (total)	358 548	-0.01	9.58	8.23	0.00	9.58	8.22	7.23	12.12
Agricultural products	12 191	0.12	109.01	50.39	0.07	109.02	50.69	100.99	117.97
Non-agricultural products	346 357	-0.01	6.08	6.74	-0.01	6.08	6.72	3.93	8.40
Uniform tax multiplier (per cent)					-6.89	66.87	62.68	45.54	89.77

Notes: All figures are percentage deviations from the base values that are shown in the first column.

* Base year prices and unincorporated sector wages are normalized to one, while formal sector wages are four times those in the casual market.

** Household welfare is measured by money metric utility that is normalized to one in the base year.

Source: Computed from model simulations.

increase in the wage of the unincorporated labour cuts into its cost. Hence the supply of the non-agricultural good from that producing source also declines. The decrease in the price of the domestically produced agricultural product leads to a further overall decline in the prices of the two domestically available composites, albeit that the devaluation cuts into that. Overall, the consumer price index (CPI) declines and this leads to a decline in formal sector wages. Household welfare increases for all classes, mainly because of the decline in the prices of consumables. Real GDP increases considerably following unilateral and uniform trade liberalization, by 7.68 per cent compared to the base case. However, this does not result in increased private investment. The reason is that there is a very large loss of domestic savings that occurs because of the reduction in government revenue from the decreased tariffs. This decline of savings, of course, tends to boost current expenditures and consumption, but is detrimental for the medium run as it affects growth adversely.

Scenario 3 in Table 1 presents the results of an experiment in which the tariff on the non-agricultural product is reduced to 5 per cent, but the tariff of the agricultural product is reduced to only 30 per cent. There are, of course, no quotas on agricultural imports. It can be seen that the changes are almost all of the same sign as in the previous column, except that the price of the domestically produced agricultural good increases in this case, compared with a decline in the earlier case. The magnitudes of the key variables, such as real GDP, investment and welfare of households are somewhat smaller than those of the first column, suggesting that more rather than less agricultural trade liberalization is beneficial to the economy, as well as to all households.

The major problem with the previous analysis is that, although there is a short-term increase in real GDP and household welfare that results from the trade liberalization, both uniform and non-uniform, there is a large decline in domestic private investment, which is detrimental to growth. It was seen that the fall in investment was the result of the large reductions in public revenue and hence savings. A reasonable way to counterbalance this loss of savings and investment would be to increase domestic taxation.

Scenarios 4, 5 and 6 in Table 1 exhibit the results of the quota tariffication as well as the two trade liberalization experiments discussed under scenarios 1, 2 and 3, but where the government has changed all domestic direct tax rates (namely the direct tax rates on households and enterprises) in a uniform way so as to keep public savings constant in real terms. The change in the uniform tax rate is exhibited at the bottom of Table 1. As the bulk of domestic current taxation falls on rich and middle-income households and on formal enterprises, changing taxation in a uniform way essentially changes the taxation of the middle and rich households, as well as that of formal enterprises.

Comparing scenario 4 with scenario 1, it can be seen that tariffication of the quota with equivalent levels of protection could be combined with a lowering of the average tax rate of 6.89 per cent to leave public savings unchanged in real terms. This policy would leave most of the important magnitudes in the economy almost totally unchanged. Comparing scenario 5 with scenario 2, it can be seen that the former implies an increase of the average direct tax rate of

66.87 per cent. The major magnitudes (such as real GDP, production and prices) stay unchanged. However, what changes significantly is the variation in real private investment, which from a decrease of 13.35 per cent in scenario 2 increases by 4.19 per cent in scenario 5. Moving down the line, it is clear that this gain in investment is made at the expense of household welfare, which increases by much smaller amounts than in the earlier case. Notable in particular is the very small change in the welfare of the rich, compared with a large gain of 11.82 per cent under the no taxation trade liberalization scenario. Nevertheless, it is also significant that the reversal of the investment impact is not made at the welfare cost of any household class.

Turning to scenario 6, and comparing it with scenario 3, it can be seen that, under the taxation scenario, the impacts on the main variables are similar to those of scenario 3, with a large positive change in investment compared with a large negative change under the no taxation scenario. Again the welfare of households changes by smaller amounts compared with the no taxation case, and in fact here the welfare of the rich is seen to decline. Overall it appears that the case of uniform tariff reduction, namely similar tariff reductions for both agriculture and non-agriculture, outperforms the case of differential tariff reduction in several key magnitudes, notably in real GDP and household welfare. The growth does not appear to be affected much under either scenario as the real investment change under the two cases is quite similar.

From the above it is not clear whether other uniform rates perform better. Scenario 7 in Table 1 simulates the case where the uniform tariff rate is 10 per cent, while scenario 8 simulates the case where the uniform tariff rate is zero at completely free trade. In both cases, there are compensating tax increases in the sense outlined above. The results indicate that, the lower the uniform rate of tariff, the higher the increase in real GDP, and the higher the level of real private investment. The cost is a higher overall direct tax rate, something that entails considerable political difficulties. It therefore appears that lower uniform tariff rates, when coupled with increased taxation, are more beneficial to the economy.

SUMMARY AND CONCLUSIONS

The main findings and generalizations from the above analysis are the following. First, it has been shown that tariffication of existing quotas boosts national savings and investment. The policy of unilateral trade liberalization seems an appropriate one for the Philippines from a growth perspective, but only if it is combined with higher levels of domestic effective taxation. Otherwise, although GDP will rise in the short run, domestic savings and investment will decline, with adverse consequences on medium and long-term growth. Also there does not appear to be any reason for a differential treatment of agriculture.

Among the various trade policies examined, the ones that seem to have the best outcome in terms of the welfare of the poor are those involving the least amount of protection. This runs counter to some of the current thinking in Philippine government circles, namely that agricultural protection is needed to safeguard the welfare of the poor. It seems that, as a large segment of the poor are net food buyers, their welfare is increased by lower rather than high food prices, and by policies that enhance investments and employment creation. Such policies appear to be those with low levels of protection.

REFERENCES

Balisacan, A.M. Clarete, R.L. and Cortez, A.M. (1992), *The Food Problem in the Philippines: Situation, Issues and Policy Options*, report submitted to International Food Policy Research Institute, Washington, DC.
Clarete, R.L. (1989), *The Economic Effects of Trade Liberalization on Philippine Agriculture*, Working Paper No. 89-1, Research and Training Programme on Agricultural Policy, Department of Agriculture, Manila.
Clarete, R.L. and Warr, P.G. (1991), 'The Theoretical Structure of the APEX Model of the Philippine Economy', mimeo, APEX project, Manila.
David, C.C. (1994), 'GATT and Philippine Agriculture: Facts and Fallacies', paper presented at the Symposium in honour of Dr Celia Castillo, Philippines Social Science Center, 27–8 September, Quezon City.
deDios, L.C. (1994), *A Review of the Remaining Import Restrictions*, Research Report No. 94–08, Philippine Institute of Development Studies, Manila.
Habito, C. (1986), 'A General Equilibrium Model for Philippine Agricultural Policy Analysis', *Journal of Philippine Development*, 23 (1).
Sarris, A.H. (1994), 'Agricultural Trade Policy and Options for Implementation of the Agricultural Minimum Access Commitments of the Philippines under GATT', mimeographed report under FAO project TCP/PHI/2356, November.
Sarris, A.H. (1995a), 'Philippine Agricultural Trade Policy after GATT ratification: Issues and Options', mimeographed report under FAO project TCP/PHI/2356, March.
Sarris, A.H. (1995b), 'Philippine Agricultural Trade Policy under GATT Ratification: Issues and Options from a Macroeconomic and Growth Perspective', mimeographed report under FAO project TCP/PHI/2356, December.
Tan, E.S. (1994), *Trade Policy Reforms in the 1990s: Effects of E.O. 470 and the Import Liberalization Program*, Research Paper No. 94-11, Philippine Institute of Development Studies, Manila.

F. GÉRARD, ERWIDODO AND I. MARTY*

Evaluation of the Impact of Trade Liberalization on
Food Crop Production and Farm Income in Lowland Java, Indonesia

INTRODUCTION

Since the mid-1980s, the Indonesian economy has been progressively liberalized, following a self-adjustment process after the drop in oil prices. Despite these adverse circumstances the country managed to maintain rapid economic growth, as it had since the end of the 1960s. The agricultural sector has contributed to the dynamism of the economy. Both BULOG (the national foodcrop agency) and the Ministry of Agriculture have played a major role in that success, providing a stable environment for producers and consumers through use of various policy instruments, promoting adoption of new varieties and techniques for growing crops, and providing subsidized inputs. By maintaining rice price stability on domestic markets, BULOG, since 1967, has diminished some of the risk associated with agricultural activities and contributed to social stability by isolating consumers from sharp fluctuations in staple food prices. The importance of market regulation for the welfare of the poor is well known (Newberry, 1989; Timmer, 1992). With the intensification of international negotiations on trade liberalization, further deregulation of the agricultural sector is probable and there is an urgent need to assess the consequences both for national production and for farm income. These issues will be discussed using a micro–macro approach. The methodology is described first, the Indonesian context is then reviewed and the results of various simulations are described and analysed.

METHODOLOGY: A MICRO–MACRO APPROACH

The methodology[1] proposed in this paper is a micro–macro approach, based on a detailed representation of farming systems through opportunities and constraints relating to agricultural production as determined by agroclimatic and socioeconomic conditions for each type of system. There is then a switch to the regional level through scale parameters representing the share of each farming system. The model must reproduce farmers' behaviour, evaluate the

*ESCAP CGPRT Centre, Indonesia and CIRAD-URPA, Nogent Sur Marne, France (Gérard), Centre for Agro-Socio-Economic Research, Bogor, Indonesia (Erwidodo) and CIRAD-URPA (Marty).

response to policy and estimate the impact on economic indicators at the farm and aggregate levels.

Since production is represented by a set of farming systems, it is possible to adjust the set according to the type of policy issue to be explored (poverty alleviation, regional development and so on). A great deal of attention is devoted to the representation of market imperfections and risk is taken into account as an important factor in farmers' decision making. Agricultural production is clearly a risky activity since the production level is random and geographic correlation of risks and moral hazard make insurance difficult, while the simultaneity of borrowing and depositing lead to difficulties for the banking system. Farmers are thus very sensitive to financial risk. It is assumed that they base their decisions on expectations of gross margins and potential deviations for each activity (Hazell and Scandizzo, 1979). Some imperfections on factor markets are also considered.

To identify the main farm types (operating in a homogeneous environment and with similar production factor endowments) statistical analysis of a set of data crossing agroclimatic and socioeconomic variables was combined with interviewing experts and with bibliographical review. Each representative farm type could then be described by a non-linear mathematical programming model. It was assumed that each farmer makes choices from a set of activities and techniques, utilizing those which maximize the expected utility of wealth under simultaneous constraints.[2]

Wealth is defined as the total value of the assets at the end of the year. In order to consider risk attitudes, use was made of a mean-variance analysis (Markowitz, 1959), slightly modified to introduce endogenous risk aversion:

$$Max\ U(W_F) = E(W_F) - \frac{1}{2}\sigma^2 A_{WF}. \tag{1}$$

Here $E(W_F)$ represents the expected wealth for the farm F, σ^2_{WF} the associated expected possible deviation and A the risk aversion coefficient, which is endogenous and inversely proportional to wealth.

$$E(W_F) = \Sigma_a A_{F,a} * E(P_a). \tag{2}$$

$A_{F,a}$ represents the volume of assets (a) owned by the farm (F) and $E(P_a)$ the expected price associated with it. Thus wealth is defined as the sum of the value of assets (land, equipment, livestock, cash and savings).

The risk associated with a given wealth level depends on the portfolio of activities and assets for the period.

$$\sigma^2_{WF} = \Sigma_a(\sigma_a * E(P_a) * A_{F,a})^2 + \Sigma_{act}(\sigma_{act} * E(MB_{act}))^2 \tag{3}$$

All crop activities are covered (act) while $E(MB_{act})$ represents the expected gross margin for each activity, with σ as the associated expected deviation. Covariances between activities are assumed to be zero.

Fixed factor utilization is subject to constraints defined by endowment and other transactions. For example, the land constraint requires that the sum of land allocated for each crop $j(AL_j)$ represents a smaller area than the total land available for cropping. This variable is defined by the sum of land owned (*Laown*), land purchased (*Lp*) and land rented in (*Lrin*) minus land sold (*Ls*) and land rented out (*Lrout*). Thus for each farm:

$$\Sigma_j AL_j \leq Laown + Lp - Ls + Lrin - Lrout \qquad (4)$$

The same kind of equations hold for labour, animal traction and machine allocation.

For each period, the production cost of each activity (C_{act}) can be covered by cash flow availability coming from the last period (*Pcash*), current earning activities $(Earn_{act})$, or borrowing (*B*). If some surplus cash exists it is transferred to the next period. Family consumption (*Cons*) as well as investment and savings (*Sav*) are included in this equation.

$$\Sigma_{act} C_{act} + Cons + Inv + Sav = \Sigma_{act} Earn_{act} + Pcash + B + Tcash \qquad (4)$$

A financial cost is associated with borrowing. Access to credit can be affected by caution, or globally constrained to a fixed amount for the village or region according to conditions in the capital market. Consumption is defined as a minimum level plus part of the expected profit which is determined by a consumption propensity. Investment and savings can be negative if some decapitalization is necessary. For the costs and returns of each activity, the time of paying for production costs and the point in time of earning money have to be carefully determined in order to take account of production lags which have very important effects on farmers' liquidity. For crops, the production costs have to be paid at the beginning of the season and the associated earnings come in only at its end. For outside labour from other farms, consideration must be given to the local rules; for example, when payment is in kind after the harvest, the lag has to be taken into account. Lags can be harmful for farmers, generating cash flow problems and non-linear responses to market incentives (Boussard, 1992). Some markets have a range of influence and balanced equations may be necessary at village level, for renting land, equipment or labour.

Within the model, time has to be treated according to the local nature of agriculture; in lowland Java, for example, three seasons have generally to be considered. In order to consider links between activities of the three seasons, the optimization is calculated on a yearly basis according to the expected results of quarterly activities.

The decision process leads to a land allocation to crops and techniques, livestock activity levels, investment and borrowing, and labour allocations between farm and off-farm activities. Decisions are based on expectations of prices and yields, subject to time lags between decisions and actual production, while expectations are affected by information imperfections.[3] At the end of each production period, real prices and yields are computed by applying a random coefficient to an average value. The production level and the end of period farm endowment are then calculated with 'real variables'. In this way the results of each year are used as exogenous parameters for the next period.

The model is recursive and dynamic, despite a static optimization, because each year is linked to the preceding year. It is thus possible to incorporate the importance of past results in current decisions without using a very big model. Farm-type models are linked together through markets, for labour and land at the village level and for agricultural products at national level. Because the objective is to identify the effects of policy on decisions, the 'farm types' module is linked with a set of economic variables defining the socioeconomic environment in which farmers' decisions take place.

This model addresses policy effects in an original way both at farm level and, after aggregation across all types of farms, at regional and national level. It also gives immediate impact and time lag effects and builds in risk. These features are important primarily because farm heterogeneity will lead first to different impacts on farm income for a given policy and it is useful to evaluate these variations in order to display spatial impacts. Secondly, because the reactions of the agents are not instant and their behaviour can have delayed impacts (on the environment, for example), it is important to evaluate both short and long-term effects. Thirdly, markets for products and factors are not assumed to be perfect and risk is operationalized so that stylized farm situations can be represented as accurately as practically possible. With all the features the dynamics of agricultural supply, as defined by Nerlove (1979), are more effectively represented.

THE INDONESIAN CASE

Indonesia is the largest archipelago in the world, consisting of more than 13 600 islands, almost half of which are inhabited, stretching across some 5150 km of sea in the region of the equator and extending over 5000 km between its longitudinal extremes. The development level of various islands is quite different and explains the high diversity of agroclimatic and socioeconomic conditions faced by farmers throughout the country. Java represents 60 per cent of the total population and national foodcrop production, with only 7 per cent of the area. Within Java a highly diversified agriculture can still be found. Moreover, as the density of population is already 814 inhabitants per km^2, the policy impact on farm income and consequently on rural migration is an important concern for policy makers. For all these reasons, this paper will concentrate on the case of lowland Java.

Three broad zones were distinguished, two in irrigated areas, with one rainfed area. In the former there were divisions according to levels of water availability and the level of water management, which ranged from high and intermediate to low. On rainfed land there were two areas, one of them being drier than the other (Table 1). Three seasons were considered, one wet and two dry. The crops involved are rice, maize, soybean, mungbean, cassava and various kinds of vegetables.[4]

Irrigated land with a high level of water control obtains the highest yields. Concentrated mainly in the rich volcanic and alluvial soils of lowland Java, the characteristic pattern consists of two crops of rice, often followed during the second dry season by a secondary crop or by vegetables. A non-rice crop seems to be far more common than a third rice crop, owing to water availability, labour constraints and crop rotation to control pests. Farmers in irrigated areas use high-yielding varieties of rice, as well as large quantities of fertilizer. Yields reach more than 5.5 tonnes per hectare. Three types of farm (F1–3) were represented in this area (Table 1), mainly differing by type of land holding.

In the area with moderate water control, water availability often allows cultivation of two crops of rice, but with a lower yield level than in the sawah with high water control, especially during the first dry season. A third crop is also common. In areas with low water control, secondary crops are more developed. During the wet season, poor drainage makes the cultivation of non-rice crops almost impossible. In these areas, traditional varieties of rice can be found. The presence of small streams allows rice cultivation during the other seasons. Four types of farm were represented in this zone, of which two mainly grow soybean as a secondary crop (F4, F5) and two primarily grow maize (F6, F7).

Farmers in rainfed areas have to wait for the monsoon to grow rice, which entails considerably more risk than in irrigated areas. As the level of water control is low, the higher-yielding varieties of rice are less frequently used. Fertilizer use is also lower and the yields seldom reach more than 4.5 tonnes per hectare. Rice cannot be grown during the dry season, when soybeans is a common crop. The second dry season is usually fallow owing to drought.

TABLE 1   *Main lowland farming systems and their characteristics in Java*

Farming systems characteristics	Technical irrigated with high-level water control			Simple irrigated with moderate to low water control				Rainfed	
	F1	F2	F3	F4	F5	F6	F7	F8	F9
Area controlled (ha)	2.4	1.05	0.95	1.2	0.7	1.2	0.7	0.35	0.35
Active persons	3.2	3.2	3.6	2.5	2.7	2.5	2.7	2.0	3
Type of land	irt	irt	irt	irt	irt–irs	irt	irt–irs	rai	rai–dry
Cultivated area (%)	95	96	94	44	60	56	70	47	30
Rice	2	1.5	1.3	36	36	8	6	3	2
Soybean	0	0	0	19	4	36	24	30	29
Maize	3	2.5	4.7	0	0	0	0	20	39
Mechanization	yes	yes	yes	yes	yes	yes	yes	no	no
Yearly net income per cap (million rp)	2.5	1	0.6	1.6	0.8	1.9	0.9	0.55	0.25
Off-farm income (%)	12	26	36	17	29	18	35	37	40
Animals in total wealth (%)	0.01	6.3	0.3	3.5	8.1	3.5	7	0.2	0.3

Notes: Land 'controlled' is land 'owned' + land 'rented in' – land 'rented out'; 'irt' is 'technical irrigated', 'irs' is 'simple irrigated', 'rai' is 'rainfed land' and 'dry' is 'dryland'.

TESTING THE IMPACT OF LIBERALIZATION

Since GATT and APEC negotiations are now under intensive discussion, the characteristically strong intervention of the government of Indonesia in the agricultural sector is increasingly criticized, both within and outside the country. Hence it is interesting to attempt an assessment of the consequence of a free trade environment for food crops and inputs at both regional and farm level.

Liberalizing the food crops sub-sector will lead to changes in the level of prices and in the variability of returns.[5] According to economic theory, domestic prices will adjust to international prices unless transaction costs are significant, or if domestic production is high enough in comparison with total world production to influence prices. In the first scenario (S1) domestic prices are assumed to adjust towards international prices in the second year of simulation (Y2). For rice during 1972–89, the coefficient of variation of prices was 0.59 on the international market and 0.16 for the domestic market (Gérard and Marty, 1995). Moreover, domestic prices were somewhat higher than international prices. The same may be said for soybean and maize in terms of price variability, while the price of maize was similar to the international level and that of soybean was around 50 per cent higher than on the international market (Gonzales *et al.*, 1993).

The main result in the projections is that rice output remains stable after the assumed liberalization (S1 compared with S0 in Figure 1). By contrast, soybean production decreases sharply in the liberalization scenario (S1, Figure 2), while maize production shows a strong increase (Figure 3). The changes underline the land competition between these crops. Since rice market stabilization is so important in Indonesia, the second scenario (S2) excluded this crop from the liberalization process. The impact is important in terms of income, as shown later, but not in production (Figures 1, 2, 3).

In view of the adverse impact on soybean output in the liberalization scenario, the effects of two technical improvements were included in the third

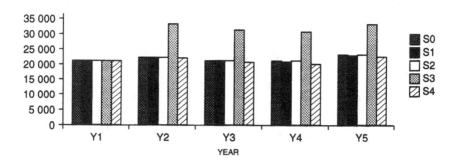

FIGURE 1 *Impact of liberalization on regional rice production*

scenario (S3) for rice and soybean (increased yield of 50 per cent for both crops, with improvement in practices and material). Resources are still being devoted to research on new varieties, which could generate further increase in yields of rice, especially in the rainfed area, while for soybean (where yields are around 800 kg/ha on average for lowland Java) the simulated increase will take yields to a medium level in comparison with international performance. Supply response is important for the two products. The increase in soybean production is higher than the yield increase because more land is allocated to the crop. In fact, the technological improvement overcompensates the loss of profitability induced by trade liberalization. In some areas, the crop becomes more profitable than maize, production of which decreases.

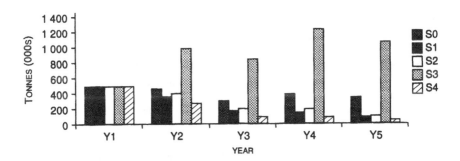

FIGURE 2   *Impact of liberalization on regional soybean production*

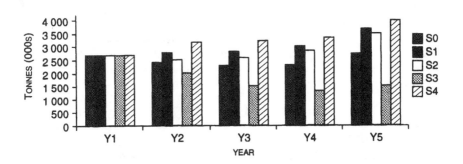

FIGURE 3   *Impact of liberalization on regional maize production*

Because the Indonesian economy experiences continuous rapid development, the last simulation (S4) assumes a quicker increase of off-farm activities in comparison with the base run (10 per cent instead of 5 per cent in the base run). There is a slightly unfavourable impact on rice production (Figure 1), a more serious negative impact on soybean (Figure 2), but a positive effect on maize output (Figure 3), underlining its low labour requirement.

One interesting feature of the MATA model is that it allows deeper analysis of income and crop allocation impacts at the farm level (Table 2). The decrease in agricultural income after liberalization of the whole food crops sub-sector is sharp for each farm type (S1), but the situation is much better if rice is excluded from the liberalization process (S2). The technical innovation scenario (S3) has different impacts from one farm type to another. For those with the high level of water control, agricultural incomes become larger than in the base run (S0), because they are highly specialized in rice and in a position to take advantage of innovation. For the farms in the rainfed area, the situation is hardly better than in the liberalized scenario (S1), since the small farm sizes do not allow much advantage to be gained from technical change. The simulation with the higher increase in off-farm activities (S4) has the worst impact on agricultural income. However, for total income this scenario is the most favourable, except on the biggest farms in the 'high level of water control' area. For this type of farm, competition on the labour market is very damaging, because there is heavy reliance on hired labour for cultivation. This analysis is confirmed by the results of the land allocation exercise, which shows that the difficulty of finding hired labour results in movement from soybean and rice to maize.

For all the other farms it is clear that the best way to increase rural income is to promote the development of off-farm activities such as processing and packaging of agricultural products or other small-scale rural industry. The farms which fared worst in the liberalization scenario (S1) were the small farmers (F3) and those in the rainfed area (F8 and F9). However, the importance of off-farm activities allowed them to maintain and not to decrease total income

TABLE 2   *Agricultural income in various scenarios after four years' simulations (000s rp)*

Farm type scenarios	Technical irrigated with high-level water control			Simple irrigated with moderate to low water control				Rainfed	
	F1	F2	F3	F4	F5	F6	F7	F8	F9
S0	1 979	664	353	1 279	541	1 586	575	183	61
S1	1 335	441	191	853	336	1 186	428	112	35
S2	1 726	606	274	1 022	434	1 370	534	146	45
S3	2 018	901	354	945	385	1 451	503	143	52
S4	1 135	384	245	705	358	1 032	408	101	33

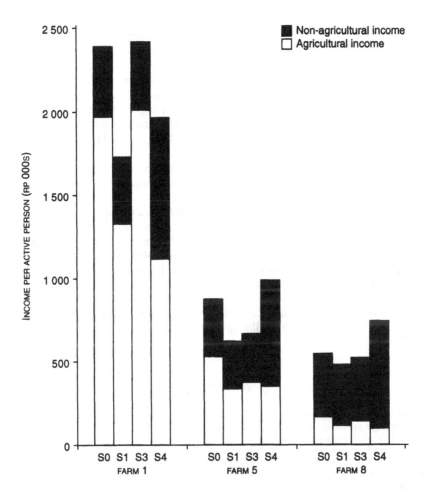

FIGURE 4   *Distribution of income after four-year simulations for three farms and three scenarios*

(Figure 4), which is significant since these three farm types represent roughly one and half million households (around four million active persons) and would have very little incentive to stay in agricultural production in the liberalization scenario.

CONCLUSION

Various scenarios concerning the liberalization of the food crop sub-sector were tested and analysed in this study. In contrast with previous analysis (Trewin *et al.*, 1993; Thorbecke, 1992), the use of a micro–macro approach enables evaluation of the impact to be made at various levels. Rice production is very stable with liberalization, while soybean production decreases sharply and maize production increases. At the farm level, the effects on agricultural income tend to be adverse, though the decrease is less pronounced if rice is excluded from the trade liberalization. Technological improvement for rice and soybean would be able to compensate partially for the impact of liberalization on income. Farms in the irrigated area could obtain higher income than in the base-run situation. Increased off-farm jobs opportunities have a strong positive effect on household income, except in the case of the largest farm type in the study.

Finally, the study highlights the importance of technical innovations, as induced by agronomic research, to maintain rural income during a trade liberalization process. It shows that claims about any favourable effects of liberalization for farmers, stemming from efficiency gains, have to be reconsidered in an imperfect market context, at least in the short term. The liquidity constraint and the existence of risk aversion would prevent farmers from specializing in the more profitable crops. The study also points out that the development of off-farm activities is necessary to increase rural income. The liberalization of agricultural trade will induce a sharp decrease in income, and for around 4 million active farm participants very few incentives will remain to keep them in agricultural production. Hence, even though liberalization could lead to a more efficient factor allocation, it could be worth considering the introduction of accompanying policies to minimize adverse effects.

NOTES

[1]This study uses the agricultural production module of the MATA model. For further details on methodology, see Gérard *et al.* (1994) and Deybe (1994).

[3]Various objective functions can be used in the MATA model. Farming system models usually use profit maximization in market economies and self-sufficiency objectives for subsistence economies. Here wealth is used as a proxy for the total value of the farm, because the model is dynamic but the optimization is static. Because we wanted to allow the level of assets to appear in the model, as well as to account for risk (it is less risky to own gold than to own buffaloes), it was better to consider the expected stock of wealth rather than flows of income. However, tests were made with expected profit (still taking risk into account) for the Indonesian case, leading to the same results. The constraints, in the Javanese case, defined a small set of activity combinations as optimum and the model is not sensitive to the formulation of the objective function.

[3]To approach the concept of rational expectations (Muth, 1961), given the fact that prices and yields are determined randomly around an average, farmers expect to obtain the average level of gross margins.

[4]For a number of reasons, sugarcane was not included in our study. The political regulation for this crop is complicated, with some forced crop allocation. Profitability is highly reliant on the proximity of sugar mill factories (Collier *et al.*, 1993) and this information was not included in the typology. In addition, the production lag is longer than the yearly optimization process used in the study.

[5]As pointed out by Koester (1993), the impact of liberalization of trade will be different according to the number of countries involved, but there is still great uncertainty about the impact on the world prices level and on instability.

REFERENCES

Boussard, J.M. (1992), *Introduction à l'économie rurale*, Paris: Cujas.

Collier, William L., Santoso, K. and Soentoro, W.R. (1993), *A New Approach to Rural Development in Java: Twenty Five Years of Village Studies*, Jakarta: Pt Intersys.

Deybe, D. (1994), *Vers une agriculture durable. Un modèle bio-économique*, Paris: CIRAD.

Gérard, F. and Marty, I. (1995), 'Les Politiques d'accompagnement de la "Révolution Verte" en Asie: République de Corée, Indonésie, Philippines et Thaïlande', *Revue d'économie du développement*, **2**, 93–114.

Gérard, F., Boussard J.M. and Deybe D. (1994), 'MATA: A multilevel analysis tool for agricultural policy', *Working Paper URPA no. 23*, Paris: CIRAD.

Gonzales, L.A., Kasryno F., Perez, N.D. and Rosegrant, Mark W. (1993), *Economic Incentives and Comparative Advantage in Indonesian Food Crop Production*, Research Report 93, Washington, DC.: International Food Policy Research Institute.

Hazell, P. and Scandizzo, P.L. (1979), 'Farmers' Expectations, Risk Aversion and Market Equilibrium under Risk', *American Journal of Agricultural Economics*, **61**, 204–9.

Koester, U. (1993), 'International Trade and Agricultural Development in Developing Countries: Significance of the Uruguay Round of GATT Negotiations', *Agricultural Economics*, **8**, 275–94.

Markowitz, H.M. (1959), *Portfolio Selection: Efficient Diversification of Investments*, New York: Wiley.

Muth, J.F. (1961), 'Rational expectations and the theory of price movements', *Econometrica*, **29**, 315–35.

Nerlove, M. (1979), 'The dynamics of supply: retrospect and prospect', *American Journal of Agricultural Economics*, **61**, 874–88.

Newberry, D.M. (1989), 'The Theory of Food Price Stabilisation', *Economic Journal*, **99**, 1065–82.

Thorbecke, E. (1992), *Ajustement et équité en Indonésie*, Paris: OECD.

Timmer, C.P. (1992), 'Food price stability and the welfare of the poor', *Indonesian Food Journal*, 42–57.

Trewin, R., Erwidodo and Huang, Y. (1993), 'Stages of Development of an Indonesian CGE Model (INDOGEM) with Application to Analysis of Key Agricultural Policies', paper presented at the Conference of Economists, 27–30 September, Murdoch University, Perth.

PANEL DISCUSSION REPORTS

PANEL 1: AGRICULTURAL HISTORY: LESSONS FROM AGRICULTURAL DEVELOPMENT

ORGANIZER AND CHAIRPERSON

Vernon W. Ruttan (University of Minnesota, USA)

PANEL DISCUSSANTS

Technical Changes in US Agricultural History: A Perspective on the Induced Innovation Hypothesis   *Alan L. Olmstead (University of California-Davis, USA)*

Contract Choice: Land and Labour Relationships in China in the Imperial, Communist and Post-Communist Period   *Lauren Brandt (University of Toronto, Canada)*

Historical Change in Land–Labour Relationships in Western Europe   *Gerd Anderson, Günther Schmitt, Heinrich Hockmann (University of Göttingen, Germany)*

Between Political Control and Efficiency Gains: The Evolution of Agrarian Property Rights in Mexico   *Alain de Janvry (University of California-Berkeley, USA), Gustovo Gordillo (FAO), Elisabeth Sadoulet (University of California-Berkeley, USA)*

Contract Choice and Tenure Relations During the Pre-Colonial, Colonial and Post-Colonial Periods in India   *Vasant Sukhatme (Macalester College, USA)*

A Comparative Perspective on Change in Technology and Land–Labour Relationships   *Hans P. Binswanger (World Bank)*

RAPPORTEUR

Regina Birner[1] *(University of Göttingen, Germany)*

---

[1]An asterisk indicates the main author or authors of the reports. Invaluable assistance in the preparation of panel material was given by Katinka Weinberger (University of Bonn).

The aim of the discussion was to confront the well known 'induced innovation' hypothesis with further evidence as to its applicability from a range of countries and of time periods. Alan Olmstead began by arguing that the available historical data are quite different from the so-called 'stylized facts' to which the induced innovation hypothesis model was applied for testing. In particular, it seems that the considerable biological innovation which occurred before the 1930s contradicts the whole notion. It is also true that there was considerable variation in what was happening within the various regions of the United States; there were great differences in interest rates and in land values, which makes any generalization impossible.

An air of scepticism about the robustness of the hypothesis pervaded the contributions of other members of the Panel, though it did become clear that there are great difficulties in formulating adequate tests since alternative specifications can be used. Heinrich Hockmann, who presented the work on Western Europe agricultural history, discussed two models which suggested that a number of variables not captured by the induced innovation hypothesis could be important in explaining developments there. It was also apparent that there can be fundamental differences in types of economic institutions which make comparisons on a grand scale distinctly problematic. Account has to be taken of such features as the Zamindar system of India with all of its principal–agent problems, mentioned by Vasant Sukhatme, and intricacies of relationships in China and Mexico.

In more general discussion, Alain de Janvry pointed out the need for clarity of definition prior to analysis. For example, access to new crops (a feature of the early history of the United States) represents a shift in the entire set of innovation possibilities. This situation differs from a 'simpler' alteration in price relationships, for which the induced innovation hypothesis was formulated. As the discussion widened to the floor, James Roumasset (University of Hawaii) suggested that the hypothesis is very useful as a starting point for analysis. The question then is to find out how much can be attributed to the facts captured within it, and how much has to be explained by other facts such as economies of scale or transaction costs. It would not be surprising if in some cases the proportion of facts which could be explained by induced innovation became small. Colin Thirtle (University of Reading) agreed with that basic proposition, noting that, in his researches, he found that the hypothesis was useful at the aggregate level, precisely as a starting point, but this was not the case in microeconomic studies. John Pender (IFPRI) was more sceptical, wondering whether factor prices are really relevant as incentives in the search for future innovations because there is a time lag involved. Past factor prices may lead to wrong expectations because they may not be good predictors of future situations. There were comments on this broad issue in the work of Hans Binswanger.

Bruce Johnston (Stanford University) noted that the whole debate on induced innovation should not now be regarded as one relating to history, important though that is in itself. It is still a live issue in relation to what he called 'late developing countries', where there is an abundant rural labour force caused by population growth and the share engaged in agriculture is still high. Using that relatively cheap resource in the optimum way remains critical for both employment and growth.

Vernon Ruttan, as co-author of the original work on induced innovation, concluded the session with the comment that, for him, the most interesting cases to investigate are actually those in which the hypothesis appears not to work, rather than those where it is more adequate. There is clearly much which remains to be done, both for history and for modern analysis.

PANEL 2: RURAL DEVELOPMENT AND AGRARIAN REFORM: INSTITUTIONAL CONSTRAINTS AND INNOVATIONS

ORGANIZER AND CHAIRPERSON

Laurent Martens (University of Ghent, Belgium)

PANEL DISCUSSANTS

Agrarian Reform in Southern Africa: Redistribution of Land and Water Use Rights   *Johan Van Zyl, Johan Kirsten (University of Pretoria, South Africa)*

Innovations in Financial Markets: Implications for Rural Development
Richard L. Meyer, Geetha Nagarajan (Ohio State University, USA)

Rural Development and Farm Structures in Transition   *Franciszek Tomczak (Warsaw School of Economics, Poland)*

Family Farms in a Globalized Economy: Fordism v. Nichism in Japanese Experience   *Yoshio Kawamura (Ryokoku University, Japan)*

RAPPORTEUR

Abdul Bayes* (Jahangirnagar University, Bangladesh)

This discussion dealt with agrarian reform, with an emphasis on institutional matters. Institutional innovations have been defined as changes in the actual or potential performance of existing or new organizations, as well as changes in the relationship between an organization and its environment. The panel looked at four separate, but interrelated, themes: land and water use rights, rural financial institutions, farm structures, rural communities and rural/urban inter-action. Each contribution was prepared with a specific regional focus: South Africa, less developed countries (LDC), Central and Eastern European Countries (CEEC) and Japan.

Necessity for reforms in South Africa

Van Zyl and Kirsten argued that reforms of land and water rights are necessary for sustainable, broad-based rural development in South Africa. The arguments centre mainly upon three issues: equity/equality, efficiency and employment/ linkage considerations. Several innovative approaches to bringing about a re-distribution of land and water rights were discussed. By following a market-assisted approach to land reform, an opportunity was created for other innovations to bring about the necessary reforms. However, while these re-forms are necessary, they are not sufficient to ensure rural development. Access to productive resources is only the starting point.

Research shows that agriculture can be the engine for rural development. This implies that the productivity of the farming sector should be increased. One of the most direct ways of increasing the real incomes of resource-poor farmers is to develop improved technology to increase the productivity of their main enterprise, staple food production. Increased staple food production may increase the per capita availability of home-produced foods, raise cash in-comes by generating a marketable surplus of grain or allow subsistence food needs to be produced with fewer resources, thus freeing land and labour to produce higher-value crops. It also allows scarce funds to be used for purchas-ing other food, which could lead to improved dietary intake. Although improved technology and related measures could be of assistance, there are a number of constraints, largely of an institutional nature, that need to be addressed in an innovative fashion, as was shown in this paper.

Innovations in rural financial markets

Meyer and Nagarajan showed that a paradoxical situation has recently emerged in rural financial markets in low-income countries. Most programmes to ex-tend the frontier of formal finance into rural areas have failed, but informal finance has thrived. This paradox can be explained in terms of asymmetric information and transaction costs. A number of innovations have been devel-oped in microfinance which involve lenders, frequently NGOs, making small short-term loans to poor urban borrowers.

In summary, through innovation microfinance has found ways to solve, or at least reduce, some of the information and transaction cost problems that have plagued agricultural lending in many low-income countries. It is not yet clear, however, how far this can really extend the financial frontier into specialized agricultural areas, or be sustainable. Some analysts argue that expanded outreach contributes to sustainability through economies of scale. Others believe that there is a trade-off between outreach and sustainability so that, over time, organizations will shift their portfolios away from poor borrowers and small loan sizes in order to reduce costs and achieve higher levels of operational efficiency.

A large amount of experimentation is being undertaken by microlenders. Several that historically made only small group loans are now experimenting with making larger individual loans to their best customers. Some organiza-tions operating exclusively in urban areas are experimenting with rural and agricultural lending. These experiments will reveal the extent to which recent microfinance innovations are capable of resolving the basic challenges of expanding financial services for agricultural and rural development.

Farm structures in transitional economies

Tomczak spoke about several issues in the transition process for agriculture and rural development in Central and Eastern European countries, in general, and for Poland in particular, relating to the choice between small-scale and large-scale farming, between agricultural and non-agricultural employment and between multifunctional and rural development. Tomczak believed that the changes which took place in Polish agriculture during the first period of transition were beneficial. However, excessive employment in agriculture remains the main problem causing low income in rural areas. Changes in this situation are expected to be slow and depend upon an increased demand for labour outside agriculture. There is a sense in which the social and political determination to finalize the construction of the new economic order is not sufficient.

Rural communities in postwar Japan

Kawamura dealt with major changes in rural communities in postwar Japan, especially focusing on developments since the 1980s, when Japan came onto the stage as a globalized economy. This has left agriculture and rural communities in a difficult position because of the lack of mobility in its major production factors, especially land. Depopulation of remote areas, as well as booming urbanization in other parts of the country, have brought serious problems to rural communities struggling to maintain basic community systems and local resources. Japanese farm households are sharply dichotomized, with a minority of full-time farms and with a large majority of part-time farm households, earning the major part of their income outside agriculture. The author recognized a positive correlation between economic and social activities at the community level, which suggests an important role for social groups and for cooperation for economic development. He also developed the concept of the 'niche' type of production, characterized by small-scale and labour-intensive production of multiple crops, suited to the environment, and with direct linkages between producers and consumers and between rural and urban populations.

Floor discussion: differences and similarities between regions

It was suggested that the characteristics of the rural financial markets in CEEC, in Japan and in South Africa are somewhat different. Nevertheless, some similarities between pre-agrarian reform in Japan and current reform in South Africa were recognized, particularly relating to the fact that the majority of the rural population existed, or exists, in a situation of extreme social, political and economic disadvantage compared with a rural elite. In relation to the transition process in Europe, it was emphasized that the reform of the rural financial markets had been delayed in some countries because of the strategic role that food plays in their economies.

It was then argued that examples of all types of innovative lending technologies, as described by Meyer and Nagarajan, can be found in South Africa, but that none of the institutions currently providing access to loan finance is even close to sustainability. Referring to the Tomczak paper, it was stated that some of the findings on Polish agriculture are shared by studies on South African agriculture. However, while the move to small farms in Poland is more direct, in South Africa the focus is rather on the removal of discriminating policies which favoured large farms or discriminated against smaller farmers.

Several participants expressed concerns over the market-based land reform approach in South Africa, and about the transfer of taxpayers' money to landowners. Diverging views were expressed concerning the role of formal banks or of NGOs for microlending to agriculture. Attention was also paid to the role of cooperatives for rural development in Japan, as well as in the transition process in Central and Eastern Europe, where the concept should not be rejected on the basis of some unfortunate experiences under the previous political system.

PANEL 3: EVOLUTION OF NATIONAL RESEARCH SYSTEMS: EMERGING POLICY ISSUES

ORGANIZER, RAPPORTEUR AND CHAIRPERSON

Derek Byerlee* (World Bank)

PANEL DISCUSSANTS

Financing Agricultural Research: International Investment Patterns and Policy Perspectives   *Julian Alston (University of California-Davis), Phil Pardey (IFPRI), Johannes Roseboom (ISNAR)*

International Agricultural Research: On Striving for International Public Goods in an Era of Donor Fatigue   *J.R. Anderson (World Bank)*

Agricultural Research Policy Issues in Latin America: An Overview   *Ruben Echeverria (Inter-American Development Bank)*

Indian Agricultural Research System: Structure, Current Policy Issues and Future Orientation   *Mruthyunjaya and P. Ranjitha (Indian Council of Agricultural Research)*

Private Sector Investment in R&D: Will it Fill the Gap?   *Carl Pray (Rutgers University, USA) and Dinah Umali-Deininger (World Bank)*

The Transformation of the Dutch Agricultural Research System: An Unfinished Agenda   *Johannes Roseboom and H. Rutten (ISNAR)*

Crafting Smallholder-driven Agricultural Research Systems in Southern Africa   *Mandivamba Rukuni (University of Zimbabwe) Malcolm Blackie (Rockefeller Foundation, Malawi), Carl Eicher (Michigan State University, USA)*

This session dealt with the recent development of national research systems, highlighting current policy issues, and their evolution into the 21st century. Four of the discussants emphasized regional or country perspectives – three from the developing world and one industrialized country. The remainder focused on particular themes: trends in financing research at the global level, the international research system and the growing role of the private sector.[2]

---

[2]The papers presented are being published in full in *World Development*, June 1998.

Trends in R&D investments

Alston, Pardey and Roseboom provided global figures on investment in agricultural research. Growth was rapid in the 1970s, averaging over 6 per cent annually in the developing world. However, in the 1980s, the rate slowed and in many cases, especially in Latin America and Africa, investment declined. Almost everywhere, expansion of staff has been more rapid than funding, resulting in a growing proportion of funds being used to pay salaries and an acute shortage of operating funds for undertaking research.

The slowdown reflects the decline in both domestic support and donor contributions over the past decade. The decline in donor support was especially felt in the Consultative Group for International Agricultural Research (CGIAR) system, which witnessed a stagnation of funding in the 1990s, despite an increase in the number of centres and in the scope of its mandate. However, in Africa, donor contributions to national systems have increased in relation to domestic support, so that nearly half of the agricultural research investment in Africa is from donors, including development banks. Rukuni, Blackie and Eicher argued that high donor dependency in Africa has undermined efforts to develop domestic political support for sustainable funding of agricultural research, especially for the smallholder sector.

The decline in funding in part reflects a re-examination almost everywhere of the appropriate role of government, and a worldwide move to privatize public-sector activities. The private sector has, in fact, sharply increased investment in agricultural R&D in recent years, but this has only partly alleviated the gap in public sector funding (Pray and Umali-Deininger). Even after a period of rapid growth in private investment, private R&D typically accounts for only 10–15 per cent of total agricultural R&D in developing countries, compared to about half in the industrialized countries (Alston *et al.*).

The result is that research intensity (R&D investment as a proportion of agricultural GDP) in developing countries remains low, at about 0.6 per cent, and has hardly increased over the past 25 years. This situation is further heightened by the increasing demands being placed on research systems everywhere. During much of the 1970s and 1980s, investment in research was largely motivated by concerns about growing population, a finite resource base, import substitution and food security at both the global and national levels that required a clear focus on increased food productivity. In the 1990s, natural resource management and environmental preservation received much higher priority, along with food safety in industrialized countries. At the international level, especially in the CGIAR system, poverty alleviation is now the main rationale for investment in agricultural research (Anderson). Thus research systems are being asked to do more with less.

The emerging paradigm for NARS

Accompanying these trends there has been a parallel shift in the institutional make-up of the national agricultural research systems (NARS). During much of the past 25 years, the public sector has depended on the national agricultural research organization (NARO) model. In this paradigm, public funds were provided as block grant, usually through the ministry of agriculture, to a centralized research department or institute which then set priorities and executed research through a network of centres under the control of the NARO. A new paradigm is now emerging for thinking about national agricultural research systems. The main elements are summarized below.

Pluralistic institutional structures   There is recognition of the variety of organizations that have the potential to participate in agricultural research, both for funding and execution. The inclusion of this wider range of organizations in the conception of a NARS enhances the quantity and quality of financial and human resources that can be tapped; for example, potential new funding sources from non-agricultural ministries or farmer organizations, and the considerable scientific talent available in universities.

Coupled with this there has been a trend towards the separation of policy making, funding and execution of research, since each requires different inputs and skills. This trend is most advanced in the Netherlands, where the Ministry of Agriculture now only concerns itself with research policy and funding; research execution takes place in a wide variety of organizations. A similar arrangement is evolving in Zimbabwe (Rukuni *et al.*) where the newly revamped Agricultural Research Council is focusing on policy and funding issues, while much of the execution of research is carried out in the Ministry of Agriculture, universities, farmer organizations and the private sector.

The growing role of the private sector   Pray and Umali-Deininger document the growing role of the private sector in R&D. The worldwide trend towards market liberalization and privatization, and much stronger intellectual property protection for biological technologies, have been major stimulants to private investment in agricultural research. However, they point out that, even with these favourable trends, there are still many factors that limit private-sector investment in R&D, including poor agroclimatic potential, small market size and restrictive policies on technology imports and release. In addition, several of the papers note that private-sector research depends to a large extent on using knowledge, methods and technologies developed in the public sector, especially products of basic and strategic research. Hence strong public support for research, especially basic and strategic research, may be one of the major stimulants to private investment in R&D. The bottom line is that, even with suitable policies in place, private-sector research has the potential to fill the gap caused by dwindling public support only in certain cases, especially in mature NARS and in areas of commercial agriculture. There is also concern about the growing role of multinationals, a concern heightened by several recent mergers of biotechnology, seed and chemical companies that have strengthened the market position of a few large multinationals (Pray and Umali-Deininger, Mruthyunjaya and Ranjitha). A strong public sector focused on more strategic research is seen as a stimulus to the development of local private R&D capacity and a competitive private sector.

A parallel development is the increasing trend towards public–private-sector partnerships in agricultural research. These take many forms, including joint ventures of public organizations with the private sector to commercialize their technologies, and private funding of research in the public sector to utilize available infrastructure and scientific skills. Farmer organizations are also becoming more active as a source of funding for public-sector research, through the use of levies on commodity output, especially for export crops.

This rise in private-sector research allows the public sector to focus more sharply on public goods and other areas where there are market failures in the provision of technologies. Alston *et al.* define such market failures as arising from several causes, especially lack of appropriability of much agricultural technology, the long-term and uncertain pay-offs to research and environmental externalities of much agricultural technology. However, they also caution that market failures are a necessary, but not sufficient, condition for public-sector intervention, since many interventions, such as the use of general tax revenue to fund research, also incur considerable welfare costs.

New mechanisms for research funding   The mechanisms for public funding of research have also evolved. There has been a universal move away from providing block grants towards the use of competitive and contractual arrangements to funding research. Alston *et al.* argue that such competitive arrangements, although more costly to manage, are likely to improve the allocation of research resources. The CGIAR system continues with block funding, but Anderson argued that it too should pilot a competitive system of funding that would encourage partnerships and participation of stronger NARS that have a cost advantage in some types of research.

Even where competitive funding is not used, contractual arrangements between research founder and research provider are becoming more common. Essentially, this reflects broader government efforts to enhance accountability and to monitor outputs rather than inputs in government-provided services. Such arrangements are managerially intensive and are most widely used, and perhaps most appropriate, in industrialized countries such as the Netherlands (Roseboom and Rutten).

Efficiency and effectiveness of public research organizations   While research systems are becoming more pluralistic, public research organizations (the NAROs), where most infrastructure and human resources are concentrated, will continue to play a key, but no longer the central, role in the national research system. All countries are searching for ways to improve the efficiency and effectiveness of their NAROs. In most cases (including India and Zimbabwe), this includes consolidation and rationalization of the existing network of research stations, and in some cases (such as the Netherlands) significant downsizing. Even the CGIAR centres have embarked on consolidation and Anderson noted the potential for more. In addition, highly centralized systems such as the ICAR are exploring options for decentralization by devolving full decision-making authority to individual centres.

Most public research organizations are also attempting to reform their management and governance to allow them more flexibility in financial, human resource and asset management. Many NAROs are attempting to shed their old bureaucratic style of management and organization, and are taking on more of the characteristics of private firms in their management styles. In some cases, such as in the Netherlands and in several countries of Latin America, NAROs have been set up essentially as private corporations, with a board of governors that represents their major stakeholders (see below). In other cases, reforms are being attempted from within the existing civil service structure, as in Malawi, where task forces are being constituted to follow research on specific high-priority activities (Rukuni *et al.*)

One of the main reasons for reform of public research organizations is to allow them greater flexibility to seek diverse sources of funding support. A common strategy is for public research institutes to commercialize research products and services, applying intellectual property protection as needed. All of the papers presented evidence of moves in this direction. While commercialization can provide valuable funds for operating costs and incentives for scientists, there are also limits to which a public organization can commercialize its products, especially if it is redefining its role to focus more sharply on public goods which by definition are not 'commercializable'.

Commercialization cannot be a substitute for the development of a local political constituency that will support public funding of agricultural research. Rukuni *et al.*, in particular, argue that the major challenge for NAROs of Southern Africa is the development of a political constituency among small-holder farmers, often bypassed by the research system in the past. The mechanisms for achieving political support are varied and include organization of smallholders to give them greater voice, stronger relations between NAROs and ministries of finance, and greater efforts by research organizations to 'market' their achievements.

Within these general reforms, public organizations are also much more concerned about setting priorities to better utilize their existing resources to achieve stated policy objectives. One approach that is being advocated to guide spending is the use of formal economic approaches to analyse trade-offs in research resource allocation and to set priorities (Alston *et al.*). Many NAROs have applied such methods in recent years, although there are, as yet, few examples of effective institutionalization of such capacity.

Another approach is to involve stakeholders in the governance, priority setting, research execution and even financial support of public research organizations in order to promote more demand-driven and responsive organizations. Governing boards of NAROs are being broadened to include major stakeholders, and various types of mechanisms are being utilized to seek farmer input into priority setting: for example, the regional farmer committees in Zimbabwe. Similar trends are appearing at the international level, where developing countries are also becoming members and contributors to the CGIAR, a healthy trend in strengthening both financial and political support and improving effectiveness, given the growing evidence of donor fatigue (Anderson).

Global scientific linkages Finally, a common thread in all of the presentations was the globalization of agricultural research and the need for all research organizations to develop strategies to keep abreast of global advances in knowledge. Spillovers of technologies and scientific knowledge across subnational and national borders have always been important, and indeed the CGIAR system was established to foster such spillovers and 'spillins'.

The rapid advances in recent years in biotechnology and informational sciences have reinforced the need for countries to participate in this global agricultural research system, if they are to keep abreast of these advances and maintain a competitive agricultural sector. The fact that many of these advances have occurred in the private sector considerably complicates access to much of the emerging knowledge and technology. This has important implications for developing countries as regards implementation and enforcement of intellectual property rights, as well as for the CGIAR centres that might play an intermediary role in helping client countries gain access to the new technologies.

The development of strong national capacity, public and private, in the agricultural sciences will be necessary for countries to exploit these scientific advances. Investment in human resources will be integral to this strategy. Even a strong NARS, such as India, has seen its human resource quality decline in recent years (Mruthyunjaya and Ranjitha). Another approach evident in several countries has been to establish national centres of excellence in basic and strategic research. One implication of the growing complexity of science is the need for research organizations to develop partnerships to gain access to complementary skills, and to participate in research networks that promote exchange of knowledge. Such partnerships and networks are rapidly increasing at both the national and international levels (Anderson).

PANEL 4: TRADE AGREEMENTS:
IMPLEMENTATION, EXPERIENCES AND IMPLICATIONS

ORGANIZER AND CHAIRPERSON

Daniel A. Sumner* (University of California-Davis, USA)

PANEL DISCUSSANTS

Perspectives from Less Developed, Food-importing Countries with Large Agricultural Industries   *Harbinderjit S. Dillon (Ministry of Agriculture,
Indonesia)*

A Perspective from Developed Countries: Subsidized Exporters in North
America and Europe   *Tim Josling (Stanford University, USA), Stefan
Tangermann (University of Göttingen, Germany)*

Trade Agreements: A Policy Maker's and Implementer's Perspective   *John
Slater, Ben Atkinson (Ministry of Agriculture, UK)*

A Perspective from a Food Importer that has Recently Joined the Developed
Countries   *Jaeok Lee (Korean Rural Economic Institute, Republic of Korea)*

RAPPORTEUR

Monika Hartmann* (University of Halle, Germany)

Trade agreements are a major issue for researchers in agricultural economics,
as well as for governments around the globe. Researchers face the challenge of
understanding the implementation of the many agreements recently negotiated,
as well as the task of providing useful information and perspectives to aid
negotiation of additional agreements in the future. Thus the analysis creates
both disciplinary and practical challenges for agricultural economists.

Trade agreements from the perspective of developed countries

Key points made by Tangermann were that the implementation of the Uruguay
Round Agreement (URA) has proceeded so smoothly in the European Union

(EU) that it has been nearly unnoticed. Although variable levies have been converted to tariffs, at most levels of world prices a large measure of protection remains. Most of the reduction in protection that has occurred has been the result of the Common Agricultural Policy reforms that were implemented in 1992, not a result of the URA as such. Export subsidy commitments have been met, but given the recent low EU output and high world prices (due to adverse weather) the impact on markets has been minimal. The EU has implemented grain export taxes to replace export subsidies. Although hardly used for grains, export subsidies for minor products (including olive oils, some dairy products, some meats and some fruits and vegetables) are near URA limits. As expected, the internal support commitments have been nowhere near binding, even though total support by some measures has been maintained. Tangermann observed that the policy shifts encouraged by the URA, and the prospects of further reductions required by the next round of negotiations, have changed the nature of agricultural policy debates within Europe. Fundamental reforms seem far more likely now than a few years ago and this change is due in part to the international trade agreements and negotiations.

Josling noted that the United States has also implemented the URA with little direct policy or trade consequence. Tariffication caused the elimination of the famous Section 22 exception to limits on unilateral institution of quantitative controls on imports, but the result is mainly symbolic. Export subsidy curbs have not been binding because of high international prices for grains and the US ability to export without subsidy. And, as expected, the internal support provisions negotiated in the URA have proved to be non-binding. The Federal Agriculture Improvement and Reform Act of 1996 made these provisions all the more redundant. Josling dealt briefly with the experience of several other countries. Canada implemented the URA import limits by replacing non-tariff barriers for so-called 'supply managed commodities' (dairy, eggs and poultry) with extremely high tariffs to ensure that significant over-tariff imports would not occur. But to meet export support limits, Canada eliminated grain transport subsidies, thus far exceeding the required reductions in this area. Mexico has made remarkable policy changes in recent years, though not mainly in response to the URA. For Mexico, unilateral reforms and the North American Free Trade Agreement have been dominant, but the URA does lock in some of these reforms. Neither Australia nor New Zealand has had difficulties in meeting URA commitments. New Zealand has been the model of far-reaching reforms, based on is experience in the 1980s. Australia was required to modify a number of policies, but no major issues arose. Both countries maintain major state trading enterprises (STEs) for commodity exports and these are likely to be a focus of debate in the next round.

Trade agreements from the perspective of developing countries

Dillon focused on the difficulties of negotiating and implementing agreements for open agricultural trade and the reduction of barriers in some less developed countries. He pointed out that in countries like Indonesia the rural population is poorer than the urban. Further, Indonesia and similar countries are likely to continue to be food importers. This signifies that relaxing import controls may put stress on those farmers who are ill-positioned to weather a loss of family income. Dillon emphasized that those pressing for additional market openings have to recognize the difficult position of nations with a large proportion of rural and poor population. He argued forcefully, not only for more understanding, but also for action to aid poor food-importing nations in their efforts to ensure food security and provide farm income relief. He expressed considerable dissatisfaction with the outcome and process of past trade negotiations. His remarks stimulated lively discussion on the role of economics and of economists' general prescription for more open markets.

Trade agreements from a policy maker's perspective

Slater, in his background paper with Atkinson, focused on EU policies with respect to preferential trading agreements (PTAs). Slater placed these agreements in the context of implementation of the URA and outlined areas where modifications were likely to be forthcoming. The General Agreement on Tariffs and Trade (GATT) has specific provisions governing preferential agreements that allow countries to move away from the GATT principle under which all members are to be treated in a way equivalent to the most favoured nation. In particular, the major GATT provision is that PTAs should work to lower barriers for members, not raise barriers for non-members, and they must cover substantially all trade. The EU has a number of PTAs, notably with other countries in Western Europe, with Eastern Europe, with former colonies of EU members and with non-EU countries of the Mediterranean. Each of these arrangements raises concerns from within the EU and from third-country competitors. Coverage is not complete and the amount of trade created is often limited. For some nations, the participation in a PTA is not a final position with respect to trade relations with the EU. As the EU is enlarged over the next decade, some nations now subject to PTAs will become new EU members. For these countries, the PTAs are a half-way stop on the road to full membership.

Trade agreements from the perspective of a major agricultural importer

Jaeok Lee outlined issues faced by major agricultural importers, such as South Korea, in implementation of trade agreements that require changes in internal support and whose markets need to be further opened to imports. In the URA, South Korea opened its rice market but was able to postpone tariffication of rice for a decade. Lee discussed major changes occurring in South Korean agriculture and agricultural policy as a response to increased globalization. Agricultural imports have continued to expand at a rapid pace and the structure of domestic production is changing as well. For example, in the period 1990–95, rice fell from 37 to 26 per cent of gross value of farm production, while fruit and vegetables revenue grew from 26 to 36 per cent.

Food security is a major concern for countries such as South Korea that rely on imports for a sizeable portion of their food and livestock feed consumption.

Koreans are concerned that thinness and variability of the international rice market cause vulnerability for nations that rely on imports. In implementing the URA, South Korea was concerned with the non-equivalence of tariffs and import quotas in a dynamic context and thus has paid close attention to safeguarding mechanisms in the agreements. Further, in order to capture rents from low duties on the within-quota imports, South Korea has been operating a state trading system for many items. Management of this state importing system is complex and a number of issues have not been resolved. Unlike the countries discussed earlier, South Korea was required to reduce its aggregate measure of support under the URA, because price support activities for rice expanded in the period after 1986, and over 90 per cent of domestic support is associated with rice. Even though under its import quota the domestic rice programme has zero impact on trade, the URA required that it be modified to reduce the World Trade Organization (WTO) measurement of aggregate support. An additional set of policy changes was stimulated by the URA, although not required. Large new public investments to improve the productivity of Korean agriculture are under way. These investments include funds for agricultural research, infrastructure and rural development to improve non-farm opportunities.

Lee ended with a suggestion (reinforcing a similar statement by Tangermann) that, in exchange for additional market openings by importers, exporting nations should commit themselves to eliminating the use of export taxes and other restraints on exports. In the past, the United States has used export embargoes and, in the current crop year, the EU has shifted from subsidies to export taxes on grain shipments. Thus food importers have a real concern about the reliability of exporters in times of short crops and high prices. An international agreement to limit export restraints would help ensure food availability in times of high world prices and would serve to stabilize international markets. As a way to help create a sense of food security among importers, such a move could be quite important.

Floor discussion

The discussion was opened by questioning the benefits to food importers of more liberalization. Then several speakers voiced scepticism about the source of political or economic pressure for more trade reform in 1999. One comment noted especially that, in the next round, agriculture and other negotiating groups would not be linked, as in the URA. Others raised the importance of the environment and food safety, and of sanitary and phytosanitary barriers to the next round of negotiations. The panel responded with a general sense of optimism that there was sufficient willingness of nations to undertake substantive negotiations on agriculture in 1999. They agreed that environmental and related issues would continue to be important.

Observations and questions raised related to anti-dumping, regional trade agreements, dispute settlement and new large members of the WTO (China and Russia). The panel agreed that dispute settlement was as yet not fully tested, but Josling responded to one question by suggesting that, when challenged, Latin American variable levies would be found to violate the URA. There was considerable discussion of the point that low-income countries and food importers were not major beneficiaries of trade agreements. Dillon asserted that the URA was a deal between the United States and the EU, and that other negotiating countries were vulnerable. He stressed that, with 46 per cent of employment in agriculture in Indonesia, some way must be found to aid those affected negatively by trade agreements. He also argued that stabilization was more important than protection. Tangermann responded that, for agriculture, there was no reason to doubt the broad economic conclusion that import protection hurts consumers and cuts national income in those countries that use protection. He also argued that less developed countries were active participants in the URA. There was a general agreement that less developed countries and new WTO members will play an increasingly important role in future negotiations.

PANEL 5: NEW APPROACHES TO 'ALTERNATIVE' AGRICULTURE IN HIGH AND LOW INCOME COUNTRIES AND THEIR ECONOMIC ASPECTS

ORGANIZER AND CHAIRPERSON

Olvar Bergland* (The Agricultural University of Norway)

PANEL DISCUSSANTS

Policy Approaches towards Alternative Agricultural Systems   *Ian Hodge and Katherine Falconer (Cambridge University, UK)*

Innovations in Alternative Agriculture Policy to Capture Full Natural Resource Values   *David E. Ervin and Elizabeth M. Higgins (Henry A. Wallace Institute for Alternative Agriculture, USA)*

Superlative Index Numbers as a Measure of the Productivity and Relative Efficiency of Alternative Agricultural Practices in Low Income Countries *Simeon K. Ehui (International Livestock Research Institute, Ethiopia)*

RAPPORTEUR

Latha Nagarajan (M.S. Swaminathan Research Foundation, India)

The background for the discussion was the concern that conventional agricultural production practices may not be sustainable in the long run. Alternative organization of agricultural production *may* reduce environmental impacts, enhance long-term productivity, improve product quality and improve living and working conditions.

Ian Hodge focused on three environmental issues relating to production agriculture: biodiversity, nitrate leaching and pesticide contamination. An approach based on transferable permits relating to environmental indicators could establish the necessary incentives for farmers to modify their production systems to meet regional environmental objectives. Such a permit system would be flexible.

David Ervin brought in the concept of 'whole farm planning' as a term describing planning and management systems which attempt to capture all resource relationships on the farm and all potential enterprises in a dynamic interplay. Whole farm planning is a voluntary effort which tends to have high initial costs, but with great potential for individual adjustments and future gains. The lack of specific agricultural environmental performance standards and indicators has not permitted whole farm planning to reach its potential in achieving improved natural resource management.

Simeon Ehui argued for the use of superlative index numbers, as expressions for total factor productivity, to measure and assess agricultural productivity and the relative efficiency of the alternative farming practices. Of particular importance is the long-run sustainability and competitiveness of different farming systems. Traditional productivity measures are biased and often misleading, which can result in inappropriate policy assessments and recommendations.

The general discussion which followed brought up the concern that whole farm planning is an on-farm tool, while agriculture-related environmental problems often have off-farm effects. Ervin acknowledged that whole farm planning is not a 'global' planning tool and that there is a certain lack of feedback with respect to environmental performance. However, these concerns are not unique to whole farm planning.

The discussion brought out views on both the principles and details of regulatory policies in agriculture. The need for flexible regulatory policies was stressed. Hodge emphasized the policy trade-off between complexity and transactions costs, reminding us that improved environmental performance, not regulatory precision, is the objective. Creation of new markets as part of regulatory policies also raises concerns about how this is to be done, and by whom.

Bergland closed the panel by pointing out that the discussion about policy instruments for 'alternative' agriculture parallels the general discussion in environmental policy, and he was pleased to see that different forms of voluntary agreements are being considered. He stated that the panel discussion had fulfilled his expectations in terms of providing some ideas for what we, as policy analysts and instrument innovators, could pursue in the future.

PANEL 6: BIOTECHNOLOGY IN AGRICULTURE

ORGANIZER, CHAIRPERSON AND RAPPORTEUR

David Zilberman* (University of California-Berkeley, USA)

PANEL DISCUSSANTS

The National Perspective   *Gerald Carlson and Michele Marra (North Carolina State University, USA)*

The Global Perspective   *Carl E. Pray (Rutgers University, USA)*

Agricultural Biotechnology: Status and Prospects   *Susanne L. Huttner (University of California-Berkeley, USA)*

The Industry Perspective   *Sano Shimoda (BioScience Securities, Inc. USA)*

The summer of 1997 was an ideal time to hold a symposium on agricultural biotechnology. In 1996, and especially in 1997, we witnessed the first widespread commercial use of biotechnology seeds in major crops. Carlson and Marra conducted a study on the productivity and effectiveness of BT cotton (an insecticide-resistant cotton variety) and Round-up tolerant soybeans (which allowed more intensive use of herbicide). The BT cotton was adopted by 30 to 40 per cent of growers in the southeastern United States, as well as other parts of the world. In most cases, Marra and Carlson's calculations suggest that it increased yields and reduced costs (more than paying for itself). While there has been some evidence of build-up of resistance, this is not likely to alter projections of continued adoption diffusion of this new variety. Growers seem to be even more receptive to herbicide-tolerant soybeans in the United States and other countries (Argentina), and diffusion was constrained only by the availability of seeds.

To counter the growth of pests' resistance to the new genetically engineered seed varieties, programmes where growers allocate about 25 per cent of their land to traditional varieties have been established. This land supports vulnerable insects that help to dilute the build-up of BT resistance in the pest population. Carlson and Marra report that the prices of these genetically engineered materials vary across locations, depending on the severity of pest problems and the relevant productivity of new varieties. Often growers are asked to pay approximately the existing seed price, but are then charged an extra fee for the use of genetically manipulated materials. These fees (which may be $30 to $40 per acre) also vary by location.

Carl Pray provided a global perspective on the development of research capacity and adoption of genetically engineered seed varieties. Major agribusiness companies have conducted global experiments on genetically engineered soybeans, corn and cotton. In both India and China, there is a widespread effort to introduce genetically engineered, high-yield varieties of rice and wheat that have improved pest-resistance capabilities. There have already been significant acreages of the new biotechnology varieties used in developing countries, and in the future biotechnology will play a major role in improving crops in the developing world. China, in particular, has conducted widespread experimentation with different types of genetically engineered materials for various field crops, and even for those of higher value.

Issues of intellectual property rights protection have already arisen in experiments and in collaboration between agribusiness firms and local organizations in developing countries. Lack of traditional intellectual property rights protection for genetic materials and their efficient pricing are causes for dispute that hamper operations. This results in extra measures to protect genetic materials where field experiments are done. Educational efforts in the economics and management of genetic biotechnology and the diplomatic and legal efforts to reach pricing formulas and intellectual property rights protection will lead to efficiency and enable future collaborative effort.

The CGIAR centres, which provide the genetic materials and seeds for many developing countries, have recognised the importance of biotechnology. They are in the midst of developing a strategy to incorporate it into their activities. The high-cost infrastructure that is needed in biotechnology and the cost of intellectual property rights required for certain key procedures make implementing biotechnology at international centres very difficult. They are considering arrangements that would include partnerships with the private sector and with other, public sector, entities such as universities. Another major issue that has to be resolved is the tradition of providing genetic materials freely to breeders all over the world. There is a growing tendency towards protectionism regarding genetic materials, and future guidelines may need to be established regarding conditions and compensation for transfer of genetic materials.

Many in the developing world resent having to pay for genetic materials that are manipulated in new seed varieties, arguing that most of the available varieties originated in the developing world, and have been preserved by farmers' efforts. Thus it is clear that the economics and policies of biotechnology are intertwined with the economics of 'biodiversity'.

In spite of the recent adoption of biotechnology varieties, Susanne Huttner stated that agricultural biotechnology is significantly lagging behind medical biotechnology. In the United States, much more public money is spent to support basic research in medical aspects than on agriculture. The budget of the National Institute of Health, which funds a substantial amount of work, has risen constantly over the last 15 years, sometimes at annual rates that are close to 10 per cent. Public support for agricultural research conducted by the Department of Agriculture and other organizations has been stagnant for long periods during the last 20 years.

More importantly, large amounts of public money have been spent to establish start-up companies that purchased the rights to develop medical innovations.

These companies provided the engine that led to the medical biotechnology industry's growth and provided some of the most important products in commercial use. They embodied much of the technological change and innovation in medical biotechnology, and their continuous emergence fostered new developments and new technologies. Obviously, many start-up companies have not survived, but some were absorbed by giant pharmaceutical firms and others have become major companies in their own right. There has been much less investment in agricultural biotechnology start-up companies. Survival rates have been very low, and most of the successful ones have been absorbed at an early stage of their lives by agribusiness firms like Monsanto. A few of them (about 10 agricultural biotechnology companies) were established in 1992, and most of the research and virtually all the developments in agricultural biotechnology were done by major agribusiness firms and pharmaceuticals.

Dr Huttner expressed concern that the control of much of the process innovation in agricultural biotechnology by a small number of firms will lead to much underinvestment and underdevelopment, since concentration leads to undersupply. Furthermore, it will give some major agribusiness firms considerable control in the pricing and production of many products. There should be increased public support for agricultural biotechnology research as well as larger development funding. She suggested that farm organizations and cooperatives build the financial muscle to obtain intellectual property rights and valuable genetic materials, thus allowing farmers to be less dependent on major companies. There is an important role for private partnership in developing innovations that may be too risky for private sectors to implement. Dr Huttner, herself, is in charge of a large effort, worth several million dollars, to develop such a partnership.

Sano Shimoda presented a different perspective. As a venture capitalist, he argued that the lack of investment in agricultural biotechnology in the 1990s was reasonable. It had seemed very promising in the late 1980s, but there had not subsequently been a spurt in the development of major development products and investors had lost confidence in the future of the industry. However, recent successes have led to its rejuvenation and revival, and he expects much more private investment in ventures that aim to develop agricultural biotechnology. Like Dr Huttner, he also suggested that the regulations governing agricultural biotechnology, established in the 1980s, served as a damper to growth. While it could be argued that control did contribute to the survival of the industry and its acceptance in the United States, both agreed that some regulations may still be too strict.

Sano Shimodo was optimistic about the commercial potential of biotechnology: it will alter agriculture, especially in states like California. Agricultural biotechnology embodies much more than new pest-resistant and pesticide-tolerant varieties. It will lead to higher quality and differentiated food products. It will produce oils, cosmetic materials and pharmaceuticals. He embraced Dr Huttner's suggestion that agriculture should invest its own funds in capturing development rights. One example is Saskatchewan, where the local agricultural community provided much of the funding for development of new canola varieties and agribusiness based on their use.

After the presentation, the audience raised some major issues. First, it was suggested that procedures of technology transfer from private and public sectors should be modified to accommodate different environments to increase the efficiency of using new knowledge. Secondly, it was recognized that the private sector (even in the United States) cannot provide the research infrastructure for biotechnology and public sector support must continue. A third conclusion, shared by both speakers and the audience, was the importance of high-quality institutions of research and learning as a breeding ground for new technology. Biotechnology provides a concrete example of the high economic value of research activities in agriculture.

On the other hand, however, concern was expressed about the environmental side-effects of biotechnology. Several people in the audience felt that biotechnology raised much uncertainty and should be developed with caution. They also suggested that emphasis on biotechnology would divert attention from technologies that may be more environmentally friendly. For example, research in better soil management practices and more precise application and input use may increase productivity and reduce environmental damage. Some felt that issues of safety and acceptance of biotechnology have still to be resolved and that they are critical for the future development of the industry. Others raised the issue of intellectual property rights. They were concerned that developing countries were being omitted in the evolution of biotechnology and urged that this should be remedied.

PANEL 7: THE FUTURE OF AGRICULTURAL ORGANIZATIONS AT GLOBAL, NATIONAL AND LOCAL LEVEL

ORGANIZER AND CHAIRPERSON

Hartwig de Haen* (FAO)

PANEL DISCUSSANTS

Agricultural Organizations: Mandates, Functions and Performance   *Daniel Bromley (University of Wisconsin, USA)*

Knowledge Networks for Augmenting Grassroots Creativity and Innovation *Anil Gupta (Indian Institute of Management, India)*

National Dimensions: The Role of Agricultural Organizations in Designing, Implementing, Monitoring and Evaluating Policies   *Wilhelm Schopen (Federal Ministry of Food, Agriculture and Forestry, Germany)*

International Organizations Affecting Agriculture: Characteristics, Environment and Challenges   *Kelley White (US Department of Agriculture)*

RAPPORTEUR

Katinka Weinberger (Centre for Development Research, Germany)

This panel dealt with the rapidly changing roles of agricultural organizations as a result of the various policy reforms and structural adjustments which many countries, developing as well as developed, have undergone in the recent past. Since the early and mid-1980s, under the pressure of a severe economic crisis and growth stagnation, many developing as well as developed countries have progressively abandoned the economic paradigm based on mistrust of markets to allocate resources, implying an active government role in the economy. The new policy paradigm assigns a much greater role to markets and a reduced role of governments in allocating resources. Governments are now expected to concentrate on areas in which markets fail and on the production of non-market goods necessary for the efficient and socially acceptable functioning of economy and society. Generally, this implies that the state, possibly in collaboration with non-governmental and private organizations, should, above all, ensure a sufficient supply of public goods and services.

An additional but related manifestation of the new paradigm is the increasing global interdependence resulting from liberalization of financial flows and the opening up of markets (including agricultural markets) as a result of the Uruguay Round of trade negotiations. Governments are expected to reduce direct market interventions and concentrate on enabling environments for markets to function more satisfactorily. In this new era governments negotiate, implement and supervise international standards, codes and trade agreements and ensure information exchange.

Together with an increased overall emphasis on participatory, decentralized and pluralistic political systems, these paradigmatic changes have had far-reaching implications for the institutional framework. The changes in paradigm promote further forces of change through the possibilities for increasing interaction between agriculture and the rest of the economy, but also with the non-farm rural economy through production and expenditure linkages. At the level of the individual farm households, labour market linkages to the non-agricultural sectors play an increasing role. At the sectoral level there are tendencies of enhanced linkages of primary agriculture to factor and product markets through upstream and downstream interactions. Together with a wide range of location-specific social and ecological functions which societies have been associating with agriculture, this diversification has resulted in traditional agricultural organizations being more and more involved with issues that go beyond agriculture itself, for example environment protection, maintenance of landscapes or rural poverty alleviation.

Finally, the diversity of mandates of agricultural organizations is being shaped by the increasing attention which consumers pay to the quality, safety and health effects of diets and foods. This process has led either to the establishment of completely new, or to the reform of existing regulatory bodies, and the strengthening of existing, or creation of new, consumer interest groups which attempt to influence policies and developments in these fields.

The above factors, along with increased budgetary constraints, are leading to revisions of mandates, structures and work programmes of agricultural organizations, including new forms of division of labour between governmental and non-governmental, international, national and sub-national organizations. The Panel topics and speakers were chosen to reflect some of the main tendencies of this process.

Diversity of agricultural organizations

An overview on agricultural organizations was given by Bromley. At the outset, he recommended maintaining a clear distinction between institutions as expressions of societal values, rules and norms, and organizations as structural entities where decisions and actions are taken within the given institutional framework. According to Bromley the provision of low-cost information to dispersed and remotely located agricultural producers provided the original *raison d'être* of most of the agricultural organizations. Bromley categorized agricultural organizations into four types, each performing a distinct role at various stages of economic and social development: private organizations at local and national level; non-governmental organizations at local, national and international level; national governmental organizations operating at national and international levels; and, finally, multinational organizations that operate at the international level.

The point was made that, over time, these organizations have evolved from having mainly an information function to having a variety of roles. Four different types are distinguished: advocating, facilitating, inducing and compelling. Depending on their place in the 'public–private continuum', the mandates of the organizations comprise a different mix of these functions. According to Bromley, all organizations have a tendency to undergo so-called 'mission drifts'. As a result of changing political and economic circumstances, they tend to move from mainly information and facilitation functions towards functions of advocating and compelling. He concluded with the recommendation that it would be more in the spirit of the current market liberalization and withdrawal of governments from direct interventions in agricultural markets if organizations, in particular governmental organizations, were to drift back to a primarily facilitating role.

Organizations in an international context

White summarized the broad range of functions of international agricultural organizations, including research, technology transfer, policy advice, information collection and dissemination, financial transfers, neutral forum and establishment and monitoring of rules and standards. Each of the principal international organizations to which he referred (CGIAR, FAO, IFAD, IICA, OECD, World Bank, UNDP) performs a particular combination of these functions, depending on their respective mandates. White analysed the changes in the global environment (end of the Cold War, pervasive adoption of markets at national level, globalization of markets, emergence of 'bottom up' and 'participatory' development initiatives, fiscal restraint, emergence of environmental concerns), all of which necessitated adaptation of missions and operations of the international organizations concerned. Typical challenges and opportunities included the need to broaden the mix of functions of these organizations, increase competition among organizations ('loss of institutional uniqueness') and redirect and sharpen their focus.

In White's opinion, many of the difficulties in which the international organizations have recently found themselves were the result of their attempt to substitute for national organizations rather than to make use of their comparative advantages. More emphasis should be on facilitating national actions than on substituting for them. In concluding, White made particular reference to the importance of international agricultural research. Globalization and liberalization of markets reduced the ability of nations to capture the benefits of 'public goods research' and thus reduced the incentive for national investment in such research. International agricultural organizations therefore had an important role in finding an institutional mechanism for taxing the global community in order to ensure a sufficient level of public goods research.

The role of agricultural organizations in industrialized countries

Schopen addressed a particular phenomenon observed in many industrialized countries, namely the declining economic importance of agriculture and the rising additional demands societies make on rural areas. These include conservation of national resources, safeguarding and maintaining rural landscapes as cultural heritage and keeping rural livelihoods attractive for the population. As many of these functions were more or less directly related to agriculture, policy approaches were needed which went beyond the strictly agricultural and took account of the agricultural to non-agricultural linkages and spatial impacts of many rural activities. Schopen's conclusion from these trends was that agricultural organizations, in particular ministries and their subordinate agencies, will only have a sustainable future if they start to reflect this integrated and multidisciplinary rural perspective in their missions and functions. 'Ministries for rural areas' were needed with mandates comprising not only traditional agricultural policy, but also agroenvironmental, regional planning, cultural and social policies for rural populations. This also implied a coordinating role of government organizations for the involvement of local initiatives and non-governmental organizations in decision making and policy implementation.

If timely action in this regard was not taken, new organizations or other ministries handling environment and regional development would fill the 'vacuum'. Schopen gave a number of examples where these new tendencies had already been realized. In the light of budget limitations, a goal-oriented allocation of funds and a pooling of hitherto sectoral policies and programmes was advised. A final point was made: that at the European level the enlargement of the EU would enhance the relative importance of integrated policies for rural areas.

Importance of knowledge networks

Gupta expressed the view that, unless the context in which the future role and functions of agricultural and rural development organizations were perceived is changed, one would not be able to change the content of organizational design, development policy and relationships between public, private and voluntary organizations. Gupta started out by referring to several challenges which are before development planners and need solution, among them the expeditious sharing of experiences and solutions of similar problems between different parts of the world, the linkage of formal and informal sciences and the scaling up of 'little innovations', that is 'converting ideas into enterprises'. Gupta believed that the development process could become sustainable only when answers to these challenges were sought more rigorously and choices for decision making were more widespread – a process in which NGOs and NGIs have been engaged very effectively so far.

Gupta emphasized the need to facilitate access to information, in particular on useful innovations, which was absolutely essential for the poor. In this context he advocated the creation of so-called 'knowledge centres/networks' which would help their members in reducing transition costs for gaining access to certain kinds of information and generate reciprocity amongst providers and receivers of information, so that incentives for problem solvers to create a network with knowledge centres would be ensured. Such organizational arrangements could liaise with other existing efforts over the globe, mobilize volunteers and donors and fulfil an ethical obligation towards poor people through appropriate arrangements, such as use of local language and protection of intellectual property and cultural heritage of local communities. Gupta expected that 'information entrepreneurs' would become more significant in the future. He concluded that markets and the state, so far, seemed to be handicapped in dealing with the problem of sustainability in agriculture and rural development.

Floor discussion: adapting to a changing environment

As the theme of this panel covered a wide range of issues, the discussion could only address a few of them. One of the main points raised was the climate of change experienced by agricultural organizations at all levels and the impact that this had on their future. Participants agreed that the mission drift observed by Bromley would have to be reversed and organizations encouraged to revisit their roles. While agreeing that the declining role of agriculture in many economies was a fact and needed to be reflected in the downsizing and/or adaptation of organizational mandates, several participants referred to the strong lobbyism exercised by the farm community in many developed countries. This might make any downsizing or adaptation of mandates of agricultural organizations rather difficult. On the other hand, it was underlined that there are many developing countries with rather weak lobbying for higher priority for the agricultural sector in overall economic policy. These countries would have to strengthen their agricultural organizations so as to ensure that agriculture be given the needed primacy in overall development priority.

Several discussants were worried by the shortage of investment in agricultural research and commented on what agricultural organizations could do to redress this trend. While recognizing that international organizations had an important role in ensuring that agricultural research reflected global public interests and also benefited the developing countries, they emphasized the need not to neglect the local research organizations. Local, national and international, public- and private-sector research had clear complementarities which needed to be tapped. A consensus developed during the debate that there is a continuous need for agricultural organizations to adapt to changing circumstances. The suggestion that the organizations have to be open for a widening of their missions and to reorient their mandates towards a broader range of rural issues was shared by a number of speakers. There was also agreement that the division of labour between the various levels and types of organizations needed to be revisited. Interaction between organizations had to be strengthened and duplication of work avoided as far as possible. Governmental as well as non-governmental organizations, including grassroots organizations, needed to build more on their complementarities and comparative advantages in order to be useful to the farmers and the societies as a whole.

PANEL 8: WORLD FOOD FUTURES: METHODOLOGICAL BASIS AND IMPLICATIONS OF LONG-TERM FOOD PROJECTIONS

ORGANIZER AND CHAIRPERSON

David Colman* (University of Manchester, UK)

PANEL DISCUSSANTS

Key System Requirements for Projecting Food Futures. Deficiencies to be Addressed   *Charles Riemenschneider (FAO)*

Why Environmentalists are Wrong about the Global Food Situation: Methods and Myths   *Mark Rosegrant, Claudia Ringler (IFPRI)*

Comparison of Medium and Long-term Projections of Food Futures   *William Myers (Iowa State University, USA)*

A Biophysical Perspective on Medium and Long-term Food Futures   *Prabhu Pingali (CIMMYT)*

RAPPORTEUR

T. Satyanarayana (Indian Society of Agricultural Marketing, India)

The formal presentations of the panel members introduced some of the key issues and some background to modelling the world's future food 'situation'. The situation is multifaceted; there is the question of the amount and types of food which will be produced and consumed in possible medium- and long-term states; there are the food security issues about the extent of malnutrition and its distribution between countries and groups; also there are questions of international trade and the macroeconomic configurations which support and lead to particular patterns; there are the issues of needed investment in agricultural infrastructure and in new technology; and there is the ever-present issue of sustainability in the face of the environmental demands made by continuing growth in agricultural and general economic activity.

Underlying the presentations and discussion was the question of whether agricultural economists are overoptimistic about the future scenarios as opposed, in particular, to environmentalists, who appear relatively pessimistic, as exemplified by Meadows *et al.* (1972; 1992), The Worldwatch Institute and Lester Brown (1996), and also by Darwin Hall who, at this conference, has presented a plenary paper reporting futures modelling concerned with the possible impacts of global warming. Although some contributors felt that it was misguided to attempt to focus the session's debate on conflict between the respective optimism and pessimism of economists and environmentalists, the impression that there is a fundamental difference was if anything reinforced by the proceedings.

Characteristics of agricultural economists' models

Myers, a leader in the FAPRI modelling team, opened the panel's account by providing a brief comparison of the characteristics of some of the main agricultural economists' (AE) models and their projected futures. He focused on the FAPRI, IMPACT (from IFPRI), AGLINK (from OECD), FAO, USDA and ABARE models. Compared to the environmentalist models, these models have relatively short time horizons, the longest being IMPACT at 2020, and FAO at 2010. Given that confidence intervals rapidly widen as the projection horizon is increased, there are strong methodological reasons for not hazarding what would be increasingly less reliable point estimates into the distant future; and there is the quasi-ethical issue that care should be taken not to provoke either panic or overcomplacency by projecting unjustifiably pessimistic or rosy futures in the form of estimates with ever-decreasing probabilities of occurring.

For the most part, the models referred to above are partial equilibrium models, but they all vary in terms of details of structure, objectives and their inputs. FAPRI and the ABARE models are based almost entirely on econometrically estimated equations, whereas the FAO and OECD models have a large input from commodity and country specialists in modifying parameters and projecting exogenous variables, the most important of which are yields.

Key system requirements

No detailed discussion took place as to the ways in which yield projections are generated but, as Riemenschneider argued in his presentation, it is the future trajectory of these which dominates the characteristic outcome of the models. The AE models do not endogenize yields but employ exogenous trends generated judgmentally or econometrically. This is where there is a major difference with the environmentalist models (Meadows *et al.*, 1992; Hall, at this meeting) where the impacts of environmental change on yields are at the heart of the exercise and where large negative impacts are projected in time frames which extend way beyond those explored in the AE model.

One of the key focuses of AE modelling is the impact of policy changes, since as a profession we are naturally fixated on the prospects for controlling events by tweaking the policy variables. Thus the FAPRI, OECD, ABARE and USDA models incorporate specific policy instruments, whereas IFPRI's

IMPACT model introduces policy changes in terms of PSEs, and the FAO model employs a more eclectic approach greatly influenced by expert inputs. This expert input is one of the strengths of this model (Alexandratos, 1995) but it entails a very labour-intensive approach, a characteristic shared by the USDA's modelling systems.

It is fair to state that the FAO model is more concerned with future food security issues than the other AE models. All of them have different levels of commodity and country disaggregation as reflect their objectives, which are dominated by issues of trade liberalization and trade rather than long-term food security. Implicit in their philosophy is that efficient markets will ensure a future food supply–demand balance with constant or falling real prices and marginal improvements in global food security for a total population increasing in line with the UN's projected medium variant.

Myth of environmentalist models?

This optimistic view was endorsed by Rosegrant and Ringler. In their presentation they attacked various positions they associate with environmentalists: they assert the superiority of commercial (and often large-scale) agriculture over 'small (is beautiful)' farming for its continuing contribution to global food security; they cite studies which indicate the limitations of organic farming, and instead state their confidence in modern farming methods and biotechnology; they address concerns about the high chemical dependency of modern farming, the issue of soil degradation and the implications drawn by environmentalists about the adverse consequences of development leading to more general adoption of the diets of the rich. Among their conclusions is the following:

> The methods and myths employed by many environmentalists when confronting the world food system have caused them to be consistently wrong in their assessment of the long-term prospects for global food security. ... incorrect prophecies of doom from environmentalists have contributed to the fatigue with agricultural issues of donors and policy makers, who point to the failed prophecies as evidence that serious concerns about future agricultural development are unnecessary. ... Environmental and resource degradation are not intrinsically limiting to the necessary growth in crop production to meet global demand in the coming decades. Nor is the current path of agricultural development a threat to the global environment.

Unsurprisingly, these views provoked lively responses from participants in the session, with some accusations of overoptimism. Nevertheless, the position was fairly well defended. Robert Thompson agreed with the proposition that Asian diets were unlikely to be transformed by economic growth into current Western ones. It was observed by Gregory Scott that environmentalists, just as much as agricultural economists, examine issues using partial analysis, and that, whereas AE models may have inadequate biophysical underpinning and environmental feedbacks, environmental models contain insufficient recognition of economic behaviour, market forces and macroeconomic relations. Darwin Hall's intervention suggested that the long-term impacts of global warming, which he projects to be considerable, are in themselves not primarily due to agricultural pollution but rather are (and will be) due to the carbon dioxide released from fossil fuels as a consequence of industrial and urban growth; of course, agriculture contributes something to this industrialization. That could be construed as supporting Rosegrant and Ringler's relatively optimistic view that agriculturally induced environmental degradation is not an overriding constraint to meeting the projected global population's food demands without increases in real prices.

Technological and biophysical limitations

However, a warning note was sounded from the platform by Pingali, chief economist at CIMMYT. He examined some aspects of the technological and biophysical assumptions for food supply growth and highlighted the point that the capacity for exploiting further yield growth for wheat and rice is now very limited. For maize, however, there is a gap between best and average yields which does provide scope for output growth, and Pingali identified other sources of potential growth, such as improved management practices, improved water management and commercialization leading to relocation of production to achieve better exploitation of agroclimatic potentials. He highlighted the need for appropriate (higher) levels of research investment in order that the yield ceilings for the main staples can be raised. This issue of research investment emerged as one of the strongest from this panel session, although it perhaps received less attention in the conference as a whole than on some previous occasions. As Charles Riemenschneider's presentation emphasized, yield projections are possibly the most critical in AE models for establishing optimistic or pessimistic scenarios (given that population projections are usually exogenous), but the basis for these projections is not greatly elaborated. Certainly, in current AE models, there is no explicit recognition of the research investments needed to maintain the past levels of yield growth which are projected into the future. Indeed, it is striking that in Alexandratos (1995) FAO has none of the emphasis on investment which was in its earlier projections in Alexandratos, 1988.

Riemenschneider addressed other desirable methodological requirements for models which are specifically designed to address food security issues. Given the problems of rural poverty, ideally models would endogenize income determination for vulnerable groups and consider in more detail root crops and other staples which often receive little or no attention in trade liberalization models but are of great importance in sub-Saharan Africa. It is also desirable to model outcome in terms of calories supplied and demanded (as Alexandratos, 1995 does) rather than to consider commodities solely in terms of tonnage.

The issues raised by Riemenschneider underline the difficulty of comparing models when the objectives of models differ: for example, prioritizing trade liberalization, as opposed to food security or environment and geoclimate feedbacks. However, many issues were addressed by the session. Among these was the issue of the future time scale to be considered. The AE models tend to focus on the short to medium term, which means their horizon does not

538   *Panel Discussion Reports*

generally stretch to that at which environmentalists' scenarios envisage major collapses in the food and economic systems. Meadows *et al.* (1992) project some scenarios from their World 3 model in which a major collapse (agricultural, population and general economic) begins around 2020, which is the outer limit for current published projections from AE models. That collapse is envisaged to occur as a consequence of environmental pollution, land degradation and loss, water shortages and global warming. Hall, at this conference, had elaborate projections up to 380 years ahead. It should be noted, however, that the scenarios reported by him carry a mixed message; for some regions, agricultural productivity would improve, but in the tropics calamitous outcomes are envisaged. These outcomes are avoidable but Hall, doubtless correctly, envisages the danger that appropriate reactions will be slowed by overcomplacency and unwillingness to face facts and make difficult choices. Economists have considerable faith in the ability of the market to drive rapid corrective responses; others are much less sanguine.

Floor discussion: emphasis lies on hypothetically possible outcomes

One message which strongly emerged from the participants is that care should be taken to avoid any impression that our models generate forecasts but to emphasize that they produce hypothetically possible outcomes. The consequences of giving the impression of making forecasts, and of getting them wrong, are damaging to modelling exercises which are an essential requirement for reaching understanding of interacting systems. AE models are a medium for fostering debate with biophysical and environmental scientists, and it is apparent that much more cooperation between them and agricultural economists is desirable if policy makers with research funds are not to receive conflicting signals.

One thing underlined by this last point is that we must take care to use appropriate criteria to judge the performance of models. Such criteria can only relate to the specific objectives of each model, and confusion will be created if models are applied to exercises strictly beyond their capacities. Since the computing capacities exist, it is in principle possible to enhance the environmental and biophysical feedback systems of AE models, but that in turn runs into the difficulty of establishing research teams with the capacity to grow and change in ways which maintain and enhance the performance of such models.

REFERENCES

Alexandratos, N. (ed.) (1988), *World Agriculture: Toward 2000, An FAO Study*, London: Behaven Press and London and New York: New York University Press.
Alexandratos, N. (ed.) (1995), *World Agriculture: Towards 2010 – An FAO Study*, Chichester: John Wiley and Sons.
Brown, L.R. (1996), *The State of the World*, London: Earthscan.
Meadows, D.H., Meadows, D.L., Randers, J. and Behrens, W.W. (1972), *The Limits to Growth*, London: Earth Island.
Meadows, D.H., Meadows, D.L. and Randers, J. (1992), *Beyond the Limits: Global Collapse or a Sustainable Future*, London: Earthscan.

PANEL 9: NEW APPROACHES TO DEMAND ANALYSIS: QUALITY, INVISIBLES, DYNAMICS IN TASTES AND PREFERENCES

ORGANIZER AND CHAIRPERSON

Ben Senauer (University of Minnesota, USA)

PANEL DISCUSSANTS

Structural Change in Demand   *Kyree Rickertsen (Agricultural University of Norway)*

Non-parametric and Semi-parametric Analysis   *Jim Chalfant (University of California-Davis, USA)*

Tastes and Quality Characteristics in Demand   *Roland Herrmann, Claudia Roeder (University of Giessen, Germany)*

Recent Changes in Food Consumption in Japan: Laying Stress on 'Dining Out' *Michio Kanai (National Research Institute of Agricultural Economics, Japan)*

RAPPORTEUR

Vasant Gandhi* (Indian Institute of Management, India)

The presentations and discussion in this session focused on a wide variety of issues on the analysis of food demand. This covered structural changes in demand, issues related to health information and product quality in demand, recent changes in food consumption patterns and non-parametric and semi-parametric analysis of food demand.

Structural changes in demand

Rickertsen discussed the issue of what constitutes structural change in demand and how to measure it. Structural change, according to him, is used broadly to imply that factors related to either preferences or aggregation across consumers have changed. If preferences are assumed to be identical across individuals, changes in income distribution may cause a structural change in demand. This usually matters for aggregate demand but frequently behaves like a trend variable and can be captured by it. If preferences vary by demographic group then demographic changes can cause structural change in demand. This involves the proportion of older to younger people, education, size of household (notably the growth of single-person households) and female participation in the labour force. These features are often too numerous to handle and might well be excluded, but this would result in a structural change being observed. There are also exogenous variables which influence demand. These include introduction of new food products, seasonality, advertising and information about health and nutrition. Advertising includes branded and generic advertising. Branded advertising is often found to increase demand, but there is no clear conclusion on generic advertising.

Tests for structural change involve parametric and non-parametric approaches. The approach through the parametric method requires assumptions about functional form, about endogeneity of prices, quantities and total expenditure, and further separability-related assumptions. The model needs to be tested for misspecification. Structural change can then be detected either by testing for violation of theoretical restrictions of demand theory, testing for parameter instability or through explicitly modelling structural change through inclusion of the responsible or indicator variables.

Tastes and quality characteristics in demand

The presentation by Herrmann and Roeder addressed some neglected issues in food demand analysis which are important in understanding recent trends in industrialized countries. On the issue of price elasticity, they report that, even though there is ample evidence that food demand in industrialized countries is price-inelastic, it is possible that retail-level elasticities may be much higher. On examining whether marketing policies influence the price elasticity of demand, they find that price discounts accompanied by marketing and promotion have a strong impact for wines. Without promotion, the elasticity may turn out to be of the order of 0.20, but with all promotion that rises to 8.29. Thus any simple hypothesis about demand for food cannot be generalized.

Another issue discussed was whether health concerns and nutritional information are important determinants of food demand. Empirical results from a German household survey suggest that food demand was influenced by income, sociodemographic variables and attitude and knowledge variables. Health and diet information, nutrition-specific knowledge and general education play an important role in explaining food consumption and food quality.

Herrmann and Roeder also considered whether demand for non-homogenous commodities is driven by objective or subjective quality. They find that, for wine, objective sensorial evaluation by wine experts cannot explain price differences across wines but subjectively assessed bottle design does. Subjective quality indicators such as familiarity and product classes influenced by image and promotion are more important than quality, as evaluated by experts in tasting and in explaining wine demand.

Recent changes in food consumption in Japan

Michio Kanai argued that significant diversification was taking place in food consumption in Japan. The two major new directions were increasing incidence of dining out and of eating prepared foods. Some important reasons for this were the rise in single-person households, due to an increase in the marriage age and the number of divorces. The consumption of organic products was also increasing.

Non-parametric and semi-parametric analysis

Chalfant dealt with non-parametric and semi-parametric methods in food demand analysis. He argued that problems arise in using parametric analysis for demand because a second-order local approximation to an unknown set of preferences does not exist and point approximations do not exist, while specification errors are hard to detect and resemble structural change. Non-parametric regression analysis is computer-intensive and attempts to avoid prediction errors by not assuming that a linear regression is appropriate throughout the data. Alternatives are non-parametric, semi-parametric and semi-non-parametric analyses of demand. Non-parametric demand analysis makes data mining more systematic. Other solutions to the specification problem are fitting several models, and nesting models. One risk of the latter is 'overparameterization' of the model. Demand systems may be overrated because choice of equations is driven by price and quantity data available, and that can make untenable separability and aggregation assumptions necessary for all other goods. Getting demand analysis right is frequently very hard because often things that are assumed not to matter actually matter substantially.

In the discussion it was asked whether there were any approaches for predicting demand for brand new food products. One possibility was to work through the demand for characteristics. Often the formulation of the problem itself led to structural change being incorrectly detected. It was also indicated that demand analysis could benefit from time-series analysis approaches: cointegration had quite a good theoretical base.

Floor discussion

In regard to the presentation of Rickertsen, it was suggested that one of the major difficulties in capturing structural change was the location of switching points. Another problem was the separation of the cause between population-related changes and utility function changes. Problems were also created because of the gap between the individual consumers and the representative consumer used in the modelling.

On the presentation of Herrmann and Roeder, it was pointed out that it was difficult to measure 'image'. It was also indicated that, given variation in storage/stock-up from store to store, price elasticity at the store level is important. The situation for wine is also complicated. Export scores for French red wines did have a positive and significant impact. The directions of causality in the three-way relationship between price, image and demand were not clear and needed to be examined.

In Japan, the fat content of the diet is gradually rising. It is possible that the food consumption pattern of older and younger Japanese is different, though there may be a trend for younger people to revert to traditional diets.

It was suggested that 'point of sale' scanner data presented a good opportunity for demand analysis. Earlier it was less useful because it was not linked to the consumers, but recently it has begun to be linked through the use of consumers cards, often for a sample of households. These also often incorporate useful demographic data. This could provide a means of more rigorous analysis, though scanner data is often not publicly available and is provided only to contracted market research firms.

PANEL 10: LABOUR IN AGRICULTURE – DIVERSIFICATION OF THE
RURAL ECONOMY, RURAL NON-FARM EMPLOYMENT,
URBANIZATION AND MIGRATION CHALLENGES

ORGANIZER, RAPPORTEUR AND CHAIRPERSON

Alberto Valdés* (World Bank)

PANEL DISCUSSANTS

Rural Employment in Industrialized Countries   *Ray Bollman (Canada) and
John Bryden (University of Aberdeen, UK)*

Labour Absorption in the Rural Economy in Transition Economics   *Ulrich
Koester (University of Kiel, Germany)*

The Rural Non-farm Sector: An Update   *Jean Lanjouw (USA) and Peter
Lanjouw (World Bank)*

Rural Poverty in Latin America: Issues, New Evidence and Policy   *Ramon
Lopez (University of Maryland, USA) and Alberto Valdés (World Bank)*

The four discussants presented recent findings relating to employment and
poverty issues affecting the rural farm and non-farm sectors. While widely
recognized as having great potential in absorbing rural labour and facilitating
agricultural structural adjustment, the rural non-farm sector is poorly understood in both developed and less developed countries. In part, this is due, not
only to the sector's great heterogeneity, but also to inadequate attention at the
conceptual and empirical level. This topic was the focal point of the presentations by Bollman and Bryden, on OECD countries, and Lanjouw and Lanjouw,
on developing countries. The paper by Koester focused on labour absorption in
transition economies, while Lopez and Valdés addressed the question of rural
poverty in Latin America.

Recent rural development trends in OECD countries

On the basis of a comparative study on industrial countries prepared for the
OECD, Bollman and Bryden examined three issues: (1) the changing context
for rural development in industrial countries, (2) the trends in rural employment between 1980 and 1990, and (3) explanation of rural employment trends.

The main issue addressed is the type of strategy that should be employed to foster an active rural non-agricultural economy. They observe that employment in services and industrial activities is becoming more predominant in rural areas (although a substantial range of situations is observed), while there is a steady and long-term decline in agricultural employment. In many OECD countries, employment in tourism has been increasing and is now exceeding that in agriculture, but the experience with employment in other services (retailing and personal services, public services including health and education) is mixed.

The authors focus on two main groups of explanations for changes in rural employment, namely the impact of globalization and restructuring, and the new consumption functions of the countryside in OECD countries. The former include the 'shrinking of distance', influenced by lower transport costs, trade liberalization, improvements in information technology and the changing role of the nation state. The latter examines how the movement of people into rural areas is determined not only by the availability of work and other economic opportunities but also by the new values placed on rural space – clean environment, community life, space for leisure, pleasant landscape, healthy lifestyles and so on – as well as, in some cases, by the availability of redundant buildings and lower-cost housing. The more rapid growth of rural employment includes a broad range of 'non-tradable' activities, including access to education and training. In discussing the policy implications, the authors concluded that rural employment problems will never be solved by agricultural policies.

The role of the non-farm sector in poverty alleviation in developing countries

On the basis of empirical analysis in many developing countries, Lanjouw and Lanjouw examined the characteristics of the non-farm sector and its role in poverty alleviation. Typically, the distinction between rural and urban employment is based on the place of residence, so that those who commute to a job in a nearby urban centre are still considered to be rural workers. 'Rural' is most often defined to include settlements of about 5000 or fewer inhabitants, but in the national statistics the authors find a wide range of definitions, such as under 10 000 in Mauritania, with Taiwan only excluding cities over 250 000. Recognizing the great heterogeneity of the rural non-farm sector, the authors suggest a distinction between two types of occupations: low labour productivity activities serving as a residual source of employment (a safety net) and the high labour productivity (and hence income) activities.

In considering policy implications, Lanjouw and Lanjouw asked what role there might be for government intervention in the non-farm sector. Historically, projects rather than policies have been the primary method of encouraging the development of small-scale rural enterprises, either through selective credit programmes (the most common) or through the creation of special enterprise zones such as in China and India; however, the record with such projects is very mixed. The authors also highlighted the importance of education, subcontracting and infrastructure (roads, electricity) in the growth of the rural non-farm sector.

Unemployment in rural areas of transition countries

In his analysis of labour absorption in transition countries, Koester provided empirical evidence on the problem of unemployment in rural regions, showing that the agricultural labour force declined significantly more than farm output. Disguised unemployment in collective farm under the previous socialist regime was high (30 per cent of the labour force in East Germany) and surpasses the absorption capacity of the new emerging private sector. Considering the magnitude and abrupt nature of the changes, and the downward rigidity in the market price of labour, Koester suggested that private market employment growth should be complemented by significant investment in 'public and merit goods' in the form of infrastructure, state-financed social security, the provision of information and investment in human capital and, for some regions, consideration of resettlement programmes. Koester makes a distinction between FSU countries (excluding the Baltics) and Central and Eastern European countries. He thought that the problem is more serious in the FSU. In addition to the broad guidelines mentioned above, his policy recommendations to promote rural employment included output and factor market liberalization, abolishing privileges granted to large-scale farms, and flexible labour markets.

Determinants of rural poverty in Latin America

Lopez and Valdés discussed preliminary findings of a study on determinants of rural poverty in Latin America. According to an econometric analysis based on recent household surveys in six countries, their findings suggest that (1) the impact of schooling on farm output and income per capita in agriculture is generally small, the higher returns to education are captured by those who migrate to urban areas; (2) there is a powerful negative effect of family size and dependency ratio on per capita income; (3) in some of the countries the per capita income of the landless is not significantly different from that of small farmers; (4) legal reforms of labour contracts providing greater job security may have slowed down employment creation in commercial farms; and (5) the contribution of land to per capita income (that is, elasticity) is small and, although land redistribution to small farmers may contribute to increasing farm output, it may have only a limited impact on household income.

Floor discussion: policy implications

In the discussion some participants argued that, given the great heterogeneity of situations in rural areas, the strategy to follow should be highly decentralized and participatory, looking at local specificity and adjusting to local capacities. By contrast, others argued that focusing too much on the heterogeneity could only cause great despair – and that we should learn from the successful cases. Regarding decentralization, some stated that certain policies have to be taken at a higher centralized level recognizing multiple goals; thus decentralization is not always the best option. One example is policies to deal with the so-called 'neighbourhood effect'. The question is to define what needs to be decentralized rather than requiring a regional and more centralized view.

There was an argument on the need to pay more attention to the rural non-farm sector, examining what kind of support is more efficient. The issue of who pays and how this effort is financed came up repeatedly. Rural unemployment will never be solved by agricultural support policies. For example, in Europe, education has been an important means of access to jobs, while subsidized selective credit policies have failed. Also in Europe, it was stated that agricultural policies have been a major generator of negative externalities on the amenity environment, leading some to argue in favour of less agricultural support and more capacity to support the rural non-farm sector. The most discussed issue regarding the rural poverty analysis for Latin America was related to education and whether the low returns in agriculture should be attributed to the absence of complementary investments in other assets such as infrastructure and research, or to the poor quality of the education offered.

PANEL 11: THE TRANSFORMING ECONOMIES (FORMER
SOCIALIST): FOOD SECURITY, DIVERSIFICATION AND RESOURCE
MANAGEMENT

ORGANIZER AND CHAIRPERSON

Csaba Forgacs* (Budapest University of Economic Sciences, Hungary)

PANEL DISCUSSANTS

Csaba Csaki (World Bank), Eugenia Serova (Institute for Economy in Transition, Russia), Natalija Kazlauskiene (Ministry of Agriculture and Forestry, Lithuania), Jerzy Wilkin (University of Warsaw, Poland), Ulrich Koester (University of Kiel, Germany)

RAPPORTEUR

Renata Ianbykh (Agrarian Institute, Moscow, Russia)

This panel dealt with food security, diversification and resource management in transforming economies, each of them looking at their home country. A common thread through all presentations was the issue of food security, which is still of relevance in all of the areas in transition. All panellists agreed that in the transforming economies the degree of food security does not depend on the level of agricultural production, but on food availability and the income of the population. Therefore one cannot conclude that countries in transformation have experienced a decrease in food security during the 1990s because of a reduction in production levels. Instead the opposite has occurred: ineffective policies of food subsidies combined with compulsory sales to the state were changed to more efficient, market-oriented policies. As the potential for food production in the region is substantial, from an economic point of view those structural changes could result in a more sustainable development of the agricultural sector and in a more rational food policy. On the other hand, from a social point of view, the socialist policy approach not only included providing for cheap food, but also helped to maintain full employment of the rural population. This led to a debate on the type of economic theory that could be used as a base for a new agricultural policy in transition economies. It was emphasized that only such policies (and theories) that take into account the local economic, social and political circumstances could provide sustainable agricultural development.

Policies for future development

Floor discussants were critical, suggesting that, although the panellists had shown a strong agreement in their assessment of the past, their attitude towards future diversification and resource management in rural economies was not clear. Since the further development of the agroindustrial sector depends heavily on investments, the promotion of new technologies (one of the dimensions of diversification) is a question of great importance. Other aspects should also be taken into account. Food and ecological security deteriorates through environmental pollution (through animal waste and chemicals utilization) and price fluctuations affect food availability. Risk-avoiding sets of sanitary norms and regulations common in developed countries should be adapted in transition countries. The question of how to avoid ineffective policies employed in the past is still acute.

Necessity for reforms

From the answers of panellists it was obvious that some five to 10 years ago national and foreign economists were not equipped with the tools needed to solve specific problems of transition. Changes are not the result of a revolution but of a collapse of the system. In most of the former socialist countries, agrarian reforms are only just beginning to be implemented, because policy makers are unwilling to move swiftly. Proficiency levels of policy makers, in general, are very low.

On the other hand, it is difficult to solve social and economic problems of the agricultural sector without a revitalization of the stability of the sector. Even more important is the stabilization of the macroeconomic sector, as investment and rural diversification will take place only in a benign environment. This is still lacking in some countries, such as Russia, where property rights in land are not yet clearly defined and a system of land collateral does not exist. Government policies, so far, do not indicate favourable conditions for investment. Apart from that, countries in transition use the agricultural sector as a pool for cheap labour resources, so productivity improvement is not gained by technological innovations.

Rural unemployment

As far as rural unemployment is concerned, a considerable share of the population in countries in transition live in rural areas (from 15 to 30 per cent). Because of this, structural changes in the agrifood sector should be supplemented by employment policies, and new jobs in alternative non-agricultural spheres should be created. Through this kind of diversification the transformation process could be mitigated and access to food be provided to a bigger proportion of the population. The experience of Poland (where Gminas – small rural units – were revitalized through a state programme) shows that small and medium business promotion could contribute greatly to rural prosperity.

PANEL 12: SUB-SAHARAN AFRICA: FOOD SECURITY, DIVERSIFICATION AND RESOURCE MANAGEMENT

ORGANIZER AND CHAIRPERSON

Willis Oluoch-Kosura* (University of Nairobi, Kenya)

PANEL DISCUSSANTS

Abating Sub-Saharan Africa's Food Insecurity Through Targeted Capacity Building   *Anthony Ikpi (University of Ibadan, Nigeria)*

The Contributions of Livestock to Food Security in Sub-Saharan Africa: A Review of Technology and Policy Issues   *Simeon K. Ehui (ILRI)*

Unrecorded Cross-border Trade in Eastern and Southern Africa: Implications for Export Diversification and Food Security   *Chris Ackello-Oguta (University of Nairobi, Kenya)*

Towards Food Security in Southern Africa: New Roles for the Agriculture Sector   *Johan Van Rooyen (University of Pretoria, South Africa)*

RAPPORTEUR

Igbekele A. Ajibefun (Federal University of Technology, Nigeria)

Food security in this session was defined as 'access by all people at all times to adequate food for a healthy and productive life and where such access is stable over the years'. Projections for the future of the sub-Saharan Africa (SSA) food situation are gloomy. It is the only region of the world where the proportion of people who are unable to consume sufficient energy has not decreased during the recent years. Owing to population growth even optimistic versions of food situation models predict that the absolute number of malnourished people in the region will increase during the years to come.

Food security through capacity building

Ikpi emphasized that lack of capacity is a major reason for food insecurity in SSA. His discussion of existing strategies for tackling food security problems and unsustainable agriculture in sub-Saharan Africa included macroeconomic strategies which involve formulation of consistent policies, thereby creating a conducive policy environment for production, distribution and consumption of food to ensure access to adequate and nutritive food at all times by households. Under this strategy, specific programmes could include the promotion of private-sector development. He identified four major areas around which sub-Saharan Africa's food security issues revolve: sustainability of agricultural production, environment and related natural resource management; the interface of agriculture and income diversification; market deregulation, development and liberalization; and sub-regional co-operation, integration and trade.

Ikpi emphasized that each of these issues is a force which cuts across ecological zones and poses challenges which are needed to abate Africa's food insecurity. Concerning natural resource management, one of the greatest challenges facing sub-Saharan Africa is the population, poverty and land degradation nexus. To address these environmental challenges effectively, SSA has to build up capacities of policy makers and analysts who can analyse the problems and tactically solve them. With respect to agriculture and income diversification, the identified challenges include ensuring that technology-driven agricultural intensification develops strong linkages with the non-farm economy and improves the transfer of resources to the agricultural sector. Under market deregulation, the challenges lie in combating uneven bargaining power and unfair competition; price instability; and getting access to food for the poor excluded from the market. Effective translation of agroecological complementarities in SSA into dynamic trade links is the main challenge under regional cooperation and integration.

Food security through increased livestock production

Ehui discussed the importance of increased livestock production to achieve food security. He identified four factors which affect food security in sub-Saharan Africa: (1) high variability of food supplies with skewed distribution of purchasing power, (2) high population growth rate, (3) limited resources, low input use and low level of technology adoption, and (4) government policy unfavourable to the agricultural sector, with rapid urbanization at the expense of agriculture. Ehui was optimistic that, overall, the reforms now being implemented by many countries in the region would continue to have a positive impact on agricultural development. Concerning the role of livestock, he distinguished several factors contributing to food security, among them the direct access of poor smallholder farmers to more food of livestock origin, reduction of prices of livestock products resulting from increased production, and reduction of imports of livestock products.

Effects of trade on food security

Ackello-Ogutu identified fluctuation in regional food production as a major factor responsible for food insecurity and argued that trade liberalization for agricultural products would contribute to greater price stability on international markets and make it easier for low-income countries to import food, thereby improving the availability of food supplies. Constraints on formal intraregional trade were discussed. Such constraints included commodity price controls which act as disincentives to farmers, cropping seasonality and differences in comparative advantage, and lack of commitment to the ideal of a free market economy.

The presenter noted that, whereas formal trade within Eastern and Southern Africa (ESA) has not been encouraging, investigations indicate that informal cross-border trade (ICBT) is thriving and may have significant employment potentials. For example, the results of an empirical study of cross-border trade between Kenya and Uganda suggest that Kenya has comparative advantage over Uganda in manufacturing and processing, while Uganda has comparative advantage in production of agricultural commodities which could be exported to Kenya.

Some issues concerning cross-border trade in ESA remain unresolved to date. These include the magnitude and direction of ICBT and whether it conforms to existing comparative advantage, how informal traders cope with restrictions and other non-tariff barriers faced by formal traders, the transaction costs of ICBT, who loses and who gains when cross-border trade becomes liberalized, and how informal trade contributes to national and regional food security. Policy makers in ESA have clearly not been successful in promoting formal trade because of inconsistent and unstable policies and trade restrictions which encourage informal cross-border trade.

Features of the agricultural sector for food security

Van Rooyen discussed the traditional roles of agriculture in a nation's economy. His conceptual framework for analysing the importance of the positive stimulation of agriculture for successful economies includes the following components: the relationship between the agricultural sector and other sectors of the economy, the way agriculture is treated in the political process and the chosen model for regionalism.

The discussion indicated that, apart from unfavourable state intervention in agriculture in the Southern African region, there has also been a range of regional political influences that have not had a favourable impact on farming and agricultural trade. The following features were emphasized: (1) rural poverty, food insecurity and lack of rural employment, where a regional approach is required to find a solution, (2) the fragile resource base of the region, with a potential of large areas that can be brought under agricultural production, but lack of physical infrastructure, (3) available opportunities to raise productivity of agriculture in the region, (4) agricultural trade and marketing, and (5) the status of regional cooperation. Owing to the diversified conditions within the continent, there is need to harmonize policies to capture the opportunities for expanded intraregional trade in sub-Saharan Africa.

Floor discussion: challenge for further research

It was suggested that SSA has a large potential to combat food insecurity. The consensus of the discussion was that SSA faces big challenges because of the need for rapid transformation of the agricultural sector. One of the challenges is that the labour force still engaged in semi-subsistence agriculture amounts to 60–70 per cent of the total. It could be contended that 'low-input' sustainable agriculture in SSA will not be able to achieve needed productivity growth in order to meet rapidly changing food needs within a socially acceptable time frame.

At a methodological level, it was noted that the use of the ratio of agriculture's value-added to GDP as a measure of the contribution of agriculture to the national economy could lead to underestimation of the sector's relative importance. This is because agricultural products are artificially under priced relative to non-agricultural products, owing to existing policies that suppress farm prices. This, however, is more than a quibble about economic statistics. Policy often does not assist farmers and provide them with real incentives. They do not even have strong lobby groups to change the situation.

PANEL 13: SOUTH AND EAST ASIA: FOOD SECURITY,
DIVERSIFICATION AND RESOURCE MANAGEMENT

ORGANIZER AND CHAIRPERSON

A. Vaidyanathan (Madras Institute of Development Studies, India)

PANEL DISCUSSANTS

Zhu Ling (Chinese Academy of Social Sciences, China) K.S. Parikh (Indira Gandhi Institute of Development Research, India), S. Osmani (University of Ulster, Northern Ireland)

RAPPORTEUR

Latha Nagarajan* (M.S. Swaminathan Research Foundation, India)

The presentations centred on various aspects of food security for the poor. Zhu Ling highlighted the role of income distribution, across and within regions, in determining food consumption, especially in the post-reform period. She emphasized the importance of policies to redress regional income disparities and of poverty reduction programmes to ensure food security for the poor. Professor Osmani reported some interesting findings, based on a micro study, regarding the influence of subsistence production, market dependence and diversification of livelihood on the level of food consumption and on ability to cope with seasonal shortages. Dr Parikh sought to demonstrate that providing additional incomes through employment guarantee programmes (combined with subsidized supply of food to the aged and the infirm) is a far more effective and cheaper way of ensuring food security for the poor than subsidizing food supply through a wide coverage public distribution system.

Floor discussion

There was then a wide-ranging floor discussion, prompted by the chairperson, about the concept of food security and its relation to income. Most discussion of the subject takes it for granted that the level of food consumption is an increasing function of income per capita. The level of income of the poor is therefore seen as the key determinant of their nutritional status. Most of us have accepted this assumption as being reasonable. However, evidence is accumulating which seriously calls this into question.

This has appeared in the plenary paper by Hanumantha Rao and Radhakrishna, which gives data from the Indian National Sample Survey to show that the mean level of calorie intake of the population as a whole has remained constant over the last two decades despite a significant increase in total consumption in real terms. There have also been substantial changes in the pattern of consumption from food to non-food items, within the food group from cereal to non cereal foods, and from 'coarse' to 'fine' cereals. What is more important, however, is the fact that these tendencies were also in evidence among the poorest 30 per cent of the population, whose mean calorie intake was only 1500–1600 per capita per day, compared with the nutritional requirement of 2200. These classes seem to have experienced changes in the consumption similar to that of the rest of the population.

It was then pointed out in discussion that a similar pattern seems to be found in several other low-income countries as well, including China, as is evident from Zhu Ling's report. That the overall calorie elasticity of even the poor with respect to other income is turning out to be very low, and that they seem to be shifting to more expensive sources of calories, was agreed to be surprising. While this phenomenon remains to be satisfactorily explained, the available evidence does call seriously into question the widely held belief that the quantum of food consumed, and therefore the nutritional status of the poor, will automatically increase, and increase substantially, as incomes increase. If higher incomes do not, for whatever reasons, lead to increased consumption of food, the superiority of employment programmes as a means to ensure food security, over direct subsidized supply of food to the poor through public distribution systems or school meals and other such interventions, is questionable.

There were also warnings that food intake estimates, derived from sample surveys of household consumption, need to be used with caution. These surveys typically seek information on the quantity of various items of food stuffs consumed by each sample household during a specified reference period. Apart from recall lapses and informant biases, food eaten outside the household (for example, meals given by employers to their workers, and meals, snacks and refreshments brought from eating houses or teashops) is not always ascertained and accounted carefully. Furthermore, informants are usually asked about the quantities of particular foodstuffs consumed in raw (for example, paddy), semi-processed (milled rice) and in processed form (flour). The information relates to gross amounts utilized by the household during the reference period. The actual amount ingested by members of the household is usually lower because of weight losses in the process of cooking and wastage on the plate. There is need to know what kind of changes have occurred in these respects and what their net impact on actual intake has been. Insofar as there are systematic changes in one or other of them, reported gross intake may not accurately reflect the level of actual food intake (and changes therein) of the sample population and more especially for its poor segments.

A further consideration is that changes in nutritional status are not uniquely determined by food intake. The efficiency with which ingested food is utilized by the body also depends, to an important degree, on the incidence and severity of infections. Given that there has been considerable improvement in water supply, control of certain mass communicable diseases and containment of infections (on account of the wider and greater use of antibiotics), we cannot rule out the possibility that nutritional status may improve in spite of the stagnation of reported gross food intake. That nutrition surveys in India show some improvement in anthropometric indices (such as the weight and body mass index) and a reduction in the extent of malnourishment points in that direction. But these data are an inadequate basis on which to judge nutritional status of even the population as a whole not to speak of the poorer segments, whose calorie intake is 30 per cent below the recommended norm. Much more detailed and careful research to monitor nutritional status in terms of outcome indicators (namely, body mass index, morbidity, mortality and nature and intensity of activity) along with actual food intake is clearly necessary to assess trends in nutritional status, especially of the poor.

The relative stagnation of calorie intake in the face of rising per capita real incomes even in low-income countries like India also has important implications for planning of production. Recent exercises in long-term projections of agricultural supply by organizations such as FAO, the World Bank and IFPRI, draw pointed attention to the decline in the income elasticity of demand for food grains. This means that the rate of growth in food grain production required to sustain a given rate of growth in the rest of economy, without risking inflation due to shortage of basic wage goods, is also lower. Does this mean that agriculture is becoming less of a constraint on the growth of the economy? Such an inference would be unwarranted. For one thing, it is necessary to allow for relatively rapid rise in the demand for grains used as animal feed. Also the composition of foodgrain demand is changing. The problems and prospects of increasing production are not the same in all cases. More important, food demand is becoming diversified towards milk, meat, eggs and fish, vegetables and fruits. The elasticity of demand for these items is much higher, while recent evidence suggests that this demand may be rising even as that for cereals is falling. Therefore the required rate of growth in their output consistent with a given overall rate of growth is also much higher. The constraints, opportunities and resource requirements of expanding production of food items other than foodgrains therefore should receive much greater attention than they have hitherto. Focusing only, or mainly, on declining demand elasticity of foodgrains can mislead policy makers into underestimating the importance of agriculture and of the resources and attention needed to ensure the requisite level and pattern of agriculture production.

PANEL 14: NORTH AFRICA AND MIDDLE EAST: FOOD SECURITY, DIVERSIFICATION AND RESOURCE MANAGEMENT

ORGANIZER AND CHAIRPERSON

Hassan Sergini (Ministry of Agriculture, Morocco)

PANEL DISCUSSANT

Food Security in the Middle East and North Africa Region   *Nour El Din Mona (Aleppo University, Syria)*

RAPPORTEUR

Claudia Ringler* (IFPRI)

This session focused on an important issue in the Arab world that includes economics as well as politics and trade. It was hampered by the fact that logistic problems meant that there was only a single opener, though her remarks did lead to a stimulating debate. Nour El Din Mona stressed that the difficulties in the region are multifarious. Agricultural production is mainly rainfed, leading to risk and uncertainty, combined with low levels of income. Problems are exacerbated by the pressure on natural resources and high population growth (2.5–2.8 per cent). As food production in the region has not been able to meet the demand, imports have increased substantially. At present this results in balance of payment problems in most countries of the region. Malnutrition and undernutrition are prevalent, especially among the landless, small farmers and the unemployed.

The contribution of agriculture to the GNP varies markedly in the different countries of the region, ranging from 5 per cent to as much as 65 per cent. Nevertheless, agriculture will have to play an important role in the future. Intensification is one necessary component in the drive to increase agricultural exports (especially the gaps in cereal, crops, dairy and livestock production) and to minimize imports. Water is seen as the major resource constraint and technologies will have to be improved in this area to avoid problems such as flooding, waterlogging and salinity.

Optimistic versus pessimistic points of view

The main point discussed during the debate was whether the issue of food security in the Arab countries is truly as dismal as it might appear to be, or whether it could not be viewed in a more positive light. The group taking the pessimistic side pointed out that there is a vicious circle of an increasing population depleting the resource base. The countries in question are politically unstable (in general, it is only those which are politically stable, such as Morocco or Egypt, which are progressing). They also tend to have policies which favour their consumers, thus reducing profits for farmers.

While the production of export crops could be a solution, protectionist European Union policies hinder exports from the Arab region. On the other hand, there is a lack of competitiveness for classic export fruits such as citrus and olive oil (Spain produces these more cheaply) while at the same time there is an increase in local demand for these products as well as a lack of continuous flow, so necessary for successful exporting. Problems in resource management in general, and water management in particular, are responsible.

The rather small number of discussants proposing a more optimistic view stressed that the food security situation is more complex. Rainfed agriculture remains important, water is not as scarce as is sometimes implied and, with better management, yields in the region could be improved. It was stressed that there is a lack of water-saving efforts and up-to-date cooperation in water management does not exist. Water is still considered a free commodity, leading, for example, to salinization in the Euphrates basin.

Few disagreed with this analysis, though the emphasis on the general merits of rainfed agriculture were probably overstated. For example, in Egypt, wheat production yields 5.2 tons per hectare, while in Morocco and other (rainfed) areas yields are only around one ton per hectare. This is likely to be particularly important in the case of higher-value crops, which offer greater opportunities for poorer farmers to obtain satisfactory incomes.

PANEL 15: LATIN AMERICA: FOOD SECURITY, DIVERSIFICATION AND RESOURCE MANAGEMENT

ORGANIZER AND CHAIRPERSON

Antonio Brandao (Fundacao Getulio Vargas, Brazil)

PANEL DISCUSSANTS

Trade Liberalization and Agricultural Reforms in Brazil's Agriculture: Implications for Food Security and the Management of Natural Resources   *Mauro de Rezende Lopes (Centro de Estudos Agrícolas, Brazil)*

Food Security, Resource Management and the Adjustment Plan in Argentina: Some Comments   *Julio A. Penna (INTA, Argentina)*

Agricultural Development and Factor Markets: Some Notes about Peru and Ecuador   *Gabriel Montes LLamas (IADB)*

Markets for Water Rights in Chile   *Eugenia Muchnik, Marco Luraschi and Flavia Maldini (CEPAL, Chile)*

RAPPORTEUR

Joaquim Bento de Souza Ferreira Filho* (Brazil)

Slow growth of agriculture is a consequence of several factors, a number of them associated with macroeconomic reforms, such as appreciation of exchange rates and increases in real interest rates. However, factor market distortions and imperfections are also important underlying factors. Tenure insecurity is pervasive and land legislation frequently restricts transactions in the land market, imperfections in the capital markets are often magnified by the lack of appropriate collateral legislation, labour costs are increased by ill-conceived legislation and water markets are not yet properly developed.

Countries are affected differently by these problems and it was impossible to do full justice to this diversity in the short time allocated to a panel. The analysis presented by the four invited discussants highlighted a wide range of issues which are at centre stage in Latin America.

Aftermath of macroeconomic reforms in Argentina

According to Julio Penna, farmers' real income in Argentina has dropped significantly since the initiation of the stabilization plan in 1991, as a result of several factors: high interest rates, tight labour regulations that keep the cost of labour at levels inconsistent with the other prices in the economy, high taxes on agriculture and, despite the reduction in the inflation rates, an increase of 30 per cent in the consumer price index between 1991 and 1996.

These changes have affected farmers differently. Large and medium-size operators took advantage of lower input prices, especially of capital goods, and upgraded their technologies, increasing the use of irrigation and new machinery as well as applying more fertilizers. This favourable development was facilitated by the relatively high levels of initial capital and education, and by the possibility of taking advantage of economies of scale. Small farmers, however, could not take full advantage of the lower input prices and were severely constrained by their lower scale of production. Starting from a high degree of indebtedness, the increase in the interest rate has further restricted their access to credit and constrained their capacity to improve technological standards and to increase their operational scale.

It is interesting to observe that Argentina's legislation apparently does not restrict the adjustments that are taking place through the land market. Even though the adjustment to the new set of relative prices is causing discomfort now, the adjustment process is probably less painful than it would be if restrictions on land transactions existed.

Aftermath of macroeconomic reforms in Brazil

The adjustment issues in Brazil have a similar macroeconomic background to that of Argentina, despite the fact that the exchange rate regimes adopted by the two countries are quite different, with the Brazilian system being more flexible and easier to adjust if the need arises.

The reforms in Brazil started with trade liberalization. The tariff reform of 1990–3 is a landmark in the process. A second important component of this process was the creation of MERCOSUL, together with Argentina, Paraguay and Uruguay. At the same time, several policies of domestic support were eliminated. In this regard the elimination of marketing boards for coffee, cocoa, sugar and wheat was important. Also significant was the discontinuation of other policies of domestic support, such as reduction (if not elimination) of interest rate subsidies, reduction of government expenditures on agriculture and discontinuation of the guaranteed minimum prices for several commodities.

The impacts on the sector have been large. First, high imports of commodities such as rice, corn, cotton, dairy products and wheat displaced domestic production and reduced employment in the sector. Second, the macroeconomic stabilization plan (*Plano Real*), with accompanying high interest rates, caught farmers with already high levels of indebtedness. Third, the process of squeezing farm income was exacerbated by the appreciation of the exchange rate with its negative impact on exports and its positive impact on imports. It should be added that MERCOSUL (with zero tariffs for trade within the region) has contributed in an important way to higher imports of agricultural commodities from Argentina.

One political consequence of this process is the appearance of the landless movement which has gained strength in the last two years. This group is composed mainly (but not exclusively) of unemployed rural workers. The movement is politically important and is pushing the government to speed up the land reform process. However, since governments (federal, state and municipal) do not have funds to provide enough resources (besides land) to guarantee minimum profitability in the settlements, the economic results have been poor. This problem is further complicated by the fact that initial endowments are quite small. Lopes, quoting results of a survey by the newspaper, *Folha de São Paulo*, notes that, in those properties invaded by landless workers, 22 per cent were illiterate, 68 per cent had no formal education, 54 per cent had no income, and 67 per cent lived on donations.

Argentina and Brazil are still coping with consequences of the reforms and facing the challenge of further deepening the process. The discontinuation of past policies has indeed been a positive development. Nevertheless, the fact that the flow of resources reaching the sector has been reduced at a time when increased interest rates have put several farmers in a financially weak position. Pressures for backtracking in the reform process can build up in the wake of the adverse initial effects, but they are unlikely to succeed. Nevertheless, the government must be quick to develop the new framework for the sector. This must emphasize infrastructure development, factor market deregulation (especially for the labour market), technological change and natural resource management, even though the latter is not yet at the forefront of discussions. This agenda has not yet been fully absorbed by many producers and producer groups and there are bureaucratic niches that still fight for the status quo, even though it is no longer feasible. While the adjustment may be painful for some groups, the government needs to create policies, in addition to those noted above, to reduce the adjustment costs for the most vulnerable groups within agriculture.

Land markets in Ecuador and Peru

Gabriel LLamas noted that in Ecuador and Peru the land reform legislation enacted in 1964 and 1969 restricted property rights in land in several ways. Interventions such as prohibitions or restrictions to purchase, sales and rentals of land, existed in the two countries, but other land market distortions were also found, such as establishment of maximum and minimum sizes. This pattern of intervention was not peculiar to the two countries. Limits to property rights in land are common in the developing world. Countries such as Bolivia, Mexico and Honduras in Latin America have had similar patterns of intervention. But similar restrictions also exist in other parts of the world.

Several countries in Latin America have started the process of modernization of their agrarian legislation. Examples are Mexico and Honduras, which began the changes at the beginning of the 1990s; more recently, Bolivia did the same. The change in Peru started in 1991 and was further advanced in 1995 with the approval of Law 26505, which eliminated plot size limits and confined expropriation only to situations related to the construction of public infrastructure and services. At the same time, Peru is improving the land administration system with a cadastral survey and modernization of the land register services. The change in Ecuador, although with a more limited scope, came with the Agrarian Development Law, in 1994. Among its provisions the law eliminated restrictions to land transactions, allowed corporations to own land and reduced the cases where land expropriation was allowed. In water management, development has been even slower. Earlier legislation did not allow any private ownership of water resources and water prices were insufficient to cover capital and operating costs. This has certainly induced uneconomic uses of this resource and, as LLamas notes, had its private benefits skewed towards large landowners. Some initiatives to improve the legislation are under consideration in the two countries.

Chile: water resources

According to Eugenia Muchnik and her colleagues, Chile has successful experience in the management of water. Private concessions of water have existed since colonial days. Some of the main features of the 1981 Water Code, which is still in effect, are as follows. Water rights are completely separated from land rights and can be freely transferred, sold and bought; applications for new water rights are not conditional on the type of use and there is no priority list for different uses of water; water rights are allocated by the state and, in the case of simultaneous requests for the same water rights, these are allocated to the highest bidder. There is no specific tax for holding water rights.

Nevertheless, at present, there are conflicts and issues related to provisions of the Water Code. One key issue refers to the need for more regulation of water markets on the grounds that water transactions usually involve externalities, that in some cases a natural monopoly arises (large dams, canal systems) and that water is in fact an intermediate case between a private and public good such as a free access good. But this view is opposed by others who argue that the system has worked well so far and that no major regulatory reform is needed. The speakers themselves defended this last position, given the advantages in terms of mobility and efficiency.

Water markets are vital to the development of a modern and efficient agricultural system. This is beginning to be understood by policy makers throughout Latin America. It can be noted that Chile has an advanced land administration system which permits land markets to work quite efficiently. On balance, the Chilean experience is remarkable and contains lessons for most countries, since it has created an effective system of water allocation which has largely avoided waste (despite the problems raised by speculation with water rights) of this increasingly scarce resource.

Concluding comment

The developments discussed by the panel provided a broad view of policy issues related to resource management and food security in Latin America. The analyses have indicated that, despite the existence of some difficulties, policies oriented to improve growth with equity in agriculture are being implemented. The process is far from finished. It will proceed at different speeds throughout the region and occasional setbacks are likely to occur. Nevertheless, it is highly improbable that market pessimism and populism in economic policy will return to Latin America. The next step of reforming input markets is under way in selected countries and will also be taken up by other countries.

DISCUSSION GROUP AND MINI-SYMPOSIUM REPORTS

INTRODUCTION*

The 1997 IAAE Conference in Sacramento, California, USA, was the 14th that included organized discussion groups. It was the third conference in which some groups were organized as mini-symposia rather than in the traditional format. At this conference, 75 per cent of the sessions were mini-symposia, while at the 1994 Harare Conference 50 per cent were mini-symposia. The leadership for the traditional format groups consisted of a chairperson, rapporteur, and one or more consultants. For the mini-symposia, the organizer made arrangements for a more formal set of presentations prior to the conference.

Attendance for the 24 topics conducted was very good, with more than 500 people participating in the sessions. Each group was scheduled for three sessions of 90 minutes each, on three separate days during the conference. The topics were selected from a list of suggestions obtained from membership responses to a request for topics and interest in leadership in the sessions. The topics selected were the following:

- Water Quality and Markets.
- Agricultural Scientists, Agricultural Economists: How Can They Cooperate?
- Is Agricultural Support Outmoded?
- Trade and Foreign Direct Investment in Food and Agriculture.
- Environmentally Beneficial Agriculture and Rural Revitalization: Perspectives from International Cooperative Studies.
- Global trends in Taste, Preferences and Composition of Food Baskets.
- Approaches to Understanding International Consumer Demand.
- Improving Food Security Through Household, School and Community Gardening.
- Sessions on Sustainable Nutritional Security for sub-Saharan Women Subsistence Farmers.
- What is the Potential for Sustainable Intensification of Fragile Lands? Empirical Evidence and Policy Implications.
- Spatial Economic Models of Land Use: Techniques for the Quantitative Assessment of Land Use Determinants and Environmental Consequences.
- Finance and Factor Market Development for the Rural Poor.
- Role of Rural Non-Farm Activities.
- Rural Financial Institutions for and with the Poor: Relating Access and Impact to Policy Design.

*Larry Sivers (United States Department of Agriculture) organized and reported the discussion groups and mini-symposia.

- The Missing Link Between Agricultural Technology Adoption and Rural Poverty Alleviation.
- Food Quality Regulation in International Markets.
- Agricultural Market Liberalization in Africa.
- Regional Agricultural Trade and Comparative Advantage in Southern and Eastern Africa.
- Improving Higher Education in Agricultural Economics in Transition Countries.
- Agricultural Transition in Central and East European Countries and the Former Soviet Union.
- Future Role of Development Assistance in Agriculture.
- Agricultural Productivity: Multilateral Comparisons.
- Political Economy Analysis in Agricultural Economics: Concepts and Experiences Among Countries.
- Quality and Environmental Management for Competitive Advantage in Agriculture and the Food Industry.

Participants were not asked to register for a session prior to the first meeting, a change from past conference procedures.

Those selected for leadership for the traditional format and the organizers for the mini-symposium were selected from a list of recommendations made by country representatives, the Executive Committee and proposals that came from people proposing mini-symposia. This process resulted in a wide geographical representation in the leadership roles.

Summary reports for each of the topics are contained in the following pages. For the convenience of those who attended meetings the group numbers are taken from the list as originally advertised. Two groups from the latter (2 and 24) were cancelled.

GROUP 1

WATER QUALITY AND MARKETS

ORGANIZERS   MAUREEN R. KILKENNY (USA), ROBERT INNES (USA)

RAPPORTEUR   MAUREEN R. KILKENNY (USA)

'The defining issue of the twenty-first century may well be the control of water resources. In the next 30 years, it is likely that water shortages will increase dramatically. While water supplies are dwindling because of groundwater depletion, waste and pollution, demand is rising fast. Currently, 338 million people are subject to sometimes severe water shortages, and by 2025 this number is projected to about 3 billion. The worsening scarcity of water threatens agricultural growth and industrial production and is likely to increase water-related health problems and degrade the environment. Policies must treat water, not as a free good, as they often do now, but rather as a scarce commodity that comes at a price' (Pinstrup-Anderson, 'Foreword', to Mark Rosegrant, *Water Resources in the Twenty-first Century: Challenges and Implications for Action*, IFPRI Discussion Paper 20, 1997).

This mini-symposium devoted one meeting to recent research, one to a round table discussion, and one to an experimental market.

Recent research

Mateen Thobani presented 'Formal Water Markets: Why, When and How to Introduce Tradeable Water Rights' (1997), *The World Bank Research Observer*, **12** (2): 161–79. In contrast to the claim that 'water is too precious to be left to markets to allocate it', he contended that marketable water rights increase the efficiency of water use, allow rapid changes in allocation in response to changing demands and can stimulate investment (as in Chile). He insisted that water rights must be separate from land rights. Also the most pragmatic initial allocation is based on existing water use – no matter how unfair or inequitable those patterns may be.

Marca Weinberg extended 'Uncoordinated Agricultural and Environmental Policy Making: An Application to Irrigated Agriculture in the West' (1996), *American Journal of Agricultural Economics*, **78** (1): 65–78. Subsidized (or relatively underpriced) water for agriculture and underpriced effluent both create incentives to overuse water. To correct these two distortions, two instruments are required: markets to price water correctly and markets correctly to price discharge. Water markets provide economic incentives to conserve water and may thus reduce agricultural effluent externalities.

Reduced drainage in conjunction with unchanged chemical use, however, can lead to increased pollutant concentrations. Jeffrey Connor's model indicates that, although perfectly competitive trade in water allocates water efficiently, the pollutant concentration associated with that allocation may worsen if (1) the value of water in alternative uses is low; (2) small reductions in water use are *not* accompanied by relatively larger reductions in pollutant loading; and (3) small reductions in water use cause large reductions in dilution capacity.

Since geology differs across locations and watersheds, the same farming practices will cause different levels of non-point pollution. Jun Jie Wu described the Regional Agricultural Policy Simulation (RAPS) model: (http://www.ag.iastate.edu/card/divisions/rep/RAPS). The RAPS model uses the United States Department of Agriculture's (USDA) National Resources Inventory detailed information in a geographic information system (GIS) database about land characteristics and farming practices at thousands of points of private land in the United States. A multinominal logit model predicts the allocation of land across crops and chemical use, with respect to government policies and market prices. A region-specific environmental simulation model estimates the environmental consequences of those predicted practices. Jun Jie showed the region-specific changes in cropping patterns and nitrogen run-off across the Midwest due to the changes in US agricultural policies.

Round table

What are the serious water problems? What are the minimum legal or social institutions (or physical systems) needed to support water markets? What are the externalities associated with water use?

David Zilberman argued that the diversion of water to low-value uses is the most serious problem. Agricultural chemical pollution, contamination of water by livestock wastes and waterlogging of soils are secondary problems. Simple solutions are preferable to sophisticated and complex government regulations, which we know always provide opportunities for corruption. He also argued that, if water rights are defined with respect to consumption, externalities associated with return flows are most often positive.

Richard Howitt distinguished rights to water *stocks* from rights to water *flows*. The first is an asset which is very difficult to price and market. Use (flow) rights are easy to price in spot or option markets. Transaction costs for trade in water use rights, however, are difficult to measure. Also there are three categories of externalities: pecuniary, technical and environmental. Citing a recent dispute between water distributors in Southern California, he noted that the ability to convey water is much more valuable than the water itself.

Bill Easter spoke of the key role of water user groups in managing the links between water providers and consumers. On the basis of their survey of water systems around the world, he argued that informal markets (supported by custom and reputation constraints) are working well. Alternatively, formal markets (supported by legal and government institutions) do not solve corruption problems. Governments still own water; tradable permits only guarantee the rights to use it. He argued that legalizing existing informal markets (for example, in India) may be more effective than imposing formal regulations.

Dr Vaidyanathan, who is sceptical about markets, expressed concern about contingent rights, 'fuzzy' water rights, lack of credible enforcement and the limitations of the conveyance system. Bill Easter noted that, particularly as a result of conveyance limitations one should expect a limited amount of trading in use rights.

Participants provided this list of 'the most serious water problem(s),' by region:

Africa   rural access, risk, drinking water quality, ecology, equity;
Armenia   scarcity, competing users, transition issues;
Australia   rising consumption/declining environment, poorly defined property rights, (un)reliable endowments;
Canada   aquatic ecology;
China   urban shortage, drinking water quality;
India   waste, fuzzy rights, inequities, income distribution;
Japan   high cost, quality of drinking water;
South Africa   equity/income distribution;
Taiwan   scarcity, competing uses, decoupling water from land rights;
Thailand   failure to exploit water endowments;
UK   urban water shortage, public good aspects;
USA (west)   (lack of) conveyance facilities, public good aspects;
(east coast)   aquatic ecology;
(corn belt)   livestock and agriculture chemical contamination.

Experimental market

Like crop field trials by agronomists, experimental markets are run by economists to investigate the behaviour of people in controlled situations. Maureen Kilkenny ran an experiment to test if/how a tradable pollution permit market (1) substitutes an excludable and rival piece of paper (permit) for a non-excludable, non-rival externality, and reveals the social value of the externality; (2) controls incidence more efficiently than an (ex-post revealed) optimal Pigouvian tax; and (3) allows for more local control of externalities, tailored to each individual producer's technological, cost, price and local citizens' preference structures, while supporting private incentives to adopt abatement technologies.

Each of the 15 participants in the experimental market assumed a well-defined role of a consumer, or one of three different types of producers of a private good. First, a double oral auction revealed the equilibrium market price (and quantity) of the private good; however, some producers generated negative externalities (in the form of paper bags over neighbour's heads). After a 'public choice' to constrain the allowable level of externalities to five (reduced from eight) by endowing each producer with a permit for one 'unit' of pollution, another double oral auction revealed the value of the externality to be (approximately) the sum of producer and consumer surplus at the margin of five units (as theory predicts).

The third auction (of private goods) showed that, even given the costs of permits, the market price of the private good increased by 13 per cent, compared to the 18 per cent increase under the optimal Pigouvian tax (based on the social value revealed in the second market). Furthermore, only one unit, rather than the permitted five units, of externality was ultimately generated, since many permits were retired by consumers, and less of the private good was sold, reflecting local preferences and income (as well as the effects of too few units of observation in the experiment). Also producers who abated expanded their market share.

GROUP 3

AGRICULTURAL SCIENTISTS, AGRICULTURAL ECONOMISTS:
HOW CAN THEY COOPERATE?

ORGANIZER   JEAN-MARC BOUSSARD (FRANCE)

RAPPORTEUR   SLIM ZEKRI (TUNISIA)

The mini-symposium was organized in two sessions with five interventions. John Dixon from FAO addressed the broad issue of 'Managing Interdisciplinarity in the Public Sector.' He stressed that there are currently a great number of professionals working in the agricultural sector. These professionals are mainly working in commodity or disciplinary organizations, which leads to more specialization of task and methods. On the other hand, he remarked that there are few multidisciplinary rewards to provide incentive for building multidisciplinary teams. The factors enhancing multidisciplinarity are decentralization, strong leadership, proximity to field, ease of communication, clarity of roles and small, long-term teams. Multidisciplinarity should be considered as a complement to disciplinary work. In order to reduce the transaction costs arising from multidisciplinary work, there is a need for common framework, modelling and electronic communications.

C.A.J. Botha, from the University of Pretoria, South Africa, stressed the need of multidisciplinarity for extension service in South Africa. The transition from large-scale farms to small family farms created new challenges. For the most part, the experienced white staff left the extension service and new black people came in with no experience. Scientists are not working together, thus not enough research results are obtained. Money put into the extension system is not adequate and small farmers are not contributing financially. Currently, closing the public extension service is being considered as an option.

Guy Trébuil from CIRAD, France, presented a study of 'Cooperation Between Agronomists and Agricultural Economists to Improve Southeast Asian Agrarian Systems: the DORAS Model in Thailand.' First, he provided a definition of agricultural production systems which he considered as the basis of development-oriented research. The study begins with a preliminary diagnostic stage leading to the planning, division of labour and explanation of the appropriate criteria. The linkages between the institutions, agrarian structures, ecosystem and available technologies are then addressed. Two case studies were later presented. These concerned the coastal rainfed alluvial plain in Southern Thailand and subsistence small farmers in an area of steep land in the upper northern part of Thailand. He concluded that this kind of interdisciplinary investigation has the potential to generate a specific field of study. The integration of modelling and simulation approaches will be necessary to improve the rapidity of answering farmers' needs under a dramatically changing world.

Guillermo Flichman from CIHEAM, France, presented a methodology based on the use of EPIC as an agronomic model coupled with a mathematical programming model (GAMS). The objectives of this methodology are the study of agricultural and environmental policies in the European Union (EU). This kind of methodology allows the simultaneous tackling of economic aspects and environmental impacts of the changing EU policy. The EPIC model determines engineering production functions as well as potential pollution from agricultural chemicals. The economic and pollution data are later introduced into a mathematical multicriteria model. Results obtained were satisfactory for both France and Spain. The model also included the management of water as a scarce resource.

Finally, Paul Dyke from Texas A&M University presented the integration of agronomic models and mathematical programming at regional or watershed levels. He stressed the fact that it takes years to build a team. He said that integrated natural modelling is a multidisciplinary approach where a great number of disciplines are needed, such as geomorphology, topography, geology, soils, vegetation, land resources, weather, wildlife, reservoirs and ponds. He remarked that in the future the integration of these different disciplines should be done in an additive way. That is, a mathematical model should be designed which would incorporate different models such as salinity, nitrate pollution, pesticides, water shortages and prices. As different periods of time are used in each process of modelling, these models could be simply added to the mathematical model.

GROUP 4

IS AGRICULTURAL SUPPORT OUTMODED?

ORGANIZER   JOHN S. MARSH (UK)

RAPPORTEUR   JOHN S. MARSH (UK)

Summary

This mini-symposium focused on agricultural policy in developed countries. Its principal conclusions were that:

- traditional arguments for agricultural support are now less valid, and they did not justify intervention in the shape of price policy;
- increased concerns about the environmental impact of agriculture, animal welfare and the quality and safety of food had combined with far-reaching geopolitical changes to change the focus of agricultural policy;
- direct payments to farmers raised questions of legitimacy. The political system had to establish accepted priorities for policy and to ensure that it was delivered efficiently. Agricultural economists had an important role in both areas.

Past reasons for support

These included food security, market stability, improving farmers' bargaining power, counteracting the impact of protectionist trade policies, shielding vulnerable farmers from market pressures and, especially, raising farmers' incomes. The weight attached to these goals had changed but it was strongly argued that, even where they remained important, price policy had shown itself to be incapable of delivering satisfactory solutions. The desirability and feasibility of stabilization was carefully explored. The jury remained out on whether US policy stabilized markets. In the EU, the CAP had stabilized prices to EU farmers but at the expense of increased instability in world markets. The rationality of stability as a goal was questioned. Stabilization at prices which raised farm revenues had increased investment and stimulated surplus production in Europe. The visibility of such surpluses and the cost of dealing with them, together with declining confidence in the ability of governments to manage economies, had undermined the consensus in favour of protection. The status quo was no longer accepted.

Agricultural policy faces new social priorities within a changed economic context

The end of the Cold War, rising income levels in many Asian economies and commitments made as part of the GATT Uruguay Round settlement had resulted in a new global market. Past policy had centred on food production, but now issues relating to public goods and externalities had come to the fore. These included climate change, biodiversity, landscape, wildlife, animal welfare and food safety. Agriculture was no longer the sole motor of the rural economy, and policy had to assist the movement of resources to these new uses. Although, in the mind of many farm lobbyists, market prices remained the most important issue, policy makers faced a new agenda. Evaluating its goals, assessing the cost effectiveness of specific policies and seeking to identify those instruments which were 'least trade distorting' represented a contemporary challenge to agricultural economists. It might be appropriate to abandon a sectoral approach, replacing agricultural policy with policies designed to cope with each type of market failure. The days when ministries of agriculture dominated rural policy may be numbered. There were no obvious or easy ways of directing resources to those uses which were most highly valued. Problems could arise in seeking to encourage the production of public goods. Farmers might perceive an incentive to farm badly if this qualified them for subsidies to change to approved farming systems. The application of the 'polluter pays principle' was impossible where the identity of polluters could not be established or where pollution was the result of the farming activity of past generations. Payments for environmental outputs could not replace revenue lost as a result of lower prices. Farmers' abilities to provide such goods did not match their past levels of production. There was a danger that lobby groups would capture such payments for sectional interests.

New policies had to be politically feasible and economically efficient

Politicians have to consider the cost to them of time spent in promoting policies, the durability of commitment to any new policy, and the extent to which policies would command the continued support of constituents. Market failure was a necessary but not sufficient basis for government intervention. There had to be a clear assurance that the benefits of policies exceeded their cost, including the cost of raising taxes for their finance. Only one voice was raised arguing that past EU policy had been a success. Within the EU there had already been a major switch to direct income payments. These now accounted for two-thirds of the disposable income of French farms. Such support needed to be decoupled. If linked to the provision of environmental goods, long-term contracts would need to be negotiated between farmers' organizations and their governments. The extent to which governments could justify direct payments was questioned. One idea was that they might be made via NGOs, proportionately to money they raised voluntarily. Some politicians might welcome the transparency of such payments. Others would see it as a vice. Farmers, such as those in New Zealand, who saw themselves as part of a commercial economy, might not welcome such payments. For some participants the question was not how to provide support but how to remove it. The possibility that some semi-public goods could be produced by the private sector was explored and attention was drawn to the relevance of the theory of clubs.[1] Regulations to protect the environment could impair the ability of farmers to compete in world markets. Payments for environmental goods, however, raised difficult trade policy issues. For some they seemed to be the thin end of a new wedge of protection; for others, an essential tool if resources were to be used in a way which reflected social as well as market values. A strongly expressed view was that policies needed to facilitate the provision of public goods but not to 'subsidize' them. Subsidies would result in an excess supply. Agricultural economists face challenges both in valuing public goods and in assessing the efficiency of environmental policies.

[1]See, for example, T.G. MacAulay, 'Games, Clubs and Models; The Economics of an Agricultural Economics Society' (1995), *The Australian Journal of Agricultural Economics*, **39** (1), April.

GROUP 5

TRADE AND FOREIGN DIRECT
INVESTMENT IN FOOD AND AGRICULTURE

ORGANIZER   STEVE NEFF (USA)

RAPPORTEUR   STEVE NEFF (USA)

International food commerce is more than imports and exports. It consists
also of foreign direct investment (FDI), licensing of foreign production and
other arrangements. Trade and foreign direct investment have both grown
faster than GDP for many countries and for the world . This is true for food
and agriculture as well as for the general economy. The mini-symposium
brought forth a range of perspectives on the globalization of the food economy.
What are the sources of globalization: for example, liberalization of trade,
deregulation of domestic markets, developments in transport and communication, and the evolution of market capitalism brought about through
developments in firm structures and strategies? What are the effects of FDI
on home and host countries in terms of domestic resource utilization? The
range of issues presented and discussed spanned firm-level decisions to
export or invest in production abroad, the role of economies of scale in
industries as firms make these decisions, the influence of intellectual property protections and other international trade rules, international investment
as a transforming influence in Central European food industries, and the
impact of regional integration on food trade and FDI. The first two sessions
each had two speakers, while the third had one presentation, allowing ample
time for discussion of issues raised by audience members as well as those
introduced by the speakers.

Following an introduction of the topic by the chairman, each member of the
group gave a brief personal self-introduction including a comment, question or
statement of interest in the topic of trade and foreign direct investment. Interests expressed by group members included, among other topics, technology
transfer through FDI, effects of outward FDI on the home country's economy,
risks associated with FDI (especially from changes in economic policies in the
host country), the effects of host country trade restrictions on FDI and the
effects of FDI on trade.

Regional integration session

Topic: Food Trade and FDI in Eastern Europe and the European Union
Tim Josling, Stanford University

Regional integration can be accomplished through trade, policy or investment. In the case of the integration of Western Europe with Central and Eastern European countries in transition from state planning, investment appear as the leading force. The presentation focused on three different business strategies for outbound FDI from Western Europe to Eastern Europe: (1) to jump over trade barriers at Eastern European borders and sell food products in the FDI host countries; (2) to invest in Eastern Europe to make food products to sell back on Western Europe markets; and (3) to make products in Eastern Europe for sale in the former Soviet Union. After a review of the data, the third strategy was deemed most important and the second strategy least significant in terms of sales value.

Topic: International Trade and FDI: A CUSTA Case Study
Mary Marchant, University of Kentucky

The speaker presented an empirical study of the relationship between trade and FDI in food industries before and after the Canada–United States Trade Agreement (CUSTA). Econometric evidence favoured a complementary relationship between trade and FDI. In discussion, group members suggested that Canadian supply management policies, such as for eggs, poultry and milk, distort firms' decisions and reduce confidence in results for those industries. A symposium participant emphasized that a change in Canadian investment laws in 1986 may have dampened responses to CUSTA.

Economics of FDI and business strategy session

Topic: Trade Impacts of Economies of Scale in the Pork and Poultry Industries
Maury Bredahl, University of Missouri

There are apparent differences in economies of scale at different stages of the vertical chain of food production. As trade becomes freer, economies of scale effects may become more prominent. Economies of scale at several levels of processing may have different trade implications across countries, depending on the relationship of firm or plant size and the size of the national market. In discussion, group members were curious about whether information on optimal plant size could be inferred from available data, and the speaker was confident that enough information would be available.

Topic: Business Strategies and FDI in the Food Industry
Dennis Henderson, Ohio State University (emeritus)

The presentation centred around nine points related to firm strategies in international commerce, among which were proprietary assets (such as brands), headquarter services such as research and development, early perception of consumer trends, and intra-industry firm rivalry. In discussion, a member of the symposium asked which of the nine points is the most important. The speaker's opinion was that proprietary assets are essential to innovation.

Regional trade and FDI session

Topic: Japanese Outbound FDI in the Food Industry
Mike Reed, University of Kentucky

The presentation focused on patterns of outward investment in the food industry. Some data on total food industry FDI were available since 1970, while other data were available in detail only for 1993. The data tended to confirm that Japanese companies invest abroad with a greater tendency to ship products back to the home market, while US and European firms tend to sell a larger share of products in the host country.

General discussion for the mini-symposium suggested that FDI data are problematical owing to different means of collection, different purposes for data collection, different definitions across countries, short time-series and non-disclosure by governments or companies of data in some cases for confidentiality or other reasons.

GROUP 6

ENVIRONMENTALLY BENEFICIAL AGRICULTURE AND RURAL REVITALIZATION: PERSPECTIVES FROM INTERNATIONAL COOPERATIVE STUDIES

ORGANIZER   **SHIGEKI YOKOYAMA (JAPAN)**

RAPPORTEUR   **SHIGEKI YOKOYAMA (JAPAN)**

Establishing environmentally beneficial agriculture is a global issue. Effective and acceptable policies for less favoured areas is a common concern in developed countries. This symposium incorporated the two issues. Case studies from EU, United States and Japan were presented. Half of them were two-country comparative studies of Japan and another country. Employing similar methodology, these studies showed areas of commonality and differences. The remaining studies reported country-specific cases. The topics covered included farm structure, technology choice, regional resource management, consumer behaviour, marketing and public policies. By exchanging reports on the experience of various countries attempting to develop environmentally beneficial agriculture for rural revitalization, a forum for cooperative research was established.

Session 1

Establishing environmentally friendly dairy farming: Japanese and US perspectives. (Chaired by Al E. Luloff.)

Topic: The Unique Potential for International Cooperation in Grazing Research
Al E. Luloff, Gregory D. Hanson, Penn State, and Shigeki Yokoyama

Family-owned dairy systems in Japan and the United States face similar economic, environmental, and social pressures that threaten their future existence. The common problems, as well as similar topography, climate and dairy production technology, permit a unique international comparison between grazing-based dairy systems in both countries. The economic returns, environmental impacts and sociodemographic characteristics provide similar implications for both countries.

Topic: Towards Differentiating Dairy Grazing Systems in the Northeastern United States
J.R. Winsten, Gregory D. Hanson, Robert L. Parsons, and Al E. Luloff, Penn State

The survey on dairy production practices focusing on grazing intensity was conducted in early 1997 in Pennsylvania, Vermont and Virginia. The intensive grazers were younger, better educated, heavier computer users, were more likely to have written farm plans, and were more satisfied with economic performance and quality of life than others. Use of intensive grazing was the most significant determinant of increasing future reliance on grazing.

Topic: Development of Hokkaido Dairy Farming and Environmental Problems
Hiroki Ukawa, Hokkaido National Agricultural Experiment Station, Japan

Hokkaido dairy farming has long been based on self-supplied feed, while the Japanese livestock industry as a whole depends heavily on imported feed. Enlarging herd size to reduce costs along with increasing dependence on imported feed has led to environmental problems in Hokkaido.

Topic: The Determinant Factors in Adoption of Manure Management among Hokkaido Dairy Farmers: Covariance Structure Analysis
Shigeki Yokoyama, Hiroki Ukawa, Al E. Luloff

Casual relationships among subjective and objective factors on adoption of manure management were examined using covariance structure analysis with data from a survey of Hokkaido dairy farms. Determinant factors in adoption of new manure management included attitude and perception of environmental problems which, in turn, was influenced by source of information and communication. The number of cows per worker and the socioeconomic context of farm location influenced farmers' attitudes.

Topic: Profitability and Expansion of Low-input Dairying in the 'My-pace Dairying' Movement of Northeastern Japan
Yoshihiko Yoshino, Rakunogakuen University, Japan

'My-pace Dairying' is a farmer group aiming at enhancing cow health and farmers' quality of life through reducing farm size. Unique features of their practices are small herd size, low use of concentrates and other purchased feeds, fewer labour hours, more grazing and better manure treatment. Though gross production and yield per cow are lower than among conventional farmers, net income is higher owing to much lower cash expenses. Their commitment to communities and environmental concerns are also high.

Session 2

Regional resource management and environmental policies towards rural revitalization. (Chaired by Gregory D. Hanson.)

Topic: Agritourism as Regional Resource Management in Less Favoured Areas: Japan–Italy Comparison
Yasuo Ohe, Chugoku National Agricultural Experiment Station, Japan; Adriano Ciani, University of Perugia, Italy

Italian and Japanese agritourism were compared. Based on high profitability, Italian agritourism was more likely to be operated on a full-time basis providing year round and diverse services. The potential of indigenous rural development is higher in Italy, reflecting the fact that Japanese rural communities are more stable due to their strong farm background. To respond to increasing and divergent demands for agritourism in Japan, more entrepreneurship is required.

Topic: Environmental Accounting: The Result of Biennial Research and Experience in Italy
Adriano Ciani, Stephan Coocco, University of Perugia

This paper reported on an approach which modified the traditional balance sheet of farming production by considering negative and positive effects on the environment and natural resources. This was illustrated with empirical results from Umbria.

Topic: A Multi-use Sustainable Water Management: Central Italy Irrigation Plan
Antonio Boggia and Gaetano Martino, University of Perugia

This paper examined the various systems of sustainable water use by focusing on irrigation projects which cover Umbria and Tuscany.

Topic: Mineral Surplus in EU Agriculture and Environmental Policies: an Approach at the Farm, Regional and National Levels
Floor M. Brouwer, LEI-DLO, The Netherlands

Mineral balances are important tools for investigating the efficiency of input use and to increase farmers' understanding of management options to reduce nitrogen surpluses. This knowledge can contribute to monitoring progress achieved in agrienvironmental policy and also for monitoring actions to meet the requirements of the EU Nitrates Directive. Two approaches, farm gate balance and surface balance, were presented.

Topic: A Comparison of Less Favoured Area Policies in the EU and Japan
Jaap Post, LEI-DLO, The Netherlands; Yoichi Matsuki, Nippon Veterinary and
Animal Science University

Both the EU and Japan have many regions with a long agricultural history of
production under unfavourable natural conditions. The necessity of a policy to
sustain agriculture in less favoured areas increases with further trade liberalization. The main objective of the less favoured area (LFA) policy in the EU is a
continuation of farming in LFA, thereby maintaining a minimum level of
population and conserving the countryside. Japanese LFA policy tends to
promote agroforestry. In both regions, future LFA subsidies will be more tied
to the environment and landscape and less to agricultural production, implying
a stronger relation between the approach to production and the level of compensation.

Session 3

Influence of consumer behavior on promotion of environmentally friendly
farming. (Chaired by Shigeki Yokoyama.)

Topic: Development of the Organic Fresh Produce Market in Japan
Kazunori Sato, National Agriculture Research Center, Japan

Organic fresh produce marketing emerged during the early 1970s in Japan,
responding to increased concern over food safety and farmer health. Currently,
marketing channels are divided into the following four types: (1) consumer
organizations which have been the major channel from the beginning; (2)
supermarkets and department stores, the second largest channel, increasing
rapidly; (3) specialist stores, with a small but stable share; and (4) farmers'
direct marketing, which is prominent in the suburbs of large cities.

Topic: Issues of Organic Farming Standards in Japan
Taichi Takahaski, National Agriculture Research Center, Japan

There are no standards with legal force on organic farm products in Japan.
Currently, the ministry prescribes complicated cultivation guidelines. Moreover, in the stores, many kinds of certificates are used arbitrarily. To avoid this
confusion, there is a need for a unified certification system.

Topic: Consumers' Consciousness about Quality of Vegetables and Fruits in
Japan
Yuji Oura, Kazunori Sato, National Agriculture Research Center, Japan

The relationship between recognition of environmental problems and purchase
behaviour was analysed using a laddering method. The tomato was the crop
studied. Consumers recognized 'growing area' and 'cultivation technique' as
indices of product safeness.

GROUP 7

GLOBAL TRENDS IN TASTE,
PREFERENCES AND COMPOSITION OF FOOD BASKETS

ORGANIZER   BHUBAN C. BARAH (INDIA)

RAPPORTEUR   BHUBAN C. BARAH (INDIA)

A group of specialist researchers from 11 countries who have been working in the area of food consumption behaviour participated in this symposium where 18 contributed papers were presented. The symposium was divided into three sections: (1) new frontiers of studies on food consumers' behaviour and conceptualization, (2) case studies, and (3) country experiences and status papers.

The emerging scenario in food consumption has generated global interest. It has also evoked serious interest among scholars for further studies of food consumption trend changes and the various implications for personal, social and global welfare. Income expenditure patterns, poverty and inequality, and the effect of agricultural diversification in the wake of diversification of food baskets are also of interest. The establishment of a global network on food consumption trends is a significant decision.

The pattern of food consumption has been drastically changing globally in recent years. The changes have multiple dimensions and varied implications. Such changes are taking place across social classes, different age groups and over all countries of the world. Older people are happy with social food while the young are fast shifting to modern and varied food. Women and working families have stronger preferences for convenience food, including processed food. Following the basic Engel's Law, the percentage of food expenditure is decreasing and the high-income societies spend a high proportion of their family income on luxury food. This has led to a rapidly rising degree of overconsumption in these nations. In contrast, the low-income countries frequently confront several issues related to deprivation and inaccessibility of food and problems of poverty and inequality loom large. The important paradox is that, while the consumption of cereals in preference to luxury food is declining for the wealthy, the same situation is occurring faster for the poor because of non-availability, lack of purchasing power and entitlement. The problem is so serious that even the consumption of coarse cereals and semi-processed food is affected.

Changes in consumption patterns have brought about interesting questions regarding, for example, what we eat, why we eat, whether all spending on food is beneficial, how to educate to eat well, the social cost of overconsumption, and the relationship between diversification of food baskets and agricultural diversification. Several methodological questions also arise in this context. There is near-unanimity on issues wherein the role of the economic variable such as income, prices and food availability becomes marginal in the conventional consumption models. In their place, a number of non-economic factors tend to occupy a dominant role. Gender, age structure of population, literacy, knowledge, class composition, food decision makers, quality and method of food production (organic versus chemical, processed or irradiated food), food marketing and advertising are some of important factors affecting food consumption behaviour. Also, in the face of widespread economic reforms, liberalization and international trade, studies on structural changes in the demand–supply scenario for food and feed warrant careful research efforts.

The impact of changes in food consumption behaviour raises several diverse and relevant issues which are regionally crucial and globally significant.

(1)   With technological advancement, demand for more caloric energy declines, which reduces the amount of cereal intake, particularly coarse cereal. For example, as the spade is replaced by the mechanical drill for digging a hole, a substantial amount of human body energy is saved and the demand for calorie-rich food is reduced.

(2)   Decline in cereal use is compensated for by a variety of non-cereals such as fruits and vegetables, milk and milk products, meat and fish. Thus a new pattern of agricultural diversification may emerge.

(3)   Diversification of the food basket leads to agricultural diversification. Grains may shift from human food to animal food. Prime agricultural land is converted to fish ponds, poultry farms, cattle ranching and other livestock activities.

(4)   Preferences for processed food derivatives and animal product-based items are increasing significantly. Processed and transformed cereals such as cake and flakes are of lesser nutritional value because vital micronutrients are destroyed in processing and the diet becomes nutritionally inadequate.

(5)   Meals eaten away from the home and processed foods are expensive and nutritionally poor.

(6)   Younger sections of the population prefer processed variety foods; older people stick to conventional food and less variety. With modern food intake increasing, the market for fast food outlets is spreading aggressively.

(7)   Women have a strong preference for convenience food and cooked food. Changing family status (working status) has reduced the liking for home-prepared food, and eating out is becoming popular.

(8)   The relationship between overconsumption and a balanced diet is inverse in nature. Overconsumption and variety of food affect health and the increasing diet-related health care cost has tremendous implications for social welfare.

(9)   Demand for food is competing hard with demand for feed.

(10) Home-produced food as a social entity is losing ground to the upcoming strong preference for food eaten away from home.

(11) Income/expenditure and price as determinants of food consumption have lost importance, with the non-economic items emerging as major determining factors.

(12) Innovative advertising strategies influence the food consumption pattern, in particular that of the younger consumers.

(13) The issues on poverty (food entitlement versus availability), inequality, deprivation and malnutrition re-emerge and re-enforce the academic debate on calorie versus protein, in more generalized form. The social dimension of food consumption and conflict resolution may gain further importance.

(14) Internationalism and liberalization of food trade warrant more careful examination.

(15) Due consideration to the high social cost of changing food habits and its influence on economic sustainability should be a part of food planning.

(16) The challenging food-related environmental issues require urgent attention.

Regional issues in relation to some of the above are addressed in various degrees, but the global ones are rarely debated. The symposium covered in some detail the issues of various regions and countries.

Conclusion

The problem of food is global in nature, affecting all mankind. Change in taste and preference of the consumers is distinctly visible, not only in the cross-country (horizontal movement) comparison but also in the intra-country experience (vertical movement). The pace of change in the food consumption pattern in recent years is very fast compared to the historical pace, which has puzzled researchers. The implication of these dynamic changes are more perplexing than ever. The wealthy nations face problems of overeating and diet-related health problems, and the other nations confront problems of poverty, inequality and social justice. The variation of food consumption patterns over age group, gender and other characteristics of the population is also observed simultaneously. The problems of food availability, distributional equity, acute malnutrition and deprivation are the typical problems of a large number of poor countries. On calorie intake, the average person in the developed world consumes two-thirds more calories (about 3700 cal per day in 1990 in the United States, up from 3300 cal in 1970) than the average person in the developing world. For example, in sub-Saharan Africa, the total number of people consuming fewer than 2200 calories per day (the poverty line) has increased from 38 per cent in the 1970s to 43 per cent in the early 1990s. The paradox of food consumption is a widespread phenomenon, as seen in a food-surplus rich nation or a food-deficit poor nation. There are approximately 800 million people in the developing world who do not have adequate quantities of food available to them, another quarter of a billion suffer periodically from inaccessibility to food and, by the year 2025, the number of malnourished people will rise to over a billion. Can such development embrace social justice and the welfare of mankind?

This symposium tried to highlight the importance of regional food issues and touched upon a few international experiences. The academic enthusiasm of the participants on the matters of security of food was extremely high and encouraging. International experiences on food security are illuminating but need more research to understand the dynamics of the modern changes. The participation of highly motivated, committed and very experienced researchers in the symposium contributed greatly to the value of the sessions.

GROUP 8

APPROACHES TO UNDERSTANDING CONSUMER DEMAND

ORGANIZER   DOROTHY PRICE (USA)

RAPPORTEUR   DOROTHY PRICE (USA)

Six papers were presented and discussed during the three sessions. The first paper estimated the increases in consumer welfare in Taiwan resulting from a reduction in tariffs in six categories of meat and seafood. Hicksian compensating variation was used to measure the benefits to consumers. Derived compensated demand elasticities were estimated. The effects of various tariff reductions were estimated using a simulation procedure. The estimates accounted for the complementarity and the substitutability among the six commodities, but did not measure the effects of tariff reductions on producers. If tariffs on all meat products were reduced by 10 per cent, the prices on all meat categories would decrease by 7 to 9 per cent, depending on the type of meat. The demand for meats would increase by 4 to 14 per cent. Consumer meat expenditure would decrease by 8.22 per cent. If all tariffs were reduced, consumer meat expenditure would decrease by 18.11 per cent.

The second paper estimated the demand for surirni-based fish products in Japan. Surirni is an intermediate product which is used to make several consumer goods. The primary tool of analysis is the AIDS model, but other methods have been used where appropriate. The results are as yet preliminary, but several hypotheses have been generated: (1) prices of surirni-based products move together because of supply; (2) the demand for kamaboko is high in December because it is used as a gift; (3) the demand for chikuwa and satsumaage is sensitive to weather; (4) food items which have a complementary relationship in Japan are considered substitutes in the United States; (5) substitute and complementary relationships differ among surirni-based products; and (6) income is an important determinant for most surirni-based products. Fish sausage appears to be a Giffen good.

The third paper estimated the effect of habit among five major food categories and among nine fresh fruit products using an annual Japanese retail level time-series data set. Habit is expected in food purchasing behaviour since such behaviour is a low cognitive process, and food is inherently tied to culture. The paper compared results using the State Adjustment Model, the Koyck lag model and the Almon lag model. Habit was significant for meat and cereal products, but non-significant for fruits and vegetables with all models. The Almon model and the State Adjustment Model also estimated a small habit effect for seafood. Habit was significant for some fresh fruits but not others; structural breaks were a problem with the fresh fruits. Some fruits showed declining popularity over time while others did not.

The fourth paper compared meat safety attitudes and expected meat purchases between US and Japanese consumers. A tri-component attitude model was used to construct the questionnaire. The three components of attitude are: affective (feeling), conative (behavioural) and cognitive (knowledge). The surveys were conducted in Seattle and Kansas City for the United States ($n = 1217$) and in Osaka and Tokyo for Japan ($n = 1149$). The dependent variables are behavioural attitudes measured by categorical responses to the question, 'How do you think your household's consumption of the following foods will change in the future?' The explanatory variables are cognitive and affective attitudes about meat safety, processing food safety, production food safety and regulation of food safety. The affective attitudes include consumer meat preferences and household demographics. An ordered logit model was used for estimation. In general, consumer preferences are important in explaining expected meat consumption. Expected increases in US chicken and fish consumption are driven by concern over the safety of pork. Future Japanese fish consumers feel that fish has a relative safety advantage over beef. Japanese consumers who expect to increase beef and pork purchase also believe that fish is a safe product. *The role of government in ensuring a safe food supply was not significant in any of the models.*

The fifth paper examined the role of Guanxi in doing business in China. Guanxi is a type of social relationship, linking two individuals to enable a social interaction and exchange. Guanxi is egocentric; it is situation-specific and there is no membership or beginning or ending date. Guanxi is different from the social networking in Western society. Social interaction in the West is based on equality, freedom and social interests, while social interaction in China is limited by the hierarchical social structure. In order to do business successfully in China, Guanxi must be built and maintained. Three strategies are suggested: (1) defining what resources one has that can be used to attract others, (2) cultivating personal relationships, and (3) developing mutual trust. All of these strategies must be used with a knowledge of Chinese culture and social interaction.

The last paper presented an overall model for understanding consumers in various societies. The model illustrates factors that affect individuals, families and larger social units in various cultures. Three major environments affect any organizational unit: the macro, the intermediate and the micro. The macro consists of the cultural, the political and the economic environments. Individuals are acted on by these external forces and react to them. In the cultural environment, people learn appropriate behaviour and general attitudinal patterns. The political system makes demands on and regulates individuals, but also benefits them. The economic system determines what and how much will be produced, and how, when and where goods and services will be exchanged. The intermediate environment is a network that links individuals and their families to the elements of the macro environment. One's goals and behaviour are affected by the elements within this environment: roles, resources, needs, values and motivation. The micro environment stems from the intermediate environment. It includes interrelated linking systems that form behaviour boundaries for individuals or social units. It includes structure, decision making and communication. The use of this model can provide an effective base for working with parties involved in international marketing. It can help in reconciling needs and welfare of importing countries with the profits of exporters. It can help delineate marketing strategies that are universal from those that are regional and/or country-specific.

The overall contribution of this symposium was to provide a broader perspective on consumer demand than is evident in the work done by much of the economics profession. Some of the contributions of other disciplines such as social psychology and sociology were elaborated.

GROUP 9

IMPROVING FOOD SECURITY THROUGH HOUSEHOLD,
SCHOOL AND COMMUNITY GARDENING

ORGANIZER   ROBIN MARSH (USA)

RAPPORTEUR   ANGELA MOSKOW (USA)

Introduction

The panel presented evidence on the costs and benefits of gardening from case
studies of community entrepreneurial gardening projects in the United States
and home and community gardens in developing countries. A key issue discussed was the financial viability and sustainability of garden projects, as
compared with other types of community development initiatives; and the
appropriate role of subsidies in supporting garden projects.

The panel addressed the role of gardens in achieving food security goals and
touched on criteria for designing sustainable garden projects and programmes,
given a variety of objectives (nutrition, income generation, employment, education, empowerment of women).

Laura Lawson, Berkeley Youth Alternatives (BYA)
BYA works with at-risk youth and their families running a landscape crew and
the Garden Patch Program. The landscaping work provides employment and
on-the-job training for at-risk youth. The Garden Patch Program, started in
1993, includes a children's garden, a demonstration garden, an outdoor class-
room, a compost area, an entrepreneurial youth garden and a tree-planting
project. Young people who are successful on the landscaping crew have the
opportunity to work in the Garden Patch Program to enhance their gardening
and leadership skills.

Elizabeth Tan, San Francisco League of Urban Gardeners (SLUG)
Slug employs at-risk youth and young adult interns in a number of community
greening and beautification projects on public lands. Additionally, SLUG interns participate in a youth leadership programme on environmental justice
issues, create lead-safe gardens, and produce and market Urban Herbals, a line
of vinegars and jams made with garden products.

Gail Feenstra, Sustainable Agriculture Research and Education Program (SAREP), University of California, Davis (UC Davis)
Feenstra presented the preliminary results from a nationwide study, conducted in 1996 and 1997 by SAREP, to assess the economic development potential of 28 entrepreneurial community gardens. Gardens were described as entrepreneurial if gardeners sold some of their produce or if the garden employed community residents. The study quantifies the costs and benefits of entrepreneurial garden projects that have pursued economic development strategies, and describes the conditions under which they thrive and fail. Most programmes included in the study were not able to cover all of their costs through the product sales. Nonetheless, they generated significant social and economic benefits for their communities.

Preliminary findings indicate that the most successful gardens have built continuing alliances with local businesses and community organizations. The more stable projects also developed business plans, devoted resources to developing a market plan and focused on high-value crops.

Robin Marsh, United Nations Food and Agriculture Organizations (FAO), Rural Development Division, Rome, Italy
Marsh presented findings from 'Household Gardening and Food Security: A Critical Review of the Literature', a paper prepared for the FAO in 1996. Marsh identified the following food security benefits of home gardening: (1) production of fresh, diverse foods seasonally or year-round; (2) production of nutrient-rich foods otherwise not consumed, or consumed in smaller quantities; (3) income earned from garden sales and/or savings on purchased foods increase cash available for buying staple foods for the family; (4) garden production may become the dominant food source in times of failed harvest or off-farm unemployment; and (5) gardening provides an opportunity for continuing 'hands-on' nutrition education. Additionally, gardening is typically a woman's activity. Gardening enhances women's control over food production and sales, and thus increases the likelihood that household nutrition will improve.

The following guidelines are important in gardens designed to meet food security goals: foremost is building on traditional gardening practices and varieties; work in areas with adequate access to water and family labour for year-round gardening; begin with community organization and nutrition education; involve and train local people to be promoters; be flexible with respect to choice of species and cropping patterns, encouraging diversity and cultivation of indigenous varieties; encourage reliance on local materials for soil and pest management as well as household/community seed production; minimize 'give aways'; and conduct regular monitoring for feedbacks and fine-tuning of project activities.

Angela Moskow, International Agricultural Development Graduate Group, UC Davis
Moskow reported on her master's thesis research conducted in Havana, Cuba, in 1995. Urban agriculture has been promoted in Havana since 1991 as a means of addressing the acute food scarcity problems which developed when

Soviet aid and trade were drastically curtailed. An important component of the government's programme is self-provision gardens, which are cultivated either on private land or on state land which the gardeners are able to use at no cost. It is estimated that Havana now has over 26 000 self-provision gardens.

Moskow determined that the quantity and quality of the food available to households was significantly incremented through garden production of plant and animal products. Furthermore, the gardens had a profound impact on household budgets, through the reduction in weekly food bills and money earned from sales of garden products, with average savings from the garden representing an impressive 40 per cent of the average household income. The study also identified five community benefits: greater food supply, food contributions to community facilities (hospitals, retirement homes), neighbourhood beautification, improved safety and enhanced urban ecology.

Desmond Jolly, Small Farm Center Director, UC Davis
In his paper, 'The Dialectics of Urban Agriculture in the Context of Hunger and Food Access Constraints,' Jolly argued that we need to address aggregate food availability and access for the poor, and the structural issues which bring about food insecurity. Gardening cannot substitute for deficiencies in earning power or the market. Urban agriculture, for the poor, is a defensive option and a 'second-best' policy. And we need to further concern ourselves with whether the role of urban agriculture and local food systems in overall food access matrices can be politically manipulated to mask a net decline in food access brought about by changes in public policies.

Discussion

Subsidy of garden projects   Gardening projects, especially entrepreneurial gardens, enable community development and training in a wide range of skills. However, it may not be feasible for market gardens to achieve social goals without consistent and sufficient external support. The evidence suggests that business and market planning are important variables in enhancing market garden economic sustainability. More research is needed to quantify the social contributions and costs associated with market gardens. In the developing country context, often only a small amount of subsidy is necessary to support garden programmes, primarily for initial technical assistance, and gardening offers clear benefits for resource-poor urban and rural families.

Food   Gardening is not a panacea for food insecurity, which stems from such factors as landlessness, underemployment, poverty and discriminating policies. However, gardening can be an integral part of a more defined food security strategy at the household, community and national policy levels. The potential is greatest in poor countries. The data from Central America and Asia show that vegetable gardening is strongly correlated with higher household consumption of vegetables, especially among young children who are most vulnerable to malnutrition.

The role of institutional catalyst In gardening projects, both in the United States and in developing countries, there seems to be a need for a strong institutional presence and committed leaders who can rally the community around the gardening efforts. Further, if a project is designed with consideration of the local context, and with substantive community input, its potential for success is greatest. The challenge for the support institution is to successfully transfer responsibility for garden management to the community.

The most successful garden projects rely primarily on local low-cost inputs, with consistent support confined to technical assistance and community capacity building. The utilization of local inputs reduces the dependency created through reliance on give-aways. A city government's stance on using vacant lands for gardening (positive or negative) can also strongly influence (enable or constrain) the potential success of a gardening programme project.

Conclusion

Gardening programmes can meet a number of social and food security needs. It is important, however, to be cognizant of the structural issues which bring about food insecurity when evaluating the benefits and costs of investing in garden projects; and to be realistic about the expected outcomes of gardening projects. Furthermore, the development of garden projects should include input from the target communities, a community capacity building component, technical transfer, business planning (when appropriate), project evaluation and continuing support for governments and private donors.

GROUP 10

SESSIONS ON SUSTAINABLE NUTRITIONAL SECURITY
FOR SUB-SAHARAN WOMEN SUBSISTENCE FARMERS

**ORGANIZERS   SYLVIA LANE (USA),
ELISABETH SADOULET (USA)**

**RAPPORTEURS   AGNES R. QUISUMBING (USA),
CHRISTINA GLADWIN (USA), ANNE THOMSON (UK)**

The three sessions focused on different aspects of the general topic. The first
session focused on women's roles as agricultural producers and income earn-
ers. Lawrence Haddad reviewed empirical studies which show that income
controlled by women has a larger impact than men's income on household
food security, child health, nutrition and education. However, Christina Gladwin
and Anne Thomson argued that attempts to increase returns to women's resources are constrained by women's roles as food provisioners and preferences
for growing subsistence crops. Since income diversification is only realizable
in the long run, fertilizer safety nets provided for poor women and expanded
efforts to increase women's access to farm and non-farm markets may be more
feasible short- and medium-term policy measures.

Agnes Quisumbing reviewed empirical evidence that lower adoption rates of
new technologies among female farmers may be due to lower levels of education and landholding sizes rather than to gender itself. However, since women
farmers are more likely to copy from other female adopters, female extension
agents and contact farmers may be more effective in reaching women. Asymmetric rights and responsibilities within the household may also reduce women's
incentives to adopt new technologies.

Michael Kevane presented the work of Tara Vishwanath and her colleagues,
who investigated whether women's weaker land rights were related to lower
productivity on women's plots in Burkina-Faso. Econometric analysis shows
that gender differentials in output and manure use cannot be explained by
differences in distance, intensity of prior land use, or inter-household insecurity. However, women in societies with higher divorce probabilities and women
with lower status within the household have less productive plots. This suggests that differences in status and bargaining power within the household may
have productivity effects.

Sara Tisch discussed the positive effects of a Winrock project involving
150 000 farmers in four countries, with 60 participating NGOs. While participatory approaches were slow to implement, they are responsible for the high

acceptability of the project among farmers and their high initial adoption of new rice technologies. However, the high initial adoption rates dropped after import liberalization led to the flood of cheaper Asian rice; farmers then moved into other crops.

Why was the Winrock project successful? While there was no specific gender focus, and project staff were mostly men, the emphasis on subsistence food crops meant that it was, in effect, aimed at women farmers. Subsequent discussion emphasized the need for anthropological work to inform economic analysis and project design. The discussion also highlighted the need to understand both men's and women's roles in African farming systems, given the diversity of cultures and agroecological conditions.

The second session revolved around nutrition and food programmes. Barbara Schneeman emphasized the need for food-based approaches to reducing malnutrition. Focusing on foods, not just nutrients, such recommendations recognize the complexity of situations in which foods are grown, prepared and consumed. Pre-harvest approaches include varietal selection, breeding and biotechnology, while post-harvest approaches consist of storage and handling, processing, fortification, dietary and lifestyle factors. Improving nutritional adequacy requires input from plant scientists, nutritionists and social scientists.

Charlotte Neumann's presentation dwelt on the nutritional status of rural African women. Lack of access to food, due to low agricultural production and vulnerability to weather risk, is a root cause of protein-energy malnutrition. Malnutrition is also exacerbated by heavy energy expenditures, high fertility, closely spaced pregnancies and infectious diseases. Reduced food intake during pregnancy leads to low birth-weight children, who face greater health risks in their childhood and adult life. Micronutrient deficiencies are also prevalent and may be linked with cultural factors which are biased against women.

Roberta van Haefton discussed US food programmes in Ethiopia, which emphasize supply-side solutions to chronic and transitory food insecurity. The short-term focus of the government is getting food to those who are in need through a grain reserve and food for work programmes. The medium-term goal to reduce the national food gap is being pursued through the promotion of improved seeds and fertilizer, as well as the liberalization of agricultural markets. Livestock income has a higher impact on women's nutritional status, but the link between agricultural production and child malnutrition is weak. Malnutrition is associated with delayed introduction of complementary feeding, morbidity and the absence of water and sanitation facilities.

The discussion focused on the need for a multisectoral approach to reducing malnutrition in sub-Saharan Africa. The expansion of the problem of food security to include nutritional security would not only improve cross-sectoral linkages but would also support food-based approaches. The discussion also highlighted the importance of livestock as a source of income for women as well as animal protein.

Two papers were presented at the third session panel. Barbara McNelly presented the results of an evaluation of Freedom from Hunger's 'Credit with Education Strategy for Improving Nutrition Security' in Ghana, based on its effect on the nutritional status of women, women's economic capacity, health behaviour and women's status. Kristy Cook presented a paper, written with George Gardiner, on USAID's approaches to nutrition security for African women farmers. This paper discussed the availability of evidence of the impact of USAID's programmes on women, including income changes for male- and female-headed households and women's participation in these programmes. The authors presented the goals and objectives of USAID's programming, noting that a direct focus on rural women's nutritional status would change programme design.

There was considerable discussion of the Freedom from Hunger programme. The supportiveness of the woman's household could contribute to the wide range of observed returns to the credit component. Exploring the possible synergism between the credit component and the education component, as well as their independent effects, was suggested. While there is tension between taking a 'cookie cutter' approach and tailoring programmes to ease specific constraints in particular villages, Freedom From Hunger is constrained to develop programmes which are potentially replicable on a large scale.

While the progress of USAID's Women in Development efforts has been slow, it is heartening to note that indicators on women are now being used in project planning. However, the separation of the AID programme into separate sub-sectors makes progress difficult. A number of contributors pointed out the difficulty of integrating different elements such as nutrition, women and agriculture into one programme, given organizational constraints, exacerbated by recent downsizing in AID.

The session emphasized that farming is only one of the activities that rural women undertake. Programmes should, therefore, be designed and evaluated in terms of how they affect both men and women and the dynamics between them.

GROUP 11

WHAT IS THE POTENTIAL FOR SUSTAINABLE INTENSIFICATION OF FRAGILE LANDS? EMPIRICAL EVIDENCE AND POLICY IMPLICATIONS

ORGANIZERS   SARA SCHERR (USA), JOHN PENDER (USA)

RAPPORTEURS   SARA SCHERR (USA), JOHN PENDER (USA)

In recent decades, there have been major increases in rural population and production in developing countries in 'fragile' areas prone to rapid degradation upon disturbance of the vegetative cover. Rural poverty is increasingly concentrated in such areas. This mini-symposium discussed the results of recent empirical studies in fragile environments, addressing three key questions: (1) to what extent did land use intensification takes place over the study period, and to what extent was it associated with land degradation or improvement; (2) what key factors explain observed patterns of resource degradation or improvement; and (3) what are the main implications for agricultural, natural resource and development policy in the fragile lands?

John Sanders of Purdue University presented findings from research with J. Vitale, B. Shapiro and O. Coulibaly in Mali on the role of fertilizer in dryland intensification. He contrasted the Sudanian zones, which is more subsistence-oriented and faces serious challenges of intensification and nutrient depletion, and the Sudano-Guinean zone, where cash crop intensification is leading to organic matter depletion.

Tom Reardon of Michigan State University presented evidence on the determinants of sustainable intensification of agriculture on hillsides in Rwanda, Ethiopia and Tanzania, based on farm survey results from D. Clay, B. Gebremedhin, Z. Semgalawe, S. Swinton and F. Byiringiro.

Stefano Pagiola of the World Bank presented evidence from a nationwide cross-sectional survey with FUSADES of farmer perceptions of erosion and use of soil-conserving practices in El Salvador.

Sara Scherr of IFPRI presented preliminary findings from a survey of 48 communities in the hillsides of Central Honduras, undertaken with J. Pender, O. Neidecker-Gonzales, G. Duron and C. Duarte.

John Pender of IFPRI presented results from a community case study representing the vegetable intensification pathway in the Central Hillside Region.

Abelardo Rodriguez of ICARDA presented a new research project with IRA Medanine in Tunisia and with WRRI in Pakistan on management of flood-prone watersheds.

Bustanul Arifiin of the University of Lampung, Indonesia, presented a regional and national scale analysis of land degradation in upland Indonesia between 1980 and 1991.

Doyle Baker of IITA summarized village survey research on patterns of intensification in the forest margins of Nigeria and Cameroon.

The general discussion raised several key issues.

(1) The dynamics of land degradation and improvement are complex, often occurring simultaneously in different spaces. Little land abandonment was reported for some high-intensity areas in Kenya and El Salvador. In Ethiopia, abandonment was more common, but typically land was brought back into production. The capacity for land recovery has been underestimated. The importance of soil erosion has been overestimated; soil nutrient depletion, compaction, organic matter loss, loss of vegetation and water constraints are usually more important causes of productivity and ecological loss.

(2) Farmers rarely pursue unsustainable pathways from failure to recognize degradation processes. Some farmers are simply too poor to invest or face binding capital or labour constraints. In many situations, land degradation is better thought of as a problem of poverty (reducing the value of the principal assets of the poor) rather than as a threat to agricultural supply. Under other conditions, incentives are insufficient. Research found that farmers did not intensify in Senegal until extensive technologies became unprofitable or in Rwanda until the alternative was abandonment. Opportunity costs of labour or capital may be higher than even well-performing conservation investments. Land-improving practices are more common for commercial, higher-value crops. Evidence on the importance of the farmers' time horizon is mixed.

(3) Policies should focus more on raising the value of farmers' production to encourage land improvement in areas where land use intensity is rising rapidly. Examples are contract farming, government provision of infrastructure, and market institutions to encourage commercialization, including new products. Extension programmes should promote production and conservation jointly, and concentrate on areas where land degradation is both documented and perceived by farmers as a challenge. Factor and product market development influence capacity to mobilize resources for land improvement.

Future research efforts should focus on the following:

● evaluation of development and conservation programmes, which have more impact on land management than most policy instruments;
● understanding how communities manage their local watershed, beyond the adoption of specific farm practices;
● understanding the actual limiting factors for land quality in different environments;
● monitoring soil nutrient changes over time at household and plot levels, with sampling across farm and microwatershed niches;

- documenting different pathways of development over time, for rural communities with different conditions, markets and institutions, and their association with land management practices and land quality outcomes;
- understanding the investment function, how conservation capital accumulates and in what sequence investments are made;
- cross-country research to capture effects of macroeconomic and other national policy variables on land management;
- assessing the 'building blocks' of sustainability, that is, what leads to increased resource use efficiency and reduced losses;
- potentials for rural non-farm opportunities to reduce land degradation pressures;
- documenting patterns and extent of land abandonment, recovery and reuse in intensively managed systems.

Methodology issues were raised. Participants emphasized the need to study the dynamics of land management processes over time, rather than depend only upon cross-sectional surveys. The definition of development pathways needs further resolution. There are measurement issues for land degradation and improvement. Farmers' own assessment of current, past and future land quality can be used in research. Multi-scale methods were used in all of the research presented. Researchers need to concern themselves more with issues of scale; what appears to be degradation on one scale may be neutral or positive on a larger scale. Village surveys offer a promising tool for analysis of intensification and degradation patterns which permit subsequent sampling for more in-depth analysis of priority issues.

GROUP 12

SPATIAL ECONOMIC MODELS OF LAND USE:
TECHNIQUES FOR THE QUANTITATIVE ASSESSMENT OF LAND USE
DETERMINANTS AND ENVIRONMENTAL CONSEQUENCES

**ORGANIZERS   GERALD NELSON (USA),
KENNETH CHOMITZ (USA)**

**RAPPORTEURS   GERALD NELSON (USA),
KENNETH CHOMITZ (USA)**

Scope and objectives of the symposium

For many years, quantitative economic analyses of the natural resource and environmental consequences of land use were hindered by lack of data. Since 1994, new data sets and new technologies to manipulate them have opened up new avenues for research. New data sets include land use data derived from satellite images for much of the surface of the earth and a wide variety of geographic information such as elevation, soil type, rainfall, locations of infrastructure such as roads, cities and ports. All of this newly available information is in digital form and amenable to manipulation with geographic information systems software. The use of these large data sets (80 megabytes is a typical file size) has become increasingly feasible as desktop computer capacity continues to double every 18 months. At the same time, land use models to exploit these data sets have been developed. Challenges include spatial autocorrelation, manipulating large files and differences in data availability (large data sets on geophysical parameters, small data sets on socioeconomic information).

This mini-symposium brought together leading researchers in this field and provided conference participants with the opportunity to see the breadth of research in this area. The following list provides titles, abstracts of presentations, where provided by the presenters, and contact information.

Roads, land, markets and deforestation: a spatial model of land use in Belize

Rural roads promote economic development, but they also facilitate deforestation. To explore this trade-off, this paper develops a spatially explicit model of land use and estimates probabilities of alternative land uses as a function of land characteristics and distance to market using a multinominal logit specification of this model. Controls are incorporated for the endogeneity of road placement.

The model is applied to data for southern Belize, an area experiencing rapid expansion of both subsistence and commercial agriculture, using geographic information system (GIS) techniques to select sample points at one kilometre intervals. Market access, land quality and tenure status affect the probability of land being agricultural, and the likelihood of its being used commercially or for subsistence. The results suggest that road building in areas with agriculturally poor soils and low population densities may be a 'lose–lose' proportion, causing habitat fragmentation and providing low economic returns. Contact: Kenneth Chomitz, kchomitz@worldbank.org.

Land use change in Jambi, Indonesia

Policy question: where is smallholder encroachment on logged-over forest most likely to be a problem? This spatial econometric analysis of land use change focuses on the peneplain and piedmont agroecological zones of Jambi province in Central Sumatra. A multivariate econometric model with a binary dependent variable (a probit) was used to control for site-specific biophysical features (fixed effects) and to estimate the effect of distance to rivers and main (asphalted) roads on the probability that logged forest would be converted to rubber agroforests and other land uses by smallholders.

The preliminary results indicate that there was substantial smallholder encroachment on logged natural forests in Jambi between the early 1980s and the early 1990s. The prototype model correctly predicts about 85 per cent of conversion of logged forests by smallholders and about 78 per cent of the cases where logged forest was not yet converted. Site-specific biophysical features are highly significant, indicating that smallholders are selective in their choices of sites for conversion. Smallholder conversion of logged forest is significantly more likely within 10km of main roads, which is consistent with a process driven by market opportunities for profitable tree crops. Contact: Tom Tomich, t.tomich@cgnet.com.

Spatial patterns of deforestation in Cameroon and Zaire

To help elucidate the causes and correlates of deforestation in tropical Africa, this paper undertakes an exploratory spatial analysis of land cover in Cameroon and Zaire. One-kilometre resolution data on land cover is merged in a geographic information system with spatial data on soils, climate, roads and rivers. A data set is generated by taking sample points at 5 km intervals within the area presumed originally to have been covered by rainforest. Using a probit model, the probability that a sample point has non-forest cover (that is, a mosaic of cultivation, secondary growth and forest, or savanna) is related to road and river accessibility, distance to major markets, soil characteristics and local climate. Controlling for agroclimatic conditions, non-forest cover is closely linked to transport access; this relationship is sharper in Cameroon than in Zaire. This may reflect the greater influence of market processes in Cameroon. In Zaire, there is an especially clear link between the presence of agriculturally suitable soils and the absence of forest cover, suggesting an important link between agriculture and deforestation. Contact: Nlandu Mamingi, n.maming@uwichill.edu.bb.

Using GIS to model rural to urban land conversion: a case study in the Patuxent Watershed, MD

Change in land use patterns in many US regions is characterized by the expansion of a highly fragmented pattern of low-density development into rural areas. The primary features of this phenomenon, sometimes referred to as 'ex-urban sprawl,' are its fragmentation and relative remoteness from urban centres.

Traditional economic models, based on the assumption that employment is located in one or several urban centres, are insufficient in explaining these emerging patterns. Using land use and market transactions data at a highly disaggregated level from a central Maryland region, we estimate a simple alternative model of land use conversion. Results show that, in addition to economic factors, such as opportunity costs and costs of conversion, several landscape pattern and government policy variables are important determinants of land use change. Contact: Elena Irwin, eirwin@arec.umd.edu.

Do roads cause deforestation? Using satellite images in econometric analysis of land use

This presentation was based on a paper of the same title published in the *American Journal of Agricultural Economics*, February 1997. The paper demonstrates how satellite images and other geographic data can be used to predict land use. A cross-section model of land use is estimated with data for a region in Central Mexico. Parameters from the model are used to examine the effects of reduced human activity. If variables that proxy human influence are changed to reflect reduced impact, 'forest' area increases and 'irrigated crop' area is reduced. Additional information on using satellite data in land use models is available at http://www.uiuc.edu/ph/www/g-nelson. Contact: Gerald Nelson, g-nelson@uiuc.edu.

Causes and effects of agricultural intensification: evidence from a case study in Central Honduras

This study explores the dynamics, determinants and implications of agricultural intensification in a study community in Central Honduras using historical recall data collected at the plot, household and community level and secondary data on prices. The community represents a pattern of vegetable crop adoption and intensification common in areas close to urban markets in Central America. Over the past 20 years, production of perishable vegetable crops has grown substantially, as has use of irrigation and chemical inputs, while traditional production of maize and beans has declined somewhat. Perceived problems of soil erosion have increased, while soil fertility is perceived to have stayed relatively constant. Based on econometric analysis of the historical data, we find that the main factors responsible for expanded horticultural production were road improvements and technical assistance. Population growth did not have a significant effect on the adoption of vegetables, irrigation or chemical inputs, although it was associated with soil erosion and lower soil fertility. Changes in national market prices did not have a measurable impact on adoption of vegetables but did affect irrigation, input use and land degradation.

The empirical findings suggest that horticultural intensification is a mixed blessing for natural resource conditions. It helped to reduce pressure to cultivate marginal lands, but the increase in continuous cropping and use of irrigation appears to have increased soil erosion problems, and use of agricultural chemicals is causing concerns about water contamination downstream. The benefits for farm incomes are a stronger rationale to promote horticultural intensification, and the results suggest the importance of infrastructure development, technical assistance and education to achieve these benefits. Improvements in market prices resulting from structural adjustment policies were not sufficient to bring this about. We believe this study demonstrates the feasibility and utility of using historical recall data to address questions about the causes and effects of agricultural intensification, although some indicators (such as changes in soil fertility) were difficult to collect historically. Contact: John Pender, j-pender@cgnet.com.

Interdisciplinary systems-based analysis for quantitative regional land use evaluation: an application for the Atlantic Zone of Costa Rica

The main thrust of the programme is the development of a methodology for analysis and evaluation of alternative scenarios for profitable and sustainable land use at the farm, (sub-)regional and possibly national level. The farm level refers to a farm household and its resources. Contact: Hans G.P. Jansen, hjansen@sol.racsa.cor.cr.

GROUP 13

FINANCE AND FACTOR MARKET
DEVELOPMENT FOR THE RURAL POOR

ORGANIZER   RICHARD L. MEYER (USA)

**RAPPORTEURS   GERHARD COETZEE (SOUTH AFRICA),
GABRIEL FUENTES (USA), DOUGLAS GRAHAM (USA)**

This mini-symposium consisted of three sessions with two papers in each. The first session, chaired by Hans Binswanger, World Bank, with Gerhard Coetzee, Development Bank of Southern Africa as rapporteur, focused on land markets and financial services. Mark Darroch and Michael Lyne of the University of Natal-Pietermaritzburg, South Africa, explored 'Broadening Access to Land Markets: Financing Emerging Farmers in South Africa'. They sampled voluntary land sales made to disadvantaged people in Kwa Zulu Natal. Only 0.09 percent of the farmland available for redistribution from commercial farmers was transferred to disadvantaged people in 1995 owing to limitations on subdividing farmland and liquidity problems. Recently, mortgage loans with graduated repayment schedules eased this problem, but they are not widely available and their impact is constrained by restrictions on farmland subdivision in the Agricultural Land Act. In the discussion, a consensus emerged that this act must be changed to facilitate broader access to land for disadvantaged farmers.

The second paper, 'Level Playing Fields and Laissez Faire: Post Liberal Development Strategy in Inegalitarian Agrarian Economies', by Michael Carter and Bradford Barham, University of Wisconsin, explored the microdynamics of the export booms of Guatemala, Paraguay and Chile. These booms led to exclusive rather than inclusive growth, emphasizing that getting prices right and property rights well defined is not enough. Small farmers were unable to take advantage of the booms because they are asset poor and rationed out of credit markets. The authors argued that highly focused policy and institutional changes are required to reduce these patterns of inequalitarian growth. In the discussion, some participants argued that focusing only on small farmer land access to fruit farms in Chile is misleading because workers on these farms enjoy increasing real wages and are better off than the small farmers. Others argued that it is necessary also to analyse various paths in the modernization adjustment process and the degree of welfare gains and losses experienced by selected population groups.

The second session, chaired by Paulo Cidade de Araujo, University of São Paulo, Brazil, with Gabriel Fuentes, Loyola Marymount University, California, as rapporteur, explored technological innovations for increasing access by the rural poor to financial services. Jonathan Conning, Williams College, reported on 'Joint Liability Loans and Innovative Private Sector Financial Technologies in Chile'. He compared the monitoring and transaction costs of joint liability loan contracts with the contracts of individual borrower–lenders and informal money-lenders who borrow to on-lend to other individual borrowers. He showed how joint liability can solve the problem derived from combining the 'monitored lending' and multi-task, principal–multi-agent problem with moral hazard and limited liability. The approach clarifies the conditions when a joint-liability contract will be preferred by borrowers to other contracts. It was agreed in the discussion that joint-liability contracts would be preferred by borrowers when the group monitoring technology offered a decided advantage over the relatively uninformed financial intermediary's monitoring technology. The case study of a Chilean sugar beet firm revealed that early in its history the firm offered joint-liability loans but later it gained monitoring experience and replaced them with other contractual forms. The discussion suggested that the study needed a longer historical record to determine how and when the contracts changed.

Claudio Gonzalez-Vega, Ohio State University, summarized best practice microfinance lending technologies and evaluated their prospects for use in lending to agricultural clienteles. These technologies, short-term loans, frequent repayment schedules, group lending, and graduated loan sizes and term maturities, do not lend themselves to agriculture because there is greater heterogeneity among farmers than among rural and urban non-farm micro entrepreneurs so that screening is more costly. Also there is a greater impact of exogenous events (bad weather, pests and so on) on farmer borrowers, so identifying moral hazard behaviour and monitoring are more expensive. Covariant income losses should also be larger, while the greater spatial dispersion of farmers increases screening and monitoring costs for lenders. The discussion highlighted the need for microfinance programmes serving agriculture to address overall household activities, not just farming; to rely on household income diversification strategies including non-farm and off-farm activities; and to incorporate more flexible repayment schedules. Still, it is likely that any microfinance programme incorporating a sizeable agricultural clientele base will face greater risks and higher costs than urban programmes.

The final session, chaired by Alberto Valdéz, World Bank, with Douglas Graham, Ohio State University, as rapporteur, explored the issue of poverty as a determinant of access to finance. Julie Stanton, Arizona State University, reported on wealth levels and access to finance among farmers in four provinces in Mexico. As expected, wealthier borrowers were heavily associated with private bank finance, but subsidized rate programmes which were specifically aimed to reach low-income, first-time borrowers with modest collateral were also exploited by all wealth levels. These two sources of finance, Banrural and Solidaridad, surprisingly recorded a significant number of borrowers from the two highest wealth quintiles. This finding highlighted the capability of wealthier rent-seeking constituencies to gain access to funding designed for poorer borrowers.

The second paper, by Richard Meyer *et al.*, Ohio State University, documented the degree to which five microfinance organizations in Bolivia reached clients at or below the poverty line. New data were presented to show how far down the basic needs poverty indicator the new micro lending technologies can reach. The evidence underlined the following: few urban poor are reached by these technologies; these organizations reach clienteles clustered just above or just below the poverty line; and group lending programmes tend to reach a slightly poorer clientele than do those making individual loans. The discussion noted that the poorest of the poor cannot be successfully reached by microfinance programmes, so other policy instruments must be utilized to alleviate poverty.

GROUP 14

ROLE OF NON-FARM ACTIVITIES

ORGANIZER   HARBINDERJIT SINGH DILLON (INDONESIA)

RAPPORTEUR   BUSTANUL ARIFIN (INDONESIA)

In introducing the topic, the organizer noted that there were currently two schools of thought on the role of rural non-farm activities (RNFA) in agricultural development. The first one holds that the rapid change and the rise in non-farm employment during the 'green revolution' was due to the failure of the agricultural sector in channelling surplus, unbridled population growth and relatively constant real agricultural wages. This deterioration trajectory is often associated with the juxtaposition of high agrarian population growth and densities, stagnant agricultural productivity growth, skewed distribution of access to land and significant numbers of rural households, nevertheless dependent on agriculture. The other school interprets the same phenomena as an indicator of successful structural transformation. The development trajectory is characterized by a relatively egalitarian distribution of land and a low incidence of rural households without access to land but dependent on agricultural production for their livelihood. These two sharply divergent views provided the stage for a lively discussion on the role of technological change, investment in rural infrastructure and enhanced agricultural productivity in understanding the dynamics of RNFA. Presenters were Jung-Sup Choi, Korea Rural Economic Institute, Korea; Mangara Tambunan, Bogor Agricultural University; Ryohei Kada, Kyoto University, Japan.

The major issues surrounding the role of RNFA in agricultural development include promotion of agroindustry, manufacture of farm equipment and machinery, small-scale industries ranging from processing of farm produce to full-fledged textile plants, and agrotourism. The transformation is driven not only by the abundant supply of labour, seasonality and urbanization, but also by the availability and quality of infrastructure. Investment in infrastructure such as rural roads, irrigation systems, communication networks, power, farm-support services, education and health delivery systems has also contributed to the growth in RNFA.

Various forms of rural non-farm activities were highlighted in the course of the discussion. In countries with abundant rural labour, such as Indonesia, Bangladesh and African and Latin American countries, RNFA are often associated with the survival strategies of rural landless labourers. Although RNFA usually involve unskilled rural labourers, this does not necessarily imply a low

level of management capacity and enterpreneurship. The failure of the manufacturing and high-value service sectors to absorb excess labour from agriculture
and the slow growth and low productivity of small and medium enterprises
have all contributed to the growth of RNFA.

Nevertheless, it was felt that the dynamics and the full potentials of RNFA
were not yet fully understood owing to a lack of rigorous research into this
topic in most developing countries. The dearth of studies concentrating on
migrant movement or the flow of resources from rural to urban areas, both
interregional and intersectoral, and those studying consumption and investment in depth was lamented.

Existing statistics indicate that rural income in most developing countries
does not originate solely from within agriculture. During the last decade, a
higher proportion of rural income has been derived from the service sector,
particularly remittances, trading and construction. The issues of non-farm activities in developing countries have moved beyond the labour seasonality
towards the utilization and allocation of rural labour. Farm land has tended to
decrease over time, even in developing countries in the wake of industrialization. Consequently, average farm size has also been declining. However, in the
absence of coherent and comprehensive industrial policies, industries now
appear to be scattered all over the rural landscape. In more advanced countries
such as Korea, Japan, the United States and Northern Europe, RNFA involve
highly skilled farm-based individuals. Furthermore, commercial entities such
as agricultural cooperatives, incorporated farm and non-farm enterprises have
located some of their more labour-intensive core businesses in rural areas; this
is very much evident in Japan and Korea. Japan has also witnessed the rapid
emergence of part-time farming. Low-income part-time farming is usually
associated with aged labourers and small farms, whereas higher-income part-
time farming is related to young individuals with larger farms who have
managed to secure high-paying urban jobs as well.

The role RNFA play is based on the economic rationale underlying household labour allocation strategies. Investment in farm equipment and agriculture
support services also led to progressive rural transformation in most developed
countries. In addition, RNFA have also functioned as risk-spreading strategies,
since full-time farming is inherently more susceptible to shocks. Recent evidence shows that RNFA serve to generate greater stability in rural employment,
as these activities also absorb an amount of disguised unemployment in rural
areas.

Developed countries such as Japan and France have seen strong pressure
from farmers and agricultural cooperatives for continued government support.
However, implementation of the Marrakesh Accord in full should serve to
mitigate such pressure in the near future. One key factor explaining the shape
of RNFA in developed countries is the high income obtained from the industrial and service sectors. In addition, a more transparent and better-defined
industrial development strategy has helped strengthen the role of RNFA in
these countries. Zoning restrictions on conversion of farmland to industrial use
and a very large tax on such conversion has also contributed to the strength of
agricultural and rural sectors, including RNFA, in a number of developed
countries.

The symposium participants felt that RNFA could play a major role in alleviating rural poverty. In this respect, it noted with satisfaction a number of policy reforms in developing countries surrounding the ability of local governments to promote investment in rural areas, to provide quality secondary education for rural youth and to reassess the city-based and capital-intensive nature of their industrialization strategies. Besides the initial investment by the government in infrastructure and other employment-generating activities, the symposium called for larger funding and a more research-focused agenda for the role of RNFA in agricultural development.

GROUP 15

RURAL FINANCIAL INSTITUTIONS FOR AND WITH THE POOR: RELATING ACCESS AND IMPACT TO POLICY DESIGN

**ORGANIZERS   MANFRED ZELLER (USA),
MANOHAR SHARMA (USA)**

**RAPPORTEURS   MANFRED ZELLER (USA),
MANOHAR SHARMA (USA)**

Summary

The objective of the symposium was to discuss policy options in providing rural finance for and with the poor in the light of empirical evidence collected so far on (1) the nature of access of the poor to existing financial institutions and (2) the impact of such institutions on their livelihood and welfare.

Session 1

Chair: Tracey Simbi, Ministry of Agriculture, South Africa. Presenters: Susan Lund (McKinsey Consulting Group), Marcel Fafchamps (Stanford University), Franz Heidhues, Gertrud Schrieder and Belle-Sossoh (University of Hohenheim). Discussant: Anand Swamy (University of Maryland).

Lund and Fafchamps, as well as Heidhues *et al.*, showed how small groups of people can collectively obtain access to credit. Fafchamps and Lund showed how this can be done informally, whereas Heidhues *et al.* analysed more formal group lending schemes. Lund and Fafchamps' study of four villages in the northern Philippines tested for pareto-optimal risk pooling at the village level. They reject this hypothesis but find that risks are shared within smaller networks of relatives and friends. Within these networks, risk sharing takes place through repeated informal transactions based on reciprocity, and mutual insurance takes place through a mix of gifts and no-interest loans. However, they find that more observable shocks such as illnesses are better insured than less observable ones such as unemployment or crop loss.

Heidhues *et al.* compared transaction costs of two group lending schemes and one individual lending scheme in the Cameroon. These costs were analysed at three levels: the financial organization level, the group level and the borrower's level. They found that transaction costs are the lowest in individual lending and highest in group-based lending. However, they caution against misinterpretation of this result, as the client bases in the three programmes are quite different. The higher transaction costs of the group-based programmes may well be the result of the higher cost of screening and monitoring more risky clients as well as other factors.

Session 2

Chair: Monique Cohen (USAID). Presenters: Anjini Kochar (Stanford University), Aliou Diagne (IFPRI). Discussant: Anna Paulson (Northwestern University).

Papers by Diagne and Kochar discussed the impact of access to rural financial services on household income and welfare. Diagne argued that amount borrowed is not a good measure of access to credit as individuals and households often do not borrow to the full extent of their credit limits. Using data on credit limits and credit transactions from Malawi, he showed that this was the case both in the formal and the informal sectors. Using credit limit as a measure of access, Diagne found that formal credit programmes reduce households' dependence on informal credit but, apart from that, have little impact, direct or indirect, on household income, food security and nutritional status of credit programme members. He concluded that access to land and the availability of market infrastructure are the most constraining factors on per capita household income. Returns to credit services, therefore, importantly depend on the access and use of these complementary inputs. Furthermore, return to credit services was low in the two survey years owing to drought.

Kochar used a panel data from Pakistan to examine the effects of income uncertainty and anticipated changes in income and health on the saving patterns of households. She found that ill-health, especially that of young males, is far more likely to contribute to poverty through adverse portfolio shifts than is either anticipated change in income or income uncertainty. This was the case for both intergenerational and nuclear households. She also found that, while intergenerational households are able to increase saving in response to an anticipated reduction in work days due to illness, nuclear households appear unable to do so. Nuclear households, therefore, were more likely to use informal credit to protect consumption from episodes of illness. Given the importance of illness in affecting saving decisions of households, Kochar concluded that improvements in health infrastructure are likely to have a substantial impact not just on improved health but also on income levels.

Session 3

Chair: Mahabub Hossain (International Rice Research Institute). Presenters: Julia Paxton and Carlos Cuevas (World Bank), Jacob Yaron and McDonald Benjamin (World Bank). Discussant: Zhu Ling (Chinese Academy of Social Sciences).

Paxton and Cuevas, as well as Yaron and Benjamin, discussed policy/programme options in rural finance. Paxton and Cuevas compared the performance of village banks and credit unions in a number of countries in Latin America. The two offer different financial products to different target groups: while the village banks concentrate on the very poor, the women, and the uneducated, credit unions have a much more heterogeneous client base consisting of both the poor and the non-poor. In addition, credit unions also provide voluntary microdeposit instruments. The analysis of Paxton and Cuevas indicated that, compared to the credit unions, village banks scored higher on outreach but lower on measures of financial sustainability, suggesting a possible trade-off between outreach and financial sustainability. However, they argued that this may not necessarily be so, since village banking is a relatively newer lending methodology and that experience, innovations and economies of scale will strengthen its financial status in due time.

Yaron and Benjamin reviewed recent international experiences in rural financial development. They suggest that new policies for strengthening rural financial markets aim at improving the macroeconomic environment, removing urban-biased policies and introducing legal and regulatory changes affecting financial transactions. They also stress the need for adopting sound performance criteria based on measures of outreach as well as financial sustainability to evaluate financial institutions. They argued that, with these kinds of measures, not only can financial services be provided to low-income rural clients at lower costs, but they can also be provided in many cases while reducing or even eliminating the need for subsidies.

The session concluded with a joint meeting with the participants of a concurrent mini-symposium on 'Finance Factor Market Development for the Rural Poor', where remarks summing up were made by Manfred Zeller and Douglas Graham (Ohio State University). One overall conclusion was that further research leading to a better understanding of the institutional processes of microfinance would be instrumental in coming up with new methods of financial intermediation that reduce the trade-offs between outreach to the poor and financial sustainability.

GROUP 16

THE MISSING LINK BETWEEN AGRICULTURAL
TECHNOLOGY ADOPTION AND RURAL POVERTY ALLEVIATION

ORGANIZER   GANESH RAUNIYAR (NEW ZEALAND)

RAPPORTEUR   JILL FINDEIS (USA)

Rural poverty remains a persistent problem, particularly in developing countries. While much research has been conducted on the characteristics and
causes of rural poverty as well as on policies to alleviate poverty, one issue that
is not well understood is the role of the new agricultural technologies in
reducing the poverty problem. The four presented papers and discussion by
participants in the mini-symposium focused on the issue of the missing links
between agriculture and poverty alleviation.

The symptoms of rural poverty are clear: a poor living environment, a poor
resource base, unemployment and underemployment of resources including
human resources, and inadequate food production and consumption, among
other problems. The causes of poverty are also well known and include lack of
economic opportunities, low levels of human capital, and social and political
instability. Strategies to alleviate rural poverty have included a variety of
approaches that have met with varying degrees of success. Common programmes include integrated rural development programmes, rural credit, food
for work programmes, programmes to encourage diversification of agricultural
households into off-farm work and microenterprise development, market reforms and development programmes designed using the local participatory
approach.

But do missing links exist that deserve more attention? The four presentations in the mini-symposium focused on possible links that are not recognized
or not well understood. The chairperson and organizer of the mini-symposium,
Ganesh Rauniyar, initially reviewed the symptoms and causes of poverty and
strategies to alleviate poverty. Potential missing links that were identified in
this presentation included gender roles, access to service delivery institutions,
(excessive) emphasis on credit as an instrument without fully recognizing
minimum thresholds for household consumption requirements, lack of technologies suitable for smallholders who often have different resource
endowments, and the role of off-farm income in access to and utilization of
technologies. For agricultural households, barriers to technology adoption on
small farms still exist and limit the extent to which many agricultural households can enhance their incomes through the use of the new agricultural

technologies. One particularly problematic issue emphasized in the Rauniyar presentation is the operation of agricultural credit programmes to enable households to adopt new technologies or develop other income-enhancing enterprises. Agricultural credit programmes are often based on the assumption that credit is used for productive investment. In practice, the population in poverty tends to allocate production loans (at least partially) for consumption and energy needs.

Issues identified by the other papers presenters as missing links included (1) lack of sufficient knowledge regarding the welfare effects of the agricultural technologies on society as a whole, as well as for different sectors or groups, (2) lack of understanding of the direct and indirect impacts on rural labour, and (3) lack of development of markets. While the principal goal of the new agricultural technologies is to improve human welfare, two issues arise. First, the new technologies may serve to improve absolute welfare measures, but increase the relative welfare differences between the higher income groups, more able to adopt and utilize the new technologies, and households in poverty. Second, there may even be absolute declines in welfare, particularly for certain sub-groups of the rural population. Many studies of the new agricultural technologies have focused on adoption decisions and the returns to agricultural research. Suggestions for further research to understand better the welfare impacts of the new technologies include insertion of explicit welfare measures into models of technology adoption, explicit consideration of dynamics, and integration of technological change into multi-market analyses (including financial markets and labour markets).

Furthermore, it was pointed out that the effects of the new agricultural technologies on rural labour markets are generally not well understood. Since households in poverty are typically dependent on wage labour, the indirect effects of agricultural technology adoption on hired farm labour and off-farm (non-agricultural) labour markets are particularly relevant. Additional research is needed on, first, the long-run effects of the agricultural technologies on hired farm labour markets, both for agricultural products enhanced by the technologies (such as rice, maize and wheat) and for secondary crop and non-crop farm enterprises, and second, the long-run effects of the agricultural technologies on local agricultural processing employment and wages.

Finally, the important role of further development of efficient markets in rural areas was emphasized. Without access to markets for different agricultural enterprises, even poor farmers able to use the new technologies are unable to benefit. One aspect of this issue that generated much discussion by the mini-symposium participants was whether or not access to efficient markets was a necessary and sufficient condition for alleviating poverty among poor farm households.

The discussion during and following the presentations focused on the missing links identified by the presenters as well as on other possible missing links identified by the mini-symposium participants. The mini-symposium concluded with plans to establish a network to examine further the technology–poverty issue.

GROUP 17

FOOD QUALITY REGULATION IN INTERNATIONAL MARKETS

ORGANIZERS   JULIE A. CASWELL (USA),
TANYA ROBERTS (USA)

RAPPORTEUR   JULIE A. CASWELL (USA)

The purpose of this session was to compare and discuss the role economic analysis plays in the design of food quality regulation, with an emphasis on regulation of food safety and food labelling. We also focused on the impact of this regulation on international trade in food products. We divided our discussion into the subject areas of (1) food safety regulation in international meat product trade, and (2) food standards, certification and labelling issues. Governments frequently use a combination of input, process and product performance standards to ensure the safety of meat and other food products. In contrast, certification and labelling programmes are frequently used for food attributes such as nutritional quality, region of production and processing method.

Laurian Unnevehr (University of Illinois) led the discussion on food safety regulation in international meat product trade. She noted that, as incomes rise throughout the world, demand for meat products is growing, and so is international trade in these products. Two kinds of risks from this trade are subject to sanitary regulation. Animal disease risk through trade in live animals or products is one kind of risk that is becoming more important as trade volumes grow. The second kind of risk is from microbial pathogens in meat products that cause food-borne illness. As consumers become more wealthy and more informed about the links between diet and health, they demand a higher level of safety from food products. These trends are converging to make sanitary regulation an issue of growing importance in the trade of meat products. The 1994 GATT agreement provides new guidance regarding sanitary regulations and the application of transparent, science-based border measures. Governments around the world are trying different approaches to regulating food safety in domestic and international trade.

Unnevehr discussed the move towards newer process certification approaches to insuring food safety, such as hazard analysis critical control point (HACCP) systems. In the United States, major regulations such as the recently adopted HACCP rule for meat and poultry must be subjected to benefit/cost analysis. This analysis, and consideration of the economic incentives of new rules, played an important role in the final form of the HACCP rule.

Kenneth Forsythe (USDA/APHIS) then discussed the process that the Animal and Plant Health Inspection Service of USDA is using to make regulatory decisions regarding animals and animal products, particularly quarantine decisions. In setting up a programme that is responsive to WTO requirements, APHIS has shifted from using a blanket approach which categorizes animals or products from specific geographical regions as acceptable for admission to the United States to using a case-by-case approach that weighs the benefits and costs of allowing import of specific animals or products. He noted that the SPS Agreement under the WTO does not specifically say whether or how economic costs must be evaluated in making regulatory decisions.

Takuji Sakurai (Shiga Prefecture Department of Agriculture, Forestry and Fisheries, Japan) discussed the scope and effects of recent outbreaks of food-borne illness in Japan. His presentation indicated that problems with *E. coli* 0157:H7 have been evident for some time in Japan but recent outbreaks of illness have greatly increased concern. The Japanese and local governments are taking a number of actions to improve safety assurance, as well as conducting programmes to inform consumers on safe food-handling practices. The discussion that followed focused on the operation of regulatory systems and the extent to which economic analysis does or does not play a role in policy formulation.

The second area the discussion group focused on was food standards, certification and labelling issues. This approach is frequently used for food quality attributes that are not safety-related. Julie Caswell (University of Massachusetts) introduced the topic area noting that labelling is backed up by standards and certification programmes that define the labelled attributes. Labelling's main roles are to change the information environment for consumers by increasing the amount and type of information they have about products and to influence companies' decisions on which product to offer for sale.

Jean-Christophe Bureau (INRA-Station d'Economie et Sociologie Rurales, France) led the discussion by describing and analysing the use of labels for quality attributes such as place of origin and production method in the European Union. He noted that several labelling schemes coexist, qualifying for particular labels is often complicated and imported products usually may not qualify. The labelling schemes may be becoming too complex for consumers to use effectively, weakening the labels' impact and increasing the importance of brand names. Discussion focused on what role government should play in supporting various labelling schemes whose main impact may be to provide protection to certain production interests, while at the same time, perhaps, protecting traditional foods and production practices. Stephan Marette (INRA-Station d'Economie et Sociologie Rurales, France) discussed the trade impacts of the quality labelling schemes. He thinks their trade impacts are minor because the labels are not exclusive and other sources of information, such as brand names, play important roles in consumers' choices.

Caswell discussed the use of labelling for nutritional quality in the United States. The inclusion of a nutrition information panel has been mandatory for nearly all food products since 1994. In addition, the use of voluntary nutrient and health claims such as 'low fat' and 'reduced sodium' is strictly regulated. The labelling programme has been effective in improving the amount and quality of nutrition information available to consumers. Discussion of standards, certification and labelling programmes focused on the great variety of these programmes across countries; which attributes should be the priority of government-sanctioned programmes; and the impact of labelling on markets for consumer products.

The discussion group identified several contributions economists can make to regulatory decisions for food products: analysis of market imperfections and failures (rationales for regulation); analysis of programme effects on demand and supply; estimation of national-level benefits and costs; an economic overview of risk management strategies; and analysis of the trade impacts of regulatory policy.

GROUP 18

AGRICULTURAL MARKET LIBERALIZATION IN AFRICA

**ORGANIZERS	RAISUDDIN AHMED (USA),
STEVEN BUCCOLA (USA)**

**RAPPORTEUR	STEVEN BUCCOLA (USA)**

In the first session, Steven Buccola discussed progress under way in Malawi to privatize smallholder coffee marketing. He recounted strategies the government-owned Smallholder Coffee Authority has used to resist the government's move to eliminate agricultural parastatals. Strategies include alliances with key ministry personnel, delays in issuing required memoranda and farmer misinformation campaigns. Buccola pointed out that the Coffee Authority's costs have been extremely high relative to the quantity of coffee they have purchased from farmers. The model he proposed to explain these costs is that a marketing board naturally seeks to *maximize* its marketing costs subject to the restriction that net losses do not exceed the limit imposed by the government and donors, and that the quantity supplied by farmers be a function of the prices the marketing board offers. He outlined a set of first-order conditions that can be used to test the model. Raisuddin Ahmed commented that thin markets and natural monopolies are a common problem in Africa, and that the principal solution is to integrate markets by reducing transport and transactions costs.

Glenn Rogers discussed regional markets for illicit payments to public agents along roads in West Africa, using 10 years of data from Niger, Burkina-Faso and Côte d'Ivoire. A model of optimal demands for illicit payments suggests that public agents who ask for these payments do respond to market incentives but sometimes extract the payments excessively, causing the market to collapse. National governments have reduced legal trade taxes to promote exports, but illicit payments have increased, partly offsetting the benefits of market liberalization. This encourages governments to reimpose legal trade taxes. Increased transparency and provision of information, in combination with increased enforcement of regulations, has temporarily reduced illicit payments. However, greater competition in the market for these payments will be required to sustain significant reductions in the payments, enabling more rapid economic growth in West Africa. Eric Crawford recommended further examination regarding who bears the cost of the illicit payments.

On the second day of the mini-symposium, Michael Kevane and Leslie Gray discussed the effects of land tenure security and ethnicity on manure and fertilizer use in Burkina-Faso. They reported on a two-period profit maximization model of manure and fertilizer demand, estimated using cross-sectional data. The strongest determinants of manure and fertilizer demand are the plot's productivity potential, slope and distance from the household. The effects on manure use of the farmer's ethnicity and strength of claim to the plot were weaker than were the distance and slope effects. The first discussant, Jayashree Sil, questioned whether tenure status and ethnicity are the principal issues in manure use and whether the effect of crop mix is not more important. She also criticized the model's assumption of perfect input substitution. The second discussant, Will Masters, suggested that better proxies be used for the household's labour abundance, real wage and implicit consumption discount rate.

Marcel Fafchamps reviewed his thesis that the emergence of markets in a newly liberalized environment depends upon the process whereby a potential trader gathers information about other potential market participants. The main way he does so is to engage in initial exchanges to test a potential partner's reliability. The easier it is to engage in these initial exchanges, the less costly it is to gather the information sought and, thus, the more quickly the market becomes efficient. Fafchamps employs parameters representing screening costs and the proportion of 'competent' to total traders known to a given agent. Among other things, he shows that trades between anonymous individuals – in which neither partner knows anything about the other – are impossible. Facilitating information flows about the traders' histories, therefore, becomes crucial to improving market efficiency. Jayashree Sil commented that the policy implications of these results would be improved by characterizing the magnitude of screening costs relative to the potential gains from trade. Will Masters asked why some markets are full of competent traders while others are not and suggested that we pay attention to the parameter values that lead to such results.

On the third and final day of the mini-symposium, Francesco Goletti (delivering a paper of his with Mylene Kheralla) reviewed the response of input markets to liberalization in five African countries: Malawi, Ghana, Benin, Senegal and Madagascar. His presentation results from an extensive random survey of farmers and input traders. Principal inputs included in the survey were fertilizer, seed and credit; principal farm commodities were maize and rice. Much of the survey concentrated on the intensity of use of these inputs and the reasons farmers and traders give for levels of use. For example, only 10 per cent of Madagascar rice farmers have access to credit; the main reason given for failure to obtain credit is the height of the interest rate and the requirement of forming a cooperative loan association. In the other countries studied, similar reasons were given for failure to obtain credit. Overall, Goletti finds that liberalization has had some success in the cash crop sector but has not been as successful in the food crop sector. In his comment, Buccola pointed out that this result is consistent with the fact that pre-reform regulatory regimes tended to subsidize food crops at the expense of cash crops.

Eric Crawford (in a paper written by Thom Jayne, John Staatz, Michael Weber, Stephen Jones and himself) discussed a reduced-form econometric model of productivity growth rates in seven African countries. Productivity growth was measured by value of crop output per hectare. The explanatory variables were farmer-to-land ratio, rainfall, fertilizer-to-land ratio, a warfare dummy variable in two countries and a reform dummy variable. The authors find that structural reform improved productivity growth in five of the seven countries examined. Much of the improvement has come about because of increased use of fertilizer and because of a reform-induced switch to higher-value crops. In some cases, especially in East and Southern Africa, reform has, however, led to reduced fertilizer use following the removal of fertilizer subsidies. The authors say that a key policy objective now should be for governments to help reduce marketing costs by investing in road and communication infrastructure, further liberalizing the policies of existing marketing boards and improving provisions for contract enforcement. In his comments, Buccola suggested recasting the reduced-form model as a profit-function model in which the dependent variables are rainfall, the reform dummy variable, and border prices of products and inputs.

GROUP 19

REGIONAL AGRICULTURAL TRADE AND COMPARATIVE ADVANTAGE IN SOUTHERN AND EASTERN AFRICA

ORGANIZER   RUVIMBO CHIMEDZA (ZIMBABWE)

RAPPORTEURS   EMMANUEL ACQUAH (USA), BRIAN D'SILVA (USA)

The mini-symposium included participants from at least 10 East and Southern African countries who are involved in the 'Regional Trade Analytical Agenda for East and Southern Africa', which is being funded by USAID.

The opening theme was 'The Policy Environment, Trade and Transport Issues in East and Southern Africa' and was chaired by Dr Ruvimbo Chimedza (Zimbabwe). The initial presentation focused on 'The Overview of the Program of Work for the Regional Trade Analytical Agenda' by D'Silva and Carvalho of USAID. Emphasis was placed on the theme of the agenda which was 'From Analysis to Policy Change Through Dialogue'. The manner in which the agenda was developed was discussed, as well as the major thematic areas: policy change in trade and agriculture; reduction of transport costs; estimates of unrecorded cross-border trade in East and Southern Africa; and changing agricultural comparative advantage in Southern Africa. Participation of researchers, policy makers and policy analysts from the region was emphasized in the sessions, with 22 East and Southern Africans involved in implementation of the agenda participating with presentations in this mini-symposium.

'Changes in the Policy Environment in Trade and Agriculture in the Greater Horn of Africa' was presented by Professor N'Geno (Kenya). Emphasis was placed on the pace of reform in different countries as well as the impact of civil strife on achievement of objectives related to reforms. All of the Greater Horn of Africa countries except Somalia were covered in this report. The Southern Africa report was presented by Professor Van Rooyen (South Africa). The approach taken in Southern Africa was different, in that key researchers and policy analysts in each of five countries were asked to analyse the structure of reform and look at anticipated reforms in the future. Countries covered were Zimbabwe, Zambia, Malawi, Mozambique and South Africa. Then a cross-country synthesis was developed. The in-depth knowledge of country researchers was highlighted in this process. Subsequent to the completion of the report, the SADC free trade protocol was signed as a way of encouraging regional integration in the region. Efforts will be made to expand coverage of this report to all of the SADC countries.

In the Greater Horn of Africa, the issue of transport costs as an impediment to regional trade and food security was highlighted with the presentation of results from two studies: one on East Africa and the other on the northern tier of the Greater Horn. These two studies were conducted by Anyango (Kenya) and reported on by Nimrod Waniala (Uganda). The studies showed that between 50 and 70 per cent of the c.i.f. costs of imports for landlocked countries in the region were related to transport costs. As a result of these analyses, a process is now in place where the recommendations from the studies are being implemented by bodies in the region. Key to the dialogue and implementation of the findings is a group called the East African Transport Initiative which is working with national-level policy makers in implementing policy reforms which will lead to reduced costs of transport in the region.

The second day of the mini-symposium focused on 'Unrecorded Cross-border Trade in East and Southern Africa: Implications for Food Security'. Chair of the session was Nimrod Waniala (Uganda). The overview of the programme of work which started in 1995 and the development of the methodology was presented by Chris Ackello-Ogutu (Kenya). For each of the sites that data were reported on, monitoring had taken place over a 12-month period. Results were then presented from monitoring of the different sites, beginning with the Kenya/Uganda border by Protase Echessah (Kenya); Tanzania and its neighbours by Echessah (Kenya); Malawi and its neighbours by Isaac Minde (Malawi); Mozambique and its neighbours by Jose Macamo (Mozambique). Future plans are to cover Zambia and its neighbours and Ethiopia and its neighbours in 1998. The overall results showed the magnitude of unrecorded trade in both agricultural and non-agricultural commodities. Food commodities were dominant in trade across the Kenya/Uganda border. Agricultural inputs like fertilizer, petroleum products and used and new clothes were also traded in large quantities. Similar to the work on transport costs, the next phase of this activity involves the setting up of regional groups who will utilize the data for dialogue with policy makers on the importance of informal unrecorded trade in meeting food and non-food needs, especially in border areas. Transport and comparative advantage issues were seen as key factors in determining both the direction of trade and the magnitude of unrecorded trade.

The third day of the mini-symposium focused on results from the research on 'Comparative Advantage in Southern Africa: An Agro-ecological Zone Approach', Glenn Magagula (Swaziland), who coordinates all of this work, chaired the session and described the overall organization of the research. Country teams are currently undertaking country-level work in seven countries in Southern Africa. The unifying methodology being utilized by all seven countries was presented by Rashid Hassan (South Africa). This methodology utilizes GIS techniques to link spatially data and analyses within each country. Country-level results were presented by Johan Van Zyl (South Africa), Hamid Faki (Swaziland), Teddy Nankhumwa (Malawi), Firmino Mucavele (Mozambique), Faustin Mwape (Zambia) and Chrispen Sukume (Zimbabwe). The next steps are for the regional analyses to be completed by early 1998, which will link all of the country-level work.

Discussion on all three days was excellent. Recognition was given to the fact that this capacity-building exercise is not only making a major effort at producing significant research results and capacity but is also making important contributions to the role of research in policy dialogue in the region. Consequently, it fits very well into the principles of USAID's Greater Horn of Africa Initiative and the Initiative for Southern Africa, which expects people from the region to provide the leadership in both identifying and analysing problems and their solutions. In addition, the topic of regional trade and food security was important, not only for East and Southern Africa, but for all of Africa.

GROUP 20

IMPROVING HIGHER EDUCATION IN
AGRICULTURAL ECONOMICS IN TRANSITION COUNTRIES

ORGANIZER   **KLAUS FROHBERG (GERMANY)**

RAPPORTEUR   **KLAUS FROHBERG (GERMANY)**

The discussion was divided into three parts: (1) what kind of qualifications do agricultural economists need for their employment in transition countries; (2) how can this demand be met in terms of curricula and teaching methods; and (3) what kind of assistance from Western countries is expected and also necessary?

The profile required of agricultural economists in transition countries is now substantially different from what it was in socialist times. During the socialist period, most agricultural economists graduating from universities worked in administration and on farms. Now they are largely employed in private enterprises of which farmers make up only a relatively small share. This change is indicative of the necessity to adjust the system of higher education for agricultural economists.

There was general agreement that demand for agricultural economists is similar in all transition countries, and structure of employment will approach that which is typically found in Western countries. Enrolment in agricultural economics is very high. It was argued that this may also be because the sudden upsurge in demand for studying economics cannot be met by universities. Therefore some students might enrol in agricultural economics. If this holds true, it can be expected that enrolment will decline in the near future. Otherwise, a gradual reduction in the number of students in agricultural economics is likely.

In transition countries, universities offering degrees in agricultural economics are rather diverse, with respect to the kind of degrees offered. Not all have a PhD programme. The 'Doctor of Science' degree is hardly awarded any more. Also the quality of the programme varies considerably. In Russia, many institutes formerly belonging to the Academy of Agricultural Sciences changed their name so as to have the word 'university' included. The bachelor's degree was not offered during socialist times. While some countries recently introduced it (for example, in the National University of the Ukraine in Kiev), it is not accepted at all in others (for example, in Russia).

Curricula are usually not coordinated and certified by a central agency. In almost all countries, universities are completely free to determine the content of their study programmes. This also leads to a high degree of diversity among them. Some harmonization is suggested, but on the other hand, it does allow for specialization.

Some of the leading universities in transition countries make quite an effort to get the degrees offered acknowledged by universities in Western countries. The rate of success, so far, seems to be rather low. Just a few universities have signed such agreements, including only one or two degrees and not the entire spectrum. However, since the harmonization process is far from being over, a continuation of these efforts is to be expected. This will be advantageous for all concerned.

The problems universities in transition countries face are numerous. Therefore they need assistance in finding solutions and implementing them. One major problem is the lack of sufficient knowledge on the part of teachers and researchers. This knowledge is available in Western countries. To transfer it takes human and financial resources and time. The financial support required can be relatively small if the right strategy is chosen.

One aspect is helping the transition countries to adjust their curricula: synergy effects may be utilized once the basic approach is developed. On the other hand, experts from different Western countries are engaged in such activities. This will lead to some diversity in the curricula, because the differences existing among Western countries will also be transferred. More effort in coordinating this work is desirable.

A rather successful approach in spreading knowledge is courses organized by colleagues from Western countries in which postgraduates are taught basics of agricultural economics. Thereafter, these students will become lecturers themselves. Participants from transition countries have pointed out that providing support for modernizing libraries is also urgent. Teachers, as well as students, lack access to most recent textbooks as well as to Western literature on research. Another bottleneck seems to be the lack of funding for postgraduates to do research in Western countries. Of great concern to all participants from transition countries is the decline in quality of education at all levels, but especially with regard to the PhD degree. There was no general solution to this point.

GROUP 21

AGRICULTURAL TRANSITION IN CENTRAL AND EAST EUROPEAN COUNTRIES AND THE FORMER SOVIET UNION

ORGANIZER   LIONEL HUBBARD (UK)

RAPPORTEURS   NATALIJA KAZLAUSKIENE (LITHUANIA), WILLIAM H. MEYERS (USA)

The sessions focused on three topics: (1) Price and Support Policies in the CEEC and the FSU, (2) Trade Agreements and Trade Relations, (3) Policy Implications of the CEEC Accession to the EU. Secondo Tarditi opened the first session with a provocative discussion of free market policies in Estonia in the context of distorted world market prices. Estonia, up to the present, has used no tariff protection for food and agricultural products or any other products and has had very little support of any kind for domestic producers. Two circumstances in which free market policies may not be optimal under current conditions are where the exchange rate is overvalued owing to the currency board arrangement in Estonia or where world market prices are distorted downwards by the policies of other countries. Alternative policies to offset these potential distortions include flexible exchange rates, countervailing duties, CAP-like policies and structural adjustment programmes.

Hartell and Swinnen compared agricultural support instruments in Central and East European countries and evaluated the similarity of phases in development of these policies from broad liberalization to introduction of various forms of protection and support. The explanation for these similar paths may lie in a desire to emulate CAP policies of the EU or in political pressures that could explain these developments in an endogenous political economy paradigm. While not conclusive, there is some evidence that political economy analysis can explain some of these similarities.

Bojnec discussed the role of exchange rates and exchange rate appreciation in evaluations of CEEC price levels and levels of protection. Purchasing power parity (PPP) exchange rates were compared to nominal rates in terms of different results obtained for protection levels. Exchange rate appreciation has helped to raise the domestic prices in CEEC relative to values in international markets but has slowed price growth in real domestic currency.

Discussion of these topics focused on the interplay of agricultural policy measures, political forces and market forces as policies in CEEC evolve from forms common to central planned economies to those forms common to market economies.

The second session was opened by Kazlauskiene in a discussion of motivations for regional trade arrangements, their effects on trade liberalization and policy harmonization, and the advantages and disadvantages of these arrangements. The reasons for forming regional trading blocks are often more political than economic, but there can be economic benefits. For emerging markets in transition economies, regional trade agreements can be a good context in which to improve competitiveness within an expanded but still limited market and to develop trade and negotiating institutions and procedures. Difficulties include reconciling differences in trade and domestic policies across member countries and conflicting trade agreements with non-member countries.

Serova presented views on Russia's trade agreements with other CIS countries. Historically, Russia has been extremely reluctant to depend on trade with the 'far abroad'. This attitude has continued to influence trade arrangements with other countries and led to a focus on trade agreements with NIS countries. There is also still an emphasis on government-to-government agreements. Even with other CIS countries, there are huge differences in trade regimes that hamper the development of normal trade relations.

Cela presented the evolving trade and related policy measures for Albania in its efforts to develop a market economy and deal with a very large trade deficit in food and agricultural products. Even the mechanisms for measuring trade flows are in a poor state of development, not to mention the trading and market institutions that are still in their infancy.

The discussion in this session revealed the wide dispersion of experience and development of trade relations, agreements and institutions in CEEC and the CIS. There is a pattern of moving from state control, to quantitative measures, to tariff measures in trade policy and from government-to-government agreements to trade agreements as countries progress in the transition to market economy systems.

Rabinowicz opened the third session with views on the policy implications of CEEC accession to the EU. There is still debate on whether accession means expansion or contraction of CEEC agriculture and what kind of integration is desirable. Current policies and membership conditions were designed by rich countries for rich countries, and their application to poorer new aspirants is difficult. Options are the full application of the current CAP, reform of the CAP prior to accession, a long transition period for CEEC, or a partial renationalization of support programmes. The Commission would oppose renationalization, and the Agenda 2000 proposals indicate the direction reforms are likely to take prior to new accessions.

Meyers discussed market structure problems and the variation in market protection policies in the CEEC. Competitiveness is clearly the most important issue facing acceding countries, since they are far from matching the efficiency of the food and agricultural industry in the EU. Low farm prices do not make an industry competitive if the product quality is inferior and the marketing chain is inefficient. Though they are poor measures of protection in CEEC, the wide dispersion of producer subsidy equivalents (PSEs) across countries in the region show the wide variation in prices and policies that still exist.

Mathijs evaluated farm restructuring and structural policies in view of accession. There is a 'convergence of divergence' when comparing farm structure in the EU and CEEC. Both have coexisting family and part-time farms and large commercial farms. Support policies are not neutral to farm structure, and CAP policies have favoured large farms rather than small ones. Policy development needs to recognize the farm structure that exists and to anticipate the impacts on this structure. The best rural development policy is actually to stimulate non-agricultural activities and employment in rural areas.

Discussion of these various aspects of accession highlighted the still uncertain processes in early stages of development and the variations in outcomes that could obtain. Both the EU and the CEEC have a great deal of difficult work ahead in preparing for and implementing a process of enlargement that is, at the same time, inevitable and unpredictable.

GROUP 22

FUTURE ROLE OF DEVELOPMENT ASSISTANCE IN AGRICULTURE

ORGANIZER   MICHEL GRIFFON (FRANCE)

RAPPORTEUR   GERSHON FEDER (USA)

The session was opened by the organizer, who reviewed the background and objectives of the mini-symposium. He observed that donors' aid programmes are changing owing to a number of factors: the collapse of communism, the accomplishment of the 'green revolution' and the overcoming of the debt crisis. Four sets of issues affect future aid: (1) local conflicts, (2) direct commodity channels between some donors and recipient countries, (3) incidence of wide scale poverty and malnutrition, and (4) environmental issues linked to global effects or local sustainability.

While aid is viewed as a solution to some of these issues, it is subject to various criticisms and often lacks a significant local constituency within the donor country. As a consequence, aid has declined in recent years. Aid to agriculture has been declining as well. It has gone from a focus on irrigation, and subsequently on extension/ research, to emphasis on infrastructure. Variations between donors are present, however, and the session attempted to clarify donor strategies.

Alex McCalla described the World Bank approach. He pointed out that past Bank agricultural activities were characterized by high volume but low performance (one-third unsatisfactory). As a result, there was a realization that some of the projects supported were not very effective and a recognition of the importance of policies and incentives. Generally, the volume of lending for agriculture development projects has declined, while social sector lending has increased significantly. The Bank has now developed a vision for its rural assistance activities, stemming from the emphasis on poverty alleviation, and the recognition that the key to poverty alleviation is rural development, broadly defined. The action plan adopted by the Bank emphasizes the importance of the policy environment, and avoids past failures such as overly complex projects. Emphasis is shifting from projects to programmes, and partnership and donor coordination are sought. The Bank has now initiated the implementation of the action plan, and some increase in the volume of agricultural lending is already evident.

Shirley Prior outlined US assistance to agricultural development. She noted that there has been a marked decline, related to a perception that agriculture was not important. There has also been a general decline in public support for foreign aid. As a result, technical competence in aid administration has declined. While a major increase in aid to agriculture is not envisaged, there has recently been some renewed interest. An advisory board and leading agricultural economists are trying to affect USAID's strategy so as to put greater emphasis on agriculture, observing that such a strategy is in the US interest.

Gunter Dresrusse's presentation on the German aid programme pointed out that, because of major transfers to the former East Germany, the volume of assistance to developing countries has declined. About a third of ODA is channelled through the UNDP and a significant amount through the European Community and the World Bank's IDA programme. The overall objective of German ODA is global sustainable development, with priority to poverty alleviation, the environment and education. A focus on Africa and Eastern Europe characterizes the programme. The share of support for agricultural development has declined from 40 per cent to 30 per cent. There is a sense that the assistance to agriculture failed to link the activities to growth, employment, environment and equity. Current strategy emphasizes programmes more than projects, less state control, flexibility in decision making, 'up-front' strategy discussion and staff performance.

In a discussion among participants, several generic points emerged. Is aid through technical assistance still useful? Is it contributing effectively to the build-up of local knowhow? Speakers stressed the importance of greater involvement of NGOs and of cultivating the private sector in the donor country as a constituency supporting aid.

Shiro Okabe's presentation on Japanese aid stated that the most distinctive feature of the Japanese ODA is its enormous volume (US$14.5 billion in 1995). Approximately 48 per cent is supplied in the form of Yen-credits (mostly infrastructure) and the rest through a grant aid. During the period of the 1950s–70s, the principle of request-based aid provided the Japanese private sector with opportunities for export business. This partly contributed to forming a local constituency for aid. Another principle of Japan's ODA was a policy of non-intervention in recipients' domestic affairs. The major objective of agricultural ODA since that time has been to transfer production technologies and to improve relevant infrastructure, particularly irrigation facilities. Under the changing global conditions, since the 1980s, the principles of Japanese ODA have had to be modified. Accordingly, the government established an ODA charter in 1992. Special attention is now paid to social equity of the ODA benefits in rural areas, greater support for the poorer sections and undernourished people, and maintenance of the limited natural resources and environmental conservation. Towards such quality improvement of the Japanese ODA in agriculture, special strategic arrangements for the initial step are required. Most importantly, the will of the Japanese government has to be firmed up in promoting improved agricultural ODA programmes to integrate economic, social and technological developments in rural areas.

The French ODA programme was discussed by Bruno Vindel. Aside from the support to multilateral aid agencies, aid and development credit are also provided directly by the Ministry of Cooperation, the Ministry of Foreign Affairs and the Caisse Française de Développement. While agriculture is not a specific area of emphasis, it is addressed through priority given to poverty alleviation, natural resources management and overall growth. There is significant focus on sub-Saharan Africa. About one-third of bilateral aid is going to agriculture and rural development. Assistance to agriculture highlights programmes enhancing food security, the formation of regional markets for agricultural commodities and the improved competitiveness of commodity chains. Programmes attempt to make a rational delineation of the roles of the state vis-à-vis other players, highlight policies for more efficient agriculture and establish a regulatory climate that maintains the sustainability of investments. Experience has shown that success in assistance programmes requires farmers' participation.

William Anderson outlined the Canadian development assistance programme in the area of agriculture. He noted a significant decline in support to agriculture between the 1980s and the 1990s. Areas of priority are environmental protection, basic needs, private-sector development, human rights and women in development (WID). He pointed out that past agricultural support programmes have failed to pay attention to WID aspects, but CIDA has had positive experiences with community-based development projects. Sub-Saharan Africa is emerging as an area of focus, where agriculture will be a priority area. A shift to country-specific programmes (away from multi-country projects) is envisaged.

In the discussion which ensued, views were expressed that beneficiary participation is not by itself a guarantee of success (although it is a necessary ingredient). It was also pointed out that political interference can often stifle the sense of empowerment and self-governance that is initiated by some projects. To promote greater donor support for agricultural development, it is important to demonstrate that agriculture has important linkages to other sectors and can contribute significantly to overall growth, in particular in an open economy. In fact, in the early stages of development, agriculture can be the lead sector. Furthermore, it is a key to poverty alleviation. It was suggested that institution building and capacity enhancement should be the focal areas for development assistance. Assistance to agriculture should avoid a narrow sectoral approach and should recognize intersectoral linkages, with due attention to the overall macroeconomic and policy environment.

GROUP 23

AGRICULTURAL PRODUCTIVITY: MULTILATERAL COMPARISONS

ORGANIZERS   SHANKAR NARAYANAN (CANADA),
COLIN THIRTLE (UK)

RAPPORTEUR   JEFF CORMAN (CANADA)

Led by Colin Thirtle, Reading University, UK, the group spent the first 20 minutes introducing themselves, relating their experience and their expectations for the discussion group and adopting a tentative agenda covering the following areas: (1) background and motivation for total factor productivity (TFP) analysis, (2) issues and problems surrounding international comparison of TFP, (3) miscellaneous issues such as integration of environment impacts within a TFP framework, TFP analysis and country's competitiveness, TFP of food processing sectors and inclusion of varying quality differences for both outputs and inputs.

Background and motivation

Colin Thirtle began by asserting that the techniques employed in developing TFP indices were not all that onerous; the true value and pay-off is in explaining why certain TFP behaviour happens. Initial impetus for this work in Britain occurred as a result of Margaret Thatcher's demand for justification of the use of public money in agricultural research rather than having it done by the private sector. The biological scientists were at a loss to provide this justification, which created the demand for agricultural economists and their analysis of TFP growth.

Measurement of productivity uses basic accounting techniques and national income accounts data. The inevitable goal is to estimate consistent and unbiased aggregate measures for outputs (Q) and inputs (X). On the output side, TFP index calculation demands production-based data. In Britain, use of national accounts data (farm income data) presents problems in terms of proper account for inventory changes. This adjustment needs to be made to determine actual production within the year. In the United States, the situation is better since farm production data are available. In general, it was agreed that the analysis has to have a good idea of what is contained in national farm-level data, paying particular attention to timing problems and data sources (that is, appropriateness of FAO data for TFP development).

The issue of accounting for environmental benefits and costs of product/commodity qualities provoked an interesting discussion at this point. It was noted by Johannes Roseboom that, unless the environmental impacts have a price consequence, they will have no impact on farmers' behaviour. However, Heinrich Hockmann pointed out that, although immediate impacts may not be evident, change in environmental factors (such as land) could result in longer-term changes in productivity. This led to a general discussion of failings of production function theory. In particular, Jim Hildreth noted that the management factor has never been adequately incorporated within the theory. This observation led to speculation concerning how management might be captured within a production function arrangement, with suggestions that beers drunk and time spent in bars may be a better proxy for the level of farmers' production knowledge than years of schooling or number of PhDs involved in agriculture.

The discussion returned to the issues surrounding the aggregation of inputs. Colin Thirtle grouped inputs into three general classes: fundamental inputs, land and labour; intermediate inputs, chemicals, feed and seed; and capital items, financial capital and machinery. The discussion about the inputs produced a familiar roster of issues: adjustment for quality differences, the basis of measurement and the maintenance of a consistent accounting framework.

There are certain technical advantages in including both a land and a labour component in agriculture for calculating a TFP index. Quality adjustments are typically made for the labour component, and recent work within USDA is trying to extend this to land. The intermediate goods must be treated in the same way. Jim Hildreth pointed out that interaction between intermediate inputs are important, and this led to a discussion regarding appropriate functional form. The use of the Cobb–Douglas function came under critical discussion.

The accounting for capital items caused the greatest technical problem. Ideally, the goal is to measure the true flow of service emanating from a capital item. Real interest rates are fine for calculating an economic depreciation; however, things quickly fall apart when real interest rates are negative. Johannes Roseboom indicated that similar problems are encountered in accounting for capital subsidies.

A second major approach to estimate aggregate output and input is by the use of econometrics. Using duality, profit functions can map to production functions, and positive estimates can be obtained. Programming offers yet another alternative, with the results being used to develop Malmquist indices. The advantage of the programming technique is that no prices are needed, the amount of aggregation is limited and no behavioural assumption need be imposed. Best-practice isoquants are developed and programming leads to estimates of how far farmers are from these. There are, nevertheless, real problems with this type of aggregation.

Session 2

Robert Townsend reported on the technical aspects and advantages/disadvantages of different indices: Malmquist and Tornquist. Jean-Christophe Bureau also reported on techniques and problems in doing international comparison of TFP.

Session 3

Terry Veeman began by asking about approaches to handling private as opposed to social productivity growth. Specifically, how does one adequately account for social amenity values and environmental damages in calculating productivity indices? The major drawback identified was the paucity of longitudinal data on environmental impacts. Although this was accepted as a problem, suggestions were made to measure the decline in recreation activity around plants (pulp and paper in this instance) as a proxy for environmental damage.

Colin Thirtle then related the work of David Hudley, a PhD student at Reading University. Hudley used farm cost surveys from 1200 farms over an eight-year period, together with a GIS system which could match water quality (nitrate levels) to individual farms. Using techniques of distance functions, duality (the Horowitz Theorem) and inclusion of a negative (constrained) output, Hudley was able to determine an individual farm's willingness to pay to carry on its polluting activity. The question was whether this overestimates or underestimates the 'true' social cost of the farms' polluting activity.

David Schimmelpfennig concluded the session by relating some work on research and development spillover and the relationship to national agriculture productivity growth. The motivation for looking at this arose from trying to understand why countries like the United States and France recorded production growth rates of 3 per cent annually for the period 1973–93, whereas the United Kingdom produced an average annual growth rate of 1.6 per cent. In fact, the rate of productivity growth rates of one group of nations (including the United States and France) converge at this higher level, and those of a second group (including Britain and Germany) converge at lower levels.

Initial attempts to explain the differences in TFP growth rates used a more traditional function which included the levels of public and private R&D, extension system, level of education of farmers and weather. Results of regressions were poor and indicated an incorrectly specified functional form. Another function was employed which attempted to get at the stock of knowledge, the quality of labour and weather as major explanatory factors. In this specification, the idea of learning by doing (endogenous growth) and learning by sharing knowledge (external growth) appeared to have better explanatory power. Convergence of various factors in the two growth country groups lead to the conclusion that knowledge spillovers from one country to another helped explain the patterns of TFP growth.

There still seems to be the question why some countries hang together and achieve higher TFP growth rates and other countries achieve lower TFP growth rates. All manner of explanations are postulated, greater sharing among national public research institutes and a common approach to intellectual property rights being a couple. However, in the end, it would appear that similar research culture and R&D spending offer the best explanation. An interesting implication of this work for international competitiveness is that, with research spillovers benefiting not only the country doing the research but its partners as well, arguments for isolating a nation's R&D cannot be supported.

GROUP 25

POLITICAL ECONOMY ANALYSIS IN AGRICULTURAL ECONOMICS:
CONCEPTS AND EXPERIENCES AMONG COUNTRIES

ORGANIZER   ROBERT G. SPITZE (USA)

RAPPORTEUR   MICHELE VEEMAN (CANADA)

The presentations and discussion in this group focused on the processes by which agricultural policy is made. Contrasting examples of the differences in the procedures and outcomes of agricultural policy making in different nations were provided by the participants. These illustrated the wide range of differences between nations in the political and economic structures within which agricultural policy is developed. The associated discussion illuminated the impact of different political, legal and social structures and institutions in agricultural policy-making processes.

The discussion encompassed outlines of the policy-making process in the European Union (J. Bryden, G. Allaire, J. Anton and A. Fantini), Canada (M. Veeman and R. Bollman) and the United States (R. Spitze and J. Wells). The procedures by which agricultural policy is formulated were also outlined for Laos (P. Warr) and Nigeria (A. Ikpi). Features of the current approach and outcomes of agricultural policy in Indonesia were outlined (P. Warr), as were features of the policy environment and outcome for agriculture for Brazil (E. Teixeira).

One facet of discussion was the broad issue of the inconsistency in the approach to agricultural policy between many developing and developed countries. This discussion noted the low, frequently negative, levels of protection for agriculture in many developing nations in which agriculture often constitutes the major component of economic activity. In contrast, in most high-income countries, in which agriculture constitutes a relatively low proportion of national output and employment, this sector is typically protected and supported. One point of this discussion was the lack of power and influence of individual farmers in many developing countries. However, there are relatively low costs of organization and considerable motives for rent seeking associated with protection in high-income societies. The incentives to organize and seek sectoral protection were concluded to be particularly evident in agriculture, because of the immobility and importance of the fixed factor of the land input in this sector.

The discussions of the group included instances of both effective and ineffective agricultural policies. For example, contrasting outcomes of top-down planning approaches to agricultural policy pursued by two oil-rich developing nations, Nigeria and Indonesia, were cited. The Indonesian policy to encourage increased domestic supply of rice, focused on provision of inputs through development of reliable irrigation, as well as on high-quality education in rural areas, was noted to have been very effective in contributing to rural employment and in achieving substantial increases in food supplies. In contrast, instances of lack of consistency and effectiveness of some nations' policies to encourage food self-sufficiency were also cited. One example is the restriction on food trading across national boundaries, as in areas of Africa. Similarly, attempts to limit 'slash and burn' agriculture by limiting the land that villagers can use in Laos has been counterproductive and has led to rapid land degradation.

Another theme of discussion was related to the relative importance of different farmers' associations in North America and Western Europe in influencing the formation of policy for agriculture. Participants saw a tendency for increasing political and economic influence of commodity-specific farmers' organizations and some decline in the influence of general farm organizations which had been of more importance in earlier years. The importance of the institutional structure, within which agricultural policy is developed, was highlighted in a discussion of the differing political viewpoints relating to the agricultural sector in some of the nations of the European Union. The necessity for compromise between different national interests that is embedded in the institutional structure of the European Union was elucidated. Similarly, the institutional structure of agriculture policy making in the United States and Canada was outlined in some detail.

Overall, from the discussions, it was evident that both political and economic objectives and constraints are powerful influences in the development and application of agricultural policy. In general, however, there is a tendency for an increasing influence of external constraints and stimuli on agricultural policy, arising from the internationalization of the global economy. The growing importance of regional and multilateral trade agreements on the formation of national agricultural policy is continuing expression of this tendency. Nonetheless, there are wide differences in the political economy of national policy making for agriculture and the approaches to farm policy taken in different nations. Participants agreed that economic analysis of agricultural policy requires an understanding of the social and political structures within which agricultural policy is developed; the discussions were helpful in contributing to this.

GROUP 26

QUALITY AND ENVIRONMENTAL MANAGEMENT FOR COMPETITIVE ADVANTAGE IN AGRICULTURE AND THE FOOD INDUSTRY

ORGANIZER   GERHARD SCHIEFER (GERMANY)

RAPPORTEUR   GERHARD SCHIEFER (GERMANY)

Introduction to the subject

Agriculture and the food industry face increasing requirements on the quality of its products and the environmental consciousness of its production and trade activities. These requirements are only partly due to administrative regulations, being primarily a result of changes in consumer preferences and the society's evaluation of agriculture and the industry's impact on the environment. These requirements pose a major challenge to management in today's competitive food markets, leave little room for problem solutions and increase costs.

Improvements in the organization, control and management of processes in enterprises and throughout the vertical chain of production and trade (agrifood supply chain) are the major focus of research and management to cope with the challenge. Such improvements include the following:

- the establishment of management systems (management routines) which might follow the schemes outlined in the international standards for the organization and documentation of quality management systems (ISO 9000) and environmental management systems (ISO 14001 or the European Environmental Management and Audit Scheme (EMAS));
- the identification and reduction of the costs associated with quality production and environmental protection;
- the identification and elimination of potential hazards and failures in food production;
- the identification, evaluation and reduction of negative effects on the environment.

The mini-symposium involved five presentations which introduced participants to the subject and served as a basis for further discussion.

Overview presentations

The presentations started with a tutorial by G. Schiefer (University of Bonn) on quality and environmental management, followed by an overview on the relevance of 'metasystems' and 'metastandards' for the food industry by M. Bredahl (University of Missouri). The definition of metasystems and metastandards incorporated the standard series ISO 9000/14001 for management systems and involved the consideration of system and transaction costs. This introductory discussion emphasized the relevance of the subject for (1) individual enterprises (farms and industry), (2) the structural development in the agrifood sector, (3) market structures, and (4) agricultural policy. It was argued that one possible line of development would lead to a restructuring of the sector towards competing agrifood production chains in which farms, processing and trade cooperate closely. The chains, and not the farms, might become the principal economic units to be addressed in the not-so-distant future.

It was obvious that the broad aspect of the possible consequences of the developments could not be covered by the mini-symposium and warranted a much broader consideration.

Focused presentations

The second group of presentations did focus on approaches to identifying and reducing quality costs. A. Starbird (University of Santa Clara) elaborated on the potential cost advantages of adversarial or cooperative relationships between members of a supply chain. C.A. da Silva (University of Vicosa) presented a framework for a decision support system which aimed at cost reductions through process improvements.

Apart from gains in product quality, possible gains in efficiency through savings in costs are a driving element in today's quality management efforts. They build on improvements in process efficiency and on appropriate chain management activities. The papers did focus on management support aspects to reach the goal. Some of the discussion focused on empirical evidence which supported the claim of cost effectiveness of quality management. A study by M. Bredahl and his research group among British food companies supported the claim. A study by G. Schiefer and his group among agrifood companies, which had introduced quality management systems, showed that, in an initial phase, companies might face increases in costs (training and so on) but that the introduction of quality management systems supported initiatives for process improvements which would eventually lead to a reduction in costs.

R. Huirne (Wageningen Agricultural University) introduced a model for chain optimization which was implemented in industry and elaborated on problems surrounding the distribution of financial gains among participants in the supply chain. The presentation demonstrated the potential of process improvement initiatives, but also showed the need for farms to strengthen their position within chains. This includes access to the results of improvement initiatives as well as the ability to reserve an 'appropriate' share of the outcomes for the farms.

A last paper, presented by R. Helbig (University of Bonn), introduced the limits of today's environmental management initiatives and the need for further research in the subject area.

Concluding discussion

The group considered further advances in the implementation of quality and environmental management systems in the agrifood sector, the most probable development at least for Europe and the United States, and emphasized potential trade barrier effects that might arise.

It was also made clear that the implementation of a certified management system was of little value for customers as long as it was not combined with a clear description of the implemented level of quality or environmental protection which, in principle, could be introduced through an appropriate labelling policy.

Members of the group expressed their astonishment that the majority of agricultural economists did not seem to realize the potential impact of the developments on the sector and, in consequence, for the profession. A close cooperation among those working in the field was considered a means to promote knowledge about the developments and the possible consequences of quality and environmental management initiatives in agriculture and related industries.

POSTER PAPER ABSTRACTS

POSTER PAPER ABSTRACTS*

AFRICA

Kizito Langha, AARS-RUDARC Group, Bamenda, Cameroon – *Population pressure, technological change and agricultural growth in sub-Saharan Africa: the farming systems evolution approach*

The study examines the impact of demographic pressure on agricultural practices under four farming systems at various levels of intensification. It then explores the effects of intensification on the adoption and profitability of animal traction under these systems and assesses the impacts of intensification and technical change on household welfare levels.

Solomon Bellete, Consultant, Addis Ababa, Ethiopia – *Privatization of animal health services: the Ethiopian situation*

The efforts being made to promote private veterinary practice in Ethiopia through the PARC project are considered. A brief assessment is made of the level of veterinary services, their economic nature and the objectives, needs and constraints involved. Policy options for the delivery of veterinary services and strategies adopted for promoting private veterinary practice are analysed.

Berhanu Gebremedhin, Michigan State University, East Lansing, USA – *Effectiveness of food-for-work targeting in Tigray, Ethiopia*

For food-for-work (FFW) to meet short-term food security needs, it should be aimed at those in greatest distress and minimize 'leakages' to non-needy households. This study deals with the relationship between participation in FFW and indicators of poverty at the household level in Tigray. A probit model was used to examine factors affecting household eligibility for FFW. Double-hurdle regression was applied on eligible households to examine separately factors affecting a household's choice to participate in FFW (probit regression) and the factors affecting the decision on days worked (truncated regression). Results for 1992–5 were based on a survey of 247 households from 30 villages. FFW targeting appears to be effective in isolating wealthy households, who cultivate more land per capita, and those with higher family labour. However,

*As mentioned in the Introduction, the organization of poster paper sessions was undertaken by Arie Oskam (Wageningen Agricultural University, The Netherlands). They are arranged here under headings which, in the main, are geographical (Africa, Asia, The Americas, General, Western Europe, Transition Economies), with countries then appearing in alphabetical order. Judith Peters was responsible for the bulk of the text editing.

643

targeting failed to exclude those who claim to have adequate animal work. Days supplied to FFW relate positively to literacy and household size. The only eligible households who failed to participate were unable (rather than unwilling) to do so, and were generally small, headed by elderly women. An alternative food assistance programme in the form of free food distribution is available for this needy group.

Steven J. Staal, International Livestock Research Institute, Nairobi, Kenya – *Public policy and incentives to peri-urban dairying in Addis Ababa, Ethiopia*

This paper uses PAM methodology to examine the impact of public policy on smallholder dairy producers in Addis Ababa, Ethiopia. Domestic milk prices were lower than export-parity prices, owing to past exchange rate policies, to the detriment of producers. Regardless of policies, dairying was shown to provide above-normal profits.

Nico Heerink and Arie Kuyvenhoven, Wageningen University, The Netherlands, **and K. Yerfi Fosu**, University of Ghana – *Extension services reform and agricultural production in Ghana*

The extent to which agricultural extension in Ghana can be provided by the private sector is examined and empirical evidence is given about the effect of public extension on farm production. The results have relevance for decisions on public expenditure priorities and regulatory measures to accompany privatization programmes. Theory relating to public goods and market imperfections is used to analyse the appropriate roles of public and private sectors in providing extension services. The reform of the system following the introduction of structural adjustment is evaluated. It is argued that supplementary policy measures are needed to remove some of the undesirable effects of input supply privatization. Data from the Agricultural Economics Survey is used to examine the effect of public extension on maize output using separate production functions for contact and non-contact farmers. It appears that modern input provision by the public sector has not been successful. The supply of general agricultural information has, however, enhanced farmers' efficiency.

Johannes Jütting, Humboldt University, Berlin, Germany – *Empirical analysis of price shifts for rice after the devaluation of the CFA-Franc in the Ivory Coast*

A case study of the effects of the CFA devaluation in 1994, conducted in the Ivory Coast, shows the ambivalence of social compensatory measures by examining observed price changes for local rice. The results from ARIMA and intervention models indicate that the theoretically grounded expectations for the effect on local rice prices after the devaluation were not realized. The models suggest a significant price effect that is stronger in rural than urban markets and occurs only after the liberalization of the import rice sector. This means that the expected price incentive for local rice production actually took effect one year later, at the beginning of 1995. The price controls on rice imports, implemented as a social compensatory measure, helped to reduce adverse social impacts on vulnerable urban consumers, whereas rice producers were disadvantaged.

Wachira Kaguongo, Steven J. Staal and Chris Akello-Ogutu, ICRISAT and International Livestock Research Institute, Nairobi, Kenya – *Risk with intensification of Kenyan smallholder dairying*

The effects of risk facing smallholder dairy farmers in highland Kenya were examined through qualitative analysis and simulation modelling. Stochastic dominance tests showed that intensification of dairying through increased use of inputs tended to reduce risk-adjusted farm welfare. Market outlet and production risks thus remain impediments to increasing farm productivity.

Joseph Karugia and Michele Veeman, University of Alberta, Edmonton, Canada – *Quality factors affecting the value of beef in Kenya: an assessment of relevant grading attributes*

Experimental choice data were collected and analysed, using a multinomial logit model of butchers' contingent behaviour, in order to identify and estimate the implicit values of certain quality attributes of Kenyan beef. The results show that those of carcass conformation (shown to be the most important), fatness and weight are crucial in determining the value of a carcass at the wholesale level. This information can be used by farm managers to adjust production systems to meet market requirements, substantially increasing the value of their animals by improving conformation. The results indicate that animal breeders should breed for large animals with good conformation and intermediate fatness. Fat carcasses are preferred to lean ones, though there is discounting of overfat carcasses.

Bradford F. Mills, ISNAR, The Hague, Netherlands – *Ex ante research evaluation and regional trade flows: maize in Kenya*

This paper develops a dynamic spatial-equilibrium model to estimate adaptive research benefits when transaction costs are associated with commodity trade among regions. Adaptive research is usually aimed at one specific region, though the associated benefits could include pecuniary spillovers to other regions if inter-market transaction costs permit trade. Such research requires an extended time horizon to evaluate the impact of agricultural technologies. The application of research, as well as other factors influencing supply and demand for agricultural commodities, may, over time, affect the trends in commodity prices. Movements in relative prices can change, or even reverse, trade flows between regions. The study of maize in Kenya highlights the impact of trade flow reversals on the magnitude and distribution of research benefits. The analysis also highlights the challenge to national self-sufficiency posed by rapid population growth.

Daniel Ngugi, Charles Mataya and Davies Ng'ong'ola, Bunda College of Agriculture, Kenya – *The implications of maize market liberalization for market efficiency and agricultural policy in Kenya*

Liberalization of the domestic maize market in Kenya was completed almost three years ago as one of the conditions of Structural Adjustment Programme (SAP) funding. The motive was to promote market efficiency. Correlations of price differences and cointegration techniques were employed to study market integration, here used as an efficiency indictor, while an error correction model was used to test for causality among markets and examine the occurrence of central markets. Weekly retail prices of maize in 13 locations made up the data set. Results suggested that there were more integrated markets after liberalization than before and there was also more unidirectional causality. This conclusion lays to rest past fears that the private sector would be unable to run the liberalized market efficiently.

Angelos Pagoulatos, Georges Abbey, Tulin Ozdemir and Stephan J. Goetz, University of Kentucky, Lexington, USA – *Efficiency and safety: a joint hypothesis in farm portfolio decisions among Settat farmers, Morocco*

The poster examines empirically the trade-off between crop production efficiency and safety (survival) among a sample of 207 limited resource farmers in the Settat Region, Morocco. A comparison of alternative chance-constrained expected utility functions shows that exponential and power functions lead to the closest approximation of actual crop mixes.

Daphne S. Taylor and Truman P. Phillips, University of Guelph, Canada – *Household food security assessments in Mozambique and Laos*

Household food security is the ability of household members to ensure for themselves sustained access to sufficient quantity and quality of food to live healthy active lives, both now and in the future. Food security has two components, relating to the current situation and to the future. The aim here is to summarize survey results from Laos and Mozambique. Household food security results from Laos (316 households) are compared with anthropometric indicators for children under five years old. The results from Mozambique (2160 households) are used to demonstrate the dynamic nature of food insecurity and identify target groups in need of assistance. The assessment tool used is unique, rapid and can be replicated.

Truman P. Phillips and Daphne S. Taylor, University of Guelph, Canada – *Estimating food aid needs using household-level data*

A representative food security survey of 2160 households in 12 districts in the Zambezi Valley and Central Mozambique was undertaken from August 1995 to October 1995. Monthly food requirements by district and food commodity were estimated using information about food group insufficiencies, the season and duration of insufficiencies and the contribution to current consumption from food aid sources. Four alternative formulations of food needs were estimated and compared to World Vision (WV) estimates for 1995/96. The four alternatives contained values equivalent to WV estimates of food needs in maize, legumes and vegetable oil for the surveyed areas, although some redistribution between districts following more accurate identification of targets may be required.

Glenn R. Rogers, USAID, Washington, DC, USA – *Maximizing illicit payments and restricting trade in West Africa*

The market for illicit payments to public agents along roads in West Africa is described using data from Niger, Burkina-Faso and Côte d'Ivoire. Efficiency measures for illicit payments show that public agents respond to market incentives but sometimes extract excessive payments which cause market collapse. Agents in Côte d'Ivoire captured an increasing percentage of illicit payments on onions over the last decade and caused significant loss of income to the region. National governments have reduced legal trade taxes to promote exports, but illicit payments in other countries increased and offset the benefits of initial market liberalization, thus encouraging countries to reimpose legal trade taxes. It is argued that legal taxes and illicit payments, as trade constraints, must be addressed together on a multi-country basis using market and non-market incentives. Greater transparency and provision of information, in combination with enhanced enforcement of regulations, has temporarily reduced illicit payments. However, increased competition in the market for these payments will be required to achieve significant reductions that will foster more rapid economic growth. This is the necessary next step in the liberalization of agricultural markets.

G.B. Ayoola, University of Agriculture, Mekurdi, Nigeria – *Intervention policy in agriculture: a theoretical model of the two-sector developing economy*

The implicit need for a distinct theory of agricultural policy in a developing economy is predicated upon the widespread view that fundamental differences exist, in terms of structure and function, between developed and developing areas. The tenability of the view is established in development economics literature. Yet knowledge about the structural and functional character of the developing economy is generally overlooked, or taken for granted, when experts explore options for appropriate policy intervention for sustained growth of agriculture. Using Nigeria as a typical example, it is argued that a definite structure can be ascribed to the developing economy giving scope for effective policy intervention. The aim is to establish a theoretical framework for manipulating policy instruments to assist agriculture.

Hiroki Inaizumi and Akinwumi A. Adesina, International Institute of Tropical Agriculture, Nigeria – *Determinants of rapid dissemination of an improved cowpea variety in Northern Nigeria*

Cowpea is one of the most popular and important legumes in West Africa. There are many irrigation schemes to allow the utilization of residual moisture for dry season farming in Northern Nigeria, which were focused initially on cereals like wheat and rice. However, these cereal systems have faced many constraints, including commodity price uncertainty. A cowpea crop has potential as part of a rotation system for dry season cropping. Major constraints identified by farmers are insect pests, hence IITA developed what appeared to be the most promising resistant variety (IT89KD-288). Between 1993 and 1996, this variety was adopted, without external intervention, by over 200 farmers in Bunkure village, and the number is still increasing. Information from about 600 households has been collected to study the main factors responsible for adoption and the impediments which exist.

G.G. Antrobus, G.C.G. Fraser and S.P. Mowat, University of Fort Hare, South Africa – *The effects of economic incentives in controlling pollution in the South African leather industry*

Pollution of the environment is becoming an increasingly serious problem, a major contributor being industries generating effluent as a by-product of their production process. Two methods of avoidance are the so-called 'command and control' techniques and 'economic incentives'. In theory, the latter promise a more economically efficient and equitable means of pollution control. This paper sets out to ascertain whether this would hold in practice, by applying environmental economic theory to the practical problem of controlling effluent generated by the South African leather industry.

Johan Kirsten and Rob Townsend, University of Pretoria, South Africa – *Measurement and determinants of household nutritional status: the role of farm and non-farm activities in KwaZulu-Natal, South Africa*

There is a relationship between household nutritional status and agricultural production amongst a sample of rural households in KwaZulu-Natal. The results from multivariate analysis and a logit model indicate a positive contribution of agricultural activities to household nutrition.

Michael Lyne and David Thomson, University of Natal, South Africa – *Adapting customary institutions to promote an efficient rental market in tribal land: an empirical study in KwaZulu*

In a study conducted on tribal land in KwaZulu-Natal, the aims were (a) to reinforce tenure security and to reduce transaction costs in the rental market for farmland, and (b) to monitor the effect of rental transactions. Small institutional changes had a marked impact on market activity, bringing idle land into production and improving the welfare of both lessors and lessees.

Nico Meyer and Tommy Fenyes, Development Bank of South Africa, Halfway House, South Africa – *The impact of agricultural marketing policy on the agricultural sector*

The impact of agricultural marketing policy on farm production in South Africa is explored in this paper. Although a new player on the international scene, there is no evidence to suggest that it is experiencing anything different from what is generally found. A linear programming model was developed to project changes in production, prices and welfare brought about by market liberalization.

Johan van Rooyen and Simphiwe Ngqangweni, University of Pretoria, South Africa – *Farm worker participation schemes as a mechanism for reform in South Africa*

It is likely that large commercial farms will remain a predominant feature in South Africa. It is therefore logical to seek ways of increasing rural livelihoods and access to land on such properties through new ownership relations as part of agrarian and land reform. The participation model discussed proposes the rearrangement of ownership to include farm workers and thus involve them in the mainstream economy.

Cesar Guvele and Allen Featherstone, Kansas State University, USA – *The determination of steady-state cropland: a numerical analysis for Sudan*

Water from the Sennar reservoir (which originates in the Blue Nile) for Sudanese agriculture is scarce. This poster examines how to allocate water to the 2.1 million feddans in the Gezira gravity irrigated scheme. The objectives involve determining optimal intertemporal water allocation, the stability of crop allocation over time and the optimal cropping strategies under different scenarios. A dynamic optimal control model (50-year period) is used to 'allocate' water. The current cropping constraints imposed by the Sudan Gezira Board result in distortions relative to free water allocation by farmers, reducing potential income. At the same time, the amount of water used would not increase significantly. It is argued that returns to farmers would be greater, under the current cropping constraints, if yields were higher. If the government was to move towards free market prices for products, farmers would need greater freedom in crop allocation.

Cesar Guvele and Allen Featherstone, Kansas State University, USA – *Gains from crop diversification in the Sudan Gezira scheme*

This study examines crop diversification in the gravity-irrigated Gezira scheme, where farmers encounter many forms of uncertainty. Although government price and crop land regulation aims at its reduction, it may not do so because prices are announced after planting. The control of cultivable area also inhibits diversification. This study determines optimum crop combinations for this multi-crop production system. The mean-variance model is used for both cross-sectional and time-series farm-level data. Farmers' risk attitudes are often represented with a utility function, such as the negative exponential, which postulates a specific algebraic form to represent risk preferences. The mean variance model certainty equivalents range from 600 to 721 Sudanese pounds per feddan and marginal effects range from 0 to 84.84 Sudanese pounds for cotton, 0 to 467.35 for wheat, 0 to 378.94 for groundnuts and 223.62 to 586.63 for sorghum (which is excluded at all levels of risk aversion).

Samba Sall, David Norman and Allen Featherstone, Kansas State University, USA – *Farmer preferences and the adoption of improved rice varieties in the Casamance, Senegal*

This study applied a technology characteristic approach to the adoption of improved rice varieties in Southern Senegal. The objective was to test the hypothesis that not only farm and farmers' characteristics, but also farmers' perception of technology-specific characteristics, significantly influence the technology adoption decision. Earlier studies have not quantitatively incorporated the farmers' perceptions of the technology in the analysis of adoption. Farmers' attitudes towards rice varieties were elicited quantitatively on the basis of a method developed in industry. Based on a stratified random sample of 400 farmers, the results showed that farmers used different discriminatory criteria. They demanded rice varieties with a short maturation period, tall stature, good resistance to soil-related constraints and good cooking quality. A Tobit model indicated that farmer-specific variables (initial impression of the variety, information acquired, participation in village-level organization and age) and the technology-specific factors were significant in explaining the adoption of improved varieties. The results also showed that the response to changes in these technology-specific attributes was relatively more elastic than the response to changes in the farmer-specific factors. Therefore research and extension efforts concerned with the adoption of improved technologies need to consider farmers' perceptions of technology-specific attributes.

Samba Sall, Cesar Guvele, Allen Featherstone and David Norman, Kansas State University, USA – *Efficiency measures, farming systems research and extension activities in Southern Senegal and the Sudan Gezira*

Farming systems research and extension (FSR/E) involves tailoring research, extension and developmental/policy initiatives to the needs of different types of farmers classified into research/recommendation domains. Using primary data from Southern Senegal and the Sudan Gezira, non-parametric programming is used to estimate different efficiency indices. The mean levels of the indices suggest that there is much room for improvement, while the variation and range in their values indicate considerable heterogeneity in the farming population. Regression (Tobit) analysis on the Senegalese data showed that improvement in efficiency would require specific action in research, extension and development/policy initiatives. The results not only justify the basic FSR/ E tenet of taking into account the heterogeneity of the farming population, but also point to the need for close interactive linkage between farmers and research and extension personnel. Although the non-parametric approach has some value in FSR/E under specific circumstances (for example, to demonstrate need for interaction between the developmental actors or to convince sceptics of the importance of understanding the local production environment), it is not a substitute for other techniques currently used (such as participatory rural appraisal).

Anacleti K. Kashuliza, Sokoine University of Agriculture, Morogoro, Tanzania – *Participatory plant breeding and impact studies of the bean (CRSP) in Tanzania*

This presentation discusses the participatory plant-breeding model which has guided the bean (CRSP) breeding programme at Sokoine University for the past 5 to 10 years and assesses the outcomes of the approach. There is also a brief review of the adoption of this particular bean variety and of impact studies which have been conducted in Tanzania since 1994.

Angelos Pagoulatos, Aida Isinika, David L. Debertin and Stephan J. Goetz, University of Kentucky, Lexington, USA – *The effect of agricultural research and extension expenditures on the productivity of crop production in Tanzania*

Results are reported of a study measuring the effects of spending on agricultural research and extension on crop production in Tanzania. The study uses Tornquist–Theil–Divisia indices and is based on a production function estimation using data for the period 1972–92.

Ntengua Mdoe, Sokoine University of Agriculture, Morogoro, Tanzania – *Environmental hazards of agricultural chemical use in the southern highlands of Tanzania*

The haphazard sale and use of agricultural chemicals in the southern highlands of Tanzania, since the implementation of market reform policies, has potential environmental risks. The aim is to present empirical findings of a recent study on agrochemical use and environmental effects in the southern highlands.

Biruma Abaru, Allen Featherstone and David Norman, Kansas State University, USA – *Credit to low-income women in Uganda*

Because lack of credit was viewed as a limiting factor preventing women farmers in Uganda from increasing agricultural production, the Rural Farmers Scheme (RFS) was introduced aiming to give them 60 per cent of its credit. To increase the participation of women, some of the normal RFS credit eligibility requirements were relaxed (for example, character loans are made, women borrowers need not be old customers of the bank, and the loan is for any agricultural enterprise). The study evaluates participation of women by examining and comparing loan sizes, loan repayments, credit needs of borrowers and relative loan losses of borrowers. A sample of 1012 borrowers from 1987 to 1995 indicates that RFS approved higher loan amounts to women than to men, but for actual disbursements women received less. Results showed poor repayments by both men and women, but loan losses revealed that men were worse. Regression analysis (GLS and Tobit) identified a number of factors, apart from gender, as important. Unless major changes are made in the approach used by RFS, women will not benefit from the programme.

Jim Wright and Stephen W. Gundry, University of Edinburgh, United Kingdom – *Local indicators of food security and the use of growth-monitoring data in Zimbabwe*

The relationship between long-term patterns of malnutrition and the infrastructure and socioeconomic characteristics of Zimbabwean districts is investigated. Principal components analysis of household and district-level variables is combined with regression analysis of time-series of malnutrition rates. The analysis confirms that persistent malnutrition is related to lack of rural development.

Godfrey Mudimu, Jim A. MacMillan and Lovemore Rugube, University of Zimbabwe, Harare, Zimbabwe – *Crop diversification, food security and sustainable soil and moisture tillage among smallholder farmers in Zimbabwe*

A case study has been conducted analysing incentives for widespread adoption of soil and moisture conservation practices by smallholder farmers in a high rainfall zone in Zimbabwe. The study quantifies the relationship between conservation practices, total crop production and farm household income. The study tests the hypothesis that intensive agriculture, based on cash crop production and application of soil and moisture conservation practices, increases land and labour productivity with positive effects on household food output and income. The results show that sustainable cropping systems are profitable and improve household food security and incomes at the farm level. This provides a basis for widespread adoption by small farmers.

Stephen W. Gundry, Jim Wright and Prabhat Vaze, University of Edinburgh, United Kingdom – *An integrated model of the food system in a region of Zimbabwe*

The malnutrition–infection complex provides the basis for a systems dynamics model of household food access and its interaction with health. Temporal variability of production, sales and purchases of staples by households is modelled and compared with household nutritional requirements to provide an estimate of nutritional sufficiency.

Caroline Younger and Stephen W. Gundry, University of Edinburgh, United Kingdom – *Perceptions of livestock value in Zimbabwe's communal lands*

The study explores relative values associated with livestock in semi-arid areas, indicating that economic motives underpin farmers' actions. This finding questions previous suggestions that livestock management is based on biological survival and cultural influences. Such understanding of the crucial role of livestock in complex livelihood systems will aid the attainment of goal congruency between farmers and developers.

ASIA

H. Basavaraja, University of Agricultural Sciences, Dharwad, India – *Land use dynamics in India: An agricultural perspective*

Land use in India was appraised over 40 years, starting in 1950–51 and dividing time into three sub-periods. An exponential growth model was then applied. Mutual transferences among land use categories were identified using correlation analysis. Net area sown registered an overall growth of 0.33 per cent per annum. Growth was 0.93 per cent during Period 1, with the growth in forest cover at around 2 per cent. However, the same tempo could not be maintained during Period II and it was negative in Period III. In the latter period the amount of fallow land increased at the expense of the area under crops (it grew from 10 million hectares to 15 million hectares), while the area under non-agricultural use rose at the expense of pastures and grazing land.

Ramachandra Bhatta and Mahadev Bhat, Florida International University, Miami, USA – *Irreversible environmental development and survival of subsistence agriculture in coastal India*

The paper formulates an ecological–economic model of interactive agriculture and aquaculture sectors in India to examine the impacts of shrimp pond development on economic variability and hydroecological sustainability of the coastal environment. The model identifies circumstances in which it remains feasible to encourage crop-to-shrimp land conversion. The analysis shows that some of the government's own policies may push the development threshold downwards and weaken the ability to protect the environmental basis of traditional agriculture.

Amar S. Guleria, Himachel Pradesh University, Shimla, India – *Trade and price analysis of forest products in India*

An attempt has been made to analyse recent Indian policy changes in general and their impact on the trade of major forest products. Forest resources are 98 per cent government-owned, which is contrary to the overall economic policy measures of price liberalization and competitiveness. However, since the adoption of these measures there has been a decrease in the trade deficit of wood products. The growth in exports and export value is now fairly impressive, even after accounting for the devaluation of the rupee. From regression analysis it appears that demand for the majority of wood products is price-inelastic, though the benefits of higher competitive prices did not accrue to forest managers.

Kiyotada Hayashi, Department of Integrated Research for Agriculture, Fukuyama, Japan – *Evaluating labour-saving production systems by multi-criteria models with interval numbers*

A methodology is presented for evaluating new farm production systems using multi-attribute value models with interval numbers. The technique is applied to the evaluation of labour-saving production systems at farm level and is based on the elicitation of values and weights. The main features are (1) introducing interval computations to deal with imprecision and uncertainty; (2) distinguishing between strict preference, weak preference and indifference; (3) representing preferences among alternatives using graph theory; (4) combining interval numbers with sensitivity analysis to examine stability of preferences and effects of technical improvements; (5) utilizing swing weights to properly treat the relationship between weights and ranges for evaluation measures. For Daikon (*Raphanus sativus L.*) new production systems (introducing a self-propelled harvester and eliminating thinning) are being developed and compared with the conventional system in terms of profitability and farmwork characteristics. The results indicate that, although the new production systems at the present level of techniques are not preferred to the conventional system, they would become viable if further improvements in cultivation and mechanization could be achieved.

S.B. Hosamani, G.K. Hiremath and K.N. Ranganatha Sastry, University of Agricultural Sciences, Dharwad, India – *Institutional reforms in agricultural finance in India: a case study of performance of regional rural banks (RRBs)*

In view of divergent opinion about the performance of RRBs, and amid controversy over their continuance, a rigorous evaluation of their position was felt necessary at this time of marked change in India's economic policies. Analysis of primary and secondary data using financial ratio analysis revealed favourable liquidity, solvency and strength, though use of an exponential growth model indicated weaknesses in profitability despite the growth in other indicators.

Keishito Itagaki, University of Agriculture, Tokyo, Japan – *Food processing industries in East Asian countries*

The aim is to examine the dynamic structure of processed food trade among East Asian countries. Emphasis is placed on the nature of the market structure and the extent and effectiveness of the linkage between the food processing industry and the farm sector as supplier of basic food inputs.

Tamotsu Kawamura and Jin Shen He, Iwate University, Japan – *Measuring the productivity of multi-purpose agricultural cooperatives*

On the basis of productivity measurements for Japanese multi-purpose agricultural cooperatives, it is suggested that (1) total factor productivity of the cooperatives had grown by 10 per cent per annum in the 1960s and the first half of the 1970s; (2) it was stagnant in the later 1970s and 1980s; and (3) it has been decreasing in the 1990s.

S. Lakshmikanthamma, Bangalore, India – *Economic impact of watershed development on dryland agriculture in Karnataka, India*

A watershed development programme (WDP) has been initiated in Karnataka to improve and sustain the productivity and production potential of dryland agriculture through adoption of appropriate conservation and production technologies. It is a holistic approach to improve the economic and natural resource base of the dry regions. The paper assesses its impact on cropping patterns and intensity, crop yields, income and employment. The results show that the WDP has led to greater crop diversification, a shift from low- to high-value crops, with improved cropping intensities and crop yields. The per hectare productivity of aggregate crops was distinctly higher in the watershed project area as compared with the non-project area among all size groups of holdings. The programme also resulted in higher per hectare investment followed by higher returns from crop production for most strata of farms. This programme has led to an improvement in household incomes as well as a reduction in poverty among small farmers. WDP thus offers a ray of hope to the poor and disadvantaged regions of India which could benefit from a development alternative addressing concerns linking growth with equity and sustainability.

C. Lapenu and M. Benoit-Cattin, CIRAD, Montpellier, France – *An interpretation of the restructuring of the Indonesian rural financial system using the theory of contestable markets*

The evolution and performance of the Indonesian rural financial system is impressive and the state has played a key role since liberalization. Its action can be interpreted as creating a contestable market: the entry of new actors forces the incumbents, most particularly the public institutions, to be efficient and perform well. This theoretical framework highlights the possibilities for improvements to the financial system.

Pramod K. Mishra, Gujarat Electricity Board, Baroda, India – *Political economy of electricity supply to agriculture: a case of resource mismanagement*

In many countries the pricing of electricity supplied to agriculture is devoid of economic logic, ignores incentive effects and is influenced by political considerations. Consequently, there is not only less than optimal allocation but also mismanagement of resources, which poses a threat to sustainable agricultural growth. The analysis is based on empirical data from Gujarat (India).

Rolf A.E. Mueller and Edward S. Prescott, University of Kiel, Germany – *Hired hooves: An empirical investigation of village markets for bullock services in the semi-arid tropics of India*

Efficient production requires that factors of production be used in optimal combinations. Since farmers rarely own factors in their most productive proportions, markets, for the leasing of factors, are formed to facilitate adjustment of availabilities to desirable proportions. Bullocks are widely used as draught animals in India. Bullock to labour proportions are technically determined; generally, one bullock pair is driven by one driver. Bullock to land ratios may be adjusted through tenancy transactions or by hiring bullock services. The literature on agricultural factor markets frequently claims that bullock to land proportions are adjusted through the land market because of poorly developed markets for bullock services. The study provides evidence to the contrary. Key results are that (1) despite covariate demand for bullock services, an active market exists, (2) bullocks are hired by farmers who own bullocks as well as those who do not, (3) spot contracts for single operations dominate, (4) despite variable demand, cash prices are virtually constant, and (5) there is much monitoring, but contract enforcement is not a concern.

Ryo Nakajima and Ryohei Kada, Kyoto University, Japan – *Cointegration analysis of government agricultural expenditure growth in Japan*

This paper analyses the government preferences influencing the growth of agriculture expenditures in postwar Japan. Assuming that the government's aim was utility maximization, a cointegration approach is used to estimate parameters of the utility function. A well-specified long-run relationship between agricultural expenditure, government total expenditure and the agricultural population rate in Japan is found.

Yasuo Ohe, Chugoku National Agricultural Experiment Station, Hiroshima, Japan – *The characteristics of the tourists visiting farms in Japan for recreation*

Tourist characteristics were analysed by focusing on visitors to pick-your-own farms using a nationwide survey. They are found to have a higher academic background and respect for cultural matters than tourists in general.

Katsuhiro Ota, University of Agriculture, Tokyo, Japan – *Asian rice security*

Rice is an essential food for most Asian people. For them 'rice security', based on sustainable development of rice production and trade, implies 'food security'. The poster examines the development path and pattern of the rice industry in Asian countries and explores the implications for 'rice security'.

M.A. Razzaque and Mafizul Islam, Bangladesh Agricultural Research Council, Dhaka, Bangladesh – *Planning for research and development in hill farms in Bangladesh through the application of PRA*

Participatory Rural Appraisal (PRA) was conducted to identify constraints, opportunities, needs and potential for hill farming in Bangladesh. The exercise generated useful guidelines for research, development and policy issues for the development of hill farming on a sustainable basis. Given farmers' perceived needs and taking account of the significant risk factors involved, integrated production plans for agroforestry and livestock have been developed and an operational strategy has been suggested. The testing and transfer of system-based technologies, which are closely linked to market and rural agribusiness enterprises, are advocated to augment the income and welfare of hill farmers, the most unprivileged community of Bangladesh.

Abelardo Rodrigez, Centre for Agricultural Research in Dry Areas, Aleppo, Syria – *Can groundwater be managed sustainably in Syria?*

Modern irrigation systems introduced in Syria during the 1970s have increased and stabilized farm income in semi-arid areas. Farmers are aware of declining water tables, but appear resigned to a return to rainfed agriculture. More well drilling is seen as a rational response to increasing water scarcity. The absence of efficient monitoring systems for irrigation practices, the land tenure and water rights situations, and farmers' perception and attitudes, dissuade cooperative irrigation scheduling or water sharing. Current economic incentives to produce agricultural commodities, tilting preferences towards the present rather than the future value of water, compound the unsustainable choices made by farmers.

Seiichi Sakurai, Chugoku National Agricultural Experiment Station, Hiroshima, Japan – *Direct roadside marketing by farmers to consumers in Japan*

Many Japanese farmers' groups are now engaged in selling their products to consumers directly at roadside markets. This development has brought changes in the organizational structure and the management systems of markets, notably in the employment of sales clerks and later in the growth of more sophisticated management systems to provide farmers with information about market trends. On the basis of survey evidence, it is suggested that direct marketing has advantages of flexibility in pricing and grading and offers good opportunities for communication between suppliers and purchasers. Although it has some problems, it has had positive effects on farmers' incomes. Though it is likely to be a secondary channel, it could be an effective one in Japanese conditions.

K.L. Sharma, University of the South Pacific, Suva, Fiji – *Constraints on agricultural development in Fiji*

The characteristic features of the Fiji economy emphasize the importance of agriculture in economic development. Some socioeconomic and institutional constraints affecting the performance of agriculture are identified during the period 1970–95. Specific policies on technology, agricultural research and extension, land tenure and infrastructural development need to be instituted to increase agricultural productivity.

Teruyuki Shinbo, Koto Asano and Ryohei Kada, Kochi and Kyoto Universities, Japan – *Hedonic evaluation of the amenity of paddy fields in Japan*

Recently in Japan, much attention has been paid to the importance of the externalities of agriculture and forestry for neighbouring areas; hence the number of studies using the hedonic approach in evaluating the amenity of agriculture and forestry land in monetary terms is increasing. The hedonic method, based on a capitalization hypothesis, estimates the shadow price of the environmental factors through a regression analysis. In applying this method, however, there are various theoretical and methodological problems. The current study addresses the issue of model selection of a hedonic rent function by non-nested testing. It is crucial to specify correctly since use of an unsuitable model leads to unreliable evaluation. The advantage of using a diagnostic test is that it makes it possible to analyse the specification of the hedonic rent function by a test of a statistical hypothesis.

C.A. Tisdell and S.R. Harrison, University of Queensland, Australia – *Control of foot-and-mouth disease in Thailand: improving CBA assessment*

Foot-and-mouth disease (FMD) is endemic to Thailand but, while it causes considerable loss, no satisfactory analysis exists of the costs and benefits of control. The government has adopted measures to increase the coverage of livestock vaccination by subsidizing vaccine supplies, providing assistance from Department of Livestock officers, provision of information to farmers particularly through village headmen, as well as requiring vaccination of cattle travelling significant distances to market or arriving from neighbouring countries. Estimates of the benefit–cost ratios of controlling FMD vary greatly (from 1 to 5; 11.75 to 1 and 7.35 to 1) owing to paucity of data and the scale of the problem considered. Studies are reviewed and it is concluded that the quality of CBA assessment will not improve until many problems are overcome. Attention is also given to the economies of regulating cattle movements in Thailand in order to control FMD.

C.A. Tisdell and Ren Zhuge, University of Queensland, Australia – *Slash-and-burn agriculture in Asia: sustainability issues and transitional problems*

Estimates indicate that 300–500 million people worldwide depend on slash-and-burn agriculture. It is widespread in Asia, but is becoming unsustainable because socioeconomic changes are reducing the length of the fallow period, with adverse economic and biophysical consequences. Population pressure, withdrawal of land from villagers practising the technique, rising income aspirations of participants and their increasing involvement in the market economy have all played a role in the process. While shifting agriculture is often associated with environmental problems, food shortages and poverty, the transition to settled farming causes problems because it is difficult to change institutional arrangements governing property rights. Furthermore, suitable sustainable forms of settled agriculture are not always available, particularly in hilly or mountainous areas. Examples from Yunan, China (the Jingpo) and Northeast India illustrate these issues.

Jessica D. Tjornhom and Victor Gapud, University of Minnesota, Minneapolis, USA – *Pesticide policy dimensions of integrated pest management in the Philippines*

Pesticide use has increased worldwide, resulting in a growing set of problems related to human exposure and environmental contamination, pest resistance to pesticides and pest resurgence. Pesticide prices can influence producer decisions to apply pesticides as opposed to non-chemical means of pest control. Those prices in turn are influenced by agricultural and exchange rate policies. The aim is to present the case for assessing pesticide price distortions as part of the agenda for agricultural economics research in integrated pest management. It is illustrated by the application of pesticide policy analysis to Philippine data to assess the direct and indirect subsidies and taxes on pesticide use in that country.

Pei-Ing Wu and Heng-Chi Lee, National Taiwan University, Taipei, Taiwan – *Trade and environment: pollution control of hog production in an open economy*

The intention is to develop a theoretical linkage between trade and environment. The theoretical framework is applied to the case of pollution control of hog production in Taiwan. Values of social welfare under different policy combinations are computed and compared. The results indicate that various trade restrictions have different impacts on producers, consumers, and government expenditure. Free trade results in the highest value of social welfare.

Xu Xiang and Wang Kai, Nanjing Agricultural University, R.R. China – *China: Can the awakening giant feed a wealthier population?*

There is considerable interest in the future relationship between food supply and demand in China and in the related issue of food security for the next three decades. The questions are examined in five parts: 1. An introduction to the great debate; 2. Factors affecting the demand for grain, including population analysis, income growth, changes in the diet pattern; 3. Projections of grain demand in 2030; 4. Supply prospects, including area projections, yield projections, food security analysis; 5. The way ahead: self-sufficiency or comparative advantage?

Zhang-Yue Zhou, University of Sydney, Australia and **Liang-Biao Chen**, Ministry of Agriculture, Beijing, China – *China's grain distribution system and its reforms*

A non-specific grain rationing system in China (in place for about four decades) ensured fair distribution of grains among consumers, but it also caused some problems which led to recent changes. This paper provides an overview of the system, highlights the problems resulting from it and addresses its recent reforms. Attention is drawn to related issues emerging as a result of the reforms. It is emphasized that, while the reforms are necessary, they should not be allowed to jeopardize the food security of the poor and that the distribution of government-subsidized grains should be aimed at the poor.

THE AMERICAS

Godfrey C. Ejimakor and Jimmy Zuniga, A and T State University, Greensboro, NC, USA – *Socioeconomic changes and evolution of agricultural policy*

Survey respondents were grouped and profiled by choice of agricultural policy. The relationships between selected socioeconomic variables and the indicated policy choices were estimated. Levels of group characteristics seem to affect policy preferences. Agricultural policy is expected to keep changing in response to changes in these variables.

Arthur M. Havenner and Daniel A. Sumner, University of California, Davis, USA – *Time-series analysis of a policy-created asset: the case of the California dairy quota*

A forecasting model of the California milk quota is fitted for monthly observations. The multivariate model uses quota milk price, overbase price and the value of the quota asset to characterize the dairy farm portfolio. The model predicts well out of sample.

Ruud Huirne, Wageningen University, The Netherlands – *Goals, critical success factors and information needs of Dutch and US dairy farmers*

One of the major problems for farm-level information system users and developers is to determine farmers' goals, critical success factors and information needs. These are generally based on their management strategies with respect to important decisions. The identification of goals, critical success factors and information needs of individual farmers must be followed by an investigation of their similarity and consistency according to region and time, respectively.

Hans G.P. Jansen, André Nieuwenhuyse, Leedert't Mannetje, Muhammad Ibrahim, Sergio Abarca Monge and Mark Joenje, REPOSA, Costa Rica and Wageningen Agricultural University, Netherlands – *The economics of improved pasture and silvipastoral technologies in the Atlantic zone of Costa Rica*

Capital budgeting models were used to investigate the profitability of alternative ways to increase beef production: grass–legume mixtures, silvipastoral systems and supplementary feeding. Profitability depended on meat prices, stocking rates and length of investment period. Financial benefits of the silvipastoral system were significantly lower than those based on use of grass–legume mixtures, though no effort could be made to incorporate non-monetary benefits of including trees within farm systems. Supplementary feeding constitutes an attractive option only on poorer soils and in capital-scarce environments.

Mary A. Marchant, Ravichandran Munirathinam and Michael R. Reed, University of Kentucky, Lexington, USA – *International trade and foreign direct investment*

The impact of the Canada–United States Trade Agreement (CUSTA) on the trade of bulk, intermediate and consumer-oriented processed foods between the United States and Canada is considered. The research also seeks whether exports of these products and foreign investment in the sector are complements or substitutes. Results indicate that US exports to Canada more than doubled, while Canadian exports to the United States nearly doubled after CUSTA's implementation in 1989. Regression results using the covariance model on panel data show that US food processing firms use both exports and direct foreign investment as complementary marketing strategies in selling into Canadian markets. This is also true of some Canadian firms, though others use exports and FDI as substitute market strategies in gaining access to US markets. In the case of bulk and intermediate products, it is not possible to determine whether exports and foreign investment are substitutes or complements.

Shankar Narayanan, Agriculture and Agri-Food Canada, Ottawa, Canada – *Canadian agricultural growth: trends, policy relevance and comparisons with the United States*

The highlights of the recent updating of total factor productivity estimates for Canadian and US agriculture over the 1961–93 period are discussed. In the post-1980 period, Canadian agriculture productivity rebounded strongly, supported by government policies of large subsidy programmes to bolster output, accompanied by a sharp fall in labour input in all regions and a general decline in all input categories in eastern Canada. The long-term (1961–93) productivity growth (technical progress) for Canada stood at an annual rate of 2.3 per cent, against 2.0 per cent in the United States – a slight competitive edge narrowing significantly from the 1960s and the 1970s.

Bo Ohlmer, Kent Olson and Berndt Brehmer, University of Minnesota, St Paul, USA – *Understanding farmers' decision-making processes and improving managerial assistance*

Farmers' decision making is described as a matrix of phases (detection, definition, analysis, implementation) and sub-processes (information and attention, planning, evaluation and choice, and bearing responsibility). Farmers used continual updating, qualitative methods, 'quick and simple' methods, incremental implementation and feed-forward evaluation. Implications for management assistance are discussed.

John L. Pender, IFPRI, Washington, DC, USA – *Causes and effects of agricultural intensification: evidence from Central Honduras*

The causes and effects of agricultural intensification in Central Honduras are investigated using three-stage least squares. Contrary to Boserup's theory, population pressure is not associated with adoption of labour-intensive land improvements, inputs or higher-value crops. Access to markets, technical assistance and irrigation are associated with such intensification.

Anne Villamil and Laurian Unnevehr, University of Illinois, Urbana, USA – *Measuring the value of food product health attributes with experimental auctions*

Experimental auctions are used to test whether consumers will pay more for food products with health benefits; how information about health benefits and consumer health endowments influence willingness to pay; and whether there is a gap between willingness to pay and willingness to accept for products with health benefits.

John Westra and Kent Olson, University of Minnesota, St Paul, USA – *Farmers' decision processes and adoption of conservation tillage*

Farmers were surveyed about adopting conservation tillage. Logit analysis showed the following factors to be significant and positive: farm size, erosion concerns, recent investments in the farm, management skills, production goals, physical setting and other farmers. Negative significant factors were found to be ease of obtaining information and amount of control over the decision.

Zhikang You and Wojciech J. Florkowski, University of Georgia, Griffin, USA – *Factors influencing the frequency of consumption of selected nuts*

Frequency of consumption of selected nuts was examined on the basis of local survey data using a multi-ordered probability model. Results suggested that female, white, full-time employed or older respondents had a higher probability of selecting pecans than walnuts or peanuts. Male or urban residents were more likely to choose peanuts than pecans or walnuts, while farmers, non-white, or not full-time employed preferred walnuts.

GENERAL

Ralph Blaney and Richard Bennett, The University of Reading, United Kingdom – *What price animal suffering? The role of economics in the farm animal welfare debate*

In addressing farm animal welfare issues, there are inextricable linkages between animal science, moral philosophy and economics. The approach adopted by economists depends upon the choice of ethical stance. The welfare of animals can be seen as important only as far as it affects human utility, its level being determined by its value to society relative to the value of farm animal products. If this ethical view is followed, further work using existing methodologies should result in adequate information on which to base decisions on the optimum level of farm animal exploitation. An alternative ethical view is that animal welfare is important in its own right, requiring that both human and animal preferences/utility be considered. Many experiments have been conducted to measure animal preferences using approaches akin to consumer demand theory. If the ethical premise that animal utilities have independent value is considered valid, the challenge facing economists is to incorporate both animal and human preferences into an economic framework.

Elias Dinopoulos and James Oehmke, Michigan State University, USA – *A neo-Schumpeterian model of agricultural innovation and growth*

A neo-Schumpeterian model of agricultural research and endogenous growth addresses growth linkages, optimal financing of agricultural research and general equilibrium impacts of research. Results indicate private-sector overinvestment in non-agricultural research, systematic bias in partial equilibrium measures of research benefits and an alternative method for determining optimal research investment.

Julio Garrido-Mirapeix, Queen Elizabeth House, University of Oxford, United Kingdom – *Food security and the World Food Summit*

Following the World Food Summit (WFS) in Rome, organized by the Food and Agriculture Organization of the United Nations (FAO) in November 1996, food security is back on the agenda. The paper argues that there is likely to be much sympathy with the WFS goals, though the crucial question remains about the real impact of the summit in effectively reducing food insecurity in coming decades. Consideration of a number of issues (summit fatigue; conceptual, participatory and implementational issues; the commitment of FAO members) leads to a pessimistic view of the impact of the WFS Action Plans in terms of national household food security. It is suggested that additional research on a number of key food security areas is necessary before there can be any move forward.

Luciano Gutierrez, University of Sassari, Italy – *On the determinants of food consumer price inflation in open economies*

A simple two-sector model can be used to examine the determinants of food consumer price inflation in open economies. Starting from cost-push and monetary models, an eclectic model is formulated which allows for direct effects of cost factors plus imported inflation and money supply effects.

T.M. Horbulyk, University of Calgary, Canada – *The social cost of labour in rural development: job creation benefits re-examined*

Governments in developed and developing countries are attempting to implement policies which favour rural economic growth and simultaneously reduce existing unemployment, or underemployment, of labour. By referring to recent published examples, this paper shows that some analysis has not paid sufficient attention to the social cost of labour employed when job creation is pursued in the private or public sector. In specific instances, policy analysis has confused the social cost of labour with the distributional benefit potentially achieved through job creation. Correct analysis is important both in choosing alternative development proposals and in the choice of labour-intensive versus capital-intensive technologies. The paper illustrates these issues using static, partial equilibrium analysis of labour market adjustment, with and without regional migration. When correctly conceptualized, the social costs and benefits of job creation policies can best inform a range of rural policy decisions.

Douglas Horton, ISNAR, The Hague, The Netherlands – *Assessing institutional impacts of an international organization: the case of ISNAR*

The poster illustrates how an international agency – The International Service for National Agricultural Research – has organized and conducted an evaluation of its achievements and its impacts on client organizations in developing countries. It presents the methodology used for the evaluation and the main substantive findings. It assesses the outcomes of the evaluation process, and draws lessons for future organizational assessment exercises.

Oyvind Hoveid, Norwegian Agricultural Economics Research Institute, Oslo, Norway – *Policy analysis when history matters: from temporary equilibria to intertemporal ones*

A theoretical model comprising learning is used to study the movement from temporary towards intertemporal equilibria. Such models are needed for policy analysis when the economy is not presumed to develop in a unique intertemporal equilibrium path.

Michael Kirk, University of Göttingen, Germany – *Challenges for future cooperation in developing countries*

As cooperative self-help has proved to be efficient in phases of rapid economic change, it is an interesting option for developing countries undergoing structural adjustment and/or transformation. Against the background of reduction of official intervention and divestiture, the paper explores the concepts of new institutional economics for use in the design of cooperative types of agrarian institutions.

Maria de Belem Martins, Evora University, Portugal – *The use of linear programming to support animal breeding programmes*

Numerous features contribute to the efficiency of animal production systems and the evaluation of their relative economic weight is important for success in animal breeding programmes. Although there are several studies of genetic improvements and of meat production systems, no attempt has yet been made to utilize bioeconomic models to quantify economically the effects of selection modification on technical coefficients. This is attempted in the poster.

Severine Mateo and Daniel Deybe, CIRAD/URPA, Nogent-sur-Marne, France – *Interactions between deforestation and capital accumulation: an analytical model*

Understanding deforestation processes is a challenge. In the region studied in the Ecuadorian Andes, farmers seem to arbitrate between deforestation to accumulate livestock and conservation of the forest for future uses. A dynamic analytical optimal control model is used to formalize this process in order to obtain theoretical growth paths within the farm.

Ludwig Nellinger and Ralf Helbig, Institute of Farm Management, Bonn, Germany – *Costs of machinery and farm structure*

The properties of cost functions in agriculture require a declining annual use of machinery of increasing age. As a result, a mixture of farm sizes and the trading of machines in a second-hand market becomes beneficial. The poster outlines the theoretical background and empirical results with respect to this issue.

Ernst-August Nuppenau and Ousmane Badiane, University of Kiel, Germany – *A model of agricultural transformation through policy reforms and public investment*

This contribution focuses on the modernization of agriculture as an intertemporal process which includes pricing policies. It describes a market-oriented policy that cares about public goods provision and investigates the potential for the complementary provision of public goods in infrastructure and farm technology. Increased knowledge and quality of farm operation due to public investments allow modernization to take place.

Quirino Paris and Richard E. Howitt, University of California, Davis, USA – *Dealing with scarce and incomplete information by maximum entropy methods*

In many fields of economic inquiry the available information may not be sufficient to allow estimation of the desired structure of a model by means of traditional econometric techniques. Maximum entropy methods can, however, deal with ill-posed problems (number of observations smaller than number of parameters) and ill-conditioned problems (multicollinearity).

May Mercado Peters and Shahla Shapouri, USDA-ERS, Washington, DC, USA – *Factors affecting income distribution and food security*

Income inequality is one of the major factors contributing to the severity of chronic undernutrition in low-income countries. The objective of this study was to identify the key factors affecting income inequality by estimating the relationship between the income inequality measure and selected economic and social variables. The results of the analysis indicate that increasing the rate of economic growth and the development of the agriculture sector will significantly reduce the degree of income inequality in low-income countries.

E. Wesley F. Peterson and Siva Rama Krishna Valluru, University of Nebraska, Lincoln, USA – *Agricultural comparative advantage and policy interventions*

International trade patterns are often explained using the concept of comparative advantage based on variations in factor endowments. Government intervention in agricultural markets may distort patterns predicted by relative factor endowments. This study tests the proposition that agricultural and environmental regulations offset the effects of factor endowments in agricultural trade.

Punya Prasad Regmi, Asian Institute of Technology, Pathumthani, Thailand – *Sustaining agriculture through ecorestructuring: a holistic approach to strategy development*

Mounting population pressure has been creating economic and environmental problems and causing unsustainable development, particularly in Third World countries. Ecorestructuring is a holistic approach to evolving strategies for sustainable development. Ecosystem capabilities and ecosystem governance are two fundamental aspects of ecorestructuring.

Stacey Rosen and Shahla Shapouri, USDA-ERS, Washington, DC, USA – *Food security outlook for developing countries*

The paper attempts to project food availability and access in 60 lower-income developing countries (36 in sub-Saharan Africa, 4 in North Africa, 9 in Asia and 11 in Latin America) during the next decade. The results show that sub-Saharan Africa is the most vulnerable region in terms of both lack of adequate food supplies and the share of the total population affected.

Guenter Schamel, Humboldt University, Berlin, Germany – *Agricultural trade and the environment: domestic versus global perspectives*

Alternative environmental and trade policies are modelled, distinguishing abatement and output reduction. Terms of trade effects resulting from domestic/border policies determine optimality. Even without trade taxes, large importers (exporters) can raise their welfare by taxing production below (above) marginal external costs created, while subsidizing abatement above (below) marginal social damage avoided.

Ulf A. Stolzke, University of Kiel, Germany – *New approaches in commodity futures trading exercises: preparing students for changes in agricultural trade*

Kiel University offers Europe's first agricultural commodity futures trading exercise. Students from Western and Eastern European universities competing in a speculative game learn to use and evaluate commodity futures. Lectures given by scientists, speeches made by business people and the trading exercise prepare students to become decision makers in an agribusiness sector likely to be confronted by an increasing price risk.

Bonny Sylvie, INRA-ESR, Grignon, France – *New technologies in agriculture: are they a way to sustainability?*

Are new technologies (NT) in the position to make a positive contribution in promoting sustainable agriculture? The aim is to examine developments such as those in biotechnology and information handling for their potential effects, taking into consideration the different elements of sustainability in agriculture:

- environmental soundness: will NT lead to a greater respect for the environment and the preservation of resources?
- economic viability: will it be increased by NT adoption?
- sufficiency and quality of food: will NT improve the situation for everyone?
- social acceptability: will NT lead to acceptable forms of agriculture?
- equity: will disparities diminish or strengthen?

New technologies often appear double-edged since they may increase or decrease sustainability, depending on how they are used. With the development of ever more powerful tools, greater control is necessary. An essential condition for a sustainable development model is that technological progress does not widen the gap between those who have access to it and those who do not.

Scott R. Templeton and Sara J. Scherr, University of California, Berkeley, USA – *The effects of demographic change and related factors on hilly–mountainous land in developing countries*

Concern about environmental impacts are frequently expressed in debates about population growth in upland areas of developing countries. However, a review of more than 100 studies indicated that population change can lead to either decreases or increases in tree cover, erosion or conservation of soil on agricultural land, and degradation or enhancement of grazing areas. These polar outcomes are possible because people not only use land more frequently for production but also substitute capital- and labour-intensive methods for land-intensive ones. They also create property rights which increase the expected pay-offs from land-improving investments and production methods. Increases in local labour supply and demand, larger families and smaller land holdings are the microeconomic consequences of population growth inducing these changes. Our review indicates that population decline usually leads to degradation of agricultural and pastoral land and that better non-farm income opportunities have a similar impact. In both cases, higher labour costs are the reason, but improvements in these opportunities can also induce people to plant trees as a labour-saving strategy and enable them to finance investments in farming land. Property rights do not always affect investments as expected. What matters for sustainable land use is not only the number of producers but also what, where and how they produce. The challenge to researchers and policy makers is to understand and configure incentives for production which enhance human welfare as well as land quality.

Detlef Virchow, University of Kiel, Germany – *How to optimize the conservation of plant genetic resources in different property regimes*

In the last decade, the importance of natural resources for sustainable agricultural development has been increasingly discussed. More recently, the problem of erosion of genetic resources and its consequences for global welfare in general, and for agricultural and pharmaceutical production in particular, were introduced into the debate. Since the 1930s, systematic surveying, collection and conservation of plant genetic resources has been conducted; hence, by today, their conservation for food and agriculture is a complex international and national operation. While the political discussion is focusing on the issue of 'fair and equitable sharing' of benefits derived from the use of plant genetic resources for food and farming, an intensive analysis of the costs of conservation has been neglected. The aim here it to analyse conservation costs at the private, national and global level. Two basic scenarios are outlined and their overall cost impact is discussed.

WESTERN EUROPE

Stefan Bojnec and Cecilia Alexandri, FAO, Budapest, Hungary – *The European Union and Eastern Europe: agricultural and food integration*

The costs of accession are likely to cause many problems for agricultural policy adjustment during the integration of central European countries into the Common Agricultural Policy of the European Union. It is suggested that there is likely to be convergence of agricultural policies on both sides which will be accompanied by a more global approach in an enlarged European Union.

Ludo Peeters, Limburg University, Belgium – *The use of the maximum entropy method to estimate input–output coefficients from farm business accounting data*

This paper applies the generalized maximum entropy (GME) method to estimate input-output coefficients from farm business accounting data. The GME technique uses Shannon's information measure as a basis for estimation and inference, and allows the introduction of additional consistency and/or calibration constraints on the system of equations. The performance of the GME method is compared with three other methods: ordinary least squares (OLS), Bayesian estimation and LP. The various methods are tested by using an empirical example based on a set of RICA data from beef/dairy farms in one particular region of the EU.

François Colson and Vincent Chatellier, INRA-LERECO, Nantes, France – *CAP reform and direct payments to French farms*

The aim is to examine the distribution of farm subsidies in France before and after the CAP reform and to evaluate the level of subsidies for three types of farming by taking economic performance into account. A possible scenario for the limitation of direct subsidies per agricultural worker is tested.

Michaela Hoffmann and P. Michael Schmitz, Justus-Liebeg University, Giessen, Germany – *Agriculture and the macroeconomy: modelling linkages using the VAR approach*

A vector-autoregressive system (VAR) and vector-error-correction model (VECM) are developed to capture the dynamic interactions between macroeconomic and agricultural variables in Germany. Impulse-response functions can portray the reaction of the variables to unexpected shocks. It is shown that there are inverse relationships between German food exports and a real revaluation of the Deutschmark (DM), and between the inflation rate and exports, though the interest rate has no clear influence. Producer prices for agricultural products are sensitive to shocks in the real value of the DM in spite of the agrimonetary system of the European Union and also tend to relate to inflation. Interest rates again have little effect. The performance of the food industry is very important for the agricultural sector as prices are increased markedly when a positive shock to food exports occurs. On a less aggregated basis, it can be shown that the livestock sector is more exposed to macroeconomic influences than plant production.

Hiltrud Nieberg, Institute of Farm Economics, Braunsweig, Germany – *Economic impacts of conversion to organic farming in Germany*

The Institute of Farm Economics monitors 107 farms which began their conversion to organic farming in the crop year 1990/91. The selected farms are scattered over the territory of former West Germany. In order to assess the structural and economic changes, the development of organic farms is compared annually with results of a similarly structured group of conventionally managed reference farms. After four years, a wide variety of changes can be observed. Because organic farming prohibits the use of chemical inputs, crop rotation and the cultivation of legumes becomes more important. Furthermore, the land use system depends strongly on the marketing possibilities of organically grown products. Livestock numbers show a declining trend, while labour requirements increase. In crop production, yields decrease strongly. At this point in time, higher prices can only be realized for plant products. The conversion to organic farming has led to positive income effects for the majority of farms. However, the profitability of organic farming depends largely on the extensification premium and the marketing possibilities for organic products.

Benedetto Graziella and Pulina Pietro, University of Sassari, Italy – *The role of agriculture in Italian local systems of production*

The intention is to present the early results of research on the role of agriculture within different territorial systems of production. Specifically, the characteristics of agriculture in so-called 'Industrial Districts' and in other local systems are compared, using a multivariate discriminant analysis applied to data on population, industry and agriculture available in Italian census results. In Industrial Districts, agriculture and related activities make up only a small percentage of the labour force, many workers are over 55 years of age and there is concentration on cropping for local markets. Elsewhere, greater importance attaches to permanent crops (fruit, olives and vineyards, for example) more reliant on waged labour.

Maroeska Boots and Jack Peerlings, Wageningen University, The Netherlands – *Consequences of a two-tier price system for Dutch dairy farms*

The effects of a two-tier price system, as an alternative to the present milk quota system, are simulated. The main result is that farmers produce B-milk only if the price of B-milk – or the world market price – exceeds marginal production cost.

Alison Burrell, Wageningen University, The Netherlands – *The trade argument for eradicating Aujeszky's disease: effects of export restrictions on the Netherlands pig industry*

Market outcomes and pig producers' returns are simulated under different assumptions about the closure of export markets for live piglets and hogs. If The Netherlands failed to eradicate Aujeszky's disease before its trading partners, live piglet exports would be banned, reducing industry revenue and export earnings by 9 per cent and 10 per cent, respectively, in the medium term. If live hog exports were also banned, the reductions would be 26 and 32 per cent, respectively. Piglet producers are less severely affected than hog fatteners.

Folkhard Isermeyer, Torsten Hemme, Claus Deblitz, Ron Knutso and John Miller, Institute of Farm Economics, Braunsweig, Germany – *The International Farm Comparison Network (IFCN) technology and policy impact calculations for typical farms worldwide*

IFCN is a permanent international network of scientists, advisors and farmers which conducts farm-level economic analyses for policy makers, agribusiness and agricultural organizations. Dairy farm results include cost of production comparisons for dairy farms worldwide (12 countries in 1996), policy analyses of dairy farms in the United States, Canada and Mexico, and quota policy analyses of dairy farms in Germany, The Netherlands, the UK and France.

Tassew Woldehanna, Mekelle University, Ethiopia – *Farm household consumption and borrowing constraint: a test of Euler equations on Dutch farms*

Euler equations were derived from a constant relative risk aversion utility function for the total consumption expenditure, household expenditures and other expenditures (which includes that on durable goods). The equations were estimated using the method of three-stage least squares (3SLS). The results indicate that farm households are not optimizing utility of consumption in the way suggested by the Euler equations. Households do not respond to income uncertainty and they are not constrained in borrowing. Instead, households are non-optimal and myopic, following a simple consumption rule based on their current income. The growth of family size has a significant influence on household expenditures, but not on the durable goods expenditure, implying that there are economies of scale in the consumption of durables. The growth of household expenditure and that of other expenditure are found to be complementary.

Olvar Bergland, NLH, Ås, Norway – *Valuation of landscape elements using a contingent choice method*

Agricultural activities provide important amenities for direct and/or indirect enjoyment by the public, plus environmental services to the economy such as waste receipt, wildlife habitat, recreation opportunities and biodiversity. Before making recommendations about optimal provision of these amenities, knowledge is required both of their economic value and of their production costs. Assessment of the economic value of changing landscapes must allow for multidimensional trade-offs in various attributes, which will require specialized methods. Changes to the contingent ranking method, which take into account some of the cognitive difficulties with ranking experiments and also address the reversibility paradox of ranking, are suggested. The methods are used for valuation of countryside amenities in Norway.

Javier Calatrava, Junta de Andalucia, Granada, Spain – *Economic marginality, social depreciation of agriculture and the disappearance of farming in depressed areas in south-eastern Spain*

Three effects of farming in the Alta Alpujarra have been analysed, namely, the abandonment of farming, farmers' relative welfare within the rural community and social regard for agriculture. Finally, some conclusions are drawn concerning the recent evolution of farming in the area and the factors determining farmers' resistance to marginality.

Francisco Del Campo Gomis, Juan F. Julia Igual, Nigel Poole and Fernando Vidal Gimenez, University Miguel Hernandez, Alicante; University Politecnica Valencia, Spain; Wye College, University of London, United Kingdom and University Politecnica Valencia, respectively – *Producer–buyer transactions in the Valencian citrus industry*

Transaction costs are endemic in the fresh produce industry because the technical and economic characteristics of the products give rise to high levels of uncertainty and the need for close control in the supply chain. This study uses a new institutionalist economics approach to investigate the citrus fruit industry in Valencia and to consider whether the use of contracts would facilitate producer marketing decisions, thus reducing uncertainty and transaction costs. The results suggest that, in addition to the negotiated price, marketing factors are important determinants of the terms of the transaction. Specifically, the relationships between security and uncertainty and between trustworthiness and lack of confidence are more important than the negotiated prices. The work lends support to arguments for standardized citrus marketing contracts.

Lucinio Judez, Polytechnic University of Madrid, Spain – *Survey design for application of dichotomous choice contingent valuation to recreation in the 'Tablas de Daimiel' National Park*

A procedure is described for drawing up the sample for dichotomous choice contingent valuation of the recreational value of the park, using a truncated mean as a welfare measure. Data are used to analyse the accuracy (bias and variance) of the estimate of the welfare measure from different values and sub-sample size vectors.

Joaquin Lombán and Joaquin A. Millán, UPM/ETSEAL, Lleida, Spain – *Regional preferences in demand for meat and fish in Spain*

A diverse demand model illustrates regional differences in consumption patterns in Spain. There is particular emphasis on the use of Allais' coefficients to analyse the structure of substitution and complementarity.

Albayrak Nursen, Harper Adams College, United Kingdom – *Modelling agricultural output response: a time-series analysis with GARCH, cointegration and ECM techniques*

The provision of the 'right' price incentive to promote increased supply has been repeatedly emphasized in development literature and is an important concern to policy makers. The empirical evidence on supply response reflects developments made over time in econometric methodology, especially in time-series analysis. The main purpose is both to review existing information and to provide further empirical evidence on supply response to prices and risk. This will enable assessment of the importance of price variables on agriculture. The data used are from district level and the time period analysed is 1950–90. The empirical results confirm that the price mechanism has a role to play in the reduction of price risk and resource allocation and the case for a positive price policy for agricultural development is strong. However, instead of the price mechanism being regarded as the sole instrument to promote growth and efficient resource allocation, it is also concluded that further provision of technological change will stimulate output.

Abigail Tiffin, University of Durham, United Kingdom – *Measuring oligopolistic distortion in the UK frozen potato product sector: a calibration modelling approach*

This paper compares competitive levels in the UK and Dutch frozen potato product sectors over the period 1980–92, using a calibration model and conjectural variation analysis. Estimates are obtained of the trade and welfare effects of oligopolistic distortion in the UK frozen potato product sector.

TRANSITION ECONOMIES

Tanja Jaksch and Rosemarie Siebert, Socioeconomic Institute, Muncheberg, Germany – *Agriculture and rural areas in Eastern Europe: extreme scenarios after the year 2000*

Two extreme scenarios describe the potential future, in the next millennium, of rural areas in eight selected countries, using 11 indicators (for example, agricultural production, population, unemployment, farmland area, importance of environmental protection). Delphi analysis is used to generate the scenarios.

Hermann Lotze, Humboldt University, Berlin, Germany – *Foreign direct investment in Central and East European food industries: a general equilibrium analysis*

Foreign Direct Investment (FDI) is expected to contribute significantly to the process of economic restructuring in Central and Eastern Europe. In this paper the combined effects of capital and technology transfers are modelled in a CGE framework. Factor movements, trade and growth effects are analysed.

Marian Rizov, Department of Land Management and Agricultural Development, Sofia, Bulgaria – *The problem of collateral in conditions of underdeveloped factor markets in the transitional economies of Central and Eastern European countries*

The large demand for investment credit in CEECs is likely to continue, simultaneously with the processes of banking reform and the consequent difficulties in meeting agricultural credit. Lenders also face considerable risks, since newly established farmers are difficult to rate, and bankers' expectations of positive net returns on loans can only be achieved by making default costly to the borrower or cheap to themselves. The viability of non-traded assets as collateral is explored (since creditors are willing to accept greater risk when the collateral is valuable to them) and will depend on the bank's ability to establish values placed on assets by individual debtors. A reliable forecast of future market values, however, is almost impossible in the underdeveloped CEEC land markets. Nevertheless, since such information asymmetries exist in most lending transactions worldwide, collateral should always be a necessary, but not a prime, consideration in lending.

Ararat Y. Melkonyan and Tigran A. Melkonyan, Iowa State University, USA – *Multiple uses of water: power, irrigation and amenity*

As in many countries, the Republic of Armenia has limited fresh water. Waters of Lake Sevan are used to generate power for irrigation, for industry and drinking. We present static and dynamic models of efficient allocation under institutional arrangements varying from rationing to a free market. Environmental impacts are analysed.

Tomas Doucha, Agricultural Economics Research Institute, Prague, Czech Republic – *Farm structure and farm managers in the transition period Czech Republic*

Czech farm structure, emerging after privatization, restitution and transformation, is dominated by large-scale farms such as cooperatives, joint stock and limited companies and private estates. Private farms, including family farms, occupy one-quarter of agricultural land. As a consequence of ownership fragmentation, the share of leased land is extremely high (70–100 per cent). About 500 000 hectares of state-owned land is being prepared for further privatization. The most serious problems are transformation debts and insufficient restructuring, applicable across each organizational type (transformed, restituted, privatized). The total rate of indebtedness reached 83.8 per cent in 1995. Future development strongly depends on adopting an agricultural policy which will prepare for accession to the European Union. Surveys which examine the behaviour of farmers and farm managers under the new conditions are being made to aid successful implementation of further reforms. The most conservation behaviour is that of collective farm managers who, whatever their personal feelings, aim in the main to preserve their powerful positions without causing social unrest on farms.

Valdek Loko, Institute of Agrarian Economics, Saku, Estonia – *The impact of liberal economic policy on Estonian agriculture*

After restoration of independence in August 1991 and the introduction of a new Estonian currency in June 1992, the country has been in transition, moving towards a market economy. The problems of transition in agriculture and the possible future scenarios of agricultural policy are examined.

József Alvincz and Endre Tanka, AKII, Budapest, Hungary – *The changing proprietary structure in Hungarian agriculture and food processing during 1990–95*

Outlining the main tendencies of agricultural privatization, the presentation covers three topics. A historical background analyses the basic facts and legal institutions of privatization. Secondly, the current position and expected trends of privatization are examined. Finally, the newest trends and issues affecting the privatized land use system are considered.

Péter Halmai and László Velikovszky, Gödöllő University of Agricultural Sciences, Budapest, Hungary – *The dilemmas and alternatives for agricultural market regulation in the transition countries: the Hungarian case*

This paper tries to clear up the sometimes mysterious, but at the same time quite real, disorders of agricultural economies under transition in Central and Eastern Europe. There may be reasons why short-term foresight, speculation, fluctuations of demand and supply, and cyclical or periodical over- or undersupply are present in the system. There appears to be many similarities between the countries in the whole Eastern–Central European region.

Sándor Mészáros, Research and Information Institute for Agricultural Economics, Budapest, Hungary – *Analysis and projection of value and diversification of Hungarian agricultural and food exports*

Agricultural and food exports have a foreign exchange earning role in Hungary which assumes added importance because of the country's international debts. The annual growth rate of export value was 2.3 per cent in the period 1989–94, associated with shifts in product pattern. Projections assuming eight scenarios have been made up to 2005, the latest foreseeable date of accession to the European Union.

György Neszmélyi, AKII, Budapest, Hungary – *Development of the agricultural information system in Hungary*

The main tasks required to modernize the agricultural information system in Hungary are discussed. Development is to be implemented with the participation of AKII. A strategic plan for an elaborate agroinformation system includes three main fields: broad agricultural statistics, farm management analysis and market information systems.

Sandor Somogyi, Pate Georgikon University, Keszthely, Hungary – *Economic policy and competitiveness: a case study of the Hungarian food industry*

In Hungary, food production plays an important role in foreign trade and in supplying the domestic market. Based on stable COMECON exports, considerable state subsidy and a safe position on the home-market there was rapid development over a number of decades. The sudden collapse of COMECON, import liberalization and declining purchasing power have created a new situation. The suggestion here is that the reconstruction of the food sector should be based on improvement of competitiveness. Using Porter's approach, it is pointed out that a fundamental condition for increasing competitiveness lies in exploiting the possibilities, deriving from the present comparative advantage, more expediently.

Benon Gazinski and Phillippe Burney, Agricultural University of Olsztyn, Poland – *Transformation of Polish agriculture: a study of potato marketing*

The potato sector is challenged by the nature of Poland's transition towards a market economy and by increased international competition. Trends in cultivation, disposal, storage, processing and market organization are discussed. Clear signs of recovery after the initial shock of the collapse of the former system are observed.

Steffen Noleppa, Humboldt University, Berlin, Germany – *Agricultural policy making and policy-making support in transition countries: some lessons to be learned*

The paper focuses on policy making and the contribution of scientific policy advice regarding agriculture in transition. In view of inadequate theory, the problem of agricultural policy formulation is acute. For Russia, problems in agriculture and related policy approaches are evaluated. Finally, factors are discussed that hinder successful East–West cooperation in scientific agricultural policy making.

Eric P. Thor, Olga Melyukhina, Renata Ianbykh, William E. Scott and Alexander Hristov, Arizona State University, Institute for Economies in Transition, Russian Academy of Agricultural Sciences and Agland Investment Services – *Russian farm credit, rural finance and agricultural conditions*

Economic reforms in Russia led to dramatic changes in agriculture and in the farm credit system, with the latter having faced a number of serious shocks since 1990. The commercial banks serving farmers and agribusiness are attempting to adopt new credit mechanisms and to refocus their commercial, financial and social objectives. There are a number of credit mechanisms which could succeed, with some of them being provided by models which have operated in the past. However, changes are not going to come easily for a nation in which macroeconomic, financial and trade problems create serious obstacles. Discussions at the 1997 Gore-Chernomyrdin meeting highlighted these issues. Agricultural and agribusiness strengths and weaknesses across the different oblasts are also beginning to force regional changes. Despite problems, there are signs of restructuring, with the sale of Agroprombank to SBS-Agro being an indicator that we may be at the beginning of a new era in farm financing.

Peter Wehrheim, University of Kiel, Germany – *The Russian food marketing chain in transition*

Institution building in the Russian agricultural sector needs to be complemented by new downstream marketing institutions to make the food chain more efficient. This is particularly true for domestic food products, which often do not reach the consumer or do so only at non-competitive prices because of high transaction costs. Case studies on food marketing chains for three Russian oblasts are discussed. First, results indicate that Russian farms have generally diversified their marketing channels during transition. Furthermore, marketing chains used by farms differ by products and regions. Larger farms have the more varied arrangements. Items which need substantial further processing are sold via less diversified marketing channels. At the same time, many farms try to sell their products directly to the consumer. Generally, small farms are disadvantaged most by high transaction costs. It is shown that broad features such as path-dependence, uncertainty and cultural and psychological effects are major factors shaping change. Many institutional innovations indicate a lack of market principles and market openness. The dearth of coordination between federal and regional governments is another impediment to improvement in efficiency.

Cecilia Alexandri, Institute of Agrarian Economy, Bucharest, Romania – *The relation between the demand for food and incomes in Romania*

The demand for staple foods according to the distribution of real incomes among the main socioprofessional groups in Romania is analysed. The main aim is to estimate Engel curves for 15 staple foods. Relationships considered were linear, double-logarithmic, semi-logarithmic, log inverse and double-log inverse. The elasticity coefficients obtained, using the double-log and semi-log functions, are presented and discussed. The main conclusions are that (1) in wage earner households, the link between food purchases and incomes is very strong for all products except bread, milk and potatoes; (2) in farm households, income does not influence purchases in the case of all of those products which can be obtained within the farm; and (3) in both types of household, meat, citrus fruits and alcohol show high demand elasticities.

Geetha Nagarajan and Richard L. Meyer, Ohio State University, USA – *Determinants of firm growth in the transition economy of Romania*

An attempt is made to explain the recent growth, and the associated role of finance, in Romanian private firms. A composite score capturing the multidimensional aspects of growth was regressed upon several firm, entrepreneur and financial characteristics. Econometric results suggest that female entrepreneurs who own and operate only one business, particularly if it is located in Bucharest, achieve significantly higher growth. External finance did not positively influence firm growth, possibly because of cash flow problems and underutilization of assets obtained through loans. Options, such as leasing or renting assets rather than purchasing them, are suggested which could help during the early years of development.

Vladimir Grbich, Economics Institute, Beograd, Yugoslavia – *The future of part-time farming in Serbia*

The aim is to estimate the future development of part-time farming in Serbia. A shift in agrarian policy priorities, as well as high unemployment elsewhere in the economy, will prompt many people to engage simultaneously in more than one occupation, including part-time farming. Analysis of family farm behaviour suggests that investments in part-time farms do not lag behind those which are full-time. In addition, unlike the situation in some countries, part-timers have an important stake in farmland ownership and considerable potential for development.

CLOSING SESSION

DOUGLAS D. HEDLEY*

Synoptic View

It is a very great privilege to present the closing synoptic view of the Twenty-Third Conference of the International Association of Agricultural Economists. Let me immediately recognize the tremendous effort made by many people in organizing a very successful meeting, beginning with Joachim von Braun, for undertaking the huge task of arranging the programme. The conference continues to change its shape, with new ideas and design. It has been shortened to six days, but it has more papers than any previous meeting. We all owe Joachim a debt of gratitude for his innovations and efforts to improve the quality of the papers while, at the same time, maintaining the intimacy and opportunity for discussion in these gatherings which has been a valuable tradition of the IAAE.

I also want to applaud the work of Peter Hazell for his role in organizing the contributed papers. His task has increased substantially from previous conferences, going from about 45 contributed papers in Harare three years ago, to 111 at this conference. Similarly, Arie Oskam has organized the poster sessions, as well as introducing computer-based presentations. The IAAE was one of the first associations to have poster papers and has now been followed by many others in using this presentational method. Arie has set a standard for others to follow. Finally, in terms of programme development, I must acknowledge Larry Silvers for his continuing work in once again organizing the workshops and symposia. These elements in our programme set our conferences apart from others, they strengthen the dialogue among our membership, foster network building around the world and, above all, forge professional friendships which last through our lifetimes.

In preparation for our meetings, the work of the host country organizing committee is of critical importance. Led by Jerry Siebert, the group has made us all feel welcome, provided excellent facilities and offered a wonderful glimpse of the agriculture and processing industry located in central California. I need also to praise the work of Nicole Ballenger, Chair of the US Organizing Committee, in turning the concept of a meeting in California into reality for all of us.

I also want to recognize the untiring dedication of Bernard F. Stanton (Bud, to all of us) in leading the Fund for the International Association of

*Agriculture and Agri-Food Canada, Ottawa, Canada. Reference will be made to papers presented at the Conference, some of which are being published in this Proceedings volume (designated as P), or in the Special Issue of *Agricultural Economics* (shown as S). Papers presented on the floor (F) are listed elsewhere in this volume.

Agricultural Economists. For a number of years, Bud has taken the lead in raising funds to ensure support for attending this conference for many from the developing world. With help from others, particularly our Vice-President Programme, Joachim von Braun, Bud has raised a record amount of funding, involving a wider array of donors and with more individuals supported for attendance than ever before.

Our conference attendance is about 760 members, one of the largest ever held. This is a tribute to a strong association representing all parts of the world, the attraction of California as a location and the quality of the presentations over the past week. To the many people involved in making the event a success, I want to express my appreciation and to extend on your behalf our heartfelt thanks for a job extremely well done.

Finally, I welcome the members of the new Executive Committee of the IAAE. I look forward to working with each of you over the next three years, both to maintain the momentum established under our more recent Past Presidents, Bob Thompson, Csaba Csaki, John Longworth, Michel Petit and Glenn Johnson, for continuing change to meet the needs of our members around the world, as well as to prepare for our next triennial conference in Berlin, Germany, in August 2000.

I have taken the time and space in this address to recognize these individuals and teams because of the tremendous work they have done. Of more importance, however, is that our conferences offer the vehicle for the renewal of personal and professional friendships among all of us and provide the venue for exchange of ideas and the dissemination of the foremost thinking in our profession from all corners of the earth. This basis of friendship and understanding was the central purpose expressed by Leonard K. Elmhirst and his colleagues in 1929: 'to bring together agricultural economists and research methods that were of common interest, to discuss national and international problems in the field of agricultural economics and to promote a more effective and more rapid exchange of agricultural economics information'. Our organizers have met that goal with creativity, hard work and dedication to our organization.

THE CHALLENGES

The Synoptic View is a unique feature of the IAAE. In preparing for it, I became curious about the word 'synoptic'. The *Concise Oxford* offers the following definition: 'adjective, of or forming a synopsis; taking or affording a comprehensive mental view; of the Synoptic Gospels (Matthew, Mark and Luke); giving a general view of weather conditions'.

Since I do not intend to add to the Scriptures, or to comment on the near perfect weather here in the Sacramento Valley, my talk today will attempt to combine synopsis with overview. In previous Synoptic Views, the full range can be found. Some make little if any reference to the conference content; others carefully mention most papers, pulling together the many strands of ideas presented and debated. Some have offered their own framework or context within which some of the papers are noted. One (Glenn Johnson) has even suggested that the Synoptic View is included to assure everyone that the President-Elect has done his homework.

Since there is no standard format, I begin with some comments on both the Association and our conference. As I have indicated, the workshops and mini-symposia were originally intended to offer open debate without lengthy presentations. Indeed, in the course of these sessions over many conferences, I have made and maintained many friendships that I would not have been able to establish otherwise. At this conference, a number of the workshops became paper presentation sessions, without so much debate, discussion and friendship building, and without the benefit of peer review required for access to other parts of the programme. I look forward to your views through the survey enclosed in your conference materials about the workshops. My personal view is that I would like to see the debate and friendship-building opportunities increased and the paper presentations decreased.

Second, the panel sessions instituted by Joachim von Braun in this conference are a new and different way to survey and synthesize the knowledge in various fields of interest to our profession. I am excited by them because they offer a creative avenue for our members to bring together materials and ideas in different ways. While there is the risk that the panels also become unreviewed paper sessions, the opportunity also exists for maintaining the high quality begun at this conference and, with some entrepreneurship on the part of organizers, potentially stand-alone monographs or edited volumes could result. I hope we can build further on what Joachim has begun at this conference. Again, I look forward to hearing your views through the survey.

Third, during the past three years, the Executive has spent considerable time examining future directions and strategies for the IAAE. We have identified many challenges and opportunities for streamlining our costs, better serving our membership in creative ways, ensuring access to the Journal, the membership and the Executive from all parts of the globe. I most sincerely appreciate the support which will be provided by the IAAE Council to the Executive in addressing these issues over the course of the next three years. Your views on specific issues and ideas are most welcome. Getting in touch with me or any member of the Executive will ensure that your views are heard and considered.

The theme of this year's conference, 'Food Security, Diversification and Resource Management: Refocusing the Role of Agriculture?', offers an excellent opportunity to assess progress and discuss the continuing challenges to the profession articulated by Bob Thompson in his Synoptic View three years ago (Thompson, 1995). In responding to these challenges, I want to divide my remarks into five sections: Food security, development and transition; Environment; Technology; the Management of resources and farms; and Diversification. My concluding remarks will address the question embedded in the theme on refocusing the role of agriculture.

Food security, development and transition

At the 1982 IAAE Conference in Jakarta, Indonesia, the topic of growth and equity in agricultural development was the centre of the debate (Maunder and

Ohkawa, 1983). The rapid growth in food supplies through the 1970s, based on the 'green revolution', as well as high cereal prices particularly in the first few years of the decade, gave rise to increased concerns about equity around the world in access to food. The general conclusion from that conference was that growth and equity could coexist, and that maintenance or improvement in one of those elements did not necessarily attenuate the other. Supporting that conclusion was the growing conviction that hunger and poverty were closely related if not identical phenomena, and that resource and technology access were the most important means for improving the condition of the poor and the hungry.

The 1982 conference came after a two-to-three decade effort in increasing food supplies, particularly in the developing world. There was great optimism and opportunity coming from that meeting 15 years ago. Since then, we have seen the most significant change in the world trading regime in several decades with the completion of the GATT Uruguay Round, the rise of the regional trade agreements, considerable expansion of the European Union, an opening of the markets in Eastern Europe and the former Soviet Union, and considerable domestic and trade policy change in China, India, Latin America and, more recently, in Africa. At the same time, we have witnessed a substantial shift in the priorities of the development agencies towards structural adjustment, declining expenditures in research on agriculture, and substantially shorter time horizon expectations for results from developmental investment than those which characterized the period before 1982. By the mid-1990s, we had also experienced a seemingly tighter world food supply than even during the crisis days of the early 1970s.

This span of 15 years has also led to a very considerable expansion in the range of issues we face. Among them are questions about price stability in more open international markets, the use of biotechnology to meet problems in developing and developed countries, how change in China will affect internal food production and world markets, future levels of farm resource availability and the impact of emerging and transition economies on the rest of the world. The dichotomy between those who have argued that immense quantities of additional food will be required in the next two decades and those who expect there to be food adequacy if greater attention is given to access to food for the poor, wherever they may be, has also been very obvious. For nearly a decade our profession and other specialists have been trying to find an agreed position on these issues and to decide on the priorities for agricultural and food development across areas of the world with great diversity in climate, income levels, technology and resource capacity, and environment. The World Food Summit, held in 1996 in Rome, was designed to explore these emerging priorities and the conflicting views on them.

Many papers at this conference offer quiet optimism that a substantial and stable agenda for action is re-emerging after some years of discussion in terms of food security, diversification and resource management, as well as in the role of agriculture in these matters. At the global level, the Pinstrup-Andersen and Pandya-Lorch (P) paper, arising from the IFPRI study exploring food supply, demand and the related resource issues up to year 2020, provided an outstanding foundation for much of the work of the conference. There are several related papers that extend and strengthen many of the conclusions of the IFPRI study. These provide an array of evidence on the emerging or transition economies of Central and Eastern Europe, noting the difficulties in the economic transformation to a market economy, particularly the slow progress in the institutional, legal and contractual arrangements needed as a foundation for a market economy.

Institutional economics forms a major part of many papers at this conference. This includes the institutional organization in developing and transitional economies, as well as in trade development. The best way to sum up is to say that we are relearning that Adam Smith's invisible hand must be attached to a highly visible and well respected 'long arm of the law', and the civil institutions that go with it throughout the body politic.

The paper by Ke Bingsheng (P) gives a rare overview of the breadth of change and continuing challenge in mainland China. Distribution remains a critical determinant of food security for China, being allied with the closely related infrastructural and institutional needs. He clearly notes that, without greater attention to the latter two issues, China cannot expect to resolve her internal distributional problems. Additionally, the consequences of failing to solve them could have a very heavy impact on markets around the world. The conclusion drawn is that China's grain balances are likely to require increased imports, though not on the massive scale suggested in other literature. In their discussion of India, Rao and Radhakrishna (P) make a similar set of points, but also express some concern about the results of structural adjustment which are now beginning to be displayed. Many other papers, as well as the regional panels, offer insights and updates on issues and directions for sub-Saharan Africa and Latin America.

Food security at the household and intra-household level has also been explored. Senauer and Roe (P) offer considerable insight into the variation in food availability among members of the household, even though food adequacy at the household level exists. Similarly, the Umeh, Amali and Umeh (F) paper calls attention to the interaction between endemic disease problems and labour productivity. These two papers suggest considerably more work needs to be done to better define and direct food and nutrition programmes.

Collectively, these and other conference papers offer the view that food demand is unlikely to outstrip world capacity to produce it. Nonetheless, food insecurity is likely to remain entrenched in South Asia and in parts of Latin America, and become worse in sub-Saharan Africa. Sustained and sustainable growth in food supply continues to represent the greatest challenge in research, extension, human capital development, infrastructure and economic policy. To make improvements, there are a number of conditions which will have to be met. First, the continued and possibly larger commitment to agricultural research on a sustained basis is vitally necessary. The appropriate public–private roles in research and technology transfer need more attention by our profession. Second, the institutional arrangements within each country represent a critical component of development, particularly the legal bases of land ownership, contracting, marketing arrangements and pricing. Third, the infrastructure base for distribution within much of the developing world is a growing cause for concern in meeting the needs of the poor and hungry, contributing to the stability of domestic and international markets, as well as the creation of markets for exchange. Fourth, household-level food security and health status among household members are obviously important in themselves, but also affect labour capacity and productivity at work. Finally, a number of new and different constraints need increased attention. Water policy and access to new materials deriving from biotechnology are examples of significance in the developing world.

Environment

Keith Campbell's 1982 Elmhirst Lecture presented a strong case for increased involvement of agricultural economists in the growing issues regarding the environment:

> governments in the next 25 years are going to be increasingly pressed to make trade-offs between the use of modern technologies to boost food production and the avoidance of damage to the environment. But they cannot afford to accede in an irresponsible way to the wishes of urban based environmentalists or the scientifically illiterate. (Campbell, 1983, p. 16)

In reflecting on previous conferences, we have been somewhat slow in trying to dispel the illiteracy noted by Campbell. I was pleased, then, to see the range and extent of papers at this conference addressing environmental issues.

The paper by Hall (P) provides the broadest mass of evidence for the existence of global warming, including some of the generalized effects we can measure and verify, as well as many of the relationships that elude precision and quantification. What it suggests is that we have not pushed back the illiteracy very far on issues of global scale changes in climate. But the work is under way.

Several papers explore environmental issues on less than a global scale, at farm and regional level, thus representing the emerging literature on specific environmental effects of farming systems in particular parts of the world. An example is the paper by Zeddies and Lothe (F) examining the greenhouse gas balances in crop and dairy farms. As an aside, I note that one of the IAAE inter-conference symposia was held in The Netherlands in 1996, focusing on chemicals in agriculture. A publication from that symposium, edited by Wossink, van Kooten and Peters (1998), will be available shortly.

It is particularly interesting to observe the growing recognition of the fact that annual and perennial crop agriculture shares the land resources of the world with forestry, and the water resources with fisheries and other non-agricultural demands. Bringing these aspects to bear on longer-term food supplies is increasingly important to our understanding of the balance between expanding food supply and sustainable food security.

Finally, on the topic of environment, I want to note the growing body of work on the trade-offs between pesticide use, research to develop varietal resistance and its maintenance, integrated pest management and the new pesticide-tolerant varieties now coming on the market. Papers at the conference

(Widawsky, Rozelle, Jin and Huan (S), for example) suggest that there is substantial overuse of pesticides in some regions, coupled with obvious incentives for increased integrated pest management, research in varietal resistance and more sustainable production practices.

In general, we appear to be addressing the scientific illiteracy issue identified by Campbell. The task is taking us into new and different areas, stretching our economic theory and substantially extending it, creating the development of cross-disciplinary, problem-solving approaches, and forcing us to rethink earlier conclusions which were drawn without the inclusion of environmental variables. There is no evidence from the papers that dealing with environmental problems need prevent growth or that it is inimical to the improvement of the human condition, a fundamental concern of Campbell. It is clear, however, that it does add to the complexity, the human capital requirements and the breadth of disciplines required for all of our research and policy endeavours.

Technology

I am including technology as a heading because of its very great importance in the agriculture and food industries over the past several decades. The original work of Hayami and Ruttan (1971), which is familiar to all of us, offers both theory and descriptive underpinnings for technological change for nearly three decades. More recently, the review by Anderson and Herdt (1989) in the 1988 IAAE Conference in Buenos Aires about the state of our technology generation for agriculture provided an excellent summary of the range of work to date, primarily under the CGIAR but also by the NARS. The conclusion is worth recalling: 'There may be many important (often life-threatening) distributional problems to be overcome, but our growth scenarios suggest relative ease for the human world to feed itself quite adequately into the next century' (Anderson and Herdt, 1989, p. 691). Since this was written before the huge growth in research on transgenics, one would infer that their statement would continue to hold today. Indeed, it is a similar conclusion, based on a somewhat different body of evidence, to that of Pinstrup-Andersen and Pandya-Lorch (P).

Some papers at this conference add to the evidence summarized by Anderson and Herdt, going beyond the adaptability and development of new varieties and their associated inputs. Pender (S) explores the application of neoclassical growth theory to population growth and agricultural intensification, suggesting that induced innovation occurs in both resources and man-made capital. This paper expands the scope of earlier work by bringing sustainability into the equation, as well as looking at the results in terms of income and productivity improvements. The work by Thirtle, Bottomley, Palladino and Schimmelpfennig (S) provides an interesting disaggregation of the returns to specific varietal development in wheat in the United Kingdom, implying that a higher rate of return had been obtained than was usual in the more general studies across all research. It suggests that more work needs to be done on rates of return to specific transgenic varietal development and on the public–private balance of investment and returns on new materials. The Masters, Bedingar and Oehmke (S) paper reviews a large number of studies in Africa, concluding that three-quarters of them report returns to research of over 20 per cent, although the results have largely been seen only in the past decade because of the delay in implementing policies to stimulate the use of new technologies. The paper appears to confirm the more general conclusion that macroeconomic and industrial policies need to be designed to encourage technology adoption, once technology exists. This represents an extension of the conclusion by Yair Mundlak (P) that agricultural development is a necessary condition for overall economic growth. Other papers continue to explore the technologies for the more different agricultural dryland environments, such as the Sahel. Progress appears substantially slower than for the more favourable production conditions.

In 1991, at the IAAE Conference in Tokyo, one of the plenary sessions included a talk by a biological scientist, describing in layperson terms the methodology behind gene splicing and transgenics (Peacock, 1992). This fascinating presentation laid the groundwork for what many of us are now increasingly familiar with, both in products we consume and in the research and policy issues we face. The papers at this conference certainly cover a wider span of issues in technology than ever before, ranging from the investment in, and dissemination of, technology at farm and national level, to the regulatory issues arising from the new technologies.

I draw attention to the emerging regulatory issues surrounding these new technologies. In the recent Uruguay Round, member states agreed to a science-based and risk-based approach to regulation of technologies and processes. With the general public having a growing distrust of science, I foresee increasing difficulty in finding public policy which is simultaneously acceptable to citizens, acceptable to World Trade Organization panels, and encouraging to the development and application of the new biotechnologies. Similarly, the rejection of policy and regulation based on science, in either general or specific cases, generates the opportunity for countries to retreat from the trade liberalization in the face of public opinion. I think the profession has a great deal of work to do in overcoming this distrust of science, to allow safe, practical and productivity-enhancing technologies for the benefit of food security and the human condition. The paper by Bureau, Marette and Schiavina (F) is one of the first attempts to explore the economic welfare impacts of consumer acceptance or distrust of new technologies, specifically, the beef hormone question in Europe.

The management of resources and farms

There are a large number of papers at this conference which fall into this category – not surprisingly, since the issues of efficient use of scarce resources form the basis of the work in our profession. I would add that many poster papers also address issues of resource use and farm management. Many of these papers draw linkages to other topics, including food security, trade, technology, environment and diversification.

A number of papers, including Moore and Nieuwoudt (F), De Klerck, Townsend, Kirsten and Vink (F) and Mbowa and Nieuwoudt (F), explore the emerging land distribution problems in Southern Africa and their impact on economic efficiency. This topic was initially explored in Harare at our conference three years ago. Others, like Pender and Kerr (S) and Chakravorty and Umetsu (F), examine the allocation of water among competing use, a growing concern in many developing countries, as well as in Europe (Varela-Ortega *et al.*, (S)). Li, Rozelle and Brandt (S) contribute to the evidence that payments for property rights are a necessary component of policy, both to preserve commonly held resources and for efficiency in resource use. Doss (P), Schreiner, Graham and Miranda (P), and Bresnyan (F) add to our knowledge of household behaviour. Other papers add to our methodological tools in examining and solving allocation and efficiency problems at farm and household level (Peter Witzke, (F)).

This work substantially enriches our understanding of specific allocation and efficiency issues around the world. While generalizations about land tenure, farm size, water allocation, property rights, research and extension utilization can often be made, based on many years of research, the detailed measurement and knowledge of these specific situations are of immense value to local and national policy makers, as well as international institutions.

Diversification

The Delgado and Siamwalla (P) and the McCalla and Valdés (P) papers draw similar conclusions about whether diversification is a product of policy, or an objective of policy, in developing countries. Essentially, they argue that getting policy distortions removed from both the domestic economy and the trade regime results in product diversification. The corollary is that diversification cannot be an effective policy objective as such. The only diversification policy objective noted is that of market and product expansion or development in response to trade liberalization. Somewhat different conclusions are drawn for developing countries, where technology and its adaptation and transfer at farm level are often designed to address diversification away from traditional cropping methods and the industrial crops.

A different view of diversity and diversification is taken by Zilberman, Yarkin and Heiman (P), in exploring the parallels and differences between the emergence of medical biotechnology and new products and processes of biotechnology for agriculture. Of particular note is the conclusion that the complexity of institutional arrangements for approvals of these products and processes could substantially slow or impede the access by the agricultural community to productivity-enhancing opportunities. I would add my concerns again that acceptability to the body politic of biotechnology products and processes is an equally critical element.

REFOCUSING THE ROLE OF AGRICULTURE?

Our Elmhirst Lecturer, Yair Mundlak, offered us a tightly argued, theoretically rigorous and empirically substantiated discussion about the dominating role that agriculture plays in the development of a nation's economy. His work builds on the extensive body of literature on economic growth, much of it coming from the World Bank over two or three decades. Productivity improvements in agriculture result in the release of labour from agriculture for employment in the non-agricultural sector, the decline in the proportion of the population required for local food supply, the creation of capital in both the agriculture and non-agricultural sectors and the strengthening of agricultural surpluses for export and regional trade. It is not a new conclusion, although it represents one of the most elegant statements of the proposition to date. Clearly, agriculture in all types of economies is of critical importance in addressing the theme of our conference.

The Presidential Address (Thompson, (P)) systematically reviewed each region of the world, exploring the resource constraints and opportunities, prospects for improvements in food security, the role of technology in these issues and the causality between food security and trade liberalization. He reaches similar conclusions to those of other papers at this conference, such as Pinstrup-Andersen and Pandya-Lorch: specifically, that with wise investment in research and development, technology transfer, human capital development, trade liberalization and improved civil institutions we can achieve global and regional food security. Some debates have taken place at this conference about whether the rate of increase in food supplies will lead to rising real prices or continue their long downward trend, although most experts appear to accept that global food adequacy can be achieved.

Certainly, it can be achieved. What is disturbing about this conclusion is that, even under the best of the supply scenarios of global food adequacy and decreasing real prices, we will continue to have an immense number of hungry people in the world in 20 years, the vast majority in rural areas. This is both an economic as well as a gigantic moral problem regarding the well-being of mankind, affecting not just the hungry, but each and every one of us.

Mundlak points out the central role that research plays in achieving productivity gains, the basis of overall growth, in agricultural and non-agricultural sectors. He notes the corollary that there is a strong argument for public funding in agricultural research both nationally and internationally, for both developed and developing nations. With the growing industrialization of agriculture and the consequent product differentiation through privately funded research, it is less clear that such agricultural research leads to the growth conclusion of Mundlak. This is particularly important where public funds are used in combination with private funds for this research. Requiring that public funds for research find matching private-sector moneys may increase overall spending on research, but it can also lower the amount of funding of public good research for agriculture. Both Canada and the United States, for example, are now urging public-sector research managers to seek private-sector matching dollars, directed to industry-driven research, the results of which can be captured in private benefits. The emerging products and processes of biotechnology are causing an acceleration of this trend. In the process, fewer dollars are left for purely public goods, for which no privately captured benefits can be found. Environmental issues represent a good example.

This is only one aspect of the growing endogeneity among governments, international institutions and the private sector in agriculture. We heard much at this conference about institutions, both public and private, national and international, and their roles in agriculture, growth, policy establishment and food security. We have only begun to understand this complex set of arrangements which no longer allow the assumption of an exogenous government, remote from private-sector markets. Our theory needs expansion, empirical and qualitative evidence needs to be assembled, and our methodologies must be greatly enhanced. It is towards this set of issues that we must focus much greater attention.

REFERENCES

Anderson, J.R. and Herdt, R.W. (1989), 'The Impact of New Technology on Foodgrain Productivity to the Next Century', in A.H. Maunder and A. Valdés (eds), *Agriculture and Governments in an Interdependent World*, Aldershot: Dartmouth.

Campbell, K.O. (1983), 'Agricultural Economists and World Conservation Strategy', in A.H. Maunder and K. Ohkawa (eds), *Growth and Equity in Agricultural Development*, Aldershot: Gower.

Hayami, Y. and Ruttan, V.W. (1971), *Agricultural Development: An International Perspective*, Baltimore: Johns Hopkins University Press.

Maunder, A.H. and Ohkawa, K. (eds) (1983), *Growth and Equity in Agricultural Development*, Aldershot: Gower.

Peacock, W.J. (1992), 'Key elements of modern biotechnology of relevance to agriculture', in G.H. Peters and B.F. Stanton (eds), *Sustainable Agricultural Development: The Role of International Cooperation*, Aldershot: Dartmouth.

Thompson, R.L. (1995), 'Synoptic View', in G.H. Peters and D.D. Hedley (eds), *Agricultural Competitiveness: Market Forces and Policy Choice*, Aldershot: Dartmouth.

Wossink, G.A.A., van Kooten, G.C. and Peters, G.H. (eds) (1998), *The Economics of Agro-Chemicals: An International Overview of Use Patterns, Technical and Institutional Determinants, Policies and Perspectives*, Aldershot: Dartmouth.

Sanitary and Phytosanitary (SPS)
  measures 453–6
Sarris, A. 482–90
Satellite imaging 602
Sato, K. 582
Satyanarayana, T. 534
Savings 348, 349–54, 406, 435, 484–5
Schamel, G. 666
Scherr, S.J. 597, 667
Schiefer, G. 638, 639
Schiff, M. 121–2
Schimmelpfennig, D. 634, 687
Schmieding, H. 244
Schmitt, G. 249
Schmitz, P.M. 237–59, 296, 669
Schneeman, B. 595
Schnytzer, A. 414
Schopen, W. 529, 532
Schreiner, M. 348–54, 689
Schrieder, G. 610
Schultz, T.W. 32
Schulze, R.E. 208
Schwartz Criterion (SC) 339
Scott, G. 536
Scott, W.E. 676
Seigniorage 403, 406
Semgalawe, Z. 597
Senauer, B. 97–106, 110, 539, 685
Senegal 208
Serghini, H. 162, 556
Serova, E. 547, 626
Sewage 4
Shapiro, B. 597
Shapouri, S. 665, 666
Sharma, K.L. 657
Sharma, M. 610
Shaw, D. 201
Sheep 6
Shelf life 153
Shephard, R. 383
Shiells, C.R. 285–6
Shimoda, S. 525, 527
Shinbo, T. 657–8
Shively, G.E. 122
Shortages 21
Shreeve, J. 186
Siamwalla, A. 126–40, 162–3, 689
Siebert, J. 681
Siebert, R. 673
Sil, J. 619
Da Silva, C.A. 639
Silvers, L. 681
Simbi, T. 610

Simon, L.K. 248
Siquera, O.E. de 208
Slater, J. 518, 520
Slovak Republic 240, 246, 288, 413, 419
Slovenia 240, 245
Small country hypothesis 402
Smith, A. 685
Social accounting matrix (SAM) 403–4,
  433–5, 475, 476–7, 483
Soil degradation 60, 62, 174–5
Soil structure 6–7
Solow, R.M. 25
Somogyi, S. 675
Sorghum 317, 322
Sossoh, B. 610
Soto, R. 122
South Africa 42, 208, 356–63, 508–11
South America *see* Latin America
South Asia 52, 54–5, 63–4, 73
  deficits 108–12
  diversification 553–5
  literature 114
  non-farm employment 301–2
  poverty 104
  productivity 174
  water demand 176, 178
South Korea 282, 297, 520
Southeast Asia 4–5, 8, 91, 93
  diversification 127, 133
  post-GATT liberalization 482
  productivity 174
  water demand 176, 179–80
Southern African Customs Union 135
Soviet Union (former) 9, 52, 66, 104
  inflation 242
  literature 114
  productivity 174
  resources 168
  transformation 245–6, 296
  transition 626–8
  water demand 178
Spain 281, 326, 328–30, 333
Spatial market integration (SMI) 421–31
Special stock system 266
Spitze, R.G. 636
Sri Lanka 114, 181
Srinivasan, T.N. 285–6
Staal, S.J. 644, 645
Staatz, J. 619
Stanton, B.F. 681, 682
Stanton, J. 605
Starbird, A. 639
Start-up companies 145–6, 153